BEHAVIOR MODIFICATION

Walter Mischel • Stanford University   *Consulting Editor*

BEHAVIOR MODIFICATION

BEHAVIORAL APPROACHES TO HUMAN PROBLEMS

William H. Redd
Albert L. Porterfield
Barbara L. Andersen
University of Illinois at Urbana-Champaign

RANDOM HOUSE NEW YORK

First Edition
98765432
Copyright © 1979 by Random House, Inc.

Library of Congress Cataloging in Publication Data

Redd, William H.
  Behavior modification.

  Includes bibliographical references and index.
  1. Behavior modification.   2. Behavior therapy.
3. Psychology, Pathological.   4. Mental health laws.
I. Porterfield, Albert L., joint author.   II. Andersen,
Barbara L., joint author.   III. Title.
RC489.B4R38   616.8'914   78–9327
ISBN 0–394–32134-0

Book Designed By Dana Kasarsky

Manufactured in the United States of America

PERMISSIONS ACKNOWLEDGMENTS

PERMISSIONS ACKNOWLEDGMENTS

TO OUR PARENTS

James and Mildred Redd
Leroy and Evelyn Porterfield
Edgar and Gladys Andersen

PREFACE

Within the past two decades, the application of behavioral principles to human problems has grown from a small, rebellious movement to become a major force in clinical psychology. This explosive growth has been accompanied by significant changes in both theory and practice in behavior modification. Most behavioral psychologists now find themselves dealing with factors that not so long ago would have fallen within the exclusive domain of more traditional psychological theories. Behavioral approaches can no longer be considered either radical or simplistic. In fact, the study of behavior modification is in many ways inseparable from the study of contemporary clinical psychology.

Our goal in this text is to present a rich introduction to behavior modification. By that we mean we have attempted to give readers some appreciation of the complexities of clinical intervention beyond merely describing the procedures involved. Hence, the text is formidable both in size and scope. But we believe that it will give the beginning student a rather sophisticated understanding of what behavior modification is—and is not.

This text is appropriate for use in both undergraduate and beginning graduate level courses in behavior modification offered by schools of psychology, education, social work, nursing, and professional schools of medicine and dentistry. It can also be used as an adjunct to practica in psychotherapy and counseling. Students who have had only an introductory psychology course should find the material manageable, but we feel that readers who have also had a course in abnormal psychology will get more out of the text for a given amount of effort. Course work in experimental psychology would also be beneficial, but by no means mandatory.

The book is divided into four sections: introduction, applications with children, applications with adults, and legal issues and new directions. In the first section, we examine the origins of the behavior modification movement and attempt to provide a historical perspective for these early developments. In order to help students gain an appreciation of the difficulties that confronted the behavioral pioneers when they broke with prevailing psychological thought, we asked some of the movement's founders

(Jones, Mowrer, Skinner, Wolpe, Lazarus, Eysenck, Bijou, and Keller) to describe what it was like when it all began. These personal statements appear at the end of Chapter 1.

The first section also reviews the basic principles of respondent and operant conditioning which are the foundation for many aspects of behavior modification. We devote considerable attention to recent reinterpretations of these principles and to the controversies raised by the ever-broadening influence of cognitive theories on behavioral thought. In the final chapter of this section, we provide a detailed examination of the processes involved in all behavioral interventions. We focus on assessment, emphasizing the role of functional analysis. We also discuss factors related to the implementation of behavior change programs and ways in which the therapist can go about evaluating such programs.

Both application sections are organized according to problems rather than procedures. We have adopted this organizational structure for a very important reason. A "procedures" approach encourages a view of the behavior therapist as a technician with a "bag of tricks" who sits and waits for some problem to come along that is appropriate for his or her techniques. This picture is held by many of behavior modification's detractors. It is, however, quite the opposite of the way things really are. The behavior therapist is, first and foremost, a clinical psychologist whose skills exist for understanding and alleviating the problems of the people who seek his or her help. When faced with a client with a particular complaint, the behavior therapist must first determine exactly what the nature of the difficulty is. Only then can he or she formulate a treatment strategy that has the best chance of helping the client. Our approach in the applications sections of the text introduces students to the same process. They first learn about behavioral conceptualizations of the problem area under study; only then can they fully appreciate the logic behind treatment procedures developed to eliminate that problem.

These comments should not be taken to mean that we have deemphasized the procedural aspects of behavioral intervention. On the contrary, we have taken considerable time to describe what the treatment procedures "look like" when they are applied, so that the student is left with more than a vague impression of what the behavioral clinician really does. To help readers develop a "clinical feel" for the procedures discussed, each chapter in the applications sections is followed by two or more detailed synopses of case reports drawn from the behavior modification literature.

The last section of the text is devoted to legal issues surrounding behavioral interventions and to new directions. The legal chapter focuses on current mental health case law as it relates to the implementation of behavioral programs in institutional settings. The final chapter reviews some of the promising new applications of behavioral procedures.

Recognizing the complexity of the subject matter, we have made every effort to "demystify" it. For this reason we have adopted an informal, conversational style of writing. With regard to our "biases": we have not tried to "sell" or "whitewash" behavior modification, nor have we sought to diminish its contribution. We have tried to present a *critical* account of the current status of theory, research, and practice in behavior modification.

As behaviorally oriented psychologists, we have undoubtedly let pride in our colleagues' accomplishments distort our objectivity from time to time—in spite of our efforts to the contrary. But readers will find no lack of criticism in the pages that follow. Indeed, as we reviewed the evidence on which our "empirically derived science of behavior change" is based, we found little about which to be smug. Students would do well to avoid expectations that they are about to learn the "one true way," and be satisfied instead with an understanding of one of the more promising approaches to human problems.

William H. Redd
Albert L. Porterfield
Barbara L. Andersen

ACKNOWLEDGMENTS

Rachel Dyal and Rachel Bermingham for their editorial assistance and dedication to our project.

Jeannine Ciliotta for her editorial contributions, Fern Chertok for her work on the glossary, and Norman Baxley for his photograph.

Our colleagues who made valuable comments on earlier drafts of the manuscript—Nancy Emmel, Stephen Golding, Frederick Kanfer, Lowell Krokoff, Robert Lentz, Barbara Licht, Gordon Paul, Ralph Riesner, Edward Seidman, William Sleator, Steven Stern—and those individuals whom Random House secured to review the manuscript, George Allen (University of Connecticut), Dorothea Braginsky (Fairfield University), Karen Calhoun (University of Georgia), David R. Evans (University of Western Ontario), Jerome R. Feldman (College of Optometry, State University of New York), Rex Forehand (University of Georgia), Julia R. Heiman (State University of New York at Stony Brook), Kenneth P. Hillner (South Dakota State University), Rosemary Nelson (University of North Carolina), Douglas E. Robie (University of Vermont), Leonard P. Ullmann (University of Hawaii), Lyn Weis (University of Kansas), and Patricia Wisocki (University of Massachusetts).

Sidney Bijou, H. J. Eysenck, Mary Cover Jones, Fred Keller, Arnold Lazarus, Hobart Mowrer, B. F. Skinner, and Joseph Wolpe for their contributions to our account of the early history of the behavior modification movement.

Marsha Healy, Phyllis Jones, Jan Palumbo, and Donna Schmidt for their help in preparing the manuscript.

And finally, the editorial and promotion staff at Random House for their professionalism.

CONTENTS

CONTENTS

PART I

INTRODUCTION

one

THE BEHAVIOR
MODIFICATION MOVEMENT

Writing in the *Washington Post*, Nicholas Kittrie, author of *The Right to Be Different*, notes, "There is a behavior modification revolution upon us, which with its magnitude is not unlike the industrial revolution of 200 years ago. . . . The new revolution aims at direct reform and control of man himself." By means of a deceptively simple strategy of teaching people new ways of behaving and then changing how the social environment responds to what they do, longstanding habits and patterns are being radically altered. Behavioral techniques are being applied to almost every facet of our lives. Weight Watchers International now teaches its members how to set up behavior modification programs for losing weight. Psychologists using behavioral techniques are enabling severely disturbed children and adults to lead more fulfilling and productive lives, migraine sufferers to reduce their headaches, and frustrated parents to deal with their children more effectively. In many metropolitan areas, behavioral psychologists offer courses to teach people constructive and satisfying ways of asserting their wants and needs in their daily interactions. Father Flanagan's Boys' Home is now hiring behavioral psychologists as counselors. Behavior modification has even invaded the arts (Jellison, 1973; Madsen, Greer, & Madsen, 1975). Music teachers have adopted many of the techniques and are now capable of turning out orchestras of 100 five-year-olds all playing the violin together and, mercifully, playing in tune. Office managers, prison guards, factory work supervisors, and hospital nurses are discovering how effective its methods can be. It is, in fact, mushrooming to the extent that its popularity could well be interpreted as a fad.

Actually, the principles we will be discussing in this book are not new; they have been around since the beginning of time. As will become obvious very shortly, they are commonsense facts of life. What *is* new, however, is that psychologists have taken these everyday principles and analyzed, systematized, and pursued endless manifestations of them. What they have emerged with seems to be a revolutionary new perspective on human behavior, one that by-passes for the most part the traditional theories of inner states of the mind.

Behavior modification has gained a tremendous respectability within the academic community. There are six professional journals devoted entirely to the study of behavior modification. The Association for Advancement of Behavior Therapy has over 2,000 members and regional societies have been formed. Courses in behavior modification are now routinely included in most university psychology departments as well as in professional schools of education, social work, and nursing. Even medical and dental schools offer training in behavioral psychology. In a recent re-

3

port, the American Psychiatric Association formally acknowledged the importance of behavior therapy and behavior modification:

> The work of the Task Force has reaffirmed our belief that behavior therapy and behavior principles employed in the analysis of clinical phenomena have reached a stage of development where they now unquestionably have much to offer informed clinicians in the service of modern clinical and social psychiatry. (p. 64)

Although behavior modification is widely accepted by professionals, its extraordinary effectiveness frightens many people. This concern is expressed by former North Carolina Senator Sam J. Ervin in the preface to a report on behavior modification prepared by the staff of the Senate Subcommittee on Constitutional Rights. Ervin writes:

> To my mind, the most serious threat posed by the technology of behavior modification is the power this technology gives one man to impose his views and values on another. In our democratic society, values such as political and religious preferences are expressly left to individual choice. If our society is to remain free, one man must not be empowered to change another man's personality and dictate the values, thoughts and feelings of another. (*Individual Rights and the Federal Role in Behavior Modification,* U.S. Senate, 1974, iii)

There is no denying that behavior modification has the potential of delivering a powerful weapon into the hands of the few—it offers the possibility of control. We all know that we influence, or in a sense control, one another. Clearly, the mother exerts great influence on the child, and the child influences her in return. But there is danger when control is not balanced. Classic examples are the practice of slavery and the regimes of totalitarian governments. With behavior modification at its disposal, there is practically no limit to the control that one group of people could exert over another. This possibility is exactly what most concerns many proponents of behavior modification—that the techniques might be used as a weapon (Skinner, 1974; Holland, 1974). Recently, the American Civil Liberties Union and the American Psychological Association have been in-

vestigating alleged abuses of behavior modification.

Many people argue that behavior modification must be stopped. And yet there are individuals with serious problems for whom these techniques offer great hope. The problem, therefore, is how to prevent misuse of the tool without denying people the right to effective treatment.

The goal of the first three chapters is to provide a thorough introduction to behavior modification. In this chapter we will outline the history of behavior modification and explain what it is. We will begin by discussing the pioneering efforts of Mary Cover Jones and Hobart and Molly Mowrer. They actually applied principles of behavior modification thirty years before the term or the "movement" even existed. The next topic will be the more recent origins of behavior modification. We will identify three separate sources during the 1950s and early 1960s: Joseph Wolpe and his colleagues in South Africa, H. J. Eysenck and his staff at the Maudsley Hospital in London, and B. F. Skinner and his associates in the United States. We will also discuss the evolution of the terms "behavior modification" and "behavior therapy" and the problems these terms have created. Then we will examine the five approaches to behavior modification: behavior analysis, learning (conditioning) theory, social learning theory, cognitive behavior modification, and eclectic behaviorism. In the last part of this chapter we will identify commonalities among the approaches.

PIONEERING EFFORTS

One of the earliest published accounts of the use of behavior modification techniques appeared in 1924; it involved the treatment of a three-year-old boy who had an intense fear of rabbits. The therapist was Mary Cover Jones, a young graduate student at Columbia University. No one knew why, but the child showed severe anxiety when in the presence of a variety of furry objects, including small animals, fur coats, wool rugs, feathers, and especially rabbits. Jones did not use the Freudian psychoanalytic approach of deep and lengthy probing into the child's unconscious in an effort to try to discover the hidden origin of his fears. Instead, she simply taught him not to be afraid.

She started out by presenting him with the rabbit in a way that did *not* frighten him. While he was eating some of his favorite foods, she placed the caged rabbit far enough away from him so that, although he was aware of its presence, it was not alarming enough to interfere with his enjoyment of the food. Every day the rabbit was moved just a little bit closer, but never close enough to be frightening. Eventually, it was let out of the cage and gradually brought close to the child. By the end of the treatment the boy was even able to play with it affectionately.

Through Jones's treatment the child learned that the rabbit was not going to hurt him; as a result, his fear of the rabbit was eliminated. What's more, his fear of other furry objects disappeared. This procedure was straightforward, really nothing more than a systematic application of common sense.

Another interesting early example of the application of learning principles to psychological problems involves the treatment of enuresis (bedwetting). The Freudians had (and, in fact, still do have) a number of fascinating explanations for this particular problem. It has been interpreted as a demand for love, a "weeping through the bladder," as well as a form of aggression toward the parents. Two early behaviorists, Hobart and Molly Mowrer (1938), dispensed with all such analyses and treated bed-wetting as merely the child's inability to control the bladder. Whatever the reason, the child had not learned how to control it, and their objective was to teach him or her to do so.

What they did was to design a pad which was placed on the bed or in the child's pants and sounded a buzzer when any moisture touched it. In other words, as soon as the child began to urinate, the buzzer would sound and continue until he awoke and turned it off. The idea was that, through repeated associations of the distended bladder and awakening, the child would learn to awaken rather than void in response to the sensation of a full bladder. This method was successful in "curing" enuresis to the point that the child learned to hold his urine through the night.

Behaviorists now look back on the achievements of Jones and the Mowrers as classic examples of a behavioral approach. But at the time the reports were published their efforts were not recognized as revolutionary.

THE MOVEMENT

During the fifties many clinical psychologists and psychiatrists were becoming increasingly dissatisfied with what they perceived to be the limited effectiveness of traditional psychotherapy. This sentiment, coupled with the great interest among academic psychologists in learning theory explanations of human behavior, led to speculation and research on the application of learning principles to psychopathology and its treatment. At least three groups of investigators began research in this area at approximately the same time. Interestingly, each group worked independently and was generally unaware of the others' research.

One group consisted of Joseph Wolpe, Arnold Lazarus, and their colleagues in South Africa. As they note in the statements which appear at the end of this chapter, they looked to experimental psychology and laboratory research for methods that could be validated empirically. In 1958 Wolpe published an extremely influential book, *Psychotherapy by Reciprocal Inhibition,* in which he rejected psychoanalytic theory and techniques and introduced rather straightforward behavioral techniques for eliminating irrational fears and phobias. Wolpe suggested that rather than trying to remove the phobia by analyzing its possible symbolic meaning, anxiety reactions would be better eliminated through conditioning principles developed by Pavlov, Guthrie, and Hull. This approach culminated in the technique of systematic desensitization, today one of the most widely used behavior modification procedures.

Working in a similar vein, H. J. Eysenck and his colleagues in London sought to make clinical psychology more scientific. In his account of the history of behavior therapy, Aubrey Yates (1970) has pointed out that Eysenck believed the role of the clinical psychologist was that of an applied researcher, not a junior psychiatrist. He maintained that rather than giving batteries of projective tests, which Eysenck considered to be of little value, the clinical psychologist should employ the methods of scientific inquiry to determine the factors affecting the individual's abnormal behavior. Yates credited Eysenck's colleague M. B. Shapiro with delineating how the practitioner might go about this inquiry. Although Shapiro really did not carry out his own suggestions, many of the methods he proposed (for instance, empirical analyses) have been widely used and have come to be hallmarks of behavior modification.

Perhaps the greatest effect that Eysenck had on the behavior modification movement was to spur the growing dissatisfaction with traditional methods of psychotherapy. Eysenck (1949, 1950, 1952) provided a series of analyses of the validity and reliability of projective techniques and psychoanalysis. Eysenck's conclusion was clear: traditional one-to-one psychotherapy in a doctor's office is not very beneficial.

Although Eysenck's conclusions have become part of the collective wisdom within many professional circles (Smith & Glass, 1977), his research has also generated much controversy. It has been criticized on methodological grounds; the major criticisms concern the small number of studies analyzed (6), and the pooling of studies without adequate consideration of specific problems treated, length of treatment, and therapist qualifications (Cartwright, 1955; Luborsky, 1954; Smith & Glass, 1977). Nevertheless, at the time Eysenck published his findings, many clinicians and researchers were eager to discover an alternative to traditional methods, and his conclusions captured their attention.

Unknown to Wolpe, Eysenck, and their colleagues in South Africa and Great Britain, Skinner and his associates in the United States were also investigating the application of behavior principles to psychological problems. They were experimental psychologists whose previous research had focused on the study of animal behavior in laboratory situations. Now they became interested in the possibility that their findings with laboratory animals might be relevant to the behavior of severely disturbed adult mental patients. Their initial goal was to determine how psychotic individuals respond to reinforcement and whether the patient's behavior would change in relation to

how the reinforcers were delivered. Like most laboratory psychologists, they began with a very simple response that they could easily observe and measure. The patients were seated in a small room; in front of them was a lever that produced candy and treats when it was pressed. By recording when and how often the patients pressed the lever in relation to how the lever was programmed to produce reinforcers, the psychologists were able to analyze the patients' behavior. They found that it followed the laws of behavior, and the experiment replicated Skinner's laboratory results with animals.

Following this rather theoretical research in the early fifties, Skinner's colleagues (Sidney Bijou and Fred Keller) began to study behaviors that had more clinical relevance. Bijou and a group of psychologists and teachers at the University of Washington started testing some of these ideas with young children who had been referred for special help. Their strategy was to devise ways of motivating these children to behave more appropriately; their primary "tools" were the praise of adults and chocolate candies.

Also working at the University of Washington, Montrose Wolf, Todd Risley, and Hayden Mees (1964) used similar techniques with a severely disturbed six-year-old boy to eliminate his temper tantrums and self-injurious acts. What they did essentially was to reward him lavishly for engaging in constructive activities and totally ignore him whenever he had a tantrum. It worked. With a great deal of training and therapy, his behavior improved to the extent that, at the age of ten, he was able to attend a regular elementary school. The success they had with these and other problem children prompted them to continue their work with all types of children.

At about the same time that Bijou and his colleagues at Washington were trying out these new methods with children, Keller at Arizona State University was formulating plans for a behaviorally based psychology course for undergraduates. His goal was to develop an instructional method by which students could be taught in an effective and reinforcing manner. Keller's more personalized system of instruction involved students' completing class assignments and tests at a rate commensurate with their abilities. To motivate students, Keller used lectures and demonstrations as special events; only after students had mastered a unit of lessons could they attend those events. Students learned the material quickly and, according to their reports, enjoyed the experience as well (Keller, 1968).

The early research of Bijou, Keller, and others generated great enthusiasm within the educational community, and other psychologists in the United States and Canada successfully extended their work. It was clear that the techniques were truly effective.

DEFINING THE TERMS

The terms "behavior modification" and "behavior therapy" are almost as familiar to students of psychology as "learning" and "motivation." However, both within and outside the ranks of academic psychology there is a great deal of confusion regarding their exact meaning. With every new book and status report comes a new definition.

The term "behavior therapy" was introduced quite independently by three separate groups of researchers. It first appeared in a 1953 report by Ogden Lindsley, B. F. Skinner, and H. C. Solomon on the application of operant conditioning to psychotic patients at the Metropolitan State Hospital in Waltham, Massachusetts. They used the term to refer to the application of conditioning principles to psychological problems. Apparently, Lindsley suggested the term "behavior therapy" because of its simplicity and linkage to other methods of treatment. The term was appropriate; it specified both the focus (observable behavior as opposed to psychological states) and purpose (remediation) of their new methods.

Without being aware of the earlier usage of the term or of each other's work, Lazarus (1958) and Eysenck (1959) also coined the term "behavior therapy." Eysenck's definition was similar to Lindsley's, although somewhat broader. He viewed behavior therapy as the application of all modern learning theory to the treatment of psychological disorders. For Eysenck, the new approach was not limited to Skinnerian principles of operant conditioning. It included behavioral pro-

cedures developed by Pavlov, Hull, and Mowrer, as well as by Skinner.

Lazarus used the term "behavior therapy" to refer to the addition of objective, laboratory-derived techniques to traditional psychotherapeutic methods. Whereas other "early behavior therapists" believed that traditional methods should be discarded in favor of these new techniques, Lazarus felt that behavior therapy should serve as an adjunct to traditional psychotherapy. According to Lazarus (1971), "the behaviorist or objective psychotherapist employs all the usual psychotherapeutic techniques, such as support, guidance, insight, catharsis, interpretation, environmental manipulation, etc., but in addition . . . the behavior therapist applies objective techniques which are designed to inhibit specific neurotic patterns" (p. 2).

In their discussions of the history of the behavior modification movement, Lazarus (1971), as well as David Rimm and John Masters (1974), pointed out that none of the original definitions of the term "behavior therapy" gained widespread usage. Until recently, the term was linked almost exclusively to the treatment of anxiety-related problems and techniques derived from Wolpe's original formulations.

The term "behavior modification" was first introduced by Robert Watson in 1962 and then popularized by Leonard Ullmann and Leonard Krasner in two influential books published in 1965 (*Case Studies in Behavior Modification* and *Research in Behavior Modification*). The emphasis was on the application of learning principles to clinical problems:

> Behavior modification is the application of the results of learning theory and experimental psychology to the problem of altering maladaptive behavior. The focus of attention is overt behavior, and, in terms of both the development and change of behavior, no distinction is made between adaptive and maladaptive responses. (Ullmann & Krasner, 1965, p. 2)

This definition, which was very similar to Eysenck's, was widely accepted until the early 1970s. But with the rapid growth of the movement and the application of behavior modification methods to varied sorts of human problems, many people (including Ullmann & Krasner, 1975) found the strict "learning theory" definition too limited and not an accurate statement of the current status of the field. As we pointed out earlier, since 1965 the definitions have been revised and broadened numerous times.

For convenience, we will make a distinction between the terms "behavior modification" and "behavior therapy" and will use the definitions found in the fifth edition of the *American Handbook of Psychiatry* (Bijou and Redd, 1975). **Behavior modification** refers to the application of behavior principles to many human situations, including child rearing, education, psychotherapy, vocational preparation, business, and social movements. **Behavior therapy** is a special case of behavior modification and refers to the application of these principles to psychological problems, disturbances, and disorders in adults and children.

Even if academics and clinicians could agree on a set of definitions, ordinary people might still be confused. The problem is that the dictionary definitions refer to a broader set of techniques than those psychologists associate with the area. The terms literally include all methods used to change behavior—psychosurgery, drugs, torture, and coercion—as well as psychotherapy based on empirically derived principles of behavior. Because of this situation, many ordinary people and journalists have looked on behavior modification with suspicion.

In order to set things straight, there has been a recent move to stop using the terms (for instance, Goldfried & Davison, 1976; Bijou, 1976). Two recent reports, one from the National Institute of Mental Health and the other from the American Psychological Association, have avoided the terms altogether. Some behaviorists have suggested the terms "applied behavior analysis" or "environment modification." But, as we will discover in the next section, these may also introduce confusion and may not accurately reflect everything that "behavior interventionists" do.

FIVE APPROACHES TO BEHAVIOR MODIFICATION

As is evident from the preceding discussion, behavior modification is not evolving toward a unitary approach to human problems; rather, it has been integrated into the mainstream of clinical psychology. In their 1975 review of behavior therapy with children, Bijou and Redd identified four theoretical models of behavior modification: (1) behavior analysis, (2) learning (conditioning) theory, (3) social learning theory, and (4) eclectic behaviorism. To this list we might now add a fifth model: cognitive behavior modification. Of course, this grouping is not absolute or exclusive, but it does provide an ordered perspective on the current status of the field.

Behavior Analysis

The behavior analysis model originated with the assumptions and laboratory findings of Skinner (1938, 1953, 1969), the research methodology of Murray Sidman (1960), and the developmental theory of Bijou and Donald Baer (1961, 1965, 1976). It represents most clearly the application of radical behaviorism to clinical psychology and was for at least a decade the primary approach. Although Ullmann and Krasner have modified their conception of behavior modification over the years (1965, 1969, 1973, 1975) to the point of now being eclectic, their original formulation captures the theme of behavior analysis: "The basis of behavior modification is a body of experimental work dealing with the relationship between changes in the environment and changes in the subject's response . . . the focus of modification is behavior" (Ullmann & Krasner, 1965, p. 1). The basic premise is that the subject matter of psychology is the *observable* interaction between the individual and the environment. Behavior analysts do not deny the existence of "private events" (for instance, thinking and emotion), but they do question the utility of introducing such constructs as explanations. They argue that the only way to understand a behavioral phenomenon is to manipulate it by altering observable aspects of the environment and then recording observable changes in behavior. This approach is characterized not by a particular theory of learning or motivation, but rather by a methodology. The method is the experimental analysis of the environmental factors that control the individual's behavior.

Learning (Conditioning) Theory

The learning (conditioning) approach is associated with Wolpe's (1958, 1969) techniques for the treatment of neurosis in adults and with Lazarus's (1959) clinical work with children. The major difference between the learning theory approach and behavior analysis is that the former employs unobservable, hypothetical states, such as anxiety, to explain behavior and the latter does not. These hypothetical states are always operationally defined and directly tied to specific theories of learning. In a sense, Wolpe and his colleagues might be considered theoretical behaviorists, whereas Skinner and his followers are antitheoretical behaviorists.

The learning theory approach accepts the general notion of the law of effect, which assumes that adaptive behavior will be maintained and maladaptive behavior weakened. However, this law does not always apply when the habit in question has a large anxiety component. In such cases, the habit will show resistance to extinction even though it is clearly maladaptive. For example, a person who has a pathological fear of dirt and germs may spend ten or twelve hours each day disinfecting his or her house. In objective terms, the person's housecleaning behavior is maladaptive (the person cannot hold a regular job, have friends over, go to a restaurant, and so on), but it does not diminish. The behavior continues to be emitted because it reduces anxiety; that is, cleaning the house makes the person feel calm and relaxed. In this reductionistic theory, neurotic behavior is primarily a matter of autonomic conditioning; hence treatment techniques are based primarily on the Pavlovian paradigm. Behavior deficits, on the other hand, require operant procedures in which clear response contingencies are present.

Social Learning Theory

The foremost spokesman for the social learning model is Albert Bandura (1969). Bandura and his colleagues make even greater use of hypothetical, unobservable processes to explain behavior than does Wolpe. The social learning approach adopts the basic tenets of conditioning theory and adds cognitive mediation.

According to Bandura, all behavior is acquired and maintained by one or more of three regulatory systems. The first pertains to external stimulus control: stimuli and events in the environment elicit and evoke responses. Autonomic and emotional responses can be brought under the control of stimuli through their continuous association (as in Pavlovian conditioning) either by direct or by vicarious affective experiences. If a stimulus is repeatedly associated with a fearful situation (for example, the odor of the dentist's aftershave lotion and the pain of the drill), then a previously neutral stimulus (the lotion) may come to elicit many of the same reactions as the feared situation (the pressure of the drill).

Operant behavior is also regulated by external stimuli by means of a similar association. A previously neutral stimulus (for instance, the sound of the school bell) can come to evoke operant behavior through the stimulus's association with contingencies of reinforcement (for instance, rewards for getting down to work). That is, the stimuli can control behavior because they signify the consequences that will occur when certain behaviors are emitted.

The second way in which behavior is controlled is through feedback processes, which are principles of reinforcement and punishment. That is, behavior is controlled by its consequences. The third, and for Bandura the most important, regulatory system pertains to cognitive mediational processes. Bandura (1969) writes:

> At this higher level stimulus inputs are coded and organized; tentative hypotheses about the principles governing the occurrence of rewards and punishments are developed and tested on the basis of differential consequences accompanying the corresponding activities; and, once established, implicit rules and strategies serve to guide appropriate performances in specified situations. Symbolically generated affective arousal and covert self-reinforcing operations may also figure prominently in the regulation of overt responsiveness. (p. 63)

According to Bandura, much of behavior modification is achieved through symbolic processes, notably observational learning. In such learning the individual acquires new behaviors merely by observing the behavior of others: "Later, reinstatement of these representation mediators, in conjunction with appropriate environmental cues, guide behavioral reproduction of matching responses. Performance of an observationally learned response is largely regulated by reinforcing outcomes that may be externally applied, self-administered, or vicariously experienced" (Bandura, 1969, p. 202).

Cognitive Behavior Modification

The newest behavioral approach might be considered by many traditional behaviorists as not being "particularly behavioral." Although the cognitive approach does not deny the important role of basic conditioning principles in the control of behavior, it emphasizes the role of the cognitive mediation of behavior. Cognitive behavioral clinicians suggest that the way individuals interpret the things that happen around them determines how they will react to them. According to this model, how people react to a particular situation is determined as much by how much control they feel they have over the outcome of the situation and how they label their own emotional reactions as it is by the objective aspects of the situation (Meichenbaum, 1976).

Followers of this approach believe that individuals have stereotypic interpretations which they use across situations and that these "set interpretations" are the cause of most "behavior problems." Consider the optimist and the pessimist, for example. Each would react differently to the situation of taking a test for a new job. The optimist would be eager and confident and begin to work as soon as he gets the test materials. The pessimist, we need hardly explain, would be considerably more anxious and less eager to try because he is already convinced he is not going to do well. The goal of the cognitive behavioral clinician would be to change the pessimist's set.

This "broadened" approach to behavior modification does not mean that behavioral psychologists are now adopting Freudian notions of hidden conflicts within the psyche or are turning to techniques such as free association and dream analysis. What it does mean is that there is a clear movement toward more traditional methods of psychotherapy (for instance, analyzing the client's

attitudes, personal constructs, style of communication, and resistance to change) within behavior modification and a willingness to accept a less publicly observable subject matter (for instance, feelings, attitudes).

Combination
Eclectic Behaviorism

As one might expect, the largest group of behavioral clinicians cannot be identified with a single theoretical position. Rather, they adopt what Lazarus (1971) has called "broad spectrum" or "multimodal" behavior modification. According to Lazarus, the therapist should be free of all theoretical biases and use whatever is effective. The therapist is not a radical behaviorist or a learning theorist—the therapist is a pragmatist who is willing to use any technique that has been empirically validated. This approach might be thought of as modern clinical psychology in which behavioral postulates have been accepted and integrated into other dynamic and client-centered techniques. The eclectic behavioral clinician does not feel restricted by any single approach to intervention or research methodology. The therapist's clinical techniques might include, depending upon the person, nonnormative assessment procedures such as interviews and informal surveys of skill levels, as well as standardized tests of intelligence and personality.

Although it is true that each of the five models has evolved from earlier models, it is not correct to assume that each successive approach has replaced those that came earlier. It is also important to recognize that it is extremely difficult, if not impossible, to categorize individual behavioral psychologists. The main function of our grouping is to delineate the various facets of behavior modification.

COMMONALITIES AMONG APPROACHES

All the behavioral approaches are tied together by faith in the ability of the scientific method to solve human problems. This *zeitgeist* showed itself in clinical psychology's disenchantment with traditional dynamic methods of psychotherapy and its acceptance of the empirical methods of experimental psychology. In the early 1960s this took the form of radical behaviorism; today it is still present but in a more moderate form—eclectic behaviorism. In the midst of a proliferation of new models of behavior modification, certain commonalities emerge.

Focus on Maladaptive Behavior

According to traditional psychological and psychiatric thinking, "sick" behavior is the symptom of some underlying conflict. Behavioral psychologists, on the other hand, reject the notion that "disturbed" behavior is a manifestation of some deeper psychological state, and regard the disturbed or maladaptive behavior itself as the problem. They believe that more adaptive ("healthy") behavior patterns can be *learned* in order to replace neurotic ("sick") ones, and that they can bring this about by training the client in certain specialized ways, without having to explore the psyche.

Traditional psychiatric theory claims that if a purely behavioral strategy is used for treating the problem, another problem will appear. Take the problem of insomnia, for example. According to traditional thinking, insomnia is merely a symptom of some underlying psychological disorder or conflict. In order to eliminate the problem the underlying conflict must be resolved. If the problem behavior is somehow removed without resolving the conflict then another symptom will be substituted because the real "cause" of the problem is still there. In the case of insomnia, if the person is taught some behavioral techniques for falling asleep rapidly and does not go into lengthy psychological analysis, then another symptom (for instance, headaches, nail biting) will take its place. Only when the underlying conflict is resolved, this theory insists, can its outward manifestations be eliminated. According to this thesis, **symptom substitution** (as it is called by psychiatrists) would be inevitable when behaviorists treat people's problems.

The behaviorioral psychologist's answer to this criticism is that on a purely empirical basis, symptom substitution rarely, if ever, occurs. Rachman (1963) reported 0 to 5 percent frequency of such spontaneous occurrence of disorders following treatment with behavioral techniques. In their review of the literature, Ullmann and Krasner (1969) concluded that symptom substitution is the exception rather than the rule. Even many psychiatrists are now coming to the same conclusion. In fact, a committee of the American Psychiatric Association (1973) recently informed the membership that they had found very few instances of symptom substitution, despite a careful search.

Behavioral psychologists have, however, recognized that new maladaptive behaviors may appear or that the original problem may reappear if the intervention is ill conceived or if the individual experiences new stress from the environment. One condition under which new maladaptive behaviors might develop is if individuals are not reinforced for performing more desirable behaviors, possibly because they do not know how to carry them out, or because their social environment does not offer enough support for more desirable behaviors. To prevent such a situation, the psychotherapist would have to focus on somehow altering the reinforcement contingencies in the client's "natural environment" and provide adequate skills training. For example, in the case of a client who is anxious around women and does not know how to make light conversation, the therapist would give him specific training and practice in how to talk to a woman on the telephone, how to ask for a date, and in other skills. Another situation in which new problems might arise after therapy has terminated is the individual's confronting unfamiliar situations. Again, the therapist's job would be to give the client coping strategies for dealing with new experiences.

Functional Analysis and Continuous Assessment

Along with the dissatisfaction with dynamic approaches to psychotherapy came the rejection of traditional methods of psychiatric diagnosis. Researchers as well as clinicians found that most classification systems were of little prognostic value (Freedman, 1958). In clinical practice, consensus as to what label to give a patient was rare (Kostlan, 1954; Schmidt & Fonda, 1956). It is not unusual for a patient in a mental hospital to have three or four diagnoses. Even in cases where practitioners agree as to the proper diagnosis, there is tremendous overlap in the maladaptive behaviors emitted by people placed in different categories (Zigler & Phillips, 1961; Lorr, Klett, & McNair, 1963). What is more, traditional psychiatric diagnosis fails to do what diagnosis is intended to do, namely, specify a proper treatment. It is indeed rare for traditional psychotherapists to agree on the "treatment of choice" even when they agree on the diagnosis. Thus, diagnosis is for all intents and purposes useless.

Another important, though secondary, factor in the rejection of traditional diagnostic systems is that in many cases diagnosis stigmatizes individuals and compounds their problems. Some have suggested that "a psychiatric label has a life and influence of its own" (Rosenhan, 1973, p. 253). Once labels are given, individuals are marked, regardless of how they behave subsequently. Labels often result in others avoiding the individuals. In the case of young children, this situation is especially tragic. For example, children who are diagnosed as mentally retarded are often cut off from educational opportunities and social interactions that promote learning and are placed in a sterile "retarding" environment that may magnify any handicaps they might have. Another problem is that labels often become self-fulfilling prophecies. In many cases, once patients accept the diagnosis as true, they give up responsibility for their own behavior because they are "possessed by mental illness" and cannot do anything about it.

Finally, a diagnostic category indicates model characteristics that, in an individual case, may have little resemblance to the person's behavior problems or to his or her repertoire of positive behaviors.

The general consensus among behavioral psychologists is that people are too complex and varied to permit broad generalizations based on severely limited data. Rather than trying to assign individuals to specific diagnostic categories and therapeutic techniques, behavioral clinicians adjust their methods to their clients' problems. There is no presumption that one technique will serve as a cure. Rather, the notion is that not until the therapist has determined what factors are

supporting or maintaining the problem can a program of treatment be devised. This process is called assessment.

The therapist does not try to diagnose the client's underlying, unconscious problem, but rather attempts to make an assessment of the factors generating the maladaptive behavior. This assessment necessarily involves the systematic manipulation of variables in order to determine what changes must be made. Frederick Kanfer and George Saslow (1969) have identified five features of this functional analysis approach to assessment:

1. Since the individual operates in a complex system, psychological variables are not the only ones considered in the assessment; biological, economic, and social factors are also included in the analysis.
2. Since it is probable that many of the individual's behaviors are operants (maintained by the consequent stimulation provided by the social environment), the client's behaviors can be organized in terms of the consequences they produce.
3. Since individual behavioral repertoires are limited by individual biological, social, and intellectual attributes and by the norms of peer groups, knowledge of the client's history, of the limits of his or her capacities, and of reference group norms is necessary.
4. Assessment is always individualized.
5. Assessment does not necessarily lead to psychological intervention. If the analysis indicates that the controlling factors are economic, for example, the recommended intervention would be economic.

Since the only way therapists have of determining whether or not their intervention is effective is the outcome, assessment is ongoing. Therapists continue to gather data that are used as feedback to permit refinement in the procedures to better meet the needs of clients.

Commitment to Empirical Validation

In contrast to psychoanalytic techniques, many of the procedures used by the behavioral clinician are derived from empirical research. To the extent that the methodology is rigorous, the techniques have been scientifically validated. This validation is also carried out in individual treatment. The therapist adjusts and modifies the techniques in accordance with feedback regarding the client's behavior. If a particular procedure results in positive change, it is continued; if it results in no change or in deterioration, the therapist alters it.

To most students, this idea may appear quite unremarkable—of course the procedures are tested before they are put to use. But, unfortunately this is not the tradition in psychiatry. As Rimm and Masters (1974, pp. 16–17) have pointed out:

In the writings of orthodox analysis [for example, Fenichel, 1954] it is common practice to cite the edicts of Freud and other prominent analysts, much the way medieval scholastics cited Aristotelian proclamations as incontrovertible proof for their positions. Frequently, when cases are cited in the psychodynamic literature, no mention whatsoever is made of outcome, as if this were simply not an issue (see Astin, 1961).

Although empirical validation of procedures is a goal, it is not fulfilled in all instances. As we will discover when we discuss applications of behavior modification, a sizable number of behavioral procedures are derived from theory without being empirically validated.

SUMMARY

Behavior modification is a new approach to psychology that has not only become widely accepted in clinical and academic circles, but is also being applied to almost every facet of our daily lives. Although it offers effective solutions to many serious problems, it also has the potential of delivering a powerful method of control into the hands of the few. It is important for laypeople, as well as psychologists, to understand its techniques so that they can be used effectively and limited when necessary.

The behavior modification movement grew out of a disenchantment with traditional methods of psychotherapy and the belief in the utility of the scientific method for solving problems. The modern origins of the movement can be traced to three independent sources during the 1950s. One source was Skinner and his associates Lindsley, Solomon, and Bijou. These radical behaviorists were interested in testing laboratory-derived principles of behavior on the behavior of disturbed adults and children. The other two sources were clinical psychologists who turned to techniques of experimental psychology to develop more effective psychotherapeutic methods. One of these groups included Wolpe, Lazarus, and their colleagues at the University of Witwatersrand in Johannesburg, South Africa. The other was a group of psychologists under the direction of Eysenck and Shapiro at the Maudsley Hospital in London.

As behavior modification has been brought into the mainstream of clinical psychology it has become increasingly difficult to specify a clear set of assumptions and/or procedures that all who call themselves behavioral clinicians would accept. There is even controversy regarding what is meant by the word "behavior."

The wide proliferation of behavioral principles has resulted in the emergence of at least five distinct behavior modification approaches: (1) behavior analysis; (2) learning (conditioning) theory; (3) social learning theory; (4) eclectic behaviorism; and (5) cognitive behavior modification. These approaches differ mainly in terms of the extent to which they regard various inner states as behaviors that can be accurately observed and modified.

At the present time, there appear to be three characteristics that distinguish the behavior modification approaches from more traditional models of psychology. They are (1) the subject matter of behavior modification is maladaptive behavior, not presumed deep-seated psychological conflict; (2) assessment of the problem behavior involves a functional analysis of the conditions that maintain the problem behavior, and this analysis is continuous and always individualized; and (3) the techniques that are used to modify behavior are empirically derived.

REFLECTIONS AND COMMENTARY:
THE PIONEERS

As we researched and thought about the history of behavior modification, we became curious about how the early pioneers came to make such a radical departure from prevailing psychological thought. We also wondered how it felt to be in the midst of such controversy. To explore these issues, we asked some of these researchers to share their experiences. We are indeed honored by their enthusiastic response.

STATEMENT 1 · MARY COVER JONES

g. Paul Bishop

Mary Cover Jones

Born 1896, Johnstown, Pennsylvania. A.B. Vassar, 1919; M.A., Ph.D., Columbia, 1920, 1926. Research associate, Institute of Human Development, University of California, since 1927; professor emerita, University of California, since 1960.

I entered Vassar College in 1915 and, although I had no way of knowing it at the time, it was an outcome of this event which led to my professional association with John Watson 5 years later. Our weekends away from the campus were limited by edict, but postwar New York, only 2 hours away by train, was an exciting place. It was on one of these weekends in 1919, the spring of my senior year, that instead of the usual theater outing, a friend steered me to Watson's lecture and films reporting his work with infants. He told us that infants at birth could respond with three basic emotions—

fear, rage, and love—which were called out by specific but limited stimuli. More elaborate emotional responses were learned by association or conditioning. Watson had chosen 11-month-old Albert, "a child with a stolid and phlegmatic disposition" as the subject of a conditioning experiment which demonstrated his thesis. As is well known to you, a loud sound which called out the fear response was coupled with Albert's positive response of reaching interestedly for the white rat of which he showed no fear. After several associations of the startling sound with the presentation of the rat, Albert not only withdrew in fright from the rat, but this negative reaction to the rat eventually persisted without reinforcement of the loud sound. So far as we know, this was the first laboratory attempt to condition an emotion in a child. Transference has also occurred: to a white rabbit, to other furry objects, even to a Santa Claus mask with a white fuzzy beard!

The possibility of using the learning approach in the modification of behavior appealed to me. If fears could be built in by conditioning, as Watson had demonstrated, could they not also be removed by similar procedures? The next year at Columbia I well remember the excitement with which we doctoral candidates greeted Watson's textbook, *Psychology from the Standpoint of a Behaviorist* (1919). It pointed the way from armchair psychology to action and sold behaviorism to us.

I believe I was the last graduate student fortunate enough to work with Watson. If there is any value in having me write this, it is to illustrate how events may shape lives and how one's dignity, in the Skinnerian sense, evaporates when the fortuitous causes of one's destiny are revealed.

John Watson, after his "sensationally publicized divorce" (Woodworth, 1959), had left Johns Hopkins University and was associated with the J. Walter Thompson Advertising Company in New York City. I was at Columbia. Rosalie Rayner-Watson, the second wife, a student and assistant of Watson's, who figured in the divorce, had been a Vassar classmate and friend of mine. It was through our association that I met and had the opportunity to work with John Watson.

Watson suggested that for my Ph.D. dissertation I extend his observations of infants' developmental activities to a larger and more representative sample in order to provide normative data. This research culminated in *The Development of Behavior Patterns in Young Children* (Jones, 1926), in which I compared my measures based on data for over 300 children from well-baby clinics in New York City with those of baby biographers—from Pestalozzi in 1784, Darwin, 1877, and Shinn, 1900, to Gesell's tests on 24 children published in 1925. Many of these behaviors have continued to figure in developmental schedules. My concurrent work, under Watson's supervision, reported in *The Elimination of Children's Fears* and *A Laboratory Study of Fear: The Case of Peter* (Jones, 1924a, 1924b) was not considered by my Columbia doctoral committee to be suitable for a Ph.D. thesis because of the limited number of cases. They shared the opinion recently expressed by one of my students who commented in regard to a case history, "I am not impressed with a N of one." On the other hand, a case study does provide the opportunity to try out a principle in a new way.

With reference to the treatment of Peter, Watson wrote in *Behaviorism* (1924, p. 132), "Finding that emotional responses could be built in with great readiness (Albert) we were all the more eager to see whether they could be broken down and if so, by what methods." Watson paid us a professional visit on many Saturday afternoons throughout the conduct of the therapeutic experiments with Peter. The experiments occurred in a natural setting, since Peter lived in the institution where the study was carried on, as did I, with my husband and daughter. (This was the Hecksher Building on Fifth Avenue, over the door of which was the inscription, "The Children's Home for Happiness." An admirable sentiment, but it carried no guarantees!) The patient, meticulous, painstaking procedures used in the experiments with Peter reflected the methodological style of John B. Watson, who faithfully followed Peter's progress, reverses, and final freedom from his fear.

I was recently asked whether, if I were to begin my psychological career over again, but with my present background experience, I would repeat my 1924 research. My answer would be, "Probably, yes," provided John Watson were here to incite me, as he did 50 years ago, if my husband, Harold Jones, were here to help with interpretations as he did in the early 20's and for 40 years thereafter, and if Peter, the frightened child, were here needing help.

Now I would be less satisfied to treat the fears of a 3-year-old, or of anyone else without a later follow-up and in isolation from an appreciation of him as a tantalizingly complex person with unique potentials for stability and change. This would require a receptive attitude toward various treatment methods in order to select the one, or combination of several, most likely to benefit the individual. Einstein warned us that even in the field of physics there is no privileged position from which to make scientific observations, but that there is a responsibility to be aware of our positions in time and space (Macfarlane, 1971, p. 140).

Dr. Jones's statement is an edited version of a paper published in the *Journal of Behavior Therapy and Experimental Psychiatry*, 1975, **6**, 181–187.

j thompson studio

Born 1907, Unionville, Missouri. B.A. University of Missouri, 1929; Ph.D. Johns Hopkins University, 1932. Research fellowships, 1932–1936; Yale Institute of Human Relations, 1936–1940; Harvard University, 1940–1948; University of Illinois, since 1948.

Not long ago, on the CBS late afternoon news, there was a "profile" of John Philip Sousa. Everyone knows Sousa as "The March King of the World" and, perhaps, as the inventor of the Sousaphone (the big brass horn with the shiny gold bell). Sousa, it seems, regarded these as the least of his accomplishments. What he really wanted to be known and remembered for were the 17 light operas he wrote and three published novels. Well, it looks as if my one most enduring claim to fame may be an apparatus and method for treating bed-wetting, about which, in some ways, I couldn't care less.

Between 1934 and 1940 I was on the staff of the Institute of Human Relations at Yale University, in New Haven, Connecticut; and during the same period my wife, "Molly" (Willie Mae C. Mowrer), was psychologist at the Children's Community Center, at 1400 Whitney Avenue, a beautifully modernized version of the old New Haven Orphanage. Together we were to be the "house parents" of one of the Center's four residential "cottages," the Children's Cottage, which could accommodate 24 children between three and 11 or 12 years of age. Diagnostically, these children were a heterogeneous lot: delinquent, autistic, "neurotic," victims of parental neglect or abuse, some awaiting foster-home placement, and others with a history of several unsuccessful such placements.

The Children's Cottage itself was built on the bungalow plan, long and spacious, well staffed, clean, and with an apartment at one end where my

18

wife and I were to live. The food was abundant and good, and we ate as many meals with the children and staff as our other duties permitted. There was just one drawback: the place stank to high heaven of rancid urine, and upon inquiry we were told that about half of the Cottage's inhabitants were enuretic. This did not, however, keep us from joining the CCC staff in the capacities indicated; but from the outset, my wife and I were resolved we were going to do something—we didn't know what—about the endemic bed-wetting, which the Cottage staff found a great burden but seemed to accept fatalistically.

During the middle and late 1930s there were a number of members of the IHR staff—Clark Hull, Neal Miller, Don Marquis, Kenneth Spence, Ivor Hovland, and others—who were much interested in the psychology of learning, a relatively new field to me. And gradually I became convinced that there was a good chance that the enuresis problem at the Children's Center could be solved by simple, Pavlovian conditioning. All we had to do, I reasoned, was to make bladder distention a conditioned stimulus for the response of waking instead of an unconditioned stimulus for urination during sleep. The instrumentation seemed quite simple (Mowrer, 1938). Two pieces of copper window screening 18 by 24 inches, with a piece of heavy bedspread material between to insulate them electrically and another piece of this material on top, to be next to the sleeping child's body, were quilted together and nicely hemmed around the edges, with one strand of twisted electric-light cord soldered to one of the screens and the other strand to the other screen. The opposite end of the cord was connected to a telephone plug and this, when inserted into a matching jack in the end of a small metal box, would make an ordinary electric doorbell ring whenever a slight electric contact was established between the two pieces of copper screening by a small amount of urine on the pad (about the size, someone has observed, of a "pea").

The first child we treated was an 11-year-old boy named Walter. We chose Walter partly because his room was near our apartment and also because he was easily the champion bed-wetter in the Cottage. Over the course of two or three days, in a rather low-key manner, we explained to this boy what we were proposing to do; and since he was very ashamed of his enuresis and genuinely wanted to get rid of it, he was fully cooperative, even enthusiastic.

The first night we were very excited and hoped we would still be up and about when Walter wet his bed so we could see what happened. He did not disappoint us. It was not more than half an hour after he retired until we heard the bell ringing rancorously in the metal box, and we rushed into his room, only to find him sleeping placidly through all the clatter. Obviously the bell hadn't wakened him, so we spoke to him, shook him gently, and finally got him into a sitting position on the edge of his bed and said: "Walter, Walter, wake up! You need to go to the bathroom." Highly indignant and disgruntled, he said: "But I've just *been* in there." We said, "no, you were just dreaming, so go on to the bathroom," which he did.

Already there were two interesting findings: (1) As we were later to discover in some German literature, children often have "toilet dreams" (*klosett traume*) just before they wet the bed, thus legitimating it; and (2) we also found that although our bell did not suffice to waken Walter, it inhibited his urination after the first few drops. However, in a few nights, the bell was awakening him and he would quickly go to the bathroom; and soon he was awakening *before* he urinated at all.

We then had our apparatus duplicated, and over the course of a year or so we used it with 38 children in all. The pattern of reaction and recovery varied from child to child, but the end result was the same: a dry-bed habit. I combed the literature and found literally dozens of treatments that had been proposed for enuresis, some the exact antithesis of others, but none of them seemed to have worked in any significant percentage of cases. And at the 1937 meeting of the American Orthopsychiatry Association, in New York, Molly and I reported our findings to an over-flow audience. We apparently "covered the bases" pretty thoroughly and had, as I recall, no serious criticism or heated objections in the discussion period.

Some writers have generously referred to our enuresis study as the beginning of what is now known as Behavior Therapy, but this is an overstatement. Yates (1970) lists 27 studies, all carried out and published before 1940, which represented attempts to apply learning principles to clinical problems, so Behavior Therapy has a much broader historical base than our enuresis study; but with the exception of Mary Cover Jones' 1924 experiment with counterconditioning (which was one of the inspirations for Joseph Wolpe's conception of reciprocal inhibition and "systematic desensitization," Wolpe, 1958), our work on enuresis is the only one of these early explorations that has stood the test of time and continued application. Also, within the specific realm of enuresis, we can, I think, claim complete originality. A German pediatrician by the name of Pfaundler had previously developed, in a hospital maternity ward, a means of signaling to nurses when a baby needed changing; but the instrumentation was quite different from ours, the goal was not to eliminate enuresis, but merely to alert a nurse, and we didn't even know of Pfaundler's work until *after* we had completed ours. In 1939, J. J. B. Morgan and F. J. Witmer, of Northwestern University, published a paper on enuresis in which they used an apparatus and method very similar to ours; and according to third-hand reports, Professor Morgan felt some bitterness about our 1938 publication, with plausible but not valid justification. During the academic year 1932–33 I had been a National Research Council Fellow in Franklin Fearing's laboratory at Northwestern; and apparently the Morgan-Witmer work on bedwetting was in progress at that time, and I might easily have heard about it. To the best of my knowledge and belief, this, however, was not the case. I barely knew Morgan and, so far as I can recall, was completely unaware of his interest in enuresis. For this and other reasons, I have no hesitance in accepting, with my wife, the accolade of originality in this connection, but neither do I question the possibility that Morgan and his students were independently working along these lines before we began our work. By the accident of prior publications, however, we have gotten the lion's share of the credit for developing and carefully testing the method. I grant that this was to some extent unfortunate, but I want to attest that there was no scientific dishonesty in the situation as far as we were concerned.

When Molly and I published our original paper in the *American Journal of Orthopsychiatry* (1938), our supply of 500 reprints was exhausted in two or three weeks; and despite the fact that the piece has been reprinted, in whole or in part, a number of times, we still, after nearly 40 years, get occasional reprint requests. My wife and I haven't done any work on enuresis since our original publication; but just our reminiscences on the subject seem to be in hot demand.

All of which I regard as a little absurd, since, for the last 15 years, I've devoted myself almost exclusively to the development of something that we call "Integrity Groups," and I can publish an article or monograph on *that* subject—which I regard as vastly more important than bed-wetting—and not get a single request for a copy. Certainly this is not because the integrity of the average citizen (not to mention political and industrial leaders) is so perfect that it couldn't do with a little improving, or that loss of integrity is unrelated to the problem of identity crisis (formerly misnamed "neurosis"). Perhaps the difficulty is that clinical psychologists (and other mental-health professionals) aspire to being scientists; and since science is said to be value-free, you can't have anything to do with people's moral or ethical problems without becoming unscientific, even antiscientific. But the tide seems to be slowly turning.

During the early 1960s, after Wiley & Sons had published my two volumes (representing 25 years of work) on the psychology of learning, I was often asked: "With your background, why haven't you become active in Behavior Modification and Learning Therapy?" The simple answer was, I just didn't want to—I had found something (interpersonal relations) which interested me far more and which seemed clinically and culturally more significant in the long run. But there was a lot more to it than just this. Early in my career I had tried "radical behaviorism" as John B. Watson had promulgated it, and it took 20 years to recover my sanity (see *Learning Theory and Personality Dynamics,* 1950, as well as the two 1960 books), and I wasn't about to get on the same merry-go-round which Fred Skinner had started. Moreover, I didn't like what seemed to border on chauvinism.

Skinner created new terms for old phenomena: e.g., he spoke of "operant conditioning" when Hilgard and Marquis had already suggested "instrumental learning" and, even earlier, Thorndike had written at length about "Habits" and "Trial-and-Error Learning." He "invented" *behavior shaping* long after Thorndike had worked on animal training through *successive approximation,* not to mention the methods used by circus animal trainers for hundreds of years. And the Skinnerians, if not Skinner himself, also speak of "time out" as if it were something new. My fourth-grade teacher in 1917 sometimes banished me and other miscreants to the "cloak room" for a spell. What's the difference?

I've already noted that Watsonian behaviorism gradually evolved into a neo-behaviorism which was pretty subjective. The same thing seems to be happening to Skinnerian behaviorism. Some of his most devoted followers are now talking about "self-control," contracts, and imagery. Reaction against it has stimulated renewed interest in cognitive psychology; but I don't see much interest on anybody's part—except members of Alcoholics Anonymous, Recovery, Inc., Synanon Foundation, and other lay mutual-aid movements—in interpersonal relations, in a word "character," "responsibility," "ethics," "integrity." It's here, in my opinion, that we're going to make it or lose the whole game. Bed-wetting, in comparison, seems relatively unimportant.

STATEMENT 3 • JOSEPH WOLPE

Born 1915, Johannesburg; medical qualifying degree, University of Witwaters-rand, South Africa, 1939; private practice until 1942; South African Medical Corps, 1942–1946; psychiatric training and research, since 1946. Professor of psychiatry, University of Virginia, 1960–1965; Temple University, since 1965.

A tortuous route brought me to the experimental work that has generated most present-day behavioral techniques for overcoming neurotic anxiety. During my early years as a medical student, I thought the theories of Freud ridiculous and could not understand how serious people could accept such flights of fancy as truth. My attitude was sharply changed by the following experience with a patient in 1939 while I was a medical intern at Johannesburg General Hospital.

A girl of 20, named Hetty, had for about 4 months been treated in the ward with a diagnosis of chorea (St. Vitus' dance)—a severe and unusual variety, characterized by marked athetoid movements. She had improved markedly under sedative drugs. One day she told me that she often dreamed of swimming in a lake towards a man on a distant shore that she could never reach. I recounted this dream to a psychoanalytically-oriented friend, who made the "obvious" interpretation that the man represented Hetty's father, and suggested that I try the effects of "wild analysis"—essentially, confronting the patient with this "insight." Accordingly, the next day, I told Hetty that the dream meant that she had a desire one day to meet a nice young man like her father. She made no immediate response to this information, but a few minutes later, when I was out of her room, began to display a very marked exacerbation of her symptoms that continued until the end of my internship some weeks later. I was deeply impressed by the powerful impact of the interpretation, negative though its direction was. My skepticism about psychoanalysis gave way to an eager interest.

Cold logic cannot in fact derive a confirmation of psychoanalytic theory from these events. Many a girl would probably be so upset at the suggestion that she desires her father that any nervous distress she might have would worsen—whether or not she actually had such a desire. But at the time, fired by the change in Hetty, I avidly read books on psychoanalysis and for several months made a practice of writing down all my dreams and free associating to them—an adventurous and enjoyable experience, whose record I still have.

After about two years in general practice, I joined the South African Medical Corps in April, 1942; and later that year was assigned to a military hospital near Kimberley that was receiving casualties from the Western Desert. Among these were numerous war neuroses. I was one of several medical officers in that hospital who routinely treated these cases by narcoanalysis, which at the time was regarded as a shortcut to the release of Freudian repressed conflicts. While this treatment often produced excited and exciting narrations, and usually led to the soldier being calmed for a day or two, it was plain to all of us after a few months that no lasting effects of magnitude were achieved. This, in conjunction with the fact of the nonacceptance of psychoanalysis by the Russians (then our allies), made me start a search for another way. The logical first thing to look at was the work of the Russian, Pavlov—although the available literature suggested that his only imprint on Russian psychiatry was in the use of bromide and caffeine combinations for neuroses.

During the next two years I studied Pavlov intensively, writing a summary and a critique of each of the experiments in Anrep's translation of his work. I also read a great deal of the English and American literature on conditioning, and found in the *Principles of Behavior* by Clark L. Hull a fitting framework for all this knowledge. I studied with great care all published experiments on the production and treatment of experimental neuroses, before starting in 1947 to work on my own experimental neuroses of cats, following in a general way the model of Dimmick, Ludlow, and Whiteman (1939) and Masserman (1943). My observations contradicted the belief previously held by all other experimenters in this field—that conflict plays a necessary part in the production of experimental neuroses. I showed that these neuroses are actually strong anxiety responses that are conditioned to a situation in which high anxiety is repeatedly evoked—*either* by conflict *or* by noxious stimulation. The experimental neuroses were very resistant to ordinary extinction. Neurotic anxiety inhibited eating, but it could, reciprocally, be inhibited and in consequence progressively and lastingly eliminated if eating could be made to take place in the presence of relatively weak anxiety.

This finding suggested that reciprocal inhibition might be a general mechanism for psychotherapeutic effects. I later found that it could be successfully applied to human neuroses, using a variety of anxiety-inhibiting responses. Beneficial changes were noted in most patients with gratifying rapidity—a fact that I zealously brought to the attention of my psychiatric colleagues in Johannesburg at every opportunity. The usual reaction was outright disbelief, the most favorable benign tolerance. Despite this, from time to time, colleagues did send me cases with whom they were having no success; but even the demonstration of recovery or marked improvement in many of these did very little to raise my credibility in their eyes.

My first paper in an American psychiatric journal in 1954 elicited more than 100 requests for reprints, mainly from the United States. When I came to the United States in 1956 to spend a year at the Center for Advanced Study in the Behavioral Sciences at Stanford, I found more willingness to listen and consider than I was accustomed to in South Africa, mainly in psychologists, but also to a considerable extent in psychiatrists—in spite of their being much more strongly indoctrinated than their South African counterparts in the psychoanalytic viewpoint. This receptiveness fostered in me an extravagant optimism about the future of behavior therapy. When asked after a lecture at Stanford in 1956 when the behavioristic view of neuroses (which the questioner found irresistible) would be generally accepted, I replied—"Give it five years!"

Born 1932, Johannesburg, South Africa; B.A., M.A., Ph.D., University of Witwatersrand, South Africa, 1956, 1957, 1960; private practice, 1959–1963 and 1964–1966; Stanford University, 1963–1964; Behavior Therapy Institute, Sausalito, California, 1966–1967; Temple Medical School, 1967–1970; Yale University, 1970–1972; Rutgers University, since 1972.

The year was 1955. As a graduate student at the University of the Witwatersrand, in Johannesburg, South Africa, one of my senior lecturers, Mr. C. A. L. Warffemius, taught me to develop a critical perspective regarding all psychological theories, and to have respect only for notions that could be verified or disproved. He also arranged for Joseph Wolpe to present seminars and clinical demonstrations on his theories and methods of "reciprocal inhibition." In this way I was slowly won over to a "behavioral" perspective and began to feel disenchanted with psychodynamic theories and methods. I received my M.A. degree in 1957 and served as a predoctoral intern at the Marlborough Day Hospital in London, England. There the orientation was primarily Adlerian, and I saw several warm, deeply concerned therapists helping patients in quite remarkable ways which seemed to have little bearing on their psychodynamic underpinnings. While learning that Adler had been very "behavioral," I also fully experienced the value of treating people with unusual kindness and special sensitivity—an offshoot of Adlerian philosophy. But I grew impatient with the fact that so many clinicians overlooked significant behaviors while focusing on inferred dynamics.

In 1958 while in a clinical doctoral program at the University of the Witwatersrand and while obtaining further experience as an intern at Tara

Hospital in Johannesburg, the need to examine behavior in its own right became more and more evident to me. At the time, Wolpe was supervising my Ph.D. dissertation research, and I remarked to him that since we were interested primarily in changing maladaptive behavior rather than in treating "psyches," we should call ourselves *behavior therapists* rather than psychotherapists. Wolpe, however, was strongly opposed to giving up such a well-known and convenient term as "psychotherapy," a fact that he strongly emphasized in an article published in the May 1963 edition of *Behavior Research and Therapy*. Nevertheless, in 1958 I published a case study in the *South African Medical Journal* and used the terms "behavior therapy" and "behavior therapist" for the first time.

By 1960, I had received my Ph.D. and had established myself in full-time private practice in Johannesburg as a "behavior therapist." While several physicians were impressed by this time-limited, structured, and goal-oriented approach to therapy and referred more patients to me than I could handle, the psychiatric establishment remained extremely hostile and were often openly belligerent. One exception was Professor L. A. Hurst, who was head of the Department of Psychiatry in Johannesburg, but he was never able to obtain more than a part-time lectureship for me due to the pervasive antagonism of the establishment. Nevertheless, we formed a coterie of psychologists and psychiatrists interested in behavioral methods and techniques, and we held meetings at least once a month. Many graduate students in psychology and some residents in psychiatry attended these meetings, but they asked us not to mention this to any of their supervisors or formal teachers.

When I returned to South Africa in 1964 after spending a year at Stanford University, I offered to give free talks at various hospitals and clinics, as well as at the University of the Witwatersrand, on some of the latest research and on the academic and clinical areas of work that were ongoing at Stanford. Nobody was interested! One of the clinical heads of the Johannesburg Child Guidance Clinic actually said: "We are quite satisfied with our results and do not need further outside advice." However, I was asked to present a lecture in Johannesburg to the local branch of the South African Psychological Association. A large number of people were present (over 150 colleagues), but during the question and answer period it became obvious that the majority had attended mainly to offer disclaimers and to attack Wolpe (who had left South Africa in 1960). I left South Africa in 1966 to launch the Behavior Therapy Institute in Sausalito, California, and to join Wolpe at Temple University Medical School in 1967, where I was given a full professorship. But when I last visited South Africa in 1971, I was invited to give several talks, I was welcomed, warmly received, and many of my previous critics claimed me as their special pupil!

Born 1916, Berlin, Germany. Bachelor's and Ph.D. degrees, University of London. Left Germany 1934: Fellow of British Psychological Society and American Psychological Association; Institute of Psychiatry, The Bethlehem Royal Hospital and The Maudsley Hospital, University of London; visiting professor, University of Pennsylvania and University of California at Berkeley.

The classical development of the theories and methods which I elaborated on the basis of Herzberg's work was much delayed through the hostility of my psychiatric colleagues to both my anti-Freudian stand and to the notion of psychologists doing any kind of therapy. I could tell many horrifying stories of the efforts that were made to make it impossible for me to carry out any kind of work in this field, including efforts to close down the Department entirely, and a resolution by the governing body of the hospital that psychologists should not be allowed to carry out any form of treatment. This may explain the rather late date at which our early pioneering studies, many of which are reprinted in my book on *Behaviour Therapy and the Neurosis,* were published. Wolpe was of course more fortunate in having medical training and a private practice, so that he did not have the same difficulties as we in getting any patients at all to try our methods on. Usually what we got from some friendly consultants were cases so bad and so deteriorated that no one else could do anything with them; it still seems a miracle to me that we so often succeeded where everybody else had failed. Let me give you just one example of the kind of hostility we faced. One consultant who had been particularly hostile to the very notion of behaviour therapy one day offered us a patient for treatment; our surprise was short-lived when we found out that this was one of the least tractable cases ever to appear at the Maudsley Hospital, and that everything practically had been tried with him without success. It appeared clear that the consultant had merely referred him to us in order to be able to tell his registrars that behaviour therapy was quite useless as no success was expected. Oddly enough our methods were quite successful in a very short period of time in rehabilitating this patient, and there was every chance of his being cured when the consultant suddenly decided that enough was enough. He took the patient back into his own care, had him leucotomized and that was the end of that. This is just one example; I could give many more. Whenever I wrote a paper criticising Freudian methods, there would be a long queue of psychoanalytically minded consultants at the door of Sir Aubrey Lewis who was the Director of the Institute, complaining about that fellow Eysenck and demanding his dismissal! The position in England was probably much worse than in America where psychologists had long since gained the right of treating patients so that this was no longer an issue over there; here it was very much an issue although by now we have gained the point and my Department has about 250 patients under treatment under any one moment of time.

I recall first introducing the concept, and the term behaviour therapy, to a psychiatric audience at the meeting of the Royal Medical-Psychological Association in London. The talk, which was later published in the *Journal of Mental Science* in 1959, produced an uproar which almost became a lynching party; the Chairman, a Freudian himself, had to appeal to the participants to calm down and behave more courteously towards a guest! On another occasion, about 10 years previously, I read a paper at the General Annual Meeting of the British Psychological Society at Oxford, which was very well attended, on the Effect of Psychotherapy; this was later published in 1951 in the Journal of Clinical Psychology. At the end of the paper a Professor of Psychiatry got so enraged that he raced up the aisle shouting traitor, traitor, and tried to engage me in fisticuffs, which was rather unwise as he was both old and fat, whereas I had been boxing for the university team! Fortunately he was restrained by some friends who pointed out to him that rational arguments are not negated by displays of physical aggression.

Joel Stern

B. F Skinner

Born 1904, Susquehanna, Pennsylvania. B.A. Hamilton College 1926; M.A., Ph.D., Harvard 1930, 1931. Research fellowships, 1931–1936; University of Minnesota, 1936–1945; Indiana University, 1945–1946; Harvard University, since 1948.

I had been interested in the operant behavior of psychotic patients long before the Metropolitan State Hospital research began. In the middle thirties I was in contact with David Shakow and Saul Rosenzweig, who were then at Worcester State Hospital. I discussed some of my work before the staff at the Hospital and Shakow and Rosenzweig actually tested my Verbal Summator (which they preferred to call the tautaphone) on psychotic subjects. I believe they published two papers on their results. Together we considered setting up an operant laboratory and some construction was begun, but the carpenter on the job was himself a patient and went into a considerably less than manic phase and the work was never completed.

In the early fifties an enterprising dean at the Medical School, Henry Meadows, brought me into contact with several different people at the Medical School and two of these contacts were very productive. One of them led to the association between Dr. Peter Dews and my laboratory at Harvard and much of the early work on psychopharmacology using operant methods. The other was with Dr. Harry Solomon, head of Psychiatry, who later became Commissioner of Mental Health in Massachusetts. Dr. Milton Greenblatt, who succeeded him as commissioner, was also interested in the project at the time. Together they persuaded the administration of the Metropolitan State Hospital to make some space available in the basement of one of the buildings and to provide a few back ward patients. Ogden Lindsley, then a graduate student in the Department of Psychology, came into the project almost at the very beginning and was very largely responsible for all that happened at Met. State. We began with two rooms with modified vending machines, but the project was greatly expanded and a photograph of the eventual laboratory with Dr. Lindsley appears as Figure 20, page 154, of the third edition of my *Cumulative Record.*

Dr. Lindsley surveyed available reinforcers and explored a number of schedules of reinforcement on a number of different types of psychotics. A fairly clear picture emerged of differences between normal and psychotic behavior together with considerable evidence that when contingencies of reinforcement are clear-cut, the behavior of psychotics is brought under effective control. Lindsley is a better authority on these results than I.

Sidney W. Bijou

Born 1908, Baltimore, Maryland; B. S. University of Florida, 1933; M. A. Columbia University, 1937; Ph.D. University of Iowa, 1941; post-doctoral work, Harvard University, 1961. University of Washington at Seattle, 1948–1965; University of Illinois at Urbana-Champaign, 1965–1975; University of Arizona at Tucson and professor emeritus, University of Illinois, since 1975.

In the summer of 1955 I was exploring some simple schedules of reinforcement in normal preschool children, using a variety of contingently delivered trinkets and bits of candies and cookies. The research was being conducted in a newly designed and equipped trailer laboratory at the University of Washington. In the far wall of the laboratory room as one entered was a large one-way glass, and beneath it a lever for responding (actually an O'cedar mop handle). Above the lever was a recessed light bulb and below the lever was a small opening for delivering "goodies." Also in the room were a juvenile chair, placed in front of the lever; a free play toy on a table to one side; and a young woman sitting behind a partition near the wall opposite the apparatus wall. (She had no role in the studies. Her only function was to make the child feel that he or she was not alone in the room.)

A child's responses on the lever were carried to a circuit which was programmed so that each reinforced response was accompanied by a light flash and a short buzz from the dispenser motor, indicating that a goodie was being delivered. The experimenter operated behind the wall with the one-way glass and apparatus. The trailer was parked alongside a private day care center which provided—with parental consent—the children for the study.

One day I invited Bill Verplanck, a visiting professor in the Department of Psychology at the University of Washington, to join me in observing the performances of the children. He was impressed with what he saw: children responding in a fairly orderly fashion to fixed and variable ratio and interval schedules of reinforcement. I say fairly orderly because now and again there were short breaks in responding that were not easily accounted for by the experimental conditions.

About halfway through the session, Verplanck suggested that we explore the shaping of operant behavior. We decided to see whether we could establish pulling the cord of the window shade on the window at the far side of the room, which was about fourteen feet away from the wall where the lever was situated. The procedure consisted of hand-shaping successive approximations to the final task, i.e., reinforcing getting off the chair, moving farther and farther away from the lever, raising the hand, grasping and then pulling on the window shade cord. Initial movements away from the lever were a bit slow in developing because each time the child was reinforced for moving away, he had to turn back or run back to get the goodie lodged in the receptacle. In a relatively short time, however, the response was well established: after snatching up a goodie, the child would run across the room, pull on the shade cord, and as soon as he heard the motor buzz, he would dash back to the receptacle and retrieve the goodie.

This was an amazing display! It had much more of an impact on me than our findings on schedules of reinforcement in children (e.g., *Psychological Reports*, 1957, **3**, 243–250). The general findings on schedules were that children, like infra-human subjects, could, with training, coordinate their operant behavior with the timing of reinforcing contingencies. But delivering reinforcers contingent on the topography of successive behaviors clearly showed how new operant behavior—any kind of new operant behavior—is probably established. I had just witnessed a dramatic demonstration of what we had for years been telling our students in introductory psychology, namely, that the implication of a scientific analysis of behavior is predication and control of individual behavior.

I found myself overwhelmed with thoughts about the ethical problems that could emanate from applying behavior principles to the development of children, so much so that for several years I kept this troubling observation from my colleagues and students alike. But gradually, as I began to realize that, after all, the social and ethical problems of a scientific psychology are no different than those of a scientific biology, chemistry, or physics, I freely told the story. I am confident now, as I was not in 1955, that society, through its professional organizations and its governmental agencies, must evaluate the implications of behavior applications and must institute safeguards to assure that practices in the home, school, clinic, and community are always oriented to the enhancement of the individuals within the context of their social structure.

STATEMENT 8 · FRED S. KELLER

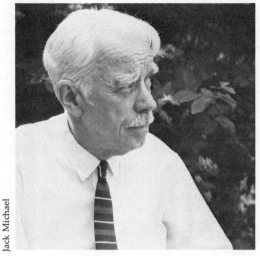

Jack Michael

Fred S. Keller

Born 1899, Rural Grove, New York; B. S. Tufts College, 1926; M. A. Harvard University, 1928; Ph.D Harvard, 1931; Colgate University, 1931–1938; Columbia University, 1938–1964; Arizona State University, 1961–1967; Institute for Behavioral Research, Maryland, 1967–1968; Western Michigan University, 1968–1973; Georgetown University, 1973–1975; since 1976; retired.

During World War II, with the help of numerous colleagues and pupils, I developed a "code-voice" method for teaching men and women to receive International Morse code. This method provided that every "copying" response by every student to a Morse-code signal be followed within a few seconds by a voiced identification of the signal just transmitted. I described the technique, in 1943, as "a modification of the well-known procedures of 'paired associates' and 'regular reinforcement'"—a technique which has recently been characterized as a "premature application" of reinforcement theory to practical affairs. However premature it may have been, it was quite successful as a method and found later use with several other simple skills.

This instance of "behavior modification" had significance for me, but I do not think of it as in the mainstream of the movement. My major role was of another sort, that of a catalyst or promoter. As a teacher of reinforcement theory, Skinner style, to undergraduates at Columbia University, and as co-author (with W. N. Schoenfeld) of a textbook for those students, I was always on the lookout for applications of the system to practical affairs —clinical, pharmacological, military, industrial, or educational—to anything that might impress my pupils with the "value" of our science. An effective classroom demonstration dealt with the generalization of Morse-code signals; in two laboratory sessions we taught Braille to all the students

33

with a modification of the code-voice method; in one lecture I discussed the principles of differentiation and discrimination as they bore upon the training of "deaf-mutes" to speak; and I often encouraged students to attempt "extrapolations" of their own. One especially enterprising student, Lewis Robins, developed an excellent method of training Navy personnel to type.

In general, our little group of reinforcement theorists at Columbia showed great caution in interpretation and great restriction in our practical reach. Our emphasis was always on laboratory research rather than the realm of application, no matter how much we enjoyed the latter. We limited ourselves to simple problems and simple explanations. I can still remember my concern, in 1953, when Skinner treated wage and salary schedules as instances of fixed-interval and fixed-ratio reinforcement; and for a long time I worried about the nature of the reinforcer in the code-voice method!

REFERENCES

American Psychiatric Association. *Task Force Report 5: Behavior therapy in psychiatry.* Washington, D.C.: American Psychiatric Association, 1973.

Astin, A. W. The functional autonomy of psychotherapy. *American Psychologist,* 1961, **16,** 75–78.

Bandura, A. *Principles of behavior modification.* New York: Holt, Rinehart and Winston, 1969.

Beck, A. Cognitive therapy: Nature and relation to behavior therapy. *Behavior Therapy,* 1970, **1,** 184–200.

Bijou, S. W. Methodology for an experimental analysis of child behavior. *Psychological Reports,* 1957, **3,** 243–250.

Bijou, S. W. *Child development: The basic stage of early childhood.* Englewood Cliffs, N.J.: Prentice-Hall, 1976.

Bijou, S. W., & Baer, D. M. *Child development: A systematic and empirical theory,* Vol. 1. Englewood Cliffs, N.J.: Prentice-Hall, 1961.

Bijou, S. W., & Baer, D. M. *Child development: The universal stage of infancy,* Vol. 2. New York: Appleton-Century-Crofts, 1965.

Bijou, S. W., & Redd, W. H. Behavior therapy for children. *American Handbook of Psychiatry,* Vol. 5. New York: Basic Books, 1975.

Cartwright, D. E. Effectiveness of psychotherapy: A critique of the spontaneous remission argument. *Journal of Counseling Psychology,* 1955, **2,** 290–296.

Dimmick, F. L., Ludlow, N., & Whiteman, A. A study of "experimental neurosis" in cats. *Journal of Comparative Psychology,* 1939, **28,** 39.

D'Zurilla, T., & Goldfried, M. Problem solving and behavior modification. *Journal of Abnormal Psychology,* 1971, **78,** 107–126.

Ellis, A. *Reason and emotion in psychotherapy.* New York: Stuart, 1962.

Eysenck, H. J. Training in clinical psychology: An English point of view. *American Psychologist,* 1949, **4,** 173–176.

Eysenck, H. J. Function and training of the clinical psychologist. *Journal of Mental Science,* 1950, **96,** 710–725.

Eysenck, H. J. The effects of psychotherapy: An evaluation. *Journal of Consulting Psychology,* 1952, **16,** 319–324.

Eysenck, H. J. Learning theory and behavior therapy. *Journal of Mental Science,* 1959, **105,** 61–75.

Eysenck, H. J. *Behaviour therapy and the neurosis.* London: Pergamon, 1960.

Freedman, D. A. Various etiologies of the schizophrenic syndrome. *Diseases of the Nervous System,* 1958, **19,** 1–6.

Garcia, J., & Koelling, R. A. Relation of cue to consequence in avoidance learning. *Psychonomic Science,* 1966, **4,** 123–124.

Goldfried, M. R., & Davison, G. C. *Clinical behavior therapy.* New York: Holt, Rinehart and Winston, 1976.

Holland, J. G. *Behavior modification for prisoners, patients, and other people as a prescription for the planned society.* Unpublished address to the Eastern Psychological Association, 1974.

Homme, L. E. Perspectives in psychology: XXIV. Control of coverants, the operants of the mind. *Psychological Record,* 1965, **15,** 501–511.

Jellison, J. A. The frequency and general mode of inquiry of research in music therapy, 1952–1972. *Council for Research in Music Education Bulletin,* 1973, **35,** 1–8.

Jones, M. C. A laboratory study of fear: The case of Peter. *Journal of Genetic Psychology,* 1924, **31,** 308–315(a).

Jones, M. C. The elimination of children's fears. *Journal of Experimental Psychology,* 1924, **7,** 383–390(b).

Jones, M. C. The development of early behavior patterns in young children. *Journal of Genetic Psychology,* 1926, **33,** 577–585.

Jones, M. C. A 1924 pioneer looks at behavior therapy. *Journal of Behavior Therapy and Experimental Psychiatry,* 1975, **6,** 181–187.

Kanfer, F. H., & Phillips, J. S. A survey of current behavior therapies and a proposal for classification. In C. M. Franks (Ed.), *Behavior therapy: Appraisal and status.* New York: McGraw-Hill, 1969.

Kanfer, F. H., & Saslow, G. Behavioral diagnosis. In C. M. Franks (Ed.), *Behavior therapy: Appraisal and status.* New York: McGraw-Hill, 1969.

Keller, F. S. A personal course in psychology. In R. Ulrich, T. Stachnik, & J. Mabry (Eds.), *Control of human behavior,* Vol. 1. Glenview, Ill.: Scott, Foresman, 1966, pp. 91–93.

Kostlan, A. A method for the empirical study of psychodiagnosis. *Journal of Consulting Psychology,* 1954, **18,** 83–88.

Krasner, L. *The utopian theme in the history and future of behavior therapy.* Psi Chi Invited Address, Eastern Psychological Association. Atlantic City, N.J., April 1970.

Krasner, L. On the death of behavior modification: Some comments from a mourner. *American Psychologist,* 1976, **31,** 387–388.

Krasner, L., & Ullmann, L. P. *Research in behavior modification—New developments and implications.* New York: Holt, Rinehart and Winston, 1965.

Krasner, L., & Ullmann, L. P. *Behavior influence and personality.* New York: Holt, Rinehart and Winston, 1973.

Lazarus, A. A. New methods of psychotherapy: A case study. *South African Medical Journal,* 1958, **32,** 660–663.

Lazarus, A. A. The elimination of children's phobias

by deconditioning. *Medical Proceedings* (South Africa), 1959, **5,** 261–265.

Lazarus, A. A. *Behavior therapy and beyond.* New York: McGraw-Hill, 1971.

Lindsley, O. R., Skinner, B. F., & Solomon, H. C. *Studies in behavior therapy. Status Report I.* Waltham, Mass.: Metropolitan State Hospital, 1953.

Locke, E. A. Is "behavior therapy" behavioristic? (An analysis of Wolpe's psychotherapeutic methods). In C. M. Franks & G. T. Wilson (Eds.), *Annual review of behavior therapy,* 1973. New York: Brunner/Mazel, 1973.

Lorr, M., Klett, C. J., & McNair, D. M. *Syndromes of psychosis.* New York: Macmillan, 1963.

Luborsky, L. A note on Eysenck's article "The effects of psychotherapy: An evaluation." *British Journal of Psychology,* 1954, **45,** 129–131.

Macfarlane, J. W. Perspectives on personality consistency and change from the Guidance Study. In M. C. Jones, N. Bayley, J. W. Macfarlane, & M. P. Honzik (Eds.), *The course of human development.* New York: Wiley, 1971.

Madsen, C. K., Greer, R. D., & Madsen, C. H. *Research in music behavior: Modifying music behavior in the classroom.* New York: Teachers College Press, Columbia University, 1975.

Masserman, J. H. *Behavior and neurosis.* Chicago: University of Chicago Press, 1943.

Meichenbaum, D. Cognitive behavior modification. In J. T. Spence, R. C. Carson, & J. W. Thibaut (Eds.), *Behavioral approaches to therapy.* Morristown, N.J.: General Learning Press, 1976.

Mowrer, O. H., & Mowrer, W. A. Enuresis: A method for its study and treatment. *American Journal of Orthopsychiatry,* 1938, **8,** 436–447.

Paul, G. L. Outcome of systematic desensitization. I: Background and procedures, and uncontrolled reports of individual treatment. In C. M. Franks (Ed.), *Behavior therapy: Appraisal and status.* New York: McGraw-Hill, 1969.

Rachman, S. Spontaneous remission and latent learning. *Behaviour Research and Therapy,* 1963, **1,** 133–137.

Rescorla, R. A. Predictability and number of pairings in Pavlovian fear conditioning. *Psychonomic Science,* 1966, **4,** 383–384.

Rescorla, R. A., & LoLordo, V. M. Inhibition and avoidance behavior. *Journal of Comparative and Physiological Psychology,* 1965, **59,** 406–412.

Rimm, D. C., & Masters, J. C. *Behavior therapy—Techniques and empirical findings.* New York: Academic Press, 1974.

Rogers, C. R. *On becoming a person: A therapist's view of psychotherapy.* Boston: Houghton Mifflin, 1961.

Rosenhan, D. L. On being sane in insane places. *Science,* 1973, **179,** 250–258.

Schmidt, H. O., & Fonda, C. P. The reliability of psy-

chiatric diagnosis: A new look. *Journal of Abnormal and Social Psychology,* 1956, **52,** 262–267.

Sidman, M. *Tactics of scientific research.* New York: Basic Books, 1960.

Skinner, B. F. *The behavior of organisms.* New York: Appleton-Century-Crofts, 1938.

Skinner, B. F. *Science and human behavior.* New York: Macmillan, 1953.

Skinner, B. F. *Contingencies of reinforcement: A theoretical analysis.* New York: Appleton-Century-Crofts, 1969.

Skinner, B. F. *Cumulative record,* 3rd ed. New York: Appleton-Century-Crofts, 1972.

Skinner, B. F. *About behaviorism.* New York: Knopf, 1974.

Smith, M. L., & Glass, G. V. Meta-analysis of psychotherapy outcome studies. *American Psychologist,* 1977, **32,** 752–760.

Ullmann, L. P., & Krasner, L. *Case studies in behavior modification.* New York: Holt, Rinehart and Winston, 1965.

Ullmann, L. P., & Krasner, L. *A psychological approach to abnormal behavior.* Englewood Cliffs, N.J.: Prentice-Hall, 1969.

Ullmann, L. P., & Krasner, L. *A psychological approach to abnormal behavior.* 2nd ed. Englewood Cliffs, N.J.: Prentice-Hall, 1975.

U.S. Congress. Individual Rights and the Federal Role in Behavior Modification. Prepared by the Staff of the Subcommittee on Constitutional Rights of the Committee on the Judiciary, U.S. Senate, 93rd Cong., November 1974. Washington, D.C.: U.S. Government Printing Office.

Watson, J. B. *Psychology from the standpoint of a behaviorist.* Philadelphia: Lippincott, 1919.

Watson, J. B. *Behaviorism.* New York: People's Institute, 1924.

Watson, R. I. The experimental tradition and clinical psychology. In A. J. Bachrach (Ed.), *Experimental foundations of clinical psychology.* New York: Basic Books, 1962.

Wolf, M. M., Risley, T., & Mees, H. Application of operant conditioning procedures to the behavior problems of an autistic child. *Behaviour Research and Therapy,* 1964, **1,** 305–312.

Wolpe, J. *Psychotherapy by reciprocal inhibition.* Stanford, Calif.: Stanford University Press, 1958.

Wolpe, J. *The practice of behavior therapy.* New York: Pergamon Press, 1969.

Woodworth, R. S. Obituary of John Broadus Watson. *American Journal of Psychology,* 1959, **72,** 301–310.

Yates, A. J. *Behavior therapy.* New York: Wiley, 1970.

Zigler, E., & Phillips, L. Psychiatric diagnosis: A critique. *Journal of Abnormal and Social Psychology,* 1961, **63,** 607–618.

two

BASIC PRINCIPLES OF BEHAVIOR

The domain of behavior modification has been broadened; radical behaviorism and the learning/conditioning approaches are no longer dominant. But, as we stressed in Chapter 1, the new approaches do not reject these earlier points of view. Rather, they seek to expand them. And although the specific methods vary widely across approaches, all rely heavily on basic principles of respondent and operant conditioning. Behavioral psychologists have employed concepts and principles from respondent conditioning in the treatment of anxiety-related problems such as phobias and maladaptive emotional responses. Even though many researchers (for instance, Locke, 1971; London, 1972) question the validity of the conditioning assumptions of certain behavioral techniques, the direct application of respondent conditioning techniques has been enormously effective (Paul, 1969). Operant conditioning principles have been applied to almost every type of human problem from energy conservation to sexual dysfunction. They are, in fact, the foundation of many behavior modification programs.

To ensure that the student understands the processes assumed to be crucial in programs of behavioral intervention, in this chapter we will review the basic principles of respondent and operant conditioning and consider some of the recent philosophical and experimental advances in the area of learning theory. We will also consider cognitive factors in behavior modification.

RESPONDENT CONDITIONING

Floyd, a rather well-fed and pampered cat, sits on the kitchen floor waiting for his supper. When the electric can opener starts making noises, he begins licking his chops; within a few seconds he is eating his supper.

Rachel is sitting in the doctor's office, and the nurse cleans her arm with alcohol so he can give her a shot. As the nurse works, Rachel smells the alcohol and starts to feel nauseous and weak.

Involuntary responses

Tom is listening to his transistor radio as he tries to do his homework. Suddenly, he feels his stomach churning, notices that his hands are sweating, and for a second wonders what's wrong. Then he realizes that the last time he heard the song now playing was the night he was in the horrible auto accident with his father. Tom turns to a different station.

In each of these examples there is an "automatic" reaction to a stimulus that in itself is neutral, but that as a result of certain experiences has acquired important meaning. The sound of the can opener signals food, the scent of the rubbing alcohol means a shot in the arm, and the song on the radio is a potent reminder of an accident. For Floyd, the previously neutral stimulus means something good, whereas for Rachel and Tom, the important stimuli cue pain and danger. The process by which previously neutral stimuli come to elicit reflexes is the subject of **respondent condi-**

37

tioning (also referred to as **classical** or **Pavlovian conditioning**).

Pavlov's Original Work

During the early 1900s the Russian physiologist I. P. Pavlov was studying the secretion of various stomach fluids. He was especially interested in the mechanisms that regulate the production of saliva in reaction to food. In the course of his research, he encountered what he initially considered an annoying phenomenon. As the dogs that he used as subjects became familiar with the laboratory procedures, they began to salivate "prematurely," before they ingested the food. The mere sight of food, the rattle of the food dish, and even Pavlov's entering the laboratory would elicit salivation. Pavlov called this premature salivation "psychic" secretion. However, he quickly reconsidered the importance of this annoying behavior when he discovered the responses were as regular as the processes he originally set out to investigate.

Pavlov's (1927) research on respondent conditioning is now classic. A dog was held in a harness and isolated as much as possible from extraneous stimulation. With the dog comfortably quiet in the apparatus, Pavlov struck a tuning fork that produced a tone and then gave the dog food. In order to record the salivation reflex, he inserted a small tube into the dog's cheek; it drained saliva into a cup. Pavlov repeated the procedure many times. At first, the dog salivated only when the food was actually placed in its mouth. But with repeated pairings of the tone and the food, salivation occurred immediately after the tone and before food was placed in its mouth. Finally, after many trials, the presentation of the tone alone elicited the salivation reflex.

Pavlov believed that through the repeated pairing of a neutral stimulus (the tone) and the naturally eliciting stimulus (food in the mouth), a neural connection was formed between the neural stimulus and the reflex (salivation). He called this process conditioning.

The terms "conditioned" and "unconditioned stimulus" and "response" are used to identify the critical components in the process described by Pavlov. An **unconditioned stimulus (US)** is a stimulus that naturally elicits a particular response, the **unconditioned response (UR).** The classic examples of the US and UR have just been mentioned: food in the mouth (US) elicits salivation (UR). Another example is the knee-jerk reflex. A tap just below the kneecap (US) elicits a jerk of the leg (UR). The response to the US is involuntary and automatic, occurring without any cognitive mediation. When a bright light is flashed in your eyes (US), you do not *decide* to constrict the pupils (UR); it simply happens. In fact, the UR is sometimes referred to as the unconditioned *reflex,* to emphasize the reflexive, involuntary nature of the response to the US. Cognitive factors can, in some instances, modify the nature of the UR: when tapped below the kneecap, you can suppress the natural response by holding your leg rigid; or you can choose to kick along with the reflex, thereby increasing the response. But for the most part, higher cognitive processes play little or no role in the US-UR relationship.

The **conditioned stimulus (CS)** is an initially neutral stimulus that consistently precedes the presentation of the US. In Pavlov's studies the sound of the tuning fork was the CS, since it was consistently followed by the US, food. The CS, through its repeated association with the US, eventually comes to elicit a response that is almost identical in form and intensity to the UR. This new response, the **conditioned response (CR),** is then elicited when the CS is presented alone, without the US. Conditioning has occurred.

Pavlov, like many experimental psychologists, believed that his discovery held the key to understanding all learning. His position was that we are all born with a sensitivity to a certain set of unconditioned stimuli and that our reactions to these stimuli are innate (for example, salivation to food, withdrawal from extreme heat). And as we go through life, all our learning involves the acquisition of more and more conditioned stimuli. According to Pavlov, even the most complex mental processes, such as problem solving and creating great art, would some day be proved to be simply a long series of unconditioned and conditioned reflexes (Rachlin, 1976). Like most grandiose predictions based on theory, however, it has not worked out that way.

Tests of Pavlov's Formulations

Many of Pavlov's original formulations regarding the critical components and mechanisms in the respondent conditioning process have been challenged, for the process does not appear to be as automatic and as pervasive as was once thought.

One major change has been the reconceptualization of the role of CS-US pairings in the conditioning process. In a series of studies, Robert A. Rescorla and his colleagues (Rescorla, 1966, 1967; Rescorla & LoLordo, 1965) found that the strength of the CS is a function of the contingency of the CS-US relation, rather than the number of pairings, as Pavlov originally proposed. In Rescorla's research, a CS that reliably predicted the occurrence of a US (100 percent correlation) acquired greater strength than another CS that was paired with the US a greater number of times but not as reliably (that is, less than 100 percent correlation). As the predictive value of the CS diminished (that is, as the correlation approaches zero) the strength of the CS decreased, regardless of the number of pairings. Rather than being an automatic, neurological linkage of the CS and US, respondent conditioning appears to involve information processing. The CS gains stimulus value as a function of the information it relays, that is, according to the accuracy of its predictions.

Another challenge to Pavlov's original notion of conditioning as an automatic process is the research on differences in associability of stimuli. Pavlov believed that conditioning occurred whenever any two stimuli were repeatedly paired closely in time. That is, according to Pavlov, any neutral stimulus could function as a CS with any US. But this is not the case. There are definite limitations in the kinds of stimuli that can be paired together to produce conditioning. In what has now become a classic study, John Garcia and Robert Koelling (1966) found that rats quickly learned to avoid a gustatory CS that was paired with sickness (produced by X rays) but failed to learn to avoid an auditory CS associated with sickness. When the US was electric shock, the animals learned to avoid the CS if it was auditory but not if it was gustatory. That is, auditory CSs worked with electric shock as the US but not with sickness as the US; gustatory CSs worked with sickness as the US but not with shock as the US.

The third major modification in the Pavlovian theory of behavior is the rejection of the notion that all learning can be explained by simple CS-US pairings. Learning theorists readily acknowledge an operant component in many respondent conditioning situations. In many cases, the organism is clearly rewarded by the environment for acquiring a CR, especially when it somehow protects the organism from pain. When the CS predicts aversive stimulation, the CR often makes the US less aversive and is thereby reinforced by the avoidance of pain (as in the example of Benjamin, below). This shift in thinking has resulted in a blurring of the distinction between respondent and operant conditioning.

OPERANT CONDITIONING

A fourth-grade student gets a star beside her name for scoring 100 on a spelling test. That night she diligently studies the words for the next day.

It is the fifth time John R. has phoned Susan M. to ask her for a date. She's perfectly pleasant, as usual. But, also as usual, she tells him she has a previous engagement that she can't get out of. It is the last time John phones Susan.

Two-year-old Benjamin is playing in the kitchen. He touches the hot stove and is burned. He does not touch the stove again.

These situations are all examples of the **law of effect.** In each case, the probability that the individual's behavior will occur again in similar circumstances increases or decreases depending upon the consequences of his or her actions. If the consequences are pleasurable or in some way adaptive, the behavior will be strengthened; if the consequences are unpleasant or maladaptive, the behavior will be weakened. This principle is an obvious fact of life.

Thorndike's Law of Effect

The law of effect proposed by Edward L. Thorndike in 1898 clearly shows the influence of the Darwinian notions of "survival of the fittest" and "natural selection by successful adaptation." Thorndike based his law on the results of research on problem solving in which a hungry dog or cat was confined in a small box and had to get out of it to get a piece of food. On the top of the box was mounted a latch or string that had to be manipulated in order to open the trap door permitting access to the food. Thorndike observed that each animal eventually learned how to escape. Each time the animal was placed in the box, it would solve the problem more quickly, until finally it acquired the successful response and could get to the food as soon as it was placed in the box. Thorndike was impressed by the gradualness of the learning process: irrelevant, unsuccessful responses dropped away and successful responses were strengthened. He believed that the animal first enters the box with a hierarchy of stimulus-response (S-R) connections and tries out various responses until a successful one is found. Then one connection between the stimulus (that is, the problem box) and the successful response is strengthened and stamped in because it is rewarded by quick access to the food. Unsuccessful connections are weakened and stamped out because they are not associated with food.

Skinner's Reformulation

Although B. F. Skinner (1938) agreed with Thorndike's observations of the powerful effect of environmental consequences on behavior, he rejected Thorndike's notion that learning involves the strengthening of stimulus-response connections. Skinner's position was straightforward: Why introduce hypothetical mechanisms that researchers cannot observe and that do not aid their predictions regarding subsequent behavior? Skinner's criterion for understanding behavior was the accurate control and prediction of the future probability of that behavior. Since Thorndike's stimulus-response connections did not facilitate the experimenter's ability to control behavior, it was considered by Skinner to be excess baggage. Skinner's position was a real departure from traditional S-R learning theory and a clear example of radical behaviorism.

Skinner argued that environmental consequences affect behavior directly regardless of hypothesized stimulus-response connections. To study the relation of behavior and its conse-

quences, he devised an apparatus that permitted an animal to make an easily measurable response which could be followed by predetermined events (food, shock, and so on). His procedures and apparatus are as famous as Pavlov's. A food-deprived rat or pigeon was placed in a small cage in which was mounted a bar or button (this apparatus is often called the Skinner box). Depending upon how the apparatus was programmed to operate, a press of the lever or button produced small amounts of food. As with Thorndike's puzzle box, the animal quickly learned how to get food. But Skinner's work extended Thorndike's by showing that the animal's behavior was controlled by the **contingencies of reinforcement.** For example, an animal would press the lever rapidly when food was delivered according to how many times it pressed the lever, and not so rapidly when the food was delivered according to the time elapsed since the last response.

Basic Principles

The principles of operant conditioning specify the relationship between behavior and environmental events that are presumed to control that behavior. Although most research has focused on the effects of consequences, antecedent events are also crucial in the control of behavior. Ogden Lindsley (1964) has delineated four components for what behaviorists call the **functional analysis of behavior.** They are (1) the antecedent stimulus or stimulus setting in which the behavior occurs, (2) the actual behavior of interest, (3) the contingencies of reinforcement, and (4) the environmental events (for instance, rewards and punishment) that follow the behavior. To this list many behaviorists (for instance, Bijou & Baer, 1966) add what J. R. Kantor (1959) calls **setting factors** or **events.** These factors refer to physiological states of the organism (for example, conditions of satiation or deprivation) that affect the functioning of antecedent and consequent events.

The remainder of this chapter will be devoted to a discussion of the research on the role of each of these components in controlling behavior. It is important to remember that in operant conditioning research, as well as in behavior modification for that matter, terms are *functionally defined.*

That is, a stimulus or an event is considered in terms of its functional properties for the individual—what it means or signifies to the individual. For example, for one child a school playground may be an aversive stimulus, one that produces strong escape and avoidance reactions because during a previous recess period he may have fallen off a swing, or been ridiculed by his classmates; for another child the playground may be a pleasant place where she can have freedom and fun. Although a stimulus may be assumed to have fixed physical properties (at least for practical purposes), its functional properties vary across individuals depending on their past interactions with it and the circumstances at the time of analysis. In principle, the only way to determine what an object, a person, or a situation "means" to the individual is to observe and analyze that person's behavior in relation to it.

Reinforcing Consequences. Consequent events are defined in terms of the effects they have on behavior. *Reinforcement* refers to any procedure whereby the presentation **(positive reinforcement)** or withdrawal **(negative reinforcement)** of a stimulus following a response results in an increase in the frequency and/or probability of occurrence of that response. Psychologists do not claim that they necessarily know what the reinforcing stimuli are in a particular situation. In practice they might be pretty sure why most of us engage in simple behaviors like eating and sleeping, but when it comes to more complex behaviors they do not always know. For example, the behavioral psychologist may not know why a particular child plays with his blocks. It could be because his mother gives him praise and attention whenever he plays quietly, or because his mother scolds him for *not* playing with the blocks, or simply because he finds them interesting. But behavioral psychologists would argue that a child plays with blocks because such play yields pleasant consequences or removes aversive ones. Such consequences are known as **reinforcers,** events which increase the likelihood that the behaviors they follow will be repeated. Thus, reinforcement can involve either obtaining something pleasant or eliminating something aversive.

Of course, some things are reinforcers for almost everyone—such as food, water, and sex. These have been called **primary,** or **unconditioned, reinforcers.** A stimulus that functions as a primary reinforcer does not depend upon special training to acquire its reinforcing value. However, its value is rarely constant; it varies depending upon such setting factors as satiation and deprivation. For example, a child might be eager to do a favor for her mother if her mother will give her a piece of gum for it, but after she has filled her mouth and pockets with Dubble Bubble she will not be so willing any more. But if, for some reason, she were deprived of gum for a period of time, it is likely that it would gain reinforcing value.

There are also reinforcers, such as money, grades, praise, and fame, that are not automatically reinforcing but have acquired reinforcing value because of the individual's learning history. These are called **secondary,** or **conditioned, reinforcers.** By their repeated association with primary reinforcers or with other conditioned reinforcers they become reinforcers in themselves. Because we all share certain common experiences and biological equipment, there are certain stimuli, such as money and high grades, that become reinforcers for most of us. But there are exceptions. Some people really do not care about grades; what is more, many of us have idiosyncratic conditioned reinforcers. Because of differences in personal history, tastes, and "chemistry," there is no list of "universal" reinforcers. A powerful reinforcer for one person may be of no value for another. A fourteen-year-old boy may find the ear-splitting sound of hard rock very pleasant and may work after school in order to buy records, whereas his forty-five-year-old father may find the sounds aversive and spend his hard-earned money on soundproofing. For the fourteen-year-old the music is reinforcement; for the father, it is punishment. Likewise, Brahms and a glass of sherry may be reinforcement for the father and punishment for the son.

The opportunity to engage in certain behaviors can also serve as a positive reinforcer. In a series of laboratory studies, David Premack (1959, 1965) discovered that behaviors performed by an individual at a relatively high frequency when given the opportunity to choose among various activities will serve as reinforcers for behaviors performed at a lower frequency. In one experiment, Premack first gave children free access to candy and pinball machines; he found that many of the children spent more time playing with the pinball machines than they did eating candy. He then tested his hypothesis that a higher-frequency behavior (playing pinball) could serve to reinforce a lower-frequency behavior (eating candy) by allowing the children to play with the machines only after they had eaten a certain amount of candy. Under these contingencies, the frequency of eating candy increased. The behavior that occurred at a higher frequency functioned as a reinforcer for the lower-frequency behavior. This phenomenon has come to be called the **Premack principle.**

Behavior can also be strengthened (reinforced) by the removal of unpleasant or aversive consequences. Putting on a coat in the winter is reinforced by the elimination of cold, turning down the stereo is reinforced by the termination of the loud noise, and going to the dentist is reinforced by the relief of a toothache. This process is called negative reinforcement because the removal of a stimulus contingent upon a behavior increases the probability that the behavior will be emitted in the future. Perhaps because the stimulus removed is aversive, many people confuse negative reinforcement with punishment. They are *not* the same.

Punishing Consequences. Punishment comes in many forms and from many sources. If we break one of nature's laws we often get hurt, and if we violate society's laws and are caught we may be fined or imprisoned. There are also less obvious forms of punishment such as sarcastic comments from others, failure, and humiliation. Gasoline taxes, import tariffs, and fines have the same effect. The negative side of the law of effect involves either loss of something good or the occurrence of something bad; in all cases, the result is to discourage certain behaviors.

Like the term "reinforcement," the term "punishment" is defined in terms of the effects it has on behavior—that is, it is functionally defined. Punishment does not refer to a specific set of procedures (for instance, spankings and reprimands),

but rather to the reduction in the frequency of response by the presentation or withdrawal of a stimulus following the occurrence of that response. Therefore, like the concepts of positive and negative reinforcers, we have the concepts of positive and negative punishers. **Positive punishment** refers to the contingent presentation of a stimulus to suppress a response. This is the familiar type of punishment we all know and probably use: reprimands, spanking, and natural consequent events like getting burned by touching a hot stove. Positive punishers are, for all intents and purposes, aversive stimuli. **Negative punishment** is the contingent removal of a stimulus to suppress a response. The term **response cost** is often used to describe the withdrawal or loss of material reinforcers contingent upon a behavior. Parking fines, taxes, and tariffs (that is, the loss of money) and the loss of privileges for misbehaving are all examples of response costs.

Timeout—or, to be technically correct, timeout from positive reinforcement—is the most popular form of negative punishment. The term refers to removal of the opportunity to obtain positive reinforcement for a certain period of time. In laboratory research timeout often involves the equipment being turned off for a fixed period of time contingent upon an animal emitting an incorrect response. As we will discuss later in the book, timeout is incorporated into many behavior modification programs. For example, a teacher might withdraw attention from a child when the child misbehaves, or may place the child in the corner or in the hall until the child "quiets down." When he or she is in the corner, the child misses an opportunity to earn reinforcement. In order for timeout to be effective, the situation from which the individual is withdrawn must be enjoyable or "reinforcing." That is, timeout must mean the loss of something "good." Unfortunately, for many children being put in the corner or out in the hall is more reinforcing than being in the classroom. In such cases, rather than being a punisher, the procedure is a reinforcer. Therefore, before a therapist or teacher incorporates a timeout contingency, he or she must determine its function for the individual being treated.

Another issue that has been debated is whether timeout actually involves the absence of positive reinforcement contingencies or the presentation of aversive stimuli. Of course, this depends on the person who is being subjected to timeout. For example, being in a small room or seated in the corner for 5 minutes may be neutral for one person, aversive for another, and pleasant for a third. In some programs aversive stimuli have been intentionally introduced along with the timeout (for example, loud noise in the timeout area, no illumination) in order to increase the punishing effect of the procedure. Although the addition of aversive stimuli is not incompatible with timeout, it is *not* included under the original definition of the procedure.

Figure 2–1 specifies the operations we have been discussing. It is important to stress that reinforcement always refers to procedures whose effect is to *strengthen* behavior—to increase frequency and future probability of occurrence. Punishment, on the other hand, always refers to procedures whose effect is to *weaken* behavior—to reduce frequency and future probability of occurrence. Positive and negative refer to the presentation and withdrawal of stimuli, respectively.

Extinction. Behavior can also be eliminated by the withholding of reinforcement: quite simply, if behavior no longer yields the reinforcement that maintains it, the behavior will eventually stop. This process is called **extinction.** Extinction is functionally defined as the reduction and eventual cessation of a response as a result of the removal of the reinforcement contingencies that maintain it. There are many examples of extinction in our daily lives. Our description at the beginning of this section of John R's response to Susan M's excuses of previous engagements is an example of extinction. Susan did not reinforce John's calls with acceptance of his invitations, and John's "calling behavior" ceased.

The most common examples of extinction involve "ignoring": the parent ignores a child's whining, a wife ignores her husband's nagging, a secretary ignores the boss's complaining. In each case, it is assumed that the attention the individual would normally receive is what maintains the behavior. If the assumption is valid and individuals are not given attention when they emit the undesirable behavior, then they will stop. But if

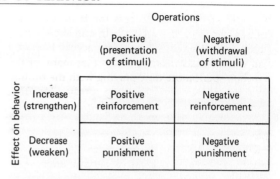

Figure 2–1. The four consequent operations and their effects on the behavior they follow. A stimulus can be presented (positive) or withdrawn (negative) contingent upon a behavior. The operation can increase (reinforce) or decrease (punish) the future probability of occurrence of the behavior.

the contingencies withheld are not the ones that maintain the behavior, the operation will not have the desired effect. As with all methods of behavior modification, the functional reinforcers must be identified before the operation is carried out.

Schedules of Reinforcement. In the natural environment, reinforcement is usually intermittent, and this fact has a tremendous effect on behavior. In an especially influential book, *Schedules of Reinforcement* (1957), Skinner and his colleague Charles Ferster identified specific patterns of behavior associated with different criteria for dispensing reinforcers. The term **schedule of reinforcement** refers to the rule used to determine which occurrence of a response will be reinforced (Reynolds, 1968).

Reinforcement can be scheduled according to the ratio of responses or according to the time elapsed since the last reinforcement. These requirements can be fixed or variable. For example, reinforcement can be delivered after a fixed number of responses (**fixed-ratio reinforcement, FR**) or after a varying number of responses (**variable-ratio reinforcement, VR**). Thus, for example, we speak of a fixed-ratio-5 schedule in which every fifth response will be reinforced, and a variable-ratio-5 in which, *on the average,* every fifth response is reinforced. With a variable-ratio-5 schedule, sometimes reinforcement will occur after three responses, sometimes after seven, and so on. But the average number of responses per reinforcement will be five. Of course, a reinforcer can be delivered following every response (fixed-ratio-1). This is referred to as **continuous reinforcement** and is abbreviated **CRF.**

Psychologists also speak of **fixed-interval reinforcement (FI)** and **variable-interval reinforcement (VI).** These refer to the delivery of reinforcers contingent upon the occurrence of a particular behavior after a specified period of time. For example, fixed-interval-30 seconds means that the first response after 30 seconds has elapsed will be reinforced. The next reinforcer will not be delivered until another 30 seconds has elapsed and the organism has emitted a response. Variable-interval reinforcement refers to the schedules in which reinforcers are delivered for the first response after a varying period of time. For example, variable-interval-10 seconds means that, *on the average*, the first response after 10 seconds will be reinforced.

Each of these schedules can be characterized by the effect it has on behavior. In terms of applied work, the relevant issue is the effect different schedules have on performance "during extinction" (that is, after reinforcement has been terminated). A behavior previously reinforced on a fixed schedule (whether ratio or interval) will be extinguished rapidly when reinforcement stops. We will not keep putting money into a candy machine after it stops delivering candy. (Candy machines are supposed to work on a FR-1 schedule.) However, behavior that has previously been reinforced on a variable schedule is much more resistant to extinction. We *will* keep on putting money into a slot machine that does not deliver instantly because we know that, unlike candy bars, jackpots are unpredictable. This machine works on a variable schedule; once reinforcement stops, it will take longer for our behavior to be extinguished.

Antecedents. Contingencies of reinforcement and punishment are not always in effect: sometimes a particular behavior is reinforced, but sometimes it isn't. Whether or not a reinforcement schedule is in effect is often signaled by stimuli in the environment. People, places, and situations often serve as cues. We quickly learn what kinds of behaviors are expected in each situation. The sophisticated adolescent knows that swearing in front of her grandparents at the dinner table will be severely punished, whereas using the same words with her friends after school brings respect and status. The young child also makes these kinds of discriminations. If, for example, the father likes to roughhouse and lauds his son's fearless stunts, but the mother gets upset and scolds him for playing rough, the child is likely to behave quite differently in the presence of each parent. He may be boisterous in the backyard with his father, but he settles down as soon as he notices his mother on the scene. The presence of each parent is a cue that indicates what kinds of behaviors will be reinforced or punished.

Even finer discriminations than these occur in our everyday lives. When we know someone fairly well, the expression on her face alone is enough to enable us to predict how she will react. Sometimes the cues we have learned are so subtle that we may not even be able to describe what they are, but they affect our behavior nonetheless. Two people who have been living together for a while can tell pretty accurately when a romantic overture is likely to be met with success, though each might not be able to explain exactly what it is about the other's behavior that is the cue.

These **discriminative stimuli (S^Ds),** as they are called, come to control our behavior through their association with contingencies of reinforcement. The onset of the stimulus evokes the previously reinforced behavior. The control that S^Ds have on behavior is called **stimulus control.** Thus, in the example above of the child playing in the backyard with his father, the mother exerted strong stimulus control over the child's behavior. Her presence indicated that new contingencies of reinforcement were in effect. A particularly clear example of stimulus control is a study (Redd & Birnbrauer, 1969) in which adults took turns supervising mentally retarded children in a playroom. One adult dispensed candy and praise to the children freely, without regard to their behavior (noncontingent), whereas the other adult gave candy and praise only if the children were engaged in cooperative play (contingent). The children quickly showed clear discriminations between the two adults. When the adult who gave out free, noncontingent goodies entered, the children remained passive and asocial. However, within less than one minute after the adult who dispensed contingent reinforcers entered, the children began playing cooperatively and continued to do so until that adult departed. The contingent adult's presence served as a discriminative stimulus and controlled the children's behavior.

Stimuli in the environment can also serve to indicate when certain behaviors will *not* be reinforced. We take advantage of this type of cue every day. For example, we know that the bowed head of the person sitting next to us in church means that talking will not evoke a positive response. Similarly, we know that loud music at a party means that serious conversation will probably not evoke much interest. Stimuli that indicate reinforcement is *not* available are referred to as **S deltas (S^Δs)**.

Response Differentiation and Shaping. Until now we have been discussing those factors that control behavior in the individual's repertoire. But in many cases the task for the behavioral clinician is to establish new behaviors. This is achieved by the gradual modification of the form and intensity of already existing behavior by either response differentiation or shaping.

Response differentiation is the refinement of a behavior by reinforcing the individual only when the behavior meets certain requirements. As the individual's behavior begins to resemble the target behavior, the reinforcement criteria are gradually increased until the desired behavior is established. The process actually involves reinforcing a subset of existing behaviors that fall within certain predetermined limits, and then making the limits more exacting. For example, if the goal is to teach someone to throw a ball accurately from a long distance, one could begin by reinforcing the individual whenever the ball landed within a certain predetermined target area. Once the individual had met these requirements, the target would be gradually made smaller until the individual had learned how to throw the ball accurately.

Parents often engage in response differentiation when they try to teach young children how to pronounce new words. For example, when the infant is babbling and the parents hear "mama," they immediately react with affection and excitement. Their child has really said a word and they are now on the lookout for it. Any time they hear "mama," they react with enthusiasm. But as the "mamas" become more frequent, the parents become more discriminating and require clearer and clearer articulations. They start holding back their smiles and hugs until the sound can be easily heard. Only when the "mama" is loud and clear do they get excited. Without necessarily planning to, the parents have developed a very effective method of teaching speech. They have used response differentiation to refine the child's babbling into a clear utterance.

Often, however, the goal behavior is not contained within a subset of existing behaviors. In such cases, the training process is more difficult because the behavior must be prompted and then refined. This process is called **shaping** and is analogous to a sculptor's shaping a figure out of the clay she has to work with. The first step in shaping behavior is to evoke (that is, prompt) a behavior and then reinforce it. This may involve physically moving the individual through the desired behavior or giving explicit instructions and demonstrations. Then the prompts are gradually withdrawn and the individual is required to emit the behavior on his or her own to receive a reinforcer. As in response differentiation, the requirements for reinforcement are gradually increased until the goal behavior is achieved. Through the reinforcement of successive approximations of the goal behavior, the individual's repertoire is increased.

We can understand how shaping works in practice by outlining a self-feeding program for a severely retarded child. Before the program is begun, the child grabs food with his hands and consistently spills it on himself, the table, and the floor. Eating neatly, with spoon and fork, is not in his repertoire and must be prompted and then reinforced.

At the beginning of the program the teacher sits near the child and physically helps him through the motions of eating. She places a spoon in the child's hand, guides him through the tasks of filling it with food and then bringing it up into his mouth. The child consumes the spoonful of food and the process is repeated. Once the training program has begun, the child is never allowed to stuff food into his mouth with his fingers. The teacher repeats the process with every bit of food. As the child becomes more comfortable with the task, the teacher gradually removes her help. She might begin by releasing her hand as the child gets the spoon to his lips; if the child succeeds in getting the spoon into his mouth without the teacher's help, she fades out another part of her assistance. As the training progresses she gradually withdraws all help until finally the child is entirely on his own. This training process is much like the way one teaches a child to ride a bike. At first one gives complete support and guidance. As the child becomes able to balance himself, the support is gradually removed, almost without the child realizing it. *Shaping*

COGNITION AND CONDITIONING

A seldom-stated but clearly implicit assumption that pervades the behavioral literature has to do with the involuntary, unconscious, automatic nature of the conditioning process. This so-called **automaticity assumption** (Mahoney, 1974) applies to both respondent and operant conditioning. For respondent conditioning, the assumption is that the response elicited by the CS is automatic; that is, the organism cannot inhibit the CR. Regardless of whether the organism is a dog or a human being, the repeated pairing of the CS with the US conditions the organism, whether he or she likes it or not. Once conditioned, presentation of the CS elicits the CR—just like that. Higher cognitive functions, such as thoughts, attitudes, or expectancies, are presumed to have no effect on this process. In operant conditioning, the automaticity assumption supports the notion that reinforcement functions as a "habit stamp." Each time a particular behavior occurs and is reinforced, it becomes more heavily stamped into the nervous system in such a way that the organism has no choice but to perform the behavior again. This process is also believed to be involuntary: individuals need not even know what response

earns them reinforcement. They respond to the contingency.

The automaticity assumption no doubt grew out of Watsonian behaviorism. In behaviorists' efforts to dissociate themselves from the "unscientific" method of introspection and the unmeasurable concept of "mind," they seized on the Pavlovian conditioned response as the basis for a new psychology. In the process, they ruled out the possibility that conditioning may be cognitively mediated by declaring that cognition was not the proper subject matter for psychology—only behavior was. When Skinner (1938) explicated the principles of operant conditioning, he too placed the inner psychological processes of the organism outside the realm of science, and instrumental behavior also became "nonmentalistic" by fiat. This assassination of the organism's ability to think led quite naturally to a conceptualization of all behaviors as some type of unmediated, automatic reflex.

Just how automatic is conditioning? In the past three decades there has been much research directed toward answering this question. William Brewer (1974) has reviewed much of this work, and the title of his paper summarizes his conclusion: "There is no convincing evidence for operant or classical conditioning in adult humans." What Brewer was referring to specifically is the notion that conditioning is an automatic, noncognitive process. A complete analysis of the research that led Brewer to this conclusion is beyond the scope of this book. But in order to clarify this issue, we will look briefly at a representative study of both respondent and operant conditioning.

The Automaticity Assumption in Respondent Conditioning
Classical

A frequent focus of respondent conditioning research with humans is the galvanic skin response (GSR). The GSR refers to the fluctuation in the electrical resistance of the skin, which is thought to be associated with sweat gland activity (Edelberg, 1972). These fluctuations, which can be measured on a polygraph, provide an indirect measure of certain kinds of nervous system activity. Although the relationship is by no means perfect (see, for example, Lang, Rice, & Sternbach, 1972; Sternbach, 1966), states of quiet and relaxation tend to produce stable levels of high resistance. The presentation of certain stimuli (usually electric shock) produces a precipitous drop in skin resistance, followed by a gradual rise to the previous level when the stimulus is terminated. In other words, shock is a US that elicits a drop in skin resistance. A stimulus that normally does not affect the GSR will, if consistently followed by shock, become a CS. This process is known as *GSR conditioning,* and the CR is called the conditioned GSR.

When individuals respond to a shock with a GSR, they do so automatically. The automaticity assumption holds that a conditioned GSR is also an automatic, unmediated response to the CS. Let us describe an experiment and see what the automaticity assumption would predict as to its outcome. The study we will describe was conducted by Glenn D. Wilson (1968). A group of high school students were presented with either a blue light or a yellow light while their skin resistance was monitored. After determining that there was no difference in the way the subjects responded to the two lights, differential conditioning was carried out. On 50 percent of the presentations of the blue light, subjects received a painful shock; presentation of the yellow light was never followed by shock. After numerous conditioning trials, presentation of the blue light without shock produced a clear conditioned GSR, while no change in GSR occurred following the yellow light. At this point Wilson told his subjects that the procedure would be reversed—that is, the *yellow* light would now be followed by shock in place of the blue light. But instead of changing the procedure as he had told his subjects he would, he put them through a series of extinction trials during which the lights were presented without shock. Shock was never given again.

What happened to the GSR that was conditioned to the blue light? If the automaticity assumption is correct, the instructions given to the subjects about the reversal of experimental procedures should have no effect. The subjects' nervous systems should still automatically respond to the blue light with the conditioned GSR. This response should then gradually extinguish over repeated trials, since the US (shock) is no longer being delivered. A second prediction—not drawn from the automaticity assumption per se, but related to a noncognitive view of conditioning—is that no change should be observed in the subjects' response to the yellow light. While the threat exists that this light will be followed by shock, such conditioning will not actually occur. Thus, no GSR response should be elicited by the yellow light.

What Wilson's subjects actually did was quite different from these predictions. After learning that the experimental contingencies were to be reversed, subjects showed immediate cessation of their GSR responses to the blue light, and immediate acquisition of a "conditioned" GSR to the yellow light. What is more, the magnitude of the GSR response to the yellow light *increased* with each trial until it was larger than that previously elicited by the blue light even though shock was never again delivered. Clearly, there was nothing "unconscious" about the subjects' reactions to the blue light. Instead, their understanding of what the light meant mediated their physiological response to it. When the subjects were told the blue light was "safe," they simply stopped responding. Similarly, the threat that the yellow light would mean shock was enough to establish it as a "CS" without the subjects' ever actually experiencing the conditioning effects of the US (shock). It is interesting to note that the threat of shock, and the subjects' increasing uncertainty as to whether it would appear, were more effective in establishing a GSR to the yellow light than shock had been in conditioning the blue light. Obviously, a simple, noncognitive view of conditioning is inadequate to account for these findings. Apparently, the thoughts people have about the things that happen to them *do* exert a profound influence on the way they behave. This is a bitter pill for the radical behaviorist to swallow.

The Automaticity Assumption in Operant Conditioning

In operant psychology the automaticity assumption has run into similar difficulties. The clearest example is in the area of verbal conditioning

(Greenspoon, 1955). The experimental task in verbal conditioning studies requires the subject either to free associate (that is, name words at random) or to construct simple sentences by selecting a pronoun (I, we, you, he, she, or they) to go with a given verb (for instance, went) (Taffel, 1955). The experimenter reinforces particular words (for example, singular nouns in the free association task or plural pronouns in the sentence construction task) with a nod or a smile, or by saying something like "Good" or "Um-hmm." Subjects do not know at the outset of the experiment that the experimenter's responses are systematically related to the things they say, since they are usually informed that the study has some other purpose. What often happens during the experiment is that subjects increase their use of the words or types of words the experimenter has reinforced. This is the phenomenon of *verbal conditioning*.

Of course, as the experiment progresses some subjects become aware that the experimenter's seemingly random responses are, in fact, related to their own behavior ("It seems like everytime I begin the sentence with 'we' or 'they,' this guy says 'uh huh.'"). However, many subjects fail to realize what the experimenter is doing. How does reinforcement affect the verbal behavior of these "unaware" subjects? The automaticity assumption for operant conditioning holds that reinforcement acts unconsciously and automatically to strengthen the behavior that it follows. Individuals need not be aware of the contingency between their responses and the events that follow them. Thus, in verbal conditioning studies, even unaware subjects should respond to the experimenter's nods, smiles, and comments by increasing their use of the "target" words.

An overwhelming amount of evidence indicates that persons who remain unaware of the reinforcement contingencies—those who do not form even a tentative hypothesis that "When I do X, Y seems to happen"—do *not* become conditioned (Brewer, 1974). Although many of the early studies of verbal conditioning lent support to the automaticity assumption and appeared to demonstrate "learning without awareness" (Krasner, 1958), those results may reflect inadequacies in the assessment of subjects' awareness rather than the absence of awareness. A simple question such as

"What do you think was the purpose of this experiment?" often fails to reveal the subject's hypothesis. What is more, although the subject's hypothesis may not be totally accurate, it may nevertheless serve to prompt increased responding.

One of the first studies illustrating subjects' operating on an incorrect hypothesis that renders them unable to state the reinforcement contingency but does increase their performance was reported by Donald Dulany, Jr. (1961). Subjects in Dulany's study were asked to emit single words and were reinforced with "Um-hmm" when they said a plural noun. This procedure produced a significant conditioning effect, and none of the subjects could state the reinforcement contingency. Was this conditioning without awareness? Not quite. When Dulany assessed subjects' hypotheses regarding the contingency, he discovered that some subjects believed they were being reinforced for giving words in a particular category, like "furniture" ("chairs," "tables," and so on). Although this hypothesis was incorrect, it did focus the subjects' responses on *noun* categories (to the exclusion of verbs, adjectives, and so on), and thereby increased the number of plural nouns they produced. Dulany reanalyzed his data and found that only subjects who had formed this type of "correlated hypothesis" showed the conditioning effect.

Automaticity Strikes Back

Similar refinements in experimental procedures have resulted in the accumulation of a large body of evidence in support of the role of cognition in operant conditioning and against the automaticity assumption. But, like many issues in contemporary psychology, this conclusion must be tempered; some evidence favoring the automaticity assumption does exist. For example, Howard Rosenfeld and Donald Baer (1969) developed an experimental task so devious that it was almost impossible for the subjects to become aware of the reinforcement contingency. A graduate student in psychology was told he was to be the experimenter in a learning-without-awareness study. (Interestingly, the student had just read a review on the topic, and expressed considerable doubt that the study would produce the learning-without-awareness phenomenon.) The graduate student was to interview another student concerning his opinions on a variety of current issues. The interviewer was asked to reinforce the interviewee's idiosyncratic chin-rubbing response by nodding his head each time it occurred during their discussion. But, unknown to the interviewer, the supposed subject of this conditioning was an *experimenter* in cahoots with Rosenfeld and Baer. He was actually using his chin-rubbing response (which the interviewer thought *he* was conditioning) to reinforce the interviewer for saying the word "yeah." In other words, each time the interviewer said "yeah," the interviewee would reinforce the response by rubbing his chin; then the interviewer would nod, thinking that he was reinforcing the chin rubbing.

Over the course of the interviews, the interviewer (the real subject) was frequently questioned by Rosenfeld and Baer. The purpose of these discussions was to determine (as unobtrusively as possible) the interviewer's awareness of what was really going on. It was clear from these assessments that the interviewer believed his subject (the real experimenter) was becoming conditioned, since his chin-rubbing responses were occurring more frequently. In fact, this was true, but only as a natural consequence of the increase in the interviewer's "yeah" responses produced by the chin-rubbing reinforcement. Several reversals of the contingency (that is, extinguishing "yeah's" by withholding chin-rubbing a short time, or applying reinforcement to "Um-hmm" instead) clearly demonstrated that the verbal behavior of the interviewer was under the control of the interviewee's reinforcement. Nevertheless, the interviewer continued to see himself as the controller until just prior to the termination of the experiment. He later reported that when he finally became aware of the contingency being applied to *him*, he suppressed saying "yeah" in order to avoid breaking into laughter when his "subject" rubbed his chin. Rosenfeld and Baer (1970) used this same "double agent" procedure on thirteen more unaware subjects, but found evidence of conditioning in only two. Clearly, the phenomenon is elusive.

There are other reasons for not abandoning the automaticity assumption of conditioning at this time. Perhaps most compelling is the fact that be-

havioral clinicians are frequently consulted by people who appear to have automatic reactions to particular stimuli, or who behave in ways they find themselves unable to understand. A man who is afraid of mice may know full well that they will not harm him, and he may frequently tell himself so. Nevertheless, the sight of a mouse produces panic in him instantaneously. Or a woman may be unable to explain her frequent crying spells, although it is obvious to the therapist that her crying is reinforced by the attention and reassurance of the people around her.

Perhaps the inconsistencies between clinical and experimental findings represent fundamental differences in real-world and laboratory experiences. People go through life reacting to an almost infinite number of stimuli, and they do not have time to hypothesize about the relationship between each of these stimuli and their own behavior. A subject in a laboratory who is wearing shock electrodes and watching a light is in quite another circumstance. Perhaps it is easier for automatic, unconscious conditioning to occur in the real world or, as Rosenfeld and Baer's research suggests, maybe only certain people are predisposed to developing true conditioned responses.

Results from experimental investigations of the role of cognition in conditioning have made behavioral clinicians aware of the need to deal with their clients' thoughts, attitudes, and beliefs. And, as we pointed out in Chapter 1, behavioral psychologists are becoming increasingly interested in the role of cognitive processes in behavior modification.

Where Does All This Controversy Lead?

How are we to regard the basic principles of behavior? Respondent and operant conditioning are still extremely useful concepts. They describe processes by which organisms acquire new behaviors—that much has not changed. But our assumptions about the nature of these processes must be revised. In the case of human beings, we would do well to recognize their complexities, and to question our simplistic notions about their behavior. As we discuss the application of behavior modification throughout the book, we will consider elaborations of this controversy.

SUMMARY

Although behavior modification is in a continual state of flux and is becoming more eclectic, the basic principles of respondent and operant conditioning remain the foundation of most approaches to behavioral intervention.

Both types of conditioning focus on the effects of stimuli and events in the environment on behavior. In respondent conditioning the subject matter is the development of more or less automatic reflexes to stimuli through the repeated pairing of a previously neutral stimulus and a naturally elicitory stimulus. The primary focus of operant conditioning is the effect of events and stimuli that follow behavior (that is, consequences). Most laboratory research in the area has dealt with schedules of reinforcement and punishment. Operant conditioning principles also deal with the effects of stimuli that precede and evoke behavior as well as with the transitory conditions that influence the particular function of stimuli. Although many researchers now question the validity of conceptualizing maladaptive reactions solely in terms of the respondent operant conditioning process, most behavior modification programs are based on principles of conditioning.

The distinction between respondent and operant conditioning has become blurred within the ranks of both laboratory and applied psychology, and simple models of conditioning that emphasize their automatic, unconscious nature have come under strong attack. Although the true nature of these processes remains unclear, it has become obvious that cognitive factors play an important role in conditioning. This realization has prompted behavioral psychologists to expand their conceptualizations of human behavior. Rather than setting out to find the "critical conditioned stimulus" or the "reinforcing relationship" maintaining a particular behavior problem, most behavioral clinicians begin their intervention with an individual analysis of the behavior problem in question.

As will become evident in subsequent chapters, the extent to which these principles are applied in intervention programs varies greatly depending upon the problem, the client, and the therapist.

REFERENCES

Bijou, S. W., & Baer, D. M. Methods in child behavior and development. In W. K. Honig (Ed.), *Operant behavior: Areas of research and application.* New York: Appleton-Century-Crofts, 1966.

Brewer, W. F. There is no convincing evidence for operant or classical conditioning in adult humans. In W. B. Weimer & D. S. Palermo (Eds.), *Cognition and the symbolic processes.* Hillsdale, N.J.: Erlbaum (Wiley), 1974.

Dulany, D. E., Jr. Hypotheses and habits in verbal "operant conditioning." *Journal of Abnormal and Social Psychology,* 1961, **63,** 251–263.

Edelberg, R. Electrical activity of the skin: Its measurement and uses in psychophysiology. In N. S. Greenfield & R. A. Sternbach (Eds.), *Handbook of psychophysiology.* New York: Holt, Rinehart and Winston, 1972.

Ferster, C. B., & Skinner, B. F. *Schedules of reinforcement.* New York: Appleton-Century-Crofts, 1957.

Garcia, J., & Koelling, R. A. Relation of cue to consequence in avoidance learning. *Psychonomic Science,* 1966, **4,** 123–124.

Greenspoon, J. The reinforcing effect of two spoken sounds on the frequency of two responses. *American*

Journal of Psychology, 1955, **68**, 409–416.

Kantor, J. R. *Interbehavioral psychology.* Bloomington, Ind.: Principia Press, 1959.

Kimble, G. A. *Hilgard and Marquis' conditioning and learning.* New York: Appleton-Century-Crofts, 1961.

Krasner, L. Studies of the conditioning of verbal behavior. *Psychological Bulletin*, 1958, **55**, 148–170.

Lang, P. J., Rice, D. G., & Sternbach, R. A. The psychophysiology of emotion. In N. S. Greenfield & R. A. Sternbach (Eds.), *Handbook of psychophysiology.* New York: Holt, Rinehart and Winston, 1972.

Leitenberg, H. Is timeout from positive reinforcement an aversive event? A review of the experimental evidence. *Psychological Bulletin*, 1965, **64**, 428–441.

Lindsley, O. R. Direct measurement and prosthesis of retarded behavior. *Journal of Education*, 1964, **147**, 62–81.

Locke, E. A. Is "behavior therapy" behavioristic? *Psychological Bulletin*, 1971, **76**, 318–327.

London, P. The end of ideology in behavior modification. *American Psychologist*, 1972, **27**, 913–919.

Mahoney, M. J. *Cognition and behavior modification.* Cambridge, Mass.: Ballinger, 1974.

Paul, G. L. Outcome of systematic desensitization: Controlled investigations of indivdual treatment, technique variations, and current status. In C. M. Franks (Ed.), *Behavior therapy: Appraisal and status.* New York: McGraw-Hill, 1969.

Pavlov, I. P. *Conditioned reflexes.* New York: Macmillan, 1927.

Premack, D. Toward empirical behavior laws: Positive reinforcement. *Psychological Review*, 1959, **66**, 219–233.

Premack, D. Reinforcement theory. In D. Levine (Ed.), *Nebraska symposium on motivation.* Lincoln: University of Nebraska Press, 1965.

Rachlin, H. *Behavior and learning.* San Francisco: Freeman, 1976.

Redd, W. H., & Birnbrauer, J. S. Adults as discriminative stimuli for different reinforcement contingencies with retarded children. *Journal of Experimental Child Psychology*, 1969, **7**, 440–447.

Rescorla, R. A. Predictability and number of pairings in Pavlovian fear conditioning. *Psychonomic Science*, 1966, **4**, 383–384.

Rescorla, R. A. Pavlovian conditioning and its proper control procedures. *Psychological Review*, 1967, **74**, 71–80.

Rescorla, R. A., & LoLordo, V. M. Inhibition of avoidance behavior. *Journal of Comparative and Physiological Psychology*, 1965, **59**, 406–412.

Reynolds, G. S. *A primer of operant conditioning.* Glenview, Ill.: Scott, Foresman, 1968.

Rosenfeld, H. M., & Baer, D. M. Unnoticed verbal conditioning of an aware experimenter by a more aware subject: The double-agent effect. *Psychological Review*, 1969, **76**, 425–432.

Rosenfeld, H. M., & Baer, D. M. Unbiased and unnoticed verbal conditioning: The double agent robot procedure. *Journal of the Experimental Analysis of Behavior*, 1970, **14**, 99–107.

Skinner, B. F. *The behavior of organisms.* New York: Appleton-Century-Crofts, 1938.

Skinner, B. F. *Science and human behavior.* New York: Free Press, 1953.

Sternbach, R. A. *Principles of psychophysiology.* New York: Academic Press, 1966.

Taffel, C. Anxiety and the conditioning of verbal behavior. *Journal of Abnormal and Social Psychology*, 1955, **51**, 496–501.

Thorndike, E. L. Animal intelligence: An experimental study of the associative processes in animals. *Psychological Review, Monography Supplement*, 1898, **2**, 28–31.

Wilson, G. D. Reversal of differential GSR conditioning by instructions. *Journal of Experimental Psychology*, 1968, **76**, 491–493.

three

INTERVENTION STRATEGIES

Behavior modification principles are deceptively simple. Despite the existence of many behavioral entrepreneurs and promoters of weekend workshops, the therapeutic methods derived from these principles cannot be learned overnight or merely by reading a do-it-yourself manual. Effective behavior modification requires a sensitivity to the most subtle cues. What is more, many, if not all, of the "nonspecific" factors (rapport, trust, empathy, and so on) associated with more traditional psychotherapeutic methods are equally characteristic of behavior modification (Lazarus, 1971; Locke, 1973; Gottman & Leiblum, 1974; Goldfried & Davison, 1976).

In this chapter, we will examine the strategies and decision processes used in behavior modification. We will organize our discussion according to the specific operations performed during the course of intervention: initial interview, goal setting, assessment and evaluation, and implementation. We will also identify the factors that must be considered at each stage of program development and the problems that can arise when they are ignored. Other important issues we will examine are the roles of rapport, resistance, and trust. The purpose in this chapter is to provide an accurate account of the complexities of implementing behavior modification programs.

THE INITIAL INTERVIEW

The initial interview is quite similar to the interview that might be conducted by a traditional psy-

chotherapist. Its purpose is to give the client the opportunity to learn what to expect from therapy, to alleviate any misconceptions or apprehensions the client might have, to make the client feel at ease with the therapeutic process, and to determine the problem.

Determining the Problem

The therapist usually begins by asking the client to identify the problems that are at issue. Most clients speak in generalities; for example, they may complain about being unhappy and depressed, misunderstood and unfulfilled in a relationship, or unable to get along with others. They rarely articulate their troubles in terms of specific undesirable or maladaptive behaviors. At this point, the therapist must attempt to clarify what a client means by feeling depressed, misunderstood, or whatever. The therapist might ask the client to give examples of feeling depressed or anxious, to explain exactly what his or her spouse would have to do to make their relationship more fulfilling, or to identify those situations in which he or she has the most difficulty getting along with others.

Behaviorally oriented therapists often use such traditional techniques as reflection and clarification of feelings. They express concern for and acknowledge the validity of clients' feelings. The goal is for clients to recognize the therapist's basic respect for them and to realize that their "hurt" and pain are appreciated. By reflecting clients' feelings, the therapist offers reassurance and, at the same time, gets feedback as to the accuracy of his (the therapist's) understanding. The therapist can also redirect a client's frame of reference toward a behavioral interpretation.

Therapist-Client Interaction

Perhaps because behavior modification focuses on concrete behavioral problems and the factors that maintain them, many clinicians have the idea that the behaviorally oriented therapist is cold and mechanical, unresponsive to the client's feelings. Although it is true that, as a rule, behavioral psychologists do not consider the therapist-client relationship as primary, it is not the case that they regard rapport and empathy as unimportant. In fact, most behavioral clinicians believe that rapport is necessary for effective treatment (Dalton & Sundbiad, 1976). If there is strong rapport between client and therapist, then the client will be more likely to trust the therapist and carry out the recommendations. In addition, the therapist's praise and attention should be of greater reinforcing value if the client has warm, positive feelings about the therapist. Rapport facilitates the implementation of other change techniques.

Research on the "quality" of therapist-client interaction has found that behaviorally oriented therapists are compassionate and accepting with their clients. In fact, in a recent study comparing the client-therapist interaction patterns of behavior therapists and psychoanalytic therapists (matched in terms of years of experience dealing with clients), behavior therapists were found to have especially good relationships with their clients (Staples, Sloane, Whipple, Cristol, & Yorkston, 1975). Although both types of psychotherapists were rated by clients as warm and accepting, the behaviorally oriented therapists were considered to show higher levels of what nondirective Rogerian psychotherapists call accurate empathy, interpersonal contact, and therapist self-congruence.

Moreover, they were more personal and self-disclosing than the psychoanalytic therapists. In the context of a warm, affectional atmosphere, the behavior therapists were direct and exerted considerable control over the issues discussed in the sessions. A content analysis of audiotapes of ses-

sions revealed that the behavioral clinicians gave explicit advice as to what the client should do, whereas the more traditional psychotherapists did not. The behavior therapists also spent, on the average, twice as much time talking during therapy sessions. Thus, it appears that the behaviorally oriented therapist, like any good psychotherapist—or, for that matter, like anyone in whom we would place trust—tries to communicate genuine understanding and acceptance.

Little research, however, has been directed toward identifying the ingredients of rapport. In fact, there is not even a consensus about what the concept really means. We somehow "know" when we have it, but we have difficulty explaining what it is or teaching others how to establish it. Eye contact during conversation, obvious interest in what someone is saying, reflection of feelings, and appropriate degree of self-disclosure are generally considered important in establishing rapport, but many psychotherapists believe that other factors are involved as well. At this point in the evolution of behavior modification, all that can be said is that a good therapist-client relationship is considered crucial to effective intervention.

ESTABLISHING PRELIMINARY GOALS

Client and therapist jointly decide on the goals of the treatment program. In contrast to other methods of psychotherapy, in which there is some a priori notion of "good mental health" that serves as the goal of therapy, behavior modification does not provide the therapist with an "end product" that treatment should achieve. The behavioral clinician has no plans to "self-actualize" clients or to free them of "neuroses." The purpose is to help the client alter what the client considers to be his or her particular difficulties. There is no requirement that the therapist reinforce conformity to society's or the therapist's view of "good adjustment" or "normality." If, for example, someone sent a truly "happy hooker" to a behavior therapist, the therapist would not necessarily try to get her to change professions. (A happy ax murderer, however, or those who are dangerous to themselves or others would, of course, be a different story.)

The issue of value judgments affecting treatment goals has received a great deal of attention in relation to the therapeutic process, particularly concerning treatment with homosexuals (Begelman, 1975; Bieber, 1976; Davison, 1976), involuntary prison inmates (Cohen, 1974; Holland, 1974; Saunders, 1974; Kennedy, 1976), and public school children (Winett & Winkler, 1972; Rappaport, 1977). As we will discuss later in the book, behavioral psychologists have begun to analyze their own clinical work in light of their commitment *not* to be a tool of the status quo.

More than any other approach to psychological intervention, behavior modification lets the client determine the goals of treatment, but it is incorrect to assume that the behavior therapist does not directly or indirectly influence that decision. By professional status alone, the behavior therapist is often viewed as an expert and an authority figure, and therefore can exert control or at least affect the client's decision-making process (Merbaum & Southwell, 1965; Truax, 1966; Halleck, 1971). The therapist may begin by encouraging a client to conceptualize problems and treatment goals in behavioral terms (Goldfried & Davison, 1976). Concurrently, the therapist may model certain attitudes and opinions regarding what behaviors could or should be changed. These factors in turn affect a client's expectations regarding change (Frank, 1961; Goldstein, 1962). The therapist, perhaps without being aware of it, can communicate his or her values to the client.

As in our absurd example of the happy ax murderer, occasionally the client's goals are clearly incompatible with or compromise the therapist's personal ethics or the best interests of other individuals. Such situations have occurred in cases where psychologists have been brought into prisons and public schools as consultants. These are difficult situations, because the person who is "paying the bill" and requesting the services is not the person receiving the services. For example, a teacher might want a program that can be used to create a classroom full of docile children. The psychologist might feel that such a goal may be convenient for the teacher but not good for the children, and express disagreement and suggest

alternatives. If that were still the teacher's only goal, then the psychologist might refer him elsewhere. Although therapists may avoid making obvious ethical decisions for clients, they may nevertheless be unwilling to embark on programs that conflict with their own professional values.

ASSESSMENT AND EVALUATION

In order to devise an effective intervention program, the behavioral clinician must determine which variables in the client's life must be changed. This requires a detailed assessment of conditions associated with the occurrence and nonoccurrence of the target behavior(s). Directly related to the necessity of conducting a careful assessment is the issue of program evaluation. In order to be sure the intervention program is having the desired effect, the clinician must evaluate it. In many ways assessment and evaluation are the same thing.

Detailed Behavioral Assessment

The factors behavioral psychologists consider important in assessment vary depending upon their specific orientations. One issue that divides behavioral psychologists is the extent to which cognitive factors, such as the client's interpretation of events and stimuli, are considered in the assessment. As we indicated in our discussion of the five approaches to behavior modification in Chapter 1, the behavior analysis approach is much more conservative than the cognitive and eclectic approaches. All approaches, however, stress the role of the following factors in assessment:

1. Antecedent stimuli that may evoke or elicit the problem behavior
2. The magnitude of the maladaptive behavior (that is, its intensity, frequency, duration, and latency)
3. Interaction patterns that might involve the reinforcement of the problem behavior and the extinction or punishment of adaptive behavior
4. Client variables that might affect the function of naturally occurring events (these variables include such nonbehavioral factors as

physical health and social relationships)
5. The client's behavioral assets and deficits

Assessment also involves a plan for program implementation. For example, the therapist must find out if family members or significant others will assist or perhaps sabotage the program, if certain client social values or commitments will restrict what the therapist can do, and so on.

Because there is such great variance in the constellation of variables interacting to affect the client's behavior, categorization by symptoms does not yield clear understanding. Each behavior and each stimulus event must be considered in functional terms for the individual. Stimuli and events have different meanings for different people, as in the example in Chapter 2 of the forty-five-year-old father for whom rock music was punishment, whereas for his fourteen-year-old son it was reinforcement. Similarly, singing in the shower may be a way of relaxing for one person, whereas for someone else it may be a means of "keeping the evil spirits away." The only way to determine the function of a behavior or event is to assess the actual impact it has on the individual's behavior.

Antecedent Stimuli. After the therapist and client have identified the *presenting problems* (that is, those behaviors that prompted the client's seeking professional help), and before the therapist can suggest strategies for change, he or she must determine any possibly relevant antecedent conditions that affect the occurrence of the behavior. For example, if the problem is an anxiety reaction, the therapist must focus on the stimuli that elicit the maladaptive response. This might be accomplished by simply asking the client to list the situations in which he feels most anxious. In some cases, the client may readily point out the feared stimuli; at other times, identification may be more difficult. With *"pervasive"* or *"free-floating"* anxiety, the client may not be able to identify the specific stimuli that he fears. For example, the client may say he is always upset or feels extremely nervous most of the time but not be able to specify the exact aspects of the situations that elicit the anxiety. The therapist would have to question the client in order to determine the actual stimuli

that elicit anxiety reactions. The client might also be requested to identify the stimulus conditions under which the anxiety was first acquired. The therapist might even suggest that the client confront certain situations to determine what components cause the greatest anxiety.

If it turns out that the presenting problem is a maladaptive operant pattern of responding, it is still crucial to determine antecedent stimuli that may be setting the occasion for the problem behavior. In such situations the therapist tries to identify the critical discriminative stimuli. It is a rule, rather than the exception, that the problem behaviors are dependent to a large extent upon the situation (Mischel, 1968; Redd, 1969, 1970; Wahler, 1969b). Sidman's (1970) account of the dramatic change in behavior he observed on the wards of a large state school for the mentally retarded demonstrates our point.

Residents of the institution were involved in an intensive program in which clear reinforcement contingencies for constructive learning were in effect for only part of the day. The remainder of the day they were idle on their home wards. When they were in the special learning unit area they were active and alert, participating in the planned activities. However, when they went back to their own wards their "psychotic-like" behavior returned. "Upon passing through the door into the unprogrammed part of the building some of the children would sit down on the floor, head on drawn-up knees, and begin to rock incessantly; others took off the clothes they had been wearing all day and ran around naked; others suddenly became incontinent" (Sidman, 1970, p. 269). The assessment information provided by Sidman's observations is clear: the home ward was a powerful antecedent event that controlled the children's regressive behavior.

In the ideal case, the therapist would assess the role of antecedent stimuli by direct observation. This is what is usually done in cases involving institutionalized individuals or classroom children. With adults it is often impossible, so the therapist must rely on the client's self-report.

Magnitude of Maladaptive Behavior. Determining the magnitude of the problem is important for at least two reasons. First, it provides a clear indication of the client's or referring agency's criteria of acceptable behavior. Occasionally, the therapist discovers that the "problem" really is not particularly extreme. For example, young parents may be concerned about their child's tantrums when, in fact, their frequency is not atypical. Of course, making judgments regarding what is "normal" is difficult given that for most behaviors no formal norms exist (Bijou & Peterson, 1972); thus therapists must rely on previous cases and their knowledge of the problem area. One strategy is to observe the client's peers and see how they behave under similar circumstances (Nelson & Bowles, 1975). If the client's behavior is not grossly different from that of peers, the therapist might reconsider the problem and focus on the expectations of the referring source.

The second reason why it is important to ascertain the baseline level of the problem behavior is that it provides a means to evaluate subsequent change. As the program continues, the therapist can check client progress against the baseline measures. Only by doing so can he or she know whether the procedures are effective. One's subjective judgments (as well as those of the client) regarding improvement following intervention are often unreliable (Kazdin, 1973; Loeber, 1971). Still, by continuing to measure the magnitude of the problem throughout the intervention period, the therapist has a built-in feedback mechanism. If the problem does not diminish as the program is applied, then procedures are adjusted until improvement is observed. Moreover, this gives the therapist an objective means of determining when the program has met the original goals.

The actual assessment of the magnitude of the behavior problem can be achieved by recording (1) the frequency of occurrence of the response, (2) the duration of an occurrence of the behavior, (3) the intensity (that is, strength or force) of the response, or (4) the latency of the response. The measure selected primarily depends upon the problem in question. For example, if the therapist is dealing with an aggressive child, frequency and intensity of the target behavior would be appropriate; if the problem involves social withdrawal and isolation, duration may be more appropriate. Of course, the measure the therapist

selects is also dependent upon practical considerations such as human resources and observation equipment.

Consequent Variables. An important facet of assessment is the identification of naturally occurring contingencies of reinforcement and punishment that might affect the client's behavior. These controlling contingencies are usually incorporated in the client's interpersonal relationships and, in the case of family members, may involve long-standing patterns of interaction. Although the therapist is often able to generate fairly accurate hypotheses from discussions with the client, it is usually the case that clients cannot identify the "dynamics" of their relationships—that is, the contingencies of reinforcement and punishment operating in their interactions. Parents and teachers often reinforce the exact behavior they are trying to suppress because they are unaware of the reinforcing function of their reprimands and attention (Madsen, Becker, & Thomas, 1968; O'Leary & Becker, 1968; Wahler, 1969a; O'Leary, Kaufman, Kass, & Drabman, 1970). Of course, the therapist cannot be sure that a hunch is valid until he or she tests it out by actually altering the social contingencies and observing the effects on the client's behavior. Therefore, the therapist's initial assessments of the role of consequent variables is only tentative.

Client Variables. Most behavioral psychologists acknowledge the role of setting factors (Kantor, 1959), or what some (Goldfried and Davison, 1976) have called *organismic variables,* in the control of human behavior and take them into account when they do assessment. The therapist must determine if there are any physiological factors (for instance, current drug usage, physical fatigue, and hormonal imbalances) or conditions of external stress (for instance, problems associated with work, education, or financial matters) contributing to the problem. If the assessment indicates that organismic variables are a possible cause, a consultation with another professional might be indicated.

Behavioral clinicians are becoming increasingly interested in the possibility of cognitive-mediational factors affecting client behavior. In the assessment the therapist might try to determine if the client has certain stereotyped ways of interpreting events and responses from others. For instance, does the client label or categorize events in irrational and maladaptive ways (Ellis, 1973; Beck, 1971)? Does the client "catastrophize" (that is, always blow things out of proportion)? Does he or she have unrealistically high standards of achievement? The therapist may ask the client to examine his or her feelings in hopes of understanding how the client views the world.

Behavioral Deficits and Assets. The therapist must also determine what behavior deficits and assets the client has that might contribute to the problem and affect the course of treatment. Because much of behavior modification involves strengthening positive behaviors and giving the client alternative (and more adaptive) ways of getting reinforcement, the therapist's knowing what the client can do is just as important as his or her knowing what the client cannot do. Generally, the therapist focuses this part of the assessment on areas that are functionally relevant to the behavior problem. For instance, if the client is a child who is aggressive in school and is rejected by her peers, the therapist might find out whether the child has skills that her peers highly value that could serve as a means of gaining peer reinforcement (for instance, special talents in a sport, game, or hobby). The therapist would also check to see if the client had any academic skill deficits, such as reading deficiency, that might contribute to her negative reaction to school (Bijou & Peterson, 1972). In the case of a depressed adult, the therapist would determine what skills and talents the individual might utilize to bring him positive social interaction to help reduce the despondency (Ferster, 1973; Lewinsohn, 1975).

A Behavior Classification Scheme

As is evident in the foregoing discussion, behavioral psychologists reject traditional methods of diagnostic classification. In their place, many professionals (Bandura, 1969; Kanfer & Phillips, 1969; Sherman & Baer, 1969; Bijou & Peterson, 1972; Ross, 1971; Goldfried & Davison, 1976) have

suggested that the presenting problem be categorized in terms of what the therapist hypothesizes to be "the variables that are probably maintaining them" (Goldfried & Davison, 1976, p. 28). In this system, problems are identified as involving behavioral excesses, behavioral deficits, or inappropriate stimulus control.

Behavioral excesses are characterized by their atypical intensity, duration, or frequency. For example, children who are considered to have behavioral excesses are typically "conduct problems," "hyperactive," "disobedient," and so on. The most common behavioral excess in adults is anxiety. **Behavioral deficits** refer to problems related to lack of skill or to unusually low rates of responding. Social withdrawal, academic deficiencies, and depression are classified as behavioral deficits. The third category, **inappropriate stimulus control,** includes behaviors that are topographically acceptable, but according to what society expects, occur at the wrong time or in the wrong place. That is, the individual possesses the necessary skills but does not respond to socially appropriate discriminative stimuli. For example, a child may know how to talk but does not direct her conversation to other people; a bright graduate student may be an active and valued member of a scholarly seminar but becomes tongue-tied in the presence of attractive women.

Advocates of this fairly popular "diagnostic" system argue that it helps the therapist determine what variables to manipulate and where to begin the program. However, the system has recently come under criticism (Bijou & Redd, 1975; Kanfer & Grimm, 1977). First, the system classifies behaviors according to what the therapist "assumes" to be the controlling variables. But the assumption is only a hypothesis and cannot replace an empirical (functional) analysis. The second criticism is that, to a great extent, classifying behaviors in such a way is nothing but a semantics exercise. For example, why is it not just as valid to view aggression as a deficit in prosocial approach behavior as it is to call it an excess of antisocial behavior? Does not social withdrawal represent as much an excess of antisocial behavior as it does a deficit of prosocial behavior? And since most programs involve both the weakening of certain behaviors and the strengthening of others, what difference does it make if something is labeled an excess or deficit?

Factors in Program Implementation

Kanfer and Saslow (1969) have identified a series of factors that the therapist must consider before embarking on an intervention program. These factors are not necessarily related to the genesis of the problem, but they are important to its remediation. The major issue is how the client's social and physical environment will influence the effectiveness of the intervention program. Given that all behavioral programs are implemented in the context of complex networks of interpersonal relationships, economic and cultural restrictions, and physical and medical conditions, it is crucial that the therapist take these factors into consideration. A program may be beautiful on paper but a total failure when put into effect because the therapist is unaware of the milieu in which the client functions. The following list is a composite of Kanfer and Saslow's decision guides in a functional (behavior analysis) assessment:

Competing Contingencies. The first set of factors concerns the clarification of the circumstances under which the client's problem behaviors occur. These include such questions as: Who in the client's immediate social environment objects to (that is, is punished by) the client's troublesome behaviors? Will these individuals be better off in some meaningful way if the client improves? Will positive changes in the client's behavior cost him or her anything (in terms of loss of parental attention, sympathy from friends, greater responsibility, and so on)? Are there any extra benefits that the client will receive by changing (for instance, greater peer esteem, increase employment opportunity, or better interpersonal relationships)? Answers to these questions provide some indication of the probability that the program will succeed and how it might be adjusted to the client's unique situation.

For example, if, through the program, the client would lose the special status and concomitant attention of being a person in need of tender loving care (which undoubtedly we all need, but not

through being emotionally helpless and dependent), chances are the program would not work. What the therapist would have to do is to teach the client other, more adaptive means of getting attention and affection. If, for instance, the only real meaning a lonely and withdrawn parent gets out of life is caring for a "helpless" mentally retarded son or daughter, it is possible that the parent would show some resistance when the child began to show signs of independence as a result of the program. Again, the therapist would have to help the parent obtain fulfillment in other ways before the program would be maximally effective.

Consideration of the social pressures and environmental contingencies that might be antagonistic to the methods and goals of the intervention program involves what some have referred to as the *analysis of client systems.* This is the notion that individuals, families, and all social groups have systems of checks and balances that somehow allow them to continue to function even though there are problems. Thus, any intervention within that unit can disrupt the system and cause new problems. For this reason, the therapist must understand the system and the effects his or her intervention might have on it. One of the therapist's major goals is to institute positive change in the system while at the same time ensuring that the needs satisfied under the old system are still met, albeit in different ways.

Clients' Personal Values. Another issue closely related to the first is the extent to which the proposed program is consistent with the clients' social and ethnic values. If the procedures are in some way offensive, problems are likely to arise. Clients may simply express their disagreement or end treatment. In either event, the therapist's credibility as a person with insight and solutions to problems will be lost, and clients will quickly come to discount whatever the therapist suggests.

There are numerous situations in which therapists can encounter difficulty if they are insensitive to these factors. In the treatment of sexual dysfunction, it is obvious that therapists must be aware of clients' attitudes regarding sex (Masters & Johnson, 1970). When working in a neighborhood-based program, it is critical that therapists recognize local mores, and that the people who are served have a voice in determining the focus of the program. Well-intentioned young professionals can easily "turn off" clients and substantially diminish their effectiveness by failing to consider the clients' frame of reference. Even in situations where the behavior therapist has formal authority as the staff psychologist or program director, insensitivity to the values and attitudes of the direct-care staff can result in their nullifying any technique that is introduced (Tharp & Wetzel, 1969; Reppucci & Saunders, 1974).

Reinforcer Hierarchy. A third consideration is the determination of the client's hierarchy of reinforcers. If the program is to involve contingencies of reinforcement, the therapist must know what the client "likes." Even if the therapist is working with the most eager and all-American six-year-old, he or she would not automatically assume that chocolate candy is a powerful reinforcer. When working with adults and most children, the therapist can simply ask clients what they like and dislike, but with severely disturbed or retarded individuals it is often necessary for the therapist to test out various items.

Biological Functioning. An especially important and often overlooked issue is the assessment of factors in biological functioning that might relate to the problem behavior. Occasionally, the problem stems from residuals of illness, congenital defects, defective vision and/or hearing, or metabolic abnormalities. Unfortunately, it is often difficult for the behavior therapist to recognize these conditions. But if the therapist works in the context of an interdisciplinary team in which the client can easily be seen by a number of professionals (neurologist, educator, physical therapist, nutritionist, and so on), then this reduces the problem.

Even if other "causes" can be identified with some reasonable confidence, often at least some of the client's maladaptive behaviors may be strengthened by the *secondary gains* (such as special attention and sympathy) they produce. Also, it is not unusual for problems that were initially the result of some physical or genetic malady to be perpetuated by the social reinforcement they bring. That is, the original physical condition alters the individual's behavior so much that it comes under the control of social reinforcement contingencies and persists after the original cause is gone.

Program Feasibility. Another consideration is the viability of the treatment program. Can it be carried out? Will the client have the opportunity to participate in the prescribed activities? Is there someone in the client's life who can function as an "agent of change" (that is, implement the program in the client's daily life)? Does the client possess the necessary skills to carry out a self-control program? Because behavior modification requires environmental change that cannot be achieved in a weekly fifty-minute session, there must be some mechanism within the client's natural environment to back up the program. Somehow, somewhere, something must change. If there is no opportunity for the client to emit more adaptive behavior, if there is no one to administer the required instructions, reinforcement, or punishment, then there can be no program. Cooperation is a necessity.

Client Control. The final item in our list of issues in implementation is the role of clients' perceptions of their control of their own behavior and what happens to them. This is especially important with programs in which a client must take responsibility for implementation. If the client is to learn self-control strategies or alter styles of interacting, then he or she must believe that one can, in fact, take charge of one's own behavior. Does the client feel helpless, a victim of bad luck or fate? Does he or she blame others for misfortunes?

The therapist is of course interested in knowing how a client has dealt with self-control problems in the past. Has the client learned to avoid situations that encourage problem behavior? Does behavior vary greatly depending upon the situation? How responsive is the client to the influence of others?

Answers to these questions determine how much responsibility the therapist can give a client. If a client appears able to change, a self-control program may be realistic without preliminary training. If not, it may be necessary for the therapist to enlist the help of friends or family.

Assessment Methods

Three methods are used to obtain information relevant to the initial assessment: the interview, role playing, and direct observation in the natural environment. Since we have already covered interviewing in detail, we will limit our present discussion to the other two methods.

Role Playing. This technique involves asking a client who is sitting in the therapist's office to pretend he or she is someone else for a few minutes, to reenact an unpleasant incident, or to imagine how he or she would react if faced with a particular situation. This technique is not new in clinical psychology. Traditional approaches have used role playing to effect behavior change for years (for instance, Lazarus, 1966; Sturm, 1965). Behavioral psychologists, on the other hand, have only recently begun using the technique, and they have used it in a new way. Although occasionally a behavioral clinician may role play in order to demonstrate a certain skill to a client, the major function of role playing in behavior therapy is as a means of re-creating problem situations to get some idea of how the client handles them (McFall & Lillesand, 1971; McFall & Marston, 1970). For example, in order to determine how a person who complains that people always take advantage of him deals with social dominance, the therapist might ask the client to imagine someone asking an inconsiderate favor and then say how he would react. The therapist might ask an adolescent who is referred by school officials because of conduct problems to pretend that a teacher has just reprimanded her for something she did not do and to explain what she might say or do to the teacher. Of course, the clinician would present numerous hypothetical situations and ask the client to role play each one before being able to offer any hypothesis.

Of course, simulated situations are not the "real world," and there is the distinct possibility that clients' role playing may have only limited resemblance to their behavior outside the office. Nevertheless, role playing may help the therapist formulate hypotheses that he or she can explore with the client.

Direct Observation in the Natural Environment. This method is by far the most "face-valid" means of gaining assessment information. In the ideal situation, either the therapist or a trained observer records the clients' behavior, but because of practical limitations usually parents, spouses, or clients themselves do the observing.

Although the notion of observing what the clients do in their daily interactions seems quite simple, devising a system that will yield valid and reliable data requires considerable sophistication and knowhow. The therapist must first decide what behaviors to record. In the case of a child who has social as well as academic difficulties in school, for instance, the therapist must determine what behaviors of the child, his peers, and his teacher are relevant to the problem. With an adult who is depressed, the therapist would focus on a variety of situations such as job, marriage, and social life. The therapist must also decide what categories of antecedent stimuli and setting events to record. The next issue is the determination of the appropriate measure (that is, frequency, intensity, duration, and latency) for each target behavior. At each point in the decision process, the therapist must also consider the feasibility of the observation system. That is, can the observer obtain this information reliably?

After determining the appropriate target behavior(s) and selecting the measures, the therapist devises a recording system. For example, in classroom settings frequency of various behavior may be recorded on a scorecard. The teacher merely notes each instance of the target behavior. If a trained observer is used, observation can be more systematic. The observer might use a stopwatch and make a note of the antecedent stimuli, the behavior of the child and the teacher, and the consequences of those behaviors (from peers and teacher) on a systematic basis (for instance, once every 15 seconds). If the problem involves self-control, the observation system might require, for example, the client to record the time and setting in which the undesirable behavior occurred. As with other facets of behavioral intervention, the observation system is tailored to the presenting problem.

Although direct observation is an extremely important method of assessment, it is not without its limitations. As with interviewing and role playing, these limitations relate to issues of reliability and validity. That is, are the results the observer obtains accurate? Is the observer biased? Would another observer's records agree with those obtained? (All questions concerning reliability.) Are the behaviors and stimuli that are the focus of the observation truly relevant to the presenting problem? Does the fact that the client is being observed affect his or her behavior? Is the sample of behavior that is observed truly representative of the client's natural way of acting? (These three questions are concerned with validity.)

Behavioral psychologists are aware of these problems and take steps to maximize the reliability and validity of the observations. First, observers (whether they are behaviorally trained technicians, parents, or peers) must be given specific instructions on how to use the obervation system. Second, the therapist can determine the reliability of the observation by having a second individual independently observe the client at the same time. One common way of calculating the interobserver reliability is to divide the number of times the two observers agree on what occurred by the number of agreements plus disagreements. This figure multiplied by 100, gives the percentage of interobserver agreement (that is, reliability). For example, if the observers recorded behavior for 200 thirty-second intervals and agreed on 150 and disagreed on 50 then the reliability would be 75 percent [(150/150 + 50) × 100 = .75)]. If the therapist is satisfied with the reliability obtained, he or she then goes on with the program. Most professional journals require interobserver reliabilities of at least 80 percent; however, with extremely complex observational systems, lower reliabilities are often accepted. If the percentage of agreement is low (often a subjective judgment on the part of the therapist), then the observer is given additional training and another reliability check is made.

Third, the observer must be as inconspicuous as possible. He or she must not initiate conversation with the client or intrude on what is happening. In most settings the observer becomes "part of the woodwork" fairly rapidly. Fortunately, most people quickly adapt to the presence of an observer. Even in an elementary classroom, children quickly stop attending to the observer and act as if he or she were not present (Bijou, Peterson, & Ault, 1968).

Fourth, the frequency and timing of the observations must be appropriate to the presenting problem. If, for example, the problem involves a mentally retarded child's eating behavior, then observations must be scheduled at meal times. Or, if a child has trouble getting along with peers, then observations made during recess might be much more useful than those obtained during the reading period. By carefully analyzing the presenting problem and the practical limitations of the setting in which the program is to be carried out, the therapist can individualize the assessment.

Having the client do the observing often results in improvement without the therapist intervening in any other way. Recording incidences of the problem behavior as well as occurrences of desired behavior can serve to prompt positive change.

The Relation between Assessment and Intervention

It is impossible to separate assessment from intervention. The functional analysis of the presenting problem is not complete until the frequency of the problem has been significantly reduced. Only by effecting a positive change is there any assurance that the causes are understood. For example, observation conducted in the natural environment may show that the parents immediately respond to their three-year-old child's tantrums with attention, but this does not prove the parents' attention is the critical factor influencing the child's misbehavior. It is only a hypothesis. Not until the child's tantrums have been eliminated by changing the parents' way of responding can the therapist be confident that he or she understands the nature of the presenting problem. Only then is the assessment complete. And when that is achieved, so are the goals of the program.

TREATMENT EVALUATION

Assessment by continuous monitoring of the client's behavior is directly relevant to program evaluation. In fact, it is the most commonly used method of evaluating intervention programs. If, following the implementation of a program, the desired behavior increases and problematic behavior decreases, both therapist and client are usually satisfied. But in such cases one cannot be sure that the programmed intervention produced the observed changes; other factors may have been at work. Of course, the client may not care what produced the change. But for the therapist, the question of whether the program or some extraneous influence was responsible for the improvement is an important one. Moreover, there is increasing concern among mental health professionals and legal authorities that psychotherapists be held accountable for the treatments they provide. Therapists should be able to produce evidence which demonstrates that their methods are the best alternatives available and that their services benefit clients. Such concerns, coupled with behavioral psychologists' commitment to empirical validation of therapeutic methods, have made program evaluation an important issue in behavior modification.

The most widely accepted method of treatment evaluation is the group experimental design. In this strategy, a group of individuals who receive a particular treatment are statistically compared to other groups of individuals who receive an alternative treatment, a placebo treatment, and/or no treatment. However, the group experimental method is inappropriate for use by the individual therapist who wants to evaluate the impact of a particular program with a specific client or small group of clients. In such cases, an *individual analysis* or *single-subject design* is used. The client's behavior is examined under various treatment conditions. In contrast to a statistical analysis which compares the performances of different groups of subjects, the performance of an individual client is measured under one set of circumstances (that is, treatment) and compared to his or her performance under another set of circumstances.

Individual analysis can be carried out in a variety of ways. In the discussion that follows we will briefly consider two basic methods of individual analysis: **ABAB reversal** and **multiple baseline.** For a more detailed discussion of this topic, a number of excellent references can be consulted— for example, Hersen & Barlow, 1976; Kendall & Nay, 1978; Sidman, 1960.

ABAB Reversal

This method involves repeated comparison of the client's behavior under baseline (no treatment) and treatment conditions. The letters A and B are used to refer to baseline and treatment conditions, respectively. During the initial phase (A) the client's behavior is measured to obtain an estimate of the "natural" frequency of the problem behavior(s). This baseline observation is continued until a relatively stable pattern of behavior is obtained. During the next phase (B), treatment procedures are introduced and observation continues. If, as illustrated in Figure 3–1, the problem behavior is reduced, the therapist might conclude that the treatment has had the desired effect.

However, it is also possible that some coincidental extraneous factor is responsible for the change. To eliminate this hypothesis and to increase the therapist's confidence that the treatment is having the observed effect, the treatment procedures are withdrawn. If this *return to baseline,* or *reversal,* is accompanied by an increase in the problem behavior, the therapist can more readily conclude that the treatment procedures were effective. Finally, the treatment is reintroduced and its effect on problematic behavior (one would hope) replicated. An especially clear example of ABAB reversal program evaluation is provided in Case Study 5–3 (Chapter 5).

In cases in which there is no clear change in behavior during the B condition, the therapist would reconsider the treatment plan and alter it in some way. As with the evaluation of the first treatment plan, the therapist would implement the revised treatment and observe the client's behavior. When a particular treatment method produces clear changes in responding, a second baseline phase is introduced, followed by a second "effective" treatment phase. Here again, the goal is to obtain at least two replications of the treatment effect. Thus, depending on the outcome of the treatments, the therapist might eventually have conducted an ABCAC or an ABCDAD reversal

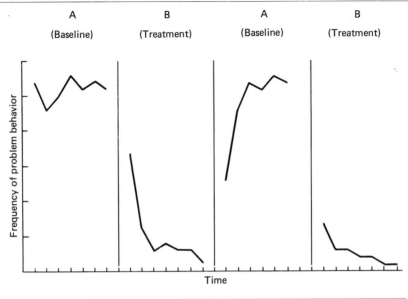

Figure 3–1. An idealized example of an ABAB reversal design.

evaluation. (C and D refer to application of different treatment techniques.)

Although the ABAB reversal design is widely used, there are situations in which it is inappropriate. One limitation is that the behaviors which are modified must be reversible. That is, in order to conclude from an ABAB reversal evaluation that the treatment was effective, the target behaviors must reliably increase or decrease with changes in conditions. This is not difficult with programs that seek to modify a relatively simple operant behavior (for instance, cooperation in a young child) through positive reinforcement (for instance, adult approval and attention). But when the behavior being modified is not as malleable (for instance, some acquired skills), reversing treatment effects is difficult if not impossible.

One could not, for example, use an ABAB reversal design to evaluate a program to train children to do long division. Although in such an instance the target behavior would be expected to increase following the introduction during the first B phase, it would not be expected to decrease following the return to baseline conditions. In certain cases there is also an ethical/practical problem involving the use of the reversal method. When the target behavior is extremely maladaptive, it would be unwise—or even dangerous—to terminate treatment and allow the problem behavior to return to baseline levels. One example is the elimination of self-injurious behavior in emotionally disturbed children. Once the self-injuries are eliminated, the therapist does not want to do anything to allow them to return to their former rate. Other methods of individual analysis have been devised to evaluate programs that deal with behaviors the therapist would be unable or unwilling to reverse.

Multiple Baseline

This method avoids the problems associated with returning the target behavior to pretreatment baseline levels. With the multiple baseline method, comparisons are based on the effects of treatment across individuals or across behaviors in the same individual. When the evaluation is based on replications with different individuals, we speak of *multiple baseline across individuals;* when evaluation is based on different behaviors

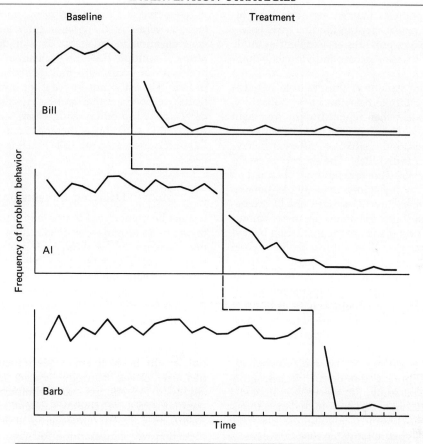

Figure 3–2. An idealized example of a multiple baseline across individuals design.

of the same individual, we speak of *multiple baseline across behaviors*.

For multiple baseline across individuals, the first step is to obtain stable baseline measures of some problem behavior in two or more individuals. Treatment is then implemented for one person, while baseline observations continue for the other(s). This situation is maintained until the first individual's problem behavior again shows stability; then the *same* treatment is applied to the second individual. This strategy is followed for any remaining clients. If the treatment is effective, the result illustrated in Figure 3–2 will be observed: each individual will continue to emit the problem behavior at stable baseline rates until the treatment is focused on them.

The multiple baseline allows the clinician to see treatment effects replicated in different individuals, thereby increasing confidence that the effect observed in the first client was not just a fluke. In addition, if the clients under observation are all in the same treatment environment (for instance, children in the same classroom or mental patients on the same hospital ward), the multiple baseline helps to eliminate the hypothesis that extraneous changes in the environment were responsible for the effects observed. Any significant environmental change *should* affect all the clients at about the same time. If nontreated individuals maintain their baseline performances while treatment is applied to others and do not show change until the treatment is shifted to them, the hypothesis that an environmental alteration is the causal agent in the change is weakened. Figure 5–1 provides an excellent example of a multiple baseline across individuals (Chapter 5).

An important variant of the multiple baseline design is the multiple baseline across behaviors. In this case, rather than replicating the treatment effect in different individuals, the therapist attempts to replicate the effect on different behaviors in the *same* individual. The strategy is essentially the same: Baseline measures are obtained on several problem behaviors in a single person. Treatment is then directed toward one of the behaviors, and the other behaviors are merely monitored. If an effect is seen in the first target behavior, the treatment is then applied to the second behavior, and so on for any remaining behaviors. The logic is the same as that for the multiple baseline across individuals. If the treatment is effective, each behavior should remain at baseline rates until treatment is implemented for it. When treatment is implemented, that behavior, and only that behavior, should change.

Case Study 8–2 (Chapter 8) provides a good example of multiple baseline evaluation across behaviors. In that study, the therapist evaluated a self-control treatment program by having the client apply self-control techniques sequentially with different types of fattening foods. After stable baseline measures were obtained for three types of foods, the treatment package was implemented with one type of food. Observation for all types of food continued. After stable measures were reestablished, treatment was implemented for the second type. Finally, self-control treatment was applied to the third type of food. Since consumption decreased for the targeted food following each implementation of treatment, the therapist concluded that the treatment was effective.

The major limitation of the multiple baseline method is the requirement that the behaviors used in the analysis be independent—that change in one behavior does not affect the other behaviors. In the example just cited (Case Study 8–2) it would have been impossible to draw firm conclusions if the client's consumption of *all* fattening foods had decreased when she was first given self-control training. But frequently behaviors are not

independent and the effects of treatment generalize. In terms of therapeutic intervention, such generalization is ideal; but it is undesirable in terms of multiple baseline evaluation. The same problem can occur with multiple baseline across individuals. It is not unusual for individuals to learn from one another and be affected by treatment applied to others with whom they interact. Again, this situation is therapeutically desirable, but unfortunate for a multiple baseline evaluation.

Drawing Conclusions

It must be pointed out that in individual analysis there are no formulas for determining whether or not a change in behavior is clear and clinically meaningful. Of course, the smaller the variation during baseline the easier it is to discern changes associated with treatment, but there are other complex factors involved. One issue relates to the type of behavior being modified. With some behaviors, anything less than total elimination is inadequate, whereas with others even a small reduction might be sufficient. For example, in the treatment of self-injurious behavior in emotionally disturbed children, total elimination of face slapping and head banging is mandatory. In the treatment of obesity, however, a 30 or 40 percent reduction in consumption of fattening foods might be satisfactory. Other factors include the goals of the client, the environment in which the client must function, and the reliability of the measurement instruments being used. When drawing conclusions from an individual analysis, therapists rely on clinical experience, knowledge of the client and of the nature of the problem, and an examination of trends in baseline responding.

It is also important to recognize the limitations of individual analysis in establishing the effectiveness of a treatment procedure for clinical populations in general. The demonstration of a strong treatment effect in two or three individuals does not "prove" a procedure is generally effective. Multiple replications are important in lending confidence to the therapist's conclusions; the more replications the better. But individual analysis with only a few replications is often an important first step in the introduction of a treatment procedure.

IMPLEMENTATION TACTICS

In our discussion of assessment we specified the variables considered relevant to effective behavioral intervention and the kind of information the behavioral clinician uses to evaluate the client's progress. Before reviewing the application of behavior modification to specific problems, it is important that we discuss the procedural tactics central to all behavioral intervention. They are establishment of the therapist-client contract, intervention in the natural environment, monitoring client progress, maintenance of client cooperation, and programming generalization. These tactics follow directly from basic behavioral assumptions regarding the factors controlling human behavior. Our discussion of the first four tactics will be brief, since much of this material has already been presented under assessment. Programming generalization will receive greater attention.

Therapist-Client Contract

After the initial assessment is completed and the client's goals have been identified, the therapist summarizes the observations and outlines the techniques that appear to be the most appropriate for the case. Although the therapist might suggest her hypotheses regarding the factors that may have generated the problem, she focuses on the things that she and the client might do to improve the client's situation. They discuss their expectations, review the client's initial goals, and evaluate the proposed program in light of the client's needs. The therapist carefully explains each facet of the program in order to ensure that the client fully understands what he might encounter in treatment. The client is also encouraged to consider carefully whether or not the therapist's ideas are compatible with his own.

Intervention in the Natural Environment

As we pointed out in Chapter 1 and in our discussion of assessment, direct intervention in the client's natural environment is one of the hallmarks of behavior modification. Regardless of the client's problem, level of sophistication, or the therapist's approach, treatment usually means chang-

ing the environment in which the client lives. Depending upon the client, this might mean intervening in the client's home, school, or institutional ward. The basic point is that the actual variables impinging on the individual in the course of daily activities are the "things" that must be changed. These changes may be instituted by the therapist, by significant others, or by the client.

The rationale for intervening in the client's everyday life should be clear from our preceding discussion. At a theoretical level, behavioral psychologists generally presume that behavioral problems are primarily related to undesirable social contingencies or learning histories. They maintain that only by changing these conditions and "reeducating" the client can the problem be alleviated. At a practical level, even if the therapist's advice and counsel were the active component in the therapeutic process, fifty minutes once a week is insufficient to change patterns of behavior. This requires input within the context of the client's daily life. Since much of behavior modification involves the delivery of social reinforcers, significant others (whose praise and attention are usually of greater value than the therapist's) may be enlisted as "therapists." For this reason, the therapist's role is often that of a consultant and teacher.

Monitoring Client Progress

In order for the therapist to tailor the treatment methods to the needs of the client and to know how fast to proceed, feedback in terms of observations of the client's behavior is necessary. Experience, "clinical intuition," and excellent training may help the therapist come up with novel ways to effect change, but without ongoing assessment the therapist would be driving with eyes closed.

Client Cooperation

As with any therapeutic or educational program, cooperation of the client is crucial. In contrast to psychoanalytic approaches, client resistance is not viewed as indicating progress toward "recovery." Rather, it is a signal that something is wrong with the program. If the client breaks appointments, fails to fulfill obligations to the program, and so on, the therapist must alter the program in some way. This requires additional assessment. Perhaps some component of the program is aversive, or the program's incentive system is no longer valued, or new problems have arisen, or the client does not possess the skills to meet certain criteria. Perhaps the problem was assessed incorrectly in the first place. The therapist must check out these possibilities and make the needed changes in order to maintain client cooperation.

Programming Generalization

One of the most important issues in behavior modification is the long-term impact of intervention programs. Unfortunately, gains are often short-lived. Unless generalization is explicitly "programmed," the individual may quickly return to old ways of behaving or emit the new behavior only in particular situations (Baer, Wolf, & Risley, 1968; Bijou & Redd, 1975; Kazdin & Bootzin, 1972; O'Leary & Drabman, 1971; Walker & Buckley, 1972).

Research has shown that changes in behavior are often limited to the time, place, and personnel associated with the program; when these "conditions" (that is, stimuli) are not present, the behavior deteriorates (for instance, Lovaas & Simmons, 1969; Redd, 1969, 1970; Rincover & Koegel, 1975). For example, in a study involving two disruptive and oppositional children (five- and eight-year-old boys referred to an outpatient psychological clinic by school personnel), the positive effects of the behavior management program instituted in the boys' homes were limited to the home setting (Wahler, 1969b). Their behavior in the classroom remained disruptive. Only after the contingency system was carried out by the teacher was there any positive change in their classroom behavior.

Even within the same setting, gains may be limited to those activities and times of the day when the program is in effect. An example of this phenomenon comes from a case report on a classroom program for delinquent adolescent girls (Meichenbaum, Bowers, & Ross, 1968). The reinforcement program was first implemented only during the afternoon session, during which period there was marked improvement. The girls did more work,

were less disruptive, and showed academic progress. But the improvement in the girls' behavior was evident only in the afternoons. During the morning sessions they behaved in the way they always had; there was no change. Given our discussion of stimulus control in Chapter 2, these results are not surprising. In each case the children quickly identified either the time or place in which the reinforcement contingencies were in effect and behaved accordingly. That is, positive change in behavior was limited to those situations in which the contingencies of reinforcement were rearranged.

Although this problem has not been extensively researched, behavioral psychologists have devised methods to foster the transfer of newly acquired behaviors to new situations. The essential component of all these methods is to make the conditions under which treatment occurs as much like the natural environment as possible. This is achieved either by altering the treatment setting so that it resembles the natural environment or by changing the client's natural environment so that it has many of the characteristics of the conditions associated with treatment. The ideal goal would be to have the treatment setting so much like the natural environment that the client could not tell them apart. Of course, this is close to impossible, but steps can be taken to reduce the differences between the two settings.

Selection of Target Behaviors. The most effective method of ensuring the maintenance of gains following the termination of the intervention program is to teach behaviors that are likely to be reinforced during the client's daily interaction, that is, behaviors that will be "naturally" reinforced. For example, if one were teaching language to a mentally retarded child, the best words to teach would be those that would bring the child reinforcement when he speaks. One might teach the child to ask for a cookie or to greet a stranger with a friendly "hello" rather than teach him how to pronounce his ABCs or some other group of words that would be unlikely to evoke praise and attention from those around him. Similarly, one would expect self-help skills and prosocial behaviors to be maintained more readily than academic and nonsocial behaviors.

Changing Reinforcement Contingencies in the Natural Environment. Unfortunately, many clients live in situations in which reinforcement of appropriate behavior is infrequent and reinforcement contingencies run counter to program goals. For example, the client's spouse may be away from the home most of the day or have social problems of his or her own; or the client may reside in an institution where staff attention is lacking or where the only way to get attention is through misbehavior. In each case, it is unlikely that the natural environment will help implement any intervention program. It is also clear that this situation must be changed if generalization is to occur.

Behavioral psychologists have handled this kind of problem in three ways: (1) training parents and significant others in techniques of reinforcement (for example, Axelrod, Hall, & Maxwell, 1972; Becker, Madsen, Arnold, & Thomas, 1967; Pomerleau, Bobrove, & Smith, 1973; Wahler, 1969a; Walker & Buckley, 1972); (2) introducing new agents of natural reinforcement in the client's life (for example, Phillips, 1968; Ullmann, 1976); and (3) placing the client in a new "therapeutic" living environment that will reinforce the desired behavior change (for example, Kelley & Henderson, 1971; Lovaas, Koegel, Simmons, & Long, 1973; Phillips, 1968).

Varying the Conditions Associated with Treatment. By varying the time, setting, materials, and personnel associated with the intervention program, the probability that these factors will gain stimulus control of the target behavior is reduced.

In a social rehabilitation program for delinquent adolescents, the effects of varying the conditions of training on the transfer of newly acquired prosocial behavior were studied (Emshoff, Redd, & Davison, 1976). Those clients who were reinforced under conditions that varied in terms of the time of day, personnel, and setting showed greater transfer of prosocial behavior to new situations than clients who were trained under a constant set of conditions. In one intervention program for severely retarded children, there was greater transfer of learning from a one-to-one tutoring setting to the classroom when children were trained under varying stimulus conditions than when they were trained under constant conditions (Pomerantz & Redd, 1978).

Changing the Form and Schedule of Reinforcement. Another method for making the conditions of treatment more like those of the natural environment is to change the magnitude, frequency, and form of reinforcement. The therapist may initially have to use very powerful reinforcers dispensed after each response, but if the newly acquired behavior is to transfer to the natural environment, it must be resistant to extinction. That is, the behavior must be maintained under conditions in which reinforcement is infrequent.

In many institutional programs, reinforcement is systematically faded out as the client progresses through what are called levels or steps. Each subsequent level better resembles the real world in that the client is required to do more in order to get less reinforcement. As the program continues, the form of reinforcement is also gradually changed to resemble the kind of reinforcement present in the natural environment. For example, during the beginning stages of treatment tangible reinforcers may be used, but as the client progresses, social reinforcers are substituted.

Training Clients in Self-Control. One method that is often effective is to teach clients to be their own behavior modifiers. Clients can be taught to set up programs, monitor their own behavior, reinforce themselves, and most important, change their social environment so that it will encourage progress (Turkewitz, O'Leary, & Ironsmith, 1975).

Changing Clients' Cognitive Sets. Changing how clients interpret events and stimuli in their daily lives has been suggested as a means of increasing the probability that new ways of behaving will be maintained after the program is ended (Bandura, 1969; Meichenbaum, 1976). Essentially, this involves teaching individuals more rational interpretations of events in their lives. If, by changing clients' cognitive sets, reactions from others that were once irrationally interpreted as punishment are viewed as inconsequential or even as positive, then behavior in the natural environment should change. Although the actual contingencies remain unchanged, because of changes in clients' cognitive sets their impact has been altered.

SUMMARY

Effective behavioral intervention is a complex process requiring scientific rigor on the one hand and refined clinical sensitivity on the other. Although the behavioral clinician displays many, if not all, of the interpersonal qualities associated with traditional supportive psychotherapy, empathy and rapport are not considered to be catalysts for therapeutic change in and of themselves. Rather, they are viewed as conditions that facilitate the implementation of other techniques.

Two important facets of behavioral intervention are assessment and evaluation. The goal of assessment is to determine the variables that affect the client's behavior. This assessment involves a functional analysis of the effects of (1) antecedent stimuli that may evoke or elicit the problem behavior, (2) the magnitude of the maladaptive behavior (that is, its frequency, duration, intensity, and latency), (3) interaction patterns that might involve the reinforcement of the problem behavior and the extinction or punishment of adaptive behavior, (4) client variables that might affect the function of naturally occurring events (these variables include such nonbehavioral factors as physical health and social relationships), and (5) the client's behavioral assets and deficits. Assessment also involves a plan for program implementation. For example, the therapist must find out if there are family members or significant others to assist or perhaps sabotage the program, if certain client social values or commitments will restrict what the therapist can do, and so on.

Evaluation of the effects of treatment has become a critical feature of behavioral intervention. The most widely accepted method is the group experimental design. However, this method is inappropriate for use by the individual therapist who wants to evaluate the impact of a particular program with a specific client. In such cases, an individual analysis strategy is used. In contrast to statistical analysis, which compares the performance of different groups of subjects, the performance of an individual client is measured under one set of circumstances (that is, treatment) and compared to his or her performance under another set of circumstances. Individual analysis can be carried out in a variety of ways. Two basic methods of individual analysis are ABAB reversal and multiple baseline.

Regardless of the client's problems or level of sophistication, treatment ultimately means changing the environment in some way. These changes may be instituted by the therapist, by significant others, or by the client. The rationale for intervening in the client's everyday life is quite simple: (1) At a theoretical level, behavior modification presumes that behavioral problems are primarily related to undesirable social contingencies or learning histories, and only by changing these conditions and "reeducating" the client can the problem be removed. (2) At a practical level, even if the therapist's advice and counsel were the active component in the therapeutic process, fifty minutes once a week would not be enough to change patterns of behavior. This requires input within the context of the client's daily life. (3) Since much of behavior modification involves the delivery of social reinforcers, significant others (whose praise and attention are usually of greater value than the therapist's) may be enlisted as "therapists." For this reason, the therapist's role is often that of a consultant and teacher. The therapist devises programs and teaches the client and/or significant others how to carry them out.

One of the most important issues in behavior modification is the long-term impact of intervention programs. Behavioral psychologists have devised methods to foster the transfer of newly acquired behaviors to new situations. The essential component of these methods is to make the conditions under which treatment occurs as much like the natural environment as possible. This is achieved either by altering the treatment setting so that it resembles the natural environment or by changing the client's natural environment so that it has many of the characteristics of the conditions associated with treatment.

REFERENCES

Axelrod, S., Hall, R. V., & Maxwell, A. Use of peer attention to increase study behavior. *Behavior Therapy,* 1972, **3,** 349–351.

Baer, D. M., Wolf, M. M., & Risley, T. R. Some current dimensions of applied behavior analysis. *Journal of Applied Behavior Analysis,* 1968, **1,** 91–97.

Bandura, A. A social learning interpretation of psychological dysfunctions. In P. London and D. Rosenhan (Eds.), *Foundations of abnormal psychology.* New York: Holt, Rinehart and Winston, 1968.

Bandura, A. *Principles of behavior modification.* New York: Holt, Rinehart and Winston, 1969.

Beck, A. T. Cognition, affect, and psychopathology. *Archives of General Psychiatry,* 1971, **24,** 495–500.

Becker, W. C., Madsen, C. H., Arnold, C. R., & Thomas, D. R. The contingent use of teacher attention and praising in reducing classroom behavior problems. *Journal of Special Education,* 1967, **1,** 287–307.

Begelman, D. A. Ethical and legal issues of behavior modification. In M. Hersen, R. M. Eisler, & P. M. Miller (Eds.), *Progress in behavior modification, 1.* New York: Academic Press, 1975.

Bieber, S. A discussion of "homosexuality: The ethical challenge." *Journal of Consulting and Clinical Psychology,* 1976, **44,** 163–166.

Bijou, S. W., & Peterson, R. F. The psychological assessment of children: A functional analysis. In P. McReynolds (Ed.), *Advances in psychological assessment,* Vol. 2. New York: Science and Behavior Books, 1972.

Bijou, S. W., Peterson, R. F., & Ault, M. H. A method to integrate descriptive and experimental field studies at the level of data and empirical concepts. *Journal of Applied Behavior Analysis,* 1968, **1,** 175–191.

Bijou, S. W., & Redd, W. H. Behavior therapy for children. *American Handbook of Psychiatry,* 5. New York: Basic Books, 1975.

Cohen, H. L. *The person: To be or not to be.* Address given to the Association for Advancement of Behavior Therapy, Chicago, 1974, unpublished.

Dalton, R. F., & Sundbiad, L. M. Using principles of social learning in training communication of empathy. *Journal of Counseling Psychology,* 1976, **23,** 454–457.

Davison, G. C. Homosexuality: The ethical challenge. *Journal of Consulting and Clinical Psychology,* 1976, **44,** 157–162.

Ellis, A. *Humanistic psychotherapy: The rational-emotive approach.* New York: Julian Press, 1973.

Emshoff, J. E., Redd, W. H., & Davison, W. S. Generalization training and the transfer of treatment effects. *Journal of Behavior Therapy and Experimental Psychiatry,* 1976, **7,** 141–144.

Ferster, C. B. A functional analysis of depression. *American Psychologist,* 1973, **28,** 857–870.

Frank, J. D. *Persuasion and healing.* Baltimore: Johns Hopkins Press, 1961.

Goldfried, M. R., & Davison, G. C. *Clinical behavior therapy.* New York: Holt, Rinehart and Winston, 1976.

Goldstein, A. P. *Therapist-patient expectations in psychotherapy.* New York: Pergamon Press, 1962.

Gottman, J. M., & Leiblum, S. R. *How to do psychotherapy and how to evaluate it.* New York: Holt, Rinehart and Winston, 1974.

Halleck, S. L. *The politics of therapy.* New York: Science House, 1971.

Hersen, M., & Barlow, D. H. *Single case experimental designs.* New York: Pergamon Press, 1976.

Holland, J. G. *Behavior modification for prisoners, patients, and other people as a prescription for the planned society.* Address given to the spring meetings of the Eastern Psychological Association, 1974, unpublished.

Kanfer, F. H., & Grimm, L. G. Behavioral analysis: Selecting target behaviors in the interview. *Behavior Modification,* 1977, **1,** 7–28.

Kanfer, F. H., & Phillips, J. S. A survey of current behavior therapies and a proposal for classification. In C. M. Franks (Ed.), *Behavior therapy: Appraisal and status.* New York: McGraw-Hill, 1969.

Kanfer, F. H., & Saslow, G. Behavioral diagnosis. In C. M. Franks (Ed.), *Behavior therapy: Appraisal and status.* New York: McGraw-Hill, 1969.

Kantor, J. R. *Interbehavioral psychology.* Bloomington, Ind.: Principia Press, 1959.

Kazdin, A. E. Role of instructions and reinforcement in behavior changes in token reinforcement programs. *Journal of Educational Psychology,* 1973, **64,** 63–71.

Kazdin, A. E., & Bootzin, R. R. The token economy: An evaluative review. *Journal of Applied Behavior Analysis,* 1972, **5,** 343–372.

Kelley, K. M., & Henderson, J. D. A community-based operant learning environment II: Systems and procedures. In R. D. Rubin, H. Fernsterheim, A. Lazarus, & C. Franks (Eds.), *Advances in behavior therapy.* New York: Academic Press, 1971.

Kendall, P. C., & Nay, W. R. Treatment evaluation strategies. In W. R. Nay (Ed.), *Multimethod clinical assessment.* New York: Gardner Press-Wiley, 1978.

Kennedy, R. E. Behavior modification in prisons. In W. E. Craighead, A. E. Kazdin, & M. J. Mahoney (Eds.), *Behavior modification: Principles, issues and applications.* Boston: Houghton Mifflin, 1976.

King, G. F., Armitage, S. G., & Tilton, J. R. A therapeutic approach to schizophrenics of extreme pathology: An operant-interpersonal method. *Journal of Abnormal and Social Psychology,* 1960, **61,** 276–286.

Kreitman, N. The reliability of psychiatric diagnosis. *Journal of Mental Science,* 1961, **107,** 876–886.

Lazarus, A. A. Behavioral rehearsal vs. non-directive therapy vs. advice in effecting behavior change. *Behaviour Research and Therapy,* 1966, **4,** 209–212.

Lazarus, A. A. *Behavior therapy and beyond.* New York: McGraw-Hill, 1971.

Lennard, H. C., & Bernstein, A. *The anatomy of psychotherapy.* New York: Columbia University Press, 1960.

Lewinsohn, P. M. The behavioral study and treatment of depression. In M. Hersen, R. M. Eisler, & P. M. Miller (Eds.), *Progress in behavior modification.* New York: Academic Press, 1975.

Locke, E. A. Is "behavior therapy" behavioristic? (An analysis of Wolpe's psychotherapeutic methods). In C. M. Franks & G. T. Wilsons (Eds.), *Annual review of behavior therapy, 1973.* New York: Brunner/Mazel, 1973.

Loeber, R. Engineering the behavioral engineer. *Journal of Applied Behavior Analysis,* 1971, **4,** 321–326.

Lorr, M., Klett, C. J., & McNair, D. M. *Syndromes of psychosis.* New York: Macmillan, 1963.

Lovaas, O. I., Koegel, R., Simmons, J. Q., & Long, J. S. Some generalization and follow-up measures on autistic children in behavior therapy. *Journal of Applied Behavior Analysis,* 1973, **6,** 131–166.

Lovaas, O. I., & Simmons, J. Q. Manipulation of self-destruction in three retarded children. *Journal of Applied Behavior Analysis,* 1969, **2,** 143–157.

Madsen, C. H., Becker, W. C., & Thomas, D. R. Rules, praise, and ignoring: Elements of elementary classroom control. *Journal of Applied Behavior Analysis,* 1968, **1,** 139–150.

Masters, W. H., & Johnson, V. E. *Human sexual inadequacy.* Boston: Little, Brown, 1970.

McFall, R. M., & Lillesand, D. V. Behavioral rehearsal with modeling and coaching in assertive training. *Journal of Abnormal Psychology,* 1971, **77,** 313–333.

McFall, R. M., & Marston, A. An experimental investigation of behavior rehearsal in assertive training. *Journal of Abnormal Psychology,* 1970, **76,** 295–303.

Meichenbaum, D. Cognitive behavior modification. In J. T. Spence, R. C. Carson, & J. W. Thibaut (Eds.), *Behavioral approaches to therapy.* Morristown, N.J.: General Learning Press, 1976.

Meichenbaum, D. M., Bowers, K., & Ross, R. R. Modification of classroom behavior of institutionalized female adolescent offenders. *Behaviour Research and Therapy,* 1968, **8,** 343–353.

Merbaum, M., & Southwell, E. A. Conditioning of affective self-references as a function of the discriminative characteristics of experimenter intervention. *Journal of Abnormal Psychology,* 1965, **70,** 180–187.

Mischel, W. *Personality and assessment.* New York: Wiley, 1968.

Nelson, R. O., & Bowles, P. E. The best of two worlds —observation with norms. *Journal of School Psychology,* 1975, **13,** 3–9.

O'Leary, K. D., & Becker, W. C. The effects of a teacher's reprimands on children's behavior. *Journal of School Psychology,* 1968, **7,** 8–11.

O'Leary, K. D., & Drabman, R. Token reinforcement programs in the classroom: A review. *Psychological Bulletin,* 1971, **75,** 379–398.

O'Leary, K. D., Kaufman, K. F., Kass, R. E., & Drabman, R. S. The effects of loud and soft reprimands on the behavior of disruptive students. *Exceptional Children,* 1970, **37,** 145–155.

Phillips, E. J. Achievement Place: Token reinforcement procedures in a home-style rehabilitation setting for "predelinquent" boys. *Journal of Applied Behavior Analysis*, 1968, **1**, 213–223.

Pomerantz, D., & Redd, W. H. Programmed generalization with severely retarded children, 1978, unpublished.

Pomerleau, O. F., Bobrove, P. H., & Smith, R. H. Rewarding psychiatric aides for the behavioral improvement of assigned patients. *Journal of Applied Behavior Analysis*, 1973, **6**, 383–390.

Rappaport, J. *Toward a community psychology: The search for new paradigms.* New York: Holt, Rinehart and Winston, 1977.

Redd, W. H. Effects of mixed reinforcement contingencies on adults' control of children's behavior. *Journal of Applied Behavior Analysis*, 1969, **2**, 249–254.

Redd, W. H. Generalization of adults' stimulus control of children's behavior. *Journal of Experimental Child Psychology*, 1970, **9**, 286–296.

Reppucci, N. D., & Saunders, J. T. Social psychology of behavior modification—problems of implementation in natural settings. *American Psychologist*, 1974, **29**, 649–660.

Rincover, A., & Koegel, R. L. Setting generality and stimulus control in autistic children. *Journal of Applied Behavior Analysis*, 1975, **8**, 235–246.

Ross, A. D. *Behavior disorders in children.* New York: General Learning Press, 1971.

Saunders, A. G. *Behavior therapy in prisons: Walden II or clock-work orange?* Paper presented at meetings of the Association for the Advancement of Behavior Therapy, Chicago, November 1974, unpublished.

Sherman, J. A., & Baer, D. M. Appraisal of operant therapy techniques with children and adults. In C. M. Franks (Ed.), *Behavior therapy: Appraisal and status.* New York: McGraw-Hill, 1969.

Sidman, M. *Tactics of scientific research: Evaluating experimental data in psychology.* New York: Basic Books, 1960.

Sidman, M. Behavior-shaping with the mentally retarded. In N. Bernstein (Ed.), *Diminished people.* Boston: Little, Brown, 1970.

Staples, F. R., Sloane, R. B., Whipple, K., Cristol, A. H., & Yorkston, N. J. Differences between behavior therapists and psychotherapists. *Archives of General Psychiatry*, 1975, **32**, 1517–1522.

Sturm, I. E. The behavioristic aspect of psychodrama. *Group Psychotherapy*, 1965, **18**, 50–64.

Tharp, R., & Wetzel, R. *Behavior modification in the natural environment.* New York: Academic Press, 1969.

Truax, C. B. Reinforcement and non-reinforcement in Rogerian psychotherapy. *Journal of Abnormal Psychology*, 1966, **71**, 1–9.

Truax, C. B., & Carkhuff, R. R. *Toward effective counseling and psychotherapy, training and practice.* Chicago: Aldine, 1961.

Turkewitz, H., O'Leary, K. D., & Ironsmith, M. Generalization and maintenance of appropriate behavior through self-control. *Journal of Consulting and Clinical Psychology*, 1975, **43**, 577–583.

Ullmann, R. K. Social side effects of contingent reinforcement: Children's adult preferences and instruction following. M.A. thesis, University of Illinois, 1976, unpublished.

Wahler, R. G. Oppositional children: A quest for parental reinforcement control. *Journal of Applied Behavior Analysis*, 1969, **2**, 159–170(a).

Wahler, R. G. Setting generality: Some specific general effects of child behavior therapy. *Journal of Applied Behavior Analysis*, 1969, **2**, 239–246(b).

Walker, H. M., & Buckley, N. K. Programming generalization and maintenance of treatment effects across time and across settings. *Journal of Applied Behavior Analysis*, 1972, **5**, 209–224.

Winett, R. A., & Winkler, R. C. Current behavior modification in the classroom: Be still, be quiet, be docile. *Journal of Applied Behavior Analysis*, 1972, **5**, 499–504.

Zigler, E., & Phillips, L. Psychiatric diagnosis: A critique. *Journal of Abnormal and Social Psychology*, 1961, **63**, 607–618.

PART II

APPLICATIONS:
CHILDREN

four
PROBLEMS OF NORMAL CHILDHOOD DEVELOPMENT

The relationship between parent and child is as intense and as potent as any relationship in a person's life. Each individual is extremely sensitive to the other's reactions and each affects the other's behavior in profound ways. We have already presented one classic example: the crying infant and the parent who picks the baby up. The baby's cries elicit caretaking behavior in the parent that serves to reinforce the child's crying. Likewise, the cessation of the crying negatively reinforces the parent's picking up the child. The parent is heavily reinforced for doing so and probably does not realize the long-term effect of these actions. In this case, the parent's actions actually strengthen behavior the parent would like to eliminate. This reciprocal influence is present in many situations. A young child grins when her father makes funny noises, so the father makes more silly sounds and faces. A mother hugs her three-year-old son when he climbs into her lap, and the next day the child does it again. In a sense, both the parent and the child are naturally placed in roles of "behavior modifiers."

Most behavioral psychologists contend that children do not misbehave because they are "bad" or because they have some deep psychological complexes, but rather because at times the payoff is greater for misbehaving than for being good. In many instances, the social environment reinforces children with attention when they misbehave and ignores them when they are well behaved.

In this chapter we will discuss problems often encountered in normal childhood development and show how many of these problems can be eliminated, or at least minimized, by parents' systematically changing how they respond to the child's behavior. We will begin our discussion with a brief review of research on infant social behavior and parent-child interaction in order to show how the very nature of the human species makes social interaction a powerful mechanism for behavioral influence. This discussion will lead into issues in parent training and the parent's role as teacher. Behavior problems will be considered in the order in which they may appear as a child develops: problems of feeding and tantrums, toilet training, enuresis, phobias, and social problems such as aggression. Our coverage here will primarily focus on problems that occur in children before they reach first grade. Problems of older children will be considered in subsequent chapters.

PARENT-CHILD INTERACTION

We are social, not by accident or desire, but by design. In a chapter aptly titled "The Social and Socializing Infant," Harriet Rheingold (1971, p. 798) observes:

The human infant is born into a social environment upon which he is dependent for survival. Although he is physically helpless during the first few months, he has several effective procedures for insuring that he receives the care he requires. He is socially responsive and he invites social responses from others. By means of his cry and smile, and to a lesser extent by means of his contented vocalizations, he modifies the caretaking behavior of his parents to suit his needs. They, furthermore, find their caretaking operations reinforcing not only in themselves but also because they result in a diminution of the infant's fretting and in an increase of his social responsiveness.

The perceptual and motor systems of the infant are well suited to the social relationship into which he or she is born. From the first moments of life, even before the first feeding, the infant is responsive to social stimulation from adults (Freedman & Freedman, 1969; Korner & Grobstein, 1967). Infants selectively attend to the bandwidth of frequencies that include voices (Eisenberger, Griffin, Coursin, & Hunter, 1964), can discriminate between voices and prefer a female voice (Boyd, 1975; Kagan & Lewis, 1965), and are best able to focus at the distance adults normally present their faces when holding or attending to an infant (seven to nine inches) (Stern, 1974). Some data suggest that perhaps as early as eleven minutes of age the infant is differentially responsive to the human face (Goren, Sarty, & Wu, 1975). A general consensus exists that by three and one-half weeks of age the infant quickly fixates on adults' faces and typically responds by smiling (Gibson, 1969; Wolff, 1963).

In addition to being especially responsive to adult social stimulation, the newborn has a host of behaviors that elicit adult attention and caretaking. One of the strongest "controlling behaviors" is crying. Researchers have observed that in natural settings, almost without exception, adults immediately respond to an infant's cry (David & Appell, 1961; Dennis & Dennis, 1951). What is more, mothers are usually able to recognize different types of crying. In one study (Wolff, 1969), researchers found that mothers and hospital nurses could actually discriminate four distinct types of crying and responded to each differently.

The young child's ability to affect and be affected by others increases with age. Studies have shown that children control their parents' behavior in a variety of ways—by being coy and cute as well as by being oppositional and aggressive (for instance, Marvin, Marvin, & Abramovitch, 1973; Wahler, 1969; Williams, 1959). Parents, in turn, control children's behavior by their varied reactions (Bijou & Baer, 1965).

Perhaps one of the clearest and most fascinating demonstrations of the subtle but powerful impact of adult attention on the behavior of the young child is a series of studies on vocal behavior in three-month-old infants conducted by Kathleen Bloom (Bloom, 1974, 1975, 1977a, 1977b; Bloom & Esposito, 1975). Bloom found that adult social stimulation (that is, smiles, gentle touches, and soft words such as "tsk, tsk") elicits prosocial behavior in the infant. In a carefully controlled laboratory setting, adults provided such stimulation on a predetermined, response-independent schedule, and the infants' rates of vocalizing decreased dramatically. Consistent with research on the infant's differential responses to adults' eyes (Wolff, 1963), Bloom found that the social elicitation was dependent upon the infant seeing the adults' eyes.

Adult attention also has a powerful reinforcing value for almost all children. In a classic study by Yvonne Brackbill (1958), rates of smiling in three- and four-and-a-half-month-old infants increased significantly when an adult reinforced their smiles by smiling and picking them up. The infants' rates were directly related to the ratio of social reinforcement: smiling increased as the ratios of reinforcement were increased. The more smiles that were required in order to obtain reinforcement, the more the infants smiled.

Infant crying has also been subjected to systematic analysis. Barbara Etzel and Jacob Gewirtz (1967) studied the crying behavior of two "problem" infants (six and twenty weeks of age) residing in the well-baby unit of a children's hospital prior to foster-home placement. Both infants exhibited high rates of crying—three times that of the other infants. Etzel and Gewirtz observed that the staff would typically try to quiet the two infants by holding them. In order to investigate the effect of adult attention on the infants' crying, Etzel and Gewirtz decided to deliver attention (a two-second full smile, coupled with soft words and a gentle nod toward the child) contingent upon responses observed to be incompatible with crying. For one child, smiling was reinforced; for the other, smiles and eye contact were reinforced. Whenever the child cried, the experimenter immediately withdrew her attention and gave a neutral face.

Within seven daily sessions, each lasting fifteen minutes, the infants' rates of crying decreased dramatically and the smiling increased (as much as fourfold). Etzel and Gewirtz's account of how one of the infants, Anthony, behaved during the extinction phase of the study, when the experimenter withheld all social reinforcement, gives some indication of the reinforcement strengths of adult attention with even very young children. "Anthony would look at E, smile, receive no reinforcement, wrinkle up his face as if to cry but without vocalizing, look at E again and smile, and so on" (p. 314). He shifted from one behavior to another as if to be trying out all the ways he knew to get adult attention.

Unfortunately, parents are often unaware or misinformed about the impact their actions have on the child, with the result that they are unable to affect their children in the ways they want. In fact, certain of their actions have the opposite effect of what they intended. One of the most common examples of parental reactions "backfiring" is the reinforcing effect that reprimands and adult attention can have. In numerous cases it has been observed that an adult's criticism and/or scolding can result in an increase in the frequency of the undesirable behavior the scolding was meant to suppress (Becker, Madsen, Arnold, & Thomas, 1967; Madsen, Becker, & Thomas, 1968; O'Leary & Becker, 1968). Robert Hawkins and his colleagues (Hawkins, Peterson, Schweid, & Bijou, 1966) reported a case that clearly demonstrates this problem. The child was a four-year-old boy whom psychologists described as oppositional. The presenting problem was his frequent tantrums and disobedience. The boy's mother reported that he would get angry and kick objects, rip his own clothing, annoy his younger sister, and make threats. The parents were discouraged and sought help.

In the course of their assessments, Hawkins and his colleagues observed the mother and the child in the home and quickly noticed that the boy's un-

desirable behaviors resulted in immediate parental attention. When he misbehaved, the parents would typically try to reason with him, distract his attention by suggesting a new activity that he might enjoy, and if all else failed, scold him. When he was cooperative and pleasant, however, he was virtually ignored. Given the absence of positive attention from the parents, the child, not surprisingly, discovered other ways to get attention (even though negative attention might have been "second best," it was better than nothing). The strategy of Hawkins and his co-workers was to have the mother systematically ignore the disruptive behavior while prompting and reinforcing incompatible positive behaviors. Within five days, the child's antisocial behaviors decreased markedly and prosocial behavior increased.

PARENT TRAINING

Given the potency of parents' influence on their child's development, it follows that teaching them how to direct their influence toward beneficial ends may well be one of the most important contributions of behavior modification.

During the last five years, at least two dozen behaviorally oriented how-to manuals for parents have been published (Hawkins, 1972). Each manual follows a slightly different format, but all focus on two basic techniques: reinforcement and timeout. Parents are urged to consider the actions of their child in terms of the benefits each behavior brings the child. Do Johnny's crying and tantrums result in your giving him immediate attention? Do you give him candy in the supermarket to keep him happy and to prevent his making a scene? What happens when he sits quietly playing with his toys?

Our coverage of parent training will be organized according to the specific behavioral techniques parents learn: positive reinforcement, punishment, and timeout.

Positive Reinforcement

Sometimes all that is necessary is for the parents to be reminded to take notice of good behavior. A good example of this principle is the report by

Emily Herbert and Donald Baer (1972). They asked mothers of problem children to record the number of times each day that they responded to their children's good behavior with praise and attention. Mothers were given golfers' wrist counters and told to press them each time they took special notice of good behavior. These instructions served to prompt positive interaction by making them aware of positive behaviors they had previously ignored. The children's behavior improved dramatically. The children became more cooperative, and their tantrums and aggressiveness diminished. In this case, parent training simply involved reminding parents to do something they already knew how to do.

The use of positive reinforcement also has some important positive side effects. It tends to change the whole atmosphere of the family. Not only does one pleasant comment usually lead to a pleasant comment in return, but the child's general attitude toward the parents also improves. As one might expect, children prefer adults who make their wishes clear (Redd, Morris, & Martin, 1975; Morris & Redd, 1975). What is more, the parents' overall view of their children seems to change when they start focusing on good behavior; often they are surprised at how well behaved their children really are (Herbert & Baer, 1972).

Parents are not told to be positive and to dispense goodies no matter what the child does. Rather, praise and attention are supposed to be given only when the child is well behaved. If children are rewarded regardless of how they act (that is, receive noncontingent reinforcement), then their behavior will not improve and may, in fact, get worse. Noncontingent reinforcement is useless. To be effective and meaningful, positive comments and attention must be "functionally" related to the person's behavior. Even with a child who is frequently inept, parents can still be positive without being noncontingent. They must begin by prompting the desired behavior and then reinforce it.

Parent training is also concerned with situations in which using positive reinforcement is not enough. Parents are advised to ignore the child's misbehavior. This suggestion is based on the notion that many children misbehave because it gets them lots of attention; and, as we have said before, adult attention, regardless of how it is intended, is usually a powerful reward for children. If parents are able to make good behavior really pay off so that it is a more attractive alternative than misbehavior, then misbehavior should diminish if the parents consistently ignore it. The idea is that good behavior should become so pervasive that it literally smothers misbehavior if contingencies are correctly established.

It is important to point out that when behavior is systematically ignored, there is often a "burst" of responding. That is, the initial response to extinction is typically a rapid increase in the frequency of the targeted behavior. This burst is temporary, and is followed by a gradual decline in the rate of the behavior. Parents are often confused by this burst phenomenon and believe that the "ignoring" is not having the desired effect. For this reason, the therapist must make sure the parents understand that this effect is expected and that it is only temporary.

In some situations, however, just ignoring a behavior does not result in its extinction. Certainly, the desire for attention is not the only reason why children misbehave, and if attention is not what a child seeks, then merely withholding it is irrelevant to the behavior and will not affect it. Even if a child is seeking attention, on some occasions ignoring the child just will not work. Bashing-at-the-stereo-with-a-baseball-bat behavior may well be reinforced by the attention the child receives as the parent drags her away. Nevertheless, it is necessary to protect the equipment, and just sitting there calmly and ignoring what is happening will not suffice. This behavior cannot be ignored; it must be stopped. One alternative comes to mind: punishment.

Punishment

No topic is more taboo in behavior modification than punishment. Although parents do use punishment, most parent-training manuals do not mention it and those that do discourage its use. This strong opposition to punishment is based on "beliefs" held by many behavioral psychologists. We use the term "beliefs" because little empirical research has been done on the effect of punishment with humans (Johnston, 1972). The arguments against the use of punishment may be emotionally compelling, but they represent extrapolations from animal research that may have only limited relevance to the application of punishment in clinical work.

Three beliefs about punishment are prominent. One objection to punishment concerns emotional side effects. The child may become very upset and cry. Another fear is that individuals who are punished might come to avoid those people and situations they associate with the punishment. Children who are severely and repeatedly punished by their parents might begin to resent and fear them. Or children might try to figure out ways to avoid their parents' punishment. They might lie or "hide the evidence" of their misbehavior. A third and very real objection is that inflicting pain on someone is repugnant. Most clinicians just do not like the idea of punishing people in order to modify behavior.

Timeout

So, behavioral psychologists do not recommend physical punishment. Instead, they advise timeout. Take the example of the child who keeps picking on his sister and won't leave her alone. In using timeout the parent, without yelling or getting upset, might put the child in a chair in the corner of the room. The child would not be given any toys or access to television, and no one would talk to him. He would just have to sit alone *for a short while*. If the parents find the child will not stay in the chair without scolding or force, timeout might have to involve removing the child from the scene and putting him in a place where the sources of reinforcement are limited. Of course, care is taken to choose a location that doesn't frighten him and one in which he cannot harm himself. The child might be placed in a room by himself and, if necessary, with the door shut. The isolation and lack of access to television, toys, and attention constitute a timeout from reinforcement.

Robert Wahler (1969) presented an example of the effectiveness of timeout. Two sets of parents had young school-age boys with whom they could not cope. The boys were stubborn and negative, threw tantrums, refused to cooperate with their

parents or follow instructions. Since their many attempts at reasoning with the boys had not worked, the parents vacillated between letting the children have their own way and resorting to spankings, a system that did nothing to improve the children's behavior. Finally, they brought the boys to a local mental health clinic. After observing the children and parents interacting with one another, Wahler taught the parents how to identify good behavior and how to use positive reinforcement and timeout—lots of praise and approval whenever the boys were cooperative, and isolation in their bedrooms for five minutes when they were disobedient. Whenever the child began to have a tantrum, the parents did not argue or get upset, but were simply told to take the child immediately to his room. After five minutes they were to let him return to his previous activities. Whenever their child cooperated, they were to dispense warm praise and attention. Both boys reacted well to their parents' new ways of responding to them: the boys' misbehavior diminished rapidly. Moreover, everyone involved appeared to benefit in other ways. Parents reported that they liked being with their children more, and the two boys had a more positive attitude toward their parents.

In addition to the general, "all-purpose" training that most behavior modification training manuals provide, behavioral psychologists have taught parents to function as interventionists in the treatment of specific childhood problems. The list of problems is extensive, ranging from the elimination of tantrums (for instance, Williams, 1959) to enuresis (for instance, Bucher, 1972), and from the teaching of self-help skills to mentally retarded children (for instance, Walder, Cohen, Breiter, Daston, Hirsch, & Leibowitz, 1969) to teaching remedial reading.

According to research, parent training has been highly effective (O'Dell, 1974; Rinn, Vernon, & Wise, 1975). When parents apply the techniques, their children's behavior changes (Hawkins, Peterson, Schweid, & Bijou, 1966; Johnson & Lobitz, 1974; Zeilberger, Sampen, & Sloane, 1968). However, broad-scale implementation of such training has not been tested (O'Dell, 1974). For example, it is not known whether all parents are amenable to such training. In the research reported, parents were carefully selected; but what about parents who refuse to participate? Is it necessary, as some researchers have suggested, to provide monetary reinforcement for attending training sessions? Research does indicate that, for some parents, payment for participation is an effective method of motivation (Patterson, McNeal, Hawkins, & Phelps, 1967). How does one deal with client resistance (Gottman & Leiblum, 1974)? Another issue that remains is long-term maintenance. How long do parents keep applying their new skills in behavior modification? How well are the children's gains maintained? These unanswered questions do not discredit the parent-training enterprise; they merely point out the fact that not all complexities associated with training parents have been solved or, for that matter, totally identified.

PROBLEMS OF CHILDHOOD

Although most of us make it through the complex social and intellectual development of the first five years of childhood with only a few scars, certain areas of development are nevertheless problematic. These include the acquisition of such basic skills as feeding and toileting and the learning of effective social skills such as cooperation. In the remainder of the chapter we will consider behavioral methods for treating problems of normal development.

Feeding

Although most children accept simple baby foods with a minimum of resistance and do not have any difficulty learning how to feed themselves, in a number of cases cited in the literature, otherwise normal children have developed serious, and in at least one case, life-threatening problems. Two such cases treated through behavior modification are presented here.

The first example of the application of behavioral approaches to feeding problems is a case reported by Martha Bernal (1972) of a four-year-old girl who refused to feed herself or eat normal foods. The etiology of the problem was unclear. The difficulty first appeared at age nine months when she choked on a piece of string bean. In response to the incident, the mother started giving her strained baby foods that would be easier to eat. When the mother tried to reintroduce solid foods a few weeks later, the child balked and refused to eat anything but strained food. Because the parents were concerned about her health, they acquiesced. When the child was twenty months old the pediatrician recommended that they force her to eat regular foods by simply withdrawing the baby food until she became sufficiently hungry to eat regular foods. After thirty-six hours of not eating, the child started to have dry heaves. The frightened parents immediately gave her the strained baby food. In the process, the child also managed to coerce her parents into feeding her. From that time on they fed her baby food.

The goal of the intervention program was to have the child feed herself a variety of table foods. The parents had been unable to withhold food from their child, and Bernal feared that another failure would extinguish their interest in working with their daughter. Thus, she devised a program that involved the parents' gradually weaning the child off baby food while reinforcing successful approximation of normal eating behavior. The program did not include a direct confrontation between the child and her parents because the child would have surely won.

The multifaceted program began with the child's receiving her most preferred strained food at meals, the only requirement being that she feed herself. The mother was to wait until the child picked up the spoon. As soon as the child put a bite of food into her mouth and swallowed it, the mother was to give her lots of attention. By the same token, she was to withhold smiles and attention as long as the child did not feed herself. The mother was not to coax, nag, or pressure her into eating. After the mother was able to modify her child's behavior with social reinforcement and timeout, the reinforcement requirements were increased. Bites of her favorite foods and eventually access to the television were made contingent on the child feeding herself regular table foods. Reinforcement requirements were continually increased so that within a period of twenty weeks the girl was feeding herself a variety of table foods.

In addition to demonstrating the application of reinforcement contingencies to reduce problem behavior associated with feeding, the case shows how undesirable behavior can be easily "taught" by the social environment. Perhaps because of guilt, devotion, and misguided notions of what is best for their child, the well-meaning parents appear to have reinforced undesirable behavior. This, coupled with the powerful reinforcement control the child exerted on her parents, made intervention with the family a difficult task.

The second example of the use of behavior modification to eliminate a severe feeding problem is reported by Peter Lang and Barbara Melamed (1969). The case is of a nine-month-old infant whose life was endangered by persistent vomiting and rumination. (When he was taken to the hospital he weighed only twelve pounds.) Up to five months of age the infant showed no abnormalities —pregnancy and delivery were normal and he made normal weight gains (nine pounds, four ounces at birth to seventeen pounds at age six months). But during the fifth month he started an unusual pattern of behavior following each meal; it included vigorous thumb-sucking, blotchiness of the face, and approximately ten to fifteen minutes after a meal, vomiting and ruminating. Extensive medical tests conducted in the hospital failed to disclose any organic basis for his persistent regurgitating, and no clear psychological cause could be identified. Prior to the behavioral intervention, numerous other treatment methods had been applied, all without success. Dietary changes, the administration of antinauseants, changes in methods of feeding (such as changes in form and amount of food), prevention of thumb-sucking via arm and hand restraints, and intensive nursing care (that is, close and warm nurturance for the purpose of providing secure feelings) did not affect his behavior.

The infant was placed in a private hospital room and carefully monitored for two days prior to treatment. Treatment involved severe punishment of vomiting. As soon as the infant started to vomit, brief and repeated shocks (approximately one-second duration with a one-second interpulse interval) were delivered to the calf of his leg via electrodes. As soon as he stopped vomiting, the shock was terminated. Lang and Melamed subjected themselves to the shock and reported that it was indeed unpleasant. In order to reduce the probability of the infant associating the treatment with a specific situation, treatment sessions were conducted at different times of the day and in different settings.

The treatment was almost immediately effective. After only two sessions the frequency of vomiting decreased dramatically, and by the sixth session the infant ceased vomiting altogether. After five days in which no vomiting or ruminating was observed, the infant was discharged from the hospital to the care of his parents. At both one-month and five-month followup evaluations there was no report of vomiting and the infant showed dramatic weight gains. After only one month he had almost doubled his weight (one-month followup weight was twenty-one pounds), and at the sixth-month followup he weighed twenty-six pounds, one ounce. The examining physician reported that he was alert, active, and attentive and that he appeared free of any new problems. The child is now attending regular elementary school and is well adjusted (personal communication, Lang, 1977). Figure 4–1 shows the infant before and after treatment.

Tantrums

The elimination of tantrums and excessive crying in young children was one of behavior modification's earliest victories. The standard procedure is to ignore or "timeout" the behavior and differentially reinforce positive behaviors that are incompatible with tantrums. Since we have already mentioned how timeout procedures are used to control such problem behaviors, the present discussion will be brief and focus on a classic example of the use of extinction procedures.

The case, reported by Carl Williams (1959), was of a twenty-one-month-old boy who had violent tantrums at bedtime if someone did not stay with him. He would cry and fuss until they returned. He would not even tolerate their reading a book while they sat with him; he required their complete attention. The parents reported that the child appeared to "enjoy" the control he had over them and that he fought off going to sleep as long as he could. As a result, they were spending from

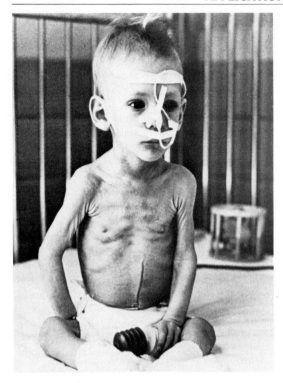
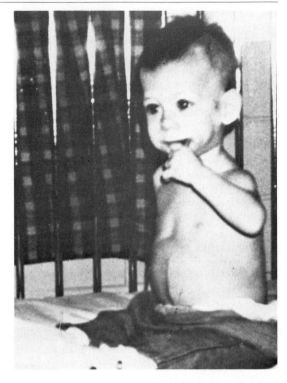

Figure 4–1. The photograph at left was taken during the observation period just prior to treatment and clearly illustrates the child's debilitated condition. The photograph at right was taken on the day of discharge from the hospital, thirteen days after the first photo. The 26 percent increase in body weight is easily seen in the full, more infantlike face, the rounded arms, the more substantial trunk. From P. J. Lang & B. G. Melamed, Case report: Avoidance conditioning therapy of an infant with chronic ruminative vomiting. *Journal of Abnormal Psychology*, 1969, **74**, p. 3, fig. 1. Copyright 1969 by the American Psychological Association. Used by permission.

one-half to two hours each bedtime sitting with their child. Needless to say, the situation was intolerable for the parents involved.

After having received medical reassurance that the child did not require such constant supervision, they instituted a simple extinction program. Once the child was put to bed and given a few loving exchanges, the parents were to leave the room and shut the door. Regardless of how loudly the child cried they were not to reenter his room. Figure 4–2 shows the effect of this procedure on the child's tantrums. After the first night, in which he cried for forty-five minutes, his bedtime behavior improved dramatically. However, on one occasion, approximately one week after the extinction program was put into effect, an aunt reinforced his crying by returning to his room and the problem returned. The same extinction procedure was employed and the tantrums subsided. Williams reported that at a two-year followup evaluation, the child showed good adjustment: the original problem had not returned nor had new problems developed.

Toilet Training

In a series of studies with both normal and mentally retarded children, Nathan Azrin and Richard Foxx (Azrin & Foxx, 1971; Azrin, Sneed, & Foxx, 1973; Foxx & Azrin, 1973) developed an effective method for toilet training. Although the method incorporates eighteen distinct components, it achieves its goals in remarkably short order. With only four hours of a therapist's time children have become toilet trained. As we will discover shortly, the techniques are derived directly from principles of operant conditioning. The general strategy involves an intensive learning experience in which prompts and reinforcement are heavily used to establish the desired behavior and then gradually eliminated as the child acquires the desired skills.

We will summarize their method by enumerating their eighteen components and then discuss their research on the effectiveness of their method.

1. Training is carried out in an environment "free of distraction." Toys, television, and other activities are removed during training. Parents and siblings are asked to leave the home the day that training is initiated.

2. In order to have many opportunities to reinforce the desired behavior, large quantities of liquid are served. At least once every five minutes throughout the day of training the child is required to take a drink of some preferred beverage (for example, soft drink, milk, or juice) so that the child's intake is approximately two cups per hour.

3. Every instance of correct toileting is reinforced.

4. Each behavior leading up to using the toilet correctly is also reinforced. Approaching the potty chair, lowering the pants, sitting on the potty chair, wiping, emptying the pot, flushing the toilet, and so on, earn reinforcers.

5. Care is given to selecting powerful reinforcers. By interviewing the parents, the child's favorite edibles are determined. Other reinforcers, like praise, hugs, and smiles, are also used.

6. Reinforcers are varied.

7. Reinforcement is immediate. Although visual observation of the child seated on the potty chair would probably permit the trainer's immediate detection of the desired voiding response, Azrin and Foxx recommend a special seat that rings musical chimes as soon as liquid enters the bowl.

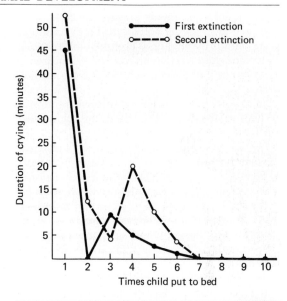

Figure 4–2. Length of crying in two extinction series as a function of successive occasions of being put to bed. From C. D. Williams, The elimination of tantrum behavior by extinction procedures. *Journal of Abnormal and Social Psychology,* 1959, **59,** p. 296, fig. 1. Copyright 1959 by the American Psychological Association. Used by permission.

8. During the initial phase of training, reinforcement is continuous.

9. If necessary, the trainer manually guides the child through all the components of correct toileting.

10. The child also receives specific instructions as to how to carry out the operations.

11. The child is provided with a "wet doll" that the trainer uses to demonstrate the correct behaviors. The trainer puts the doll through all the motions of correct toileting. The doll is given the liquid, put on the seat, and then praised by the trainer when the water passes into the toilet.

12. The child's pants are checked once every five minutes. Each time a check reveals that the pants are dry the child receives a treat.

13. The child is mildly punished for accidents; if his pants are wet, the child is reprimanded, forfeits a treat on the next check, and is required to change his pants himself.

14. In order to provide practice the child is required to sit on the potty chair for five minutes (or until urinating) once every ten minutes.

15. The child who has an accident is required to go through all the components of correct toileting.

16. In order to increase the intrinsic reinforcement value of correct toileting, the trainer discusses with the child how happy parents, friends, and relatives will be when they hear about his or her new skills. The positive reactions of Santa Claus, Batman, and other favorite storybook characters are also used as support for the child's progress.

17. Prompts and reinforcers are gradually withdrawn after the child has experienced repeated success using the potty chair and keeping the pants dry.

18. Posttraining maintenance of correct toileting is provided. For the first few days after training the parents are to check the child's pants before each snack, meal, and at bedtime and to give lavish praise if the child's pants are dry. If an accident has occurred they are to reprimand the child, make the child change his or her pants, and practice using the potty chair.

Using thirty-four normal children (twenty-two boys and twelve girls) ranging in age from twenty to thirty-six months (mean age twenty-five months) as subjects, Foxx and Azrin obtained impressive results. Before training, the children averaged six accidents per day. After only one day of training, the frequency of accidents decreased to one per week. At the four-month followup, there was almost perfect success. Moreover, 30 percent of the children stopped wetting their beds at night immediately after they completed training. Foxx and Azrin reported that most of the children reacted very positively to the training.

Enuresis

Enuresis is the involuntary voiding of urine by individuals who have no known defects in their nervous or urogenital systems. Although the problem can occur when the individual is asleep or awake, by far the most common type of enuresis is nocturnal. Diurnal enuresis is extremely rare. An arbitrary age of three years is used in diagnosing enuresis: if the bed-wetter is younger than three, the problem is not labeled enuresis.

Bed-wetting is a well-known problem to the general practitioner, pediatrician, child psychiatrist, and clinical psychologist. The primary problem for approximately 26 percent of all children referred for psychiatric treatment is nocturnal enuresis (Kanner, 1972).

A variety of nonbehavioral methods have been employed in the treatment of enuresis, but most have not met with success. In two long-term studies of the effectiveness of psychotherapy with enuretics (Deleon & Mandell, 1966; Werry & Cohrssen, 1965), one-to-one counseling did not have a significant impact on the problem. Drug therapy has also been used. Although amphetamine (for the purpose of lightening the child's sleep) and imipramine (for the purpose of increasing bladder capacity) have yielded statistically significant treatment effects, the actual cure rates with both drugs have not been clinically meaningful (only 23 to 30 percent success) (Forrester, Stein, & Susser, 1964; Kardish, Hillman, & Werry, 1968).

The Mowrers' Conditioning Method. The conditioning approach to treating enuresis originally suggested by Hobart and Molly Mowrer in 1938 (Mowrer & Mowrer, 1938) is now recognized as a milestone in the history of behavior modification, as well as in the treatment of enuresis. The Mowrers viewed enuresis as simply the child's absence of bladder control, and argued that this control is a skill which can be learned in accordance with basic principles of conditioning. As we will point out later, their conceptualization of the problem was and still is a radical departure from prevailing psychiatric thinking.

The Mowrers reasoned that involuntary voiding was an unconditioned reflex to bladder tension, and that if awakening could be substituted as a conditioned reflex to the tension, the problem would be eliminated: instead of voiding, the child would awaken when his bladder was distended. Their procedure was designed to facilitate this conditioning. The apparatus they used consists of a pad composed of layers of cotton cloth and bronze gauze connected to a small battery and bell. Any liquid passing through the pad completes the circuit and sounds the bell. With the pad inserted under the child's bedsheets, voiding activates the bell, which awakens the child. The child must be fully awakened when the bell sounds, get out of bed, and go to the bathroom. He or she is not scolded or punished, but merely required to reset the bell and make up the bed before retiring again.

Their procedures worked: all thirty children who participated in the original study progressed from bed-wetting nightly to the Mowrers' criterion of fourteen consecutive dry nights within two months. Subsequent studies using the same apparatus have achieved moderate positive results; success rates are generally between 70 and 80 percent (Deleon & Sacks, 1972; Doleys, 1977). The relapse rate (after six months) is approximately 32 percent (Doleys, 1977). The greatest problem with the Mowrer method seems to be parental cooperation (Doleys, 1977). At least five research studies have indicated that the most common reason for failure is the parents' refusal to carry out the procedure (Collins, 1973; Forsythe & Redmond, 1970; Fraser, 1972; McConaghy, 1969; Young, 1969).

Despite the relative effectiveness of the pad and bell, most child psychiatrists and pediatricians rejected the method when it was first introduced and some practitioners still will not use it. The major fear was symptom substitution: if the problem is somehow eliminated via conditioning techniques, then perhaps some other problem will replace it since the "real" (underlying, unconscious) problem is still there. But research has shown that symptom substitution is not a concern with the Mowrer treatment. For example, Bruce Baker (1969) obtained a sample of ninety elementary schoolchildren in the New Haven, Connecticut, area: thirty enuretics and sixty nonenuretic controls. The enuretic sample consisted of ten girls and twenty boys with a mean age of eight years and a range of six to twelve years. All but four of the children had been troubled with bed-wetting since birth, and more than half were wet seven nights a week. Enuretics were matched on demographic data obtained during parent interviews and assigned to treatment conditions in triads.

Conditions were (1) the Mowrer procedure, (2) child awakened by parents at a fixed time throughout the night and taken to the bathroom, and (3) no-treatment, waiting list control. In addition to direct behavioral measures of frequency of bed-wetting, both objective and projective indices of each child's adjustment were obtained from parents, teachers, and children.

Children trained by the Mowrer device showed a significantly greater decrease in bed-wetting than children in the wake-up and control groups. Measures of personal adjustment revealed *no* negative side effects or symptom substitution in those who received the Mowrer treatment. In fact, these children were reported to be "happier, less anxious, and more grown-up, assuming responsibility and venturing into new activities" (Baker, 1969, p. 49). If anything, the Mowrer method had positive side effects. Even though research has not indicated the presence of symptom substitution in the behavioral treatment of bed-wetting, many practitioners are still opposed to using the Mowrer apparatus. For example, pediatrician Linus Salk (1972) warns that such treatment may affect the child's personality, and child psychiatrist Leo Kanner (1972) does not even mention behavioral procedures in his discussion of enuresis in his 1972 edition of *Child Psychiatry*. This attitude is indeed disappointing, given the proclaimed commitment to empiricism in modern psychology and psychiatry.

Retention Control Training. The **retention control training** technique (Kimmel & Kimmel, 1970; Paschalis, Kimmel, & Kimmel, 1972; Starfield, 1972) is based on research which has found that enuretics have weak bladder capacity. Enuretics urinate 50 percent more frequently than normals. Retention control training involves increasing children's ability to hold their urine during the day. The children are instructed to tell their parents whenever they need to relieve themselves, and when they do, the parents ask them to wait a few minutes before they go. After they wait, the parents give them cookies or special treats and they are allowed to go to the bathroom. The waiting period is gradually increased until the children can wait for thirty minutes before going to the bathroom. As the children learn to retain their urine during the day, there is a corresponding decrease in bed-wetting. Of the first thirty-one enuretic children who received retention control training, twenty-three (74 percent) showed significant improvement within twenty days. A nine-month followup evaluation indicated no relapses or new problem behaviors. Unfortunately, there has been no controlled research on the long-term effectiveness of this procedure.

Dry-bed Training. The third method used to treat enuresis was devised by Azrin, Sneed, and Foxx (1973) and combines the other two methods with intensive prompting and shaping. The unique feature of **dry-bed training** is an hourly awakening procedure that the parents follow for one or two nights at the beginning of the program. At one-hour intervals throughout the night the parents get the children out of bed, send them to the bathroom, and reinforce voiding. If the children wet the bed during the night, the buzzer sounds and they are awakened. They go to the bathroom to finish voiding and then return to their rooms for **full cleanliness training.** This procedure is actually a form of punishment in which the children must change their pajamas and sheets and clean the mattress pad. In addition to this overcorrection procedure, the children receive **positive practice,** which involves going through the motions of correct toileting twenty times.

Azrin, Sneed, and Foxx (1974) studied the dry-bed procedure with a group of 26 six-year-old enuretics. After one night of intensive training, the frequency of bed-wetting diminished dramatically. Results for children who received dry-bed training were superior to those for children who received standard pad-bell training. Subsequent research (Doleys, Ciminero, Tollison, Williams, & Wells, 1977) has shown that this method is also more effective than retention training. As has been the case with many behavior modification methods, before definitive conclusions can be drawn, long-term followup research is necessary.

Encopresis

Encopresis is involuntary defecation not due to organic illness. The problem has received much less attention than enuresis, and its treatment is less complicated. Treatment programs have typically involved ignoring "accidents" and positively reinforcing each occurrence of the desired behavior (Edelman, 1971; Keehn, 1965; Neale, 1963; Young & Goldsmith, 1972). Case Study 4–1 provides a clear example of the use of positive reinforcement in the elimination of encopresis. Another interesting case involved an otherwise normal and healthy nine-year-old boy whose soiling (two or three times each day) appeared to be maintained by the attention he received from his mother. Treatment simply involved the mother's ignoring accidents (that is, not reinforcing them with attention) and refusing to change his clothes immediately following an accident. This strategy was immediately effective; after soiling himself on the first day of the program, the child's problem behavior never reappeared (Conger, 1970).

Another procedure is full cleanliness training (Doleys, McWhorter, Williams, & Gentry, 1977). As with the treatment of enuresis, training involves children washing their clothes and bodies after an accident. In cases in which full cleanliness has been used, children were required to wash their soiled underpants and trousers for at least twenty minutes and bathe in cool or cold water for an equal length of time. (One might well question the use of such a strong punishment before first attempting to modify the behavior with nonaversive procedures.) Parents were instructed not to give the children attention during training and to ignore crying and other attempts to get out of the chore. Although controlled outcome research on the effectiveness of full cleanliness training has not been conducted, results from case studies suggest that the procedure is quite effective (Doleys, McWhorter, Williams, & Gentry, 1977).

Children's Fears

Like the treatment of enuresis, the elimination of children's fears and phobias has been an important issue throughout the history of behavior modification. As we mentioned in Chapter 1, one of the first applications of behavioral principles to clinical problems was Mary Cover Jones's work on a two-year-old child's fear of rabbits (Jones, 1924a, 1924b). Today clinical researchers are investigating the use of prepackaged videotapes showing children happily playing with dogs in order to eliminate dog phobias (Bandura, 1971).

Jones: Direct Conditioning and Modeling. Much of the current work on behavioral treatments of children's phobias is a direct extension of Jones's original work. Most, if not all, present-day procedures were suggested by Jones in her 1924 article entitled "The Elimination of Children's Fears." Because of the importance of Jones's early work, we will organize our presentation around her research and show how her procedures have been validated and refined. We suggest that the student turn back to Chapter 1 and reread Jones's account of the factors that affected her thinking.

Jones presented her work in a series of brief case studies organized according to the methods used to eliminate fear. Her subjects were selected from seventy children from three months to seven years of age who resided in a temporary-care facility. They were all normal children who had been placed in the home for "situational" reasons; for instance, illness in the family, parents who were separated, a mother whose work made it impossible for her to care for her children. From Jones's description, the home served many of the same functions as a modern day-care center. The children Jones selected showed extreme fear and agitation under conditions that normally elicit pleasant or only slightly distressed reactions. Assessment was systematic: each child was placed in a series of situations that might elicit fear (such as being alone in a dark room or in the presence of a snake, rabbit, and frog) and the child's reactions were observed. Those children who showed strong distress were chosen to participate.

Jones investigated seven methods for eliminating the children's fears. They were

1. The method of elimination through disuse (not subjecting the child to the fear-eliciting stimuli).
2. The method of verbal appeal (connecting the feared stimuli with positive images through conversation).
3. The method of negative adaptation (repeatedly presenting the feared stimuli).
4. Method of repression (punishing the fear response with mild reprimands).
5. Method of distraction (offering the child a substitute activity).
6. Method of direct conditioning (gradually introducing the feared stimuli in association with positive stimuli, in vivo systematic desensitization).
7. Method of social imitation (having the child observe another child contact the feared stimuli).

Only two of the methods, direct conditioning and social imitation, resulted in the elimination of fear responses. Jones used both methods in her classic case of Peter, a healthy and well-adjusted child of two years and ten months of age whose only problem was an extreme fear reaction to rabbits. Peter's fears extended to white rats, feathers, fur, and soft cloth such as wool and cotton. Whenever any of these objects was present, he would start to cry and scream. In one instance he was quietly playing in his crib when Jones presented a white rat. As soon as he saw the animal, he fell flat on his back and started crying; when the rat was removed, he became relaxed.

The primary treatment involved direct conditioning. Once or twice each day Peter was placed in his high chair and given some food. While he ate, a white rabbit was brought into the room. Jones first placed the rabbit four feet from Peter's chair; he then started to cry, insisting that the animal be removed. He continued to cry until the animal had been moved twenty feet away. He fussed again and Jones moved the animal farther away until it did not disturb him. During successive sessions the animal was gradually brought nearer to the high chair. Jones carefully observed Peter's reactions in order to determine exactly how fast to move the rabbit. It was crucial that the positive value of eating always outweigh the fear reactions to the rabbit. If she had introduced the rabbit too quickly and the fear reaction overcame the positive reaction to food, then the program might have backfired and Peter could have learned to be afraid of eating in his high chair. After two months of intensive treatment, Peter's fears were eliminated and replaced with positive reactions.

Jones's social imitation was a rather straightforward procedure involving the phobic child's observing peers happily playing with the feared object and then being given the opportunity to play along with them. (The term **modeling** is now more frequently used than **social imitation.** Both refer to the same general set of procedures.) In the three cases she reported, treatment began with the phobic child and nonfearful peers playing together. While they played, Jones quietly introduced the feared object (a small animal). When the other children saw the animal, they would immediately go over to see it. In no instance was the phobic child forced or even asked to join them; he was free to watch or participate, as he wished. After only a few play sessions, each of the phobic children asked to play with the animal.

Jones's work was clearly ahead of its time. It is unfortunate that she did not continue her research in the area, because it took psychology over forty years to rediscover the principles she explicated in two brief articles.

Refinement of Jones's Methods. Although the direct conditioning method has been incorporated into procedures for eliminating anxiety reactions in adults, it has not been extensively utilized in the treatment of children's fears. Our review of the literature revealed less than a dozen published reports on its application. They involved the treatment of school phobia (e.g., Lazarus, Davison, & Polefka, 1965; Leventhal, Weinberger, Stander, & Stearns, 1967) and fear of loud noises (e.g., Tasto, 1969; Wish, Hasazi, & Jurgela, 1973). Case Study 4–2 shows the use of direct conditioning to eliminate a young child's extreme fear of bathing.

Peter Wish and his colleagues J. E. Hasazi, and A. P. Jurgela (1973) modified Jones's direct conditioning procedures in their treatment of an eleven-year-old boy who was afraid of loud noise. Whenever he heard thunder, fireworks, or other loud noise he would become agitated and try to hide. His fear reactions produced a variety of somatic complaints, including headaches and nausea. Treatment involved systematically associating feared sounds recorded on a tape and deep muscle relaxation, which has been found to be incompatible with anxiety. The child was first given specific training in muscle relaxation. Then, while he was relaxed, the sounds were pre-

sented according to a hierarchy based on the child's ratings of degree of disturbance produced by the sounds, which ranged from surf and a popping balloon to thunderstorms and fireworks.

The stimuli were presented during thrice daily sessions for a period of eight days. If the child experienced any anxiety, the tape was stopped and replayed after he was again relaxed. At each successive session the volume was increased until, by the last day of treatment, he was able to hear all the feared sounds at high volume without experiencing anxiety. In order to determine if the treatment had resulted in the elimination of his fear reaction in the natural environment, the child was subjected to the sounds of live fireworks and a real thunderstorm. He showed no anxiety: he did not cry, complain, or attempt to hide. At a nine-month followup evaluation, the child was still free of any fear of loud sounds.

Modeling has become a popular means of eliminating children's fears. Albert Bandura and his associates (Bandura, 1971; Bandura, Grusec, & Menlove, 1967; Bandura & Menlove, 1968) have refined Jones's procedures and developed a series of videotapes in which peers model a positive approach response toward phobic stimuli—in this case, dogs. The children shown in the film are similar to the phobic child in age and sex in order to facilitate the child's identification and subsequent imitation of the fearless children's behavior (Rosekrans, 1967). This research with dog-phobic children is impressive. Within only eight sessions, the children who displayed extreme anxiety at even the sight of a dog were able to approach a large dog without being afraid.

Emotive Imagery. Arnold Lazarus and Arnold Abramovitz (1962) devised a variant on Jones's method of verbal appeal called **emotive imagery.** Their rationale was that if strong anxiety-inhibiting emotive images could be elicited in the context of feared stimuli, the anxiety reaction to those stimuli would be reduced. By telling a story that involved favorite storybook heroes interacting with the phobic stimuli, the child should come to associate these stimuli with positive feelings of self-assertion, pride, affection, and mirth. As the therapist tells the story he introduces the feared stimuli in a hierarchical fashion, from least to most distressing. Lazarus and Abramovitz reported one case of a ten-year-old boy who was afraid of the dark. Whenever his parents left the house at night, he became extremely anxious. In order to protect himself from the dark, he insisted on sharing a bedroom with his brother and kept a light on next to his bed. Before the program, the therapist interviewed the boy and his parents to determine the exact components of his fear and to ascertain his favorite radio hero. The following quotation demonstrates how the therapist employed emotive imagery (Lazarus & Abramovitz, 1962, p. 193).

> The child was asked to imagine that Superman and Captain Silver had joined forces and had appointed him their agent. After a brief discussion concerning the topography of his house he was given his first assignment. The therapist said, "Now I want you to close your eyes and imagine that you are sitting in the dining room with your mother and father. It is night time. Suddenly, you receive a signal on the wrist radio that Superman has given you. You quickly run into the lounge because your mission must be kept a secret. There is only a little light coming into the lounge from the passage. Now pretend that you are all alone in the lounge waiting for Superman and Captain Silver to visit you. Think about this very clearly. If the idea makes you feel afraid, lift up your right hand."
>
> An ongoing scene was terminated as soon as any anxiety was indicated. When an image aroused anxiety, it would either be represented in a more challengingly assertive manner, or it would be altered slightly so as to prove less objectively threatening.
>
> At the end of the third session, the child was able to picture himself alone in his bathroom with all the lights turned off, awaiting a communication from Superman.

Lazarus and Abramovitz reported that the program was successful; in addition to ridding the child of his specific phobia, his schoolwork improved. An eleven-month followup interview with the child's mother found the child well adjusted with no new problems.

Lazarus (1971) also reported a case of an eight-year-old boy who was afraid of the dentist. Using Batman and Robin as heroes, the therapist asked the child to imagine his heroes visiting the dentist while he watched them, and then to imagine himself in the chair as Batman and Robin observed him. After engaging in such fantasies five times daily for one week, the child was able to visit the dentist's office without resisting.

Unfortunately, Lazarus's emotive imagery has not been subject to detailed experimental evaluation. All data on its effectiveness are derived from case studies. Thus, although the method certainly appears promising, firm conclusions regarding its value cannot be drawn.

Prosocial Behavior

In the area of social behavior, behavioral psychologists have focused on the problems of social isolation and aggression. Intervention has typically involved relatively straightforward reinforcement programs in which parents and/or nursery school teachers are trained to reinforce prosocial behavior and extinguish antisocial acts.

Social Isolation. The treatment of shy, withdrawn children has received a great deal of attention, first during the 1960s by Sidney Bijou and the staff at the University of Washington Nursery School, and more recently by John Gottman and Steven Asher at the University of Illinois.

The initial studies conducted at the University of Washington involved changing the conditions under which adults give such children attention. For example, in a case of a withdrawn four-and-a-half-year-old girl, the nursery school teacher was instructed to pay attention and give her appropriate praise *only* when she was interacting with other children and to ignore her in a natural way (extinction) when she was by herself (Allen, Hart, Buell, Harris, & Wolf, 1964). Initially, if the child showed any approximation of social interaction, such as sitting near another child, the teacher immediately attended to her. As the child began to interact more readily with other children, the teacher increased the requirements for reinforcement and attended to the child only when she was engaging in cooperative play. After the prosocial behavior occurred at a high frequency, the teacher gradually reduced the density of her reinforcement. As a result of the program, the child's percentage of peer interactions per session increased from 15 to 60.

Another technique for increasing social interaction involved the teacher reinforcing behaviors that required social interaction (Buell, Stoddard, Harris, & Baer, 1968). The teacher first reinforced approximations of the target behavior (the use of previously avoided play equipment) and then gradually increased the requirements for reinforcement until the child was vigorously using the equipment. Since peer interaction was a corollary of the reinforced play behavior, there was a concomitant increase in social interaction. In a similar case study (Kirby & Toler, 1970), a nursery school teacher reinforced a five-year-old isolate boy with nickels and praise for distributing candy and treats to other children in the class. Following this training there was a marked increase in the child's peer interaction in other school settings as well.

Social imitation is also used in the treatment of social isolates. One example is a case (Ross, Ross, & Evans, 1971) of a six-year-old boy whose extreme social withdrawal from peers was eliminated following such a treatment program. The therapist began by reinforcing the child for imitating simple motor responses. After the child readily imitated, the therapist modeled positive social interaction and discussed the positive aspects of peer interaction. During subsequent play periods, the child was reinforced by the therapist for successive approximations of the desirable social behavior. Treatment continued through a graduated series of social interaction phases until the child's social behavior resembled that of his peers. At the end of the seven-week program, there was dramatic reduction in the child's social withdrawal.

Gottman's techniques focus on general problems of social isolation. He and his colleagues have developed social skills training "packages" for children who do not have close friends and who appear unable to initiate social interaction. Treatment consists of a coach (that is, a therapist) first observing the child in the child's classroom or family setting and then providing instruction in how to make friends and communicate more effectively. In the first stage of coaching, the child watches a ten-minute videotape of a child trying to join in play with other children. As the child watches, the coach suggests a series of appropriate coping self-statements. For example, the coach discusses the child's worries about being accepted, what the child might say to the other children, and how the child might get the other children to share. During the second phase of coaching, the coach and the child engage in role playing. Here the focus is on teaching the child how to show interest in what someone else is doing, how to share, and how to make friends (Gottman, Gonso, & Rasmussen, 1975). In the third stage, the therapist deals with techniques of effective communication.

The coaching program devised by Asher and his colleague Sherri Oden (Oden & Asher, 1977) is similar to Gottman's. In their program the therapist relies on role playing, didactic instruction, and constructive feedback; videotapes are not used. Instruction focuses on four skill areas: (1) participating in a game or activity; (2) cooperating (for instance, taking turns and sharing); (3) communicating (for instance, listening as well as talking); (4) validating and supporting (for instance, giving attention or help, being friendly).

Preliminary results are quite encouraging. In the one study in which Gottman's program has been evaluated (Gottman, Gonso, & Schuler, 1976), peer sociometric ratings for isolate third-grade children who were coached were significantly better than those for isolate children who were not coached. That is, peers indicated greater interest in interacting (playing) with the children who had been given social skills coaching. Oden and Asher (1977) also obtained significant increases in peers' interest in playing with children (third and fourth graders) who received social skills training. A one-year followup evaluation indicated continued progress in terms of sociometric ratings. Although these results are indeed impressive, both Gottman and Asher feel their procedures must be refined: individualized programs might yield even greater improvement.

Aggression. Interpersonal aggression among children has received a great deal of attention, first during the 1960s from Bijou and his colleagues at the University of Washington and more recently from Gerald Patterson at the Oregon Research Institute. The work carried out at the University of Washington focused on individual children with specific problems. Most of the published research by Bijou and his associates were single case studies and today are considered classic in the behavior modification literature. Their strategy was quite simple: aggressive behavior was "timed out" or put on extinction, and prosocial behavior was prompted and immediately reinforced.

For example, in a case involving the treatment of a four-and-a-half-year-old boy's aggressive biting, hitting, and kicking, the nursery school teacher reinforced cooperative behavior with praise and attention and removed the child from activities (timeout) immediately following aggressive behavior (Sloane, Johnston, & Bijou, 1967). Timeout consisted of placing the child in an adjacent room free of all objects that could provide a source of reinforcement. A teacher stationed behind a one-way-vision screen observed his behavior and returned him to the classroom after he had remained quiet for two minutes. As the frequency of the child's aversive behaviors decreased, there was a corresponding increase in his prosocial behavior.

The most extensively researched program for the elimination of aggressive behavior in children is that developed by Patterson and his colleagues (Patterson, 1976). During the last ten years they have treated over 150 highly aggressive children. Most of their published research concerns the treatment of thirty-five families referred to the Social Learning Program at the Oregon Research Institute by community agencies. Each of the families had at least one son between the ages of five and fifteen who had been identified as a severe conduct problem. These boys were typically in trouble at school, aggressive toward their siblings, and noncompliant. Their parents reported that

the problems were longstanding, and that they had previously sought professional assistance in child management.

The behavioral intervention was multifaceted and involved parents as well as teachers. All the families received at least one month of intensive training that included: (1) required reading of a manual on the behavior modification approach to child management (Patterson & Gullion, 1968; Patterson, 1971); (2) instruction in how to define, track, and record relevant child behaviors; (3) participation in a parent-training group in which behavioral techniques were discussed; and (4) instruction in how to devise reciprocal behavioral contracts with their children. In each case, a behavior therapist followed the family closely, meeting with them in their homes, providing specific recommendations regarding particular problematic situations, and making sure the parents were consistent in their use of contingent positive reinforcement and punishment. In many cases, reinforcement programs were also initiated in the boys' classrooms. Teachers were instructed to heavily reinforce cooperation and academic achievement.

Approximately two-thirds to three-fourths of the boys showed significant reductions in aggressive behavior at home and at school. Moreover, parents' perceptions of their children became significantly more positive by the end of the intervention program. Long-term followup evaluations generally indicated that treatment gains were maintained, although not at the same level as observed immediately following the intervention.

Unfortunately, not all families benefited from Patterson's intervention program. Some of the most severely disturbed families dropped out before completing the program. As Patterson has pointed out, there is still a need for more effective methods of intervention.

SUMMARY

Without necessarily being aware of it, both parent and child modify each other's behavior in profound ways. The actions and reactions of each have both eliciting and reinforcing functions. This reciprocity is even present during infancy. In the context of this potent relationship, desirable as well as undesirable patterns of behavior in the child are established.

One of the major issues in behavior modification with children is parent training. During the last five years at least two dozen behaviorally oriented manuals for parents have been published. The goal of this type of training is for parents to be able to apply basic behavioral principles in rearing their children. Parents are taught to recognize the effect their actions, as well as their "inactions," have on their children's behavior. By changing how and when they respond to their children, parents can eliminate many of their children's undesirable behaviors. Most manuals focus on parental use of positive reinforcement and timeout; they generally discourage the use of physical punishment. Research has clearly shown that, with adequate training and supervision, parents can be taught to be very effective "behavior change agents" even with relatively severe social and intellectual problems.

There is almost no area of the young child's life that has not been subjected to behavior modification. In addition to methods for teaching basic self-help skills to children, researchers in behavior modification have devised procedures for dealing with such social problems as tantrums, social isolation, and aggression. Perhaps one of the most impressive and far-reaching self-help programs is Azrin and Foxx's (1971) rapid toilet-training method. Through the use of prompts, reinforcement, and modeling, children less than two years old can be effectively trained in only one day. Their program has also been successfully used with mentally retarded individuals.

There is growing interest in the problems of children who do not readily interact with others or who are disliked by peers. The initial work of Bijou and his associates dealt with preschool children who avoided interaction with classmates and who were especially attached to adults. By making their attention contingent upon peer interaction and ignoring dependent acts, teachers were able to establish prosocial behavior in these children. More recently, researchers have studied the use of social skill training and behavioral contracting with school-aged isolate children. Preliminary results in this area are quite encouraging.

Behavior modification techniques have also been effective in eliminating potentially serious problems such as enuresis, encopresis, and childhood fears and phobias. Many of these procedures, such as the Mowrers' conditioning techniques for the treatment of enuresis, were rejected for many years because professionals feared new symptoms would develop to replace the problems eliminated by behavior therapies. Interestingly, this fear was not subjected to empirical investigation until thirty years after the Mowrers first published their findings. Many of the procedures used today follow directly from the early work of the Mowrers and of Mary Cover Jones. Although their procedures have been refined, the original conceptualizations and intervention strategies remain unchanged.

CASE STUDY 4–1

AYLLON, T., SIMON, S. J., & WILDMAN, R. W., INSTRUCTIONS AND REINFORCEMENT IN THE ELIMINATION OF ENCOPRESIS: A CASE STUDY. *JOURNAL OF BEHAVIOR THERAPY AND EXPERIMENTAL PSYCHIATRY*, 1975, **6**, 235–238.

Quiet and well-behaved, Reggie was the youngest of three boys. School officials referred him to the therapist for treatment of his encopresis. At least two or three times each week, Reggie would soil himself and have to be sent home from school. The mother reported that when he arrived home she would give him a bath, change his clothes, and let him go outside to play for the remainder of the day. She was upset about Reggie's problem and said the only thing she could do was urge him to remember to use the toilet. Unfortunately, her request had little effect on his behavior.

Since Reggie was able to use the toilet and understood what was expected of him, the therapist did not have to devise an elaborate training program. The plan was simply to establish a procedure that would ensure that *not* soiling would be reinforced. But before initiating a reinforcement system, the therapist attempted to establish rapport with Reggie. On two separate occasions, the therapist took him on special outings for hamburgers. Reggie seemed to enjoy being with the therapist. When the therapist arrived at the child's home for the second outing (seven days after the first), he was surprised to learn that Reggie had soiled himself only once since the last visit. When the therapist made a third visit to the home the following week to explain the reinforcement program, the mother reported, to her amazement, that Reggie had gone an entire week without soiling himself.

Something strange was happening: without instituting any systematic program, Reggie's problem vanished. The therapist then questioned the mother to determine what might account for this immediate change. She noted that during the preceding week Reggie would come home and proudly ask her to tell the therapist that he did not do it (soil) that day. The therapist was still puzzled; how did he know what the therapist wanted him to do since they had never discussed it? The mother said she had told Reggie why the therapist came to visit him and also told him the therapist would not take him out if he had had any accidents during the week. Reggie cooperated; he wanted to go out for a hamburger. What is especially interesting is that the therapist had not suggested the mother use his visits as a reinforcer for not soiling. But she seized the opportunity and it worked. It was clear that, even though the therapist did not know it at the time, an effective reinforcement program had been instituted. Using stars on a chart to record Reggie's successes, and the therapist's visit as reinforcement, the program was continued. Only once did Reggie miss going to get hamburgers with the therapist.

After approximately two months of weekly contact, the therapist gradually removed himself. The mother reported that she continued to use the chart and outings as reinforcement, but on a very informal basis. An eleven-month followup interview with Reggie's mother revealed that Reggie's problem had not returned and that the school personnel were happy with the change.

The reinforcement program was successful, without a doubt, but it is likely that other methods might have worked as well. For instance, perhaps if the mother and school authorities had stopped reacting to his soiling by sending him home, soiling might have extinguished. Although there is no way of knowing, it is quite possible that the mother's behavior toward Reggie when he came home with soiled pants served as a positive reinforcer. If the reinforcement had been withdrawn, his misbehavior might have extinguished. But such a program was, in fact, not feasible. The school obviously could not tolerate a six-year-old with soiled pants sitting in the classroom. The practical constraints of the classroom may have served to maintain the problem. The only way to counteract this control was to introduce a systematic reinforcement program.

CASE STUDY 4–2

BENTLER, P. M.   AN INFANT'S PHOBIA TREATED WITH RECIPROCAL INHIBITION THERAPY. *JOURNAL OF CHILD PSYCHOLOGY AND PSY-CHIATRY*, 1962, **3,** 185–189.

At age eleven months, Margaret enjoyed wading in a small pool and having a bath.   However, during one evening bath, she tried to stand up and slipped.   She immediately started screaming.   The mother quickly rescued her and assured her that everything was all right.   But from that moment on, Margaret refused to have a bath.   She reacted violently not only to the bathtub and the faucet, but also to being bathed anywhere or wading in the pool.

Treatment involved the systematic association of positive activities and playthings with the bathtub and bathing.   The first step was to place Margaret's favorite toys in the empty bathtub and give her free access to them. Her response was to enter the bath, grab the toys, and take them away. She did not play with them in the bathtub.   As this process was repeated, she gradually showed less fear of the tub.   The second step involved her toys being placed in and around the kitchen sink, which was filled with water.   At first she cried and refused to go near the water, but as she played, she moved toward the water to get more toys.   After several vacillations, she entered the water.   The third step was washing the child in the kitchen sink while she held a favorite toy.   This step was managed with little resistance.   The final step was to bathe Margaret in the bathtub.   Her initial reaction was to cry and scream, but her mother's hugs and firmness eliminated the crying.

After approximately one month of what Jones might have called direct conditioning, Margaret's phobia was eliminated.   She displayed no fear in reaction to water, the bathtub, or being bathed.   Followup conducted six months later found Margaret happy and well adjusted.   Her phobia had completely disappeared.

REFERENCES

Allen, K. E., Hart, B. M., Buell, J. S., Harris, F. R., & Wolf, M. M. Effects of social reinforcement on isolate behavior of a nursery school child. *Child Development*, 1964, **35**, 511–518.

Ayllon, T., Simon, S. J., & Wildman, R. W. Instructions and reinforcement in the elimination of encopresis. *Behavior Therapy and Experimental Psychiatry*, 1975, **6**, 235–238.

Azrin, N. H., & Foxx, R. M. A rapid method of toilet training the institutionalized retarded. *Journal of Applied Behavior Analysis*, 1971, **4**, 89–99.

Azrin, N. H., Sneed, T. J., & Foxx, R. M. Dry bed: A rapid method of eliminating bedwetting (enuresis) of the retarded. *Behaviour Research and Therapy*, 1973, **11**, 427–434.

Azrin, N. H., Sneed, T. J., & Foxx, R. M. Dry-bed training: Rapid elimination of childhood enuresis. *Behaviour Research and Therapy*, 1974, **12**, 147–156.

Baker, B. L. Symptom treatment and symptom substitution in enuresis. *Journal of Abnormal Psychology*, 1969, **74**, 42–49.

Bandura, A. Psychotherapy based upon modeling principles. In A. E. Bergin and S. L. Garfield (Eds.), *Handbook of psychotherapy and behavior change*. New York: Wiley, 1971.

Bandura, A., Grusec, J. E., & Menlove, F. L. Vicarious extinction of avoidance behavior. *Journal of Personality and Social Psychology*, 1967, **5**, 16–23.

Bandura, A., & Menlove, F. L. Factors determining vicarious extinction of avoidance behavior through symbolic modeling. *Journal of Personality and Social Psychology*, 1968, **8**, 99–108.

Becker, W. C., Madsen, C. H., Arnold, C. R., & Thomas, D. R. The contingent use of teacher attention and praise in reducing classroom behavior problems. *Journal of Special Education*, 1967, **1**, 287–307.

Bernal, M. E. Behavioral treatment of a child's eating problem. *Journal of Behavior Therapy and Experimental Psychiatry*, 1972, **3**, 43–50.

Bijou, S. W. What psychology has to offer education—now. *Journal of Applied Behavior Analysis*, 1970, **3**, 65–71.

Bijou, S. W., & Baer, D. M. *Child development: The universal stage of infancy*, Vol. 2, New York: Appleton-Century-Crofts, 1965.

Bloom, K. Eye contact as a setting event for infant learning. *Journal of Experimental Child Psychology*, 1974, **17**, 250–263.

Bloom, K. Social elicitation of infant vocal behavior. *Journal of Experimental Child Psychology*, 1975, **20**, 51–58.

Bloom, K. Operant baseline procedures suppress infant social behavior. *Journal of Experimental Child Psychology*, 1977, **23**, 128–132(a).

Bloom, K. Patterning of infant vocal behavior. *Journal of Experimental Child Psychology*, 1977, **23**, 367–377(b).

Bloom, K., & Esposito, A. Social conditioning and its proper control procedures. *Journal of Experimental Child Psychology*, 1975, **19**, 209–222.

Boyd, E. F. Visual fixation and voice discrimination in 2-month-old-infants. In F. D. Horowitz (Ed.), *Visual attention, auditory stimulation and language discrimination in young infants. Monographs of the Society for Research in Child Development*, 1975, **39**, 63–77.

Brackbill, Y. Extinction of the smiling response in infants as a function of reinforcement schedule. *Child Development*, 1958, **29**, 115–124.

Bucher, B. D. Learning theory. In B. B. Wolman (Ed.), *Manual of child psychotherapy*. New York: McGraw-Hill, 1972.

Buell, J., Stoddard, P., Harris, R., & Baer, D. M. Collateral social development accompanying reinforcement of outdoor play in a preschool child. *Journal of Applied Behavior Analysis*, 1968, **1**, 167–173.

Collins, R. W. Importance of bladder-cue buzzer contingency in the conditioning treatment of enuresis. *Journal of Abnormal Psychology*, 1973, **82**, 299–308.

Conger, J. C. The treatment of encopresis by management of social consequences. *Behavior Therapy*, 1970, **1**, 386–390.

David, M., & Appell, G. A study of nursing care and nurse-infant interaction. In B. M. Foss (Ed.), *Determinants of infant behaviour I*. London: Methuen, 1961.

Deleon, G., & Mandell, W. A comparison of conditioning any psychotherapy in the treatment of functional enuresis. *Journal of Clinical Psychology*, 1966, **22**, 326–330.

Deleon, G., & Sacks, S. Conditioning functional enuresis: A four year follow-up. *Journal of Consulting and Clinical Psychology*, 1972, **39**, 299–300.

Dennis, W., & Dennis, M. G. Development under controlled environmental conditions. In W. Dennis (Ed.), *Readings in child psychology*. New York: Prentice Hall, 1951.

Doleys, D. M. Behavioral treatment of nocturnal enuresis in children: A review of the recent literature. *Psychological Bulletin*, 1977, **84**, 30–54.

Doleys, D. M., Ciminero, A. R., Tollison, J. W., Williams, C. L., & Wells, K. C. Dry-bed training and retention training: A comparison. *Behavior Therapy*, 1977 (in press).

Doleys, D. M., McWhorter, A. Q., Williams, S. C., & Gentry, W. R. Encopresis: Its treatment and relation to nocturnal enuresis. *Behavior Therapy*, 1977, **8**, 77–82.

Edelman, R. I. Operant conditioning treatment of encopresis. *Journal of Behavior Therapy and Experimental Psychiatry*, 1971, **2**, 71–73.

Eisenberger, R. B., Griffin, E. J., Coursin, D. B., & Hunter, M. S. Auditory behavior in the human neonate: A preliminary report. *Journal of Speech and Hearing Research*, 1964, **7**, 245–269.

Etzel, B. C., & Gewirtz, J. L. Experimental modification of caretaker-maintained high-rate operant crying in a 6- and a 20-week-old infant (*infans tyrannotearus*): Extinction of crying with reinforcement of eye contact and smiling. *Journal of Experimental Child Psychology*, 1967, **5**, 303–317.

Forrester, R. M., Stein, Z., & Susser, M. W. A trial of conditioning therapy in nocturnal enuresis. *Developmental Medicine and Child Neurology*, 1964, **6**, 158–166.

Forsythe, W. I., & Redmond, A. Enuresis and the electric alarm: Study of 200 cases. *British Medical Journal*, 1970, **1**, 211–213.

Foxx, R. M., & Azrin, N. H. Dry pants: A rapid method of toilet trainng children. *Behaviour Research and Therapy*, 1973, **11**, 435–442.

Fraser, M. S. Nocturnal enuresis. *The Practitioner*, 1972, **208**, 203–211.

Freedman, D. G., & Freedman, N. A. Differences in behavior between Chinese-American and European-American newborns. *Nature* (London), 1969, **224**, 1227.

Gibson, E. *Principles of perceptual learning and development.* New York: Appleton-Century-Crofts, 1969.

Goren, C. C., Sarty, M., & Wu, P. Y. K. Visual following and pattern discrimination of face-like stimuli by newborn infants. *Pediatrics*, 1975, **56**, 544–549.

Gottman, J., Gonso, J., & Rasmussen, B. Social interaction, social competence & friendship in children. *Child Development*, 1975, **46**, 709–718.

Gottman, J., Gonso, J., & Schuler, P. Teaching social skills to isolated children. *Journal of Abnormal Child Psychology*, 1976, **4**, 179–197.

Gottman, J. M., & Leiblum, S. R. *How to do psychotherapy and how to evaluate it.* New York: Holt, Rinehart and Winston, 1974.

Hall, R. V., Axelrod, S., Tyler, L., Grief, E., Jones, F. C., & Robertson, R. Modification of behavior problems in the home with the parent as observer and experimenter. *Journal of Applied Behavior Analysis*, 1972, **5**, 53–64.

Hawkins, R. P. It's time we taught the young how to be good parents (and don't we wish we'd started a long time ago?) *Psychology Today*, 1972, **6.**

Hawkins, R. P., Peterson, R. F., Schweid, E., & Bijou, S. W. Behavior therapy in the home: Amelioration of problem parent-child relations with the parent in a therapeutic role. *Journal of Experimental Child Psychology*, 1966, **4**, 99–107.

Herbert, E. W., & Baer, D. M. Training parents as behavior modifiers: Self-recording of contingent atten-

tion. *Journal of Applied Behavior Analysis*, 1972, **5**, 139–149.

Johnson, S. M., & Lobitz, G. K. Parental manipulation of child behavior in home observations. *Journal of Applied Behavior Analysis*, 1974, **7**, 23–31.

Johnston, J. M. Punishment of human behavior. *American Psychologist*, 1972, **27**, 1033–1055.

Jones, M. C. The elimination of children's fears. *Journal of Experimental Psychology*, 1924, **7**, 383–390(a).

Jones, M. C. A laboratory study of fear: The case of Peter. *Journal of Genetic Psychology*, 1924, **31**, 308–315(b).

Kagan, J., & Lewis, M. Studies of attention in the human infant. *Merrill-Palmer Quarterly*, 1965, **11**, 95–127.

Kanner, L. *Child psychiatry.* Springfield, Ill.: Thomas, 1972.

Kardish, S., Hillman, E., & Werry, J. Efficacy of imipramine in childhood enuresis. *Canadian Medical Association Journal*, 1968, **99**, 263–266.

Keehn, J. D. Brief case report: Reinforcement therapy of incontinence. *Behaviour Research and Therapy*, 1965, **2**, 239.

Kimmel, H. D., & Kimmel, E. An instrumental conditioning method for treatment of enuresis. *Journal of Behavior Therapy and Experimental Psychiatry*, 1970, **1**, 121–124.

Kirby, F. D., & Toler, H. C. Modification of preschool isolate behavior: A case study. *Journal of Applied Behavior Analysis*, 1970, **3**, 309–314.

Korner, A. F., & Grobstein, R. Individual differences at birth: Implications for mother-infant relationship and later development. *Journal of the American Academy for Child Psychiatry*, 1967, **6**, 676–690.

Lang, P. J., & Melamed, B. G. Case report: Avoidance conditioning therapy of an infant with chronic ruminative vomiting. *Journal of Abnormal Psychology*, 1969, **74**, 1–8.

Lazarus, A. A. *Behavior therapy and beyond.* New York: McGraw-Hill, 1971.

Lazarus, A. A., & Abramovitz, A. The use of "emotive imagery" in the treatment of children's phobias. *Journal of Mental Science*, 1962, **108**, 191–195.

Lazarus, A. A., Davison, G. C., & Polefka, D. A. Classical and operant factors in the treatment of a school phobia. *Journal of Abnormal Psychology*, 1965, **70**, 225–229.

Leventhal, T., Weinberger, G., Stander, R. J., & Stearns, R. P. Therapeutic strategies with school phobics. *American Journal of Orthopsychiatry*, 1967, **37**, 64–70.

Lovibond, S. H. The mechanism of conditioning treatment of enuresis. *Behaviour Research and Therapy*, 1963, **1**, 17–21.

Madsen, C. H., Becker, W. C., & Thomas, D. R. Rules,

praise, and ignoring: Elements of elementary classroom control. *Journal of Applied Behavior Analysis,* 1968, **1**, 139–150.

Madsen, C. H., Hoffman, M., Thomas, D. R., Koropsak, E., & Madsen, C. K. Comparison of toilet training techniques. In D. M. Gelfand (Ed.), *Social learning in childhood.* Belmont, Calif.: Brook/Cole, 1969.

Marvin, R. S., Marvin, C. N., & Abramovitch, L. An ethological study of the development of coy behavior in young children. Paper presented at the meeting of the Society for Research in Child Development, Philadelphia, 1973, unpublished.

McConaghy, N. A controlled trial of imipramine, amphetamine, pad-and-bell conditioning and random wakening in the treatment of enuresis. *Medical Journal of Australia,* 1969, **2**, 237–239.

Morris, E. K., & Redd, W. H. Children's performance and social preference for positive, negative, and mixed adult-child interactions. *Child Development,* 1975, **46**, 525–531.

Mowrer, O. H., & Mowrer, W. A. Enuresis: A method for its study and treatment. *American Journal of Orthopsychiatry,* 1938, **8**, 436–447.

Neale, P. H. Behavior therapy and encopresis in children. *Behaviour Research and Therapy,* 1963, **1**, 139–149.

O'Dell, S. Training parents in behavior modification: A review. *Psychological Bulletin,* 1974, **81**, 418–433.

Oden, S., & Asher, S. R. Coaching children in social skills for friendship making. *Child Development,* 1977, **48**, 495–506.

O'Leary, K. D., & Becker, W. C. The effects of a teacher's reprimands on children's behavior. *Journal of School Psychology,* 1968, **7**, 8–11.

Paschalis, A. P., Kimmel, H. D., & Kimmel, E. Further study of diurnal instrumental conditioning in the treatment of enuresis nocturna. *Journal of Behavior Therapy and Experimental Psychiatry,* 1972, **3**, 253–256.

Patterson, G. R. Direct intervention in families of deviant children. Eugene: Oregon Research Institute, 1968.

Patterson, G. R. *Families: Applications of social learning to family life.* Champaign, Ill.: Research Press, 1971.

Patterson, G. R. Aggressive child: Victim and architect of a coercive system. In E. J. Marsh, L. A. Hamerlynck, & L. C. Handy (Eds.), *Behavior modification and families.* New York: Brunner/Mazel, 1976.

Patterson, G. R., & Gullion, M. E. *Living with children: New methods for parents and teachers.* Champaign, Ill.: Research Press, 1968.

Patterson, G. R., McNeal, N., Hawkins, N., & Phelps, R. Reprograming the social environment. *Journal of Child Psychology and Psychiatry,* 1967, **8**, 181–195.

Redd, W. H., Morris, E. K., & Martin, J. A. Effects of positive and negative adult-child interactions on children's social preference. *Journal of Experimental Child Psychology,* 1975, **19**, 153–164.

Rheingold, H. L. The social and socializing infant. In D. A. Goslin (Ed.), *Handbook of socialization theory and research.* Chicago: Rand McNally, 1971.

Rinn, R. C., Vernon, J. C., & Wise, M. J. Training parents of behaviorally-disordered children in groups: A three years' program evaluation. *Behavior Therapy,* 1975, **6**, 378–387.

Rosekrans, M. A. Imitation in children as a function of perceived similarity to social model and vicarious reinforcement. *Journal of Personality and Social Psychology,* 1967, **7**, 307–315.

Ross, D. M., Ross, S. A., & Evans, T. The modification of extreme social withdrawal of modeling and guided participation. *Journal of Behavior Therapy and Experimental Psychiatry,* 1971, **2**, 273–279.

Salk, L. *What every child would like his parents to know.* New York: McKay, 1972.

Sloane, H. N., Johnston, M. K., & Bijou, S. W. Successive modification of aggressive behavior and aggressive fantasy play by management of contingencies. *Journal of Child Psychology and Psychiatry,* 1967, **8**, 217–226.

Starfield, B. Enuresis: Its pathogenesis and management. *Clinical Pediatrics,* 1972, **11**, 343–349.

Stern, D. N. Mother and infant at play: The dyadic interactions involving facial, vocal, and gaze behaviors. In M. Lewis & L. A. Rosenblum (Eds.), *The effect of the infant on its caretaker.* New York: Wiley, 1974.

Tasto, D. L. Systematic desensitization, muscle relaxation and visual imagery in the counter-conditioning of a four-year-old phobic child. *Behaviour Research and Therapy,* 1969, **7**, 409–411.

Wahler, R. G. Oppositional children: A quest for parental reinforcement control. *Journal of Applied Behavior Analysis,* 1969, **2**, 159–170.

Walder, L. O., Cohen, S. I., Breiter, D. E., Daston, P. G., Hirsch, I. S., & Leibowitz, J. M. Teaching behavioral principles to parents of disturbed children. In B. G. Gurney (Ed.), *Psychotherapeutic agents: A new role for non-professionals, parents and teachers.* New York: Holt, Rinehart and Winston, 1969.

Werry, J. S., & Cohrssen, J. Enuresis—an etiological and therapeutic study. *Journal of Pediatrics,* 1965, **67**, 423–431.

Williams, C. D. The elimination of tantrum behavior by extinction procedures. *Journal of Abnormal and Social Psychology,* 1959, **59**, 269.

Wish, P. A., Hasazi, J. E., & Jurgela, A. R. Automated

direct deconditioning of a childhood phobia. *Journal of Behavior Therapy and Experimental Psychiatry*, 1973, **4**, 279–283.

Wolff, P. Observations on the early development of smiling. In B. M. Foss (Ed.), *Determinants of infant behaviour II*. London: Methuen, 1963.

Wolff, P. H. The natural history of crying and other vocalizations in early infancy. In B. M. Foss (Ed.), *Determinants of infant behaviour IV*, London: Methuen, 1969.

Yates, A. J. *Theory and practice in behavior therapy*. New York: Wiley, 1975.

Young, G. C. Conditioning treatment of enuresis. *Developmental Medicine and Child Neurology*, 1969, **7**, 557 –562.

Young, I. L., & Goldsmith, A. O. Treatment of encopresis in a day treatment program. *Psychotherapy: Theory, Research and Practice*, 1972, **9**, 231–235.

Zeilberger, J., Sampen, S. E., & Sloane, H. N. Modification of a child's problem behaviors in the home with the mother as therapist. *Journal of Applied Behavior Analysis*, 1968, **1**, 47–53.

five

BEHAVIORAL INTERVENTIONS IN EDUCATIONAL SETTINGS

Even a superficial look at the history of the American educational system reveals that teachers have been delegated more and more responsibility for children's development, and that the public schools have been the battlefront for many controversial social issues. The good old days when schoolteachers taught readin', writin', and 'rithmetic are long since gone. Today, teachers need to be experts in broad curriculum areas (for instance, health, math, science, art, music), child management, as well as the workings of large bureaucratic structures. Indeed, education almost becomes a peripheral issue when administrators, teachers, and parents are embroiled in such controversial topics as busing, sex-education programs, teacher strikes, and budget cuts.

Schools can exist in the midst of these dramatic changes and turmoil, but this does not mean our children's education remains unaffected. Although no single solution exists for solving the problems facing educators, behavioral psychologists have offered a number of alternatives. In this chapter we will examine the variety of intervention strategies that have evolved during the last fifteen years. We will begin by discussing briefly the behavioral approach to classroom intervention. Next we will examine strategies for controlling problem behavior and improving academic performance and instructional materials, including a discussion of two special problems: hyperactivity and learning disabilities. Finally,

we will review the available evaluative data on behavioral interventions and some issues frequently arising from intervention in educational systems.

A BEHAVIORAL APPROACH TO EDUCATIONAL INTERVENTION

During the early 1960s, behavior modification procedures for classroom intervention were first used. Projects at the University of Washington (Bijou, 1965) and the University of Arizona (Staats, 1969) combined B. F. Skinner's (1938, 1953) notions about learning and education with the rapidly developing strategies for behavioral intervention. By the mid-1960s, researchers had moved their work from the laboratory or preschool to classrooms in the public schools. By now, behavioral techniques have been applied more extensively in the classroom than in any other setting.

Behavioral psychologists working in educational settings offer services that are considerably different from those of traditional school psychologists. Rather than serving as psychometricians administering projective and intelligence tests or as clinicians counseling individual students, behavioral psychologists work in close alliance with teachers and students. Sidney Bijou (1970) has discussed three ways that behavioral psychologists can do this. First, they can help teachers as-

103

sess the academic and social skills of children entering school and arrange appropriate individualized educational programs. They can also assist teachers and classroom aides in using behavioral principles to deal with problems in classroom management. Finally, they can aid in devising instructional materials. Behaviorally oriented school psychologists typically do not function as "testers" or counselors, but rather as those skilled in the use of behavioral techniques for all aspects of learning and teaching.

When behavioral psychologists are called on to resolve particular problems in a school, they follow the same basic strategy used in working with individual clients (see Chapter 3). Here, too, the process begins by delineating the goals for intervention. However, a unique problem that can be encountered at this point is determining who in the educational system is "the client"—that is, who are the services meant to benefit? For example, a behavioral psychologist may be asked to assist an exasperated teacher whose threats of phone calls to parents and after-school detention go unheeded by his desk-pounding, textbook-shredding students. Not only does this situation give the teacher the feeling that his role is that of a policeman, but students believe school is something of a cross between the Spanish Inquisition and extended recess. In such a situation, the "client" could be the teacher, particular students, or even the entire class. Ideally, everyone's goals would be similar. But when there is a conflict, the behavioral psychologist should act as a mediator between interests rather than as an agent of one party against the other.

Once intervention goals are established, the behavioral psychologist can begin a detailed assessment to determine potential problem areas. In the example just cited, areas of intervention might include bringing the children's behavior under more appropriate control, increasing the teacher's frequency of reinforcement for improved behavior or academic performance, altering the contingencies of reinforcement between individuals, and/or improving the academic program. Once the problem areas are defined, an intervention program can be formulated. As is the case with any intervention, agreement between the psychologist and client(s) on the tactics of intervention is

crucial. When the program is implemented, continual assessment allows the psychologist to see the impact of the intervention, and to modify the program where necessary.

CONTROL OF CLASSROOM PROBLEM BEHAVIORS

Teacher Attention: Praise and Ignore

In the context of a busy, crowded classroom where children may go unrecognized for long periods of time, it is not surprising that teacher attention of the "Get back to work" and "Stop talking" variety may unintentionally encourage students' misbehaviors and act paradoxically as a positive reinforcer. For this reason, helping teachers alter their patterns of attention to students is a central component of classroom management programs.

Using attention effectively requires particular skill on the teacher's part. He or she first selects the types of behavior that should benefit the child's progress if they occurred more frequently. For example, one teacher might want a child to follow verbal instructions, complete assignments, and raise her hand when she has a question. This teacher then reinforces the child's appropriate behaviors with positive comments. As easy as this sounds, sometimes it is difficult for teachers to praise students. When a teacher begins to increase the frequency of praise, it may at first feel somewhat awkward, artificial, and even difficult with those children who have been particularly troublesome. To make sure of not getting "stuck" and using the same words over and over, the teacher can be more genuine and individualize comments by specifying the child's appropriate behavior (for example, "Thank you, Mary, for raising your hand," "Finished your assignment already!"). The teacher also needs to be aware of what type of attention is effective for particular children. Instead of, or in addition to, verbal praise, some children may appreciate a hug or a pat on the back; others may find it aversive.

As the teacher praises students for appropriate behavior, he or she also withdraws *all* attention from problem behaviors. Again, this is a new strategy for many teachers and may take a bit of practice to perfect. It is often difficult to consistently ignore behavior that is annoying. And, although a teacher may be able to stifle verbal reprimands, students may still be able to catch his eye by being disruptive. Finally, since research indicates that ignoring is often insufficient to reduce inappropriate classroom behavior (Madsen, Becker, & Thomas, 1968), teachers may also find it helpful to reinforce students for behavior incompatible with the ignored behaviors (for example, praising a child for working quietly at her desk while ignoring her whispering across the aisle to friends) as well as praising other appropriate behavior.

There are numerous examples in the literature of the effectiveness of differential teacher attention (Becker, Madsen, Arnold, & Thomas, 1967; Cossairt, Hall, & Hopkins, 1973; Hall, Lund, & Jackson, 1968; Madsen, Becker, & Thomas, 1968; Madsen, Becker, Thomas, Koser, & Plager, 1968; Schutte & Hopkins, 1970; Zimmerman & Zimmerman, 1962). Even though research in this area consists primarily of single-subject designs with multiple replications, the existence of functional (that is, cause-effect) relationships between teacher attention and student behavior appears well established.

Peer Influence

One conclusion that can be drawn from the teacher attention studies is that disruptive classroom behavior can often be eliminated by systematically altering the teacher's response. Sometimes, however, this is insufficient. Even if a teacher consistently ignores the attention-getting antics of the class clown, this may have little effect if classmates are roaring with laughter. The impact of a child's peers is considerable. They can model appropriate and inappropriate behavior as well as respond contingently to their classmates' actions (O'Leary & O'Leary, 1977).

Peer competition can also serve to disrupt children's classroom behavior. "Doing better than Jeff, the class brain," can be a strong motivation for some children, but it can also be the source of many unpleasant and destructive exchanges between classmates. Recognizing these conditions, behavioral psychologists have employed peer in-

fluence to modify the behavior of children in the classroom.

"Spillover" Effect. A rather indirect yet frequently used procedure is to praise a target child's peers for appropriate behavior with the hope that the target child will then behave similarly. A number of studies have demonstrated that this procedure often produces desirable changes in the behaviors of nonreinforced peers (Christy, 1975; Drabman & Lahey, 1974; Kazdin, Silverman, & Sittler, 1975; Strain & Timm, 1974; Broden, Bruce, Mitchell, Carter, & Hall, 1970).

One study that clearly demonstrates this phenomenon was conducted by Phillip Strain, Richard Shores, and Mary Kerr (1976). Three children in a class of ten were prompted and reinforced for appropriate social behavior. Two of the children, Dan and Hank, were physically abusive when they interacted with their peers. Another child, Ricky, was extremely isolated and spent most of his time sitting in the corner. All three children received prompts (for instance, being moved to where others were playing, receiving verbal comments such as "Let's play with your friends") and reinforcement (for instance, pats on the back, comments such as "I like it when you play with your friends, Hank") to increase appropriate social interactions. Figure 5–1 indicates that the strategy reliably increased positive social behavior and decreased negative behavior. Data were also obtained on the social behavior of Dan, Hank, and Ricky's classmates. Figure 5–2 shows that increases in positive behavior clearly "spilled over" and affected the frequency of positive interactions among peers even though only three children were directly reinforced. The other children may have behaved better because appropriate behavior was modeled by peers, because they had heard the teacher specify what behaviors she would reward, or both. In any event, the "spillover" effects from such interventions are certainly encouraging.

Group Consequences. Rather than changing a child's behavior indirectly, teachers can also successfully reduce classroom disruptions through **group consequences.** This can be done in one of two ways. The first involves the teacher's focusing on one child's behavior and delivering conse-

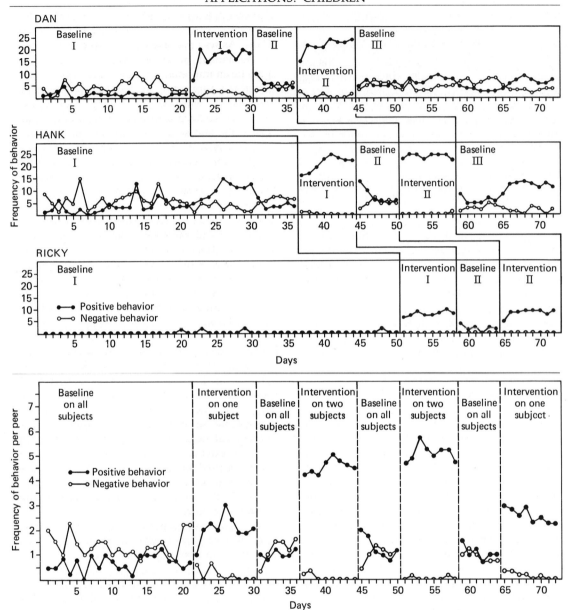

quences (positive or negative) to the entire class, depending on how that child behaves. In this case, the most disruptive class member is usually selected as the target. For example, if the child's running about and talking out of turn is kept to some specified minimum level during the morning hours, then the entire class may be granted fifteen extra minutes of recess in the afternoon. If a number of class members are about equally disruptive, the second alternative—group consequences contingent on the entire group's behavior —can be employed (Hayes, 1976). For example,

Figure 5–1. Three boys exhibiting socially inappropriate behavior who were sequentially exposed to intervention conditions involving prompting and reinforcement for increased positive social behavior. From P. S. Strain, R. E. Shores, & M. M. Kerr, An experimental analysis of "spill-over" effects on the social interaction of behaviorally handicapped preschool children. *Journal of Applied Behavior Analysis,* 1976, **9,** p. 37, fig. 1. By permission of the Journal of Applied Behavior Analysis, Department of Human Development, University of Kansas, Lawrence.

Figure 5–2. Frequency of positive and negative behavior among nonreinforced classmates across baseline (all), intervention on one subject, and intervention on two subjects' conditions. From P. S. Strain, R. E. Shores, & M. M. Kerr, An experimental analysis of "spill-over" effects on the social interaction of behaviorally handicapped preschool children. *Journal of Applied Behavior Analysis,* 1976, **9,** p. 37, fig. 2. By permission of the Journal of Applied Behavior Analysis, Department of Human Development, University of Kansas, Lawrence.

points determining extra recess for the class can be accumulated as each child refrains from disruptive activity during the day.

There are several accounts in the literature of the use of group consequences for individual behavior (Brooks & Snow, 1972; Carlson, Arnold, Becker, & Madsen, 1968; Coleman, 1970; Patterson, 1965; Rosenbaum, O'Leary, & Jacob, 1975). An advantage of group reward cited by researchers is that peer influence can add to the reinforcement the target child receives. Classmates have often cheered and encouraged the child whose behavior controlled rewards for them (Patterson, 1965; Carlson, Arnold, Becker, & Madsen, 1968). On the other hand, peer influence may also escalate into peer pressure and increase inappropriate social behavior between classmates. Thus, although the disruptive behavior of target children may decrease through group consequences, the potentially destructive influence of peer pressure on the target child must be taken into consideration.

Several studies have also been conducted with group consequences for group behavior (Barrish, Saunders, & Wolf, 1969; Harris & Sherman, 1973a;

Medlund & Stachnik, 1972; Greene & Pratt, 1972; Schmidt & Ulrich, 1969; Sulzbacher & Houser, 1970). As was the case with group consequences for individual behavior, peer interactions can again be an important variable. Instead of laughing at and applauding each other's pranks, children start to work on time and urge disruptive classmates to keep the noise down, complete assignments, and so on, so they can all have their special activity or treat. In this manner, individual children receive social reinforcement from peers for behaving appropriately in addition to sharing the rewards administered to the entire group. A problem has occasionally arisen when a few class members have found it reinforcing to misbehave and sabotage rewards for the rest of the class (Harris & Sherman, 1973a; Barrish, Saunders, & Wolf, 1969). Usually, problems of this type can be managed by adding individual contingencies for the oppositional child until he or she can effectively rejoin the group system (Hayes, 1976).

Peer Contingency Management. A final strategy for employing peer influence to reduce the disruptive behavior of classmates is to have peers directly responsible for contingency management for the target child. Peers can observe and record data on the relevant behaviors as well as dispense reinforcers. Although the use of peers in this manner has been extensively investigated in special programs for predelinquents (Bailey, Timbers, Phillips, & Wolf, 1971; Phillips, Phillips, Wolf, & Fixsen, 1973), this procedure has rarely been used in classroom research.

One of the few studies (Surratt, Ulrich, & Hawkins, 1969) employed a fifth-grader as an observer to record the disruptive behavior of four first-graders. In another example, the five most popular students in a sixth-grade class were taught to praise and ignore the behavior of five disruptive classmates (Solomon & Wahler, 1973). Obviously, we cannot judge the effectiveness of peer contingency management from these two studies. However, the substantial influence that peers have, both when they receive praise while target children observe and when they are involved in group contingencies with target children, indicates they may also function effectively as contingency managers.

Token Economies

Changing the way the teacher and peers attend to a child does not always alter the behavior of a child who is disruptive in school. Many children are only minimally influenced by the "normal" classroom reinforcers such as teacher attention, grades, honor lists, and the like. Such children may need an extra "push" or motivation to behave more appropriately or to improve their academic performance. A token reinforcement program often provides just the right conditions for change.

Token reinforcement programs are really quite simple. A monetary system is established in which the children earn tokens (plastic chips, stars, checks on a page, and so on) contingent upon desired behavior. These tokens are then used by the child to purchase various items and/or special privileges at a classroom "store." A token economy is merely a miniature version of the system we all live under: children work, get paid, and then spend their pay as they wish. Although the tokens may not be valued by the children initially, the association of tokens with **backup reinforcers** (things the children can buy with their tokens) makes them highly valued within a short period of time. Games, candy, books, tickets to school events, and extra recess time are among the most common backup reinforcers.

The rules for receiving tokens vary from class to class and usually from child to child. In the ideal situation, the requirements for reinforcement depend on the individual child's level of ability. If, for example, Danny has trouble working independently and takes a long time to finish his assignments, the teacher would set his work requirements much lower than those for Jodi, who is much less distractible. Working for five minutes might earn Danny a token, whereas his classmates would need to work longer and complete their assignment to earn the same reward. The idea is to motivate all the children to work at their full potential, regardless of their ability level. If the same reinforcement schedule were applied to all children, Danny might have to work all day to complete his lesson and would most likely be discouraged before he earned his first token. Yet, Jodi, who works rapidly, might get tokens so fast

that she would become satiated and stop trying. It is assumed that with a flexible and individualized system, both children would experience success and be challenged at the same time.

In addition, there are other, less obvious benefits of token economies. For one thing, a pocketful of tokens is a good reminder to the teacher to use positive reinforcement. In fact, researchers have noted that teachers' rates of positive comments increase and negative comments decrease following the institution of a token system (Breyer & Allen, 1975; Iwata & Bailey, 1974). Furthermore, since the teacher has to pay close attention to each child in order to know when tokens should be given, the system often ensures greater teacher attention and more frequent contacts (Mandelker, Brigham, & Bushell, 1970). It is encouraging to note the positive changes in classroom atmosphere that can result from token systems.

Many teachers question whether a token program is not just a way to bribe children for working. Instead of being motivated by the desire to collect chips and trade them in for treats, should not a child want to learn and perform well in school? But token economies are no closer to bribery than any other incentive system. The word "bribery" implies corruption, and one hardly speaks of "bribing" teachers with money to make them teach their students. Most behavioral psychologists and teachers would probably agree that it would be ideal if all children were motivated by academic achievement. However, since each child is different, token reinforcement may provide the extra encouragement to those students not "turned on" by school.

The initial educational token economy studies, conducted by Arthur Staats and his associates (Staats, Finley, Minke, Wolf, & Brooks, 1964; Staats, Staats, Schultz, & Wolf, 1962), demonstrated that token reinforcement systems could maintain children's performance for long periods of time. Since Staats' early work in the 1960s, token systems have been used in many institutional and public school classrooms. Teachers are usually instructed to ignore such behaviors as getting out of seat without permission, talking out of turn, and disturbing classmates while praising children and giving them tokens for following instructions, raising a hand to speak, looking at the task assigned, or completing assignments. Usually, a token program coupled with ignore procedures adequately reduces disruptive behavior. However, investigators have also used time-out (Birnbrauer, Wolf, Kidder, & Tague, 1965; Walker, Mattson & Buckley, 1971) and **response cost** (that is, disruptive behavior *costs* a child tokens) procedures (Iwata & Bailey, 1974; McLaughlin & Malaby, 1972b) instead of ignoring.

Most research with token programs has employed single-subject designs with multiple replications. Following a baseline period in which teachers conduct their classes as usual, a treatment phase is instituted in which they praise their students and administer tokens for appropriate behavior. The token program may be withdrawn for a time and later reinstated to evaluate its effectiveness. A great many investigators have reported large decreases in disruptive behavior with token programs that reinforced nondisruptive appropriate behavior (for instance, Main & Munroe, 1977; see also reviews by Kazdin, 1977; O'Leary & Drabman, 1971).

As with most interventions, the behavior changes produced by token programs will not necessarily be maintained when the program is withdrawn or the child moves on unless specific procedures are employed to foster transfer of training. For example, the use of backup reinforcers that are indigenous to the classroom, such as extra recess, early dismissal, library trips, and special projects, encourages maintenance of new behavior because these rewards remain available when the token program is gone. In contrast, backing up tokens with toys, candy, or other reinforcers that may disappear with the program is unwise.

Another way to help maintain behavior changes is to remove token reinforcement gradually rather than abruptly. This can be done by gradually "thinning" the token reinforcement schedule until the tokens are not needed at all. Also, the delay between performance and delivery of tokens or between getting a token and exchanging it for a backup reinforcer can be gradually increased until the new behavior has become relatively independent of token reinforcement. Perhaps most important, however, the teacher must remember that new behavior will *not* be maintained in the absence of reinforcement. Withdrawing a token

program eliminates one type of reinforcer, but other types must remain. The most readily available maintenance reinforcer in the classroom is praise and attention. If teachers have been careful to pair praise with the disbursement of tokens, they may find that praise has become an effective reinforcer even though it may not have been before the token program was introduced.

Although there has been remarkable improvement in many classrooms when problematic behaviors are reduced, these changes are not necessarily accompanied by improvements in academic performance (Ferritor, Buckholdt, Hamblin, & Smith, 1972; Harris & Sherman, 1973b; McLaughlin & Malaby, 1972a). Disruptive behavior can also be reduced by reinforcing academic performance (Ayllon & Roberts, 1974), but this route is infrequently taken; some investigators feel disruptive behavior is all too often the sole focus of intervention (Winett & Winkler, 1972). Behavioral psychologists have directed considerable attention toward improving academic performance through both classroom management interventions and improved instructional materials. We will examine these efforts in detail.

IMPROVING ACADEMIC PERFORMANCE

Teacher Attention: Praise and Ignore

As we discussed earlier, teachers can decrease the frequency of student disruptions and misbehavior in the classroom by systematically praising task-oriented activities while ignoring noise making, daydreaming, or any other activity incompatible with learning. Although the more frequent intervention for children's academic problems is to modify teachers' instructional methods or program materials, praise and ignore strategies have been helpful in this area as well. Teachers have increased students' productivity simply by praising them for the number of problems completed or words written (Houten, Hill, & Parsons, 1975); they have also improved the accuracy of students' completed assignments with praise (Felixbrod & O'Leary, 1973; Hasazi & Hasazi, 1972; Kirby &

Shields, 1972; Zimmerman & Zimmerman, 1962). Case Study 5–3 is an unusually clear example of the way in which teacher attention can maintain an academic problem and how systematically altering the teacher's behavior can eliminate the difficulty.

Peer Influence

Although peer influence is most commonly used to alter disruptive behavior, elementary school children can also improve their classmates' academic performance through participation in group contingencies, contingency management, or tutoring programs. Group rewards have been used successfully to improve target children's performance on daily lessons (Evans & Oswalt, 1968; Hamblin, Hathaway, & Wodarski, 1971). Children have even dispensed tokens and praise for the academic work of their classmates (Greenwood, Sloane, & Baskin, 1974). Most research in this area has involved children providing academic tutoring to lesser-achieving students (Harris & Sherman, 1973b; Johnson & Bailey, 1974; Robertson, DeReus, & Drabman, 1976; Willis, Morris, & Crowder, 1972). The children who are tutored are not the only ones who benefit from such extra attention; the tutors themselves also profit from the lesson rehearsals and additional responsibility (Dineen, Clark, & Risley, 1977). Although only preliminary work has been done in this area, the use of peer influence to improve academic performance might prove to be helpful to busy classroom teachers as well.

Token Economies

Token reinforcement has been used to improve a wide variety of academic skills. Many programs aimed at academic performance often focus initially on improving children's attentive behavior. Sitting in one's chair, listening to the teacher, or looking at and studying one's lessons are all behaviors that have shown improvement when children have received token reinforcement (Broden, Hall, Dunlap, & Clark, 1970; Bushell, Wrobel, & Michaelis, 1968; Ferritor, Buckholdt, Hamblin, & Smith, 1972; Hewett, Taylor, & Artuso, 1969).

As we mentioned, reinforcing attentive behavior alone often does not improve academic achievement. Thus, many researchers have reinforced the correct following of instructions (Zimmerman, Zimmerman, & Russell, 1969); lesson completion (Rickard, Melvin, Creel, & Creel, 1973; Willis, 1974; Wolf, Giles, & Hall, 1968); or accuracy (Birnbrauer, Wolf, Kidder, & Tague, 1965; Ferritor, Buckholdt, Hamblin, & Smith, 1972; Knapczyk & Livingston, 1973; Walker & Hops, 1976) instead. When this strategy has been used, academic improvements have been accompanied by increased attentiveness and reduced disruption (Ayllon, Layman, & Burke, 1972; Kirby & Shields, 1972; Marholin, Steinman, McInnis, & Heads, 1975). The results of these studies suggest that the problems of student inattention and disruption, often the major complaints of classroom teachers, may be altered indirectly by reinforcing academic performance.

Self-Control

There is growing interest among educators and behavioral psychologists in the possibility of teaching young children certain behavior modification techniques so that they can exercise greater control over their own behavior. The interest is not so much in teaching self-control techniques as ends in themselves, but rather as skills a child might use to facilitate success in the classroom.

Such self-control training has focused on four areas. The first involves the child determining his own performance goals and criteria to dispense reinforcers. For example, a child doing workbook problems would decide exactly how many problems he should do in order to earn a reinforcer. The second area includes self-monitoring and evaluation of behavior. A child literally keeps records of his own progress and then evaluates the adequacy of his work against some standard. The child working on arithmetic problems might count the number of problems he completes in a class period and then compare his performance against the standards that he set for himself earlier.

The third self-control skill is self-reinforcement. Exactly as the term implies, the child gives himself the reinforcers he has earned. This might involve a child assigning himself redeemable points or taking treats from the classroom storage closet. The fourth skill that is often included in self-control training is self-instruction and problem solving. This is typically more complex than the other skills and involves teaching the child how to assess new situations, determine the options that are available and the possible consequence of each course of action, and instruct himself as to the way in which the task should be approached.

Research evaluating the feasibility of self-control training with children has been limited to laboratory studies and a small number of experimental classroom programs. It has shown that elementary school-age children can learn how to become their own behavior modifiers and master the components of effective self-control. They can be taught to set their own performance standards (Bandura & Perloff, 1967; Drabman, 1973; Felixbrod & O'Leary, 1973; Glynn, Thomas, & Shee, 1973; Turkewitz, O'Leary, & Ironsmith, 1975), and dispense reinforcers to themselves (Bolstad & Johnson, 1972). In fact, children learn these skills quite easily. The problem is that in most cases young children require close supervision if they are to carry out these operations (O'Leary & O'Leary, 1976). Although children will readily emit self-control behaviors if a teacher checks up on them (Felixbrod & O'Leary, 1973) or if an adult experimenter explicitly rewards them for correctly doing so (Salzberg, 1972), many children adopt lenient standards (Felixbrod & O'Leary, 1973) or incorrectly score their work to their own advantage if left to themselves (O'Leary & O'Leary, 1976).

In contrast to these rather discouraging findings, researchers have found that teaching children self-control techniques in the context of an ongoing token reinforcement program can facilitate the generalization and maintenance of behavioral gains (Bolstad & Johnson, 1972; Drabman, Spitalnik, & O'Leary, 1973; Turkewitz, O'Leary, & Ironsmith, 1975). In one after-school remedial reading class that operated on a token economy, disruptive behavior decreased and academic output increased after students were taught to evaluate their own behavior and to assign themselves redeemable points for satisfactory performance (Drabman, Spitalnik, & O'Leary, 1973). The eight nine- to ten-year-old boys in the class were first taught how to rate their conduct and academic behavior. To encourage "accurate" self-evaluation, the teacher gave bonus points when a student's evaluation matched her own. As the students mastered the self-evaluation task, the teacher removed the bonus-point contingency. After approximately four weeks of training, students were evaluating their own behavior and assigning their own points without the teacher's checking for accuracy. Under these conditions, the students' disruptive behavior remained quite low—significantly less than during the preintervention baseline period. Moreover, the students' improved behavior generalized to other times during the day when the token/self-control system was not in operation.

Another aspect of self-control training involves teaching children self-instructional and problem-solving skills (Douglas, Parry, Marton, & Garson, 1976; Meichenbaum & Goodman, 1971). Similar to work done earlier (Lovitt & Curtis, 1968), this procedure involves teaching children to provide themselves with a set of instructions that help them to size up a problem and concentrate on solving it. The procedure may be particularly helpful to "impulsive" children who are easily distracted and who have difficulty seeing a task through to completion. Working with a child in a one-to-one setting, the teacher demonstrates a task (such as copying a simple line drawing) while verbalizing questions and instructions that help to complete it. The teacher's verbalizations are aimed at clarifying the problem, developing a plan, checking other alternatives, monitoring the work and correcting errors, coping with frustration, and, finally, delivering self-reinforcement. For example, the teacher might say the following things when copying a simple drawing:

"Okay, what is it I have to do? You want me to copy the picture with the different lines. I have to go slow and be careful. Okay, draw the line down, down, good; then to the right, that's it; now down some more and to the left. Good, I'm doing fine so far. Remember go slow. Now back up again. No, I was supposed to go down. That's okay. Just erase the line carefully. . . . Good. Even if I make an error I can go on slowly and carefully. Okay, I have to go down now. Finished. I did it." (Meichen-baum & Goodman, 1971, p. 117)

In more complex tasks, the teacher would spend time verbalizing a plan of action and planning alternatives before starting to work.

Once the teacher has modeled the task and the self-instructions, the child tries the same task while the teacher provides instructions. Next, the child tries again, this time giving himself a set of instructions out loud. On subsequent trials, the child is asked to talk to himself less and less audibly, and eventually to *internalize* the self-instructions (that is, *think* them without verbalizing). The child practices on a variety of simple tasks and problems to generalize the new skill.

Self-instructional and problem-solving training are intended to interrupt impulsive children's usual unplanned way of responding to tasks and increase the probability that they will consider a variety of ways of dealing with problem situations. Controlled investigations indicate that children labeled both "impulsive" (Meichenbaum & Goodman, 1971) and "hyperactive" (Douglas, Parry, Marton, & Garson, 1976; Palkes, Stewart, & Freedman, 1972; Palkes, Stewart, & Kahana, 1968) show improved performance on simple cognitive and visual-motor tasks, and preschoolers can also show improvements in printing following self-instructional training (Robin, Armel, & O'Leary, 1975). However, the utility of such procedures for making significant and lasting improvements in classroom behavior or academic performance has not yet been demonstrated.

Programmed Instruction

Almost eighty years ago, in his *Talks to Teachers on Psychology*, William James said (1899, p. 12):

You make a great, great mistake, if you think that psychology, being the science of the mind's laws, is something from which you can deduce definite programs and schemes and methods of instruction for immediate schoolroom use. Psychology is a science, and teaching is an art; and sciences never generate arts directly out of themselves.

Writing in the 1900s, James was probably correct in his analysis of psychology's contribution to education. Since then, however, psychology has produced a technology of teaching that provides "programs, schemes and methods of instruction" (Skinner, 1968). Many of us have become aware of this technology through recent developments in programmed workbooks and texts, teaching machines and computer-assisted instruction, and personalized systems of instruction (PSI). These three innovations represent some of psychology's contribution to the "art" of teaching.

Although programmed materials and machines have become big business only in the last twenty-five years, they have been around for a relatively long time. Sydney L. Pressey (1926, 1927) first designed a machine for automated teaching during the mid-1920s. Pressey's device was about the size of a small typewriter. In addition to presenting both informational and drill material, it also administered and scored tests. If the student pressed the key for the correct answer on Pressey's machine, it advanced to the next item; if the student's selection was incorrect, the machine scored an error and did not advance until the correct answer was chosen. Despite Pressey's innovations, it was not until 1958 that the real impetus for research and development of individualized programmed instruction came with the publication of B. F. Skinner's (1958) article, "Teaching Machines."

Regardless of the mode of presentation, the same general strategy is used for constructing all programmed materials. First, the skills that the student is to learn from the program are clearly specified. Next, the information to be presented is broken down into small units, which are then carefully put in order so that each lesson builds on the work that has come before. As a student progresses through the material, he or she must demonstrate learning at each step. The student must respond to the material by pointing to a correct answer, pressing the correct button, or typing an answer on a computer terminal typewriter. This format gives the student an opportunity to receive *immediate* feedback. Many programs are written on a straight-line format; that is, new subject matter is introduced very gradually in order to enable every student to proceed through the program virtually error free. Other programs are "branching"; that is, when the student makes an error, he or she is instructed to go back to or over a particu-

				Teacher Instruction	Child Response
WR 6-6	————	——	ball	"This is the word 'ball' (pointing). Point to it and read it."	"Ball" (pointing)
WR 6-7	I	ball	fk	"Point to the word 'ball' and read it."	"Ball" (pointing)
WR 6-8	ball	kxt	a	"Point to the word 'ball' in this line and read it."	"Ball" (pointing)
WR 6-9	eii	ball	1b	"Find 'ball' here and point to it."	"Ball" (pointing)
WR 6-10		ball		"Read the word."	"Ball"

Figure 5–3. Five lines from an Edmark Reading Program lesson that teaches the word "ball." © 1972 Edmark Associates, Bellevue, Washington 98005.

lar section designed to deal with the specific error. As students progress through the program, extra help and prompts are gradually removed so that on completion of the program they eventually produce the criterion skills unaided.

Individualized instructional materials can be presented in a variety of formats. The most common is the **programmed lesson manual** or **text.** Manuals have been developed for teaching everything from handwriting (for instance, Skinner & Krakower, 1968) to neuroanatomy (for instance, Sidman & Sidman, 1965). An area that has seen particular expansion is the development of academic materials for schoolchildren. Edmark (1972) is one such program designed for remedial reading. The Edmark program consists of 150 word-recognition lessons, each of which introduces one word to the beginning reader. Figure 5–3 illustrates five lines from a lesson teaching the word "ball." The teacher begins by pronouncing each new word as the child points to and repeats it. The word is then presented visually along with two "distractors" (groups of letters or words), and the child is instructed to point to the correct word and read it. Finally, the child is asked to read the word aloud without prompting when it is presented alone. In subsequent word-recognition lessons the word is reviewed in phrases and sentences. Each word is also reviewed using supplementary materials (such as matching phrases with pictures, following written instructions, and reading aloud stories constructed only of the words taught) that are interspersed with the word-recognition lessons in a prescribed order. Other programs similar to Edmark have been constructed for areas such as mathematics and language arts.

Another format for individualized instruction consists of **teaching machines.** Teaching machines can come in many shapes and sizes. One of the simplest is the Mini-Max, a plastic box with a roller and a display window. A page of programmed material (for instance, a page from an Edmark lesson) is inserted in the box and rolled forward. Children see the question and write their answers in the display opening, roll the sheet forward, observe both their answer and the correct one simultaneously, and roll the sheet to the next question. Other teaching machines are considerably more complex and expensive. Computer technology has made possible the development of whole "libraries" of programmed courses of instruction. At the University of Illinois, for instance, 300 courses are available in the PLATO (Programmed Logic for Automatic Teaching Operation) system.

The third innovation, a **personalized system of instruction (PSI),** attempts to bring to classroom instruction all aspects of the other programmed materials. Fred Keller (1966, 1968) first developed the PSI format when he and his colleagues were involved in setting up a new department of psychology at the University of Brasilia. Dissatisfied with conventional teaching approaches, Keller decided to combine what he knew about programmed instruction with the application of reinforcement principles. Keller has summarized the features of PSI that seem to distinguish it from conventional teaching: (1) A "go-at-your-own-pace" feature permits students to move through the course at a rate commensurate with their own abilities and other time demands. (2) The "unit perfection requirement" permits students to go on to new material only after demonstrating mastery of the preceding material. (3) Lectures and demonstrations are used as vehicles of motivation, and students are eligible to attend only after they have completed their assignments. (4) Stress is placed upon the written word in student-teacher communications (short written quizzes and assignments accompanying all lessons). (5) Student proctors assist in testing, immediate scoring of exams, and assistance, which enables all students to benefit from continuous feedback on their performance and from personalized assistance.

For many students, the PSI courses are certainly very different from the traditional three-lectures-per-week, two-exams-per-semester college courses. During the last fifteen years, PSI course offerings have become very popular in many universities. Along with this flurry of enthusiasm, research comparing the benefits of the various program components of the PSI format is being conducted (Alba & Pennypacker, 1972; Born & Davis, 1974; McMichael & Corey, 1969; Semb, 1974).

Numerous studies have been directed at evaluating particular components of programmed materials or entire "packages" in comparison with more traditional forms of instruction. Unfortunately, the studies have extensive methodological problems such as insensitive measurement instruments, lack of equation of the instructional content, and uncontrolled student and teacher differences. Although reviews of programmed and computer-assisted instruction conclude that these innovations seem as effective as more traditional instructional methods (Jamison, Suppes, & Wells, 1974), they generally do not provide adequate information to enable the teacher or school administrator to make practical decisions regarding which instructional materials to use. Nevertheless, programmed courses are being implemented across the country. A consistent finding is that programmed materials typically save the student time, and "slower" students may improve more rapidly. For many students and teachers, such

findings may be encouraging enough for them to give programmed instruction a try.

HYPERACTIVITY AND LEARNING DISABILITIES

Children defined by the schools as hyperactive or learning disabled pose a paradox. In most respects they are viewed as normal, yet they present serious behavioral and academic problems. These children do not easily fit into the categories school systems traditionally use ("retarded" or "emotionally disturbed") to identify children with problems (Lahey, 1976). It is for this reason, plus the great interest psychologists, educators, and school personnel have taken in these problems, that we discuss their treatment under a special category. They are indeed special problems.

Definition and Characteristics

Although both categories are often narrowly defined, children labeled hyperactive or learning disabled are extremely heterogeneous in their behavioral characteristics. With regard to hyperactivity, teachers may respond to a particular problem behavior in a child such as excessive movement and activity in the classroom. Or a teacher might note a number of problems, such as short attention span, impulsivity, distractibility, emotional lability, and general academic deficits, that may lead to school failure. This diversity of behavior problems has led some researchers to characterize hyperactivity as a behavioral syndrome (Sleator & Sprague, 1977). Estimates indicate that between 3 and 20 percent of school-age children are labeled hyperactive (Cantwell, 1975), whether or not they exhibit one or several problem behaviors.

Characteristics of children labeled learning disabled are equally unclear. In fact, even traditional definitions have emphasized the heterogeneity of this population. A learning-disabled child may be overactive or underactive, may or may not have visual problems, may be too concerned with academic work or completely uninterested, and so on (Lahey, 1976). The various conceptualizations of learning disabilities are captured in the following definition:

Children with special learning disabilities exhibit a disorder in one or more of the basic psychological processes involved in understanding or in using spoken or written languages. These may be manifested in disorders of listening, thinking, talking, reading, writing, spelling, or arithmetic. They include conditions which have been referred to as perceptual handicaps, brain injury, minimal brain dysfunction, dyslexia, developmental aphasia, etc. (National Advisory Committee on Handicapped Children, 1968)

Another area where speculation largely outweighs data is in estimates of the incidence of learning disabilities. Figures are as variable as those for hyperactivity, ranging from 1 to 5 percent. Thus, it appears that the number of children and the types of behavior problems exhibited by either hyperactive or learning-disabled children vary considerably.

Traditional Treatment Approaches

Once a child is labeled hyperactive, the most common treatment recommendation is psychostimulant medication, usually methylphenidate (Ritalin) or dextroamphetamine (Dexedrine). For many children as well as adults, these drugs seem to make it easier to attend to a task and work effectively. In many cases, the effects are immediate, and teachers often recognize dramatic improvement in children's behavior within twenty-four hours of taking the drug (Sleator & Sprague, 1977). Although the drug literature is far too extensive to review here, researchers have consistently reported improvements in classroom behavior for between 60 and 90 percent of children taking stimulant medication on a daily basis (Whalen & Henker, 1976). Unfortunately, it is not known why, with whom, or for how long the positive effects will last (Cantwell, 1975). Because of these limitations, some researchers have recommended behavioral treatment strategies used alone or in conjunction with an ongoing drug program (Ayllon, Layman, & Kandel, 1975; Christiansen & Sprague, 1973; O'Leary, Pelham, Rosenbaum, & Price, 1976; Sprague & Werry, 1974).

Traditional approaches to remediating learning disabilities vary according to the deficit or impairment that is believed to cause the difficulty. For instance, brain dysfunction theories hypothesize neurological impairment, which presumably results in the child being unable to focus on relevant stimuli to the exclusion of others. Thus, the solution is to remove all competing stimuli from the child's environment (a classroom without colors or decorations, individual cubicles for each child, and so on). Other researchers view disorders of perception or perceptual-motor integration as the primary cause of learning disabilities. For instance, if visual perception is believed to be problematic, children might be asked to draw large blackboard letters and pronounce the words as they write them. Children who confuse and reverse letters presumably did not learn the orientation of their own bodies in space, so they are required to practice walking on balance beams to develop this sense. Benjamin Lahey (1976, p. 184) quite aptly summarizes the status of these traditional procedures:

> The consistent lack of evidence on the effectiveness of these traditional training programs is not at all surprising when they are evaluated according to basic principles of learning. Individually, and as a group, these methods violate virtually everything that is known about the way behavior changes. They require children to practice drawing visual abstract forms, perform calisthenics, repeat sentences, and the like, in the absence of systematic feedback or reinforcement, and expect to find improvement in reading skills as a result. The fact that these training programs are extensively used in the United States in spite of glaring inadequacies of design and evaluative research is surprising only to those who expect the world to be rational.

Behavioral Approaches

Behavioral programming with hyperactive or learning-disabled children combines many of the elements of interventions designed to improve academic performance and eliminate disruptive behavior. Typically, individual children are given praise and attention from their teachers for sitting quietly in class, paying attention, and reducing their disruptive behavior (Patterson, Jones, Whittier, & Wright, 1965; Shafto & Sulzbacher, 1977). Token reinforcement is also often used to increase appropriate behavior (Doubros & Daniels, 1966; Novy, Burnett, Powers, & Sulzer-Azaroff, 1973; Twardoz & Sajwaj, 1972; Wagner & Guyer, 1971; Wulbert & Dries, 1977) and to increase academic achievement (Ayllon, Layman, & Kandel, 1975; Haring & Hauck, 1969). Results from two group studies have demonstrated reductions in seat movements in hyperactive children receiving tokens for sitting quietly (Christiansen & Sprague, 1973) and improvements in teacher ratings of individual children following the introduction of token reinforcement programs for improved academic and social behavior (O'Leary, Pelham, Rosenbaum, & Price, 1976).

In addition to the preliminary work in the area of classroom management, a number of researchers have suggested teaching hyperactive children the kinds of self-control techniques we described earlier in this chapter (Bornstein & Quevillon, 1976; Douglas, Parry, Marton, & Garson, 1976; Meichenbaum & Goodman, 1971; Palkes, Stewart, & Kahana, 1968). Studies that have evaluated the effectiveness of these procedures have obtained significant improvements in children's performance on criterion tests requiring fine motor coordination and prolonged attention.

Thus, although behavioral techniques with so-called hyperactive and learning-disabled children are at a preliminary stage of development, the findings are remarkably encouraging when compared to the outcome of more traditional techniques. Further research must use more rigorous experimental designs and more sensitive dependent measures.

BEHAVIORAL INTERVENTIONS WITH "DISADVANTAGED" CHILDREN

The Impact of Head Start

In 1964 Congress passed the Economic Opportunity Act (EOA) as the key element in President Lyndon Johnson's antipoverty program. The purpose of the EOA was to create several social service programs to help the nation's poor. One such program was Head Start. For years, data

from academic achievement tests had indicated that poor children entered school less well prepared than their middle-class peers, and as the years passed they fell farther and farther behind. The Head Start strategy was to inject millions of dollars into local centers that could provide poor preschoolers with educational, nutritional, and medical services that had previously been unavailable to them. It was believed that this "head start" for the nation's "disadvantaged" children would boost their academic achievement levels so they could successfully begin the primary grades and continue to do well.

Local Head Start programs varied tremendously. The time each child spent at the center, the number of weeks the program operated, teacher qualifications, teacher-student ratios, techniques, and goals were all idiosyncratic. Despite this variability, a national evaluation was undertaken that attempted to assess the "overall effectiveness" of the entire Head Start effort (Westinghouse Learning Corporation/Ohio University, 1969). The methodology of the study has been seriously questioned, defended, and questioned again, but there appears to be considerable agreement with regard to its general conclusions (Rappaport, 1977): Although Head Start helped some children begin school better prepared, the improvement did not last. The performance of Head Start graduates in later grades was indistinguishable from that of poor children who had not been in the program.

Follow Through

The implications of the findings, released before official publication of the report, were highly controversial. Considerable pressure was placed on the Johnson administration to do something to correct the situation. In 1967 the EOA was amended to provide for a new program, Project Follow Through. Unlike Head Start, which had involved only preschoolers, Follow Through was designed for children from kindergarten through third grade. The plan was to develop approximately twenty-five educational programs, each based on a different theory of elementary education and child development. An evaluation component was also built into the program (rather than being tacked on afterwards) to determine which programs worked and which did not.

Two of the Follow Through programs had a decidedly behavioral approach. One program, Direct Instruction (DI), was developed by Siegfried Engelmann and Wesley Becker at the University of Oregon. The other, Behavior Analysis (BA), originated with Donald Bushell and Eugene Ramp at the University of Kansas. Both programs placed primary emphasis on the basic academic skills of reading, arithmetic, and language or writing, and sought to maximize the students' exposure to these subject areas during the school day. To increase human resources in the classroom, teacher aides (many of them parents) provided extra help and tutoring. All teachers and aides were trained and observed to ensure quality instruction. Throughout the programs, student progress was monitored so that the entire academic program could be individualized.

Despite these similarities, the models differed with respect to specific program materials and instructional methods. The DI authors developed their own packages of materials in arithmetic, language, and reading (now published by Science Research Associates under the trade name DISTAR). Children were instructed in small groups, with the teacher seated in the middle, within arm's reach of any student. The teacher presented lesson material and then went around the group drilling the students on the basic concepts. The DISTAR program indicated *exactly* what the teacher was to say and do for each lesson. These teacher "scripts" were used for a number of reasons. They eliminated any possibility of the teacher using wording that might be unfamiliar to lower-performing students, inappropriate examples, or lengthy presentations that might lead to loss of student attention. The scripted presentations allowed a teacher to use tried and proved directions, sequences of examples, sequences of subskills, and wordings (Engelmann & Becker, 1977). This strategy also ensured that lessons were broken down into small units, and that the children received lots of verbal feedback and praise during drill exercises.

Unlike the DI developers, the BA authors chose primarily existing curriculum materials that could be individualized. The main programs selected were *Programmed Reading* (McGraw-Hill), *Set and Numbers* (Singer), and the *Behavior Analysis Handwriting Primer*, which the BA team developed. Also different was the operation of the BA classrooms, which were based on a token economy to provide needed incentives for each student to begin and carry through on learning tasks (Ramp, 1977). Tokens were dispensed for progress and achievement and later exchanged for such reinforcers as free time, stories, attractive materials, or a chance to select a favorite activity. In addition, teachers used praise and ignore strategies to maintain appropriate classroom behavior.

Both programs have been evaluated as part of the national study of all Follow Through models. The test battery included measures of basic academic skills, cognitive-conceptual skills, affect, and self-image. Since both behavioral models ranked on or near the top on virtually every measure in the evaluation, we will present only the academic skills measures as an illustration.

The four measures of academic skills are from the Metropolitan Achievement Test (MAT) Elementary Level, Form F: MAT total reading, MAT total math, MAT spelling, and MAT language. These percentile data are presented in Figure 5–4 for the three most successful models. The Bank Street College of Education (BSC) model, a humanistic approach where the major goal is for children to become confident, inventive, and responsive through the teacher functioning in a variety of roles (good mother, therapist, value trainer, and master teacher), is the only model that even approached the academic gains made by the DI and BA models. As indicated, both the latter programs appeared successful and resulted in greater academic gains for their students than other Follow Through models. And the DI scores consistently approached or equaled the national norms.

One can also see that the data in Figure 5–4 reveal the large differences between the two behavioral programs. Of course, we can only speculate on the reasons for the DI program's fine showing. It may be the DI's small-group drills and constant demand for verbal output from the students produced greater gains in reading and language than BA's reinforcing the children for progress and improvement. Or the complete package of materials the DI teams developed and the BA spelling pro-

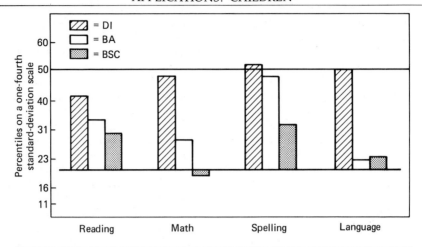

Figure 5-4. Performance of Follow Through students in the Direct Instruction (DI), Behavior Analysis (BA), and Bank Street College (BSC) programs on the Metropolitan Achievement Tests in reading, math, spelling, and language. The figure shows the difference between models on a one-fourth standard deviation scale. The data were drawn from the 20th percentile, the average expectation for "disadvantaged" children without followup assistance. The 50th percentile is the average expectation for all children. From S. Engelmann & W. C. Becker, *Forward from basics: The case for direct instruction.* Book in preparation; © S. Engelmann, 1977.

gram may have been more effective than materials previously on the market. In any event, it is encouraging to note that behavioral-based interventions may be very helpful for less academically prepared students entering the schools.

A FINAL COMMENT

When a behavioral psychologist is called on to resolve a particular problem in school, the process begins with the delineation of the areas of intervention. A critical issue involves determining who in the educational system is "the client." When there is a conflict between the goals of the teacher, particular students, or the entire class, the behavioral psychologist needs to act as a mediator between interests rather than as an agent of one party against another. However, some researchers have argued that those engaged in behavioral intervention have too often used their procedures to serve only the goals and values of

the school systems. In their article, "Current Behavior Modification in the Classroom: Be Still, Be Quiet, Be Docile," Richard Winett and Robin Winkler (1972, p. 501) summarize this position:

Just what do these present goals seem to be? Taken as a fairly accurate indicator of what public schools deemed as the "model" child, these studies described this pupil as one who stays glued to his seat and desk all day, continually looks at his teacher or his text/workbook, does not talk to or in fact look at other children, does not talk unless asked to by the teacher, hopefully does not laugh or sing (or at the wrong time), and assuredly passes silently in halls. Unfortunately, this description seems to fit perfectly with Silberman's cogent observations of just what is wrong with our schools. We are thus forced to conclude that as currently practiced, behavior modification has done very little to change the deplorable state of our schools.

If one looks only at the efforts of behavioral psychologists in eliminating disruptive classroom behavior, a considerable degree of credibility can be given to Winett and Winkler's position. Several studies involve children receiving either tangible or social reinforcers for "attending," yet there is often little or no related improvement in academic performance. Certainly, many parents and educators would feel that improvement in academic performance is at least as, if not more important than, whether a child sits quietly at a desk and looks at a book or teacher. However, there has been a decided shift in behavioral research (possibly as a result of Winett and Winkler's article) toward focusing less on deportment and more on improving instructional materials and academic performance. As the present chapter attests, to view behavioral interventions in classrooms as focused only on problem behaviors would mean ignoring a sizable portion of the behavioral research in education.

Unfortunately, even with the increased focus on academic programming, behavioral psychologists have not come any closer to fulfilling or even balancing the goals and values of *students* with those of school systems. It is the rare exception when students are given the option of determining their own "appropriate" behavior goals or strategies of intervention. Even the self-control studies are carried out within a framework provided by an adult teacher or experimenter (Nietzel, Winett, MacDonald, & Davidson, 1977). Case Study 5–2 demonstrates one of the few occasions when children have been taught to use behavioral techniques to increase the teacher's positive contacts and decrease negative contacts. But even this strategy is one-way, focusing only on the goals of one party and totally excluding the input of others. Thus, it would appear the role of the behavioral psychologist as mediator between interests is rarely, if ever, fulfilled. Such narrowness can potentially limit the extension of behavioral interventions beyond the current small-scale "demonstration" projects or special laboratory schools.

Another problem is the extremely limited evaluation of behavioral interventions. Research must now go beyond single-subject and small-group studies to determine both how lasting and how generalizable the observed gains are. If behavioral psychologists can respond to this challenge while remaining sensitive to such thorny issues as goal setting, then the approach might well become the treatment of choice for educational problems.

SUMMARY

The use of behavioral principles to improve the quality of education in our schools and universities has focused on three areas: (1) the assessment of the student's academic and social skills in order to devise individualized programs of instruction, (2) the management of classroom behavior through the application of reinforcement principles, and (3) the development of instructional materials that allow students to progress at their own rates without experiencing repeated failure and frustration. When a behavioral psychologist or consultant is called into the classroom to help alleviate a particular problem, the strategies used are similar to those of any behavioral intervention: careful evaluation of the client's (the student's) skills and assessment of the conditions present in the environment, development of concrete goals, and so on. The particular procedures that are used depend upon the results of the detailed assessment.

Much of the research on behavior modification in the classroom has concerned controlling problem behaviors. Helping teachers systematically alter the way they attend to their students (that is, praise and ignore procedures) is the most frequently suggested first step in classroom-management programs. Peers can also be employed to alter their classmates' disruptive behavior. For children who are only minimally influenced by these "normal" classroom reinforcers, a token reinforcement program may provide extra motivation to behave more appropriately in the classroom. Finally, training in techniques of self-control has enabled some children to learn how to monitor their behavior and deliver reinforcement for their own improvements.

Praise and ignore procedures, peer influence, and token programs have also been employed to improve academic performance, but developments in programmed instruction represent the most extensive intervention in this area. Although specific format varies for programmed texts, teaching machines, or PSI courses, certain features are common to all: (1) skills that the student is to learn are clearly specified; (2) lesson material is divided into small units and sequenced so that each lesson builds on previously presented materials; (3) immediate feedback is provided at each step, and students must demonstrate complete mastery of the material as they progress; and (4) extra help and prompts are gradually removed so that at the program's completion the student eventually produces the criterion skills unaided.

Children defined by the schools as "hyperactive" or "learning disabled" present both behavior and academic problems in the classroom. Although both categories are often narrowly defined, the children are extremely heterogeneous in their behavioral characteristics. Behavioral programming for hyperactive and learning-disabled children combines many of the elements of the interventions designed to improve academic performance and eliminate disruptive behavior. Although such programs are still at a preliminary stage of development, the findings are remarkably encouraging when compared to the outcome of more traditional techniques.

Behavioral psychologists have also developed outstanding educational programs for Project Follow Through. The Direct Instruction and Behavior Analysis programs produced academic gains for thousands of children and far exceeded the outcomes of other programs.

Behavioral psychologists have become intimately involved in many controversial issues involving the education and socialization of young children. Some have expressed the concern that behavior modification has been used to keep children quiet and docile rather than to facilitate their reaching their full potential, and that the teacher's needs and goals are often considered to the exclusion of what is best for students. There is no denying these possibilities, but recent developments in the application of behavioral principles in education indicate a clear shift away from an exclusive interest in deportment toward a greater concern for the long-term social and intellectual development of children.

CASE STUDY 5-1

REDD, W. H., ULLMANN, R. K., O'LEARY, M., STELLE, C., & ROESCH, P. A CLASSROOM INCENTIVE PROGRAM INSTITUTED BY TUTORS AFTER SCHOOL. UNPUBLISHED MANUSCRIPT, UNIVERSITY OF ILLINOIS, 1977.

Numerous studies have demonstrated the use of behavioral interventions to reduce children's disruptive behavior and improve their academic skills. For many programs, the teacher's involvement is crucial. He or she must often devise appropriate consequences, record student behavior, ignore inappropriate behavior, deliver reinforcers, and provide backup reinforcers. Because it is often impossible for a classroom teacher to perform all these tasks unassisted, many professionals (Andersen, Licht, Ullmann, Buck, & Redd, 1977; Cowen, Dorr, Trost, & Izzo, 1972; Hill & Tolman, 1970; Schoeller & Pearson, 1970; Tolor, 1968) have suggested using paraprofessional volunteers as classroom assistants or tutors. The present case demonstrates a rather novel after-school role paraprofessionals can fill to promote in-class performance.

Four first-graders (two boys and two girls) were referred for special tutoring by their public school teacher because she felt they were not working up to their full potential. She reported that they were especially inattentive when desk work was assigned and rarely completed their reading and arithmetic assignments. They were falling behind their classmates.

Intervention involved undergraduate students providing tutoring and backup reinforcement for classroom performance. Each tutor met with a child two afternoons a week and gave the child a prize contingent upon the teacher's rating of classroom performance. A child who met the predetermined criterion chose a small toy such as jacks, a model car, or some other inexpensive item. The child who did not meet the criterion was instructed to try harder the next time, and the tutor then proceeded with the daily lesson. One-to-one tutoring was scheduled each afternoon the tutor met with the child. Using materials supplied by the teacher, the tutor focused on basic arithmetic and reading skills.

On alternate afternoons, another undergraduate met with the child. This undergraduate did not dispense prizes contingent upon classroom performance; rather, he served as a buddy—playing games, sharing snacks, and going on walks with the child. Regardless of how the child had done in class that day, the buddy would plan an enjoyable activity. The buddy's interaction with the child resembled the way many volunteer programs for disadvantaged children are conducted: The college student served as a special friend.

In order to evaluate the effectiveness of the tutor-based incentive program, daily classroom observations on those days the tutor met with the child were compared with observations for days the buddy met with the child. That is, the children's on-task performance for "tutor days" was compared with that for "buddy days." The intervention program was clearly successful. The children spent between 80 and 85 percent of class time working on their assignments on "tutor days" versus 30 to 60 percent on "buddy days."

The findings of this case study are similar to those of studies indicating that parents and foster parents can be effective contingency managers when delivering reinforcers at home for children's school performance (Bailey, Wolf, & Phillips, 1970; Cantrell, Cantrell, Huddlesten, & Woolridge, 1969; McKenzie, Clark, Wolf, Kothera, & Benson, 1968). This study also suggests an effective way college volunteers might be used in educational programming. Many after-school "pal" programs might easily be enhanced by using extra-classroom contingencies for recreational activities.

CASE STUDY 5-2

GRAUBARD, P. S., ROSENBERG, H., & MILLER, M. STUDENT APPLI-
CATIONS OF BEHAVIOR MODIFICATION TO TEACHERS AND EN-
VIRONMENTS OR ECOLOGICAL APPROACHES TO SOCIAL DE-
VIANCY. IN E. A. RAMP & B. L. HOPKINS (EDS.), *A NEW DIRECTION
FOR EDUCATION: BEHAVIOR ANALYSIS 1971*, VOL. 1. LAWRENCE:
UNIVERSITY OF KANSAS, SUPPORT AND DEVELOPMENT CENTER
FOR FOLLOW THROUGH, DEPARTMENT OF HUMAN DEVELOP-
MENT, 1971.

The behavior modification literature is replete with examples of procedures
to alter the inappropriate behavior of students designed for use by teachers. The present case study is one of the rare cases in which students were
taught to modify the inappropriate behavior of their teachers and classmates.

The study took place in a school with a track record of hostility toward the
special education program and the minority group children who participated in it. In the past it had been difficult to place special students in the
regular classes. They were often scapegoated by the teachers and ridiculed
by the other students. The goal of the intervention was to reintegrate the
special students into the mainstream of the regular school.

Seven of these children ranging in age from twelve to fifteen were selected and trained as behavioral engineers. The students met with their
special education teachers for half the day. During a portion of the time,
they were instructed on how to record teacher-student and student-student
comments and how to sort them into positive and negative groupings. Initially the children were unable to recognize praise as such and consistently
underestimated the amount of praise given to them. Later they were able
to differentiate comments and rate them reliably. The first intervention
phase was designed to improve interactions with teachers in the regular
classes. The children were taught to make eye contact when asking for
help, and to make reinforcing comments such as, "Gee, it makes me feel
good and work so much better when you praise me," or "I like the way you
teach that lesson." They also learned to sit up straight and nod in agreement during presentations and to show up early for class and ask for extra
assignments. Students were also taught to break eye contact with the
teachers when receiving a scolding. The regular teachers were naive to the
intervention program.

Interactions between students and teachers changed dramatically over
the course of the four-week intervention. The average number of positive
teacher contacts per student during baseline was 8. During intervention,
positive contacts increased steadily to an average of 32 after only four
weeks. The opposite trend was observed for negative comments, which
dropped from an average of 18 per week during baseline to 0 after four
weeks.

A similar program was then carried out to improve the very poor relationships between the special and regular students. Typically, the special students were ridiculed with names like "retards," "rejects from the funny
farm," and "tardos." Being teased or ignored were everyday occurrences.

The intervention began by having the special students list the names of children who made school unpleasant for them and the behaviors they found troublesome, and also the names of those children they wanted to spend more time with. The special students were then taught to break eye contact with the provocative children and ignore their insulting remarks. They were also instructed to share toys or candy, give compliments, and initiate activities with those children with whom they wanted to become friends.

As with the student-teacher study, the average number of positive contacts between the special and regular students increased from 4 to 18 and negative comments decreased from 26 to 6. Hostile physical contacts and teasing decreased, and positive behaviors, including invitations to parties and baseball games, increased.

As the authors noted, behavior modification appeared to be a powerful tool which gave "deviant" children the ability to change their own behavior and the behavior of others in their environment.

CASE STUDY 5-3

HASAZI, J. E., & HASAZI, S. E. EFFECTS OF TEACHER ATTENTION ON DIGIT-REVERSAL BEHAVIOR IN AN ELEMENTARY SCHOOL CHILD. *JOURNAL OF APPLIED BEHAVIOR ANALYSIS*, 1972, **5**, 157–162.

Well-meaning attention and concern can often reinforce the behaviors they are intended to decrease. The present case study illustrates how a teacher's misdirected special help and one-to-one tutoring actually maintained a serious academic problem.

The child was an eight-year-old boy, Bob, enrolled in a basic skills class in a regular public school. The teacher considered Bob to be one of the most capable children: he did well in most of his subjects and was well liked. The problem was that he had difficulty adding numbers whose sum had two digits. Almost invariably, he would reverse the order of the digits. For example, he would write 21 as the sum of 5 plus 7, 81 as the sum of 9 plus 9. After extensive neurological and visual examinations revealed nothing, it was decided that Bob needed special help. This help involved the teacher's taking Bob through the basic components of each addition problem he missed and prompting the correct response. A variety of teaching aids such as counters and number lines were also used, but after one year of individual tutoring Bob had not improved. The possibility that the teacher's attention might be the cause of Bob's digit-reversing behavior was suggested by several curious observations: Bob's ability to discriminate between numbers containing the same digits (12 vs. 21), his pointing out of reversals on his paper when the teacher failed to notice them, and his frequent erasure of correct sums and quick replacement with reversed digits.

The intervention strategy was quite simple. The teacher continued to work with Bob, but ignored all reversals and socially reinforced correct re-

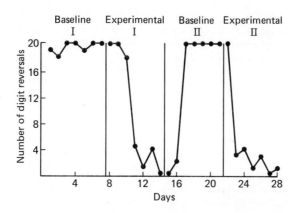

Figure 5–5. Number of digit reversals per day under baseline and experimental conditions. From J. Hasazi & S. Hasazi, Effects of teacher attention on digit-reversed behavior in an elementary school child. *Journal of Applied Behavior Analysis*, 1972, **5**, p. 160, fig. 1. By permission of the Journal of Applied Behavior Analysis, Department of Human Development, University of Kansas, Lawrence.

sponses with praise. In order to evaluate the effectiveness of the program, the procedures were introduced and then removed for seven-day periods. Bob's daily performance was determined only after he had completed 20 problems. The results of this reversal design are shown in Figure 5–5. Number of digit reversals are plotted across successive days. Experiments 1 and 2 refer to those periods in which the program was followed and baselines 1 and 2 refer to those periods in which the usual "special help" tutoring was carried out.

Altering the way the teacher responded to Bob's number reversals clearly controlled their occurrence. In their discussion of the program, Hasazi and Hasazi emphasize that they do not wish to suggest that *all* academic problems are developed by misguided teacher attention. But teachers must recognize the possibility that providing special attention in the manner described can have undesirable consequences; they must make sure they provide adequate social reinforcement for academic improvement and achievement.

REFERENCES

Alba, E., & Pennypacker, H. S. A multiple change score comparison of traditional and behavioral college teaching procedures. *Journal of Applied Behavior Analysis*, 1972, **5**, 121–124.

Ayllon, T., Layman, D., & Burke, S. Disruptive behavior and reinforcement of academic performance. *Psychological Record*, 1972, **22**, 315–323.

Ayllon, T., Layman, D., & Kandel, H. J. A behavioral-educational alternative to drug control of hyperactive children. *Journal of Applied Behavior Analysis*, 1975, **8**, 137–146.

Ayllon, T., & Roberts, M. D. Eliminating discipline problems by strengthening academic performance. *Journal of Applied Behavior Analysis*, 1974, **7**, 71–76.

Bailey, J. S., Timbers, G. D., Phillips, E. L., & Wolf, M. M. Modification of articulation errors of predelinquents by their peers. *Journal of Applied Behavior Analysis*, 1971, **4**, 265–281.

Bandura, A., & Perloff, B. Relative efficacy of self-monitored and externally imposed reinforcement systems. *Journal of Personality and Social Psychology*, 1967, **7**, 111–116.

Barrish, H. H., Saunders, M., & Wolf, M. M. Good behavior game: Effects of individual contingencies for group consequences on disruptive behavior in a classroom. *Journal of Applied Behavior Analysis*, 1969, **2**, 119–124.

Becker, W. C., Madsen, C. H., Arnold, C. R., & Thomas, D. R. The contingent use of teacher attention and praise in reducing classroom behavior problems. *Journal of Special Education*, 1967, **1**, 287–307.

Bijou, S. W. Experimental studies of child behavior, normal and deviant. In L. Krasner & L. P. Ullmann (Eds.), *Research in behavior modification.* New York: Holt, Rinehart and Winston, 1965.

Bijou, S. W. What psychology has to offer education—Now. *Journal of Applied Behavior Analysis*, 1970, **3**, 65–71.

Birnbrauer, J. S., Wolf, M. M., Kidder, J. D., & Tague, C. E. Classroom behavior of retarded pupils with token reinforcement. *Journal of Experimental Child Psychology*, 1965, **2**, 219–235.

Bolstad, O. D., & Johnson, S. M. Self-regulation in the modification of disruptive classroom behavior. *Journal of Applied Behavior Analysis*, 1972, **5**, 443–454.

Born, D. G., & Davis, M. L. Amount and distribution of study in a personalized instruction course and in a lecture course. *Journal of Applied Behavior Analysis*, 1974, **7**, 365–375.

Bornstein, P. H., & Quevillon, R. P. The effects of a self-instructional package on overactive preschool boys. *Journal of Applied Behavior Analysis*, 1976, **9**, 179–188.

Breyer, N. L., & Allen, G. J. Effect of implementing a token economy on teacher attending behavior. *Journal of Applied Behavior Analysis*, 1975, **8**, 373–380.

Broden, M., Bruce, C., Mitchell, M. A., Carter, V., & Hall, R. V. Effects of teacher attention on attending behavior of two boys at adjacent desks. *Journal of Applied Behavior Analysis*, 1970, **3**, 199–203.

Broden, M., Hall, R. V., Dunlap, A., & Clark, R. Effects of teacher attention and a token reinforcement system in a junior high school special education class. *Exceptional Children*, 1970, **36**, 341–349.

Brooks, R. B., & Snow, D. L. Two case illustrations of the use of behavior modification techniques in the school setting. *Behavior Therapy*, 1972, **3**, 100–103.

Bushell, D., Wrobel, P. A., & Michaelis, M. L. Applying "group" contingencies to the classroom study behavior of preschool children. *Journal of Applied Behavior Therapy*, 1968, **1**, 55–61.

Cantwell, D. P. Clinical picture, epidemiology and classifications of the hyperactive child syndrome. In D. P. Cantwell (Ed.), *The hyperactive child: Diagnosis, management, current research*. New York: Spectrum, 1975.

Carlson, C. S., Arnold, C. R., Becker, W. C., & Madsen, C. H. The elimination of tantrum behavior of a child in an elementary classroom. *Behaviour Research and Therapy*, 1968, **6**, 117–119.

Christiansen, D. E., & Sprague, R. L. Reduction of hyperactive behavior by conditioning procedures alone and combined with methylphenidate (Ritalin). *Behaviour Research and Therapy*, 1973, **11**, 331–334.

Christy, P. R. Does use of tangible rewards with individual children affect peer observers? *Journal of Applied Behavior Analysis*, 1975, **8**, 187–196.

Coleman, R. A conditioning technique applicable to elementary school classrooms. *Journal of Applied Behavior Analysis*, 1970, **3**, 293–297.

Cossairt, A., Hall, R. V., & Hopkins, B. L. The effects of experimenter instructions, feedback and praise and student attending behavior. *Journal of Applied Behavior Analysis*, 1973, **6**, 89–100.

Dineen, J. P., Clark, H. B., & Risley, T. R. Peer tutoring among elementary students: Educational benefits to the tutor. *Journal of Applied Behavior Analysis*, 1977, **10**, 231–238.

Doubros, S. G., & Daniels, G. J. An experimental approach to the reduction of overactive behavior. *Behaviour Research and Therapy*, 1966, **4**, 251–258.

Douglas, U. I., Parry, P., Marton, P., & Garson, C. Assessment of a cognitive training program for hyperactive children. *Journal of Abnormal Child Psychology*, 1976, **4**, 389–410.

Drabman, R. S. Child—versus teacher—administered token programs in a psychiatric hospital school. *Journal of Abnormal Child Psychology*, 1973, **1**, 68–87.

Drabman, R. S., & Lahey, B. B. Feedback in classroom behavior modification: Effects on the target and her classmates. *Journal of Applied Behavior Analysis*, 1974, **7**, 591–598.

Drabman, R. S., Spitalnik, R., & O'Leary, K. D. Teaching self-control to disruptive children. *Journal of Abnormal Psychology*, 1973, **82**, 10–16.

Edmark Reading Program. Seattle, Wash.: Edmark Associates, 1972.

Engelmann, S., & Becker, W. C. *Forward from basics: The case for direct instruction*. In preparation, 1977.

Evans, G. W., & Oswalt, G. L. Acceleration of academic progress through the manipulation of peer influence. *Behaviour Research and Therapy*, 1968, **6**, 189–195.

Felixbrod, J. J., & O'Leary, K. D. Effects of reinforcement on children's academic behavior as a function of self-determined and externally imposed contingencies. *Journal of Applied Behavior Analysis*, 1973, **6**, 241–250.

Ferritor, D. E., Buckholdt, D., Hamblin, R. L., & Smith, L. The noneffects of contingent reinforcement for attending behavior on work accomplished. *Journal of Applied Behavior Analysis*, 1972, **5**, 7–17.

Glynn, E. L., Thomas, J. D., & Shee, S. M. Behavioral self-control of on-task behavior in an elementary classroom. *Journal of Applied Behavior Analysis*, 1973, **6**, 105–113.

Graubard, P. S., Rosenberg, H., & Miller, M. Student applications of behavior modification to teachers and environments or ecological approaches to social deviancy. In E. A. Ramp & B. L. Hopkins (Eds.), *A new direction for education: Behavior analysis 1971*, Vol. 1. Lawrence: University of Kansas, Department of Human Development, 1971.

Greene, R. J., & Pratt, J. J. A group contingency for individual misbehaviors in the classroom. *Mental Retardation*, 1972, **6**, 33–34.

Greenwood, C. R., Sloane, H. N., & Baskin, A. Training elementary aged peer-behavior managers to control small group programmed mathematics. *Journal of Applied Behavior Analysis*, 1974, **7**, 103–114.

Hall, R. V., Lund, D., & Jackson, D. Effects of teacher attention on study behavior. *Journal of Applied Behavior Analysis*, 1968, **1**, 1–12.

Hamblin, R. I., Hathaway, C., & Wodarski, J. Group contingencies, peer tutoring and accelerating academic achievement. In E. A. Ramp & B. L. Hopkins (Eds.), *A new direction for education: Behavior analysis 1971*, Vol. 1. Lawrence: University of Kansas, Department of Human Development, 1971.

Haring, N. G., & Hauck, M. A. Improved learning conditions in the establishment of reading skills with disabled readers. *Exceptional Children*, 1969, **35**, 341–352.

Harris, V. W., & Sherman, J. A. Use and analysis of the "good behavior game" to reduce disruptive classroom behavior. *Journal of Applied Behavior Analysis,* 1973a, **6,** 405–417.

Harris, V. W., & Sherman, J. A. Effects of peer tutoring and consequences on the math performance of elementary classroom students. *Journal of Applied Behavior Analysis,* 1973b, **6,** 587–597.

Hasazi, J., & Hasazi, S. Effects of teacher attention on digit-reversal behavior in an elementary school child. *Journal of Applied Behavior Analysis,* 1972, **5,** 157–162.

Hayes, L. A. The use of group contingencies for behavioral control: A review. *Psychological Bulletin,* 1976, **83,** 628–648.

Hewett, F., Taylor, F. D., & Artuso, A. A. The Santa Monica Project: Evaluation of an engineered classroom design with emotionally disturbed children. *Exceptional Children,* 1969, **35,** 523–529.

Houten, R. V., Hill, S., & Parsons, M. An analysis of a performance feedback system: The effects of timing and feedback, public posting, and praise upon academic performance and peer interaction. *Journal of Applied Behavior Analysis,* 1975, **8,** 449–457.

Iwata, B. A., & Bailey, J. S. Reward versus cost token systems: An analysis of the effects on students and teacher. *Journal of Applied Behavior Analysis,* 1974, **7,** 567–576.

James, W. *Talks to teachers on psychology and to students on some of life's ideas.* New York: Norton, 1899.

Jamison, D., Suppes, P., & Wells, S. The effectiveness of alternative media: A survey. *Review of Educational Research,* 1974, **44,** 1–67.

Johnson, M., & Bailey, J. S. Cross-age tutoring: Fifth graders as arithmetic tutors for kindergarten children. *Journal of Applied Behavior Analysis,* 1974, **7,** 223–232.

Kazdin, A. E. *The token economy.* New York: Plenum Press, 1977.

Kazdin, A. E., Silverman, N. A., & Sittler, J. L. The use of prompts to enhance vicarious effects of nonverbal approval. *Journal of Applied Behavior Analysis,* 1975, **8,** 279–286.

Keller, F. S. A personal course in psychology. In R. Ulrich, T. Stachnik, & J. Mabry (Eds.), *Control of human behavior,* Vol. 1. Glenview, Ill.: Scott, Foresman, 1966.

Keller, F. S. "Good-bye, teacher . . ." *Journal of Applied Behavior Analysis,* 1968, **1,** 79–89.

Kirby, F. D., & Shields, F. Modification of arithmetic response rate and attending behavior in a seventh-grade student. *Journal of Applied Behavior Analysis,* 1972, **5,** 79–84.

Knapczyk, D. R., & Livingston, G. Self-recording and student teacher supervision: Variables within a token economy structure. *Journal of Applied Behavior Analysis,* 1973, **6,** 481–486.

Lahey, B. B. Behavior modification with learning disabilities and related problems. In M. Hersen, R. M. Eisler, & P. M. Miller (Eds.), *Progress in behavior modification,* Vol. 3. New York: Academic Press, 1976.

Lovitt, T. C., & Curtis, K. A. Effects of manipulating an antecedent event on mathematics response rate. *Journal of Applied Behavior Analysis,* 1968, **1,** 329–333.

Madsen, C. H., Becker, W. C., & Thomas, D. R. Rules, praise, and ignoring: Elements of elementary classroom control. *Journal of Applied Behavior Analysis,* 1968, **1,** 139–150.

Madsen, C. H., Becker, W. C., Thomas, D. R., Koser, L., & Plager, E. An analysis of the reinforcing function of "sit down" commands. In R. K. Parker (Ed.), *Readings in educational psychology.* Boston: Allyn & Bacon, 1968.

Main, G. C., & Munroe, B. C. A token reinforcement program in a public junior high school. *Journal of Applied Behavior Analysis,* 1977, **10,** 93–94.

Mandelker, A. V., Brigham, T. A., & Bushell, D. The effects of token procedures on a teacher's social contacts with her students. *Journal of Applied Behavior Analysis,* 1970, **3,** 169–174.

Marholin, D., II, Steinman, W. M., McInnis, E. T., & Heads, T. B. The effect of a teacher's presence on the classroom behavior of conduct-problem children. *Journal of Abnormal Child Psychology,* 1975, **3,** 11–25.

McLaughlin, T. F., & Malaby, J. Intrinsic reinforcers in a classroom token economy. *Journal of Applied Behavior Analysis,* 1972a, **5,** 263–270.

McLaughlin, T., & Malaby, J. Reducing and measuring inappropriate verbalizations in a token classroom. *Journal of Applied Behavior Analysis,* 1972b, **5,** 329–333.

McMichael, J. S., & Corey, J. R. Contingency management in an introductory psychology course produces better learning. *Journal of Applied Behavior Analysis,* 1969, **2,** 79–83.

Medlund, M. B., & Stachnik, J. J. Good behavior game: A replication and systematic analysis. *Journal of Applied Behavior Analysis,* 1972, **5,** 45–51.

Meichenbaum, D. H., & Goodman, J. Training impulsive children to talk to themselves: A means of developing self-control. *Journal of Abnormal Psychology,* 1971, **77,** 115–126.

Nietzel, M. T., Winett, R. A., MacDonald, M. L., & Davidson, W. S. *Behavioral approaches to community psychology.* New York: Pergamon Press, 1977.

Novy, P., Burnett, J., Powers, M., & Sulzer-Azaroff, B. Modifying attending-to-work behavior of a learning disabled child. *Journal of Learning Disabilities,* 1973, **6,** 217–221.

O'Leary, K. D., & Drabman, R. Token reinforcement programs in the classroom. *Psychological Bulletin*, 1971, **75**, 379–398.

O'Leary, K. D., & O'Leary, S. G. *Classroom management*. 2nd ed. New York: Pergamon Press, 1977.

O'Leary, K. D., Pelham, W. E., Rosenbaum, A., & Price, G. H. Behavioral treatment of hyperkinetic children. *Clinical Pediatrics*, 1976, **15**, 510–515.

O'Leary, S. G., & O'Leary, K. D. Behavior modification in the school. In H. Leitenberg (Ed.), *Handbook of behavioral modification and behavior therapy*. Englewood Cliffs, N.J.: Prentice-Hall, 1976.

Palkes, H., Stewart, M., & Freedman, J. Improvement in maze performance of hyperactive boys as a function of verbal training procedures. *Journal of Special Education*, 1972, **5**, 337–342.

Palkes, H., Stewart, M., & Kahana, B. Porteus maze performance of hyperactive boys after training in self-directed verbal commands. *Child Development*, 1968, **39**, 817–826.

Patterson, G. R. An application of conditioning techniques to the control of a hyperactive child. In L. P. Ullman & L. Krasner (Eds.), *Case studies in behavior modification*. New York: Holt, Rinehart and Winston, 1965.

Patterson, G. R., Jones, R., Whittier, J., & Wright, M. A. A behavior modification technique for the hyperactive child. *Behaviour Research and Therapy*, 1965, **2**, 217–226.

Phillips, E. L., Phillips, E. A., Wolf, M. M., & Fixsen, D. L. Achievement Place: Development of the elected manager system. *Journal of Applied Behavior Analysis*, 1973, **6**, 541–561.

Pressey, S. L. A simple apparatus which gives tests and scores—and teaches. *School and Society*, 1926, **23**, 373–376.

Pressey, S. L. A machine for automatic teaching of drill material. *School and Society*, 1927, **25**, 549–552.

Ramp, E. A. University of Kansas Follow Through Program: Behavior Analysis Model. Unpublished manuscript, University of Kansas, 1977.

Rappaport, J. *Community psychology*. New York: Holt, Rinehart and Winston, 1977.

Rickard, H. C., Melvin, K. B., Creel, J., & Creel, L. The effects of bonus tokens upon productivity in a remedial classroom for behaviorally disturbed children. *Behavior Therapy*, 1973, **4**, 378–385.

Robertson, S. J., DeReus, D. M., & Drabman, R. S. Peer and college-student tutoring as reinforcement in a token economy. *Journal of Applied Behavior Analysis*, 1976, **9**, 169–177.

Robin, A. L., Armel, S., & O'Leary, K. D. The effects of self-instruction on writing deficiencies. *Behavior Therapy*, 1975, **6**, 178–187.

Rosenbaum, A., O'Leary, K. D., & Jacob, R. G. Behavioral intervention with hyperactive children: Group consequences as a supplement to individual contingencies. *Behavior Therapy*, 1975, **6**, 315–323.

Salzberg, C. L. Freedom and responsibility in an elementary school. In G. Semb (Ed.), *Behavior analysis and education—1972*. Lawrence: University of Kansas, Support and Development Center for Follow Through, 1972.

Schmidt, G. W., & Ulrich, R. E. Effects of group contingent events upon classroom noise. *Journal of Applied Behavior Analysis*, 1969, **2**, 171–179.

Schutte, R. C., & Hopkins, B. L. The effects of teacher attention on following instructions in a kindergarten class. *Journal of Applied Behavior Analysis*, 1970, **3**, 117–122.

Semb, G. The effects of mastery criteria and assignment length on college-student test performance. *Journal of Applied Behavior Analysis*, 1974, **7**, 61–69.

Shafto, F., & Sulzbacher, S. Comparing treatment tactics with a hyperactive preschool child: Stimulant medication and programmed teacher intervention. *Journal of Applied Behavior Analysis*, 1977, **10**, 13–20.

Sidman, R. L., & Sidman, M. *Neuroanatomy, a programmed text*. Boston: Little, Brown, 1965.

Skinner, B. F. *The behavior of organisms*. New York: Appleton-Century-Crofts, 1938.

Skinner, B. F. *Science and human behavior*. New York: Macmillan, 1953.

Skinner, B. F. Teaching machines. *Science*, 1958, **128**, 969–977.

Skinner, B. F. *The technology of teaching*. New York: Appleton-Century-Crofts, 1968.

Skinner, B. F., & Krakower, S. A. *Handwriting with write and see*. Chicago: Lyons & Carnahan, 1968.

Sleator, E. K., & Sprague, R. L. Pediatric psychopharmacotherapy. In W. G. Clark and J. del Giudice (Eds.), *Principles of psychopharmacology*. 2nd ed. New York: Academic Press, 1977.

Solomon, R. W., & Wahler, R. G. Peer reinforcement control of classroom problem behavior. *Journal of Applied Behavior Analysis*, 1973, **6**, 49–56.

Sprague, R. L., & Werry, J. Psychotropic drugs and handicapped children. In L. Mann & D. Sabatino (Eds.), *The second review of special education*. Philadelphia: JSE, 1974.

Staats, A. *Development, use, and social extensions of reinforcer systems in the solution of human problems*. Paper presented at the Conference on Behavior Modification, Honolulu, Hawaii, January 1969.

Staats, A., Finley, J., Minke, K. A., Wolf, M., & Brooks, C. A reinforcer system and experimental procedure for the laboratory study of reading acquisition. *Child Development*, 1964, **35**, 209–231.

Staats, A. W., Staats, C. K., Schultz, R. E., & Wolf, M. M. The conditioning of textual responses using "extrinsic" reinforcers. *Journal of the Experimental Analysis of Behavior*, 1962, **5**, 33–40.

Strain, P. S., Shores, R. E., & Kerr, M. M. An experimental analysis of "spillover" effects on the social interaction of behaviorally handicapped preschool children. *Journal of Applied Behavior Analysis, 1976,* **9**, 31–40.

Strain, P. S., & Timm, M. A. An experimental analysis of social interaction between a behaviorally disordered preschool child and her classroom peers. *Journal of Applied Behavior Analysis*, 1974, **7**, 583–590.

Sulzbacher, S. I., & Houser, J. E. A tactic to eliminate disruptive behavior in the classroom: Group contingent consequences. In R. Ulrich, T. Stachnik, & J. Mabry (Eds.), *Control of human behavior*, Vol. 2. Glenview, Ill.: Scott, Foresman, 1970.

Surratt, P. R., Ulrich, R. E., & Hawkins, R. P. An elementary student as a behavioral engineer. *Journal of Applied Behavior Analysis*, 1969, **2**, 85–92.

Turkewitz, H., O'Leary, K. D., & Ironsmith, M. Producing generalization of appropriate behavior through self-control. *Journal of Consulting and Clinical Psychology*, 1975, **43**, 577–583.

Twardoz, S., & Sajwaj, T. Multiple effects of a procedure to increase sitting in a hyperactive, retarded boy. *Journal of Applied Behavior Analysis*, 1972, **5**, 73–78.

Wagner, R. F., & Guyer, B. P. Maintenance of discipline through increasing children's span of attention by means of a token economy. *Psychology in the Schools*, 1971, **8**, 285–289.

Walker, H. M., & Hops, H. Use of normative peer data as a standard for evaluating classroom treatment effect. *Journal of Applied Behavior Analysis*, 1976, **9**, 159–168.

Walker, H. M., Mattson, R., & Buckley, N. K. The functional analysis of behavior within an experimental class setting. In W. C. Becker (Ed.), *An empirical basis for change in education.* Chicago: Science Research Associates, 1971.

Westinghouse Learning Corporation/Ohio University. *The impact of Head Start: An evaluation of the effects of Head Start on children's cognitive and affective development,* Vol. 1 & 2. Springfield, Va.: U.S. Department of Commerce (No. PB 184329), 1969.

Whalen, C. K., & Henker, B. Psychostimulants and children: A review and analysis. *Psychological Bulletin,* 1976, **83**, 1113–1130.

Willis, J. Contingent token reinforcement in an educational program for emotionally disturbed children. In M. Rickard & H. Dinoff (Eds.), *Behavior modification in children.* Tuscaloosa: University of Alabama Press, 1974.

Willis, J. W., Morris, B., & Crowder, J. A remedial reading technique for disabled readers that employs students as behavioral engineers. *Psychology in the Schools*, 1972, **9**, 67–70.

Winett, R. A., & Winkler, R. C. Current behavior modification in the classroom: Be still, be quiet, be docile. *Journal of Applied Behavior Analysis*, 1972, **5**, 499–504.

Wolf, M. M., Giles, D. K., & Hall, R. V. Experiments with token reinforcement in a remedial classroom. *Behaviour Research and Therapy*, 1968, **6**, 51–64.

Wulbert, M., & Dries, R. The relative efficacy of methylphenidate (Ritalin) and behavior-modification techniques in the treatment of a hyperactive child. *Journal of Applied Behavior Analysis*, 1977, **10**, 21–31.

Zimmerman, E. H., & Zimmerman, J. The alteration of behavior in a special classroom situation. *Journal of the Experimental Analysis of Behavior*, 1962, **5**, 59–60.

Zimmerman, E. H., Zimmerman, J., & Russell, C. D. Differential effects of token reinforcement on instruction-following behavior in retarded students instructed as a group. *Journal of Applied Behavior Analysis*, 1969, **2**, 101–112.

six

SEVERELY DEFICIENT AND DISORDERED BEHAVIOR IN CHILDREN

Of all the experiences in life, probably only a handful are as important and as emotionally charged as the birth of a child. The arrival of a new baby is surrounded by a flurry of activity: predictions about the sex of the child, decisions on the perfect name, preparation of a nursery. But in the midst of all the excitement, the prospective parents' greatest concern is that their child be normal.

Unfortunately, for some parents the hope and joy are crushed: their baby is somehow "different." The child's arms and legs may be stunted; the face may be dull and expressionless. Or the infant might seem fine, but as he gets older it becomes obvious that he is not. Motor development might be slowed; speech may be nonfunctional or completely nonexistent. Perhaps most devastating to the parent, the child may appear to reject all expressions of affection. Some infants actively avoid contact and remain preoccupied with repetitive, self-destructive activities. Most of these children are diagnosed as mentally retarded, but they may also be labeled autistic or schizophrenic.

Irrespective of the diagnostic tag, such behavior from a child can devastate a family. Not only are the parents heartbroken and distraught, but nothing they do seems to help. They may have no life of their own if the child remains at home; and for some families, the strain of home care becomes too great and institutionalization appears the only alternative. Whether the child remains at home

or is put in an institution, the severely retarded or disturbed child places an enormous emotional burden on the parents. The father of one such child wrote, "I also know I must not try to feel more sorry for myself than for Noah, but some days I forget" (Greenfield, 1970). For their parents and the psychologists who treat them, these children present an incredible responsibility.

Although retardation, childhood schizophrenia, and autism are considered by many theorists to be quite different disorders, the *behaviors* emitted by children given any of these labels may be exactly the same. For this reason, the behavioral literature has focused largely on treatment programs for specific deficient or disordered behaviors, and less effort has gone into theorizing about retardation, schizophrenia, or autism. Controlled outcome evaluations are virtually nonexistent. Nonetheless, behavior modification does appear to present treatment strategies that have been effective in relatively well-designed single-subject studies.

In this chapter, we will begin by examining the traditional conceptualizations of the causes and diagnoses of deficient and disordered behavior in children. We will then consider specific treatment programs for controlling problematic behaviors and building normal behaviors. Finally, we will discuss the effectiveness of behavioral interventions, with special attention to the nature of the treatment environment and the benefits from such programs in relation to their cost.

TRADITIONAL DIAGNOSTIC CATEGORIES

Clinicians and researchers have offered numerous theories to explain the nature and causes of retardation and psychoses such as autism or schizophrenia in children. Each theory seems to produce a different definition and new criteria for diagnosis. This situation, plus the incredible complexity and diversity of behaviors that can be regarded as "normal," may account for the fact that professionals have difficulty in agreeing on a diagnosis for any child who is regarded as "abnormal" in some way. It is not at all unusual for a child to have as many labels as professionals who have examined him (MacMillan, Jones, & Aloia, 1974). Unfortunately, in many cases the result is overlapping diagnoses based on inferences and sweeping generalizations, all of which do little to relieve the anguished parent or help the child who desperately needs attention.

Mental Retardation

For years the diagnosis of mental retardation has been based primarily on a child's performance on a standardized intelligence test such as the Stanford-Binet Intelligence Scale or Wechsler Intelligence Scale for Children. IQ's are calculated and differing scores are presumed to indicate different degrees of "intelligence." The result of such efforts is usually a category system of mental retardation such as the one in Table 6–1, which is used

by the American Association on Mental Deficiency (AAMD). The AAMD system divides the large and heterogeneous group of mentally retarded individuals into four categories, which are often used to determine placement in treatment, training, or educational programs. For instance, children in the mildly retarded group have been eligible for special "educable" classes, whereas those moderately retarded were regarded as only "trainable." Severely and profoundly retarded children were often institutionalized and were seen as requiring constant supervision and occasional nursing care.

Recently, clinicians have relied less on IQ scores as *the* determinant for treatment and placement decisions. This has occurred in part because of their increasing recognition of the problems that plague the so-called intelligence test. Some of the problems are sampling biases in the original populations on which the tests were standardized, low test-retest reliabilities (particularly for scores at the low end of the distribution), and the great variability that can occur in IQ scores simply as the result of the conditions under which the test is administered (for example, the examiner's race, the child's familiarity with the examiner, the presence of incentives for good performance). Another critical problem with IQ tests for a handicapped population is the sheer difficulty in administering them. Many individuals are classified as severely or profoundly retarded not because they perform poorly, but simply because they are "untestable." However, the most important

Table 6–1. Incidence and Percentage of Mental Retardation by Categories Adapted

Level	IQ Obtained Stanford-Binet	Wechsler	Percentage of Mentally Retarded	Estimated Number in the United States
Mild	67–52	69–55	89.0	5,340,000
Moderate	51–36	54–40	6.0	360,000
Severe	35–20	39–25 (extrapolated)	3.5	200,000
Profound	19 and below	24 and below (extrapolated)	1.5	90,000

Source: J. F. Calhoun, *Abnormal psychology: Current perspectives*, 2nd ed. New York: Random House, 1977, Table 15.1, p. 381. Used by permission.

factor contributing to the decrease in professionals' reliance on IQ scores is the minimal amount of information that these scores actually provide as to a child's skills and deficits. IQ scores do not answer relevant questions such as: Is this child toilet trained? Can he dress himself? Does he display behaviors that would disrupt a one-to-one learning environment? This kind of information, which is so crucial to the development of an individualized program for a child, cannot be obtained from an IQ evaluation.

Professionals have recommended evaluating an individual's **adaptive behavior** in addition to administering intelligence tests. This would mean that a diagnosis of mental retardation would require deficits in *both* intellectual and adaptive behavior (that is, behaviors which are critical to functioning within general society). Adaptive behavior is measured most commonly by instruments such as the Vineland Social Maturity Scale (Doll, 1947), the Cain-Levine Social Competency Scale (Cain, Levine, & Elzey, 1963), or the Adaptive Behavior Scale (ABS) (Nihira, Foster, Shellhas, & Leland, 1969). These scales do not require formal "testing" but rely either on evaluation by individuals familiar with the child (such as ward nurses and attendants) or on direct observation. Their primary purpose is to assess important functional areas such as ambulation, self-feeding and table manners, dressing and grooming, toileting skills, stereotyped and self-destructive behaviors, and social communication. Table 6–2 presents 8 representative items from the 111-item ABS. At a conceptual level, scales of this type appear to be a viable means of determining individualized treatment options since they provide specific information about the child's skills and deficits. Unfortunately, research has not been conducted to indicate whether or not such scales are, in fact, useful in this regard.

As is the case with most human problems, professionals can only hypothesize about the causes of mental retardation. There are, however, a few readily identifiable organic disorders that can produce distinctive clinical subtypes of retardation. Perhaps the best known is Down's syndrome or Trisomy 21. Down's syndrome children possess a number of characteristic physical abnormalities

such as eyes that are slanted and almond-shaped, a nose with a flattened bridge and upward turned nostrils, and hands with a single crease across the palms and short, stubby fingers. Another common syndrome is hydrocephaly, a condition which results in the child's head becoming unusually large due to an excess of cerebrospinal fluid in the ventricles of the brain. Unusual head size also results from a condition known as microcephaly. The brain fails to grow to a normal size, the skull does not expand, and head size is typically small.

There are also a variety of well-known medical problems that can cause mental retardation: the mother can contract illnesses such as rubella and congenital syphilis, or ingest toxic substances that may be transferred to the fetus during pregnancy. Complications during birth, such as insufficient oxygen supply or injury to the newborn, can result in brain damage. A number of metabolic disorders can severely affect the development of the nervous system and lead to retardation. Abnormalities of lipid metabolism (Tay-Sachs or cerebral lipoidosis), amino acid metabolism (phenylketonuria), and carbohydrate metabolism (Hurler's syndrome or galactosemia) often produce severe retardation and, typically, early death. These identifiable problems account for a relatively small proportion of individuals who are labeled mentally retarded; the majority of such persons have no obvious neurological or physical impairment.

Childhood Schizophrenia and/or Autism

In what has been thought to be the original description of "early infantile autism," Leo Kanner (1943) described a group of eleven children characterized by "extreme autistic aloneness" (inability to relate to others or to their surroundings), delayed speech acquisition or particular language problems (pronoun reversal or echolalia), and an intolerance of even minor changes in their environment. Since Kanner's formulation, there has been considerable disagreement among researchers and clinicians regarding the nature of severely disordered behavior in children. Some see the problem as an early form of adult schizophrenia (called "schizophrenia, childhood type"),

Table 6–2. Representative Items from Adaptive Behavior Scales

1. Use of Table Utensils: Select the *one* statement that best describes the child's use of table utensils.
   - 6   Uses knife and fork correctly and neatly
   - 5   Uses table knife for cutting or spreading
   - 4   Feeds self with spoon and fork—neatly
   - 3   Feeds self with spoon and fork—considerable spilling
   - 2   Feeds self with spoon—neatly
   - 1   Feeds self with spoon—considerable spilling
   - 0   Feeds self with fingers or not at all

2. Teeth Brushing: Select the *one* statement that best describes the child's ability to brush his teeth.
   - 5   Applies tooth paste and brushes teeth with up and down motion
   - 4   Applies tooth paste and brushes teeth
   - 3   Brushes teeth without help, but cannot apply tooth paste
   - 2   Brushes teeth with supervision
   - 1   Cooperates in having teeth brushed
   - 0   Makes no attempt to brush teeth

3. Undresses Self at Night or When Bathing Without Assistance: Check "Yes" or "No." If "No," select *all* statements that apply.
   - a. Does not unbutton or unzip coat, dress, shirt, pants or skirt without assistance
   - b. Does not take off coat or dress, shirt, pants or skirt without assistance
   - c. Does not take off socks without assistance
   - d. Does not take off underwear without assistance
   - e. Does not cooperate in undressing by extending arms or legs
   - f. Other:

4. Movement Is Slow and Sluggish: Check "No" or "Yes." Select *all* statements that apply. Answer "No" if the child's physical handicaps make him slow and sluggish.
   - a. Body movement is slow and deliberate
   - b. Is a slow worker
   - c. Seems to have no energy
   - d. Other:

5. Responsibility: Select the *one* statement that best describes the child's *highest* level of responsibility.
   - 3   Very conscientious and assumes much responsibility—makes a special effort; the assigned act will always be performed
   - 2   Usually dependable—makes an effort to carry out responsibility; one can be reasonably certain that the assigned act will be performed

whereas others view severely disordered behavior in adults and in children as entirely different. Even those who agree on a separate category for childhood psychoses often disagree on any further subdivisions, such as autism. Some psychologists feel that autism develops shortly after birth and is detectable by age two or three, but that childhood schizophrenia appears much later and after a period of seeming normality. In any case, the current diagnostic confusion provides no information regarding either etiology or treatment.

Clinicians and researchers have expended con-

Table 6–2, *continued*

1 Unreliable—makes little effort to carry out responsibility; one is uncertain that the assigned act will be performed

0 Not given responsibility; is unable to carry out responsibility at all

6. Threatens or Does Physical Violence: Check "No" or "Yes." If "Yes," select *all* statements that are true of the child.
   a. Uses threatening gestures
   b. Indirectly causes injury to others
   c. Spits on others
   d. Pushes, scratches or pinches others
   e. Pulls others' hair, ears, etc.
   f. Bites others
   g. Kicks, strikes or slaps others
   h. Throws objects at others
   i. Uses objects as weapons against others
   j. Chokes others
   k. Hurts animals
   l. Other:

7. Is Profoundly Withdrawn and Inactive: Having a low level of physical activity. Check "No" or "Yes." If "Yes," select *all* statements that are true of the child.
   a. Sits or stands in one position for a long period of time
   b. Does nothing but sit and watch others
   c. Falls asleep in a chair
   d. Lies on the floor all day
   e. Does not seem to react to anything
   f. Other:

8. Has Stereotyped Behaviors: Check "No" or "Yes." If "Yes," select *all* statements that are true of the child.
   a. Drums fingers
   b. Taps feet continually
   c. Has hands constantly in motion
   d. Slaps, scratches or rubs self continually
   e. Waves or shakes parts of the body repeatedly
   f. Moves or rolls head back and forth
   g. Rocks body back and forth
   h. Paces the floor
   i. Other:

Source: K. Nihira, R. Foster, M. Shellhas, & H. Leland, *Adaptive behavior scales.* Washington, D.C.: American Association on Mental Deficiency, 1969. Used with the permission of the American Association on Mental Deficiency.

siderable effort in defining characteristics and postulating critical psychological, social, or biochemical conditions that might explain psychotic behavior in children. Nevertheless, much confusion still exists.

A variety of characteristics, the primary one being the early onset of severely disordered behavior, make physiological explanations of childhood psychosis quite plausible. Many researchers have suggested that the central nervous system (CNS) is the site of the disorder and a number of theories, many of them contradictory, have been offered. For example, hypotheses regarding intrauterine difficulties or birth complications which result in immature CNS functioning have been proposed (Bender, 1953; 1956; 1968), as well as theories suggesting advanced or accelerated CNS development (Moore & Shiek, 1971). Some researchers postulate CNS damage which results in underarousal (Rimland, 1964); others cite high-frequency electroencephalographic (EEG) data as indicating cortical overarousal (Hutt, Hutt, Lee, & Ounstead, 1964). Conclusive experimental support for any one theory is lacking, although other findings do lend support to possible physiological etiology. For instance, there is a slightly higher tendency for mothers to have experienced pregnancy and birth complications with severely disordered children (Pollack & Woerner, 1966); there is also an excess of slight motor and EEG abnormalities in severely disturbed children (Fish & Shapiro, 1965; Taterka & Katz, 1955). At the present time, no firm conclusions can be drawn about the role of the CNS in childhood psychosis.

Psychogenic theories contend that autism is directly related to certain unfortunate childhood experiences and pathological interactions with the mother. It has been argued that the child may develop a psychosis from attempts to separate himself or herself from an overly protective mother (Mahler, 1952). Or the autism may represent the child's reaction to the parents' (particularly the mother's) negative feelings about the child, or their preoccupation with other matters such as professional concerns (Bettelheim, 1967; Kanner, 1943, 1972). Charles Ferster's (1961) behavioral conceptualization of autism is remarkably similar to these notions. He suggests that the child's severely disordered behavior is a consequence of (1) ineffective secondary and generalized reinforcers (that is, the parents' smile, praise, or affection is somehow inadequate); (2) intermittent reinforcement and then extinction of the child's appropriate behavior; and (3) problems arising from competing factors in the parents' lives (for instance, somatic problems, depression, social or professional activities). It appears, then, that the psychogenic theories generally lay the "blame" for autism on the parents' lack of affection and attention for the child.

A number of difficulties arise with the psychogenic theories. For one thing, there is no evidence to suggest that mothers of autistic children have cold and rejecting personalities or are less capable of forming close emotional relationships with their children than are the mothers of normal children (Wing, 1966). Moreover, it is possible that typical parental behavior may be a *response* to the child's problems rather than a cause. Many mothers of autistic children have normal children as well and, as has been noted, "to postulate a deficiency in mothering ability severe enough and specific enough to cause the complex syndrome (autism) . . . in one child only but somehow not severe enough to involve the others, is to take speculation beyond the limits which it is clinically and scientifically useful" (Wing, 1966, p. 34). Even though the behavior of some autistic children can be changed by systematically altering social reinforcers (Ferster & DeMeyer, 1965; Lovaas, Schaeffer, & Simmons, 1965; Risley & Wolf, 1967), this does not mean autism originally developed because reinforcers were ineffective or insufficient. (Aspirin may relieve headaches, but this is not an indication that headaches result from an insufficiency of aspirin in the bloodstream [Rimland, 1964].) It would seem that in addition to indicting an already distraught group of parents, psychogenic theories have yet to receive empirical support.

Finally, other researchers have obtained results indicating that autism may be the result of a response or attentional deficit. Parents and clinicians often report extremely inconsistent responding to stimuli in autistic children; they often believe the children are blind or deaf, only to see them demonstrate keen visual or auditory acuity on other occasions. Researchers have found that these children may fail to respond (Rutter, 1968) or may respond excessively and erratically (Ornitz & Ritvo, 1968; Rimland, 1964) to sound or pain. O. Ivar Lovaas, a pioneer in the formulation of many behavioral treatment strategies for autistic children, has hypothesized that autistic children may manifest **stimulus overselectivity** and have difficulty attending to complex stimuli, particularly those involving more than one sensory modality. Research by Lovaas, Robert Koegel, Laura Schreibman, and their colleagues (Koegel &

Schreibman, 1974; Lovaas, Schreibman, Koegel, & Rehm, 1971) suggests that when presented with a stimulus complex with auditory, visual, and tactile components, autistic children selectively attend to only one component and ignore the others. Although support for any one perceptual deficit is at this time premature, later we will consider how such response or attentional deficits might limit behavioral treatment techniques that often depend on attending to complex stimuli.

A BEHAVIORAL FORMULATION

As we will see, behavioral treatment programs for mentally retarded and psychotic children are remarkably similar, since such children share a great many difficulties. First, these children may emit a variety of problem behaviors (such as self-stimulatory, self-destructive, or inappropriate antisocial behaviors) that may need to be eliminated before they can learn other, more functional ways to spend their time. Second, intellectual functioning, as indicated by formalized measures of "intelligence," is often impaired, and the children either perform at levels below those expected for their age range or behave so inappropriately that they are regarded as "untestable." Third, children labeled retarded or autistic often show profound deficits in appropriate adaptive behavior. Basic self-help skills such as feeding, dressing, bathing, or toileting are performed poorly or not at all. Their communication may consist only of echolalia, grunts, screams, or meaningless utterances. Social behavior may range from one extreme to the other, but in either case it is seldom appropriate; these children may seek affection from strangers or pull away and stare blankly at their parents. Fourth, treatment for these children is often a long and painstaking process. The severity of their difficulties usually demands a comprehensive treatment program rather than a specific, focused intervention. Unfortunately, the comprehensive programs that parents can implement in the home are only at the very earliest stages. For this reason, treatment often takes place outside the home in an institution or special school where a twenty-four-hour program can be developed.

CONTROL OF PROBLEM BEHAVIORS

One of the most bizarre and alarming characteristics of many children with severely limited behavior repertoires is their high frequency of stereotypic behavior (such as body rocking, hand waving, or head banging) and/or antisocial acts (such as physical assaultiveness or screaming). The maintenance of such behaviors can be dangerous to the children and to those near them, as well as detrimental to the children's social acceptance. Research also indicates that children engaged in stereotypic behavior are less responsive to environmental events (Koegel & Covert, 1972; Koegel, Firestone, Kramme, & Dunlap, 1974; Lovaas, Litrownik, & Mann, 1971), a factor that certainly interferes with any attempts to teach them appropriate behaviors.

Such problem behaviors are remarkably common. Walking on to a unit in any large residential facility, one would probably find many, if not most, of the children engaged in some form of bizarre, inappropriate behavior. Behavioral interventions that have been used to eliminate these problem behaviors include: (1) differential reinforcement of other (alternative or incompatible) behaviors (DRO), (2) withdrawal of positive reinforcement or the opportunity to earn positive reinforcement (extinction and timeout), (3) overcorrection, and (4) presentation of aversive stimuli (punishment). Although we have separated these procedures from those designed to build adaptive behaviors, readers should note that these techniques may be unnecessary for children who are engaged in an ongoing treatment program aimed at increasing appropriate behavior. Many bizarre behaviors simply *drop out* when an individual is taught necessary skills and reinforced for behaving appropriately. Thus, the procedures we discuss for decreasing inappropriate behavior should be used within the context of a program focused on building adaptive behavior.

Self-Stimulatory and Self-Destructive Behaviors

Self-stimulatory behaviors can take on a variety of forms (Lovaas, Litrownik, & Mann, 1971). Often the behaviors are rather gross, such as when children rock back and forth, jump up and down, pace the floor, or flap their arms. At other times, movement is more subtle, such as when children roll or cross their eyes, swish saliva in their mouths, or poke at their bodies. Children may also spin objects in front of their eyes or run their hands along a wall or fence.

Such behaviors are often referred to as self-stimulatory because these children seem to "use" the behavior to stimulate themselves (Lovaas & Newsom, 1976). Often these behaviors are so excessive or maladaptive (such as banging the head or arms against walls or furniture, beating the face with fists or knees, or biting the hands, arms, or shoulders) that they can be characterized as self-destructive or self-injurious. Although there is considerable speculation regarding the origins of such behavior, one notion that has received some empirical support is that self-injurious behaviors are learned and maintained by positive reinforcement (Carr, 1977).

It is easy to see how this might occur when children emit such violent and disturbing behaviors. A natural response for anyone might be to run and comfort the child or hold him to prevent further injury. Even someone turning and looking at a child as he begins to strike himself and cry can provide extra attention. In fact, studies have demonstrated that (1) self-injurious behavior can be reduced when social reinforcers are withdrawn (Bucher & Lovaas, 1968; Ferster, 1961; Hamilton, Stephens, & Allen, 1967; Lovaas & Simmons, 1969; Tate & Baroff, 1966); (2) self-injurious rates can increase when positive reinforcement is made contingent upon the behavior (Lovaas, Freitag, Gold, & Kassorla, 1965; Lovaas & Simmons, 1969); and (3) self-injurious behavior can come under powerful stimulus control (self-injurious behavior rates are often low when the child is alone but very high when adults are present, since adults may become discriminative stimuli for positive reinforcement) (Bucher & Lovaas, 1968; Romanczyk & Goren, 1975).

A related hypothesis states that self-injurious behavior is learned and maintained to avoid or escape from aversive stimulation (Carr, 1977; Carr, Newsom, & Binkoff, 1976). Demands for appropriate behavior or requests to perform a simple task (for instance, "Point to the door," "Touch your nose," "Say 'cookie'") may constitute aversive stimuli, and a child might "use" self-injury as an avoidance tactic. In fact, anecdotal and single-case reports have noted that such comments have "set off" injurious behavior in some children (Carr, Newsom, & Binkoff, 1976; Jones, Simmons, & Frankel, 1974; Wolf, Risley, Johnson, Harris, & Allen, 1967). If individuals working with the child withdrew their requests once the child began self-injury, the alarming pattern could be maintained.

Findings for both hypotheses are important from a treatment standpoint because they indicate that self-destructive behavior can be altered by manipulating social consequences. However, the data do not indicate the conditions under which these dangerous behaviors originally developed—important information if the behaviors are to be prevented in the future.

Differential Reinforcement of Other Behavior. DRO procedures involve reinforcing a child for performing any behavior other than the usual self-stimulatory or self-destructive acts. Lovaas and his colleagues (Lovaas, Freitag, Gold, & Kassorla, 1965) demonstrated the use of DRO procedures with a nine-year-old psychotic girl who exhibited high rates of head and arm banging, pinching, and slapping herself. Their procedure involved ignoring the girl's self-injurious acts and reinforcing her with smiles and praise for hand clapping and gesturing appropriately to music (behaviors which were incompatible with self-injury). During the first and third phases of the study, when both music and injurious behaviors were ignored, high rates of self-injury were observed and hand clapping declined. However, during the second phase, self-injury decreased as the differential reinforcement produced increases in hand clapping.

This study is one of the few examples of DRO procedures used alone. Investigators often add consequences for self-destructive acts, since just ignoring the child would lead to obvious injury before the behaviors were eliminated. (For example, in the study just cited, the child administered a total of 238 blows. On the child's worst day, Lovaas commented, "Her self destruction was extremely vicious and she was bleeding profusely from her head" [Lovaas & Newsom, 1976, p. 314].) Response cost, timeout, or punishment are typically used in conjunction with DRO procedures. Examples of response cost include the removal of food and social reinforcement contingent on injurious arm slapping and head banging in an eight-year-old retarded child (Peterson & Peterson, 1968) and withdrawal of physical contact contingent on face slapping by a retarded child during walks with his therapist (Tate & Baroff, 1966). Timeout in the form of isolation was applied to ritualistic hand movements, crying, and whining in the home-based treatment of a four-year-old child (Nordquist & Wahler, 1973). Verbal punishment (sharply saying, "No!") has been used to modify body rocking and hand movements (Repp, Deitz, & Speir, 1974) and face scratching (Repp & Deitz, 1974).

Much of the DRO research is of the single-case variety and is lacking in experimental sophistication. Taken together, however, the results of these studies indicate that differential reinforcement of some alternative behaviors supplemented by specific contingencies can produce declines, occasionally marked, in the frequency of stereotypic acts. There still remain some qualifications to this statement. As we pointed out, the severity of some self-destructive behaviors may preclude the use of DRO procedures alone. Also, a child may perform adaptive behaviors so infrequently that few opportunities exist for their reinforcement and shaping unless high-frequency inappropriate behaviors are first suppressed by punishment.

Removal of Positive Reinforcement. The use of extinction and timeout with self-stimulatory or self-destructive behaviors is based on the assumption that these behaviors are maintained by social reinforcement (that is, attention). If attention is withheld, then one should expect a decrease and eventual disappearance of the behavior. An early study by Lovaas and James Simmons (1969) demonstrates this phenomenon with two self-destructive children. John was an eight-year-old child whose self-destructive behavior dated from age two. For six months prior to the study his arms and legs had been constantly restrained to

prevent him from severe agitation and injury. Gregg was eleven years old and had been confined to a wheelchair due to shortened Achilles tendons and demineralization of his legs—a result of spending most of the prior two years in restraint. Both children had multiple scars on their heads and faces from self-injury.

Each child was observed in isolation for ninety minutes each day, and as Figure 6-1 indicates, a gradual drop in the frequency of self-destructive behavior was recorded each day. John started with a high rate of 2,750 hits to his head and body during the first ninety minutes (roughly one blow every two seconds), which declined to zero by the tenth session. John hit himself almost 9,000 times before he stopped. The data for Gregg are similar to those for John; Gregg reached a high point of more than 900 blows and then declined gradually to 30 during the last phase of extinction. The data differ in that self-injury in Gregg took much longer to extinguish and showed more irregularity in rate. (Actually, only the first seventeen days was a true extinction period for Gregg, since he also underwent certain experimental manipulations not relevant to this discussion; see Figure 6-1.) Lovaas and Simmons (1969) also indicated that extinction effects were replicated in other institutionalized children with similar but less intense self-destructive behaviors: "In each instance, the self-destructive behavior showed a very gradual drop over time, being particularly vicious in the early stages of extinction" (p. 147).

The initial "burst" of responding and slow decline characteristic of extinction procedures expose self-destructive children to the risk of severe, perhaps fatal, injury. Additionally, when extinction is used alone, it does nothing to prompt and shape other more appropriate behaviors in the child. Lovaas points out a further limitation: extinction effects appear to be highly "situation specific." In the cases of John and Gregg, "while the self-destructive behavior fell to zero in the room used for extinction, it remained unaffected in other situations. It is likely, therefore, that the child has to undergo extinction in a variety of situations" (p. 147). Finally, extinction is frequently difficult to carry out. Ensuring that everyone in a child's immediate environment ignores such disturbing behavior as head banging is almost

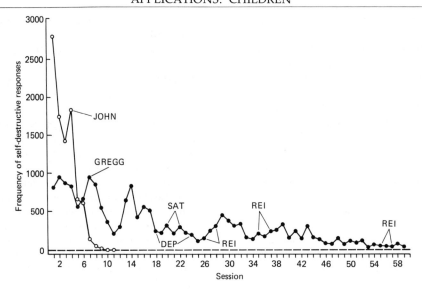

Figure 6–1. Extinction of John's and Gregg's self-destructive behaviors, over successive days of extinction, during 90-minute sessions. Within eleven days, John's self-destructive behavior extinguished; extinction procedures continued with Gregg for fifty-nine days. After two and a half weeks, however, the effect of differential social attention was also investigated in another setting. SAT (satiation) indicates days on which Gregg was given continual noncontingent attention during waking hours. DEP (deprivation) indicates days on which Gregg was left alone in his room. REI (reinforcement) refers to days Gregg received social attention contingent on self-destructive behavior. Notice that these manipulations had little effect on the rate of Gregg's self-destructive acts during extinction periods. From O. I. Lovaas & J. Q. Simmons, Manipulation of self-destruction in three retarded children. *Journal of Applied Behavior Analysis*, 1969, **2**, p. 147, fig. 1. By permission of the Journal of Applied Behavior Analysis, Department of Human Development, University of Kansas, Lawrence.

impossible, and the effects of a few individuals' misplaced attention may be deadly. For these reasons, the use of extinction as a clinical procedure seems highly questionable and perhaps unnecessarily dangerous for some children.

Several studies have indicated that timeout contingent on an occurrence of stereotypic behavior can have a suppressing effect. Montrose Wolf, Todd Risley, and their colleagues (Wolf, Risley, & Mees, 1964; Wolf, Risley, Johnson, Harris, & Allen, 1967) reduced head banging and face slapping in Dicky, a three-and-a-half-year-old autistic child, by removing him from the ward and isolating him in his hospital room whenever he struck himself. After discharge, Dicky exhibited the same self-destructive behavior during preschool, but a brief implementation of the isolation program successfully eliminated the destructive behavior in this setting as well. Other investigators have achieved similar results with timeout for other self-destructive acts (Bucher & Lovaas, 1968; Hamilton, Stephens, & Allen, 1967; Jones, Simmons, & Frankel, 1974; Tate & Baroff, 1966) and for self-stimulatory behaviors (Greene, Hoats, & Hornick, 1970; Pendergrass, 1971).

In summary, research has illustrated the clinically relevant and successful use of both extinction and timeout in the treatment of individual children, as well as pointing out their potential limitations. However, systematic evaluation of the generalization and maintenance of change in stereotypic behaviors following such procedures has yet to be accomplished.

Overcorrection. Overcorrection procedures have recently been used in the elimination of stereotypic behaviors. As we discussed in Chapter 4, overcorrection involves two components: restitution, requiring that the individual correct the consequences of his or her stereotypic act and even improve conditions existing before the act; and positive practice, requiring that the individual intensively practice correct forms of the relevant behavior. Overcorrection in some sense fits the punishment to the crime. For example, one child who continuously mouthed objects was treated with overcorrection procedures (Foxx & Azrin, 1973). Whenever she put inappropriate articles in her mouth she was told "No!" and as restitution she had to brush her gums and teeth with a toothbrush soaked in oral antiseptic to eliminate any unnecessary exposure to germs. She then had to practice this brushing following every instance of inappropriate mouthing.

Overcorrection has been used to decrease the frequency of individual cases of body rocking, head waving, and complex hand and finger movements (Foxx & Azrin, 1973; Doke & Epstein, 1975; Wells, Forehand, Hickey, & Green, 1977). However, further exploratory and evaluative research needs to be conducted on this procedure. It is difficult to know if overcorrection increases appropriate behavior or just decreases inappropriate behavior, or if there is a necessity to fit the stereotypic act to the actual practiced behavior (Epstein, Doke, Sajwaj, Sorrell, & Rimmer, 1974).

Punishment. Contingent application of an aversive stimulus has frequently been used to control or eliminate stereotypic acts. In fact, some researchers (for example, Lovaas & Newsom, 1976) regard punishment as the most successful intervention for self-destructive behavior. A variety of stimuli can function as punishers. Verbal commands ("No!" "Stop that!" and so on) (Baumeister & Forehand, 1972) and shouting and shaking a child (Risley, 1968) have been used to inhibit body rocking. Slaps have also been used to stop self-stimulation (Koegel & Covert, 1972). With self-destructive behavior, however, electric shock has been chosen almost exclusively.

Shock punishment usually consists of a .5- to 1-second extremely painful but physically harmless electric shock delivered to the child's arm or leg by a hand-held rod. As a matter of fact, the first shock devices used were cattle prods. Shock has also been delivered by a remote control device strapped to the child, thereby eliminating any delay between acts of self-destruction and punishment delivery (Prochaska, Smith, Marzilli, Colby, & Donovan, 1974). The primary advantages of shock include the ease, rapidity, and precise timing of the delivery, the wide range of intensities that can be applied, and its almost universally aversive quality (Forehand & Baumeister, 1976).

A number of case studies have supported the general conclusion that shock can rapidly suppress high-rate self-destructive behavior. The first study demonstrating such an effect involved shock administration contingent on hand waving, rocking, screaming, and self-hitting in two five-year-old retarded twin boys (Lovaas, Schaeffer, & Simmons, 1965). When shock was used, self-stimulatory and self-destructive behavior ceased almost immediately. This finding has since been replicated by a number of investigators (Baumeister & Forehand, 1972; Corte, Wolf, & Locke, 1971; Lovaas & Simmons, 1969; Merbaum, 1973; Risley, 1968; Tate & Baroff, 1966). Moreover, data have also indicated that a stimulus (for instance, the word "No!") that previously had no effect on stereotypic behavior can, when paired with shock, *acquire* aversive qualities and later function as a punisher (Lovaas & Simmons, 1969; Merbaum, 1973).

To some, the effectiveness of shock may appear baffling and unexpected. Why should shock be aversive to children who routinely and continuously bang their heads sufficiently to detach retinas, remove fingernails by the roots with their teeth, or pull pieces of skin from their faces and hands? Although any answer is purely speculative, two hypotheses may be offered. One reason may be that children gradually intensify self-directed blows or other injurious acts over time, and thereby adapt to their increasingly painful nature. Shock, on the other hand, is delivered at extremely painful levels from the very beginning, allowing no time for adaption and therefore may be subjectively more "painful" than extreme self-injury.

Another possibly important factor is that self-mutilation is completely under the children's management, whereas shock is delivered from an external source that is not under their direct control. The fact that children cannot *control* the painful shock may make it more aversive than self-injury. In fact, research has indicated that the perception of control over aversive stimuli may greatly affect their stressfulness (for instance, Pervin, 1963; Staub, Tursky, & Schwartz, 1971). But, for whatever reason, shock has changed an otherwise very bleak outlook for children whose future might have included continual chemical or physical restraints to prevent their physically harming themselves.

Another surprising finding is that children who are subjected to such treatment methods do not become generally fearful of adults who administer the punishment (Lovaas & Simmons, 1969). In addition to noting the main effect of suppressing destructive behavior, investigators have also reported concurrent decreases in crying and whining and increases in prosocial behavior (eye contact, touching, exploratory behavior, and so on) in children who have received shock punishment (Bucher & Lovaas, 1968; Lovaas & Simmons, 1969; Tate & Baroff, 1966).

As with any treatment procedure, however, it is important to consider the possible limitations and undesirable effects of the use of electric shock punishment. (1) Shock punishment does not necessarily lead to an increase in adaptive behavior. When punishment techniques appear mandatory, they should always be used in conjunction with programming that simultaneously develops appropriate behavior. (2) Although response suppression from shock is immediate, it is also highly situational and specific to both the locations and persons associated with shock presentation (Baumeister & Forehand, 1972; Lovaas & Simmons, 1969). Therefore, if shock punishment is to be employed, it should be administered by more than one person in more than one environment to ensure general effectiveness. (3) Finally, as will be discussed in Chapter 15, there is considerable concern over the use of intrusive or aversive procedures in behavior modification treatment programming. Practitioners must contend with the increasing social and legal constraints under which punishing stimuli may be used.

Even after the elimination of self-stimulatory or self-destructive behavior, some children have a long way to go before they appear "normal." However, in contrast to the alternative of physical or drug restraints, such treatment often allows children to explore their environment or at least attend to the world around them. Rather than brutalizing children, punishment may provide them with their first real freedom. Lovaas (Lovaas & Simmons, 1969, p. 149) describes John, a child who was treated with extinction and punishment procedures:

> Perhaps the most significant changes that took place in John after he was freed from restraints were the ones we were unable to quantify. He was removed from restraints and shocked at 9 A.M. He appeared extremely frightened and agitated (apparently not by the shock, but from the absence of restraints). He sat slumped on the floor, close to the wall and underneath the washbasin in a corner of his room. At 9:25 he moved out from the wall, peeked into a cupboard in the room, and then darted back to his original place of departure. He repeated this behavior at 9:40 and 9:50. At 10:00 and 10:30 he moved, in very gradual steps, from his room into the corridor and adjoining room. He became very rambunctious, running up and down the hallway, seemingly insatiable. Freedom from restraint also permitted him many other apparently reinforcing discoveries: that first afternoon he allowed himself a full hour of scratching himself, a luxury he had not been allowed while his hands were tied behind his back. He had been so self-destructive that it had been almost impossible to give him a bath in a tub. Freed of self-destructive behavior, he behaved much like a seal when he was placed in a tub, screaming in happiness and scooting underneath the water with his face up and eyes open.

Antisocial Behavior

The term *antisocial behavior* has been used to refer to those disruptive or harmful behaviors that can adversely affect children and those near them (Forehand & Baumeister, 1976). Included are assaultiveness, property damage, excessive screaming, and tantrum behavior, among others. Such behaviors are similar to stereotypic acts in that they are potentially harmful and also result in the child being regarded as deviant.

The treatment procedures that have been applied to these problem behaviors are basically the same as those used for self-stimulatory and self-injurious behaviors. When used alone, DRO procedures are often ineffective in decreasing antisocial behavior (Martin, McDonald, & Omichinski, 1971; Risley, 1968), but their effects can be enhanced by the addition of timeout contingencies for inappropriate behavior (Bostow & Bailey, 1969; Vukelich & Hake, 1971; Wiesen & Watson, 1967). In general, the removal of positive reinforcement, particularly by timeout methods, can reduce antisocial behaviors (Forehand & Baumeister, 1976). Likewise, overcorrection (Foxx & Azrin, 1972; Webster & Azrin, 1973) and punishment (Bucher & King, 1971; Hamilton & Standahl, 1969, Risley, 1968) can effectively reduce antisocial behavior. However, the researcher and clinician must again be aware that the effects of punishment procedures are often short-lived unless steps are taken to ensure the generalization of effects to other situations and at later times.

BUILDING ADAPTIVE BEHAVIOR

Once a child's bizarre and inappropriate behaviors have been decreased, training in self-care, language, social, and academic skills can be intensified. In teaching most new behaviors, a general format may be used: (1) the task is first divided into small steps; (2) correct task performance is reinforced; (3) incorrect task performance is ignored or punished, and corrective feedback is provided; (4) increasing portions of the task are then required for reinforcement; and (5) following training completion, further programming is often necessary to ensure the maintenance of the new behavior. Although this may sound rather simple and straightforward, readers should be aware that many difficulties can be encountered during these procedures.

One problem stems from the fact that little empirical information exists concerning the appropriate strategy or sequence of steps to follow in teaching most behaviors. Often clinicians must logically analyze tasks and make their "best bet" on how and where to begin. As a result, teaching plans may have to undergo much revision if a child performs erratically.

A related problem may exist when a child attends only to certain components of the training stimuli—that is, exhibits stimulus overselectivity. In training new skills, a variety of prompts and cues are usually provided to make the correct response highly discriminative to the child (Lovaas, Beberich, Perloff, & Schaeffer, 1966; Lovaas, Freitas, Nelson, & Whalen, 1967). However, the addition of such prompts has, on occasion, impeded learning in many children, particularly those described as autistic (Koegel, 1971, cited in Lovaas, 1976; Koegel & Rincover, 1976; Lovaas, 1976; Schreibman, 1975). Children may fix their attention on a prompt and be distracted from the relevant stimulus. For example, in teaching an autistic child to point to a square, a teacher may point to the square while requesting the child to do the same. Gradually, the teacher fades the pointing prompt as the child responds correctly. When the prompt is completely removed, the child responds randomly. It is as if the child learned nothing about "square" and selectively attended only to the teacher's finger. Thus, prompts can hinder the child's learning rather than aiding it.

Two suggestions have been made to remediate stimulus overselectivity (Lovaas & Newsom, 1976). One solution is to train a child on individual components of a complex stimulus prior to combining the components. For instance, in teaching a child to discriminate between a red circle and a blue square, if the child first learns to respond to each component in isolation (circle versus square, red versus blue), then he or she may be less likely to respond only on the basis of color or shape when they are later combined (red circle versus blue square).

Another way is to redirect overselective attention rather than attempt to overcome it. This can be done by incorporating the prompt within the training stimulus; the only prompt used is one that is directly relevant to the discrimination. Redundant cues are then gradually introduced. For example, this procedure was used in teaching autistic children a difficult discrimination between two stick figures (♀ and ♀) (Schreibman, 1975). In this case the only discrimination that was prompted was / versus ∧. Thus, if children *selectively* attended to the prompt they would be attending to the relevant dimension of the complete discrimination (♀ versus ♀). Once the child responded correctly to the prompt, redundant cues such as size and the "body" of the stick figure (♀) could be introduced. Such examples emphasize the need for further research on prompting and fading teaching procedures for these children.

Another problem behavioral psychologists must confront in working with children with massive deficits is the limited range of reinforcers to which such children respond. Many social stimuli, such as smiles and praise, initially do not function as reinforcers. For this reason, treatment must often be designed around the use of primary reinforcers. Although new behaviors can be established in this way, there is a drawback. The new behaviors are often limited to those environments where such reinforcers as food are available (Lovaas & Newsom, 1976). In many settings, particularly institutions, primary reinforcement is not used, and any behavior originally established with food as a reinforcer will rapidly extinguish if left unreinforced. Thus, particular care must be taken in the original selection of reinforcers. If primary reinforcers are used, either the frequency of reinforcement must be reduced or other reinforcers that can maintain the new behavior in other environments must be gradually introduced.

At this point, we will examine how each of these problems can affect teaching programs for building specific adaptive behaviors.

Self-Feeding

Mealtime with children who have undesirable or disruptive eating habits can be aversive and chaotic. If they attempt to feed themselves, one child may be grabbing food with his hands and stuffing it into his mouth, whereas another may eat directly off the plate. Invariably, food is spilled or smeared on clothes, the table, or the floor. In an attempt to prevent a mess, a beleaguered parent or nursing aide might simply restrain a child and

spoon feed him or her. Either situation places an excessive burden on caretakers and does little to engender positive feelings toward the children.

For the past decade, operant procedures have been employed to reduce disruptive mealtime behaviors and to train more appropriate eating styles. In fact, operant procedures seem to be especially appropriate for teaching self-feeding skills because powerful reinforcers (the food itself) are built into feeding programs (O'Brien, Bugle, & Azrin, 1972). Withdrawing food or the opportunity to eat could also serve as natural punishing consequences for improper behavior. Presumably, once a child learns to eat correctly, the ingestion of food would provide sufficient reinforcement to maintain proper eating skills.

Three basic procedures have been devised to train proper eating skills: manual guidance, instructions with modeling, and verbal instructions. An assessment of the child's existing self-feeding behaviors and/or ability to understand teaching prompts (verbal instructions, manual guidance) would guide selection of the procedure.

Children without any self-feeding skills may need to begin with manual guidance before they can eat properly. This fairly common procedure includes the teacher holding the child's hand closed around the spoon or fork, filling it, and bringing it to the child's mouth. As the child becomes more skilled, the teacher reduces the amount of assistance provided, possibly by moving the manual guidance from the hand to the forearm, elbow, and finally the shoulder.

For children who have some minimal self-feeding skills, the teacher may provide assistance by combining instructions with modeling or imitation of correct self-feeding behaviors (Butterfield & Parson, 1973; O'Brien & Azrin, 1972). Here the teacher would provide a visual cue by demonstrating the behavior the child is being instructed to perform. For example, as the teacher instructs the child to pick up her fork, the teacher picks up *his* fork. The teacher holds his fork correctly as he instructs the child to do the same, and so on. Finally, for some more advanced children, detailed verbal instructions about how to eat correctly may be sufficient. This would consist of the teacher closely attending to the child's behavior, telling him or her exactly what to do, and suggesting ways to improve.

In addition to teaching appropriate behavior, self-feeding programs occasionally include procedures for reducing frequent or disruptive inappropriate behaviors, such as stealing food from others, throwing food or utensils, and eating food spilled on clothing, table, or floor. A variety of punishment procedures has been used to reduce inappropriate mealtime behaviors. Briefly withdrawing the child's chair from the table (Berkowitz, Sherry, & Davis, 1971; Martin, McDonald, & Omichinski, 1971) or removing the child's food for a short time (for instance, fifteen seconds) (Barton, Guess, Garcia, & Baer, 1970; Whitney & Barnard, 1966) have been used as punishing events. Children have also been removed from the table and placed in a timeout room for offenses such as stealing food from others (Barton, Guess, Garcia, & Baer, 1970). Another remedy has been to physically restrain the child in order to interrupt a sequence of improper eating responses (O'Brien & Azrin, 1972; O'Brien, Bugle, & Azrin, 1972). This can be done by simply holding the child's hand or utensil before it reaches his mouth. However, punishment for errors is often insufficient to maintain proper eating and has, on occasion, totally disrupted all eating responses (O'Brien, Bugle, & Azrin, 1972).

While studies have provided preliminary information on self-feeding training, they have also indicated that programming the *maintenance* of correct independent eating must be included. Once children have learned to eat correctly, the reinforcement presumably obtained from food ingestion has not maintained proper eating skills (Groves & Carroccio, 1971; O'Brien, Bugle, & Azrin, 1972; Whitney & Barnard, 1966). The reason for this is simple: Food is a reinforcer for plate licking as well as for the proper use of eating utensils. Children thus revert to simpler, albeit sloppier, eating styles once training is terminated. Additionally, with rare exceptions, most training demonstrations have concerned themselves only with very low-level eating behaviors, such as using a spoon to eat food out of a bowl nailed to the table, and have not progressed to more complex behaviors, such as using a knife and fork, choosing the correct utensil, or passing food to others at a table. Thus, behavioral psychologists must continue to develop their training programs if they desire *natural* eating behavior from children with skill deficits.

✓ Toilet Training

As discussed in Chapter 4, behavioral psychologists have outlined a number of programs to teach toileting to normal children. Most notable is Azrin and Foxx's (1974) rapid (eight-hour) training method in which prompts and reinforcements are used to establish correct toileting and reprimands and overcorrection are used to punish accidents. Similar procedures have been used for children with severe behavioral deficits (Azrin & Foxx, 1971). The procedures have been modified to include: (1) additional prompting to remove or put on pants if the child has minimal dressing skills, (2) training the child to make independent toileting approaches without having to be instructed or accompanied, and (3) programming maintenance of correct toileting since training often follows years of wetting and/or soiling.

Dressing

Training children to dress themselves follows the same format used to teach many new behaviors. For example, a mother might try to teach her son how to put on and button up his shirt. On the first day, she may prompt him to put one arm through the sleeve and she reinforces him with a smile and a bit of a cookie. Once mastering this step, the child has to put each arm through a sleeve before she reinforces him, and so on. Soon the child will be putting his shirt on and buttoning it up without assistance.

Another very similar way dressing can be taught is to begin with the *last* step in the chain, that is, buttoning the last button on the shirt. Here the mother would begin by putting the shirt on her son and fastening all the buttons except the last; her son must button this one to receive his cookie. Each day the mother leaves more dressing unfinished for her son to complete. The end result of each method is the same and both seem to be equally viable strategies.

N.B. * Language Training

For years the communication problems of retarded and psychotic children were believed to be so severe that it was felt no amount of time or effort could produce significant changes (Guess, Sailor, Keogh, & Baer, 1976). Children who failed to develop speech by age five were given an unfavorable prognosis for future advances in any area of functioning (DeMeyer, Barton, DeMeyer, Norton, Allen, & Steele, 1973; Rutter & Lockyer, 1967). However, during the last ten years several researchers have devised successful intervention procedures for specific areas of language development, and clinicians have constructed comprehensive speech and language programs.

The rationale underlying the behavioral treatment of language disorders is that language is defined in terms of functional relationships between verbal behavior and the child's environment (Lovaas & Newsom, 1976; Skinner, 1957). According to this view, a child must first acquire a large number of verbal responses, including sounds (mm, ē, o͞o, and so on), words, and the combination of words into phrases and sentences. For these responses to acquire meaning, the child must next learn the appropriate stimulus contexts (time, place, and conditions) in which to use the responses.

Language training begins with the teacher obtaining the child's attention. This may take the form of reducing any incompatible or interfering behaviors (for instance, self-stimulatory or self-destructive behavior) and reinforcing the child for establishing eye contact and attending to the therapist. Once attending behavior is reliably established, the next step is establishing verbal behavior through imitation. Some investigators (Bricker & Bricker, 1970; Buddenhagen, 1971; Sloane, Johnson, & Harris, 1968) begin with training simple motor imitations, such as clapping and standing. When the children then spontaneously imitate other nontrained motor responses, a so-called general imitative skill ("generalized imitation") is said to have been acquired, which can then be used to develop vocal imitation. However, there are few data to document whether or not nonverbal imitation training facilitates the acquisition, retention, or generalization of verbal

behavior (Guess, Sailor, & Baer, 1972; Harris, 1975), even though some (Risley, Hart, & Doke, 1972) maintain that it is crucial to all language programs.

Verbal imitation training typically follows the seminal procedures developed by Lovaas and his colleagues (Lovaas, 1968, 1969, 1977; Lovaas, Berberich, Perloff, & Schaeffer, 1966). This training program involves progress through the following steps: (1) rewarding all vocalizations from the child, (2) rewarding vocalizations within a certain time (usually five to six seconds) after the therapist makes a sound, (3) rewarding only those sounds emitted that approximate or imitate the therapist's sounds during the time interval (for instance, the child says "mm" when the therapist says "mm"), and (4) introducing new sounds randomly interspersed with those already learned (for instance, once "mm" is mastered, "ē͞e" might be added). In this way, verbal imitation is taught through the development of several increasingly fine discriminations (Lovaas, Berberich, Perloff, & Schaeffer, 1966).

Despite the seemingly straightforward nature of the procedures, establishing verbal imitation in previously mute children is a long and painstaking process. The data in Figure 6–2 illustrate the acquisition of verbal imitation for Billy and Chuck, the first children to whom Lovaas taught imitation. Training was conducted six days a week, seven hours a day; the data in Figure 6–2 begin with step 3 (see above) of the imitation program. As the reader can see, both Billy and Chuck learned new words more and more easily as training progressed (they were "learning to learn"). However, hundreds of hours had to be invested before either child could reliably produce speech sounds. Several of the sounds Lovaas selected for early training were ones that permitted manual prompting (holding the child's lips together to help him pronounce "mm") or visual cues (the circular shape of the mouth as the therapist says "o͞o") to maximize cues to the child. The long period of variable responding may reflect Billy's and Chuck's attending exclusively to the prompts rather than to the sounds to be learned—that is, their stimulus overselectivity.

Once the child has a large repertoire of imitative speech, the first step toward functional language has been accomplished. Many psychotic children, however, already have this verbal imitation skill in that their speech is echolalic. For example, in response to the therapist's question, "What is this?" when shown a cookie, the child says, "What is this?" For these children, the long process of shaping verbal responses is unnecessary, and the therapist must instead establish control over the imitation before the child can shift from simple echoing to the independent naming of objects.

The procedures described by Todd Risley and Montrose Wolf (1967) best illustrate a program for establishing functional speech in echolalic children. Because a child's echolalia may often be delayed or sporadic, the therapist must first establish immediate and reliable imitation by reinforcing the echoing of a verbal prompt and extinguishing all other verbal utterances. For example, the child is reinforced for saying "cookie" after the therapist says "cookie." After the child can consistently imitate the first word, another word is alternately presented. Control is established when the child will reliably and immediately imitate any word that is presented. That is, the therapist says "cookie" and the child says "cookie," the therapist says "dog" and the child imitates, "dog," and so on. Next, the therapist presents a picture or object with the verbal prompt, and the child is reinforced for imitating the prompt. That is, the therapist holds a cookie and says "cookie" and reinforces the child when he says "cookie." The therapist then gradually fades his verbal prompt until he can simply present the object and the child labels it.

Next, the therapist presents the object and asks "What is this?" When the child looks at the object, the therapist labels it and then again reinforces the child for imitating. If at any time the child echoes, "What is this?" a timeout is programmed by the therapist withdrawing the object and looking away. On subsequent trials, the time between "What is this?" and the therapist's prompt, "cookie," is gradually lengthened, and the therapist begins to fade the prompt by speaking more softly or saying only the first syllable. Training is completed when the therapist can hold up the object, ask "What is this?" and the child responds with the correct label ("cookie"). Once a

reliable rate of naming has been attained, the entire procedure can be repeated for other new words.

The teaching of noun labels is usually the first step in making verbal behavior meaningful to the child. Generally, the words selected for labeling have been common or easily portrayed objects and events in the child's environment—for instance, nose, shoe, cookie, cup, eye. However, although several programs (for example, Cook & Adams, 1966; Salzinger, Feldman, Cowan, & Salzinger, 1965; Hewett, 1965; Sloane, Johnson, & Harris, 1968) have been designed to establish labeling, there are few guidelines for deciding the sequence for introducing nouns, more complex parts of speech such as pronouns, adjectives, or grammatical forms such as tenses (Harris, 1975). Lovaas (1977), however, has gone one step further and developed programs for establishing spontaneous speech and conversational skills in autistic children.

An outgrowth of numerous case reports and studies pertaining to the teaching of particular language components has been the publication of language training packages. Some researchers (Bricker & Bricker, 1974; Miller & Yoder, 1972, 1974; Stremel & Waryas, 1974) have based their programs and training sequences on psycholinguistic theories of normal language development. Others (Guess, Sailor, & Baer, 1972) have taken issue with this strategy due to the scarcity of information about language development in normal children. An alternate approach has been to synthesize clinical experience, research, and reinforcement theory (Kent, 1974; Lovaas, 1977; Tawney & Hipsher, 1972). Notable among the operant programs is the work of Doug Guess, Wayne Sailor, and Donald Baer (1977), whose program offers a sequence of training that can be employed once the child has developed verbal imitation skills.

A unique aspect of the program is its specific attempt to make language functional for the children. One branch of the program prepares children with language skills necessary for an academically oriented plan. Another branch provides communication training necessary for community living. Many other studies and language programs have, however, failed at this level of gen-

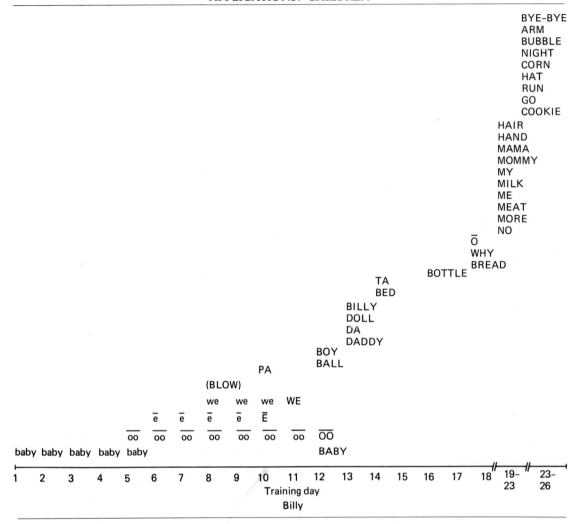

Training day
Billy

eralization (Harris, 1975). In their present state, these programs are successful in training only a small number of communication skills to formerly mute or echolalic children, although it is hoped that they will generate the types of research and conceptualizations required to more completely understand the nature of language and language training for children with severe communication deficits.

A recent innovation in language training for severely disabled children is the use of **simultaneous communication,** a combination of manually signed English and spoken language (Benaroya, Wesley, Ogilvie, Klein, & Meaney, 1977; Creedon, 1973, 1976; Fenn & Towe, 1975; Webster, McPherson, Soloman, Evans, & Kuchar, 1973). The rationale in using signing is that children appear to learn motor imitation more rapidly than verbal imitation. Once a child begins to communicate by signing, development of a verbal vocabulary might then be easier. Training begins with motor imitation, which is refined as the child learns the proper hand signs. Verbal labels are always paired with signs to prompt speech. Simultane-

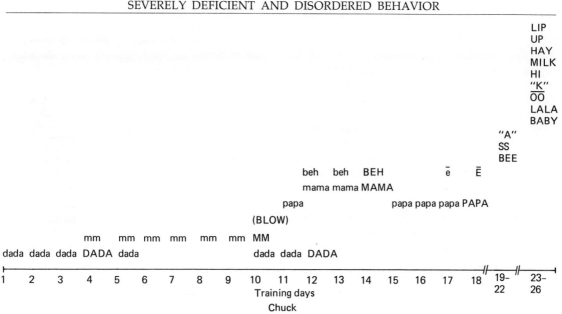

Figure 6–2. The first twenty-six days of the third step of imitation training for Billy and Chuck, who were both psychotic and mute before training. Sounds and words are shown in lowercase letters on the days they were introduced and trained, and in capitals on the days they were mastered. From O. I. Lovaas, Behavioral treatment of autistic children, in *Behavioral approaches to therapy*. Morristown, N.J.: General Learning Press, 1976, p. 193, fig. 3. © 1976 Silver Burdett Company. Used by permission.

ous communication may offer an alternative mode of communication to children, although more research in this area is necessary.

Social Skills and Play Behavior

The social behavior of many, though certainly not all, retarded and psychotic children is often inept. In certain cases, their social behavior is also bizarre. Some of these children *actively* avoid social interaction, turning away when someone looks at them, refusing to make eye contact. In fact, some of these children do not like to be touched and will struggle to get away when an adult tries to hold them or show affection. Such extreme isolative behavior is unusual. More common social "deficits" include withdrawal or, conversely, exaggerated displays of affection. Many children are extremely shy, either giving a one-word reply or saying nothing if an adult asks them a question, and rarely laughing or playing. Other children are just the opposite, lavishing affection on any adult who is present and trying to kiss and hug everyone they meet. Such behaviors present tremendous handicaps for these children because they lead people to refrain from further interactions. As these children grow up, their social behavior also limits their employment opportunities. For these reasons, it is important that they acquire more acceptable ways of relating to others.

Little research has been directed toward developing methods of teaching disturbed children social skills. Researchers have focused their attention on modifying problematic social behaviors in normal children (Gottman, Gonso, & Schuler, 1976; Hart, Reynolds, Baer, Brawley, &

Harris, 1968; O'Connor, 1969) and have generally ignored these behaviors in mentally retarded or psychotic children. Our discussion here will be limited to a review of the few available programs.

When working with severely withdrawn children, one of the first things the therapist does is make social stimuli from adults (for instance, their smiles and hellos) discriminative stimuli for positive reinforcement. For example, a child is fed only when she approaches an adult who is holding out his arms to her; this discrimination training "forces" the child to pay attention to the adult in order to receive food. Such a procedure has been found effective and necessary for some extremely withdrawn children; merely pairing saying the word "Good" with food delivery may be insufficient to establish it as a reinforcer (Lovaas, Freitag, Kinder, Rubenstein, Schaeffer, & Simmons, 1966).

Another rather controversial method of increasing the reinforcing value of social interaction is to negatively reinforce social behavior through the removal of aversive stimulation. This procedure has been used only in a very small number of cases involving severely withdrawn, self-destructive children. In one case study involving two such children, Lovaas and his colleagues (Lovaas, Schaeffer, & Simmons, 1965) paired the termination of aversive electric shock with adult contact. The child was placed in a small room equipped with an electrified grid on the floor. If the child began engaging in self-stimulation or self-injury, the shock was turned on. The therapist immediately stretched out his arms to the child and said, "Come here." As soon as the child moved toward the therapist, the shock was turned off. In three sessions both children's self-destructive behavior had been eliminated and their response to adults showed marked improvement. Although all these procedures have been demonstrated to be effective in individual cases, their effectiveness for other children and in other circumstances has not been evaluated.

Teaching retarded and psychotic children to initiate social interaction and cooperative play has received some attention from behavioral clinicians. As with the other adaptive skills we have discussed, the ultimate goal is to provide children with a behavioral repertoire that allows them to experience many of the joys of life we take for granted. Teaching these skills involves careful use of prompts, reinforcement, and modeling. For the children most immune to social attention, food reinforcement may be necessary to prompt human contact (see Figure 6–3). In many instances, it may be sufficient for a therapist to demonstrate a target behavior, such as smiling or sharing a toy with a friend, and then reinforce the children as they master the behavior (Cooke & Apolloni, 1976; Lovaas, Freitas, Nelson, & Whalen, 1967; Whitman, Mercurio, & Caponigri, 1970).

Children who already possess some play and social skills present fewer problems, and for them, refining existing behavior is often sufficient (Arnold, Sturgis, & Forehand, in press). However, as treatment and educational environments for children with behavior deficits become increasingly less segregated, procedures designed to develop more complex social skills (for example, initiating, maintaining, and terminating conversations with adults and peers) may become even more necessary. A retarded or psychotic child who attends a local public school and lives at home needs to learn a wide range of social behaviors to function effectively at school. One source of help for these children may be their classmates. In one case, two children assisted an eight-year-old autistic classmate in playing with other children on the playground (Kandel, Ayllon, & Rosenbaum, 1977). In another school, two children from a regular classroom acted as therapists for six retarded preschoolers who rarely engaged in any positive interactions (Strain, Shores, & Timm, 1977). After the older children emitted positive social behaviors toward the retarded children, the rate of social interactions with each other and the child therapists increased dramatically. Thus, behavioral programming may ease the transition of retarded or psychotic children from the special to the regular classroom.

Educational Interventions

For years, retarded and disturbed children have not received adequate educational services. These children were thought of as uneducable and thus unable to profit from a traditional "reading, writing, and arithmetic" education. However, recently, legal efforts have been made to provide

SEVERELY DEFICIENT AND DISORDERED BEHAVIOR

(a)

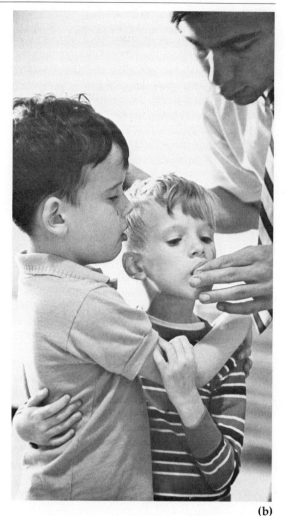

(b)

for these children's educational needs. As a result, the demand for effective educational environments and instructional materials is increasing rapidly.

Behavioral psychologists and educators have attempted to improve educational services for retarded and disturbed children in two ways. One strategy has been to create special learning environments, such as token economy classrooms, where instruction is individualized and achievement is reinforced with redeemable tokens (Birnbrauer, Wolf, Kidder, & Tague, 1965; Kaufman &

Figure 6–3. Chuck and Billy, two of the first children Lovaas and his associates treated. A variety of procedures was used to bring them into contact with each other and with those around them. Food was the key reinforcer at first. Billy balked when asked to pull Chuck around in a wagon (a). However, tastes of sherbert eventually lured them into cooperative play, and they could accept each other's closeness instead of screaming and pulling away (b). Photos: Allan Grant, from LIFE Magazine.

O'Leary, 1972; O'Leary & Drabman, 1971). The second strategy has involved designing programmed instructional materials that clearly specify the criteria for learning, gradually present increasingly complex information, and provide opportunities for both reinforcement and performance feedback (Bereiter, 1972; Bereiter & Engleman, 1966; Ellson, Barber, Engle, & Kampwerth, 1965). These two strategies also form the basis for many behavioral educational interventions with normal children (see Chapter 5 for details).

Educational programs have produced immediate gains for children in one-to-one instructional settings. However, as we have noted with other interventions, such changes are often short-lived or are only displayed in the situations in which the training was conducted. Part of the difficulty may be related to the apparent problems children have in responding to multiple stimuli (stimulus overselectivity). A classroom environment may contain so many distracting stimuli that the child is overwhelmed and unable to attend to relevant instructional cues.

One approach to this problem has involved gradually introducing stimuli present in classrooms while simultaneously making reinforcement less frequent. In the one systematic application of this approach (Koegel & Rincover, 1974), children who were later to form a class group were first taught individually or in groups of two. When these two children had reached a criterion of 80 percent correct performance in the individual setting, they were grouped with two other children who had reached the same criterion. Then, when this new group maintained an 80 percent criterion of performance, four other children were added for a final class size of eight. The reinforcement schedule was concurrently thinned from an initial FR 2 (that is, reinforcement following every second correct response) when two children were present to FR 8 when the class was complete.

This gradual reduction in the frequency of reinforcement allowed the teacher to maintain each child's responding even though she could only respond to one child at a time. The procedure was effective in enabling children to transfer responses learned in one-to-one training to the group situation. After this training, the children were able to learn new responses through the group instruc-

tion. Although these procedures may be time-consuming, they increase the possibility that subsequent training can be conducted in more typical group formats. However, the application just cited involved only the teaching of simple motor tasks. It is an open question as to whether such fading procedures are effective with the teaching of more complex skills.

SOME COMMENTS ON BEHAVIORAL TREATMENTS

The first systematic attempts to use behavioral techniques for deficits in autistic and retarded children were quite successful. By altering particular aspects of the children's lives, behavioral clinicians were able to eliminate tantrums, self-destructive acts, and self-stimulation in some children, and to teach language and imitation skills to others. Such successful results were in marked contrast to the failure of psychodynamic therapies to effect any change at all. However, most of the published research in behavioral treatment of these children has involved single case studies, and long-term followup evaluations are rare. The major exception to this trend is the research of Lovaas and his colleagues at UCLA, who have now collected treatment and followup data on twenty children treated between 1964 and 1971. (Case Study 6–2 provides an in-depth summary of the first two children treated by Lovaas and his colleagues.) Their research is the best source of information regarding the behavioral treatment of disturbed children, and much of our discussion will center on this team's report (Lovaas, Koegel, Simmons, & Long, 1973).

Although all the children Lovaas selected for treatment were diagnosed as autistic and IQ scores were all less than 50, there was considerable variation among them. The behavior of some children was more bizarre than in others, but all the children displayed the kinds of behaviors we have discussed in this chapter. In most of the cases, professionals felt that the chance for the child's improvement was essentially zero. The children whom Lovaas treated probably represent one of the most severely incapacitated groups of children ever studied.

Lovaas's treatment program can best be characterized as a massive intervention, particularly emphasizing language training. Children received as much as eight hours of one-to-one therapy, seven days a week. The first children to go through the program were treated as inpatients. Outpatient treatment was provided to later groups whose parents were given extensive training in behavioral procedures. This shift from an inpatient to an outpatient-parental treatment model came after Lovaas obtained followup data on the first four children who completed the program. Although the first children made significant gains, they deteriorated after they were placed in a state hospital where the intensive training was not continued. It was apparent to Lovaas and his colleagues that these children would require ongoing treatment to maintain their improvements, and that discharging them into the care of trained parents provided a viable solution. Figure 6–4 summarizes the outcome of the program for thirteen children who participated. Measures obtained before and after the program was initiated are presented along with followup data obtained one to four years after the children were discharged. The children who returned to their homes fared better than those who were transferred to the institution. Under parental care the children did not regress and, in some cases, improved after inpatient treatment was terminated.

Lovaas's outcome data suffer from some methodological problems that preclude determining cause-effect relationships and essential treatment elements, but they do illustrate many of the strengths and weaknesses of behavioral intervention programs with severely disturbed children. Several points are clear with regard to the benefits of such programs: (1) Self-destructive or self-stimulatory behaviors that may have existed for years can be eliminated through the application of punishment and reinforcement procedures. (2) Basic self-care and social skills can be instituted. (3) Fundamental language skills can be trained. Thus, it appears that behavioral clinicians have made the preliminary steps toward the develop-

Figure 6–4. Multiple-response measures for autistic children treated by Lovaas and his colleagues. Percentage of occurrence of the various behaviors is shown for I (average results for the four institutionalized children) and P (average results for the nine children discharged to parents' care). From O. I. Lovaas, R. Koegel, J. Q. Simmons, & J. S. Long, Some generalizations and follow-up measures on autistic children in behavior therapy. *Journal of Applied Behavior Analysis*, 1973, **6,** p. 148, fig. 7. By permission of the Journal of Applied Behavior Analysis, Department of Human Development, University of Kansas, Lawrence.

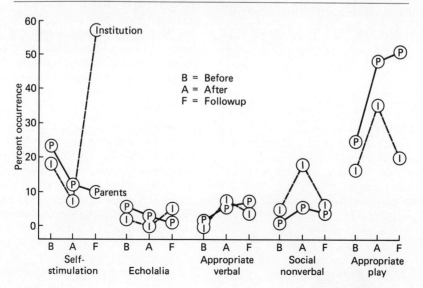

ment of powerful treatment programs for severely disturbed children.

Although behavioral programs seem to be the only effective intervention presently available, they have their limitations: (1) In the search for functional reinforcers to motivate children, behavioral clinicians have relied on food delivery and shock termination, often the only reinforcers that have any effect on such children. Unfortunately, this procedure may set up the exact conditions that result in a rapid loss of the target behavior when the contingencies are removed and equally powerful motivators are not available in the natural setting. (2) Although procedures exist for building low-level adaptive behaviors, few programs have developed methods for teaching more complex skills. If children are to progress beyond living a bit more comfortably or being more easily managed within institutions, then more *comprehensive* treatment programming and evaluation must be instituted. (3) Despite incredible expenditures of time, money, and effort, behavioral interventions still produce only minimal gains for some children. According to Lovaas (Lovaas, Koegel, Simmons, & Long, 1973, p. 160):

> Our program did not give everything to every child. Sometimes it gave very little to a particular child, but it did give something to each child we saw. The improvement was analogous to making from 10 to 20 steps on a 100 step ladder. Scotty probably started at 80 and gained 20; his treatment brought dramatic changes, he became normal and his change is irreversible. Jose, on the other hand, may have started at 10 and gained 10; the change was not all that dramatic.

Lovaas's data also illustrated that "it is not enough to help a child acquire appropriate behavior and overcome inappropriate ones; it is also necessary to provide maintaining conditions that ensure the improvements will last" (Lovaas & Newsom, 1976, p. 336). One way Lovaas chose to promote transfer and maintenance of treatment effects was to teach the child's parents to become the primary agents of change.

Another method that has been proposed is to minimize the degree to which "abnormal" persons are treated differently from "normal" persons (Wolfensberger, 1972). The basic premise is that if deviant children are segregated from the mainstream of society, they will tend to be treated differently and will behave accordingly. The strategy of **normalization,** as it is called, is to give these children the advantages of an environment that does not encourage regressed, dependent behavior, but rather encourages "normal" behavior. If training programs and environments are not designed to approximate everyday life situations, the children may not have the opportunity to acquire the skills necessary to succeed in the "natural" environment. For example, a child who only learns to eat pureed food from a bowl that is glued to the table is not likely to learn the skills necessary to eat a steak in a restaurant.

Although it is assumed that subjecting these children to "normalizing" environments is an effective strategy for generating normal behavior, the notion is still largely untested. The normalization and the behavioral approaches use different methods to establish normal behavior, but the philosophies of these two approaches are compatible, and many clinicians feel that they should merge. The degree to which procedures conform to one model or another, however, is not the appropriate basis for their evaluation; rather, a program should be judged by the benefits it affords its clients.

SUMMARY

Behavioral approaches to mentally retarded and psychotic children have substituted behavior analysis for traditional diagnostic methods and found the behaviors emitted by both groups of children to be remarkably similar. Most of these children emit a variety of problem behaviors. Intellectual functioning is impaired and children perform poorly on formalized measures of intelligence. These children often show profound deficits in appropriate, adaptive behavior. Finally, treatment is a long process often requiring twenty-four-hour programming. Behavioral strategies aim at the modification of each of these problems.

Stereotypic and antisocial behaviors must often be eliminated before other problems can be treated. Behavioral clinicians have devised four methods for treating these problem behaviors: (1) reinforcement of alternative or incompatible behaviors; (2) withdrawal of reinforcement or the opportunity to earn it contingent upon the problem behavior; (3) overcorrection; (4) presentation of aversive stimulation following the maladaptive response. All of these procedures have met with some success, but punishment techniques appear to be the treatment of choice in the elimination of severe self-destructive behavior because of their rapid suppressive effect.

Once disruptive behavior has been eliminated, the child can be taught more adaptive ways of behaving. Independent feeding, toileting, and dressing skills can be trained through prompting, shaping, and reinforcing correct responses, while ignoring or mildly punishing errors. It is particularly important to program the generalization of gains in self-care behavior, since these new responses are often specific to the settings in which they are taught.

Teaching language to nonverbal or echolalic children is a complex and arduous task. Training typically involves the building of verbal imitation (or establishing control over echolalic responding) by operant methods. When the child has acquired a large repertoire of imitative speech, noun labels are taught by pairing an object with an appropriate imitative response that is reinforced. When prompts have been faded and labeling has been established for a variety of objects, the training of other parts of speech and the formation of sentences is initiated. Although several programs for advanced language instruction are now available, they are still in the preliminary stages of development. Also at the early stage of development is teaching children to communicate through training in sign language.

With regard to other social behaviors, the "deficits" of psychotic children may range from active avoidance of all social interactions and physical contact to inappropriate displays of affection. There are two strategies for increasing attention to social stimuli: (1) make them discriminative stimuli for positive reinforcement or for the removal of aversive stimuli; (2) for the children who possess some social skills, refine existing behavior by shaping and differential reinforcement.

Behavioral psychologists and educators have created special educational environments and instructional materials to aid in the more "traditional" educational needs of retarded or disturbed children. Special fading procedures have been developed to aid children in making a successful transition from individual instruction to a classroom environment.

Behavioral approaches to the problems of severely retarded children have not been extensively evaluated, but the work of Lovaas and his team clearly demonstrates their potential in improving the lot of these children. Gains are regularly achieved through these programs; however, they appear only after long and painstaking treatment efforts. The children's improvements seem very fragile and readily disappear if programs are not continued. Parents trained in treating their children provide one possible solution to the problem of continuing treatment. Placing the children in "normalizing" environments that "demand" that they behave appropriately may be another.

CASE STUDY 6-1

WHITNEY, L. R., & BARNARD, K. E. OPERANT LEARNING THEORY AND NURSING CARE OF THE RETARDED CHILD. *MENTAL RETARDATION*, 1966, **4**, 26–29.

Children who have grown up in institutions for the retarded or psychotic often have a number of behavioral deficits. Because of years of confinement and custodial care, they have not had many of the opportunities other children have to explore and learn. In many cases, institutionalization serves to exaggerate their deficits. The case study by Whitney and Barnard illustrates an early use of multifaceted behavioral programming for a severely retarded girl who possessed many of the deficits characteristic of this population.

Ann was a fourteen-year-old adolescent who had been institutionalized much of her life. Described as a very destructive child, Ann would often remove and tear up her bedding and clothing, smear her feces, and steal food in an apparent attempt to receive attention from staff and residents. Moreover, Ann could not walk alone and responded only minimally to simple verbal commands. The only sounds she made were occasional squeals or cries.

After supervising mealtime activities on the ward for an extended period of time, a nurse noticed that other staff members made no attempt to encourage appropriate self-feeding in Ann. In fact, if Ann crawled over to less capable children to take their food, a ward attendant might look at Ann, smile, and say, "That's not a nice girl." When left alone during mealtime, Ann would overturn dishes and throw food on the floor. To teach independent feeding, the nurse took Ann to a private room with a full tray of food. Early in training the nurse reinforced Ann with bites of food for looking at the spoon. Next, Ann had to make some gesture with her right arm in the direction of the spoon in order to be reinforced. If Ann grabbed for her spoon or any food, the nurse would place Ann's hand under the table and firmly say, "No!" Finally, looking at, reaching for, and grasping the spoon were required before Ann was reinforced. After five days of continued training Ann was feeding herself. When she occasionally spilled some of her food in the process of feeding, she was taught to use her spoon to scrape it from her bib to her mouth rather than use her fingers. Self-feeding was maintained when other trained staff members joined Ann at mealtimes.

Although the bulk of the intervention program for Ann focused on teaching self-feeding, other skills (dressing, toileting, grooming, and ambulation) were also monitered to assess possible change. Four months after the initiation of the spoon-feeding program, Ann was transferred to an ambulatory ward. She ate her meals at a table with other girls from the unit. After breakfast she would practice walking with assistance from staff members. As Ann attempted walking, she received praise and attention from the staff. Although she did not learn to dress herself, Ann's pattern of undressing for attention declined to the point where she took off only her shoes and stockings. Also, staff members attempted to schedule Ann's toileting to coincide with her patterns of elimination and to stay with Ann when she was placed on the toilet to provide reinforcement for correct toileting. As Ann's behavior changed there was also considerable change in the staff members' behavior towards her. They began to expect more from her. They focused on her appropriate behavior and generously reinforced it.

The case study of Ann provides an early demonstration of reinforcement principles as a basis for establishing self-help skills in a retarded child. It also sheds light on how such behavior change can motivate staff members to continue intervention and push for even greater change from a child previously regarded as helpless.

CASE STUDY 6–2

LOVAAS, O. I. *THE AUTISTIC CHILD: LANGUAGE DEVELOPMENT THROUGH BEHAVIOR MODIFICATION.* NEW YORK: IRVINGTON PUBLISHERS, 1977.
LOVAAS, O. I., FREITAS, L., NELSON, K., & WHALEN, C. THE ESTABLISHMENT OF IMITATION AND ITS USE FOR THE DEVELOPMENT OF COMPLEX BEHAVIOR IN SCHIZOPHRENIC CHILDREN. *BEHAVIOUR RESEARCH AND THERAPY*, 1967, **5**, 171–181.
LOVAAS, O. I., KOEGEL, R., SIMMONS, J. Q., & LONG, J. S. SOME GENERALIZATIONS AND FOLLOW-UP MEASURES ON AUTISTIC CHILDREN IN BEHAVIOR THERAPY. *JOURNAL OF APPLIED BEHAVIOR ANALYSIS*, 1973, **6**, 131–165.

Although we have referred to the work of Lovaas and his colleagues throughout this chapter, it is not possible to fully appreciate the comprehensive nature of their program and the dramatic effect it had for many of the children without carefully studying their case reports. This case study traces the progress of the first two children they treated.

In June of 1964 Pamela and Ricky were admitted to the Neuropsychiatric Institute at UCLA. Both children could have been described as "classically autistic." Pamela was nine years old and had been involved in some form of psychiatric treatment most of her life. Between the ages of two and six she had received intensive psychoanalytic therapy. This was followed by two and a half years of residential treatment. When first observed, Pamela spent most of her time engaging in self-stimulation, as shown in Figure 6–5.

Ricky was eight years old when admitted and presented many of the same problems as Pamela. He responded to simple requests with blank stares, echolalia, or tantrums, as seen in Figure 6–6. On the first day of treatment one of the therapists tried to talk with Ricky about a picture in a storybook. As the therapist tried to interest him in the book, Ricky made a grab for his glasses. Below is an excerpt of the "conversation" between Ricky and the therapist (Lovaas, 1977, p. 72):

Ricky: Say please, I want your glasses (Ricky echoes *T*'s earlier statement).
T: Here, Ricky, All right, now it's my turn. Now give them back. Ricky, let go. What's this, Ricky?
Ricky: What's this, boy?
T: What's your name?
Ricky: What's your name?
T: How old are you? Ricky?
Ricky: How are you? I want my glasses.
T: Do you like my glasses?
Ricky: Do you like my glasses?
T: Say please, I want your glasses.
Ricky: Say please, I want your glasses (*T* gives Ricky the glasses).
T: All right, let me have the glasses, Ricky. Ricky, let go. I'll give them back. Attaboy. Good, good. Ricky, who's this?
Ricky: Ricky, who's this?
T: What's that, Ricky?
Ricky: What's that, Ricky?

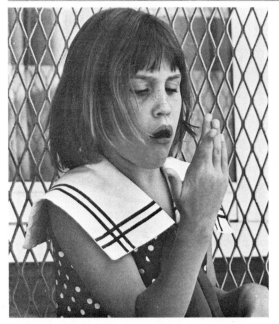

Figure 6–5. Before her treatment began, Pamela spent much of her day in isolation, flicking her fingers in front of her eyes and swishing saliva in her mouth. Photo by Allan Grant, from LIFE Magazine.

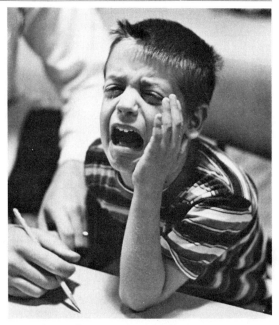

Figure 6–6. During a tantrum Ricky screams and cries. Such outbursts were common during early treatment sessions and could be triggered by Ricky's therapist requesting him to perform a simple task. Photo by Allan Grant, from LIFE magazine.

T; Look, Ricky, look where I'm pointing. Who's this, Ricky?
Ricky: Say please, I want your glasses.

During the fourteen months they were at UCLA, Pamela and Ricky spent eight hours a day, six or seven days a week in treatment. Much of the time was devoted to improving language skills. Although they were both echolalic when treatment began, Pam and Ricky made slow but steady progress during their stay. Each month Ricky's therapists made notes of his spontaneous speech. For approximately the first four months Ricky made no spontaneous verbalizations, but during the next year his speech became more frequent and more sophisticated. A few examples appear below (Lovaas, 1977, pp. 98–100):

DECEMBER

Median (typical speech): Spontaneously labeling objects.
Complex (speech): Requesting to draw a rocket ship and a merry-go-round.

JANUARY (SECOND YEAR)

Median: Saying "Hi" and interacting with therapists.
Complex: Using phrases like "kiss it and make it better." Rick hit his therapist, seemed concerned, said "How are you feeling, Joan?"

APRIL

Median: Ricky is using "I don't want to" regularly, commenting on pictures in books and coming events, commenting on things he is being trained to do.

Complex: Ricky is able to use "supposed" properly and spontaneously, e.g., "I am supposed to use my napkin." He is able to discuss events in the future using time concepts, e.g., "I am going home Thursday, three more days, no, two more days." (Two days is correct in this case.) He is also beginning to control his own behavior verbally; he says "I am not going to gag (whine, etc.) any more."

MAY

Median: Ricky is asking and answering questions and making requests of peers spontaneously. He is noticing and asking questions of strangers and verbalizing his feelings to some extent.

Complex: T allows Ricky to go on short walks by himself occasionally. After one such walk Ricky returned and told me that it was "amazing" that he had gone by himself. T told him that flowers grow up and so do people; he said, "Pour some water on my head." He understands part of the concept of growing up.

AUGUST

Median: Ricky is constantly analogizing new experiences with familiar ones: "Sprinkler is like a little shower," blowing bubbles in the bathtub water is "just like the swimming pool," "Canteloupe is just like watermelon," spinning on the swings is "just like an elevator."

Other aspects of the program were devoted to teaching the children a variety of simple tasks. This even included teaching Pam and Ricky how to play. In learning how to draw, Pam first traced with a crayon over her therapist's pencil marks. Next, she was able to copy simple line drawings as indicated in the top of Figure 6–7. As the lower portion of the figure indicates, Pam's drawing also became more complex until she was able to draw without models or assistance. Ricky also learned how to draw, dribble and shoot a basketball, cut out and color pictures, and put together puzzles. Although it took considerable effort to teach the children these activities, it was apparent that they enjoyed playing as much as any child does.

At the end of Pam's and Ricky's treatment at UCLA, Lovaas and his colleagues made a difficult decision to recommend their rehospitalization. This option was chosen for two reasons. First, the parents had not been trained to handle their children. Second, Lovaas felt that the parents had other responsibilities which could prevent their giving Pam or Ricky the kind of individualized instruction they needed. Pam's mother had other children, including a severely brain-damaged child who required continuous care. It seemed unlikely that she would be able to manage Pamela along with her siblings. Ricky's mother was divorced and needed full-time employment. Thus, both children returned to child treatment wards in a California state hospital.

In 1968, three years after leaving Lovaas's program, a followup evaluation of Pam's and Ricky's progress was undertaken. It was clear that the inter-

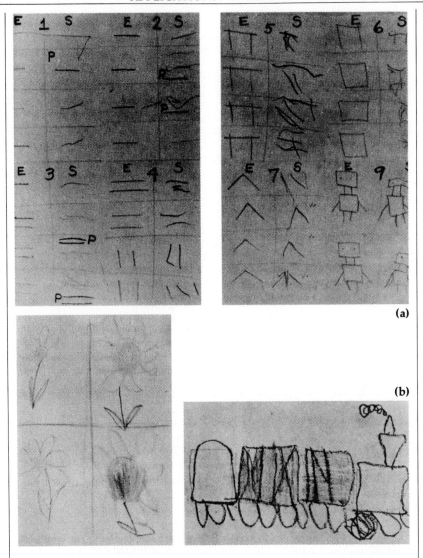

Figure 6–7. Drawings by Pamela at various points in training. Pamela's earliest attempts are shown in (a); the figures are labeled 1 through 9 and represent approximately every hundredth trial. *E* denotes the therapist's drawings, *S* Pam's copy, and *P* the occasions on which the therapist had to prompt Pam by moving her hand across the paper. Pamela's later drawings are shown in (b). Eventually, she could draw without models or prompts. From O. I. Lovaas, L. Freitas, K. Nelson, & C. Whalen, The establishment of imitation and its use for the development of children. *Behaviour Research and Therapy*, 1967, **5,** pp. 180, 181, figs. 4, 5. By permission of Pergamon Press, Ltd.

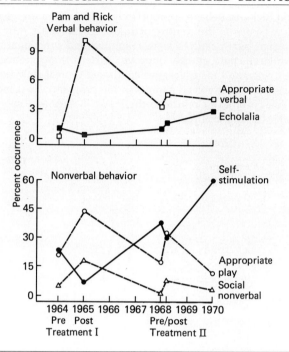

Figure 6–8. Multiple-response measures for Rick and Pam before (1964) and after (1965) first treatment, and for the first followup (1968), second treatment (1968), and second followup (1970). From O. I. Lovaas, R. Koegel, J. Q. Simmons, & J. S. Long, Some generalizations and follow-up measures on autistic children in behavior therapy. *Journal of Applied Behavior Analysis*, 1973, **6,** p. 149, fig. 8. By permission of the Journal of Applied Behavior Analysis, Department of Human Development, University of Kansas, Lawrence.

vening three years of custodial treatment had had a detrimental effect on the children's functioning. Both exhibited large decreases in appropriate behavior (such as speech, play, and social nonverbal behavior) and increases in echolalia and self-stimulation. After reviewing the children's condition, Lovaas and his colleagues decided to put them through the intensive treatment program a *second* time—twenty-four hours for Ricky and three weeks for Pamela. As indicated in Figure 6–8, this short exposure to the program resulted in some recovery of previous treatment gains. It was clear that the children had not forgotten all they had learned at UCLA. Once again the children were returned to the state hospital. A final followup was conducted in 1970. As shown in Figure 6–8, both Pam and Ricky regressed severely.

The follow up data on Ricky and Pam dramatically illustrate the importance of continuing therapeutic programming into the posttreatment environment of such children. In the state institution there was little demand for Pam and Ricky to behave appropriately, and so they regressed. Their immediate response to the reintroduction of intensive training also indicates that when contingencies were reapplied and functional reinforcers used, the children could quickly improve. After the experience with Pam and Ricky, Lovaas and his colleagues continued to treat children on an inpatient basis but also involved parents in the program. This modification enabled other children to return to their own homes and continue their progress after leaving UCLA.

CASE STUDY 6-3

WOLF, M., RISLEY, T., & MEES, H.   APPLICATION OF OPERANT CONDITIONING PROCEDURES TO THE BEHAVIOUR PROBLEMS OF AN AUTISTIC CHILD. *BEHAVIOUR RESEARCH AND THERAPY,* 1964, **1,** 305–312.

WOLF, M., RISLEY, T., JOHNSTON, M., HARRIS, F., & ALLEN, E. APPLICATION OF OPERANT CONDITIONING PROCEDURES TO THE BEHAVIOUR PROBLEMS OF AN AUTISTIC CHILD: A FOLLOW-UP AND EXTENSION. *BEHAVIOUR RESEARCH AND THERAPY,* 1967, **5,** 103–111.

NEDELMAN; D., & SULZBACHER, S. I.   DICKY AT 13 YEARS OF AGE: A LONG TERM SUCCESS FOLLOWING EARLY APPLICATION OF OPERANT CONDITIONING PROCEDURES.   IN G. SEMB (ED.), *BEHAVIOR ANALYSIS AND EDUCATION, 1972.*   LAWRENCE: UNIVERSITY OF KANSAS PRESS, 1972, PP. 3–10.

The first attempt to use behavior modification procedures for treatment of an autistic child in natural situations was reported in 1964 by Wolf, Risley, Mees, and their colleagues. The child, Dicky, was the subject of a series of studies which traced his progress from age three, when he was admitted to a children's mental institution, to age thirteen, when he was completing sixth grade. The following case study is a synopsis of Dicky's progress during these ten years. Although we have referred to aspects of this case elsewhere, its importance justifies drawing it together here.

When Dicky was first seen in the hospital his parents reported that he had progressed normally until he was nine months of age, when cataracts were discovered in the lenses of both eyes. Soon after this he developed self-destructive behavior: banging his head, slapping his face, scratching his ears and neck until they bled, and so on. Tranquilizers and restraints were tried without success. After several examinations and operations, Dicky's lenses were removed, necessitating the wearing of glasses. For a year Dicky's parents tried to make him wear his glasses but he refused, and the specialists they consulted could offer no help.

At the age of three Dicky was admitted to a children's mental hospital with a diagnosis of childhood schizophrenia. By this time Dicky had deteriorated considerably: he did not eat normally, his speech was echolalic or consisted of song singing, and he would not sleep at night. The doctors warned that his remaining vision would be lost if he did not begin wearing his glasses within the next six months. At this point Dicky was referred to the Developmental Psychology Laboratory at the University of Washington.

After assessing Dicky's condition, Wolf, Risley, and Mees decided that the first behaviors to be treated were his self-destructive acts and tantrums. Treatment involved brief timeout in his room contingent upon violent behavior and reinforcement for positive behavior. Once these problematic behaviors were eliminated, teaching Dicky more adaptive behavior began. Training Dicky to wear glasses was accomplished through shaping. Initially he was given bites of food for touching, picking up, and putting on his glasses. Later he was required to wear his glasses for longer periods of time. As Dicky progressed, contingent walks, rides, and snacks were used as reinforcers to maintain wearing of the glasses. Other programs were developed to increase appropriate speech. After seven months of intensive treatment, Dicky was released from the hospital.

Once Dicky was home, he continued to improve through management and training provided by his parents. However, at the age of five Dicky still had only minimal social skills and was not yet toilet trained. Because these problems would prevent enrollment in public school, the psychologists recommended that Dicky's parents enroll him in the University of Washington's Preschool Laboratory, where these deficits could be treated. At school, effort was focused on developing Dicky's social skills. Although contingent teacher attention and food reinforcement were not completely successful in modifying his social behavior, Dicky's rate of social interaction with his nursery school playmates did increase from near zero throughout the first year to approximately 15 percent during the second year. A timeout program was successfully implemented in the nursery school to eliminate his remaining tantrums and pinching of teachers and classmates. Dicky was also toilet trained at school by means of a simple reinforcement program.

After finishing two years of preschool, Dicky entered the public school in a special education class for the mentally retarded. He adjusted well and was soon transferred to a class for the physically handicapped. Dicky's next move was to the regular public school classroom.

Dicky's steady progress can only be regarded as remarkable. At the time of the last report, when he was thirteen, Dicky's current teacher regarded him as a considerate, socially appropriate, and responsible student. Although he occasionally displayed autistic behaviors (rocking in his seat, flapping his hands), he was accepted by his peers. Dicky was extremely fortunate to have had the benefit of such comprehensive intervention and exceptionally well-trained teachers. This case clearly illustrates the gains that can be made with severely incapacitated children through long-term behavioral programming.

REFERENCES

American Association on Mental Deficiency. *Manual on terminology and classification in mental retardation.* 1973.

Arnold, S., Sturgis, E., & Forehand, R. Training a parent to teach communication skills: A case study. *Behavior Modification* (in press).

Azrin, N. H., & Foxx, R. M. A rapid method of toilet training the institutionalized retarded. *Journal of Applied Behavior Analysis,* 1971, **4,** 89–99.

Azrin, N. H., & Foxx, R. M. *Toilet training in less than a day.* New York: Simon & Schuster, 1974.

Barton, E. S., Guess, D., Garcia, E., & Baer, D. M. Improvement of retardates' mealtime behaviors by timeout procedures using multiple baseline techniques. *Journal of Applied Behavior Analysis,* 1970, **3,** 77–84.

Baumeister, A. A., & Forehand, R. Effects of contingent shock and verbal command on body rocking of retardates. *Journal of Clinical Psychology,* 1972, **28,** 586–590.

Benaroya, S., Wesley, S., Ogilvie, L. S., Klein, L. S., & Meaney, M. Sign language and multisensory input training of children with communication and related developmental disorders. *Journal of Autism and Childhood Schizophrenia,* 1977, **7,** 23–31.

Bender, L. Childhood schizophrenia. *Psychiatric Quarterly,* 1953, **27,** 663–681.

Bender, L. Schizophrenia in childhood: Its recognition, description and treatment. *American Journal of Orthopsychiatry,* 1956, **26,** 499–506.

Bender, L. Childhood schizophrenia: A review. *International Journal of Psychiatry,* 1968, **5,** 211–220.

Bereiter, C. Conclusions from evaluation studies. In J.

S. Stanley (Ed.), *Preschool programs for the disadvantaged child.* Baltimore: Johns Hopkins University, 1972.

Bereiter, C., & Engleman, W. *Teaching disadvantaged children in preschool.* Englewood Cliffs, N.J.: Prentice-Hall, 1966.

Berkowitz, S., Sherry, P. J., & Davis, B. A. Teaching self-feeding skills to profound retardates using reinforcement and fading procedures. *Behavior Therapy,* 1971, **2,** 62–67.

Bettelheim, B. *The empty fortress.* New York: Free Press, 1967.

Birnbrauer, J. S., Wolf, M. M., Kidder, J. D., & Tague, C. E. Classroom behavior of retarded pupils with token reinforcement. *Journal of Experimental Child Psychology,* 1965, **2,** 219–235.

Bostow, D. E., & Bailey, J. S. Modification of severe disruptive and aggressive behavior using brief time-out and reinforcement procedures. *Journal of Applied Behavior Analysis,* 1969, **2,** 31–37.

Bricker, W. A., & Bricker, D. D. A program of language training for the severely handicapped child. *Exceptional Children,* 1970, **37,** 101–111.

Bricker, W. A., & Bricker, D. D. An early language training strategy. In R. Schiefelbusch & L. Lloyd (Eds.), *Language perspectives: Acquisition, retardation and intervention.* Baltimore: University Park Press, 1974.

Bucher, B., & King, L. W. Generalization of punishment effects in the deviant behavior of a psychotic child. *Behavior Therapy,* 1971, **2,** 68–77.

Bucher, B., & Lovaas, O. I. Use of aversive stimulation in behavior modification. In M. R. Jones (Ed.), *Miami symposium on the prediction of behavior, 1967: Aversive stimulation.* Coral Gables: University of Miami Press, 1968.

Buddenhagen, R. *Establishing vocalizations in mute mongoloid children.* Champaign, Ill.: Research Press, 1971.

Butterfield, W. H., & Parson, R. Modeling and shaping by parents to develop chewing behavior in their retarded child. *Journal of Behavior Therapy and Experimental Psychiatry,* 1973, **4,** 285–287.

Cain, L. F., Levine, S., & Elzey, F. F. *Manual for the Cain-Levine Social Competency Scale.* Palo Alto: Consulting Psychologists Press, 1963.

Calhoun, J. F. *Abnormal psychology: Current perspectives,* 2nd ed. New York: Random House, 1977.

Carr, E. G. The motivation of self-injurious behavior: A review of some hypotheses. *Psychological Bulletin,* 1977, **84,** 800–816.

Carr, E. G., Newsom, C. D., & Binkhoff, J. A. Stimulus control of self-destructive behavior in a psychotic child. *Journal of Abnormal Child Psychology,* 1976, **4,** 139–153.

Cook, C., & Adams, H. E. Modification of verbal behavior in speech deficient children. *Behaviour Research and Therapy,* 1966, **4,** 265–271.

Cooke, T. P., & Apolloni, T. Developing positive social-emotional behaviors: A study of training and generalization effects. *Journal of Applied Behavior Analysis,* 1976, **9,** 65–78.

Corte, H. E., Wolf, M. M., & Locke, B. J. A comparison of procedures for eliminating self-injurious behavior of retarded adolescents. *Journal of Applied Behavior Analysis,* 1971, **6,** 251–259.

Creedon, M. *Language development in nonverbal autistic children using a simultaneous communication system.* Paper presented at the Society for Research in Child Development, Philadelphia, March 1973.

Creedon, M. *The David School: A simultaneous communication model.* Paper presented at the National Society for Autistic Children meeting, Oak Brook, Ill., June 1976.

DeMeyer, M. K., Barton, S., DeMeyer, W. E., Norton, J. A., Allen, J., & Steele, R. Prognosis in autism: A follow-up study. *Journal of Autism and Childhood Schizophrenia,* 1973, **3,** 199–246.

Doke, L. A., & Epstein, L. H. Oral overcorrection: Side effects and extended applications. *Journal of Experimental Child Psychology,* 1975, **20,** 496–511.

Doll, E. A. *Vineland Social Maturity Scale: Manual of directions.* Minneapolis: American Guidance Service, 1947.

Ellson, D., Barber, L., Engle, T., & Kampwerth, L. Programmed tutoring: A teaching aid and a research tool. *Reading Research Quarterly,* 1965, **1,** 77–127.

Epstein, L. H., Doke, L. A., Sajwaj, T. E., Sorrell, S., & Rimmer, B. Generality and side effects of overcorrection. *Journal of Applied Behavior Analysis,* 1974, **7,** 385–390.

Fenn, G., & Towe, J. A. An experiment in manual communication. *British Journal of Disorders of Communication,* 1975, **10,** 3–16.

Ferster, C. B. Positive reinforcement and behavioral deficits of autistic children. *Child Development,* 1961, **32,** 437–456.

Ferster, C. B., & DeMeyer, M. K. A method for the experimental analysis of the behavior of autistic children. In L. P. Ullmann & L. Krasner (Eds.), *Case studies in behavior modification.* New York: Holt, Rinehart and Winston, 1965.

Fish, B., & Shapiro, T. A typology of children's psychiatric disorders: I. Its application to a controlled evaluation of treatment. *Journal of the American Academy of Child Psychiatry,* 1965, **4,** 426.

Forehand, R., & Baumeister, A. Deceleration of aberrant behavior among retarded individuals. In M. Hersen, R. M. Eisler, & P. M. Miller (Eds.), *Progress in behavior modification,* Vol. 2. New York: Academic press, 1976.

Foxx, R. M., & Azrin, N. H. Restitution: A method of eliminating aggressive-disruptive behavior of retarded and brain damaged patients. *Behaviour Research and Therapy,* 1972, **10,** 15–27.

Foxx, R. M., & Azrin, N. H. The elimination of autistic self-stimulatory behavior by overcorrection. *Journal of Applied Behavior Analysis,* 1973, **6,** 1–14.

Freud, A. Problems of infantile neurosis: A discussion. *The Psychoanalytic Study of the Child,* 1954, **9,** 9–71.

Gottman, J., Gonso, J., & Schuler, P. Teaching social skills to isolated children. *Journal of Abnormal Child Psychology,* 1976, **4,** 179–197.

Greene, R. J., Hoats, D. L., & Hornick, A. J. Music distortion: A new technique for behavior modification. *Psychological Record,* 1970, **20,** 107–109.

Greenfield, J. *A child called Noah.* New York: Holt, Rinehart and Winston, 1970.

Groves, I. D., & Carroccio, D. F. A self-feeding program for the severely and profoundly retarded. *Mental Retardation,* 1971, **9,** 10–12.

Guess, D., Sailor, W., & Baer, D. M. To teach a language to retarded children. In R. L. Schiefelbusch (Ed.), *Language of the mentally retarded.* Baltimore: University Park Press, 1972.

Guess, D., Sailor, W., & Baer, D. M. *Functional speech and language training for the severely handicapped,* Parts I and II. Lawrence, Kan.: H. & H. Enterprises, 1977.

Guess, D., Sailor, W., Keogh, W. J., & Baer, D. M. Language development programs for severely handicapped children. In N. G. Haring & L. J. Brown (Eds.), *Teaching the severely handicapped,* Vol. 1. New York: Grune & Stratton, 1976.

Hamilton, J., & Standahl, J. Suppression of stereotyped screaming behavior in a profoundly retarded institutionalized female. *Journal of Experimental Child Psychology,* 1969, **7,** 114–121.

Hamilton, J. W., Stephens, L., & Allen, P. Controlling aggressive and destructive behavior in severely retarded institutionalized residents. *American Journal of Mental Deficiency,* 1967, **71,** 852–856.

Harris, S. L. Teaching language to nonverbal children with emphasis on problems of generalization. *Psychological Bulletin,* 1975, **82,** 565–580.

Hart, B. M., Reynolds, N. J., Baer, D. M., Brawley, E. R., & Harris, F. R. Effect of contingent and noncontingent social reinforcement on the cooperative play of a preschool child. *Journal of Applied Behavior Analysis,* 1968, **1,** 73–76.

Hewett, F. M. Teaching speech to an autistic child through operant conditioning. *American Journal of Orthopsychiatry,* 1965, **35,** 927–936.

Hutt, C., Hutt, S. J., Lee, D., & Ounstead, C. Arousal

and childhood autism. *Nature,* 1964, **204,** 908–909.

Jones, F. H., Simmons, J. Q., & Frankel, F. An extinction procedure for eliminating self-destructive behavior in a 9-year-old autistic girl. *Journal of Autism and Childhood Schizophrenia,* 1974, **4,** 241–250.

Kandel, H. J., Ayllon, T., & Rosenbaum, M. S. Flooding. A systematic exposure in the treatment of extreme social withdrawal in children. *Journal of Behavior Therapy and Experimental Psychiatry,* 1977, **8,** 75–81.

Kanner, L. Autistic disturbances of affective contact. *Nervous Child,* 1943, **2,** 217–250.

Kanner, L. *Child psychiatry,* 3rd ed. Springfield, Ill.: Thomas, 1972.

Kaufman, K. F., & O'Leary, K. D. Reward, cost, and self-evaluation procedures for disruptive adolescents in a psychiatric hospital school. *Journal of Applied Behavior Analysis,* 1972, **5,** 293–309.

Kaufman, M. E., & Levitt, H. A study of three stereotyped behaviors in institutionalized mental defectives. *American Journal of Mental Deficiency,* 1965, **69,** 467–473.

Kent, L. *Language acquisition program for the severely retarded.* Champaign, Ill.: Research Press, 1974.

Koegel, R. Selective attention to prompt stimuli by autistic and normal children. Unpublished doctoral dissertation, University of California, Los Angeles, 1971. Cited in Lovaas, O. I. Behavioral treatment of autistic children. In J. T. Spence, R. C. Carson, & J. W. Thibaut (Eds.), *Behavioral approaches to therapy.* Morristown, N.J.: General Learning Press, 1976.

Koegel, R. L., & Covert, A. The relationship of self-stimulation to learning in autistic children. *Journal of Applied Behavior Analysis,* 1972, **5,** 381–387.

Koegel, R. L., Firestone, P. B., Kramme, K. W., & Dunlap, G. Increasing spontaneous play by suppressing self-stimulation in autistic children. *Journal of Applied Behavior Analysis,* 1974, **7,** 521–528.

Koegel, R. L., & Rincover, A. Treatment of psychotic children in a classroom environment: I. Learning in a large group. *Journal of Applied Behavior Analysis,* 1974, **7,** 45–59.

Koegel, R. L., & Rincover, A. Some detrimental effects of using extra stimuli to guide learning in normal and autistic children. *Journal of Abnormal Child Psychology,* 1976, **4,** 59–71.

Koegel, R. L., & Schreibman, L. The role of stimulus variables in teaching autistic children. In O. I. Lovaas & B. Bucher (Eds.), *Perspectives in behavior modification with deviant children.* Englewood Cliffs, N.J.: Prentice-Hall, 1974.

Laws, D. R., Brown, R. A., Epstein, J., & Hocking, N. Reduction of inappropriate social behavior in disturbed children by an untrained paraprofessional therapist. *Behavior Therapy,* 1971, **2,** 519–533.

Lovaas, O. I. A program for the establishment of

speech in psychotic children. In N. H. Sloane & B. D. MacAulay (Eds.), *Operant procedures in remedial speech and language training*. Boston: Houghton Mifflin, 1968.

Lovaas, O. I. (producer). *Behavior modification: Teaching language to psychotic children*. New York: Appleton-Century-Crofts, 1969. (film)

Lovaas, O. I. Behavioral treatment of autistic children. In J. T. Spence, R. C. Carson, & J. W. Thibaut (Eds.), *Behavioral approaches to therapy*. Morristown, N.J.: General Learning Press, 1976.

Lovaas, O. I. *The autistic child: Language development through behavior modification*. New York: Irvington, 1977.

Lovaas, O. I., Berberich, J. P., Perloff, B. F., & Schaeffer, B. Acquisition of imitative speech by schizophrenic children. *Science*, 1966, **151**, 705–707.

Lovaas, O. I., Freitag, G., Gold, V. J., & Kassorla, I. C. Experimental studies in childhood schizophrenia: Analysis of self-destructive behavior. *Journal of Experimental Child Psychology*, 1965, **2**, 67–84.

Lovaas, O. I., Freitag, G., Kinder, M. I., Rubenstein, B. D., Schaeffer, B., & Simmons, J. Q. Establishment of social reinforcers in two schizophrenic children on the basis of food. *Journal of Experimental Child Psychology*, 1966, **4**, 109–125.

Lovaas, O. I., Freitas, L., Nelson, K., & Whalen, C. The establishment of imitation and its use for the development of complex behavior in schizophrenic children. *Behaviour Research and Therapy*, 1967, **5**, 171–181.

Lovaas, O. I., Koegel, R., Simmons, J. Q., & Long, J. S. Some generalizations and follow-up measures on autistic children in behavior therapy. *Journal of Applied Behavior Analysis*, 1973, **6**, 131–166.

Lovaas, O. I., Litrownik, A., & Mann, R. Response latencies to auditory stimuli in autistic children engaged in self-stimulatory behavior. *Behaviour Research and Therapy*, 1971, **9**, 34–49.

Lovaas, O. I., & Newsom, C. D. Behavior modification with psychotic children. In H. Leitenberg (Ed.), *Handbook of behavior modification and behavior therapy*. Englewood Cliffs, N.J.: Prentice-Hall, 1976.

Lovaas, O., Schaeffer, B., & Simmons, J. Building social behavior in autistic children by use of electric shock. *Journal of Experimental Research in Personality*, 1965, **1**, 99–109.

Lovaas, O. I., Schreibman, L., Koegel, R., & Rehm, R. Selective responding by autistic children to multiple sensory input. *Journal of Abnormal Psychology*, 1971, **77**, 211–222.

Lovaas, O. I., & Simmons, J. Q. Manipulation of self-destruction in three retarded children. *Journal of Applied Behavior Analysis*, 1969, **2**, 143–157.

MacMillan, D. L., Jones, R. L., & Aloia, G. F. The mentally retarded label: A theoretical analysis and review

of research. *American Journal of Mental Deficiency*, 1974, **79**, 241–261.

Mahler, M. On child psychosis in schizophrenia: Autistic and symbiotic infantile psychosis. In *Psychoanalytic study of the child*, Vol. 7. New York: International University Press, 1952.

Martin, G. L., McDonald, S., & Omichinski, M. An operant analysis of response interactions during meals with severely retarded girls. *American Journal of Mental Deficiency*, 1971, **76**, 68–75.

Merbaum, M. The modification of self-destructive behavior by a mother-therapist using aversive stimulation. *Behavior Therapy*, 1973, **4**, 442–447.

Miller, J., & Yoder, D. A syntax teaching program. In J. E. McLean, D. E. Yoder, & R. L. Schiefelbusch (Eds.), *Language intervention with the retarded: Developing strategies*. Baltimore: University Park Press, 1972.

Miller, J., & Yoder, D. An ontogenetic language teaching strategy for retarded children. In R. Schiefelbusch & L. Lloyd (Eds.), *Language perspectives: Acquisition, retardation and intervention*. Baltimore: University Park Press, 1974.

Moore, C., & Shiek, D. Toward a theory of early infantile autism. *Psychological Review*, 1971, **78**, 451–456.

Nedelman, D., & Sulzbacher, S. I. Dicky at 13 years of age: A long term success following early application of operant conditioning procedures. In G. Semb (Ed.), *Behavior analysis and education, 1972*. Lawrence: University of Kansas Press, 1972.

Nihira, K., Foster, R., Shellhas, M., & Leland, H. *Adaptive behavior scales*. Washington, D.C.: American Association on Mental Deficiency, 1969.

Nordquist, V. M., & Wahler, R. G. Naturalistic treatment of the autistic child. *Journal of Applied Behavior Analysis*, 1973, **6**, 79–87.

O'Brien, F., & Azrin, N. H. Developing proper mealtime behaviors of the institutionalized retarded. *Journal of Applied Behavior Analysis*, 1972, **5**, 389–399.

O'Brien, F., Bugle, C., & Azrin, N. H. Training and maintaining a retarded child's proper eating. *Journal of Applied Behavior Analysis*, 1972, **5**, 67–72.

O'Connor, R. D. Modification of social withdrawal through symbolic modeling. *Journal of Applied Behavior Analysis*, 1969, **2**, 15–22.

O'Leary, K. D., & Drabman, R. Token reinforcement programs in the classroom: A review. *Psychological Bulletin*, 1971, **75**, 379–398.

Ornitz, E. M., & Ritvo, E. R. Perceptual inconsistency in early infantile autism. *Archives of General Psychiatry*, 1968, **18**, 76–98.

Pendergrass, V. E. Effects of length of timeout from positive reinforcement and schedule of application in suppression of aggressive behavior. *Psychological Record*, 1971, **21**, 75–80.

Pervin, L. A. The need to predict and control under conditions of threat. *Journal of Personality*, 1963, **31**, 570–587.

Peterson, R. F., & Peterson, L. R. The use of positive reinforcement in the control of self-destructive behavior in a retarded boy. *Journal of Experimental Child Psychology*, 1968, **6**, 351–360.

Pollack, M., & Woerner, M. Pre- and perinatal complications and "childhood schizophrenia": A comparison of five controlled studies. *Journal of Child Psychology and Psychiatry*, 1966, **7**, 235–242.

Prochaska, J., Smith, N., Marzilli, R., Colby, J., & Donovan, W. Remote-control aversive stimulation in the treatment of head-banging in a retarded child. *Journal of Behavior Therapy and Experimental Psychiatry*, 1974, **5**, 285–289.

Repp, A. C., & Deitz, S. M. Reducing aggressive and self-injurious behavior of institutionalized retarded children through reinforcement of other behaviors. *Journal of Applied Behavior Analysis*, 1974, **7**, 313–324.

Repp, A. C., Deitz, S. M., & Speir, N. C. Reducing stereotypic responding of retarded persons by differential reinforcement of other behaviors. *American Journal of Mental Deficiency*, 1974, **79**, 279–284.

Rimland, B. *Infantile autism*. New York: Appleton-Century-Crofts, 1964.

Rimm, D. C., & Somervill, J. W. *Abnormal psychology*. New York: Academic Press, 1976.

Risley, T. The effects and side effects of using punishment with an autistic child. *Journal of Applied Behavior Analysis*, 1968, **1**, 21–34.

Risley, T., Hart, B., & Doke, L. Operant language development: The outline of a therapeutic technology. In R. L. Schiefelbusch (Ed.), *Language of the mentally retarded*. Baltimore: University Park Press, 1972.

Risley, T., & Wolf, M. Establishing functional speech in echolalic children. *Behaviour Research and Therapy*, 1967, **5**, 73–88.

Romanczyk, R. G., & Goren, E. R. Severe self-injurious behavior: The problem of clinical control. *Journal of Consulting and Clinical Psychology*, 1975, **43**, 730–739.

Rutter, M. Concepts of autism: A review of research. *Journal of Child Psychology and Psychiatry*, 1968, **9**, 1–25.

Rutter, M., & Lockyer, L. A five to fifteen year follow-up study of infantile psychosis: I. Description of the sample. *British Journal of Psychiatry*, 1967, **113**, 1169–1182.

Sachs, D. A. The efficacy of time-out procedures in a variety of behavior problems. *Journal of Behavior Therapy and Experimental Psychiatry*, 1973, **4**, 237–242.

Salzinger, K., Feldman, R., Cowan, J., & Salzinger, S. Operant conditioning of verbal behavior of two young speech deficient boys. In L. Krasner & L. Ullmann (Eds.), *Research in behavior modification*. New York: Holt, Rinehart and Winston, 1965.

Schreibman, L. Effects of within-stimulus and extra-stimulus prompting on discrimination learning in autistic children. *Journal of Applied Behavior Analysis*, 1975, **8**, 91–112.

Skinner, B. F. *Verbal behavior*. New York: Appleton-Century-Crofts, 1957.

Sloane, H. N., Johnson, M. K., & Harris, F. R. In H. N. Sloane & B. D. MacAulay (Eds.), *Operant procedures in remedial speech and language training*. Boston: Houghton Mifflin, 1968.

Staub, E., Tursky, B., & Schwartz, G. E. Self-control and predictability: Their effects on reactions to aversive stimulation. *Journal of Personality and Social Psychology*, 1971, **18**, 157–162.

Strain, P. S., Shores, R. E., & Timm, R. A. Effects of peer social imitations on the behavior of withdrawn preschool children. *Journal of Applied Behavior Analysis*, 1977, **10**, 289–298.

Stremel, K., & Waryas, C. A behavioral-psycholinguistic approach to language training. *American Speech and Hearing Monography*, 1974, **18**, 96–124.

Tate, B. G., & Baroff, G. S. Aversive control of self-injurious behavior in a psychotic boy. *Behaviour Research and Therapy*, 1966, **4**, 281–287.

Taterka, J., & Katz, J. Study of correlations between electroencephalographic and psychological patterns in emotionally disturbed children. *Psychosomatic Medicine*, 1955, **17**, 62–72.

Tawney, J., & Hipsher, L. Systematic instruction for retarded children: Illinois Program, Part II. Systematic language instruction. State of Illinois, Office of the Superintendent of Public Instruction, 1972.

Vukelich, R., & Hake, D. F. Reduction of dangerously aggressive behavior in a severely retarded resident through a combination of positive reinforcement procedures. *Journal of Applied Behavior Analysis*, 1971, **4**, 215–225.

Webster, C. D., McPherson, H., Soloman, L., Evans, M. A., & Kuchar, E. Communicating with an autistic boy with gestures. *Journal of Autism and Childhood Schizophrenia*, 1973, **3**, 337–346.

Webster, D. R., & Azrin, N. H. Required relaxation: A method of inhibiting agitative-disruptive behavior of retardates. *Behaviour Research and Therapy*, 1973, **11**, 67–78.

Wells, K. C., Forehand, R., Hickey, K., & Green, K. D. Effects of a procedure derived from the overcorrection principle on manipulated and nonmanipulated behaviors. *Journal of Applied Behavior Analysis*, 1977, **10**, 679–687.

Whitman, T. L., Mercurio, J. R., & Caponigri, V. Development of social responses in two severely retarded children. *Journal of Applied Behavior Analysis*, 1970, **3**, 133–138.

Whitney, L. R., & Barnard, K. E. Operant learning theory and nursing care of the retarded child. *Mental Retardation*, 1966, **4**, 26–29.

Wiesen, A. E., & Watson, E. Elimination of attention seeking behavior in a retarded child. *American Journal of Mental Deficiency*, 1967, **72**, 50–52.

Wing, J. Diagnosis, epidemiology and etiology. In J. Wing (Ed.), *Early childhood autism*. Oxford: Pergamon, 1966.

Wing, L. The handicaps of autistic children: A comparative study. *Journal of Child Psychology and Psychiatry*, 1969, **10**, 1–40.

Wolf, M., Risley, T., Johnson, M., Harris, F., & Allen, E. Application of operant conditioning procedures to the behaviour problems of an autistic child: A follow-up and extension. *Behaviour Research and Therapy*, 1967, **5**, 103–111.

Wolf, M., Risley, T., & Mees, H. Application of operant conditioning procedures to the behaviour problems of an autistic child. *Behaviour Research and Therapy*, 1964, **1**, 305–312.

Wolfensberger, W. *Normalization*. Toronto: National Institute on Mental Retardation, 1972.

seven

JUVENILE DELINQUENCY

We should not delude ourselves; working with juvenile delinquents is tough business. Juvenile delinquency is on the rise, despite the fact that social scientists have offered elaborate theories, federal and state governments have poured millions into innovative programs, and local municipalities have enforced strict curfews and other restrictions (U.S. Department of Justice, 1977a, b). Between 1940 and 1968, the number of adolescents convicted of serious crimes has doubled (Stratton & Terry, 1968), a rate that far exceeds the growth of the adolescent population. According to 1973 FBI reports, 34 percent of all crimes are committed by persons under eighteen years of age (Neitzel, Winett, MacDonald, & Davidson, 1977). By the age of eighteen, 11 percent of all adolescents have had formal contact with the criminal justice system for some type of law violation (President's Commission on Law Enforcement and Administrative Justice, 1967). According to Saleem Shah, director for Studies of Crime and Delinquency of the National Institute of Mental Health, "the phenomena of delinquency and crime constitute one of the most critical domestic problems presently facing the country" (1973, p. 12).

Social scientists have not found the "magic cure" for delinquency. Studies of one-to-one counseling with identified delinquents, community-based prevention programs with "predelinquents," and paraprofessional volunteer companionship programs have produced disappointing results (Davidson, 1976). Although a few investigators have found benefits from such social services, the majority of studies have shown these approaches to have minimal impact. What is more, methodological inadequacies in most of the research preclude any definitive statements regarding the long-term effects of traditional treatment methods. The general consensus among authorities in the area is that such programs hold little promise for significantly reducing delinquency (McCord, McCord, & Zola, 1959; Ross, 1974; Toby, 1965).

We will begin this chapter by discussing behavioral hypotheses regarding factors that contribute to juvenile delinquency. We will then consider the four major behavioral strategies for reducing delinquent behavior. Under each topic, we will describe specific treatment programs and discuss their effectiveness. In the last section of the chapter, we will consider possible limitations in the behavioral approach and briefly discuss alternative strategies that have been suggested.

POSSIBLE ETIOLOGY

At least five distinct theories of delinquency can be identified. They are the psychoanalytic, the biological, the conditionability, the sociological, and the social learning theories. However, only the sociological and the social learning theories have really had an influence on treatment methods. We will discuss the other three theories just briefly and then consider the two more important ones in more detail.

Psychoanalytic Theory

Freudians maintain that delinquent behavior is symptomatic of underlying conflict in the psyche and represents the youth's attempt to compensate for feelings of inadequacy (Aichhorn, 1935; Lindner, 1944). According to their theories, delinquent adolescents engage in antisocial behavior in order to be punished by authority figures and to gain recognition from peers. They feel badly about themselves and want to be punished while at the same time they seek the esteem of their peers. Many behavioral psychologists agree with psychoanalysts that delinquent behavior often represents the adolescent's attempt to gain peer approval. In many neighborhoods, antisocial behavior earns high status. A number of writers (for instance, Aichhorn, 1935; Healy & Bronner, 1926; Lindner, 1944) have considered the possibility of psychoanalytic causes in cases of delinquency, but for the most part Freudian theories have not been empirically validated and have received little serious consideration.

Biological Theories

At least three theories suggesting constitutional differences in delinquents have been offered. Researchers who have tried to identify delinquent youths according to physical attributes and body types (Cortes & Gatti, 1972; Sheldon, 1949) have obtained inconsistent results. Others (for example, Lange, 1931) have looked for genetic predispositions for delinquency by investigating the incidence of criminal behavior among family members. Research in this area has involved twin studies, but as is often the case in correlational twin studies, confoundings in research design make it difficult to draw firm conclusions.

The most recent interest in possible biological factors in delinquency comes from studies of chromosomal aberration associated with violent crimes by adults. Certain aggressive criminals have been found to have an extra Y chromosome;

instead of the usual forty-six chromosomes, they have forty-seven (Jacobs, Brunton, Melville, Brittain, & McClement, 1965). When first discovered, this abnormality, called the XYY genotype, received much attention in the press and a number of sensational mass murders were directly linked to it. After the initial excitement, the research was reevaluated; among other things, researchers discovered that the XYY genotype existed in many normal, law-abiding men. Furthermore, they discovered that the incidence of the abnormality is extremely rare among the criminal population, less than 3 percent. After considerable research into the relationship of the XYY genotype to criminality, the theory is no longer viewed as an explanation of criminality and delinquency.

Conditionability Theory

A number of researchers have suggested that delinquents may be constitutionally different from nondelinquents in terms of impulsivity and reaction to threat of punishment. On a variety of laboratory tasks, delinquents have been found to be impulsive and poor at delaying gratification and judging time (Barndt & Johnson, 1955; Rankin & Wikoff, 1964; Stein, Sarbin, & Kulik, 1968). They also tend to score higher than nondelinquents on scales of extroversion (Pierson & Kelly, 1963a, 1963b). These general patterns of traits are exhibited by what some have called the unsocialized psychopathic delinquent, who is characterized by extroversion and a defiance of authority (Quay, 1964).

Related to this pattern of behavior is what Eysenck (1964) has identified as the delinquent's lack of responsiveness to punishment. In a number of experiments with adult criminals diagnosed as psychopathic, researchers have found that these individuals do not respond as rapidly to stimuli signaling shock as do normals (Hare, 1965a,b,c; 1968). The findings have led researchers to hypothesize that perhaps delinquents do not develop appropriate levels of moral judgment and behavior because they are not controlled by the threat of punishment, presumed to be an important controlling factor for nondelinquents. In other words, the conditioning theory suggests that many adolescents "misbehave" because they are not afraid of being punished.

Although this research may describe a general constellation of traits characterizing the delinquent personality, it does not necessarily describe any particular delinquent individual. When researchers (Peterson, Quay, & Tiffany, 1961) attempted a cluster analysis to determine whether delinquent adolescents could be classified according to behavior patterns, they were unsuccessful. Individual adolescents could not be typed.

Sociological Theory

One of the most popular theories of juvenile delinquency is that delinquent behavior is acquired through exposure to economic and social conditions reinforcing criminal behavior and either punishing or extinguishing law-abiding behavior. This theory was first introduced in 1939 by E. H. Sutherland, who referred to it as the theory of differential association (Sutherland, 1939).

Perhaps the most clearly articulated extension of the sociological theory of delinquency is A. K. Cohen's subculture theory (1955). According to this theory, many youths in our culture cannot "make it" by prevailing high-achievement, middle-class standards. Because of academic, cultural, and economic deficits, a large number of adolescents are punished by failure, frustration, and social rejection when they try to compete in the middle-class arena. In order to obtain reinforcement, they must find another arena in which to compete. Thus they switch to a subculture reference group that functions according to a set of standards they can meet. The specific values of such groups vary considerably, but they are characterized in general by rejection of middle-class standards. In many gangs, being tough, daring, and merciless is absolutely necessary for getting along.

We are reminded in this connection of a story one of our colleagues tells about his attempts as an adolescent to make it with a neighborhood gang. Apparently, his friends challenged his masculinity and told him to prove how tough he was by stealing a car. He remembers that he really did not want to do it and felt very anxious, but that he knew he had to in order to be accepted by the

gang. One night he did steal a car with a group of friends. After enjoying the admiration and esteem of his peers for a few hours, he carefully parked the car under a street light with the ignition unlocked. His wish came true; during the night someone stole the car from *him*, thus alleviating his fears of being caught. The contingencies were clear, the reinforcers were strong, and our friend behaved accordingly. But one might ask: What happened? How did he end up being a university professor rather than a car thief? The answer is that another reference group, namely, his family, exerted stronger control and managed to encourage (rather, force) him to do well in school and find new friends.

The subculture theory makes sense: if you cannot get reinforcement in one place, you will find another place. The subcultural group sought by the individual depends upon a number of factors: what alternatives are available, which group's standards are most compatible with the individual's skills and assets, and the presence of competing contingencies from rival groups. Although the subcultural theory has not been directly translated into a specific method of treatment, it is theoretically consistent with behavioral intervention programs in which a great deal of attention is given to teaching skills that will help youths succeed in a middle-class, achievement-oriented society.

Social Learning Theory

Many theorists contend that delinquency is directly related to patterns of child rearing. The major thesis is that violence breeds violence. In a classic volume on social development, Albert Bandura and Richard Walters (1963) proposed that many parents actually teach their children to be aggressive. This training is not intentional on the parents' part, but by modeling aggressive behavior and encouraging their children to use physical force in handling disputes with friends and adults outside the home, the parents effectively foster aggression. The following transcript of an interview with the mother of an extremely aggressive boy shows the insidious nature of this training. "I" refers to the interviewer, "M" to the mother (Bandura & Walters, 1959, pp. 115–116).

I: Have you ever encouraged Earl to stand up for himself?

M: Yes. I've taught young Earl, and his Dad has. I feel he should stand up for his rights, so you can get along in this world.

I: How have you encouraged him?

M: I've told him to look after himself and don't let anybody shove him around or anything like that, but not to look for trouble. I don't want him to be a sissy.

I: Have you ever encouraged Earl to use his fists to defend himself?

M: Oh yes. Oh yes. He knows how to fight.

I: What have you done to encourage him?

M: When he was a little boy, he had a little pair of boxing gloves. His dad has been an athlete all his life, so his dad taught him.

I: Has he ever come to you and complained that another fellow was giving him a rough time?

M: Oh yes, when he was younger. I told him, "Go on out and fight it out yourself."

I: If Earl got into a fight with one of the neighbor's boys, how would you handle it?

M: Oh, he should fight it out himself. When he was a little fellow he used to fight his own battles . . .

I: What would you do if you found Earl teasing another fellow or calling him bad names?

M: That would be up to Earl. If the other boy wants to lick him, that would be up to Earl. He deserves it.

In a number of naturalistic studies of delinquents, researchers have observed characteristic patterns of child rearing. There is typically a much higher incidence of aggressive behavior modeled by parents in homes of delinquents than in homes of nondelinquents (Glueck & Glueck, 1950). The incidence of delinquency among sons of criminals is twice as great in homes where the father is cruel and violent in his disciplinary tactics than where he is not (McCord, McCord, & Zola, 1959). The general pattern of parental behavior associated with delinquency appears to be

rejection and hostility combined with criminal and antisocial behavior modeled by the father (Bandura & Walters, 1959).

Social learning theory does have more empirical support than do the others. However, most of the research is correlational in nature and subject to certain methodological problems. Without more rigorous research in the area, the social learning theory can be viewed only as tentative.

REDUCING DELINQUENCY

Our usual method of organization has been to consider specific problem behaviors and the behavioral techniques that have been used to eliminate them. In this chapter, we will discuss general programs of treatment instead. We make this change because behavioral psychologists, like most social scientists, have tended for the most part to view "delinquency" rather than specific "delinquent behaviors" as the problem. This is not to imply that behavior therapists do not focus on particular problems with individuals. Rather, their strategy is to work with these problems in the context of a pervasive treatment program designed to effect general changes in the clients' ways of dealing with the world. One very important reason for this approach is that the criminal justice system, not behavioral psychologists, actually identifies the problem (delinquency) and the clients. Because they control sentencing and parole, the courts often have a greater role in determining many critical aspects of treatment than do the persons supposedly in charge of treatment programs.

In our discussion of behavioral strategies of intervention, we will use the categories devised by John Burchard and Paul Harig (1976), who have identified three types of behavioral programs: institutional, community-based residential, and prevention. In order to place these programs in historical perspective, we will begin by describing the pioneer behavior program conducted by Ralph and Robert Schwitzgebel. Because their program does not clearly fit under any of these three categories, we will consider it separately. After discussing behavioral programs, we will consider an offshoot, youth advocacy.

Street Corner Research

The first systematic application of reinforcement principles to juvenile delinquency was a program developed by C. W. Slack (1960) and later expanded by the Schwitzgebels and their colleagues (Schwitzgebel, 1960, 1961, 1964, 1967; Schwitzgebel & Kolb, 1964; Schwitzgebel, Schwitzgebel, Pahnke, & Hurd, 1964), who worked in Cambridge, Massachusetts. The name Street Corner Research was coined because the project was conducted out of an urban storefront. It was described to the adolescents involved as a research program designed to learn how adolescents felt about personal issues. Like many other behavioral interventions with delinquents, the program did not focus directly on delinquent behavior, but rather on the adolescents' talking to counselors about their problems. Counselors avoided giving advice and telling the youths what to do. During one-hour counseling sessions held two or three times a week, the youths were reinforced with praise and cash bonuses for dealing with emotionally charged issues and for expressing themselves openly. Participants also received monetary rewards for doing chores at the center such as answering the telephone. The average length of participation was ten months.

In order to evaluate the effectiveness of the program, the posttreatment arrest records of the first twenty participants were compared to a similar group of juvenile delinquents who did not participate. The adolescents who participated did much better than the control subjects in terms of the number of arrests during the first three years following the program, averaging 2.4 arrests as opposed to 4.7 arrests for the control subjects. Moreover, the offenses they did commit after participating were less serious than those committed by control subjects. Although the project cannot be considered a success, it did set the stage for subsequent behavioral programs.

INSTITUTIONAL PROGRAMS

Initial attempts to apply behavior modification principles to rehabilitation of juvenile delinquents were introduced in state and federal correctional facilities for adjudicated youths (those found guilty of some crime). Implementing treatment programs with these individuals was not easy because many of the rules and regulations regarding parole and access to community resources were incompatible with some of the principles that the program directors wanted to apply. Administrative regulations did not permit many powerful reinforcement contingencies that the directors might have used. Through the wisdom of hindsight, many professionals now contend that effective behavior modification is impossible under such conditions. As we will discover shortly, most rehabilitation effort is now directed toward community-based treatment and preventive intervention.

During the mid-1960s, three major institutional programs used behavior modification. One was the **CASE (Contingencies Applicable to Special Education)** program at the National Training School (NTS), Washington, D.C., under the direction of Harold L. Cohen (Cohen & Filipczak, 1971; Cohen, Filipczak, & Bis, 1970). Another project was the Intensive Training Unit at the Murdock Center for Mental Retardation, Butner, North Carolina, directed by John D. Burchard (Burchard, 1967). The third was the Youth Training Research Project, Stockton, California, directed by Carl Jesness (Jesness & DeRisi, 1973). Each project operated along similar lines. Adjudicated youths participated in token economies in which academic achievement and prosocial behavior (for instance, cooperation, good manners, and friendliness) were reinforced with money, special privileges, and adult attention. The goals of the programs were also the same: to strengthen those behaviors presumed to be critical to success in the outside world. Because of the similarity among these programs, we will limit our discussion to a detailed description of CASE.

CASE

This was a two-phase project. The first was an eight-month demonstration phase in which sixteen volunteer inmates spent five mornings each week in a specially designed education unit at the NTS. The students had severe academic deficits, performing at least four years below grade level.

All were high school dropouts who showed no interest in academic subjects. In fact, they were hostile toward any form of schooling.

After preliminary academic testing, each student was given an individualized, self-paced program that focused on basic communication and arithmetic skills. Individual contingencies were established so that each student earned redeemable points for successful mastery of the material. A variety of backup reinforcers were used: points could be exchanged for commissary items (such as candy, soft drinks, and potato chips), Polaroid snapshots, use of recreational equipment (such as a record player, television, or exercise equipment), and "rental" of special areas for limited periods of time (that is, private study offices). As the students progressed through the educational program, the opportunity to work in advanced materials became a powerful reinforcer. Much to the staff's surprise, some of the students asked if they could take their algebra books to their "home" cottages after school. From the anecdotal reports of cottage staff, it appeared that the algebra books had become status symbols. Other students in the cottages asked about how they had gone so far ahead and commented that they must really be smart. Soon other CASE students started working harder so that they might have the opportunity to use the algebra books.

Not all of the students' mornings were spent doing academic work. Approximately one-half of the area set aside for the CASE project was designed for nonacademic activities. A lounge, game room, and small student offices were made available contingent upon satisfactory progress in the academic program. All the facilities could be rented with points. Contingencies were regulated so that all students had enough time to earn points and to enjoy the reinforcers they bought.

All the students showed marked improvement in academic achievement during the eight-month period. However, since the program aimed at demonstration rather than experimentation, Cohen and his colleagues did not have control groups using other methods that might have permitted a rigorous assessment of their program.

Phase II represented an extension of the procedures used during Phase I to a full twenty-four-hour day. Again, the goal was to strengthen those academic behaviors that were presumed to help the students reenter the public school system. In addition to earning points for academic achievement, CASE II students could receive points from the correction officers at the institution for "exemplary" social behavior.

The results were clearly positive. On the average, students remained in the program eight months and improved between one and two grade levels. In order to assess the impact of the program, Cohen and his colleague J. Filipczak (1971) compared CASE II students' progress with that of other, non-CASE students at the NTS. (Before reporting their results, we must point out that subject selection was not random. It is quite possible that CASE II students were somehow different from the general NTS population. However, although the practical constraints that affected their research are quite understandable, the problem of subject selection represents a serious methodological flaw.) For the CASE II students who were discharged directly from the program into the community, the recidivism rate (percentage of individuals who were reimprisoned) was 27 percent, whereas the overall recidivism rate for the NTS was 76 percent. Recidivism rates for students who were transferred from the project to other units of the institution before finally being discharged to the community were considerably higher (62.5 percent) but still significantly lower than the NTS average. However, at the end of three years, the rate of recidivism for CASE II students was the same as for other NTS students.

Cohen's results are very important. They show the benefits that can accrue from intensive academic remediation with underachieving delinquent youths. CASE students made significant academic gains. However, as Cohen and Filipczak (1971) readily acknowledged, the program was not enough. They reasoned that the contingencies existing in the youths' natural environment outweighed the benefits associated with their academic improvement. Cohen and Filipczak's (1971) position is quite clear: "We must stop building prisons for youth and begin investing our funds and energy to establish preventive systems within our present ongoing schools and community centers" (p. 143). This is a view shared by many authorities.

COMMUNITY-BASED RESIDENTIAL PROGRAMS

During the last decade, institutional treatment of delinquents has shifted decidedly toward community-based programs designed around a family-unit model. Throughout the country, various state and local agencies have acquired large, older homes in well-established neighborhoods and turned them into residences for delinquent adolescents. These homes are similar to halfway houses in their size and operation. Houseparents, usually a young married couple, live in the house and provide supervision and training for five to ten adolescents. During the day, these youths either go to school or to work, and during the evening they engage in various recreational and school-related activities. Each youth has clearly delineated household responsibilities and specific input into decisions made regarding how the house is to be run. These group homes are different from halfway houses in that youths go to the home *instead* of a correctional facility *before* rather than *after* institutionalization. They serve as an alternative to the large training school or correctional facility.

These group homes appear to have a number of potential advantages: (1) Because the number of individuals living together is relatively small compared to that of the typical correctional facility, the staff can usually give greater attention to each youth. (2) Since the living arrangements in group homes are similar to those in many of the youths' natural environments, the experiences they have in dealing with problems there may have greater applicability to their normal lives than would those they would have in a large correctional facility. That is, by living in a homelike setting within the community, they have greater opportunities to learn basic "survival" skills such as how to budget money, use public transportation, secure medical care, and so forth. (3) Related to the second advantage is the fact that the time and energy institutions usually spend teaching the youths how to be "good inmates" can be directed to more meaningful issues. In most institutional programs, at least 25 percent of the training is directed toward behaviors related to the orderly functioning of the institution. For instance, in the Youth Center Re-search Project, 45 percent of each student's daily earnings from the token economy had to be "convenience points" (points earned for behaviors relevant to the smooth operation of the institution). Such skills are typically not important in a group home and are therefore not specifically taught. (4) The group home may alleviate some of the negative side effects of institutionalization, such as disparaging self-labeling (Burchard & Harig, 1976).

All these possible advantages lead to the conclusion that gains made by means of community-based intervention *should* show greater generalization to the natural environment than similar gains made through institutional programs. Of course these are only *potential* advantages; it is conceivable that a group home could be established in which none of the advantages was realized. Without enlightened leadership, a group home could easily become a mini-institution. A secondary, though certainly not minor, advantage of community-based programs is that they are cheaper to operate than traditional treatment programs. On the average, they cost half as much per resident as correctional institutions (Vinter, Downs, & Hall, 1975).

Achievement Place

The most successful and well-researched community-based program is Achievement Place, Lawrence, Kansas, under the direction of Elery Phillips, Montrose Wolf, and Dean Fixsen at the University of Kansas (Wolf, Phillips, & Fixsen, 1972). The program began with three boys from low-income families who had committed minor offenses and with two houseparents, Elaine and Elery Phillips, trained at the University of Kansas in behavior modification. Since the program's inception in 1967, over a dozen reports evaluating its effectiveness have been published, and the Achievement Place model has been replicated in more than eighty group homes in twelve states (Kansas, North Carolina, Nebraska, Nevada, Arizona, Texas, Montana, Missouri, Colorado, Minnesota, Maryland, and Florida) and Canada.

As of the summer of 1976, a total of forty-one boys ranging in age from ten to sixteen years (average age, fourteen years) had been admitted to

Achievement Place: 61 percent white, 29 percent black, 7 percent Native American, and 2 percent Mexican-American (Wolf, Phillips, Fixsen, Braukmann, Kirigin, Willner, & Schumaker, 1976). Sixty percent of the youths came from families whose income was below $7,000 per year; 53 percent of all families were supported on welfare. The students' academic records before entering Achievement Place were generally poor; the youths' average grade in school for the year prior to entering the program was D minus. The mean recorded IQ was 91 (range of 73 to 113). Eighty percent of the youths were labeled by school authorities as behavior problems. All the youths had been adjudicated before entering the program and had an average of three contacts with the police or courts for the year prior to entering the program. They had all received some type of social service and had been given a variety of psychiatric diagnoses ranging from adolescent adjustment reaction and psychopathic personality to childhood schizophrenia and autism.

Achievement Place: The Concept. The basic assumptions underlying the Achievement Place model of training combine Cohen's (1955) subcultural theory and Bandura and Walter's (1963) social learning theory. The presumption is that the kinds of behaviors that typically get adolescents into trouble are not the result of psychopathology, but rather of unfortunate social learning histories. Because of inadequate training and education, ineffective incentives, poor adult models of prosocial behavior, and a delinquent peer group, youths acquire a repertoire of antisocial behaviors that bring them to the attention of the courts (Wolf, Phillips, Fixsen, Braukmann, Kirigin, Willner, & Schumaker, 1976). The goal of Achievement Place is to provide these youths with training and support to enable them to acquire the social, academic, and vocational skills that are presumed to be critical to success in the community.

Achievement Place can be characterized as a relatively straightforward token economy implemented in a structured family setting. On one level, the program is really quite simple: youths receive special privileges and extra reinforcers contingent upon good behavior. However, at another level it is extremely complex: youths are encouraged to develop a close relationship with the teaching-parents who provide guidance and support. Wolf and colleagues (1976) use the term "teaching-parent" in order to emphasize the teaching role of the supervisory staff and to distinguish them from the more traditional, untrained custodial houseparent. In addition to training within the context of the living unit, the teaching-parent's major role is that of an advocate for the youth. The teaching-parent gives students assistance in coping with community agencies, getting jobs, and dealing with school personnel. The Achievement Place model clearly represents a *total* social service delivery system.

During its ten-year history, the Achievement Place concept has been modified and refined. One of the most impressive qualities of the program has been the willingness of its directors to alter their procedures in response to feedback provided by their own research and by their clients. As we discuss the program in detail, it should become clear that the evolution of the Achievement Place model parallels, in many ways, the evolution of behavior modification. It has progressed to considering more and more complex issues to be within the domain of behavioral intervention.

The Achievement Place model has four main areas of concentration: (1) skills training, (2) a token economy reinforcement system, (3) student government, and (4) relationship building. To best explain the model we review the operations of the token economy, discuss how a youth typically progresses through the program, and outline an average day at Achievement Place.

The Achievement Place Token Economy. After a new student has had a tour of the home, met the other students, and unpacked, the teaching-parents explain the operation of the home. They carefully outline the goals of the program, what is expected of each student, and the workings of the token economy. From the very first day the parents try to establish a close and positive relationship with the students. One of their primary aims is to express affection, concern, and respect for the youths in ways that they can understand and accept.

In the token economy in which all students par-

Table 7–1. Behaviors and the Number of Points Earned or Lost

Behaviors That Earned Points	Points
1. Watching news on TV or reading the newspaper	300 per day
2. Cleaning and maintaining neatness in one's room	500 per day
3. Keeping one's person neat and clean	500 per day
4. Reading books	5 to 10 per page
5. Aiding houseparents in various household tasks	20 to 1,000 per task
6. Doing dishes	500 to 1,000 per meal
7. Being well dressed for an evening meal	100 to 500 per meal
8. Performing homework	500 per day
9. Obtaining desirable grades on school report cards	500 to 1,000 per grade
10. Turning out lights when not in use	25 per light

Behaviors That Lost Points	Points
1. Failing grades on the report card	500 to 1,000 per grade
2. Speaking aggressively	20 to 50 per response
3. Forgetting to wash hands before meals	100 to 300 per meal
4. Arguing	300 per response
5. Disobeying	100 to 1,000 per response
6. Being late	10 per minute
7. Displaying poor manners	50 to 100 per response
8. Engaging in poor posture	50 to 100 per response
9. Using poor grammar	20 to 50 per response
10. Stealing, lying, or cheating	10,000 per response

Source: E. L. Phillips, Achievement Place: Token reinforcement procedures in a home-style rehabilitation setting for "pre-delinquent" boys. *Journal of Applied Behavior Analysis,* 1968, **1,** Table 1, p. 214. By permission of JABA, Department of Human Development, University of Kansas, Lawrence, Kansas.

ticipate, redeemable tokens (points) are earned or lost contingent upon the student's behavior. Desirable behaviors are positively reinforced and undesirable behaviors punished (through response costs). Table 7–1 provides a partial list of the target behaviors and their point assignments. In addition to these behaviors, students typically have others that earn and lose points. These additional target behaviors (for example, helping other students and being cooperative) are specifically related to the student's individual program.

A variety of backup reinforcers is available. They range from the privilege to go downtown (1,000 points) to use of woodworking tools (500 points). The number of points charged for most of these reinforcers is stable from week to week. Prices are adjusted for those items whose relative importance shifts from time to time. For instance, the number of points required to watch television increases during the winter months. Another exception to this fixed-price list is the cost of "one-of-a-kind" events, such as the opportunity to go to a rock concert or a college basketball game. For these events, an auction is held and the highest bidders get the reinforcers.

Exchanging points for backup reinforcers is handled in a very straightforward, businesslike manner. Each student knows how many points he has to spend and the cost of each item. Students are free to spend their points any way they wish, and often they elect to save their points to purchase a special high-priced item. In addition to serving as a powerful incentive system, the token economy gives the student firsthand experience in managing his earnings, using basic mathematics, and saving.

The first day a youth is in the program all privileges are free. After this brief orientation period, he is placed on a daily point system in which points are exchanged for backup reinforcers throughout the day at six-, three-, or one-hour intervals. The frequency of point exchanges depends on the youth's adjustment to the system. If he shows difficulty grasping the system, exchanges are scheduled more frequently. As he begins to understand how the system operates, the intervals are gradually extended until he is up to one exchange each day. After the student has succeeded in earning points consistently for one week, he is shifted to the weekly point system. Exchanges are scheduled on a weekly basis, and points earned during one week are exchanged for backup reinforcers for the following week. After the student has shown improvement on the weekly point system for four consecutive weeks, he moves to the merit system in which points are no longer used and all privileges are free. During this time, the staff carefully assesses his progress to determine how well he might do without the support of the token system. If the youth's behavior starts to deteriorate under the merit system, the weekly point system is reinstated.

The last level is the homeward-bound system to which the youth graduates after four successful weeks on the merit system. Homeward-bound involves the student's making a shift from living at Achievement Place to living in his own home. This move is gradual, beginning with the youth's spending only two or three nights a week at home. Depending on the youth's adjustment, the shift continues until finally he is spending all his nights at home. Throughout the youth's stay, the teaching-parents meet with the youth's family to discuss possible ways the parents might enhance reciprocal reinforcement and cooperation. The goals and needs of family members are discussed and clarified with the aim of arriving at agreement of expectations.

An important aspect of the point system is the daily classroom report card, which is often used with the students (Bailey, Wolf, & Phillips, 1970). During the daily and weekly point system phases, the student's classroom teacher notes whether or not the youth has done his assigned work and obeyed the classroom rules. Positive reports earn points, negative reports cost points.

A Day at Achievement Place. The typical day at Achievement Place begins with breakfast and the completion of certain housekeeping chores. Most of the students then go off to school. Since the program is community-based, the majority of the youths remain in their regular public school classes during their stay at Achievement Place. This feature of the program has many obvious advantages: (1) The youth has no problem of adjusting to a new classroom in the program and then readjusting upon returning home. (2) The teaching-parents have the opportunity to work with the classroom teacher and the student on *real* problems encountered in school. (3) The classroom teacher can serve as a valuable resource for suggestions as to the most appropriate academic and social programs and for feedback on their effectiveness.

Afternoons are spent having fun, doing homework, participating in individualized training programs, and preparing dinner. Youths typically take turns doing general household chores such as cleaning the bathrooms and taking out the trash.

After dinner all the students and the teaching-parents hold a meeting in which issues regarding the management of the house are discussed. Issues might include a reevaluation of the rules and point assignments, as well as general discussions of the day's events. During this meeting, methods of effective self-government, such as negotiation, compromise, and constructive criticism, are taught. One-to-one counseling sessions are also scheduled during the evening. The teaching-parent and the student discuss how the student is getting along with the other students, how he feels about the program, and pressing personal problems. A primary focus of these sessions is effective problem solving in the area of interpersonal relations. They might discuss an argument or conflict the student had and consider alternative ways of responding. The teaching-parents are careful to show their honest concern and affection as well as to provide strong emotional support.

Research and Evaluation

As we mentioned earlier, Achievement Place is perhaps the most carefully researched program in the country. At least thirty separate experiments have been conducted and two large outcome evaluations have been done (Trotter, 1973; Braukmann, Kirigin, & Wolf, 1976). Moreover, the directors of Achievement Place have been engaged in research to evaluate "consumer (client) satisfaction" (Wolf, 1976). They have been obtaining data on the students' subjective reactions to the program. This type of broad-spectrum research, indeed unusual in behavior modification as well as in juvenile delinquency, clearly permits comprehensive evaluation of the programs.

Almost all the thirty separate experiments have involved individual analyses of specific reinforcement contingencies in the token economy. Although these studies have conclusively demonstrated the efficacy of the token system as a means of modifying a variety of behaviors, many of the studies have been criticized on the grounds that the target behaviors changed are trivial (Burchard & Harig, 1976; Davidson & Seidman, 1974; Emery & Marholin, 1977). Indeed, it is difficult to understand how improvement in keeping a bathroom clean, being punctual, and avoiding the use of "ain't" (to name a few of the behaviors that have been studied) are relevant to the problems of the delinquent youth.

There has been a shift toward evaluating Achievement Place in terms of variables more relevant to the problems of delinquency. An example of this new focus is a study concerning methods used in Achievement Place to improve juvenile-police interaction (Werner, Minkin, Minkin, Fixsen, Phillips, & Wolf, 1975). In order to identify relevant target behaviors, police officers were interviewed and completed a questionnaire assessing their reactions to a variety of youth behaviors. Two of the most critical behavioral components were politeness and cooperation. Agreement among police officers that youths should not curse, argue, interrupt, give unclear answers, or be uncooperative when dealing with an officer reached 95 percent. The officers also felt that it was important that youths maintain eye contact, be attentive, and let the officer know that they understand what is being said. Werner and his colleagues then proceeded to teach six Achievement Place youths the positive behaviors the police had identified. The youths received instructions and rationales as well as demonstrations and practice

with feedback. Each youth was paid one dollar for participation in each session. Training was quite detailed, focusing on tone of voice, length of answer, and expression of understanding.

In order to assess the training package, police officers were asked to rate pretraining and posttraining videotapes of trained and untrained youths interacting with an officer; the officers were not told which youths had undergone training. Figure 7–1 shows the officers' mean pretraining and postratings across eight behavioral components. Except for cooperation, trained youths improved significantly more on each component than untrained youths. Although this study does not show how youths fare in actual interaction with police after training, it does suggest that such a training program improved interaction. Of course, some social critics might argue that the program was backward—the police officers might also have benefited from such training. What's more, a more worthwhile strategy might have been to teach the youths how to avoid getting into trouble in the first place.

In the most recent outcome evaluation of Achievement Place, the delinquency and reinstitutionalization records for Achievement Place students were compared with those for youths who participated in programs based on the Achievement Place model (replications) and for youths from Kansas correctional facilities *not* operated on the model (comparison homes). When youths were in the program, the rate of offenses dropped to .9 per student, whereas the rate for the comparison group increased to 7.3 per student. Results for the A.P. replication homes were mixed: the first two replication homes appear to have been less effective than the later replications.

The directors of the program have suggested that differences may be due to certain aspects of the model (personal counseling, self-government, and relationship building) not present in the first two replications but included in later ones. The rate of reinstitutionalization during the first year after termination was much lower for Achievement Place and its replications than for the comparison homes, although the rate of posttreatment offenses was high for all groups.

The directors of Achievement Place clearly recognize the limitations of their program and are using their research findings as a guide to how to

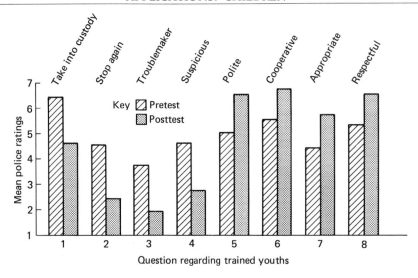

Figure 7–1. Plots of the mean ratings of five police officers for the trained youths in the pre- and posttest. This figure, drawn from "Intervention Package": An analysis to prepare juvenile delinquents for encounters with police officers, by John S. Werner, Neil Minken, Bonnie L. Minken, Dean L. Fixsen, Elery L. Phillips, & Montrose M. Wolf, is reprinted from *Criminal Justice and Behavior*, 1975, **2**, 55–84, by permission of the publisher, Sage Publications, Inc.

modify it. One strategy has been to implement an after-care advocate program. Rather than teaching-parents' terminating their involvement when the youths leave the program, they now maintain formal contact and provide continued support. The directors are also considering that these youths may need to stay in the program longer than a few months—perhaps throughout the high-risk years of adolescence. In addition, there is an increased awareness of the importance of the youths' establishing good relationships with the teaching-parents. Subjective data on the youths' satisfaction with the program indicated that the greater a youth's satisfaction with the program, the lower the offense rate during the treatment. (Offense rates during treatment and overall student/consumer ratings correlated −.71.) Prospective teaching-parents now receive specific training in how to show empathy and caring as well as how to relate to adolescents. Furthermore, the youths' subjective ratings of the teaching-parents are now used in evaluating staff for certification. By implementing these changes, the direc-

tors hope to increase the long-term effectiveness of the program.

As we stated earlier, the Achievement Place model is not static. Its procedures are continually being refined and updated. The model serves as a clear example of an empirically based intervention program.

PREVENTION PROGRAMS

The idea of correcting a problem before it becomes full-blown and leads to a more serious problem is very appealing. This hope of preventing juvenile delinquency has motivated "big brother" type companionship programs and early intervention projects. However, before we discuss the application of behavior modification principles in the prevention of delinquency, we must point out the difficulties associated with trying to identify children who may stand a high risk of becoming delinquent.

First is the problem of determining what childhood behaviors are predictive of later delinquency. Although research has shown definite correlations between later delinquency and both academic failure and poor family relationships during early adolescence (Cohen & Filipczak, 1971; Stuart, 1971), it is not known whether these relationships are in fact causal. Nevertheless, most prevention programs are predicated on the possibly false assumptions that academic failure and family conflict lead to delinquency.

Second is the problem of labeling children "predelinquents." In many cases, such labels do prejudice teachers, mental health professionals, and correctional officers. They stigmatize children and set up negative expectancies in those responsible for their well-being. A very real consideration is whether the potential benefits of most prevention programs outweigh the effects of these negative expectancies. Some critics think not (Rappaport, 1977; Schur, 1973).

In many ways, behavioral prevention programs for predelinquents are similar to the residential programs discussed above. The major difference is that prevention programs are generally directed toward younger children residing in their natural homes. Behavioral programs designed to prevent delinquency have generally focused on one or both of two areas: special remedial education and behavioral contracting within the adolescent's family.

Special Remedial Education

Prevention through early remedial education has provided predelinquents with individualized instruction and powerful material reinforcers for achievement. In one of the best-known programs (PICA, Programming Interpersonal Curricula for Adolescents), Cohen and his colleagues extended the CASE model to a day program for underachieving adolescents whose behavior problems were considered serious by school personnel (Cohen, Filipczak, Slavin, & Boren, 1971). Junior high school students spent approximately two and one-half hours each day in the program working on self-paced programs in math and English; they also received special instruction in problem areas such as social relations, sex, and legal rights and responsibilities. In addition, students partici-

pated in an individualized token reinforcement system. During the first year of the program's operation, students showed marked progress; their grades in subjects covered in the program increased an average of three letter grades, whereas grades in other subjects decreased an average of one letter grade. Although these results are impressive, Cohen and his colleagues did not determine whether the program had any effect on the probability of later delinquency—the central question. Without that information, it is difficult to assess the full impact of their prevention program.

Behavioral Contracting

The notion of actually negotiating contracts between adolescents and their parents was first proposed by Roland Tharp and Ralph Wetzel (1969). In their clinical work with delinquent adolescents, they found that often family members had such bad relationships that formal agreements had to be drawn up in which each party explicitly stated what he or she would do and what reinforcers would be expected.

Richard Stuart and his colleagues (Jayaratne, Stuart, & Tripodi, 1974; Stuart, 1971; Stuart & Lott, 1972; Stuart & Tripodi, 1973; Stuart, Tripodi, Jayaratne, & Camburn, 1976) have extended Tharp and Wetzel's original formulations in a federally funded counseling program for adolescents (Family and School Consultation Project). Most of their contracts were quid pro quo agreements in which each person agreed to change a behavior that would be a reinforcer for the other person. For example, a mother might agree to stop complaining about the length of her son's hair if he carried out the trash each afternoon. One such contract is presented in Case Study 7–2.

In a study involving 102 adolescents referred by school officials for counseling, Stuart and his associates (Stuart, Tripodi, Jayaratne, & Camburn, 1976) found that behavioral contracting improved the general quality of the adolescents' social interaction and adjustment but did not affect their classroom performance. Compared to randomly assigned no-treatment control subjects, students who participated in behavioral contracting with their parents showed significant improvement in terms of global ratings of their social-academic behavior made by parents and teachers. Unfortunately, academic performance, as measured by grades (the primary focus of the contracts) and school attendance was unaffected

The possible benefits of behavioral contracting are demonstrated more clearly in an extensive outcome study of ninety-nine families referred by the Salt Lake City County Juvenile Court (Alexander & Parsons, 1973). Psychologists at the Family Clinic at the University of Utah offered predelinquent adolescents, who had been arrested for such offenses as shoplifting and the possession of drugs, and their families a comprehensive treatment program including training in behavior management, communication skills, and behavioral contracting. Subjects matched on delinquency records were randomly assigned to one of three groups (no-treatment control, behavioral intervention, client-centered/psychoanalytic). Six to eighteen months following the six-month intervention program, all subjects received an extensive followup evaluation. The families who received the behavioral intervention demonstrated significantly greater improvement on measures of communication (greater frequency of equal verbal exchange and constructive feedback among family members) than did families in either of the other two groups. What is more, adolescents in the behavioral group showed significantly lower rates of recidivism than adolescents in the other groups. The authors concluded that the results lend confidence to the belief in the effectiveness of behavioral prevention programs in changing problematic family interactions.

Behavioral contracting can have a number of positive side effects. Stuart (1971) has reported that behavioral contracting results in a general improvement in family relations by changing the ratio of positive to negative interactions among family members. In Case Study 7–2 the exchange of positive reinforcers between family members is increased after contracts are introduced. A second possible benefit is that contracts ensure a fairer balance of power. Since all the issues covered by the contract are negotiated, arbitrary decisions and rule by fiat on the part of the parents are presumably reduced, and the adolescent should

have more effective methods of countercontrol. The introduction of a counselor into the family can also have beneficial consequences. Serving as a mediator during the initial stages of contracting, the counselor attempts to (1) create an atmosphere within the family in which each member feels free to express his or her desires, (2) present a rationale for changing behavior that does not involve family members' "losing face," and (3) teach the family basic communication skills to improve later interaction and reduce interpersonal conflict.

YOUTH ADVOCACY

Prompted by the disappointing results of institutional programs, the focus of behavior modification programs for delinquents has gradually shifted during the last three years. Although token economy programs were able to effect radical changes in the youths' behavior while they were in the institution, the gains were not maintained when the adolescents returned to their local communities. The emphasis is now on community-based intervention in which youths receive training and assistance in dealing with the actual problems they encounter in their daily lives. In line with this has come a growing interest in providing advocacy services for youths.

Youth advocacy involves helping youths to effectively manage the various service systems that they must use in order to "survive." For instance, advocacy might include assisting a youth to deal with an irate teacher, fill out a job application, or obtain special health services. Much of the effort is directed toward teaching youths effective problem-solving skills. This often involves teaching them how to work within the system in ways that will ensure that they satisfy their individual needs without antagonizing those in authority. The goal is for the person to become his or her own advocate and to learn critical negotiation skills in dealing with those individuals and community agencies that can provide relevant social support.

Although the notion of providing advocacy services for delinquent adolescents has been incorporated into at least two behavior modification

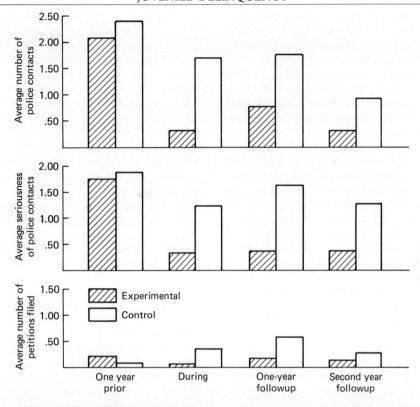

Figure 7–2. Police and court record data for youths in advocacy program and control subjects. From E. Seidman, J. Rappaport, & W. S. Davidson, Adolescents in legal jeopardy: Initial success and replication of an alternative to the criminal justice system. APA convention, Washington, D.C., 1976. Unpublished manuscript; used by permission.

programs (Achievement Place and Burchard's Hunt School Program, Burlington, Vermont), to date only one program has been specifically designed to provide advocacy services, and its outcome results are overwhelmingly positive. The program was instituted by psychologists Edward Seidman, Julian Rappaport, and William Davidson (Davidson & Robinson, 1975; Davidson & Rapp, 1976; Seidman, Rappaport, & Davidson, 1977) in conjunction with the local police in the Champaign-Urbana, Illinois, area. As will become evident, the program might best be described as a combination of early diversion from the criminal justice system and training in relationship skills, behavioral contracting, and youth advocacy. The twenty-five youths who participated had been charged with various crimes such as car theft and vandalism. Mean number of police contacts in the year prior to referral was 2.16. The age range was 11 to 17 years, and the mean age was 14.1 years; the average youth was in the eighth grade.

Referral to the program was made immediately after the youth had been charged and before any formal court action could be taken. The purpose was to divert youths from the criminal justice system as soon as possible in order to avoid its possibly damaging side effects (Rappaport, 1977). The notion was that if youths could receive services without being involved with the justice system, they would not be subjected to the negative expectations of parents, teachers, and peers that many theorists believe foster increased antisocial behavior. As soon as a youth was referred, police dropped all charges and terminated their involvement. Seidman and his colleagues also recognized the possibility that even participation in their program might result in derogatory labeling, and for that reason, were careful to avoid involving youths prematurely. Youths were referred to the program only when court action was imminent (Rappaport, 1978, personal communication).

The actual intervention involved specific training in relationship skills (that is, effective interpersonal communication), behavioral contracting, and youth advocacy. Training in the first two areas focused on how to deal with interpersonal contingencies involving parents, teachers, and other authority figures. Many of the procedures were based on Stuart's (1971) contracting project with adolescents. In the advocacy training, youths were taught how to develop legitimate means for attainment of their personal goals. In all cases, training was directly tied to the actual conflicts and situations the youths faced in their daily interactions.

Each youth was assigned an undergraduate college student who served as a counselor/advocate. During the three- to five-month intervention, the college student (who was supervised by a graduate student in clinical psychology) met with the youth on a weekly basis and provided training in contingency contracting and advocacy. In each case, the college student interventionist began by working with the youth to identify specific problems and then explored various alternatives. A major focus was on negotiation skills. The college student first modeled these skills for the youth and then provided the youth with opportunities to practice.

Figure 7–2 compares the results for students who participated in the program with those for randomly assigned, no-treatment control subjects. As is clear from the graphs, recidivism rates for youths who participated in the program were significantly lower than for control subjects; specifically: (1) youths in the program had fewer contacts with police, (2) the contacts they did have were of lesser severity, and (3) they had fewer petitions filed against them.

In their subsequent research, Seidman, Rappaport, and Davidson (1977) assessed the separate effects on similar youths of training in behavioral contracting and youth advocacy and found no differences. Both types of training were equally effective. An especially interesting finding was that youths who got into trouble with the police (regardless of the type of training they received) lacked strong social support systems. That is, they had low levels of involvement at home, with the school, and with sources of meaningful employment. Seidman and his associates hypothesized that the establishment of a strong social support system is crucial in the reduction of delinquency. Although this hypothesis must be subjected to future examination, it is interesting to note that it is consistent with many of the conclusions drawn from the Achievement Place project.

SUMMARY

Behavioral programs for juvenile delinquents can be divided into three categories: institutional, community-based residential, and preventive. The best-known institutional program is a token economy established at the National Training School in Washington, D.C., by Harold Cohen. Cohen's CASE program serves as a model for most behavioral residential programs. Adjudicated youths participated in an individualized training program in which academic achievement and prosocial behavior were reinforced with redeemable tokens. The goal of the program was to strengthen those behaviors that were presumed to be critical to success in the outside world. All the students in the CASE program showed marked improvement in academic achievement; however, their long-term (three-year) recidivism rate was no different than for other NTS students. These results led Cohen and others in the area to conclude that programs for delinquent youths must be conducted in the context of the youths' local community.

Achievement Place, originally started in 1967 by Phillips, Wolf, and Fixsen at the University of Kansas, is the most successful and well-documented community-based treatment program for delinquents and has now been replicated in twelve states. Its basic assumptions and goals are similar to those of CASE. The aim is to provide adolescents with the intellectual and social skills they need to survive in a middle-class society. At a simpler level, youths receive privileges and special treats contingent upon good behavior; at a more complex level, youths are encouraged to develop close relationships with teaching-parents who provide guidance and support. The program has four major areas of concentration: skills training, a token reinforcement system, student government, and relationship building. All students progress through four levels, daily point, weekly point, merit, and homeward bound, each of which involves successively greater independence and more responsibility for youths until they are able to manage their own behavior without the support of the token reinforcement system. Outcome results for Achievement Place are mixed. Although rates of reinstitutionalization for Achievement Place students are much lower than for youths from other, nonbehavioral programs, the records of posttreatment offenses for Achievement Place youths are no better than for other delinquents. The directors are now refining their program, focusing on youth advocacy and relationship building in an effort to increase its long-term effectiveness.

Among the various prevention programs devised, most have focused on academic and social training. One strategy has been to teach adolescents and their families how to negotiate and establish behavioral contracts in which the exchange of positive reinforcers between family members is increased. Preliminary research suggests that contracting has a positive effect on adolescent adjustment and reduces delinquency.

Recently, youth advocacy has received an enthusiastic response. Although this strategy has not been extensively researched, the one evaluation that has been conducted indicates that it may be one of the most effective ways of steering adolescents away from delinquency.

CASE STUDY 7–1

LYSAGHT, T. V., & BURCHARD, J. D. THE ANALYSIS AND MODIFI-
CATION OF A DEVIANT PARENT-YOUTH COMMUNICATION PAT-
TERN. *JOURNAL OF BEHAVIOR THERAPY AND EXPERIMENTAL PSY-
CHIATRY*, 1975, **6**, 339–342.

Interaction within families of delinquents is often characterized by hostility
and insult; positive feedback and affection are rare. Family members argue
rather than discuss, criticize rather than compliment. This case describes a
program designed to improve the quality of interaction between a 12-year-
old boy, Joey, and his mother.

Joey was enrolled in a community-based group home for boys with learning and behavior problems. He had been referred for refusing to go to
school. In addition to a number of severe academic and social deficits, Joey
viewed himself as inadequate and would often make self-deprecating remarks. His mother's reaction to him was generally negative. In discussions with the home's staff she focused on Joey's shortcomings and rarely
praised his accomplishments. She typically responded to Joey only when
he did something she did not like. She almost never expressed approval.
Baseline behavioral assessment confirmed the staff's opinions. Systematic
observation of Joey and his mother when they were engaged in structured
discussions of Joey's progress in the program revealed that the mother gave
a disproportionate amount of her attention to Joey's inappropriate behavior. Furthermore, the mother's rate of giving praise was only one-third as
high as her rate of criticism.

The intervention program was quite simple: The mother was given direct
instructions and feedback on how to be more supportive with her son. She
was told to carry on two structured discussions with Joey each weekend
during his two-day visit home. These were to center on Joey's weekly program progress report and her reactions to his weekly essay. Both conversations were recorded. During the mother's weekly conference with one of
the program's staff members, the tape of the conversation concerning Joey's
progress was played, and the staff member gave explicit instructions as to
how she might focus on his achievements, become more supportive, and
express greater approval. The staff member also discussed her negativism
and pointed out how she tended to dwell on Joey's deficits rather than his
assets.

In order to evaluate the effectiveness of the program, Lysaght and Burchard coded all the taperecordings. They noted the frequency of the
mother's praise and criticism and whether she focused on Joey's strengths
or his weaknesses. Then they compared preintervention baseline conversations with conversations made following intervention. In order to determine whether or not the effects of their feedback to the mother had generalized to other interactions, they also compared the conversations concerning
Joey's progress (which had been discussed each week by the staff member
and Joey's mother) with the conversations about his essays (which had not
been discussed). The staff's constructive feedback had an immediate effect: the mother's criticism fell to zero. This effect was not limited to the
task that was the focus of the staff's feedback; it generalized to the conversa-

tions on Joey's essays. The mother's use of praise, however, did not generalize. The rate of praise increased only after the staff member gave her specific directions about how to be more positive and supportive in the essay discussions.

In their report, Lysaght and Burchard recognized the limited focus of their case study and suggested that the question of generalization of the suppression of criticism versus the lack of generalization of the use of praise will require more research. Although limited in its scope, the case demonstrates the possibility of substantially modifying a parent's negativistic pattern of interaction by means of didactic discussion and constructive feedback.

CASE STUDY 7–2

STUART, R. B. BEHAVIORAL CONTRACTING WITHIN FAMILIES OF DELINQUENTS. *JOURNAL OF BEHAVIOR THERAPY AND EXPERIMENTAL PSYCHIATRY*, 1971, **2**, 1–11.

This case demonstrates the use of behavioral contracting to improve family interactions and behavior of a 16-year-old girl referred to a behavioral intervention project by the local juvenile court. At the time Candy Bremer (a pseudonym) was referred, she had been hospitalized for alleged promiscuity, exhibitionism, drug abuse, and home truancy. Candy came from an intact, middle-class family of modest means. Her parents reported that they could not control Candy and that most of their interactions with her were unpleasant. Most of her comments to them were antagonistic. After a series of conferences with Candy and her parents, a contract was negotiated (Figure 7–3). Essentially the contract specified that Candy would abide by her parents' curfew and take responsibility for certain household chores in exchange for specified privileges and early payment of her allowance.

Mr. and Mrs. Bremer reported that family interactions had improved following the introduction of the contract. There were many fewer arguments and when conflicts did arise, there was an effective way to resolve issues. The local court's wardship was terminated and no new problems developed.

PRIVILEGES	RESPONSIBILITIES
General	
In exchange for the privilege of remaining to-gether and preserving some semblance of family integrity, Mr. and Mrs. Bremer and Candy all agree to	concentrate on positively reinforcing each other's behavior while diminishing the present overempha-sis upon the faults of the others.
Specific	
In exchange for the privilege of riding the bus directly from school into town after school on school days	Candy agrees to phone her father by 4:00 p.m. to tell him that she is all right and to return home by 5:15 p.m.
In exchange for the privilege of going out at 7:00 p.m. on one weekend evening without having to account for her whereabouts	Candy must maintain a weekly average of "B" in the academic ratings of all of her classes and must return home by 11:30 p.m.
In exchange for the privilege of going out a second weekend night	Candy must tell her parents *by 6:00 p.m.* of her destination and her companion, and must return home by 11:30 p.m.
In exchange for the privilege of going out between 11:00 a.m. and 5:15 p.m. Saturdays, Sundays and holidays	Candy agrees to have completed all household chores *before* leaving and to telephone her parents once during the time she is out to tell them that she is all right.
In exchange for the privilege of having Candy complete household chores and maintain her curfew	Mr. and Mrs. Bremer agree to pay Candy $1.50 on the morning following days on which the money is earned.
Bonuses and Sanctions	
If Candy is 1–10 minutes late	she must come in the same amount of time earlier the following day, but she does not forfeit her money for the day.
If Candy is 11–30 minutes late	she must come in 22–60 minutes earlier the follow-ing day and does forfeit her money for the day.
If Candy is 31–60 minutes late	she loses the privilege of going out the following day and does forfeit her money for the day.
For each half hour of tardiness over one hour, Candy	loses her privilege of going out and her money for one additional day.
Candy may go out on Sunday evenings from 7:00 to 9:30 p.m. and either Monday or Thurs-day evening	if she abides by all the terms of this contract from Sunday through Saturday with a total tardiness not exceeding 30 minutes which must have been made up as above.
Candy may add a total of two hours divided among one to three curfews	if she abides by all the terms of this contract for two weeks with a total tardiness not exceeding 30 minutes which must have been made up as above and if she requests permission to use this additional time by 9:00 p.m.

MONITORING

Mr. and Mrs. Bremer agree to keep written records of the hours of Candy's leaving and coming home and of the completion of her chores.

Candy agrees to furnish her parents with a school monitoring card each Friday at dinner.

Figure 7–3. Behavioral contract. From R. B. Stuart, Behavioral contracting within the families of delinquents. *Journal of Behavior Therapy and Experimental Psychology,* 1971, **2,** p. 9, fig. 5. Used by permission.

REFERENCES

Aichhorn, A. *Wayward youth*. New York: Viking, 1935.

Alexander, J. F., & Parsons, B. V. Short-term behavioral intervention with delinquent families: Impact on family process and recidivism. *Journal of Abnormal Psychology*, 1973, **81**, 219–225.

Bailey, J. S., Wolf, M. M., & Phillips, E. L. Home-based reinforcement and the modification of predelinquents' classroom behavior. *Journal of Applied Behavior Analysis*, 1970, **3**, 223–233.

Bandura, A., & Walters, R. H. *Adolescent aggression*. New York: Ronald Press, 1959.

Bandura, A., & Walters, R. H. *Social learning and personality development*. New York: Holt, Rinehart and Winston, 1963.

Barndt, R. J., & Johnson, D. M. Time orientation in delinquents. *Journal of Abnormal and Social Psychology*, 1955, **51**, 343–345.

Braukmann, C. J., Kirigin, K. A., & Wolf, M. Achievement Place: The researcher's perspective. American Psychological Association meeting, Washington, D.C., September 1976, unpublished manuscript.

Burchard, J. D. Systematic socialization: A programmed environment for the habilitation of anti-social retardates. *Psychological Record*, 1967, **17**, 461–476.

Burchard, J. D., & Harig, P. T. Behavior modification and juvenile delinquency. In H. Leitenberg (Ed.), *Handbook of behavior modification and behavior therapy*. Englewood Cliffs, N.J.: Prentice-Hall, 1976.

Cohen, A. *Delinquent boys*. New York: Free Press, 1955.

Cohen, H. L., & Filipczak, J. *A new learning environment*. San Francisco: Jossey-Bass, 1971.

Cohen, H. R., Filipczak, J., & Bis, J. A study of contingencies applicable to special education. In R. Ulrich, T. Stachnik, & J. Mabry (Eds.), *Control of human behavior*, Vol. 2. Glenview, Ill.: Scott, Foresman, 1970.

Cohen, H. L., Filipczak, J. A., Slavin, J., & Boren, J. *Programmed interpersonal curricula for adolescents (PICA)—Project year three: A laboratory model*. Silver Spring, Md.: Institute for Behavioral Research, 1971.

Cortes, J. B., & Gatti, F. M. *Delinquency and crime: A biosocial approach*. New York: Seminar Press, 1972.

Davidson, W. S. The diversion of juvenile delinquents: An examination of the processes and relative efficacy of child advocacy and behavioral contracting. Unpublished doctoral dissertation, University of Illinois, 1976.

Davidson, W. S., & Rapp, C. A. Child advocacy in the justice system. *Social Work*, 1976, **21**, 225–232.

Davidson, W. S., & Robinson, M. J. Community psychology and behavior modification: A community based program for the prevention of delinquency. *Journal of Corrective Psychiatry and Behavior Therapy*, 1975, **21**, 1–12.

Davidson, W. S., & Seidman, E. Studies of behavior modification and juvenile delinquency: A review, methodological critique, and social perspective. *Psychological Bulletin*, 1974, **81**, 998–1011.

Emery, R. E., & Marholin, D. An applied analysis of delinquency: The irrelevancy of relevant behavior. *American Psychologist*, 1977, **32**, 860–873.

Eysenck, H. J. *Crime and personality*. London: Routledge & Kegan Paul, 1964.

F.B.I. *Uniform crime reports*. Washington, D.C.: U.S. Government Printing Office, 1973.

Glueck, S., & Glueck, E. *Unraveling juvenile delinquency*. Cambridge, Mass: Harvard University Press, 1950.

Hare, R. D. A conflict and learning theory analysis of psychopathic behavior. *Journal of Research in Crime and Delinquency*, 1965, **2**, 12–19(a).

Hare, R. D. Acquisition and generalization of a conditioned fear response in psychopathic and nonpsychopathic criminals. *Journal of Psychology*, 1965, **59**, 367–370(b).

Hare, R. D. Temporal gradients of fear arousal in psychopaths. *Journal of Abnormal Psychology*, 1965, **70**, 442–445(c).

Hare, R. D. Detection threshold for electric shock in psychopaths. *Journal of Abnormal Psychology*, 1968, **73**, 268–272.

Healy, W., & Bronner, A. L. *Delinquents and criminals: Their making and unmaking*. New York: Macmillan, 1926.

Jacobs, P. A., Brunton, M., Melville, M. M., Brittain, R. P., & McClemont, W. F. Aggressive behavior, mental subnormality and the XYY male. *Nature*, 1965, **208**, 1351–1352.

Jayaratne, S., Stuart, R. B., & Tripodi, T. Methodological issues and problems in evaluation treatment outcomes in family and school consultation project, 1970–1973. In P. D. Davidson, F. W. Clark, & L. A. Hamerlynck (Eds.), *Evaluation of behavioral programs*. Champaign, Ill.: Research Press, 1974.

Jesness, C. F., & DeRisi, W. J. Some variations in techniques of contingency management in a school for delinquents. In J. S. Stumphauzer (Ed.), *Behavior therapy with delinquents*. Springfield, Ill.: Thomas, 1973.

Lange, J. *Crime as destiny*. London: Allen and Unwin, 1931.

Lindner, R. M. *Rebel without a cause*. New York: Grune & Stratton, 1944.

Lysaght, T. V., & Burchard, J. D. The analysis and modification of a deviant parent-youth communication pattern. *Journal of Behavior Therapy and Experimental Psychiatry*, 1975, **6**, 339–342.

McCord, W., McCord, J., & Zola, I. K. *Origins of crime: A new evaluation of the Cambridge-Somerville Youth Study.* New York: Columbia University Press, 1959.

Neitzel, M., Winett, R., MacDonald, M., & Davidson, W. S. *Behavioral approaches to community psychology.* New York: Pergamon Press, 1977.

Peterson, D. R., Quay, H. C., & Tiffany, T. L. Personality factors related to juvenile delinquency. *Child Development,* 1961, **32,** 355–372.

Phillips, E. L. Achievement Place: Token reinforcement procedures in a home-style rehabilitation setting for "pre-delinquent" boys. *Journal of Applied Behavior Analysis,* 1968, **1,** 213–223.

Pierson, G. R., & Kelly, R. F. HSPQ norms in a statewide delinquent population. *Journal of Psychology,* 1963, **56,** 185–192(a).

Pierson, G. R., & Kelly, R. F. Anxiety, extraversion, and personality idiosyncrasy in delinquency. *Journal of Psychology,* 1963, **56,** 441–445(b).

President's Commission on Law Enforcement and Administrative Justice. *Task force report: Juvenile delinquency and youth crime.* Washington, D.C.: U.S. Government Printing Office, 1967.

Quay, H. C. Personality dimensions in delinquent males as inferred from the factor analysis of behavior rating. *Journal of Crime and Delinquency,* 1964, **1,** 33–37.

Rankin, R. J., & Wikoff, R. L. The IES Arrow Dot performance of delinquents and nondelinquents. *Perceptual and Motor Skills,* 1964, **18,** 207–210.

Rappaport, J. *Community psychology: Values, research, and action.* New York: Holt, Rinehart & Winston, 1977.

Ross, A. O. *Psychological disorders of children.* New York: McGraw-Hill, 1974.

Schur, E. M. *Radical non-intervention: Rethinking the delinquency problem.* Englewood Cliffs, N.J.: Prentice-Hall, 1973.

Schwitzgebel, R. A new approach to reducing adolescent crime. *Federal Probation,* March 1960, pp. 20–24.

Schwitzgebel, R. Reduction of adolescent crime by a research method. *Journal of Correctional Psychiatry and Social Therapy,* 1961, **7,** 212–215.

Schwitzgebel, R. *Street-corner research: An experimental approach to the juvenile delinquent.* Cambridge, Mass.: Harvard University Press, 1964.

Schwitzgebel, R. Short-term operant conditioning of adolescent offenders on socially relevant variables. *Journal of Abnormal Psychology,* 1967, **72,** 134–142.

Schwitzgebel, R., & Kolb, D. A. Inducing behaviour change in adolescent delinquents. *Behaviour Research and Therapy,* 1964, **1,** 297–304.

Schwitzgebel, R., Schwitzgebel, R., Pahnke, W. N., &

Hurd, W. S. A program of research in behavioral electronics. *Behavior Science,* 1964, **9,** 233–238.

Seidman, E., Rappaport, J., & Davidson, W. S. Adolescents in legal jeopardy: Initial success and replication of an alternative to the criminal justice system. In National Institute of Law Enforcement Assistance Administration, *The adolescent diversion project: A university's approach to delinquency prevention.* Washington, D.C.: U.S. Government Printing Office, 1977.

Shah, S. A. Perspectives and directions in juvenile corrections. *Psychiatric Quarterly,* 1973, **47,** 12–36.

Sheldon, W. H. *Varieties of delinquent youth.* New York: Harper, 1949.

Slack, C. W. Experimenter-subject psychotherapy: A new method of introducing intensive office treatment for unreachable cases. *Mental Hygiene,* 1960, **44,** 238–256.

Stein, K. B., Sarbin, T. R., & Kulik, J. A. Future time perspective: Its relation to the socialization process and the delinquent role. *Journal of Consulting and Clinical Psychology,* 1968, **32,** 257–264.

Stratton, J. R., & Terry, R. M. *Prevention of delinquency problems and programs.* New York: Macmillan, 1968.

Stuart, R. B. Behavioral contracting within families of delinquents. *Journal of Behavior Therapy and Experimental Psychiatry,* 1971, **2,** 1–11.

Stuart, R. B., & Lott, T. A. Behavioral contracting with delinquents: A cautionary note. *Journal of Behavior Therapy and Experimental Psychiatry.* 1972, **3,** 161–169.

Stuart, R. B., & Tripodi, T. Experimental valuation of three time-constrained behavioral treatments for predelinquents and delinquents. In R. D. Rubin, J. P. Brady, & J. D. Henderson (Eds.), *Advances in behavior therapy.* New York: Academic Press, 1973.

Stuart, R. B., Tripodi, I., Jayaratne, S., & Camburn, D. An experiment in social engineering in serving the families of predelinquents. *Journal of Abnormal Child Psychology,* 1976, **4,** 243–261.

Stumphauzer, J. S. (Ed.). *Behavior therapy with delinquents.* Springfield, Ill.: Thomas, 1973.

Sutherland, E. H. *Principles of criminology.* Philadelphia: Lippincott, 1939.

Tharp, R. G., & Wetzel, R. J. *Behavior modification in the natural environment.* New York: Academic Press, 1969.

Toby, J. An evaluation of early intervention and intensive treatment programs for predelinquents. *Social Problems,* 1965, **13,** 160–175.

Trotter, R. J. Behavior modification: Here, there, and everywhere. *Science News,* 1973, **103,** 260–263.

U.S. Department of Justice. *Children in custody.* Washington, D.C.: U.S. Government Printing Office, 1977(a).

U.S. Department of Justice. *Sourcebook of criminal justice statistics—1976*. Washington, D.C.: U.S. Government Printing Office, 1977(b).

Vinter, R. D., Downs, G., & Hall, T. *Juvenile corrections in the states: Residential programs and deinstitutionalization*. Ann Arbor: University of Michigan National Association of Juvenile Corrections, 1975.

Werner, J. S., Minkin, N., Minkin, B. L., Fixsen, D. L., Phillips, E. L., & Wolf, M. M. "Intervention Package": An analysis to prepare juvenile delinquents for encounters with police officers. *Criminal Justice and Behavior*, 1975, **2**, 55–84.

Wolf, M. M. *Social validity: The case for subjective measurement or how applied behavior analysis is finding its heart*. American Psychological Association meeting, Washington, D.C., September 1976.

Wolf, M. M., Phillips, E. L., & Fixsen, D. L. The teaching-family: A new model for the treatment of deviant child behavior in the community. In S. W. Bijou & E. L. Ribes-Inesta (Eds.), *Behavior modification*. New York: Academic Press, 1972.

Wolf, M. M., Phillips, E. L., Fixsen, D. L., Braukmann, C. J., Kirigin, K. A., Willner, A. G., & Schumaker, J. Achievement Place: The teaching-family model. *Child Care Quarterly*, 1976, **5**, 92–103.

PART III

APPLICATIONS: ADULTS

eight

HABIT DISORDERS AND SELF-CONTROL

It is the rare person who has not at some time grappled with the problems of resisting temptation, breaking bad habits, or turning a new leaf. Examples are all too familiar: refusing that piece of rich pastry and starting the diet today instead of tomorrow; getting work done on time and not procrastinating; trying to stop smoking. Alexander Woolcott's observation that "everything I like is either immoral, illegal, or fattening" is one way of describing why it is so easy to transgress. The spirit is willing, but the flesh is weak.

Psychologists' conceptualization of the problem is a bit more precise. They would characterize the above examples as involving either (1) behaviors whose immediate consequences are gratifying but whose long-term consequences are aversive or (2) behaviors whose immediate consequences are aversive but whose long-term consequences are positive. (For example, the pastry is delicious, but it will make you fat; studying may be unpleasant while you are doing it, but it may lead to success and satisfaction later.) As many researchers (for instance, Mischel, 1966; Rachlin, 1974; Rotter, 1954) have pointed out, these habit disorders really involve the issue of "now" versus "later"; the immediate consequences of the undesirable behavior (such as overindulgence) are more positive than the more desirable and incompatible alternative (such as moderation). In order to increase the likelihood that the individual will engage in the more desirable behavior, something must change. Either the undesirable behavior must be prevented or the contingencies associated with each alternative must be reversed so that the desirable behavior is more reinforcing than the undesirable behavior.

Behavioral psychologists have tackled the problem of eliminating unwanted habits in two ways: by teaching people how to manage their own behavior or through conditioning treatment in the therapist's office. The first method involves people learning to be their own "behavior modifiers." They are taught to alter factors (that is, antecedents, consequences, and setting events) in their own environments that influence their behavior. The second method involves a psychotherapist's systematically pairing the unwanted behavior with some type of aversive stimulation and pairing the desired alternative with pleasant stimulation. This method relies primarily on classical conditioning procedures.

In this chapter we will consider these two methods of eliminating common habit disorders. We will begin by discussing the processes that are presumed to be involved in one's exerting control of one's own behavior. From this theoretical discussion we will move on to describe the actual operations included in most self-control programs. We will then consider the use of classical conditioning methods. The last section of the chapter will be devoted to a discussion of the effectiveness of behavioral methods in treating problems of obesity, smoking, and alcohol abuse.

SELF-CONTROL: THE BEHAVIORAL CONCEPTUALIZATION

Behavioral psychologists generally agree that self-control essentially involves the individual's emitting certain controlling responses that alter critical features of the environment that, in turn, affect the probability of problem behavior (that is, the *controlled response*). However, there is clear disagreement regarding the extent to which cognitive processes such as covert self-reinforcement and self-punishment are involved. In a very real sense this disagreement represents the rift that we discussed in Chapter 1 between the radical and cognitive approaches to behavior modification.

Before we review the two most important models of self-control, we must point out that neither model was directly derived from empirical research. Rather, they represent theoretical extrapolations from behavior theory and common sense. Although both models have received some clinical validation and experimental analysis, neither has been thoroughly tested. Nevertheless, they have made a significant contribution to the development of effective procedures for eliminating habit disorders. These two major behavioral models are those of B. F. Skinner (1953) and Frederick Kanfer (1970, 1977).

Skinner's Model

Skinner's (1953) position is clear and straightforward:

> When a man controls himself, chooses a course of action, thinks out the solution to a problem, or strives toward an increase in self-knowledge, he is behaving. He controls himself precisely as he would control the behavior of anyone else—through the manipulation of variables of which behavior is a function. (p. 228)

According to Skinner, the reason people control themselves is that society heavily reinforces them for such behavior. The ultimate control rests with society. Because of social pressure, laws, and institutionalized contingencies of punishment we are encouraged to exert self-control. Skinner delineated various ways in which an individual can control his or her own behavior. A brief outline of his view of the processes involved follows.

Physical Restraint and Physical Aid. One way to eliminate a problem behavior is to literally prevent its occurrence. Skinner points out that, for example, we cover our mouths in order to control our own laughter, and we put our hands into our pockets to stop ourselves from fidgeting or biting our nails. A familiar example of the use of physical restraints as a means of self-control is Homer's tale of Odysseus's defense against the Sirens. Circe warned Odysseus to plug his oarsmen's ears with soft beeswax in order to prevent their hearing the seductive songs of the Sirens. To control himself, Odysseus had his oarsmen tie him to the mast and instructed them not to release him, regardless of his pleas and demands. His purpose was to make it impossible for himself to succumb to the desire to follow the songs of the Sirens and steer the ship into dangerous seas. In these examples, the individuals impose some physical restraint on themselves *before* they are faced with the conflict. By so doing, they make it easy to resist temptation.

Individuals can also physically restrain themselves by simply eliminating the opportunity to engage in the undesirable response. One way is to remove oneself from the "tempting" environment. For example, if the temptation to eat doughnuts is strong, the individual might leave the doughnut shop, or better yet, avoid going into the shop altogether. Another means of making it impossible to engage in the undesirable behavior is to remove necessary components of the response. A spendthrift might leave half his money at home or destroy his credit cards before he goes shopping. If a student finds himself listening to his stereo rather than studying in the evening, he might keep the stereo equipment in a locked closet except during predetermined relaxation periods.

The converse of the use of physical restraints to prevent or inhibit misbehavior is the introduction of physical aids and prompts to make the desirable behavior more likely. The student might lock himself in the library on Saturday afternoons instead of trying to study in his dormitory room where he can see a touch-football game going on outside. An accountant can buy a bicycle or a good pair of jogging shoes to make it more likely that she will get some exercise.

2 *Changing the Stimulus.* Another strategy is to manipulate discriminative and conditioned stimuli. Rather than making the undesirable response impossible, the individual introduces stimuli that evoke desirable behavior or eliminates stimuli that prompt undesirable behavior. For example, a person trying to cut down on eating might get rid of magazines that showed pictures of delicious desserts.

Discriminative stimuli are also introduced in order to prompt desirable behavior and distract undesirable behavior. A note on the refrigerator door or a string tied around a finger are two examples of self-control tactics. Religious medals and pictures of loved ones prominently displayed often serve to prompt good behavior.

Skinner suggests three ways of manipulating setting events in order to control one's own behavior: changing levels of reinforcer satiation and deprivation, altering emotional conditions, and ingesting drugs.

3 *Deprivation and Satiation.* Altering levels of motivation automatically changes the reinforcement value of behavioral alternatives. This self-control strategy has two sides: an individual can satiate the "needs" associated with the undesirable response or deprive those associated with the desirable behavior. Both methods would result in an increase in the probability of emitting the desirable response. For example, a person who wanted to avoid eating lots of fattening junk food at a party might satisfy his or her appetite by filling up with carrots before arriving. Then that person would be less likely to overindulge on junk food at the party because the reinforcement value of food would, at least theoretically, be reduced.

4 *Manipulating Emotional Conditions.* Establishing particular emotional predispositions is another method that Skinner suggests as a means of self-

control. We often prepare ourselves for a situation by "getting in the mood." For example, a person who has difficulty dealing with interpersonal conflict and often "loses his temper" might prepare for a rough business meeting by relaxing for a half-hour before the confrontation. Similarly, athletes might "psych themselves up" before an important game in order that they might "give their all" when they play. Skinner used the example of the weak and nonassertive employee who prepares to ask his boss for a raise by recalling all the injustices he has endured; the notion is that the employee will be more forceful and effective in confrontation if he is angered. (Of course, this is an empirical question. It is quite possible that ruminating about past injustices might make him discouraged and even more nonassertive.) Once individuals are in emotionally charged situations they can still practice self-control by altering their emotional condition. By "counting to ten" before answering in anger or by "biting their lip," they can delay the emotional reaction and thereby reduce its magnitude.

5 *Drugs.* Another means of controlling behavior by altering setting events is through the ingestion of drugs. Alcohol, tranquilizers, and other sedatives reduce inhibition and alter both the reinforcement and the punishment value of many events. Certain drugs can have the opposite effect and increase inhibition, anxiety, and arousal.

6 *Using Aversive Stimulation.* Setting an alarm clock, betting on oneself, and making a public resolution to change some behavior are ways of establishing punishment contingencies to control behavior. In each case, individuals establish a mechanism through which their undesirable behavior will be punished if it occurs. The alarm clock's ring punishes oversleeping, and the humiliation of not keeping a resolution punishes backsliding. To the extent that the aversive consequences outweigh immediate reinforcement for the undesirable response, the desirable response will be more probable.

7 *Operant Conditioning and Punishment.* Both techniques refer to individuals' delivering some consequence to themselves following a particular re-

sponse. These consequences are topographically similar to the operations a person performs when applying consequences to another person's behavior. Although Skinner readily acknowledges that such behaviors are emitted, he argues that they do not, in fact, control behavior. Rather, they are parts of behavioral chains that are ultimately reinforced by society. Individuals' self-reinforcement and self-punishment represent their evaluation of their behavior in terms of the consequences that society will deliver following that behavior. As we will discover shortly, it is this view of the role of self-reinforcement and self-punishment that separates Skinner's view of self-control from more cognitive approaches.

Doing Something Else. The last method of self-control that Skinner proposes is the act of engaging in behavior incompatible with the undesired behavior. If someone wants to avoid talking about a particular topic, he or she talks about something else. In order to be effective, the controlling response (that is, doing something else) must be executed strongly enough to be prepotent over the other response.

In a theoretical article primarily based on laboratory research with animals (Ainslie, 1974; Rachlin & Green, 1972), Howard Rachlin (1974) has extended Skinner's formulations and suggested that the most important variable is the temporal distance between the controlling response and the "to be controlled" behavior. The longer the time between the point at which individuals must modify their environment or the contingencies under which they operate and the point at which the undesirable behavior is a real option, the easier it is for them to emit the controlling response.

For example, a person who wants to avoid eating a large bowl of ice cream at midnight is more likely to discard the container of ice cream (an effective controlling response) at 7 A.M. than at 11:30 P.M. Similarly, a student trying to improve study habits by cutting down on amount of time spent watching television finds it easier to leave for the library two hours before the basketball game comes on the air than to leave as the sports commentator announces the starting lineup.

Rachlin's argument (1974, 1976) is based on Richard Herrnstein's (1970) model of choice.

Herrnstein's model states that preference varies directly with the amount of reinforcement associated with each alternative and inversely with the delay of the reinforcement. The person who has the opportunity to emit a controlling response when the reinforcement produced by the undesirable response is delayed is more likely to show self-control. Although Rachlin's position is intuitively appealing, it can only be viewed as speculative, since his results have not been replicated with humans.

Kanfer's Model

Like Skinner, Kanfer contends that environmental contingencies are the ultimate source of behavior control, and that self-control can be analyzed in terms of those contingencies. Kanfer does not reject Skinner's formulations regarding how individuals can manipulate their environments to alter their own behavior, but Kanfer gives great importance to the role of self-evaluation and to what he describes as covert self-reinforcement and punishment. According to Kanfer, how individuals evaluate their own behavior, independent of immediate environmental consequences, affects what they do. These self-generated cognitive events interact with environmental variables to control behavior.

Kanfer also identifies a third source of control, the individual's biological system. This includes conditions of deprivation and satiation of food, sleep, sex, and so on, as well as the condition of homeostatic regulation systems. Kanfer has labeled these sources of control alpha, beta, and gamma. **Alpha control** refers to the impact of environmental variables on behavior; **beta control** represents the influence of the individual's self-evaluation and covert reinforcement and punishment; **gamma control** identifies the control exerted by the individual's biological system. According to this model, these three sets of independent variables continuously interact to control behavior.

The relative contribution of each set varies from moment to moment. Although at a conceptual level it is relatively easy to determine the contribution of each source, in any particular instance it is extremely difficult to specify the absolute contribution of each. Kanfer readily acknowledges the complexity. In a recent discussion of his model of self-control (Kanfer, 1977), he provides a clear illustration of the interaction of alpha, beta, and gamma variables. A hungry and penniless man enters a bakery and smells the aroma of the freshly baked bread sitting on the counter. The question is—what factors determine whether or not he will succumb to temptation and steal the bread? Gamma variables such as level of food deprivation certainly influence his stealing behavior. Alpha variables will also impinge: stealing will depend upon the ease with which he can reach the bread and hide it under his coat or in a bag without being caught. Can the other customers see what he is doing, and if so, will they report him? Is there a one-way mirror behind the counter? Beta variables such as feelings of guilt, notions about the immorality of theft, and beliefs regarding whether a poor man's stealing from the rich is right will play a role.

The relative magnitude of each set of variables and their interaction will determine the outcome of his dilemma. If alpha and gamma variables are strong—for instance, the bread is in easy reach, no one is looking, and he hasn't eaten in three days—and beta variables are weak—for example, in the past he has felt no guilt when he has broken the law, and he feels the proprietors of the bakery deserve to be ripped off—then we might predict with some confidence that the man will steal the bread. However, the prediction might be different if the man knew that someone might walk in unannounced at any moment or if he had eaten a large breakfast three hours earlier. Depending upon the relative magnitude of the variables influencing alternative behaviors, variables interact to determine the individual's course of action.

Although the individual never ceases to be affected by alpha and gamma variables, beta variables are of primary importance in self-control. Beta control allows the individual to maintain consistent patterns of behavior across changing situations, and to be temporarily free of immediate external contingencies. According to Kanfer, only when the individual chooses to engage in one behavior whose immediate environmental and/or biological consequences favor another is that individual exerting self-control. In the example given

here, we might correctly conclude that the man in the bakery was exerting self-control if he did not steal the bread even though there was no one watching, he had a large shopping bag on his arm, and he hadn't eaten in days. Self-control means that beta variables take precedent.

According to Kanfer, individuals regulate their own behavior by a three-stage process involving *self-monitoring, self-evaluation,* and either *self-reinforcement* or *self-punishment.* Individuals must first observe their own behavior using the feedback from the external environment as well as internal bodily cues. Once people know "what they are doing," they can make a judgment regarding the adequacy of their performance relative to some standard. That is, individuals must make a discrimination between what they do and what they ought to be doing. This self-evaluation is in terms of some ad hoc performance standard. The standard is important because it serves as a statement of intention and guides future behavior. Whether persons actually set performance standards, and consequently regulate their own behavior, depends upon a number of alpha variables. Relevant factors include the aversive consequences associated with the undesirable behavior, satiation of the reinforcement value of the undesirable behavior, and social approval for setting high standards. Finally, individuals provide themselves with consequences for engaging in the behavior. This reinforcement or punishment may be covert (such as telling themselves they did well) or overt (such as indulging themselves in a long-awaited extravagance). Figure 8–1 is taken from an article by Kanfer and his colleague Paul Karoly (1972) and summarizes the Kanfer three-stage self-regulation model.

SELF-CONTROL METHODS

Researchers in the area of self-control (for example, Kanfer, 1977; Mahoney & Thoresen, 1974; Thoresen & Mahoney, 1974) recognize two general strategies of self-control, environmental planning and behavioral programming. **Environmental planning** directly follows from Skinner's (1953) formulations of self-control and involves individuals' altering the relevant situational variables that

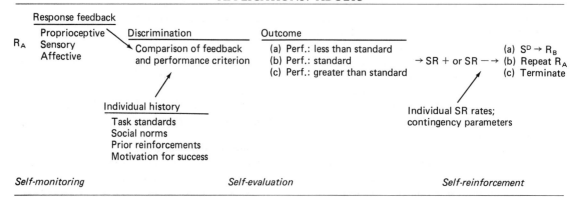

Self-monitoring   Self-evaluation   Self-reinforcement

Figure 8–1. A working model of self-regulation. From F. H. Kanfer & P. Karoly, Self-control: A behavioristic excursion into the lion's den. *Behavior Therapy*, 1972, **3**, p. 407, fig. 1. By permission of Academic Press and the authors.

influence their behavior. **Behavioral programming**, on the other hand, more closely follows Kanfer's model and involves the self-administration of reinforcing and punishing consequences. This type of programming can also involve changing cognitions that mediate behavior. Although the two strategies incorporate different operations, they are in no way incompatible and are usually combined in clinical self-control programs.

Environmental Planning

Changing factors in the environment that control behavior is the most straightforward technique of self-control and has been utilized with numerous habit disorders. The primary application involves the individual's taking advantage of naturally occurring stimulus control and contingencies of reinforcement to prompt the desired behavior change.

Altering Stimulus Control. This procedure involves the individual's removing stimuli that evoke undesirable behavior and introducing stimuli that prompt desirable behavior. In order to explain how stimulus control techniques are used, we will briefly discuss two problem areas (insomnia and studying problems) in which it has been

used. This technique will also be discussed when we review the Stuart and Davis (1972) weight-control program.

Richard Bootzin (1972) reported a case study of an adult insomniac whose problem was long-standing. When he would go to bed he would begin thinking about the day's problems and toss and turn for three or four hours. Unable to get settled, he would switch on the television and watch it until he finally fell asleep at 3 or 4 A.M. Bootzin's program was quite simple. In order to make the bed a stimulus for sleeping instead of ruminating and watching television, the client was instructed not to go to bed until he was very sleepy so that it would be extremely likely that he would quickly fall asleep as soon as he hit the bed. If, after he went to bed, he was unable to fall asleep within a short time, he was to get up and go into another room until he was again sleepy. He was not to read or watch television in bed. During the first week of the program the client got up four or five times each night before he was able to fall asleep quickly. However, during the second week, he reported that his sleeping had improved. At a two-month followup the client's insomnia had almost vanished; he was getting up less than one time per week.

Changing the stimulus control has also been used to improve study habits (Beneke & Harris, 1972; Fox, 1962). Again, the goal was to establish strong discriminative stimuli that would evoke the desired behavior. In one case study, the client was a college student who had trouble concentrating on his school work (Fox, 1962). When he went to the library he got nothing done; he would daydream, take coffee breaks, and talk to friends. The student was instructed to find a "new room" in the library and go there for a brief time each day. At the beginning he was to take materials for one subject and complete one assignment. When he found himself daydreaming or not paying attention, he was to get up from his chair and leave the room. The idea was to have the room associated with studying and nothing else. The assignments were gradually increased, with the requirement being that he not stay in the room if he was not studying. Gradually, he increased his daily study time to one hour per subject and his grades improved. Four other students also followed this program and improved at least one letter grade during the quarter the program was in effect. In a subsequent study (Beneke & Harris, 1972), stimulus control training yielded similar improvement in grades.

Changing Contingencies of Reinforcement and Contingency Contracting. Another self-control technique that involves environmental planning is altering contingencies of reinforcement and punishment. The individual enlists the help of family, friends, and therapist to rearrange environmental contingencies so that the desirable behavior is reinforced and the undesirable behavior is punished. This is usually accomplished by the individual's making agreements and contracts with significant others who will aid in the implementation of contingencies. Kanfer (1975, p. 321) has enumerated the major elements of such a contract:

1. A clear and detailed description of the required instrumental behavior should be stated.
2. Some criterion should be set for the time or frequency limitations which constitute the goal of the contract.
3. The contract should specify the positive reinforcements contingent upon fulfillment of the criterion.
4. Provisions should be made for some aversive consequence contingent upon nonfulfillment of the contract within the specified time or with the specified frequency.
5. A bonus clause should indicate the additional positive reinforcements obtainable if the person exceeds the minimal demands of the contract.

6. The contract should specify the means by which the contracted response is to be observed, measured, recorded; and a procedure should be stated for informing the client of his achievements during the duration of the contract.
7. The timing for delivery of reinforcement contingencies should be arranged to follow the response as quickly as possible.

Unfortunately, controlled studies on the effectiveness of contingency contracting are lacking. To date, case studies form the primary bases for evaluation. In such studies it is often difficult to discern the exact contribution of any single factor. Contracts are rarely used alone, but are part of a multifaceted intervention program including methods such as one-to-one counseling, relaxation training, and self-control techniques such as physical restraint.

A typical self-control contract might involve the client depositing a sizable amount of money or valuables, with the agreement that deposits will be returned in portions as the client meets new, self-determined standards. A client who fails to fulfill the requirements forfeits part of the money or goods to a previously specified source. H. M. Boudin (1972) provided an example of the use of contingency contracting within a comprehensive program for a woman graduate student who sought help in reducing her high amphetamine use. The student had become dependent on the drugs during a three-year period, and at the time she first saw the therapist she was consuming 60 to 70 mg of amphetamines a day. In order to reinforce abstinence and punish drug usage, the therapist and client drew up a contract that specified she would deposit five hundred dollars with the therapist, who would return fifty dollars to her each week she did not take amphetamines. If she did not fulfill the conditions of the contract during the week, she forfeited fifty dollars to the Ku Klux Klan. The conditions of the contract were these (Boudin, 1972, pp. 605–606):

1. Miss X had to submit a weekly schedule to the therapist, and keep him continuously informed of her whereabouts.
2. Three check-in times were established every day. Each morning, noon, and night, Miss X would call and describe her projected activities

up to the preceding check-in period. Any "potentially dangerous situations" (those situations where drugs, or drug users were in close range, which increased the probability of using drugs) were communicated to the therapist in order to be discussed at the next check-in time.

3. During any clearly "potentially dangerous situation," Miss X called the therapist so that immediate counsel could be given, resulting in one of the three following outcomes: (a) Miss X could remain in this situation under certain conditions; (b) Miss X had to extricate herself from the situation; or (c) Miss X had to be removed from the situation by the therapist.

4. Miss X had to give up all drugs which were accessible to her. Since she was living in a house with other drug users, and knew where various drug supplies were kept, these people had to be informed of our arrangement. Miss X had to make a formal announcement individually to her suppliers to remove any drugs from accessibility to her, and to refrain from giving or selling her any drugs, even if she requested them. The therapist was present at all of these interactions, to further confirm that Miss X was in earnest.

5. The therapist had to arrange his schedule so that Miss X knew where he was at all times.

6. The therapist had to agree that he was to be accessible and available in all crises, 24 hr a day.

7. A subsection of the contract dealt with the self-application of shock, as described by Wolpe (1965). Miss X was instructed in the use of a small portable shock dispenser which she carried with her at all times. Any awareness of what was termed "volitional behavior," behavior leading to the acquisition of drugs, or any drug-searching behaviors (for example, searching the medicine chest), was a discriminative stimulus for the self-application of shock.

8. A joint bank account between Miss X and the therapist was established in the amount of $500 (all of Miss X's money). Ten signed checks in the amount of $50 each were held by the therapist, who had only to sign any of these checks to make it valid.

9. It was agreed to by the therapist and Miss X that any drug use or suspected drug use by Miss X would result in the loss of a $50 check. Originally, this check was to be sent to the National Welfare Rights Organization, but since Miss X was active in supporting their work, it was decided that this would not really be an effective decelerating consequence. It was finally mutually agreed upon that a $50 check would be sent to the Ku Klux Klan for any infringement of the rules as determined in the contract.

10. Miss X would receive rent, food, and spending money from the therapist whenever necessary as long as she could account for her expenses.

During the ten-week period, Miss X broke the contract only once. The program was successful; a two-year followup evaluation indicated that she had not returned to amphetamine use.

In one of the few controlled studies in the area, Lester Tobias (1972) compared the effectiveness of environmental planning (changing stimuli associated with eating), sheer determination (willpower), and contingency contracting as aids to weight reduction. One hundred overweight women undergraduates were randomly assigned to one of five groups: weight reduction manual (which included environmental planning strategies), behavior contract, self-determination, no-treatment control, and no-contact control. Clients in the behavior contract group negotiated a legal contract with the therapist in which they agreed to surrender cash or valuables to the therapist to be returned if they met their own weekly weight-loss goals.

If they did not achieve the desired weight loss, the cash or items would be given to a previously specified "hated" organization. Care was taken that each subject establish realistic and safe weight-loss requirements. The average weight-loss requirement was two pounds per week. Weekly records were kept on each client's progress and were compared against their individual contracts to determine whether or not they should receive all their deposits. Even though half the women did not meet their original goals, the clients did lose weight.

At the end of the ten-week program and at a four-week followup evaluation, the mean weight losses for the five groups were compared. Clients in the environmental planning and contracting groups lost significantly more weight than the other clients. Questionnaires also revealed that contract clients were satisfied with their programs. Unfortunately, long-term followup data were not collected.

As with most procedures, self-control through

environmental planning is most effective when the changes are instituted within the client's natural environment (Kanfer, 1977; Kanfer & Phillips, 1970). That is, contracts made with family members who are willing to follow through in the agreement for an extended period of time hold greater promise than those made with a therapist who might see the client once a week. Likewise, stimuli that are reprogrammed must be relevant to the client in daily life. As we suggested in Chapter 3, generalization must be programmed.

Behavioral Programming

This method of self-control requires individuals to take greater responsibility for changing their behavior. They must first monitor their actions and then apply contingencies of reinforcement and/or punishment. This is no easy job. Since the goal is to reduce the occurrence of behaviors that are presumably more immediately reinforcing than the behaviors he or she wishes to strengthen, it is often difficult for the individual to execute the self-control operation. For example, it is hard to imagine a person being willing to repeatedly self-administer aversive consequences powerful enough to suppress smoking behavior by effectively competing with the reinforcement received from smoking. For this reason, it should not be surprising to the reader that behavioral programming has not yielded great breakthroughs in the quest for effective methods of self-control.

Another problem with behavioral programming strategies is that they are hard to evaluate. For one thing, many of the procedures involve covert (that is, cognitive) operations that are unobservable, thereby making precise measurement difficult. This problem is compounded by the fact that the available research involves either laboratory analogues or case studies. Laboratory studies have typically involved either children or college sophomores playing contrived games or engaging in meaningless motor tasks. Although these studies may be theoretically interesting, their relevance to clinical issues is questionable. The case studies are often confounded with other variables, such as demand characteristics (Orne, 1962), de facto instructions (Broden, Hall, & Mitts, 1971; Redd, 1974), and contingencies of social

reinforcement (Thomas, Abrams, & Johnson, 1971), which make it difficult to identify the effective components.

With this rather pessimistic introduction, we will now review the essential components of behavioral programming and the research on its utility as a method of self-control. The operations generally presumed to be involved in behavioral programming are self-monitoring, self-reinforcement (covert or overt), self-punishment (covert or overt), and covert modeling.

Self-monitoring. Monitoring one's own behavior is not new to clinical psychology—in fact, an early variant, introspection, was one of psychology's first methods. Behavioral clinicians have used self-monitoring as a means of assessment. This might be as simple as having the client wear a golfer's wrist counter and press it each time he or she engages in a particular behavior or as complicated as having the person keep records and diaries. For example, in Stuart and Davis's (1972) weight-control manual, elaborate data sheets are included for the reader to use in recording such events as food eaten, exercise, and so on. In many self-control programs, therapist and client together devise specific, individualized self-monitoring procedures.

Does self-monitoring produce meaningful data? Of course, in many situations it is impossible to determine reliability. For instance, there is obviously no way to determine reliability in monitoring self-deprecating thoughts or sexual fantasies. In studies where it has been possible to obtain reliability estimates of self-monitoring, results have been mixed. Children do not appear to be very skilled at self-monitoring (Broden, Hall, & Mitts, 1971; Fixsen, Phillips, & Wolf, 1972), whereas adults seem to be somewhat more reliable (Azrin & Powell, 1969). However, the results for adults are not consistently positive (Ober, 1968; Herbert & Baer, 1972; Goldstein, 1966).

Surprisingly enough, no clear relationship seems to exist between the reliability of self-monitoring and the actual effectiveness of the self-control program. For instance, in the study conducted by Emily Herbert and Donald Baer (1972) (Chapter 4), mothers were asked to keep records of the number of times they responded favorably

[handwritten margin note: Sometimes Self-monitoring alone can change the behavior / Self monitoring is sometimes reactive]

to their children's cooperative behavior. The reliability of the mother's self-monitoring was low (average agreement of mothers and independent observers was 43 and 46 percent), although a clinically meaningful change occurred in the mothers' behavior (they started dispensing more praise and attention) as a result of merely being asked to self-monitor.

Self-monitoring is sometimes *reactive*. That is, merely having clients monitor their own behavior often results in improvement without their being asked to do anything else. The Herbert and Baer (1972) study demonstrates this quite clearly. Richard Stuart (1967) found that having overweight individuals monitor their own eating behavior without being told to reduce food consumption or change their behavior in any way resulted in a significant though temporary weight loss. This reactivity phenomenon has also been observed with school-age children (Broden, Hall, & Mitts, 1971). However, with both adults and children, the reactive effect attenuates over time (Broden, Hall, & Mitts, 1971; Fixsen, Phillips, & Wolf, 1972; Stuart, 1967).

Self-reinforcement and Self-punishment. The role of self-reinforcement and self-punishment in the control of human behavior has fascinated many researchers, notably Bandura (1969, 1971) and Kanfer (1966, 1970, 1977). Bandura contends that many of our actions are maintained without external reinforcement. Through cognitive mediational processes, notions of what we "ought to do" prompt and direct much of our behavior. These self-generated standards of performance often represent internalized norms and values acquired through the socialization process. Individuals evaluate the adequacy of their behavior against these standards and then either reinforce or punish themselves. Bandura claims that by utilizing these two forms of self-generated stimulation (that is, cognitions) people can exercise some degree of control over their own actions. In a series of laboratory studies with children, Bandura and his colleagues (Bandura, Grusec, & Menlove, 1967; Bandura & Kupers, 1964; Bandura & Whalen, 1966) have obtained results that support this hypothesis. Kanfer's research (Kanfer, 1966; Kanfer & Duerfeldt, 1968; Kanfer & Marston, 1963)

also suggests that reinforcement people deliver to themselves can effectively control behavior and compete with immediate external contingencies of reinforcement.

Bandura and Kanfer have been credited with identifying the role of cognitive mediation in behavior control (Craighead, Kazdin, & Mahoney, 1976; Mahoney, 1974; Thoresen & Mahoney, 1974), and their formulations have had a real impact on the development of behavioral self-control programs. Unquestionably, their research merits the enthusiastic response it has received. However, as Kanfer (1977) has pointed out, these formulations must be recognized as heuristic models rather than actual statements of fact. Given the complex and unobservable nature of the variables being studied, conclusions drawn from research in this area are speculative. The problem is that these variables are, by necessity, studied in a context of subtle but potentially powerful social demands placed on the subjects to perform in certain ways (Orne, 1962; Steinman, 1976). Although subjects are of course not explicitly told what to do, the demonstrations and supervision that may be provided have often been found to communicate information relevant to the "desired" outcome (Peterson, Merwin, Moyer, & Whitehurst, 1971; Steinman, 1970). Thus, it may be difficult to separate out the effects of variables that are potentially operating.

Self-reinforcement operations have been used in the treatment of a variety of problems ranging from academic underachievement (Lovitt & Curtis, 1969; Bolstad & Johnson, 1972) and poor study habits (Beneke & Harris, 1972) to heterosexual anxiety (Rehm & Marston, 1968) and depression (Jackson, 1972). In many of the reported studies, individuals evaluate their own performance and then give themselves points or tokens that are later redeemable for special activities or prizes. For example, in a remedial reading classroom, adolescent psychiatric patients rated their classroom performance each day and then gave themselves tokens accordingly (Kaufman & O'Leary, 1972).

Imagined or "covert" self-reinforcement has also been used. In order to strengthen a particular behavior, some (for example, Cautela, 1970) have suggested instructing clients to imagine pleasurable experiences (such as tasting a favorite dessert, winning at bridge) after emitting the desired response. Results have been consistently positive: programs involving self-reinforcement operations have produced clinically meaningful results. However, in all the clinical self-reinforcement studies reported in the literature, it is impossible to determine the specific contribution of the self-reinforcement operations because self-reinforcement procedures have been confounded with other variables: for instance, graduated performance (Rehm & Marston, 1968), peer social reinforcement (Kaufman & O'Leary, 1972), and teacher supervision (Bolstad & Johnson, 1972).

Self-punishment has also been suggested as a means of self-control. For instance, in one case study of the elimination of hallucinations, a psychiatric patient was instructed to punish self-critical obsessive thoughts by snapping a heavy-gauge rubber band against his wrist whenever they occurred. Reported obsessions declined to zero (Mahoney, 1971). In a report of two cases involving the control of smoking, individuals were told to tear up a dollar bill whenever they exceeded a self-imposed daily smoking limit of fifteen cigarettes. Within fifteen days, cigarette consumption had decreased to zero; at a two-year followup evaluation, both individuals had not resumed smoking (Axelrod, Hall, Weis, & Rohrer, 1974).

Individuals have also been instructed to imagine an unpleasant event (for instance, vomiting) immediately following the occurrence of the undesirable behavior. The notion is that through this **covert sensitization** process (a term coined by Cautela, 1967), the undesirable behavior acquires aversive properties through association with the noxious image. Unfortunately, controlled research in this area is scarce. In the case studies that have been reported, confounding of variables in the procedures preclude the determination of whether improvement was the result of self-punishment contingencies per se.

Changing Cognitions. Despite the methodological problems in studying cognitive variables and the theoretical confusion associated with distinguishing between external and internal sources of behavior control, researchers and clinicians continue to be interested in the role of cognitive mediation

in behavior change. In the area of self-control, cognitive behavior modification is indeed being used.

Donald Meichenbaum and his colleagues (Meichenbaum, 1976; Meichenbaum & Cameron, 1974; Meichenbaum & Goodman, 1969, 1971) have extended Bandura's notions regarding the cognitive mediation of behavior change and suggest that people's interpretations of events around them are as important as the events themselves in determining what they do. According to Meichenbaum, "it is not the environmental consequences per se that are of primary importance but what the subject says to himself about those consequences" (Meichenbaum & Cameron, 1974, p. 264).

Consider the situation in which an acquaintance passes by but does not speak. Jamie is reading a book as she rides the commuter train into the city. The train stops in Tucker and her friend Robin gets on and takes the empty seat across the aisle. Jamie continues to read her book, but starts to wonder why she was snubbed. She is mildly annoyed, feels a little rejected, but says nothing. A few minutes later, she goes to the snack bar for some coffee and does not ask Robin to join her. But Jamie's reaction might have been quite different if she had interpreted Robin's behavior differently. Perhaps Robin was just preoccupied and really did not notice her, or perhaps Robin saw that she was reading and did not want to disturb her. If Jamie had adopted either of these two interpretations, she would not have reacted negatively; in fact, she might have appreciated Robin's consideration and invited her to go to the snack bar.

Meichenbaum's work has been directed toward teaching people more adaptive ways of interpreting events in their lives. The goal is for clients to gain insight into the ways they "talk to themselves" in problematic situations, thus exaggerating the conflict and making them react maladaptively (that is, overreact). Meichenbaum tries to show clients how these irrational thoughts are self-fulfilling and therefore self-defeating. Once clients understand the role of such self-instructions, he teaches them more adaptive self-instructions. By means of these more rational self-instructions, individuals, in essence, tell themselves how to behave. Rather than reacting impulsively, individuals stop and consider the implications of what they might do. Depending upon the situation and the behavior that they are trying to change, they might think of alternative reactions, review instructions that they and the therapist have devised earlier, or tell themselves to relax. As we will see in Chapter 10, these self-control procedures have proved to be quite effective in controlling anxiety reactions.

AVERSIVE CONDITIONING

Although training in self-control methods is the primary strategy for eliminating habit disorders, aversive conditioning in the therapist's office has also been used. This treatment typically follows the classical conditioning paradigm. The undesirable habit behaviors or stimuli associated with the behavior are repeatedly paired with a noxious stimulus. Conditioning can involve the pairing of either real (that is, physical) or imagined stimuli. The notion is that, as a result of the pairing, the "value" of the undesirable habit for the client will change. Stimuli associated with the habit should come to elicit anxiety or at least no longer elicit pleasurable sensations. In a sense, this treatment involves the therapist attempting to establish a "miniphobia" of the undesirable stimuli in order to eliminate the habit disorder. Thus, following direct conditioning the individual should avoid the undesirable activity.

Direct Conditioning

When physical stimuli are used, the client actually engages in the undesirable habit (for example, sips alcohol, inhales cigarette smoke, takes a bite of candy) or is presented with stimuli associated with the habit (for example, slides showing a bottle of whisky, a pack of cigarettes, a cake). This presentation is then immediately followed by the delivery of either painful electric shock or the aversive effects of some pharmacological agent.

Electrically Induced Aversion. This procedure involves the use of painful electric shock as the unconditioned stimulus. The client is usually seated in a comfortable chair in the therapist's office with

electrodes strapped to forearm, calf, or fingertips. Shock intensity is then carefully adjusted so that it is painful, yet not strong enough to cause any physical damage. When the shock is terminated, the discomfort immediately ends. Since most individuals adapt to shock after repeated exposure, the intensity must be readjusted before each conditioning session.

In most cases, the classical conditioning paradigm is modified by the introduction of a negative reinforcement component. This involves providing the client the option of escaping or avoiding the aversive stimuli by emitting a response that is "incompatible" with the undesirable habit. For example, if the alcoholic spits out the sip of whisky that is presented, the shock is withheld. Or, if he or she spits it out after shock is on, the shock is immediately turned off. The former is called **avoidance training** (avoidance of the electric shock serves to negatively reinforce the individual for rejecting the habit stimuli); the latter is called **escape training** (escape from the electric shock serves to negatively reinforce the individual for rejecting the habit stimuli). The assumption underlying this combining of classical and operant conditioning procedures is that the habit stimuli should become conditioned stimuli for pain and discomfort, and that the rejection and/or avoidance should be strengthened by the termination of aversive stimulation.

Chemically Induced Aversion. Drugs that produce nausea, vomiting, and momentary respiratory paralysis have been used as unconditioned stimuli in classical conditioning treatment. As with electrically induced aversion, the goal is to reduce the valence of the undesirable habit by pairing it with the noxious effects of the drugs. Much of the work in this area has dealt with the treatment of chronic alcohol abuse.

Three drugs have been used: (1) Emetine (or emetine hydrochloride, or apomorphine), (2) Scoline (succinylcholine chloride dehydrate), and (3) Antabuse (disulfiram, or tetraethylthiuram disulfide). Since each drug produces different effects and requires different methods of administration, we will discuss them separately.

1. *Emetine.* This drug was first used during the late 1930s by W. L. Voegtlin and his colleagues at

the Shadel Sanatorium for alcoholics in Seattle, Washington (Lemere & Voegtlin, 1950; Voegtlin, 1940, 1947). Emetine is taken orally or intravenously and produces severe nausea and vomiting that can last as long as forty-five minutes. The individual is seated in a quiet, relatively distraction-free room and is given a dose of Emetine orally. In many instances, this is followed by an injection of a solution of Emetine and other nausea-producing drugs. Then, just as the individual begins to feel sick, he is given a jigger of whisky to smell and sip. He is told to concentrate on its smell, color, and taste. This procedure is repeated one or two more times during the period in which the noxious effects are being experienced. Conditioning sessions are scheduled every other day for seven to ten days using various alcoholic beverages.

As the reader probably recognizes, this procedure does not follow the classical conditioning paradigm exactly. Although the smell and taste of alcohol are paired with nausea and vomiting, it is not a one-to-one correspondence. To be maximally effective (at least theoretically), every instance of nausea and vomiting should be immediately preceded by the smell and taste of alcohol. However, the effects of Emetine are continuous, whereas the presentation of alcohol is discrete; thus, there are occasions when the nausea and vomiting occur and alcohol is not present.

2. *Scoline*. This controversial drug produces brief respiratory paralysis (apnea), which is accompanied by feelings of suffocation and terror. According to those who have studied the drug (Laverty, 1966; Sanderson, Campbell, & Laverty, 1962, 1963), Scoline apnea is a horrifying experience. With the client comfortably seated, an anesthetist inserts the intravenous needle through which the drug is administered. Then the client is given a glass of his favorite alcoholic beverage and is asked to smell and sip it. As the individual smells the drink, the Scoline is injected. Within three or four seconds the drug has its traumatic effects. The client's initial reaction is a sudden drop in GSR and tension in facial muscles. Scoline also produces tremulousness and twitching in certain muscles, followed by inability to move or breathe (Laverty, 1966). Fortunately for the client, the effects last only thirty to sixty seconds. The

client is then given a few minutes to recover and the procedure is repeated. Scoline's major advantage over Emetine is that it can be more easily regulated and therefore can be paired with ingestion of alcohol more reliably.

It is important to point out that this procedure has come under a great deal of criticism, primarily on ethical grounds. Two issues are really involved. First, the patients who participated in the original research (Sanderson, Campbell & Laverty, 1962) were not properly informed as to the nature of the treatment and did not know the full impact of effects. Second, the long-term effectiveness of the procedure (which is poor) does not appear to justify the pain and suffering the clients experienced. Some of the clients experienced dizziness, headaches, and severe emotional discomfort during the first three months following treatment (Laverty, 1966).

3. *Antabuse*. This drug interferes with the metabolism of alcohol so that any amount of alcohol in the bloodstream produces nausea, vomiting, increased heart rate, and cold sweating. Antabuse is usually taken orally in the morning and stays in the bloodstream for between two and three days. This procedure can be viewed as involving either classical or operant conditioning mechanisms. The classical conditioning interpretation is that during the two days following the ingestion of Antabuse, nausea and vomiting occur whenever alcohol is ingested until alcohol eventually becomes a conditioned stimulus for nausea and vomiting even without the Antabuse. The operant conditioning interpretation, on the other hand, is that while Antabuse is in the system the act of consuming alcoholic beverages is immediately punished by nausea and vomiting. Probably both things are happening.

Although Antabuse was first viewed as the "cure" for alcoholism, recent research has dampened therapists' enthusiasm (Nathan, 1976). One problem is that Antabuse sometimes produces violent reactions to aftershave lotion, cough medicine, and any other product containing alcohol. However, the main limitation is that most (99 percent) of those treated with Antabuse refuse to take the drug when they are no longer supervised (Lubetkin, Rivers, & Rosenberg, 1971). Although Antabuse has the potential for being a very effective way of eliminating the consumption of alcohol, in practice this has not been found to be so.

Covert Sensitization

The term "covert sensitization" has been used to describe an aversive conditioning procedure in which imaginal stimuli are used. This technique was suggested by Arnold Lazarus (1958) and others (Miller, 1959; Strel'chuk, 1957) in their reports of "hypnotically induced aversion" in which clients were hypnotized and instructed to imagine some undesirable problem behavior, and then to imagine feelings of nausea and pain. Joseph Cautela (1966, 1967) systematized the procedure, eliminated the hypnotic component, and called the result covert sensitization. Following the same classical conditioning format used with electrically and chemically induced aversion, the therapist has the client comfortably relaxed and then describes scenes of the client engaging in the undesirable habit that end with the client's encountering the aversive stimuli. The following passage taken from Cautela (1967, pp. 461–462) describes the procedure vividly:

> You are walking into a bar. You decide to have a glass of beer. You are now walking toward the bar. As you are approaching the bar you have a funny feeling in the pit of your stomach. Your stomach feels all queasy and nauseous. Some liquid comes up your throat and it is very sour. You try to swallow it back down, but as you do this, food particles start coming up your throat to your mouth. You are now reaching the bar and you order a beer. As the bartender is pouring the beer, puke comes up into your mouth. You try to keep your mouth closed and swallow it down. As soon as your hand touches the glass, you can't hold it down any longer. You have to open your mouth and you puke. It goes all over your hand, all over the glass and the beer. Snots and mucous come out of your nose. Your shirt and pants are full of vomit. The bartender has some on his shirt. You notice people looking at you. You get sick again and vomit some more and more.

But Cautela also introduces an escape component (p. 462):

> You turn away from the beer and immediately start to feel better and better. When you get out into clean fresh air you feel wonderful. You go home and clean yourself up.

This procedure is repeated in the therapist's office with variations of the habit (in the case of alcoholism, for example, wine, whisky, gin, and so on), and the client is instructed to practice the scenes at home twice a day. As with traditional aversion conditioning, the presumption is that the habit acquires aversive properties as a function of its repeated association with nausea and vomiting in imagination.

Effectiveness of Aversive Conditioning

Although case studies have demonstrated the successful application of each of these procedures for the elimination of a variety of habit disorders (for instance, Blake, 1965, 1967; Cautela, 1966, 1967; Hedberg & Campbell, 1974; Miller & Hersen, 1972; Yafa, 1973), controlled research has not found strong support for the methods (for instance, Hallam, Rachman, & Falkowski, 1972; MacCulloch, Feldman, Oxford, & MacCulloch, 1976; Miller, Hersen, Eisler, & Hemphill, 1973; Wilson, Leaf, & Nathan, 1975). There are at least two problems. The first concerns whether direct conditioning actually alters the valence of the stimuli associated with the undesirable habit. In a fascinating study, R. S. Hallam, S. Rachman, and W. Falkowski (1972) examined the physiological reactions (skin resistance and heart rate) of clients to habit stimuli used in aversive conditioning trials. If conditioning had the expected effects, as described in the preceding paragraph, clients should show marked physiological reactions to these stimuli following treatment. Ten chronic alcoholics received approximately 200 classical conditioning trials in which stimuli associated with drinking (for instance, picture of a bar, bottle of whisky) were paired with painful electric shock. Following treatment, these slides were presented along with slides unrelated to drinking.

The subjects' reactions to the slides were compared to those of a group of alcoholics who had received only group psychotherapy. There was no difference in the reactions of the two groups. Moreover, the two groups showed no difference in sobriety at a four-month follow-up evaluation. The only difference appeared to be in the subjects' taste preferences. Subjects who received direct conditioning reported greater dislike for the taste of alcohol than did control subjects. Thus, as R. S. Hallam and Stanley Rachman (1976) concluded in their review of the research on aversive conditioning, researchers have yet to obtain convincing evidence regarding specific psychophysiological effects of aversive conditioning treatment. Similar inconclusive results as to the physiological effects of aversive conditioning have been obtained in research on the elimination of cigarette smoking (Russell, Armstrong, & Patel, 1976).

One possible explanation for the failure of aversive conditioning is that the aversive stimuli used in most studies are not strong enough to compete with the positive valence of the undesirable habit. However, even when more intense stimulation, like that produced by Scoline, is used, the long-term effects have not been great. What is more, the ethical problems presented by techniques are considerable. The second problem with direct conditioning treatment in the therapist's office is the distinct likelihood that the client will discriminate between what happens in the office and what happens in the real world. Clients know that they will not be shocked or be given a nausea-inducing drug when they engage in the habit in the outside world. Even if the treatment did produce conditioned emotional responses in the office, it is unlikely they will be emitted when the client is in a different setting. We will discuss these issues in greater detail in Chapter 14.

APPLICATIONS

Overeating and Weight Control

We will begin with a review of the weight-control program devised by Richard Stuart and Barbara Davis (1972). The description will be detailed because this program clearly incorporates many of the operations central to behavioral self-control programs and serves as a clear example of many of Skinner's (1953) and Rachlin's (1974) recommendations.

Overweight people spend a large part of their lives trying desperately to lose weight and rarely succeed. According to one report (Wyden, 1965), overweight individuals go on an average of 1.5 diets a year and make over fifteen major attempts to lose weight between the ages of twenty-one and fifty. Most attempts fail. Albert Stunkard (1974, p. 103) reported that most of us who are overweight do not seek professional treatment and those of us who do often drop out without losing much weight:

> We surveyed the medical literature and summarized the results of treatment for obesity. We took all reports in a 10-year period and calculated what percentages of patients who entered treatment lost significant amounts of weight. There was a remarkable unanimity in these results. No more than 25 percent of the patients lost as much as 20 pounds and no more than 5 percent lost as much as 40 pounds. That is not a very good record.

Moreover, those who somehow manage to lose unwanted weight usually gain all of it back in a short period of time.

Medical authorities realize that different people require different amounts of food to maintain an "ideal" weight, and biological factors must be considered (Stunkard and Mahoney, 1976), although glandular abnormality is rarely the cause of obesity. For example, researchers (Goldman, Jaffa, & Schachter, 1968; Schachter, 1971; Schachter & Gross, 1968) have shown that obese people are more responsive to external cues signaling eating (sight, smell, and taste of food) than are individuals of normal weight. However, the major cause of obesity is simply overeating; there is an excess of caloric intake in relation to energy expended (Stunkard, 1974).

Another fact that serves as a basis for the behavioral approach to weight control is that much of eating is controlled by the environment. We often eat not because we are hungry or are in need of nourishment, but because it is "time to eat." In many situations, eating is simply expected of us—when we are at a party, or in an ice cream parlor. Thus, in most cases, obesity is the result of overeating—which is under situational control.

Charles Ferster and his colleagues J. I. Nurnberger and E. B. Levitt (1962) are credited with first conceptualizing obesity and weight control as problems of behavior management and self-control. Five years later, Stuart (1967) reported a remarkable series of case studies incorporating Ferster's procedures. All of Stuart's clients who remained in treatment (20 percent dropped out) lost at least thirty pounds and 30 percent lost more than forty pounds within twelve months. These results were by far the most outstanding ever reported for the treatment of obesity. Subsequent experimental research (Wollersheim, 1970) confirmed the effectiveness of behavior modification in this area. These procedures have been published in a readable manual entitled *Slim Chance in a Fat World* by Stuart and Davis (1972).

The general procedure Stuart and Davis outline involves pinpointing the environmental conditions associated with eating (times, places, situations), and then devising ways to alter these conditions. As with most behavior modification procedures, the first step is careful observation in order to determine the antecedents and consequences of eating. Although the therapist might suggest probable conditions that contribute to the problem, the client must do most of this assessment.

The first suggestion Stuart and Davis make with regard to actually modifying eating behavior is to avoid "dangerous" situations that encourage overeating. Clients must reduce the number of stimuli that signal "eat" for them. The point is not for clients to go "cold turkey" and stop eating; rather, they merely set aside a limited number of places to do all their eating. Thus, instead of enjoying the midnight snack curled up with a book or in front of the television set, individuals must go to the dining room table to have the food. While they are eating, they are not to do anything else; they are not to read, or watch television, or talk on the phone—just eat. The object is to limit the situational cues that suggest food and thereby cause the person to eat. This step clearly differs from most traditional techniques because rather than trying abruptly to reduce the amount of food consumed, the goal is to develop new patterns, or habits, of eating.

Another important feature of this self-control program is a reduction in the consumption of especially fattening food. The strategy is to make it easy to resist temptation and *as difficult as possible* to succumb to "problem" foods. Obviously, if there is a half-gallon of ice cream in the freezer when a person gets hungry late at night, he or she will be more likely to eat than if the ice cream is not there at all. The best way to make sure the ice cream will not be there is, of course, not buying it in the first place—in other words, changing shopping behavior. The purpose is to remove the temptation before it becomes really strong. (This recommendation directly follows from Rachlin's conceptualization of self-control.)

Stuart and Davis recommended that food shopping be done when the stomach is full and not when the person is hungry. A person who shops just after eating, for example, is much less likely to lose control in the bakery aisle than if one who has not eaten for hours and is ravenously hungry. This recommendation follows from Skinner's (1953) observations and advises shopping when internal cues make fattening food less attractive. Stuart and Davis also suggest that the person shop from a list and bring only enough money to buy what is on the list.

Eating between meals is another bad habit that must be controlled in order to lose weight and keep it off. One way to help avoid between-meal eating is to *eat three meals a day.* Too many people skip breakfast or lunch (which usually involve less fattening foods) in an effort to lose weight, and then stuff themselves at dinner and devour fattening snacks in the evening to satisfy the gigantic hunger that has been created. The later in the day the person eats the worse it is, because the body does not have an opportunity to work off the additional calories. If a person eats a balanced breakfast and lunch, it will be easier not to overindulge at dinner or during the less active evening hours.

If individuals do snack, then they should provide themselves with nonfattening foods to snack on and do it in only one location. If all that is around to eat is raw carrots (instead of cookies or potato chips), then snacking means ingesting many fewer calories. Eating off smaller plates and dishes is another way Stuart and Davis suggest for reducing food consumption. Four ounces of lean meat and one-half cup of mashed potatoes is going to seem like more if it is served on a salad-size plate rather than on a dinner plate.

Another method is to eat more slowly. It is a well-known physiological fact that the sensation of satiation is delayed (Stunkard, 1974). The feeling that the stomach is full does not reach the brain until well after the food has reached the stomach. This means that the faster a person eats, the more that person is going to shovel down between the time the stomach is full and the time he or she is aware of the fullness. If eating can be slowed down, therefore, there will be less food in the stomach when the feeling of fullness finally comes and the person stops eating. To slow the pace of eating, Stuart and Davis suggest interposing short delays at several points. Simply put down the knife and fork and do not pick them up until a predetermined period of time has elapsed (for example, two or three minutes).

It is also suggested that individuals modify their social environment to reinforce the new self-control behaviors and help extinguish indulgence. This means getting the assistance of family and friends. For example, the wife might be asked not to bake the special dessert but instead prepare the husband's favorite roast. The husband might agree to take his wife out to a special event or buy her a new dress after she has successfully followed the weight-control program for a certain period of time. Contracts have also been written by the family, in which certain rewards and privileges are promised contingent upon the development of certain new eating habits by the obese person.

The focus is on better eating habits, not weight loss per se. Although the goal is to take off unwanted pounds, reinforcing the individual for losing weight introduces two problems. First, even a person who carefully follows a very restricted, low-calorie diet will lose weight erratically. It is possible to lose three pounds one week and then not lose anything for the next two, even though caloric intake remains the same. If reinforcement is made contingent on weight loss, the behavior that is to be strengthened (eating less fattening foods) will be reinforced on an irregular schedule —one week the dieter will be reinforced, the next he or she may not. Making reinforcement contingent upon altered eating behavior increases the likelihood that the individual will lose weight and keep it off. The second problem with reinforcing

weight loss is that the individual may find ways to meet the contingencies which may be undesirable or may circumvent the entire purpose of the program. For example, one investigator (Mann, 1972) found that individuals who were reinforced for weight loss would use extreme measures to meet the contingency requirements. These included taking laxatives, diuretics, and doing vigorous exercises just before being weighed. In addition to being dangerous to health, these techniques have no lasting effect.

Stuart and Davis recognize the importance of following a sensible diet. The object is to balance the amount of calories taken in with the amount used up through exercise, while at the same time maintaining high-quality nutrition. Toward this end, Stuart and Davis, among others, have devised methods of categorizing foods into different groups so that foods within each group can be freely exchanged for one another in different situations. Rather than trying to impose a rigid diet, they suggest a method for eating that leaves decision making (and control) up to the individual. They also suggest ways the overweight person can increase the amount of exercise and thus burn up excess calories. Once again, it is a question of situational control, of establishing the antecedents and consequences of exercise (and nonexercise), and then altering them to make the desired behavior more likely to occur.

Stuart and Davis point out that one way to strengthen the antecedents of exercise is to associate companionship with exercise, so that exercise becomes a social event. For instance, the person can have a conversation while going for a walk rather than over coffee and doughnuts. Starting out with an easy, overall exercise like walking will also eliminate the aversive consequences of sore muscles and fatigue that can result from sudden, strenuous exercise when a person is not used to it. *After* the body has gradually adjusted to more exercise is the time to arrange for more strenuous activity with others, either with friends or by going to a nearby gym.

To help keep up the balance between caloric intake and output, Stuart and Davis suggest making charts and graphs of *eating and exercise behavior* in order to compare the two, so that the dieter can see exactly what is happening at any point. In this way, the person can learn how his or her own particular metabolism works in relation to caloric intake and output.

Although this approach to weight reduction has been shown to be clearly superior to more traditional dietary and pharmacological methods, long-term followup data on its effectiveness are lacking (Jeffrey, 1976). At the present time, it is unclear whether weight losses achieved through self-control programs can be maintained. Until this research is carried out, cautious enthusiasm for the behavioral approach to treating obesity is advised.

Cigarette Smoking

Smoking shares with overeating the insidious characteristic of being immediately pleasurable while leading to long-term aversive consequences. Many people find it even harder to quit smoking than to cut down on eating. One reason giving up cigarettes is so difficult is that the long term negative consequences of smoking are extremely remote—certainly more remote than those associated with overeating. If a person continually takes in more calories than he or she burns up, it will not be long before he or she is fat—that much is guaranteed. Lung cancer and emphysema, on the other hand, take years to develop, and many smokers never contract either malady. We all know of people who have smoked for fifty years and never had any respiratory ailment. So it is quite understandable that many of us ignore the possibility of permanent damage from smoking and have the attitude that "it will never happen to me." For most smokers, it takes a specific health problem or a physician's warning that serious illness is imminent to get them to quit (Straits, 1966).

The intransigence of the smoking habit can be attributed to other reasons. One involves the issue of stimulus control. There is almost no situation in which people do not smoke. People often light up a cigarette as they dress in the morning, on the way to work, at the office, after lunch, at a party, and so on. For this reason, it is difficult to avoid stimuli that signal smoking. Another problem is the "quasi-addictive" nature of cigarette smoking. Even though there is no evidence that

people actually become addicted to nicotine (there is no single set of characteristic withdrawal symptoms, and physical dependence does not occur), a psychological dependence does seem to develop (*Surgeon General's Report*, 1964). Reactions associated with quitting vary from person to person, with the most common being hostility, aggressiveness, and irritability (Hutchinson & Emley, 1973). Another impediment to quitting is the unavailability of an effective incompatible response for smoking. An individual who wants to eat can stuff himself with carrots instead of candy bars (not necessarily an acceptable substitute, but a substitute nonetheless); but when that person wants a cigarette, nothing else will do. Chewing gum is not a satisfactory substitute.

Many techniques have been used to help people stop smoking; unfortunately, none has been completely successful. The initial effect of most procedures is an immediate and total cessation of smoking followed by a gradual relapse (Hunt, Barnett, & Branch, 1971). The pattern of backsliding is shown in Figure 8–2; by the end of three months over half of the ex-smokers have started

Figure 8–2. Relapse curves based on 84 smoking modification studies. Results of three heroin and one alcohol study are included for comparison. From W. A. Hunt, L. W. Barnett, & L. G. Branch, Relapse rates in addiction program. *Journal of Clinical Psychology*, 1971, **27**, p. 456, fig. 1. Used by permission.

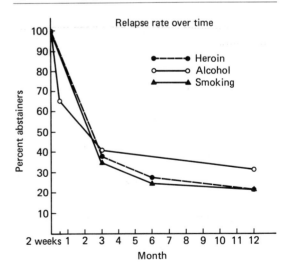

Relapse rate over time

Heroin
Alcohol
Smoking

Percent abstainers

2 weeks 1 2 3 4 5 6 7 8 9 10 11 12
Month

smoking again. Since we cannot present a fool-proof program, we will briefly review the various methods that have been employed to help people stop smoking.

Let us begin by summarizing briefly the non-behavioral approaches. Throughout the United States and Canada, smoking cessation clinics have been established to provide people with support and encouragement in their attempts to stop smoking. Although the specific techniques vary from clinic to clinic, the general format involves group meetings in which ex-smokers band together and group leaders give lectures on the hazards of smoking. In order to make stopping smoking less aversive, various drugs that produce effects similar to nicotine have been prescribed for ex-smokers. The most commonly used drug is lobeline sulfate. As with smoking cessation clinics, beneficial effects from the medication have been temporary and may have resulted from unspecified factors such as demand characteristics (Bernstein, 1969; Schwartz, 1969). Hypnosis has been used to provide "unconscious suggestions" and to uncover "personality conflicts" presumed to underlie the individual's "need to smoke" (Bryan, 1964). Research has not shown hypnosis to be effective (Johnston & Donoghue, 1971). Subjecting the smoker to periods of sensory deprivation and then providing antismoking material has also been tried, but to no avail. Based on research presently available, we must conclude that non-behavioral approaches really have very little to offer the person who wants to quit smoking.

Three different strategies have been used in the application of behavioral principles to the cessation of smoking. Clients receive either direct aversive conditioning in the therapist's office, instructions in self-control, or self-control training along with the instruction to quit smoking abruptly (that is, to pick a date to quit and then stop smoking from that day on). Although these methods have not provided a magic cure, many researchers consider the behavioral approach the most promising (Bernstein, 1969; Bernstein & McAlister, 1976; Keutzer, Lichtenstein, & Mees, 1968; Lichtenstein & Keutzer, 1971).

As we mentioned earlier, the purpose of aversive conditioning is to change the reinforcement value (valence) of the undesirable behavior. For smoking, the goal is to make inhaling cigarette smoke repugnant. This strategy involves pairing smoking with some noxious stimulus; for instance, electric shock (Best & Steffy, 1971), smoke and hot air blown in the smoker's face (Schmahl, Lichtenstein, & Harris, 1972), and nausea-inducing thoughts (Cautela, 1967). The most effective of these procedures involves the client smoking as rapidly as possible until he or she feels sick. This technique, known as **rapid smoking,** consists of having the client inhale cigarette smoke every six seconds until he or she can no longer tolerate it. Trials usually last five minutes, with the client smoking four or five cigarettes each trial. During a session, two or three trials are scheduled with five-minute rest periods in between.

Reports on the effectiveness of rapid smoking are mixed. The initial research (Schmahl, Lichtenstein, & Harris, 1972) produced promising results of 60 to 65 percent abstinence at six months (compared with the curves shown in Figure 8–2, these data are indeed impressive). However, other researchers have been unable to replicate this high rate of success (Claiborn, Lewis, & Humble, 1972; Conway, 1977; Marston & McFall, 1971). One important variable influencing the long-term effectiveness of the rapid smoking procedure is the "emotional atmosphere" in which it is employed. The probability that the ex-smoker will succeed is greatly enhanced if the therapist is supportive and provides a positive expectancy (Bernstein & McAlister, 1976).

Researchers have pointed out a possible danger associated with the rapid smoking procedure (Dawley, Ellithorpe, & Tretola, 1976; Hauser, 1974; Horan, Hackett, Nicholas, Linberg, Stone, & Lukaski, 1977; Lichtenstein, 1974). For some individuals, rapid smoking produces a temporary change in the oxygen level in the blood that could produce serious complications for those suffering from coronary disease. Therefore, it is important that clients be screened before receiving this method of treatment. It is recommended that individuals be rejected for rapid smoking if they are (1) not in good health, (2) forty years of age or older, or (3) obese (Dawley, Ellithorpe, & Tretola, 1976).

Self-control techniques have met with limited success in the modification of smoking behavior.

One procedure involves gradually reducing the number of stimuli associated with smoking. Toward this end, many clever methods have been devised. One way of trying to establish stimulus control is quite similar to a method described in modifying overeating. A "smoking place" is established—one particular chair, for instance; and the smoker is instructed to smoke only in that chair. While smoking, he or she must not do anything but smoke—no reading, watching television, or talking to others. Supposedly, the smoker will get tired of turning off the television, or stopping a conversation, and racing to the chair every time a cigarette is desired, and will therefore automatically smoke less. To increase this effect, the chair can eventually be moved to an inconvenient location. In the end, the whole situation will become too silly and troublesome, the theory goes, and the smoker will give up cigarettes.

Another method involves the use of a special cigarette case (Azrin & Powell, 1969). This tool has a time lock built into it, so that it will open only after a certain interval and offer the smoker a single cigarette. As time goes on it opens less and less, until finally it does not open at all. Another special cigarette case delivers electric shock when it is opened (Powell & Azrin, 1968).

But why would this work, one might ask? Wouldn't the smoker just go out and buy a new pack of cigarettes and ignore these contraptions? That is a real possibility: it is what Soviet Premier Leonid Brezhnev did when he tried to curb his smoking with just such a device. He confessed to the press, "I have a reserve pack in the other pocket." Unfortunately, within a short period of time, most individuals abandon such self-control procedures and return to their old habits (Bernstein & McAlister, 1976; Flaxman, 1976).

Aversive conditioning along with self-control manipulations (that is, stimulus control procedures, contingency contracts with family and friends, programming incompatible behaviors, and so on) has been found to be a relatively effective method of curbing smoking. Success rates of 50 percent at one-year followup have been reported using the above procedures in combination (Chapman, Smith, & Layden, 1971; Harris & Rothberg, 1972). In one of the few controlled studies in the area, Harry Lando (1977) obtained

76 percent success (at six-month followup) with a multifaceted behavioral program.

Treatment was carried out during weekly group sessions in which subjects received rapid smoking training, instruction in self-control, and general emotional support from each other. The subjects also signed contracts with the therapist in which they agreed to forfeit money for each cigarette they smoked (between twenty-five cents and three dollars per cigarette). After they stopped smoking, booster sessions were scheduled to help them not to begin to smoke again. Although Lando recognizes that this study does not identify the exact contribution of each component of the effective treatment package, he contends his method does offer a viable means of helping people stop smoking. The results certainly support that conclusion.

Alcoholism

There are over 10 million alcoholics in the United States today, and, according to the U.S. Public Health Service, alcoholism is the fourth most serious health problem in our country. Even after exhaustive searches for means of diagnosing the potential alcoholic and effective methods of treatment, traditional psychotherapeutic techniques have not improved the lot of the alcoholic (Hill & Blane, 1967; Wallgren & Barry, 1973). During the last decade, the application of behavioral principles in this area has received considerable interest.

Behavioral alcoholic rehabilitation programs do not involve in-depth personality analysis or the development of willpower; rather, the focus is on either directly suppressing problem drinking or increasing incompatible positive behaviors, or both. Moreover, the goal of an increasing number of behavioral programs is to teach alcoholics to drink in moderation. Total abstinence is no longer viewed as essential to successful rehabilitation (Cohen, Liebson, Faillace, & Allen, 1971; Davies, 1962; Miller, 1972). This is in marked contrast to the disease model of alcoholism, which holds that, no matter how long alcoholics have gone without drinking, once they taste alcohol they will be unable to control their "desire" and will drink to excess (Jellinek, 1960). The behavioral approach to the issue of abstinence versus moderation is empirically based. It has been shown that alcoholics do not necessarily "lose control" after having a drink (Marlott, Demming, & Reid, 1973; Sobell, Sobell, & Christelman, 1972) and that they can become social (that is, moderate) drinkers (Davies, 1962).

Three behavioral strategies have been used in the treatment of alcoholics: (1) decreasing the reinforcement value of alcohol through aversive conditioning, (2) developing adaptive coping skills that replace the use of alcohol as a crutch, and (3) rearranging the individual's social environment so that he or she is directly reinforced for activities incompatible with excessive drinking.

Aversive Conditioning. As we pointed out earlier in this chapter, electric shock, nausea-inducing drugs, and images of unpleasant scenes (covert sensitization) have been paired with the taste of alcohol in a classical conditioning paradigm in order to make drinking repugnant. As was the case with cigarette smoking, aversive conditioning has not been very successful in treating alcoholism (Miller & Hersen, 1972; Miller, Hersen, Eisler, & Hemphill, 1973; Wilson & Tracey, 1976). One problem is that the client discriminates between the situation under which conditioning takes place and the real world—thus, generalization fails to occur (Hallam, Rachman, & Falkowski, 1972; Miller & Barlow, 1973). When drugs that make the individual nauseous and dizzy upon consuming alcohol have been used, it has been necessary to monitor clients closely to ensure that they take the drugs (Bigelow, Liebson, & Lawrence, 1973).

Coping Skills Training. This method is based on the notion that, for the alcoholic, the primary function of alcohol is a means of escape. Indeed, it might be. Alcohol is an effective sedative; used in excess, it renders a person physically debilitated and thereby unable to participate. Furthermore, it provides an excuse for otherwise unacceptable behavior. According to this thesis, when faced with difficult situations they cannot handle, alcoholics escape by becoming intoxicated.

The purpose of coping skills training is to provide the alcoholic with other, more adaptive, means of coping. The alcoholic is taught first to identify specific situations that provoke excessive drinking and then to generate more effective ways of dealing with them. For instance, in a case of an overly passive and ineffectual alcoholic, teaching him how to respond more assertively to his wife's demands resulted in a marked decrease in his consumption of alcohol (Eisler, Miller, & Hersen, 1973). In a controlled study, Mark and Linda Sobell (1973a, 1973b, 1976) provided individualized coping skills training to a group of chronic alcoholics residing in a state hospital. Each patient was first required to determine those situations and times in which he typically drank to excess. He was then instructed to think of other ways he might handle such situations and to identify the long-term consequences of each coping strategy. Of course, this took a great deal of coaching on the part of the therapists. Patients were also taught how to drink in moderation (for instance, sip alcoholic beverages rather than gulp them; drink alcohol with mixers instead of straight).

In order to evaluate the effectiveness of the procedures, each patient's progress was assessed six months and again two years after he was discharged from the hospital. Patients who participated in the program showed significantly better adjustment (more days sober) than similar alcoholics who had participated in traditional psychotherapeutic rehabilitation programs in the hospital. As in almost every study we have considered in the area of habit disorders, it is impossible to determine the relative contribution of the components of the treatment program. Of course, many clinicians are pleased to find a treatment package that appears to have a significant impact on the problem, regardless of whether the effective components can be identified.

Environmental Reprogramming. Intervening in the client's natural environment so that desirable behaviors are prompted and reinforced is a common strategy in behavior modification. In fact, it is the ideal. In a controlled study, George Hunt and Nathan Azrin (1973) evaluated the effectiveness of such an intervention program with institutionalized alcoholics. Following discharge from the hospital, eight patients participated in a multi-faceted community-reinforcement program designed to rearrange vocational, familial, and social reinforcement contingencies to optimize successful adjustment. In addition to vocational and social counseling, patients and their families received training in contingency contracting and means of building more satisfying patterns of interaction. The therapist assisted the family in negotiating such issues as how household chores should be divided, how financial matters should be handled, and so on. In order to provide an emotional support system, a social club was established which held weekly functions such as bingo games, fish fries, and the like. During the first month following discharge, the therapist visited the patient once or twice each week. At these meetings the therapist reviewed the patient's progress and made recommendations as to how the patient might deal with problems that arose.

The rehabilitation of these patients was compared with that of matched controls who did not participate in the intervention program following their discharge. Across all measures, patients who participated in the community-reinforcement program did much better than those who did not. For instance, the mean monthly income for the community-reinforcement group was $355 per month versus $190 per month for the controls. Although these results are indeed impressive, the small number of participants makes one reluctant to conclude that environmental reprogramming is the total answer to the problem of rehabilitating alcoholics. Hunt and Azrin's program must be replicated with other personnel and subject populations.

SUMMARY

Behavioral psychologists have tackled the problem of eliminating unwanted habits in two ways, either by teaching people self-control techniques or through aversive conditioning in the therapist's office. Training in self-control is the more popular method.

Behavioral theorists generally agree that self-control essentially involves the individual's emitting certain controlling responses which alter critical features of the environment. This, in turn, affects the probability of the problem behavior (the controlled response). That is, the individual manipulates those variables that control his or her behavior.

Some disagreement arises regarding the extent to which cognitive processes such as covert self-instruction, self-reinforcement, and self-punishment are involved. According to Skinner (1953), people control their own behavior in precisely the same ways they would control someone else's behavior. He argues that people exercise self-control by manipulating those environmental variables that control behavior (that is, by altering antecedents, consequences, and setting events).

Kanfer (1970) also contends that environmental contingencies are the ultimate source of behavior control, and that self-control can be analyzed in terms of those contingencies. However, unlike Skinner, Kanfer gives greater importance to the role of self-evaluation and to what he describes as covert self-reinforcement and punishment. According to Kanfer, how the individual evaluates his or her own behavior, independent of immediate environmental consequences, affects what the individual does. These self-generated cognitive events interact with environmental variables to control behavior. Kanfer also identifies a third source of control, the individual's biological system, which includes conditions of deprivation and satiation of food, sleep, sex, and so on, as well as condition of homeostatic regulation systems. These three sources of control have been labeled alpha, beta, and gamma.

Researchers in the area of self-control recognize two general strategies of self-control: environmental planning and behavioral programming. Environmental planning directly follows from Skinner's (1953) formulations of self-control and involves the individual's altering the relevant situational variables that influence his or her behavior. Behavioral programming, on the other hand, more closely follows Kanfer's (1977) model and involves the self-administering of reinforcing and punishing consequences. The two strategies do incorporate different operations, but they are in no way incompatible and are typically combined in clinical self-control programs.

Although behavioral self-control programs have been devised to help people control a variety of problem behaviors ranging from procrastination and nail biting to alcoholism and depression, most of the research on self-control has focused on ways to help people reduce their consumption of fattening foods, cigarettes, and alcohol.

CASE STUDY 8–1

McCULLOUGH, J. P., HUNTSINGER, G. M., & NAY, W. R. SELF-CONTROL TREATMENT OF AGGRESSION IN A SIXTEEN-YEAR-OLD MALE: A CASE STUDY. *JOURNAL OF CONSULTING AND CLINICAL PSYCHOLOGY,* 1977, **45,** 322–331.

Larry, a sixteen-year-old high school sophomore, was referred for psychological services by his parents because of his long-standing aggressive outbursts. Whenever he was told to do something he did not want to do, challenged on something he had said, or punished, he would strike out. He might begin by yelling at the other person and then try to hit him. One incident reported involved Larry's losing his temper with a physical education teacher and the school principal. Apparently the teacher had reprimanded Larry for being late to class. Larry's response was to argue and then berate the teacher in front of the class. When the teacher took him to the principal's office, Larry became even more irrational and stormed out. Larry's parents reported similar incidents involving disputes over use of the family car and performing household chores.

Rather than trying to analyze Larry's problems in terms of unresolved conflicts and hostility towards authority figures, the therapist set out to teach Larry self-control techniques that he might use to defuse his anger and inhibit his outbursts. The aim was for Larry to recognize cues that indicated he was angry and about to lose his temper and then to emit behaviors that would be incompatible with aggression reactions.

The therapist began by helping Larry identify the antecedents of the problem behavior, which included: (1) subvocal cursing, (2) the thought that he would not cooperate, (3) a cold shiver running up his back, (4) muscle tension beginning in his feet and then moving up his body, and (5) right arm and fist tensing. Once Larry was able to recognize these antecedents, he was taught how to interrupt the chain and prevent temper outbursts.

The therapist first taught Larry how to stop his aggression-eliciting thoughts by carefully monitoring his own cognitions and then providing himself with instructions to terminate the ruminations (thought stopping). He also learned how to tense and relax his entire torso in rapid succession to inhibit the building muscle tension. If all these methods proved unsuccessful and he noticed his right arm tensing, he was instructed to leave the scene by walking away or doing something else.

The cooperation of the family and school personnel was secured, and contingency contracts between Larry and significant others were written. Teachers were informed of the self-control program and readily agreed to let Larry handle his temper in his own way. If Larry walked away while talking with them, they were not to continue the conversation until he returned and calmly expressed his interest in talking. The school counselor also agreed to collect daily reports from teachers on Larry's progress.

Teachers reported that Larry was able to control his outbursts. On one occasion, Larry nearly hit another classmate who refused to vacate Larry's assigned seat. After asking the chap to move, Larry drew back his fist, hesitated, and then walked out of the room. The therapist monitored Larry's progress for twenty-two months following self-control training. During that period, there were only two temper outbursts, and the school guidance counselor reported that Larry had made a successful adjustment.

CASE STUDY 8–2

MORGANSTERN, K. P. CIGARETTE SMOKE AS A NOXIOUS STIMU-
LUS IN SELF-MANAGED AVERSION THERAPY FOR COMPULSIVE EAT-
ING: TECHNIQUE AND CASE ILLUSTRATION. *BEHAVIOR THERAPY*,
1974, **5**, 255–260.

This case shows the ingenious use of aversive conditioning to reduce the
consumption of fattening "junk" foods. In contrast to many clinical case
studies in which it is difficult to determine exactly what factors produce the
positive change, Morganstern's use of a multiple baseline design (Chapter 3)
permitted a clear evaluation of the effectiveness of the self-control procedures.

The client was a twenty-four-year-old obese female graduate student. In
addition to three meals a day, she reported that she ate "junk" food
throughout the day. Her favorites were candy, cookies, doughnuts, ice
cream, and pizza. Despite the use of appetite-suppressant drugs and
countless attempts to diet, she was unable to control her consumption of
these fattening foods.

After monitoring her weight and food consumption for four weeks, Morganstern instituted an aversive conditioning program. Since Miss C reported that she found cigarette smoke distasteful and nauseating, a decision was made to pair cigarette smoke with the taste of the "junk" foods.
Conditioning sessions were first conducted in the therapist's office and

Figure 8–3. Mean daily consumption of candy, cookies, and doughnuts as a function of aversive contingency application. From K. P. Morganstern, Cigarette smoke
as a noxious stimulus in self-managed aversion therapy for compulsive eating: Technique and case illustration. *Behavior Therapy*, 1974, **5**, p. 257, fig. 1. By permission of Academic Press and the author.

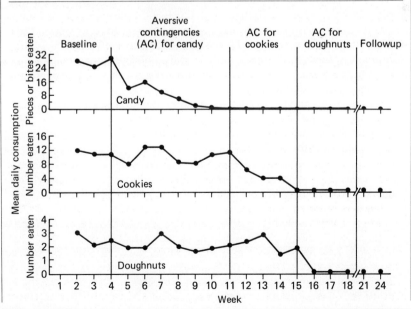

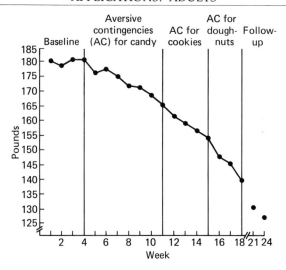

Figure 8–4. Weight as a function of aversive contingency applications to candy, cookies, and doughnuts. From K. P. Morganstern, Cigarette smoke as a noxious stimulus in self-managed aversion therapy for compulsive eating: Technique and case illustration. *Behavior Therapy,* 1974, **5,** p. 258, fig. 2. By permission of Academic Press and the author.

then carried out by the client at home. Candy was the first food to be paired with cigarette smoke. On successive trials, the client was instructed to take a bite of candy and chew it for a few seconds. Just before she swallowed it, she was to take a deep drag from a lighted cigarette. This was repeated for ten minutes two times each day for seven weeks. The aversive conditioning procedures were then applied to cookies for four weeks, then doughnuts for three weeks. Figure 8–3 shows the effect of these procedures. Consumption of each junk food diminished once aversive conditioning procedures were applied. Figure 8–4 shows the pattern of weight reduction during treatment.

Although pizza and ice cream were not paired with cigarette smoke, Miss C reported that she began reducing her intake of those foods as well. She expressed the attitude that: "If I gave up eating all that candy and other stuff, I can do anything!" (p. 258).

REFERENCES

Ainslie, G. Impulse control in pigeons. *Journal of the Experimental Analysis of Behavior*, 1974, **21**, 485–489.

Axelrod, S., Hall, R. V., Weis, L., & Rohrer, S. Use of self-imposed contingencies to reduce the frequency of smoking behavior. In M. J. Mahoney & C. E. Thoresen (Eds.), *Self-control: Power to the person*. Monterey, Calif.: Brooks/Cole, 1974.

Azrin, N. H., & Powell, J. Behavioral engineering: The use of response priming to improve prescribed self-medication. *Journal of Applied Behavior Analysis*, 1969, **2**, 39–42.

Bandura, A. *Principles of behavior modification*. New York: Holt, Rinehart & Winston, 1969.

Bandura, A. Self-reinforcement processes. In R. Glaser (Ed.), *The nature of reinforcement*. New York: Academic Press, 1971.

Bandura, A., Grusec, J. E., & Menlove, F. L. Some social determinants of self-monitoring reinforcement systems. *Journal of Personality and Social Psychology*, 1967, **5**, 449–455.

Bandura, A., & Kupers, C. J. The transmission of patterns of self-reinforcement through modeling. *Journal of Abnormal and Social Psychology*, 1964, **69**, 1–9.

Bandura, A., & Whalen, C. K. The influence of antecedent reinforcement and divergent modeling cues on patterns of self-reward. *Journal of Personality and Social Psychology*, 1966, **3**, 373–382.

Beneke, W. M., & Harris, N. B. Teaching self-control of study behavior. *Behaviour Research and Therapy*, 1972, **10**, 35–41.

Bernstein, D. A. Modification of smoking behavior: An evaluative review. *Psychological Bulletin*, 1969, **71**, 418–440.

Bernstein, D. A., & McAlister, A. The modification of smoking behavior: Progress and problems. *Addictive Behaviors*, 1976, **1**, 89–102.

Best, J. A., & Steffy, R. A. Smoking modification procedures tailored to subject characteristics. *Behavior Therapy*, 1971, **2**, 177–191.

Bigelow, G., Liebson, I., & Lawrence, C. *Prevention of alcohol abuse by reinforcement of incompatible behavior*. Miami: Association for the Advancement of Behavior Therapy, 1973.

Blake, B. G. The application of behaviour therapy to the treatment of alcoholism. *Behaviour Research and Therapy*, 1965, **3**, 75–85.

Blake, B. G. A follow-up of alcoholics treated by behaviour therapy. *Behaviour Research and Therapy*, 1967, **5**, 89–94.

Bolstad, O. D., & Johnson, S. M. Self-regulation in the modification of disruptive classroom behavior. *Journal of Applied Behavior Analysis*, 1972, **5**, 443–454.

Bootzin, R. R. Stimulus control treatment for insomnia. *Proceedings of the Eightieth Annual Convention of the American Psychological Association*, 1972, **7**, 395–396.

Boudin, H. M. Contingency contracting as a therapeutic tool in the deceleration of amphetamine use. *Behavior Therapy*, 1972, **3**, 604–608.

Broden, M., Hall, R. V., & Mitts, B. The effect of self-recording on the classroom behavior of two eighth-grade students. *Journal of Applied Behavior Analysis*, 1971, **4**, 191–199.

Bryan, W. J. Hypnosis and smoking. *Journal of the American Institute of Hypnosis*, 1964, **5**, 17–37.

Cautela, J. R. Treatment of compulsive behavior by covert sensitization. *Psychological Records*, 1966, **16**, 33–41.

Cautela, J. R. Covert sensitization. *Psychological Reports*, 1967, **20**, 459–468.

Cautela, J. R. Covert reinforcement. *Behavior Therapy*, 1970, **1**, 33–50.

Chapman, R. F., Smith, J. W., & Layden, T. A. Elimination of cigarette smoking by punishment and self-management training. *Behaviour Research and Therapy*, 1971, **9**, 255–264.

Claiborn, W. J., Lewis, P., & Humble, S. Stimulus satiation and smoking: A revisit. *Journal of Clinical Psychology*, 1972, **28**, 416–419.

Cohen, M., Liebson, I. A., Faillace, L. A., & Allen, R. R. Moderate drinking by chronic alcoholics. *Journal of Nervous and Mental Disease*, 1971, **53**, 434–444.

Conway, J. B. Behavioral self-control of smoking through aversive conditioning and self-management. *Journal of Consulting and Clinical Psychology*, 1977, **45**, 348–357.

Craighead, W. E., Kazdin, A. E., & Mahoney, M. J. *Behavior modification: Principles, issues, and applications*. Boston: Houghton Mifflin, 1976.

Davies, D. L. Normal drinking in recovered alcohol addicts. *Quarterly Journal of Studies on Alcohol*, 1962, **23**, 94–104.

Dawley, H. H., Ellithorpe, D. B., & Tretola, R. Aversive smoking: Carboxyhemoglobin levels before and after rapid smoking. *Journal of Behavior Therapy and Experimental Psychiatry*, 1976, **7**, 13–15.

Eisler, R. M., Miller, P. M., & Hersen, M. Components of assertive behavior. *Journal of Clinical Psychology*, 1973, **29**, 295–299.

Ferster, C. B., Nurnberger, J. I., & Levitt, E. B. The control of eating. *Journal of Mathetics*, 1962, **1**, 87–109.

Fixsen, D. L., Phillips, E. L., & Wolf, M. M. Achievement Place: The reliability of self-reporting and peer-reporting and their effects on behavior. *Journal of Applied Behavior Analysis*, 1972, **5**, 19–30.

Flaxman, J. Quitting smoking. In W. E. Craighead, A. E. Kazdin, & M. J. Mahoney (Eds.), *Behavior modification: Principles, issues, and applications*. Boston: Houghton Mifflin, 1976.

Fox, L. Effecting the use of efficient study habits. *Journal of Mathetics*, 1962, **1**, 76–86.

Goldman, R., Jaffa, M., & Schachter, S. Yom Kippur, Air Force, dormitory food, and eating behavior of obese and normal persons. *Journal of Personality and Social Psychology*, 1968, **10**, 117–123.

Goldstein, K. M. A comparison of self-reports and peer-reports on smoking and drinking behavior. *Psychological Reports*, 1966, **18**, 702.

Hallam, R. S., & Rachman, S. Current status of aversion therapy. In M. Hersen, R. M. Eisler, & P. M. Miller (Eds.), *Progress in behavior modification*, Vol. 2. New York: Academic Press, 1976.

Hallam, R., Rachman, S., & Falkowski, W. Subjective attitudinal and physiological effects of electrical aversion therapy. *Behaviour Research and Therapy*, 1972, **10**, 1–13.

Harris, M. B., & Rothberg, C. A self-control approach to reduced smoking. *Psychological Reports*, 1972, **31**, 165–166.

Hauser, R. Rapid smoking as a technique of behavior modification: Caution in the selection of subjects. *Journal of Consulting and Clinical Psychology*, 1974, **42**, 625.

Hedberg, A. G., & Campbell, L. A comparison of four behavioral treatments of alcoholism. *Journal of Behavior Therapy and Experimental Psychiatry*, 1974, **5**, 251–256.

Herbert, E. W., & Baer, D. M. Training parents as behavior modifiers: Self-recording of contingent attention. *Journal of Applied Behavior Analysis*, 1972, **5**, 139–149.

Herrnstein, R. J. On the law of effect. *Journal of the Experimental Analysis of Behavior*, 1970, **13**, 243–266.

Hill, M. J., & Blane, H. T. Evaluation of psychotherapy with alcoholics: A critical review. *Quarterly Journal of Studies of Alcohol*, 1967, **28**, 76–104.

Horan, J. J., Hackett, G., Nicholas, W. C., Linberg, S. E., Stone, C. I., & Lukaski, H. C. Rapid smoking: A cautionary note. *Journal of Consulting and Clinical Psychology*, 1977, **45**, 341–343.

Hunt, G. M., & Azrin, N. H. A community reinforcement approach to alcoholism. *Behaviour Research and Therapy*, 1973, **11**, 91–104.

Hunt, W. A., Barnett, L. W., & Branch, L. G. Relapse rates in addiction programs. *Journal of Clinical Psychology*, 1971, **27**, 455–456.

Hutchinson, R. R., & Emley, G. S. Effects of nicotine on avoidance, conditioned suppression and aggression response measures in animals and man. In W. L. Dunn, Jr. (Ed.), *Smoking behavior: Motives and incentives*. New York: Wiley, 1973.

Jackson, B. Treatment of depression by self-reinforcement. *Behavior Therapy*, 1972, **3**, 298–307.

Jeffrey, D. B. Behavioral management of obesity. In W. E. Craighead, A. E. Kazdin, & M. J. Mahoney (Eds.), *Behavior modification: Principles, issues, and applications*. Boston: Houghton Mifflin, 1976.

Jellinek, E. M. *The disease concept of alcoholism*. New Haven, Conn.: Hillhouse Press, 1960.

Johnston, E., & Donoghue, J. R. Hypnosis and smoking: A review of the literature. *American Journal of Clinical Hypnosis*, 1971, **13**, 265–272.

Kanfer, F. H. Influence of age and incentive conditions on children's self-rewards. *Psychological Reports*, 1966, **19**, 263–274.

Kanfer, F. H. *Self-regulation: Research, issues and speculation in clinical psychology*. New York: Appleton-Century-Crofts, 1970.

Kanfer, F. H. Self-management methods. In F. H. Kanfer & A. P. Goldstein (Eds.), *Helping people change: A textbook of methods*. New York: Pergamon Press, 1975.

Kanfer, F. H. Self-regulation and self-control. In H. Zeier (Ed.), *The psychology of the 20th century*, vol. 4. Zurich: Kindler Verlag, 1977.

Kanfer, F. H., & Duerfeldt, P. H. Comparison of self-reward and self-criticism as a function of type of prior external reinforcement. *Journal of Personality and Social Psychology*, 1968, **8**, 261–268.

Kanfer, F. H., & Karoly, P. Self-control: A behavioristic excursion into the lion's den. *Behavior Therapy*, 1972, **3**, 398–416.

Kanfer, F. H., & Marston, A. R. Determinants of self-reinforcement in human learning. *Journal of Experimental Psychology*, 1963, **66**, 245–254.

Kanfer, F. H., & Phillips, J. S. *Learning foundations of behavior therapy*. New York: Wiley, 1970.

Kaufman, K. K., & O'Leary, K. D. Reward, cost, and self-evaluation procedures for disruptive adolescents in a psychiatric hospital school. *Journal of Applied Behavior Analysis*, 1972, **5**, 293–310.

Keutzer, C. S., Lichtenstein, E., & Mees, H. L. Modification of smoking behavior: A review. *Psychological Bulletin*, 1968, **70**, 520–533.

Lando, H. A. Successful treatment of smokers with a broad-spectrum behavioral approach. *Journal of Consulting and Clinical Psychology*, 1977, **45**, 361–366.

Laverty, S. G. Aversion therapies in the treatment of alcoholism. *Psychosomatic Medicine*, 1966, **28**, 651–666.

Lazarus, A. A. New methods of psychotherapy: A case study. *South African Medical Journal*, 1958, **32**, 660–663.

Lemere, F., & Voegtlin, W. L. An evaluation of the aversive treatment of alcoholism. *Quarterly Journal of Studies of Alcohol*, 1950, **11**, 199–204.

Lichtenstein, E. Reply to Hauser. *Journal of Consulting and Clinical Psychology*, 1974, **42**, 625–626.

Lichtenstein, E., & Keutzer, C. S. Modification of smoking behavior: A later look. In R. D. Rubin, H. Fernsterhein, A. A. Lazarus, & C. M. Franks (Eds.), *Advances in behavior therapy*. New York: Academic Press, 1971.

Lovitt, T. C., & Curtis, K. Academic response rate as a function of teacher- and self-imposed contingencies. *Journal of Applied Behavior Analysis*, 1969, **2**, 49–53.

Lubetkin, B. S., Rivers, P. C., & Rosenberg, C. M. Difficulties of disulfiram therapy with alcoholics. *Quarterly Journal of Studies in Alcohol*, 1971, **32**, 168–171.

MacCulloch, M. J., Feldman, M. P., Oxford, J. F., & MacCulloch, M. L. Anticipatory avoidance learning in the treatment of alcoholism: A record of therapeutic failure. *Behaviour Research and Therapy*, 1966, **4**, 187–196.

Mahoney, M. J. The self-management of covert behavior: A case study. *Behavior Therapy*, 1971, **2**, 575–578.

Mahoney, M. J. *Cognition and behavior modification*. Cambridge, Mass.: Ballinger, 1974.

Mahoney, M. J., & Thoresen, C. E. *Self-control: Power to the people*. Monterey, Calif: Brooks/Cole, 1974.

Mann, R. A. The behavior-therapeutic use of contingency contracting to control an adult behavior problem: Weight control. *Journal of Applied Behavior Analysis*, 1972, **5**, 99–109.

Marlott, G. A., Demming, B., & Reid, J. B. Loss of control drinking in alcoholics: An environmental analogue. *Journal of Abnormal Psychology*, 1973, **81**, 233–241.

Marston, A. E., & McFall, R. M. Comparison of behavior modification approaches in smoking reduction. *Journal of Consulting and Clinical Psychology*, 1971, **36**, 153–162.

Meichenbaum, D. Cognitive behavior modification. In J. T. Spence, R. C. Carson, and J. W. Thibaut (Eds.), *Behavioral approaches to therapy*. Morristown, N.J.: General Learning Press, 1976.

Meichenbaum, D., & Cameron, R. The clinical potential of modifying what clients say to themselves. In M. J. Mahoney & C. E. Thoresen (Eds.), *Self-control: Power to the person*. Monterey, Calif.: Brooks/Cole, 1974.

Meichenbaum, D., & Goodman, J. The developmental control of operant motor responding by verbal operants. *Journal of Experimental Child Psychology*, 1969, **7**, 553–565.

Meichenbaum, D., & Goodman, J. Training impulsive children to talk to themselves: A means for developing self-control. *Journal of Abnormal Psychology*, 1971, **77**, 115–126.

Miller, M. M. Treatment of chronic alcoholism by hypnotic aversion. *Journal of the American Medical Association*, 1959, **55**, 411–415.

Miller, P. M. The use of behavioral contracting in the treatment of alcoholism: A case report. *Behavior Therapy*, 1972, **3**, 593–596.

Miller, P. M., & Barlow, D. H. Behavioral approaches to the treatment of alcoholism. *Journal of Nervous and Mental Disorders*, 1973, **157**, 10–20.

Miller, P. M., & Hersen, M. Quantitative changes in alcohol consumption as a function of electrical aversive conditioning. *Journal of Clinical Psychology*, 1972, **28**, 590–593.

Miller, P. M., Hersen, M., Eisler, R. M., & Hemphill, D. P. Electrical aversion therapy with alcoholics: An analogue study. *Behaviour Research and Therapy*, 1973, **11**, 491–497.

Mischel, W. Theory and research on the antecedents of self-imposed delay of reward. In B. A. Maher (Ed.), *Progress in experimental personality research*, Vol. 3. New York: Academic Press, 1966.

Morganstern, K. P. Cigarette smoke as a noxious stimulus in self-managed aversion therapy for compulsive eating: Technique and case illustration. *Behavior Therapy*, 1974, **5**, 255–260.

Nathan, P. E. Alcoholism. In H. Leitenberg (Ed.), *Handbook of behavior modification and behavior therapy*. Englewood Cliffs, N.J.: Prentice-Hall, 1976.

Ober, D. C. The modification of smoking behavior. *Journal of Consulting and Clinical Psychology*, 1968, **32**, 543–549.

Orne, M. T. On the social psychology of the psychological experiment: With particular reference to demand characteristics and their implications. *American Psychologist*, 1962, **71**, 776–783.

Peterson, R. F., Merwin, M. R., Moyer, T. J., & Whitehurst, G. J. Generalized imitation: The effects of experimenter absence, differential reinforcement, and stimulus complexity. *Journal of Experimental Child Psychology*, 1971, **12**, 114–128.

Powell, J., & Azrin, N. The effects of shock as a punisher for cigarette smoking. *Journal of Applied Behavior Analysis*, 1968, **1**, 63–71.

Rachlin, H. Self-control. *Behaviorism*, 1974, **2**, 94–107.

Rachlin, H. *Introduction to modern behaviorism*, 2nd ed. San Francisco: Freeman, 1976.

Rachlin, H., & Green, L. Commitment, choice and self-control. *Journal of the Experimental Analysis of Behavior*, 1972, **17**, 15–22.

Redd, W. H. Social control by adult preference in operant conditioning with children. *Journal of Experimental Child Psychology*, 1974, **17**, 61–78.

Rehm, L. P., & Marston, A. R. Reduction of social anxiety through modification of self-reinforcement: An instigation therapy technique. *Journal of Consulting and Clinical Psychology*, 1968, **32**, 565–574.

Rotter, J. B. *Social learning and clinical psychology.* Englewood Cliffs, N.J.: Prentice-Hall, 1954.

Russell, M. A. H., Armstrong, E., & Patel, U. A. Temporal contiguity in electric aversion therapy for cigarette smoking. *Behaviour Research and Therapy,* 1976, **14,** 103–124.

Sanderson, R. E., Campbell, D., & Laverty, S. G. Traumatically conditioned responses acquired during respiratory paralysis. *Nature,* 1962, **196,** 1235–1236.

Sanderson, R. E., Campbell, D., & Laverty, S. G. An investigation of a new aversive conditioning treatment for alcoholism. *Quarterly Journal of Studies of Alcohol,* 1963, **24,** 261–275.

Schachter, S. *Emotion, obesity, and crime.* New York: Academic Press, 1971.

Schachter, S., & Gross, L. P. Manipulated time and eating behavior. *Journal of Personality and Social Psychology,* 1968, **10,** 98–106.

Schmahl, D. P., Lichtenstein, E., & Harris, D. E. Successful treatment of habitual smokers with warm, smoky air, and rapid smoking. *Journal of Consulting and Clinical Psychology,* 1972, **38,** 105–111.

Schwartz, J. L. A critical review and evaluation of smoking control methods. *Public Health Reports,* 1969, **84,** 489–506.

Skinner, B. F. *Science and human behavior.* New York: Macmillan, 1953.

Sobell, L. C., Sobell, M. B., & Christelman, W. C. The myth of "one drink." *Behaviour Research and Therapy,* 1972, **10,** 119–123.

Sobell, M. B., & Sobell, L. C. Individualized behavior therapy for alcoholics. *Behavior Therapy,* 1973, **4,** 49–72(a).

Sobell, M. B., & Sobell, L. C. *Evidence of controlled drinking by former alcoholics: A second year evaluation of individualized behavior therapy.* Montreal: American Psychological Association, 1973(b).

Sobell, M. B., & Sobell, L. C. Second year treatment outcome of alcoholics treated with individualized behaviour therapy: Results. *Behaviour Research and Therapy,* 1976, **14,** 195–215.

Steinman, W. M. The social control of generalized imitation. *Journal of Experimental Child Psychology,* 1970, **3,** 159–167.

Steinman, W. M. Implicit instructions and social influence in "generalized imitation" and comparable nonimitative situations. *Merrill-Palmer Quarterly,* 1976, **22,** 85–92.

Straits, B. C. *The discontinuation of cigarette smoking: A multiple discriminant analysis.* Miami Beach: American Sociological Association, 1966.

Strel'chuk, I. V. New contemporary methods of treating patients with alcoholism. *Soviet Medicine,* 1957, **21,** 26–33.

Stuart, R. B. Behaviour control over eating. *Behaviour Research and Therapy,* 1967, **5,** 357–365.

Stuart, R. B., & Davis, B. *Slim chance in a fat world.* Champaign, Ill.: Research Press, 1972.

Stunkard, A. J. New treatments for obesity: Behavior modification. In G. A. Grady & J. E. Bethune (Eds.), *Treatment and management of obesity.* New York: Harper & Row, 1974.

Stunkard, A. J., & Mahoney, M. J. Behavioral treatment of the eating disorders. In H. Leitenberg (Ed.), *Handbook of behavior modification.* New York: Appleton-Century-Crofts, 1976.

Surgeon General's report: Smoking and health (Publication No. 1103). Washington, D.C.: U.S. Public Health Service, 1964.

Thomas, E. J., Abrams, K. S., & Johnson, J. B. Self-monitoring and reciprocal inhibition in the modification of multiple tics of Gilles de la Tourette's syndrome. *Behavior Therapy and Experimental Psychiatry,* 1971, **2,** 159–171.

Thoresen, C. E., & Mahoney, M. J. *Behavioral self-control.* New York: Holt, Rinehart & Winston, 1974.

Tobias, L. L. The relative effectiveness of behavioristic bibliotherapy, contingency contracting, and suggestions of self-control in weight reduction. Unpublished Ph.D. dissertation, University of Illinois, 1972.

Voegtlin, W. L. The treatment of alcoholism by establishing a conditioned reflex. *American Journal of Medical Science,* 1940, **199,** 802–809.

Voegtlin, W. L. Conditioned reflex therapy of chronic alcoholism: Ten years' experience with the method. *Rocky Mountain Medical Journal,* 1947, **44,** 807–812.

Wallgren, H., & Barry, H. *Actions of alcohol,* Vol. II. Amsterdam: Elsevier, 1973.

Wilson, G. T., Leaf, R. C., & Nathan, P. E. The aversive control of excessive alcohol consumption by chronic alcoholics in the laboratory setting. *Journal of Applied Behavior Analysis,* 1975, **8,** 13–26.

Wilson, G. T., & Tracey, D. A. An experimental analysis of aversive imagery versus electrical aversive conditioning in the treatment of chronic alcoholics. *Behaviour Research and Therapy,* 1976, **14,** 41–51.

Wollersheim, J. P. The effectiveness of group therapy based upon learning principles in the treatment of overweight women. *Journal of Abnormal Psychology,* 1970, **76,** 462–474.

Wyden, P. *The overweight society.* New York: Morrow, 1965.

Yafa, S. H. Zap! You're normal. *Playboy,* July 1973, pp. 87, 90, 184, 186–188.

nine

INTERPERSONAL RELATIONSHIPS

For most people, having satisfying relationships with others is crucial to personal happiness. In fact, many personality theorists contend that the need for tenderness and closeness with others is as vital to survival as are food and shelter. Harry Stack Sullivan (1953), for example, maintained that the individual's sense of emotional well-being and security depends upon experiences of acceptance and communicative intimacy. Such experiences are believed to emotionally validate one's sense of personal worth and alleviate feelings of social isolation and loneliness (Stern, 1978).

Although behaviorists might object to the terms that personality theorists have used to describe these states and conditions, the sentiments expressed undoubtedly have intuitive validity. A number of researchers have provided some preliminary support for these theoretical speculations. Harry Harlow's (1961) classic studies of infant monkeys revealed that even at the primate level "contact needs" play a major role in the formation of early attachments and in the development of security. Research on the human infant's attachment to the mothering figure (for instance, Schaffer & Emerson, 1964), experiments on the reinforcing effect of social stimulation and attention (for instance, Greenspoon, 1955; Rheingold, Gewirtz, & Ross, 1959), and demographic studies on the predictors of acute mental illness and suicide (for instance, Shneidman, Farberow, & Lit-

man, 1970) confirm the central role that interpersonal relations play in human development and emotional adjustment.

Researchers have found that deep, long-lasting relationships are characterized by uninhibited communication and self-disclosure (Levinger & Snoek, 1972; Taylor, 1968; Taylor, Altman, & Sorrentino, 1969). By pretending, speaking or behaving duplicitously, and not being sensitive to communications from others, people make it impossible for themselves to experience real intimacy. Contemporary interpersonal and "existential" approaches to psychotherapy have targeted these barriers to communication as the focal point for therapeutic intervention. Getting individuals "in touch" with their gut feelings and helping them learn to express these feelings in appropriate ways are seen as the major goals of therapy. The assumption is that socialization takes a heavy toll: suppression of feelings is reinforced and spontaneous emotional expression is punished (Goldfried & Davison, 1976).

The approach of behavior therapy to problems in interpersonal relationships is surprisingly similar. Andrew Salter (1961, p. 38) observed:

Living in society necessitates inhibition, but modern training goes too far when it teaches children to be polite at all times, not to contradict others, not to interrupt, not to be selfish, and always to consider other people's feelings. A well-adjusted person is like a housebroken dog. He has the basic inhibitions to permit him to live in society, but none extra to interfere with his happiness.

In their discussion of anxiety in interpersonal relationships, Joseph Wolpe and Arnold Lazarus (1966, p. 38) came to the same conclusion regarding factors that contribute to people's inhibition:

> A basic assumption involved in the foregoing is that people have certain rights which they are fully entitled to exercise, and that proper human adjustment includes exercising them. While self-control and tactful restraint are necessary and desirable for civilized interaction, this can be taken too far. Those parents who, bound by convention and conformity, transmit stoic and ascetic habits of self-control to their children in the name of breeding, manners, good taste and refinement create what Salter (1949) has termed "inhibitory personalities."

Suppressing one's wants and needs in the guise of "getting along" with other people does not bring real communication. Being overly assertive and imposing does not work because it alienates others. In either case, someone in the relationship is not having his or her needs met.

Many traditional approaches have been successful in getting people "in touch" with their feelings, but people must also learn how to act on these feelings. The major contribution of behavior modification has been to teach people specific ways of expressing their feelings appropriately.

In this chapter we will consider the specific behavioral techniques that have been used to improve interpersonal relations. The first topic we will discuss is assertiveness training. We will focus on its theoretical foundations, specific methods used, and research on its effectiveness. Next, we will consider social skills training in the treatment of heterosexual anxiety. In the last section, we will examine the use of behavioral contracting and communication training in marital therapy.

ASSERTIVENESS TRAINING

Salter is credited with first suggesting specific training in assertiveness, although he did not use the term "assertiveness training." In *Conditioned Reflex Therapy*, first published in 1949, he sug-

gested that most people are too well socialized. Their primary motivation is to be pleasant, maintain the status quo, and accommodate to the needs of others. Their feelings and emotions are concealed. Salter believed that this emotional inhibition produced conflict within the individual and made it impossible to achieve real emotional satisfaction with others. He considered this inhibition to be a primary component of neurosis, having the status of a trait. Salter's goal was to teach inhibited individuals how to express their feelings directly; individuals should "loosen up" and allow feelings to take precedent over convention. His treatment strategy was behavioral in that in-depth analysis of the origins of the inhibition was not conducted; rather, specific behaviors for reducing inhibitions were proposed. Salter devised six techniques:

1. *Feeling-talk.* The individual is instructed to verbalize his emotional reactions to events and situations, regardless of how trivial. For example, rather than just talking about the weather the individual should state how the weather makes him feel: "What a beautiful day, I feel great" or "This kind of weather always makes me depressed." The purpose is to give the individual experience in spontaneously expressing felt emotion.

2. *Facial-talk.* Salter also suggested that the inhibited individual practice communicating feelings by facial expressions.

3. *Contradict and attack.* Salter recommended that instead of being polite and saying nothing when he or she does not agree with someone, the inhibited person express opposition—even when the disagreement is based purely on emotion rather than reason.

4. *Deliberate use of "I."* In order to increase the probability that the individual will say what he or she feels, he suggests that clients be instructed to begin sentences with "I." For example, rather than saying "It is nice . . . ," "Fall is beautiful . . . ," and so on, the inhibited person is to practice making such statements personal: "I think it is nice . . . ," "I find the fall beautiful. . . ."

5. *Expressed agreement when praised.* He encouraged clients to express pride in their own

accomplishments. Instead of being modest and demeaning oneself when complimented, people should express pleasure in their own success. For example, the client should respond to someone's complimenting his tie by saying, "Yes, I like it, too," or "Thank you, it's one of my favorites," rather than "Oh, this old thing?"

6. *Improvisation.* Salter contended that spontaneity was essential to self-expression. He encouraged the inhibited individual to act on the first feelings that arise. Rather than planning and calculating, the individual should practice living for the moment.

For Salter (1961), "Therapy consists of getting the individual to re-educate himself back to the healthy spontaneity of which his life experiences have deprived him. Inhibitory history stops repeating itself, and excitation (i.e., spontaneity) regains its birthright" (p. 103).

Many of Salter's ideas have been incorporated in present assertiveness training, and his notions regarding the importance of feeling-talk have been widely accepted. However, Salter has been criticized for not giving enough attention to the possible negative repercussions of uninhibited expression of feeling. Conceivably, many individuals might get themselves into real trouble if they always said exactly what they thought. Today the emphasis is on socially acceptable, "responsible" assertion.

Perhaps because of the dominance of nonbehavioral theories during the 1940s and 1950s and the fact that Salter did not experimentally validate his techniques, his work went virtually unnoticed until the late 1960s. Major interest in assertiveness training has been generated by writings of Wolpe and Lazarus (Wolpe, 1958, 1969; Wolpe & Lazarus, 1966). Wolpe's conceptualization of the nature of nonassertiveness is similar to Salter's. He suggests that as young children inhibited individuals were probably punished for expressing their feelings and taught acceptable (that is, "proper") ways of responding. Regardless of their feelings, they were to emit these "correct behaviors." Inhibited individuals are typically anxious in interpersonal relationships. They may be aloof and undemonstrative, friendly without being warm. According to Wolpe, there is "a lack

of integrity of *expression of basic feelings and emotions*" (Wolpe & Lazarus, 1966, p. 39).

Wolpe disagrees with Salter on a number of points. First, Wolpe does not believe that nonassertiveness is a trait. Rather, he considers nonassertiveness situation-specific. That is, under one set of circumstances the individual may be assertive and under another nonassertive. A man who is persuasive and dominant at work may become submissive and withdrawn at home. Second, unlike Salter, Wolpe does not believe that all unhappy and poorly adjusted clients need such training. Third, whereas Salter focuses almost exclusively on individuals' expressing their feelings and does not concern himself with how clients might handle the consequences of their assertiveness, Wolpe emphasizes individuals' learning how to express their feelings in ways that minimize unpleasant repercussions. Wolpe stresses socially appropriate assertiveness.

In contrast to other behavior modification techniques such as systematic desensitization, no single set of procedures can be identified as assertiveness training. Although what is done in an effort to make people more assertive varies considerably, there is nevertheless more agreement than disagreement regarding what can legitimately be called assertiveness training.

Determining the Need for Training

Except for those who sign up for courses in assertiveness training offered by various lay groups, few people come to a therapist explicitly requesting such training. It is often the therapist who suggests the training. Such training might be recommended for individuals who are interpersonally anxious, feel that they are taken advantage of, or have difficulty communicating with others. The notion is that such individuals might have better relationships and be less anxious in social situations if communication were more open and straightforward. Assertiveness training is also used with people who are overly assertive (that is, aggressive). We all know people who have trouble getting along with others because what the person says often evokes aggression and hostility in others. Such an individual argues instead of discusses, demands instead of requests. In this case assertiveness training would focus on the use of tact and compromise.

In order to tailor the assertiveness training program to the client's needs, the therapist must determine why the individual is not assertive. There are at least three reasons. (1) The problem may represent an actual skill deficit. The requisite assertive responses may simply not be in the individual's repertoire. (2) The individual may not accurately discriminate the appropriate situations in which to be assertive. He or she may know *how* to be assertive, but not *when*. (3) Lack of assertiveness may be the result of irrational fears and/or beliefs that inhibit expression. The individual may fear possible aversive consequences of being assertive. Each of these conditions may require different training procedures.

In addition to determining the possible reasons why the individual is not assertive, the therapist must also pinpoint the exact situations in which nonassertiveness is a problem. Wolpe and Lazarus (Wolpe & Lazarus, 1966; Lazarus, 1971) have developed extensive questionnaires for that purpose. The following list is representative of the types of questions the therapist might ask. (The reader should note that the questions deal with the expression of both positive and negative feelings.)

1. Are you reluctant to change your order at a fast-food restaurant?
2. If your landlord fails to make repairs that you have requested, would you call and insist that the problems be corrected?
3. If someone owed you ten dollars and had forgotten about it, would you remind him?
4. If someone has betrayed your confidence would you express your disappointment and anger about it?
5. If someone's smoking is annoying you, are you able to ask the person to smoke elsewhere?
6. Do you find it difficult to praise someone's work?
7. If someone makes an unreasonable request, is it easy for you to say no?
8. If the person in front of you at a movie is talking, would you ask him to stop?
9. Do you find it difficult to upbraid someone working for you?

10. Is it easy for you to express your affection to your friends?

Wolpe and Lazarus are careful to point out that the therapist is not simply looking for yes or no answers. By discussing each question with the client, the therapist can determine the times and situations in which the client is unable to express true feelings.

Training Procedures

Assertiveness training is typically broken down into three parts: (1) didactic discussion, (2) behavioral rehearsal (that is, role playing), and (3) in vivo practice.

Didactic Discussion. In order to enlist cooperation and to check the validity of his hypotheses regarding a client's problems, the therapist discusses his conceptualizations with the client. Although individuals might agree that they are inhibited and do not always say what is on their minds, they may feel that it is wrong to do so. In their discussion of assertiveness training, Arthur Lange and Patricia Jakubowski (1976) point out that it is often necessary to help clients develop an "assertive belief system." They suggest that before clients can begin learning ways to be assertive, they must believe that such training will be helpful to them. The therapist begins by explaining how appropriate assertiveness brings closer and more satisfying relationships with others. Essentially, the therapist presents the ideas outlined at the beginning of this chapter and points out the illogical and maladaptive nature of the client's beliefs. Table 9–1 is adapted from Jakubowski's (1977) discussion of how mores and attitudes about what is right and wrong can inhibit assertiveness.

During the initial phases of training, the therapist discusses the distinctions between assertiveness and aggressiveness, and between politeness and nonassertiveness. Clients often fear that if they are assertive, they will be considered rude and aggressive. Here it is important that the therapist point out that being assertive does not mean being insensitive to the needs of others. The therapist also explains that assertiveness for the sake of being assertive is not desirable. Lange

Table 9–1. Beliefs and Attitudes That May Affect Assertiveness

Anti-assertive beliefs	Resulting Nonassertive Behavior	Proassertive Beliefs
Don't be selfish. Always think of others first.	When I have a conflict with someone, I give in and satisfy the other person. When I have an opinion that is different from someone else's, I do not express it because who am I to say that my ideas are better than theirs.	My needs are as important as anyone else's and they should be considered. If conflict arises, I am willing to discuss and compromise.
Be modest and humble. Never act superior. I should always avoid appearing more competent or better than other people.	When I meet other people, I focus on their accomplishments and never mention my own.	It is not good to build oneself up at the expense of others, but I have as much right as anyone else to have my talents acknowledged and praised.
Be understanding and don't get angry. Overlook irritations.	When I am talking and someone continually interrupts me, I say nothing. When someone is inconsiderate, I do not complain.	I do not let people take advantage of me. I make sure that others consider my interests.
I should not be demanding. I have no right to make requests of others.	I do not request changes or ask favors of good friends—I never borrow things.	Of course, no one should be demanding, but this does not mean that I have no right to ask people to change their behavior if it directly affects me. A request is not a demand.
Always be sensitive to other people's feelings. I have no right to do anything that might deflate someone else's ego.	I do not respond spontaneously so that I won't accidentally upset someone else. I do not say what I feel because it might hurt someone.	Although it is unkind to intentionally hurt someone, I should not be insincere. If I believe that my opinion is important I should express it. I should be tactful but not dishonest.

Adapted from P. Jabukowski, Assertive behavior and clinical problems of women. In D. Carter & E. Rawlings (Eds.), *Psychotherapy for women: Treatment towards equality*. Springfield, Ill.: Thomas, 1977.

and Jakubowski stress the concept of *responsible* assertive behavior: the goal of training is to facilitate open communication and mutually satisfying interpersonal relations, not to learn effective ways of berating others. As a result of training, clients should be able to express themselves more openly and to make it easier for others to do the same.

Behavioral Rehearsal. Based on discussions with the client, the therapist draws up a hierarchy of the situations in which the client's nonassertiveness is a problem. The list of problem situations is arranged according to the increasing degree of complexity of the skills required. The client would begin with role playing of the easiest situations and move on to more difficult situations as he or she acquired the necessary skills. The following hierarchy was devised for a male client who was nonassertive and anxious in his interactions with his employer.

1. Your boss has just explained how to complete some new order forms and you do not understand. You must ask him to repeat the instructions.
2. You have a personal long-distance call and your boss is sitting in your office. You ask him to excuse you for a few minutes.
3. You have a dental appointment and you must explain that you will not be back from lunch until 3:00.
4. You want to reschedule your vacation and you must get your boss's approval.
5. It is 7:30 P.M. and you've just finished the report your boss asked you to do. Just as you prepare to leave, he wants to discuss some trivial work. You tell him you must leave.
6. Your boss asks you to contribute to his friend's campaign and you favor another candidate. You refuse his request.
7. At the Christmas party the day before, your boss insulted you in front of the other employees. You go into his office to register your annoyance.
8. You read your boss's report on your work and feel that you have been unjustly evaluated. You want to present your side.
9. It's time for annual raises and you do not receive one. You go into your boss's office to discuss it.

In the actual behavioral rehearsal, client and therapist reverse roles from time to time so that the therapist can model appropriate assertive behavior. As is shown in the next example, the therapist gives the client direct feedback and instructions. In order to make the rehearsal more realistic, it is often conducted in a group-therapy setting. Three or four clients and one or two therapists may work together, with each client receiving and giving feedback.

What follows is an example of an assertiveness training interchange with a woman undergraduate. She is very bright and earns excellent grades despite very little study. Her sister, who is not as academically successful, continually teases the cli-

ent about her accomplishments. The client takes this ribbing good-naturedly, but is hurt and feels guilty about her good grades whenever her sister teases her.

Therapist: So your sister kids you about being smart?

Client: Yeah. It's just that every time I say, "Boy, I'm really worried about my French exam" or something, she goes "Oh *sure* Patty, you really need to worry! You could probably just ask the instructor to give you an 'A' and she would. Everybody knows how smart you are!"

Therapist: How do you respond to that?

Client: I guess I usually say something like, "Yeah, maybe I'll try that." You know, just kind of go along with it.

Therapist: But that's not what you're feeling.

Client: Oh no! It really bothers me. It makes me feel terrible that it all comes so easily. I feel . . . I feel like I'm really *different*.

Therapist: (*Sounds as if she would profit from changing some of these attitudes about her success; but I wonder if she has tried shutting her sister off.*) Have you ever told Joan that those kinds of comments hurt you?

Client: No. I'm sure she doesn't mean to hurt me. She'd feel *terrible* if she knew.

Therapist: (*Here's an opening to begin the attitude change and set the stage for an assertive response.*) And *you* feel terrible when she says those things.

Client: True.

Therapist: So who is more important, you or Joan?

Client: Well, you can't just make those determinations . . . neither of us is more important.

Therapist: Exactly! But by suffering in silence rather than asking Joan to stop making comments that hurt you, you're acting as if her feelings are more important than yours.

Client: (*Pause*) I see what you mean. I never thought of it that way.

Therapist: (*I think she's probably ready to do a bit of role playing now. I'll model a response first and see how she reacts to it.*) If you were Joan, how do you think you'd feel if you made one of these teasing comments to me and I said, "You know Joan, I know you don't mean to hurt me; but when you give me a hard time about being good in school it really upsets me. I'd appreciate it if you wouldn't do that."

Client: I guess I'd feel a little . . . embarrassed. I'd probably apologize.

Therapist: Do you think that you would stop making those comments?

Client: Oh, yeah. For sure.

Therapist: (*I think I can reverse the roles now and get her to try out an assertive response.*) OK, why don't you try it. I'll be Joan, and I'll say (*in role*), "God, Patty, you're such a brain. Why don't you frizz your hair so you look like Albert Einstein?"

Client: (*In role*) Cut it out, will you? You make me feel like a real freak when you say those things to me!

Therapist: (*That was a bit strong. She'll alienate her sister if she comes on that forcefully. I need to reinforce her for the attempt, but get her to correct. I think I can just prompt her on it; I doubt that I will need to model it again.*) OK, I'm me again. That was not too bad. You definitely got your message across. But you were a bit too sharp, given that Joan doesn't know that she's hurting you, and given that you've never mentioned this before. To Joan, that interaction might seem to have come out of the blue, and I think she would have felt hurt and probably pretty angry.

Client: Yeah, I thought of that when I was talking. I was a bit too heavy.

Therapist: Umhm. Let's give it another try. Express your feelings, but appreciate hers as well, OK? OK, I'm Joan and I say, "Patty, don't you ever get anything wrong? Doesn't it get boring being right all of the time?"

Client: (*In role*) "Joan, you know I've never mentioned this before, but when you say things like that it really hurts my feelings. I know you don't mean to be mean, but please don't do that."

Therapist: (*Out of role*) Great! You were direct and honest, yet you didn't make your sister feel like a jerk. How do you feel about it?

Client: Good. I guess it really wouldn't hurt her feelings much if I put it like that.

Therapist: I don't think so either. Now let's talk about what to do if she *doesn't* stop the teasing. . . .

Although much of assertiveness training is merely applied common sense, behavior therapists have discovered a few principles of effective assertion. Essentially, they involve ways the individual can be assertive without causing negative repercussions. The first principle is that in all situations the individual should emit the response that would accomplish the goal with minimal effort and negative emotion. In other words, say what is on your mind but do so in a way that won't get you or the listener upset. This has been called the **minimal effective response** (Rimm & Masters, 1974). The notion is that by expressing feelings in a cool and rational way, the person will not cause the listener to react defensively.

The second principle is **empathic assertion.** Here the idea is to include within the assertion an acknowledgment of the other person's feelings and rights. For instance, when asking others to stop talking in a museum, one should preface the request with a statement that lets them know that you respect their desire to share their reactions to the art. One might say, "I know that you are enthusiastic about the show, so am I, but I have trouble concentrating when you all are talking. Would you wait until you get into the corridor to talk?" Assertion is not accompanied by an insult —either expressed or implied.

The third principle involves the use of **constructive feedback.** If one person wants others to change their behavior, it is wise to suggest what they might do differently that would satisfy both parties.

The fourth principle, **escalation,** is called into play if the initial assertive statement is ignored or otherwise ineffective. In such situations, the individual should first repeat the request and then, if it does not work the second time, move to a stronger statement. The person might suggest possible negative consequences of the other's behavior. If that doesn't work, a contract or compromise might be suggested. If nothing works, the individual's only chance is to leave the situation or enlist the help of some authority. For example, if another person's talking in a movie theater is disturbing, one might first tell the person that it's difficult to hear the movie over the conversation. If that doesn't work, one might repeat the request. If the person continues to talk, one might threaten to call the manager. One should begin with a mild statement of feeling and escalate only if necessary.

In Vivo Practice. As the client shows improvement in behavioral rehearsal, the therapist introduces homework assignments. The first assignment might simply involve the client's observing how others handle interpersonal conflict. The client is instructed to note the circumstances under which others are assertive, how they actually express their feelings, and how others react (MacDonald, Lindquist, Kramer, McGrath, & Rhyne, 1975). The client also takes note of personal situations in which assertion is appropriate. After the client has completed these assignments and discussed them with the therapist, the therapist suggests that the client apply the new skills outside the office. This might mean going into a store and asking the salesperson for help in selecting an item or registering a complaint with a friend. The therapist is careful to make the initial assignment a fairly easy one that is not likely to bring rebuff or criticism. As the client successfully masters each homework assignment, the therapist suggests progressively more difficult tasks. The final goal is for the client to incorporate assertion into daily social interactions. An interesting example of the use of assertiveness training is Case Study 9–1, which involves a male homosexual's learning how to deal with others' reactions to his sexual orientation.

Effectiveness

Despite the fact that behavioral clinicians and researchers define assertion as the open expression of both positive and negative feelings (for example, Cotler & Guerra, 1976; Lange & Jakubowski, 1976; Lieberman, 1972; Wolpe & Lazarus, 1966), the research in the area has focused exclusively on the expression of negative feelings. A large body of literature indicates that assertiveness training is effective in teaching people to stand up for their own rights (Hersen, Eisler, & Miller, 1973; McFall & Twentyman, 1973; Rich & Schroeder, 1976). Most of the data in the area are based on case reports. Assertiveness training has been used to reduce such diverse problems as marital discord (Fensterheim, 1972; Macpherson, 1972), sexual disorders (Edwards, 1972; Stevenson & Wolpe, 1960), homosexual anxiety (Duehn & Mayadas, 1976), and occupational dissatisfaction (Doran, 1976; Lange & Jakubowski, 1976).

In all these cases, assertiveness training focused on interpersonal relations that cause problems. For example, in one case of a twenty-four-year-old married man who developed impotence during the first six months of his marriage, three sessions of assertiveness training led to a resolution of his sexual dysfunction (Lazarus, 1971). By interviewing the client, the therapist discovered that the client had been reared by a domineering mother whom he feared. Moreover, the client was unable to express any negative feelings to his wife. In order to reduce his interpersonal anxiety, which Lazarus reasoned produced the impotency, training involved the rehearsal of appropriate assertive responses toward his wife. Not only did the training appear to result in the resolution of the client's marital problems, it also led to more satisfying daily interactions with others.

The most experimentally rigorous research on the effectiveness of assertiveness training has been conducted by Richard McFall and his colleagues (McFall & Lillesand, 1971; McFall & Marston, 1970; McFall & Twentyman, 1973). Their work has focused on ways of teaching nonassertive college students how to refuse unreasonable demands—in other words, how to say "no." In a series of carefully controlled laboratory studies, they investigated the role of modeling, coaching, and role playing in assertiveness training.

Students were first screened on the basis of their scores on two tests of assertiveness, the Conflict Resolution Inventory (CRI) and Behavioral Role-Playing Assertion Test (BRAT). In both of these tests, situations are described in which the students' interests or rights are somehow violated. The CRI is a paper-and-pencil test which assesses students' ability to refuse an unreasonable request. One of the items, for example, describes an incident in which a roommate who constantly borrows small change for the soda machine and doesn't pay it back asks for a quarter. Students must describe how they would respond. Would they refuse, and if so, how uncomfortable would they be? The BRAT assesses general assertiveness. Students are asked to role play a variety of situations involving interpersonal annoyances (for instance, friends interrupt your studying; the laundry has lost your cleaning; a waiter brings you a cold steak). Only students who scored high on both tests of nonassertiveness were included in the study.

Training was brief (only two forty-five-minute sessions) and was specifically directed toward teaching the students how to refuse unreasonable requests. The therapist (that is, narrator) began by presenting the rationale that an individual can become more assertive by acquiring a few simple skills. Actual training consisted of the narrator describing various scenes in which assertion is called for and then applying one of the teaching strategies (depending upon the type of treatment the student received). The following are examples of the type of stimulus situation McFall and his colleagues used (McFall & Marston, 1970, p. 298; McFall & Lillesand, 1971, p. 315):

Narrator: Imagine that this morning you took your car to a local Standard station, and you explicitly told the mechanic to give you a simple tune-up. The bill should have been about $20. It's now later in the afternoon and you're at the station to pick up your car. The mechanic is walking over to you.

Mechanic: "Okay, let me make out a ticket for you. The tune-up was $12 for parts and $8 for labor. Uh, grease and oil job was $6. Antifreeze was $5. Uh, $4 for a new oil filter. And, uh, $5 for rotating the tires. That's $40 in all. Will this be cash or charge?"

Narrator: A person in one of your classes, someone whom you do not know very well, borrowed your class notes weeks ago, then failed to return them at the next class, thus forcing you to take notes on scrap paper. Now this person comes up to you again and says, "Hey, mind if I borrow your class notes again?"

The most effective training strategy was coaching and rehearsal used together. Students who received direct coaching from the therapist and were given opportunities to practice assertive responses showed the greatest improvement on both tests of assertiveness. Moreover, students who received assertiveness training were significantly more resistant to unreasonable demands during an actual telephone conversation. Posing as an unknown classmate in a large introductory psychology course, a confederate of the therapist made increasingly more unreasonable demands:

I'm Tom Blake. I don't think you know me, but I'm in (professor)'s lecture too. . . . I really hate to bother you, but I have some questions on some of the lecture material. . . . I think all I really need is to take a look at your notes. Could that be arranged? . . . Well, actually, (subject), the truth of the matter is, I haven't been to class since the 12-week exam, so I'll probably need your notes for two days. Would that be all right? . . . Oh, wait a minute! I've got a chemistry exam on Friday. Could I get them after that? That would be three days before the psych exam. . . . Now that I think about it, I'll probably need a night to recover from the chem exam, so is it all right if I get them Saturday instead, for the two days before the exam? (McFall & Twentyman, 1973, p. 212)

At the point in the conversation in which the student said "no" unequivocally to any request, the confederate terminated the conversation. Students who had had assertiveness training refused earlier in the conversation than did control subjects. This demonstrates that assertiveness training can result in meaningful changes in behaviors that generalize to novel situations.

From McFall's research it is clear that rehearsing assertive responses and getting constructive feedback are effective means of strengthening and refining assertiveness. Furthermore, such training serves to integrate the desired behavior change into the client's repertoire.

Limits of Assertiveness Training

At the beginning of the chapter we suggested that behavior therapists have developed ways of helping people express themselves more openly, and that this training would facilitate interpersonal intimacy and closeness. However, as our review of research on assertiveness training indicates, the focus of behavior modification in this area has been rather limited.

First, few investigators have determined if being assertive really makes people happier and better able to have satisfying relationships. Assertiveness training has typically been evaluated only in terms of whether it results in the client's becoming more assertive, rather than in terms of its broader goals. We do not know if being assertive makes for better marriages, better friendships, and better working relationships. Even though the notion of teaching people to be assertive may have great intuitive appeal, the value of this training must be empirically evaluated in a broader context.

A second concern is the narrow focus of most assertiveness training (Lazarus, 1971; 1973; Rich & Schroeder, 1976). Despite the fact that almost every journal article or book on assertiveness training begins by emphasizing that assertion involves the open expression of positive as well as negative feelings, most of the work in the area has focused on the latter. R. E. Alberti and M. L. Emmons (1974) propose a definition that accurately reflects the current status of behavioral approaches: assertiveness is "behavior which enables a person to act in his own best interests, stand up for himself without undue anxiety, to express his rights without destroying the rights of others" (p. 2). Although these behaviors undoubtedly facilitate our "getting what we want," the ability to emit forthright expressions of love, compassion, and appreciation seems equally important in fostering satisfying interpersonal relationships.

HETEROSEXUAL SOCIAL ANXIETY

Relating easily with persons of the opposite sex is difficult for a great number of individuals (Martinson & Zerface, 1970). In one-to-one social situations they are anxious and self-conscious, and do not know what to say. This heterosexual social anxiety, as some behavioral clinicians have labeled it, is greater among men than among women. In one survey of college undergraduates (Shmurak, 1973), 54 percent of the men and 42 percent of the women reported that, of all their social interactions, dating caused the most difficulty.

Possible Causes

The etiology of heterosexual social anxiety can only be hypothesized and, as with most psychological problems, it is unlikely that there is a single cause. Some suggest that it is a conditioned anxiety resulting from the pairing of heterosexual interactions with aversive stimuli. Through observation of others or because of unfortunate negative experiences with members of the opposite sex, the individual has come to be afraid of heterosexual relations. Quite independent of the person's social skill level, he or she is fearful. This hypothesis, although theoretically consistent with the development of phobias, has not been empirically validated.

A second hypothesis, and one that has received empirical support, is the notion that heterosexual social anxiety results from individuals' faulty cognitive appraisal of their own performances and the expectation of failure (Curran, 1977a). Before people try to perform, they "know" they are going to fail and make fools of themselves. As a result of this pessimistic expectation, they become anxious. In his review of heterosexual social anxiety, James Curran (1977b) has pointed out that because of this faulty belief system, individuals downgrade their own behavior and selectively attend to negative feedback from others. Curran supports his argument with research from various investigators working in the area of social relations.

In one study, low- and high-anxious males were asked to judge the adequacy of their own performance with females in comparison with the performance of other males. Although high-anxious subjects accurately evaluated the performances of others, they misjudged their own performances. In comparison with ratings by independent observers, the self-evaluations of high-anxious subjects were significantly lower (Clark & Arkowitz, 1975); that is, the subjects rated themselves as less successful than they actually were. These results were replicated in another study in which high-anxious males were asked to evaluate videotapes of their performances and the performances of confederates in staged interactions with women. Subjects' ratings of confederates' behavior were consistent with those of independent observers, but their ratings of their own performances were lower than the ratings of the observers (Curran, Wallander, & Fischetti, 1977).

The third hypothesis, simpler than the first two, states that heterosexual social anxiety represents individuals' reactions to the consequences of their own deficient social behavior. Because they are not skillful in their dealings with persons of the opposite sex, they experience punishment in the form of frustration and rejection. After repeated exposure to this punishment, individuals become afraid of heterosexual interaction. This hypothesis has not received the same sort of empirical support as the cognitive evaluative hypothesis, although data do suggest that such a hypothesis may apply in certain cases.

A number of researchers (Borkovec, Stone, O'Brien, & Kaloupek, 1974; Twentyman & McFall, 1975) have found that individuals who are highly anxious about their heterosexual social behavior are indeed below average on measures of social skill. Males are less responsive to approach cues projected by females (Curran, 1977a) and are awkward in their conversations with women (Fischetti, Curran, & Wessberg, 1977). Compared to low-anxious males, these men are less skilled at providing empathetic and appropriate signs of concern and interest when talking with women. Their "timing" is off (Fischetti, Curran, & Wessberg, 1977).

Treatment Methods

Four behavioral strategies have been applied to the alleviation of heterosexual social anxiety. They are: (1) systematic desensitization, (2) simple and relatively unstructured practice in "heterosexual interaction," that is, dating practice, (3) highly structured training in appropriate dating behavior using modeling, behavioral rehearsal, and coaching, and (4) modification of cognitive expectations and self-evaluations.

Most of the research in the area of heterosexual anxiety has focused on men, a situation that we find somewhat puzzling. Although the percentage of men who report problems associated with

dating exceeds that for women (54 percent versus 42 percent), this certainly does not mean that men are the only ones who might benefit from training. Traditionally, society has put the male in the dominant role in terms of making initial approaches and procuring dates; however, this does not mean that the male now (or for that matter, ever) has the full responsibility of getting relationships "started." One possible reason for the focus on men is that college-age men request such social skills training much more often than do women. If this is the case, the focus on men in research in this area merely reflects behavior therapists' response to the needs of their clients. No one has collected data relevant to this issue, but it does seem likely that the progress toward greater role flexibility will broaden the focus of social skills training.

Systematic Desensitization. In the case of severe heterosexual social anxiety, systematic desensitization has been successful with several individual cases (Bander, Steinke, Allen, & Mosher, 1975; Curran & Gilbert, 1975; Fishman & Nawas, 1973; Mitchell & Orr, 1974). This procedure will be discussed in detail in Chapter 10. At this point, our discussion of treatment strategies for heterosexual social anxiety will focus on skills training and cognitive restructuring methods.

Dating Practice. This approach presumes that one learns by doing. Treatment simply involves scheduling dates for anxious individuals (Martinson & Zerface, 1970) and, in at least one study (Christensen & Arkowitz, 1974), providing feedback to the client from his "date." This strategy has been found to result in a reduction of clients' *reported* fear of dating and an increase in *reported* frequency of dating; however, caution should be exercised in endorsing these procedures too readily. First, the studies have a number of methodological flaws that may limit the generality of results: Subjects were not adequately screened and possibly were not truly anxious when interacting with women; conclusions were based solely on self-report data, and no long-term followup evaluations were conducted. Second, if the clients were, in fact, socially anxious, going out with a perfect stranger, who may or may not have been socially skillful herself, might possibly generate even greater anxiety. What if the client's date had been abrasive or tactless? What if she had ditched him halfway through the evening? One way to reduce this possibility is to coach the "date," but in some cases that might be impossible.

3) *Structured Training.* This approach is based on the assumption that heterosexual social anxiety is the result of social skills deficits. The program developed by Curran and his colleagues (Curran, 1975; Curran & Gilbert, 1975; Curran, Gilbert, & Little, 1976) incorporates many of the same training techniques used in assertiveness training (for instance, modeling and role playing). Clients are taught such skills as how to give and receive compliments, how to handle periods of silence, and how to initiate discussions. Other topics included are nonverbal methods of communication, assertiveness, ways of enhancing one's physical attractiveness, and approaches to physical intimacy.

After a lengthy assessment phase in which clients are interviewed, complete social skill questionnaires, and are observed in mock dating situations, training is begun. Training is usually conducted in groups, with a therapist leading discussions on each topic presented. The typical format is as follows: the therapist begins by showing a videotape in which a model inappropriately performs a particular dating skill. Next, a discussion of ways in which the model could have done better is conducted. Following this, another videotape, in which the model performs more effectively, is shown. Each client in the group then role plays the skill while the others observe. All role-playing episodes are videotaped so that the client can see exactly how he did and can receive direct feedback.

When clients show improvement in role playing, homework assignments are given. Assignments are specific to the skills being taught and are carefully planned in order to ensure that the client does not encounter anxiety when he attempts to apply what he has learned. Depending upon the client's progress in role playing, the first assignment might simply be talking to a woman; subsequent assignments might require the client

to ask someone out. In order that the therapist can assess clients' progress, they are instructed to record what happens when they apply their new skills. Each client's successes and failures in completing his homework assignment are discussed at subsequent meetings.

In comparison to matched, no-treatment control subjects, individuals who received social skills training showed significant improvement. In addition to dating more, they were more skillful in a simulated dating situation test and showed less anxiety as measured by a battery of paper-and-pencil tests of general social anxiety. These gains were maintained at a six-month followup evaluation. Other investigators (e.g., MacDonald, Lindquist, Kramer, McGrath, & Rhyne, 1975; Twentyman & McFall, 1975) have replicated Curran's findings. The general conclusion is that specific training in social skills is an effective means of reducing heterosexual anxiety in college-age men.

4) *Modification of Cognitions.* The fourth method of alleviating heterosexual anxiety is based on the hypothesis that heterosexual social anxiety is the result of the individual's faulty belief system. This approach incorporates many of Donald Meichenbaum's (1976) cognitive behavior modification techniques (see Chapters 2, 8, and 10 for a discussion of his work) and focuses on changing the anxious individual's negative self-evaluations and self-defeating expectations. The argument is that many socially anxious individuals are, in fact, socially skillful; however, because they tell themselves that they cannot "make it," they are anxious and do not pursue relationships. The goal is to eliminate the beliefs and self-statements that are inhibiting positive-approach behaviors and making the individual anxious.

The techniques used to alter such self-defeating cognitions are presented in a detailed research report by Carol Glass, John Gottman, and Steven Shmurak (1976). They worked with college males who were shy and ill at ease with women. In order to ensure that their treatment package dealt with problems directly relevant to the clients' lives, the researchers asked undergraduate students to give "play-by-play" accounts of their problematic social situations and then to write down their immediate thoughts and feelings about each situation. For example, a common problem reported by the males was calling up someone with whom they were recently acquainted and asking for a date. If the woman did not remember who he was when he introduced himself on the phone or if she asked him to repeat his name, many of the students said their first inclination was to hang up.

In such a situation, the socially anxious student usually makes a number of self-defeating interpretations, such as: "I must really be unimpressive—she didn't even remember my name." "She is obviously not interested or she would have remembered who I was. It's useless." The students' accounts of difficult and anxiety-producing incidents were used in construction of the cognitive modification program. During weekly group meetings, problematic situations were presented and students' feelings and expectations in response to each situation were discussed. The therapist pointed out the irrational and self-defeating aspects of their thoughts and suggested more adaptive self-evaluative statements. Clients were taught to monitor thoughts and to be aware of making self-defeating evaluations of themselves. When they discovered themselves doing this, they were to stop and generate more positive and equally plausible interpretations.

The following are two representative transcripts taken from Glass's training materials. The first deals with the situation we just cited in which the client has difficulty handling a telephone conversation when the woman does not remember his name. The second transcript concerns initiating conversation with a stranger. The therapist describes a situation, the client role plays, and then the therapist provides constructive feedback. "Coach" and "recoach" refer to the therapist's instructions; "modeling" refers to the therapist's demonstrations.

Transcript I

Situation: Suppose that last night you met a girl at a friend's house. Now you are calling her up to ask for a date. She picks up the phone and says, "Hello." You say your name and she says, "Who?" You say:

Coaching: This is a situation where you have put yourself on the spot by calling up a girl. However, although she does not remember your name, it is not appropriate to put her on the spot by asking her, "Don't you remember me?" Rather, repeat your name and add some identifying information such as what you look like or what you talked about at the party.

Model: A thoroughly adequate response might be: "Bob Smith, we were talking at the party last night about graduate schools."

Recoach: Notice that this person didn't make an issue of her not remembering him. He simply repeated his name and added some information by which the girl could place him.

Transcript II

Situation: You have entered the dorm cafeteria to eat your lunch, but you notice that all the tables except one are completely occupied. A girl eating alone is sitting at the only table available to you. You ask if you might sit down and she says, "Sure, I'm not saving it for anyone. It's so crowded in here you better grab it while you can." You sit down and feel like you should say something. You say:

Coaching: In meeting a girl for the first time, it is a good idea to begin the conversation with what you are thinking and feeling at the moment. Be specific about yourself. Disclose, don't interrogate. Most people are anxious when beginning a conversation with a stranger. Offering something specific about yourself gives her something concrete to relate to and helps get the conversation off the ground.

Model: A perfectly adequate response would be, "Yeah, I've never seen it so crowded in here. I usually eat a half an hour earlier but that crazy psych prof held us over today."

Recoach: Notice that this person was able to listen to what she said. He responded by relating his own immediate thoughts and feelings about the crowded cafeteria. Then, by explaining how he happened to be caught in the crowd, he opened an area of conversation to which she could relate. The girl is pleased that he has made it easy for her to start getting to know him. (Glass, 1974, Appendix N–1, N–2)

Using socially anxious college students as subjects, Glass and her colleagues evaluated the effectiveness of a cognitive modification program compared to specific skills training and to the two methods used together. All three treatment packages produced significant improvement. In comparison to no-treatment control subjects, all the men who received training were more skillful in the social situations in which they had been trained. However, in novel social situations—that is, those in which they had not been trained—subjects who received cognitive modification did significantly better than subjects who received specific skills training.

The major advantage of the cognitive behavior modification approach to the treatment of heterosexual social anxiety is that the new skills show greater generalization to novel situations. Learning how to cope with negative self-evaluations and interpretations is a technique that individuals can practice on their own and apply in new situations. However, as Curran (1977a) has pointed out in his discussion of the research of Glass and others, a combined approach might be superior for socially anxious men who do have specific social skills deficits. This would give them specific skills training as well as a means of changing their self-defeating cognitive reactions and expectations.

BEHAVIORAL MARRIAGE COUNSELING

Researchers have found that marriages in which the partners report dissatisfaction are characterized by low rates of positive exchanges and high rates of punishing responses (Birchler, Weiss, & Vincent, 1975; Willis, Weiss, & Patterson, 1974). Rather than using positive methods to encourage cooperation and compliance, distressed couples use aversive control to get what they want. Moreover, the spouses' communication with one another is often ambiguous and inconsistent (Friedman, 1972), and the partners rarely express their feelings in a straightforward interpretable manner (Eisler & Hersen, 1973; Fensterheim, 1972). As a result, the two individuals become increasingly less attractive to one another.

Behavior therapists' strategy for alleviating marital strife has been to introduce means for reversing the ratio of reinforcement to punishment; that is, increase the rate of reinforcing interaction and decrease the rate of aversive interaction. This is done by teaching couples (1) communication skills that facilitate effective problem solving, and (2) contingency contracting, whereby each partner agrees to change his or her behavior in some specified way in exchange for some positive reinforcer from the other person. Although for the sake of discussion we will consider each process separately, in most cases they are used together.

Training in Effective Communication

Through didactic discussion, modeling, and role playing, couples are taught how to express their needs in a clear and unambiguous manner. Much of this is accomplished through assertiveness training. Couples are also taught to express their desires and dissatisfaction in operational terms. Instead of speaking in vague generalities, such as "You never listen to what I have to say," couples are instructed to be specific and identify problems in terms of their actual occurrences, such as "As we were driving home from work this afternoon you didn't answer any of my questions about how we should plan our vacation." In order to avoid hostile exchanges and sarcastic comments, they are not to try to determine guilt or blame. Depending upon the therapist's assessment of the clients' deficits, the therapist might also focus on nonverbal communication such as eye contact, posture, and body gestures. For example, in one case involving a depressed client and his spouse (Hersen & Eisler, 1976), the therapist provided assertiveness training as well as practice in maintaining clear eye contact when speaking, increasing the length of responses to questions during conversation, and initiating conversation. Some therapists also discuss how to have a fair and productive argument—again, the focus is on responsible assertion.

An important task is teaching couples how to listen and how to evoke honest communication from each other. In a sense, what is taught is how to facilitate the other person's expression of feelings and needs. This might be as simple as being patient and silent or asking a question so the other person has an opportunity to answer. It also involves refraining from verbally punishing the other person when he or she expresses disagreement.

Training in Contingency Contracting

A commonly used method of reversing a distressed couple's reliance on aversive control is contingency contracting. Couples begin by identifying ways each partner could change that would make the relationship more satisfying. Consistent with principles of effective problem solving, the therapist requires each partner to pinpoint specific behaviors that his or her mate could emit to improve their relationship. The couple then negotiates an agreement in which contingencies of positive reinforcement for positive behavior change are established. In order to avoid the possibility of the couple's using punishment contingencies, the focus is on increasing the frequency of desirable behaviors rather than decreasing undesirable behaviors (Weiss, Birchler, & Vincent, 1974).

There are two types of contracts: the quid pro quo (Knox, 1971; Lederer & Jackson, 1968; Stuart, 1969a, 1969b) and the good faith agreement (Weiss, Hops, & Patterson, 1973). In a **quid pro quo** (literally, "this for that") **contract,** each spouse agrees to change a particular behavior if the other spouse agrees to do the same. The agreement is reciprocal in that each spouse's change serves as a reinforcer for the other's change. For instance, the husband might agree to wash the supper dishes each night if his wife will get up with him when he prepares to go to work in the morning. Or, the wife might agree to balance the checkbook each month if her husband will pay all the utility bills. This type of contracting can create a positive snowball effect, with each partner responding to the positive behavior of the other. However, by the same token, if one partner does not meet his or her obligation, the other is affected.

The **good faith contract** differs from the quid pro quo contract in that the behavior of each partner is not used as a reinforcer. In the good faith agreement each person's reinforcer is some specific item or event such as a night on the town, a new pair of slacks, or money. The advantage of this type of contract is that each behavior change is reinforced independently, so that if one partner abdicates his or her responsibilities, the other's program is not affected.

During the initial stages of training, the therapist carefully directs the couple through contract negotiation. After the couple has drawn up and carried out one or two simple contracts under supervision, the therapist gives them homework assignments in which they take greater responsibility for completing the negotiation.

Application and Effectiveness

Most of the research on behavioral marriage counseling has been of the uncontrolled case study variety (for example, Azrin, Naster, & Jones, 1973; Stuart, 1969a, 1969b; Weiss, Hops, & Patterson, 1973). The first published account of behavior therapy treatment for marital discord was Richard Stuart's (1969a, 1969b) report of four cases in which quid pro quo contracts were used to increase the level of intimacy in the relationship. Contracts were quite simple; physical contact and sexual activity were given in exchange for time spent in relaxed conversation. All the couples who participated reported substantial increase in the frequency of the desired behavior. Gains were maintained at both twenty-four- and forty-eight-week followup evaluations.

One of the few controlled studies of behavioral marriage counseling was reported by Neil Jacobson (1977). Couples responded to a notice in the town newspaper offering a new treatment program for troubled marriages. Ages of the participants ranged from twenty-two to forty-two years and length of marriages from one to thirteen years. After preliminary screening, couples were randomly assigned to one of two groups. Control group subjects participated in all pretest and posttest assessments but were not offered treatment until after the experimental group had finished the program and all posttests had been completed. Treatment for the experimental group was begun two weeks following pretesting.

The treatment program was carried out during eight weekly sessions in which the therapist met with each couple individually. During the initial session, the therapist explained the rationale, outlined the program, and asked each couple to identify major and minor problem areas in their marriage. These problem areas were then used as the subject matter for problem-solving training during the next four sessions. At the beginning of each session, the couple was given a problem and asked to discuss possible solutions. As they talked, the therapist intervened from time to time to provide directive feedback. The therapist explicitly discouraged two classes of behavior: placing "blame" and making sarcastic comments. Couples were also taught to express criticism in more constructive ways. The therapist often role played with each partner to model compromise and acknowledgment of the other's feelings. Videotape recordings of sessions provided additional feedback to each couple. Couples were also given homework assignments in which they practiced problem solving within specific topic areas.

The last three sessions of the program focused on "good faith" contingency contracting. Again, couples identified specific problems and were asked to negotiate a contract with the therapist observing. As the couples learned how to set up equitable contracts, they were given contract-writing homework assignments that the therapist later reviewed with them. Case Study 9-2 describes how one of Jacobson's couples progressed during treatment.

On both observational and self-report measures, couples who participated in treatment showed significant improvement over control couples. Treatment couples displayed significantly fewer aversive behaviors and more positive behaviors during posttreatment problem-solving interaction tests. Self-report questionnaires completed by the couples twelve months following the termination of treatment indicated greater marital satisfaction in the treatment couples.

Clearly, learning effective problem-solving strategies and how to negotiate contracts can result in improved marital relations. The gains that have been made through the application of behavioral principles are unprecedented in the marriage counseling literature. As Jacobson and his colleague Barclay Martin (1976) stated in their review of behavioral marriage therapy, traditional approaches have received no direct empirical support (Bergin, 1971; Gurman, 1973; Olson, 1970). These results do not, of course, imply that training in contingency contracting and communication skills is the answer for *all* troubled marriages. Couples in the studies reviewed above were preselected and do not represent all distressed couples. That is, they had agreed they wanted to improve their marriage and are probably only a subset of all distressed marriages. Subsequent work in the area will likely focus on methods for determining specific problems that produce marital discord and tailoring treatment programs to meet the needs of the distressed couple.

SUMMARY

Many traditional approaches have been successful in getting people "in touch" with their feelings, but people must also learn how to act on their feelings. The major contribution of behavior modification has been to teach people specific ways of expressing their feelings appropriately.

One of the more important topics in this area has been assertiveness training. Salter (1949) is credited with first suggesting that the socialization process takes a heavy toll in reinforcing the suppression of feelings and punishing spontaneous emotional expression. For many people, being pleasant and accommodating is of primary importance. Salter's goal was to teach inhibited individuals how to express their feelings directly. His six techniques for teaching assertion were: (1) feeling-talk, (2) facial-talk, (3) contradict and attack, (4) deliberate use of "I," (5) express agreement when praised, and (6) improvisation. Many of Salter's ideas have been incorporated into present-day assertiveness training, and his notions regarding the importance of feeling-talk have been widely accepted; however, his work went virtually unrecognized until the late 1960s.

Assertiveness training is typically broken down into three parts: (1) didactic discussion, in which the rationale for appropriate assertion is explained and the client is encouraged to adopt an "assertive belief system"; (2) behavioral rehearsal, in which the therapist and client role play various problem situations and the therapist provides direct feedback; (3) in vivo practice, in which the client applies assertive skills in specified real-life situations. Much of assertiveness training is merely applied common sense, but behavior therapists have discovered four principles of effective assertion: (1) minimal effective response, (2) empathic assertion, (3) constructive feedback, and (4) escalation.

Behavior modification has also provided effective treatment methods in heterosexual social anxiety. Three strategies for training have been applied: (1) systematic desensitization, (2) simple and relatively unstructured practice in "heterosexual interaction," (3) highly structured training in appropriate dating behavior using modeling, behavioral rehearsal, and coaching, (4) modification of cognitive expectations and self-evaluations. Many of the same training techniques used in assertiveness training (for instance, role playing and modeling) have been employed here.

A third area that has generated much interest among behavior therapists is marriage counseling. Again, using didactic discussion, role playing, coaching, and in vivo practice, distressed couples have been taught techniques of effective communication and problem solving as well as how to negotiate contingency contracts. The focus of training in problem solving is to teach the couple to express their wishes in clear, operational terms, without offending the other person. Many of the skills that are taught are similar to those of effective assertion. Training in contingency contracting focuses on negotiating straightforward agreements in which reinforcement for both partners is maximized. The most common contracts are the quid pro quo and the good faith agreements.

Undoubtedly behavior modification has offered much to help people establish more satisfying interpersonal relationships, but the emphasis has been somewhat lopsided. Despite the expressed goals of assertiveness training and social skills training, almost all the work in the area has focused on teaching people how to "get what they want" and express negative feelings. Little effort has been directed toward teaching people how to express positive feelings, such as love, appreciation, and respect, more effectively. As Lazarus and others have stressed, teaching people these skills could be one of behavior modification's most valuable contributions.

CASE STUDY 9–1

DUEHN, W. D., & MAYADAS, N. S. THE USE OF STIMULUS/MODEL-
ING VIDEOTAPES IN ASSERTIVE TRAINING FOR HOMOSEXUALS.
JOURNAL OF HOMOSEXUALITY, 1976, **1,** 373–381.

During the last five years there has been a radical shift in attitudes regarding nontraditional sexual life styles; in many communities homosexuality
no longer carries the shame and embarrassment it once did. Nevertheless,
many people still experience rejection and harassment as a result of their
sexual orientation. "Coming out" can be painful and difficult. The following case demonstrates the use of assertiveness training in helping a twenty-
six-year-old businessman deal with the problems associated with publicly
acknowledging his homosexuality.

The client's request was very specific: he wanted to learn how to handle
the interpersonal problems incurred in his decision to publicly acknowledge his homosexuality. During the initial interviews, the client identified
three major problem areas. The first was the reaction of family and friends
when he informed them of his homosexual life style. His only experience
with telling "straight" friends had been disturbing—the friends became
angry, upset, and rejecting. Although he wanted to discuss his homosexuality with others close to him, he feared similar reactions. The client's second problem concerned dealing with the stereotypic reactions of strangers
who saw him with another man. Any signs of affection he might display
toward his lover would evoke ridicule and derogatory comments from
others. His third concern was his reaction to sexual overtures from other
homosexuals whom he did not find attractive. On a number of occasions
he had become involved in a sexual relationship with someone he hadn't
even liked because he was unable to reject his advances. Apart from these
difficulties, the client enjoyed his life style.

The therapist devised a hierarchy of interpersonal situations relating to
his "coming out" that were problematic. The first situation involved discussing his homosexuality with family and friends. Client and therapist
rehearsed various possible conversations he might have and discussed
what responses he might make. As the client became more skilled at handling such interchanges, he was encouraged to bring the topic up with various close friends. To enable the client to deal with hostile remarks and rejection from strangers, a videotape demonstrating assertive reactions was
used. The client was taught to hold a strong posture and to make direct eye
contact when someone insulted him. For example, rather than dropping
his head and quietly leaving a restaurant when people called him a "fag,"
he was to look at them squarely and, if they continued their harassment, to
suggest that perhaps it was *their* problem, not his. A similar videotape
demonstrated how to handle unwanted sexual overtures. Therapist and
client also role played such situations so that the client could practice effective assertion. As he became more assertive during role-playing sessions,
the therapist advised him to try out his new behaviors in real-life situations.

Throughout training, the therapist kept a detailed account of the client's
success in handling various interpersonal interactions in his daily life.

During the twelve weeks of therapy the client showed marked improvement. He found that when he told others about his homosexuality he was not anxious and felt comfortable discussing the issue. He also felt that his assertive manner during these conversations affected others in positive ways: They seemed more accepting and relaxed about his disclosures. He also indicated that he was quite effective in coping with the unpleasant reactions of strangers and dealing with sexual overtures from others. At a twelve-month followup evaluation there was no indication of any interpersonal problems. The client was involved in a satisfying relationship and did not feel that additional counseling was needed (Duehn, 1977, personal communication).

CASE STUDY 9–2

JACOBSON, N. S. PROBLEM-SOLVING AND CONTINGENCY CON-
TRACTING IN THE TREATMENT OF MARITAL DISCORD. *JOURNAL
OF CONSULTING AND CLINICAL PSYCHOLOGY*, 1977, **45,** 92–100.

This case shows the use of communication training and contingency contracting in the treatment of a common marital problem: lack of communication. The couple were in their late thirties, middle class and well educated. During the initial interview they were cooperative with the
psychotherapist and appeared eager to resolve their difficulties. Both partners reported that they were not satisfied with the relationship. After some
discussion, they became more specific in their complaints. One of their
biggest problems was that they rarely had relaxed conversations together.
The husband complained that his wife was occupied with trivial household
chores and did not relate to him and his two teen-age daughters. The wife
reported that her husband was brisk and condescending whenever he
spoke to her.

Figure 9–1. Wife's daily record of husband's demanding statements and amount
of time engaged in conversation. From N. S. Jacobson, Problem solving and
contingency contracting in the treatment of marital discord. *Journal of Consulting
and Clinical Psychology*, 1977, **45,** p. 97.

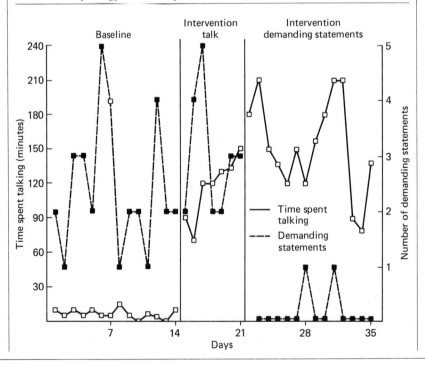

During the initial interview the husband talked incessantly and the wife said virtually nothing. Most of the conversation was controlled by the husband; he seemed to have everything organized and was clearly not interested in his wife's opinions. Until the therapist directed questions to the wife, she was passive. In order to assess the couple's problem-solving skills, the therapist asked them to discuss one of their major problems and how it might be resolved. During this discussion, the therapist observed that the husband dominated the conversation (Jacobson, 1978, personal communication).

In the first phase of treatment, the therapist had the couple go through various decision-making exercises in his office. As they talked, the therapist provided instructions for how the exercises might be made more effective. The primary recommendation was that the husband ask for his wife's opinion on every issue. This emphasis served to draw the wife into the decision-making process and to reduce the frequency of the husband's domineering comments.

The second phase of treatment focused on contingency contracting. In the first quid pro quo contract, the husband agreed to spend one hour each day in quiet conversation with his wife. In exchange she agreed to relinquish rights to the television set so that he could watch some sports event. The contract was very successful: time spent talking exceeded the contract requirement by at least 200 percent. However, frequency of demanding comments was not affected. In order to modify this behavior, a second quid pro quo contract was negotiated. In this contract the wife agreed to arrange a card game for her husband and his friends if he made no more than one demanding comment during a seven-day period. Demanding comments virtually stopped. Figure 9–1 shows the results of the two contracts.

At the twelve-month followup evaluation, the couple reported that their relationship was much more satisfying. On a standardized marriage adjustment questionnaire they showed marked improvement in their responses over responses made before therapy.

REFERENCES

Alberti, R. E., & Emmons, M. L. *Your perfect right: A guide to assertive behavior.* San Luis Obispo, Calif.: Inpact, 1974.

Azrin, N. H., Naster, B. J., & Jones, R. Reciprocity counseling: A rapid learning-based procedure for marital counseling. *Behaviour Research and Therapy*, 1973, **11**, 365–382.

Bander, K. W., Steinke, G. V., Allen, G. J., & Mosher, Q. L. Evaluation of three dating-specific treatment approaches for heterosexual dating anxiety. *Journal of Consulting and Clinical Psychology*, 1975, **43**, 259–265.

Bergin, A. E. The evaluation of therapeutic outcomes.

In A. E. Bergin & S. L. Garfield (Eds.), *Handbook of psychotherapy and behavior change: An empirical analysis.* New York: Wiley, 1971.

Birchler, G. R., Weiss, R. L., & Vincent, J. P. A multi-method analysis of social reinforcement exchange between maritally distressed and nondistressed spouse and stranger dyads. *Journal of Personality and Social Psychology*, 1975, **31**, 349–360.

Borkovec, T. D., Stone, N., O'Brien, G., & Kaloupek, D. Identification and measurement of clinically relevant target behaviors for analogue outcome research. *Behavior Therapy*, 1974, **5**, 503–513.

Christensen, A., & Arkowitz, K. Preliminary report in

250

practice dating and feedback as treatment for college dating problems. *Journal of Counseling Psychology,* 1974, **21,** 92–95.

Clark, J. V., & Arkowitz, H. Social anxiety and self-evaluation of interpersonal performance. *Psychological Reports,* 1975, **36,** 211–221.

Cotler, S. B., & Guerra, J. J. *Assertion training: A humanistic-behavioral guide to self-dignity.* Champaign, Ill.: Research Press, 1976.

Curran, J. P. An evaluation of a skills training program and a systematic desensitization program in reducing dating anxiety. *Behaviour Research and Therapy,* 1975, **13,** 65–68.

Curran, J. P. Reactivity of males of differing heterosexual social anxiety to female approach and non-approach cue conditions. Unpublished manuscript, Purdue University, 1977(a).

Curran, J. P. Skill training as an approach to the treatment of heterosexual-social anxiety. *Psychological Bulletin,* 1977, **84,** 140–157(b).

Curran, J. P., & Gilbert, F. S. A test of the relative effectiveness of a systematic desensitization program and an interpersonal skills training program with date anxious subjects. *Behavior Therapy,* 1975, **6,** 510–521.

Curran, J. P., Gilbert, F. S., & Little, L. M. A comparison between behavioral replication training and sensitivity training approaches to heterosexual dating anxiety. *Journal of Counseling Psychology,* 1976, **23,** 190–196.

Curran, J. P., Wallander, J. L., & Fischetti, M. The role of behavioral and cognitive factors in heterosexual-social anxiety. Unpublished paper presented at the Midwestern Psychological Association meetings, Chicago, May 1977.

Doran, L. E. The effects of assertion training within a career awareness course on the sex-role self-concepts and career choices of high school women. Unpublished Ph.D. dissertation, University of Illinois, 1976.

Duehn, W. D., & Mayadas, N. S. The use of stimulus/modeling videotapes in assertive training for homosexuals. *Journal of Homosexuality,* 1976, **1,** 373–381.

Edwards, N. B. Case conference: Assertive training in a case of homosexual pedophilia. *Journal of Behavior Therapy and Experimental Psychiatry,* 1972, **3,** 55–63.

Eisler, R. M., & Hersen, M. Behavioral techniques in family-orientated crisis intervention. *Archives of General Psychiatry,* 1973, **28,** 111–116.

Fensterheim, H. Assertive methods and marital problems. In R. O. Rubin, H. Fensterheim, J. D. Henderson, & L. P. Ullman (Eds.), *Advances in behavior therapy.* New York: Academic Press, 1972.

Fischetti, M., Curran, J. P., & Wessberg, H. W. Sense of timing: A skill deficit in heterosexual-socially anxious males. *Behavior Modification,* 1977, **1,** 179–194.

Fishman, S., & Nawas, M. Treatment of polysomatic or global problems by systematic desensitization. In R. Rubin (Ed.), *Advances in behavior therapy.* New York: Academic Press, 1973.

Friedman, P. M. Personalistic family and marital therapy. In A. A. Lazarus (Ed.), *Clinical behavior therapy.* New York: Brunner/Mazel, 1972.

Glass, C. R. Response acquisition and cognitive self-statement modification approaches to dating behavior training. Unpublished M.A. thesis, Indiana University, 1974.

Glass, C. R., Gottman, J. M., & Shmurak, S. H. Response acquisition and cognitive self-statement modification approaches to dating skill training. *Journal of Counseling Psychology,* 1976, **23,** 520–526.

Goldfried, M. R., & Davison, G. C. *Clinical behavior therapy.* New York: Holt, Rinehart and Winston, 1976.

Greenspoon, J. The reinforcing effect of two spoken sounds on the frequency of two responses. *American Journal of Psychology,* 1955, **68,** 409–416.

Gurman, A. S. The effects and effectiveness of marital therapy: A review of outcome research. *Family Process,* 1973, **12,** 145–170.

Harlow, H. F. The development of affectional patterns in infant monkeys. In B. M. Foss (Ed.), *Determinants of infant behavior.* London: Metheun, 1961.

Hersen, M., & Eisler, R. M. Social skill training. In W. E. Craighead, A. E. Kazdin, & M. J. Mahoney (Eds.),*Behaviour modification.* Boston: Houghton Mifflin, 1976.

Hersen, M., Eisler, R. M., & Miller, P. M. Development of assertive responses: Clinical, measurement and research considerations. *Behavior Research and Therapy,* 1973, **11,** 505–521.

Jacobson, N. S. Problem solving and contingency contracting in the treatment of marital discord. *Journal of Consulting and Clinical Psychology,* 1977, **45,** 92–100.

Jacobson, N. S., & Martin, B. Behavior marriage therapy: Current status. *Psychological Bulletin,* 1976, **83,** 540–556.

Jakubowski, P. Assertive behavior and clinical problems of women. In D. Carter & E. Rawlings (Eds.), *Psychotherapy for women: Treatment towards equality.* Springfield, Ill.: Thomas, 1977.

Knox, D. *Marriage happiness: A behavioral approach to counseling.* Champaign, Ill.: Research Press, 1971.

Lange, A. J., & Jakubowski, P. *Responsible assertive training.* Champaign, Ill.: Research Press, 1976.

Lazarus, A. A. *Behavior therapy and beyond.* New York: McGraw-Hill, 1971.

Lazarus, A. A. On assertive behavior: A brief note. *Behavior Therapy,* 1973, **4,** 697–699.

Lederer, W. J., & Jackson, D. D. *The mirages of marriage.* New York: Norton, 1968.

Levinger, G., & Snoek, J. D. *Attraction in relationship: A new look at interpersonal attraction*. Morristown, N.J.: General Learning Press, 1972.

Lieberman, R. P. *A guide to behavioral analysis and therapy*. New York: Pergamon Press, 1972.

MacDonald, M. Teaching assertion: A paradigm for therapeutic intervention. *Psychotherapy: Theory, Research, and Practice*, 1975, **12**, 60–67.

MacDonald, M. L., Lindquist, C. U., Kramer, J. A., McGrath, R. A., & Rhyne, L. D. Social skills training: Behavioral rehearsal in groups and dating skills. *Journal of Counseling Psychology*, 1975, **22**, 224–230.

Macpherson, E. L. R. Selective operant conditioning and deconditioning of assertive modes of behavior. *Journal of Behavior Therapy and Experimental Psychiatry*, 1972, **3**, 99–107.

Martinson, W. D., & Zerface, J. P. Comparison of individual counseling in a social program with nondaters. *Journal of Counseling Psychology*, 1970, **17**, 36–40.

McFall, R. M., & Lillesand, D. B. Behavioral rehearsal with modeling and coaching in assertion training. *Journal of Abnormal Psychology*, 1971, **77**, 313–323.

McFall, R. M., & Marston, A. R. An experimental investigation of behavioral rehearsal in assertive training. *Journal of Abnormal Psychology*, 1970, **76**, 295–303.

McFall, R. M., & Twentyman, C. T. Four experiments on the relative contributions of rehearsal, modeling and coaching to assertion training. *Journal of Abnormal Psychology*, 1973, **81**, 199–218.

Meichenbaum, D. Cognitive behavior modification. In J. T. Spence, R. C. Carson, & J. W. Thibaut (Eds.), *Behavioral approaches to therapy*. Morristown, N.J.: General Learning Press, 1976.

Mitchell, K. R., & Orr, T. E. Note on treatment of heterosexual anxiety using shift-term massed desensitization. *Psychological Reports*, 1974, **35**, 1093–1094.

Olson, D. H. Marital and family therapy: Integrative review and critique. *Journal of Marriage and the Family*, 1970, **32**, 501–538.

Rheingold, H. L., Gewirtz, J. L., & Ross, H. W. Social conditioning of vocalizations in the infant. *Journal of Comparative and Physiological Psychology*, 1959, **52**,

Rich, A. R., & Schroeder, H. E. Research issues in assertiveness training. *Psychological Bulletin*, 1976, **83**, 1081–1096.

Rimm, D. C., & Masters, J. C. *Behavior therapy—techniques and empirical findings*. New York: Academic Press, 1974.

Salter, A. *Conditioned reflex therapy*, 2nd ed. New York: Capricorn, 1961 (1st ed., 1949).

Schaffer, H. L., & Emerson, P. E. The development of social attachments in infancy. *Monographs of the Society for Research in Child Development*, 1964, **29** (3, Serial No. 94), 5–77.

Shmurak, S. H. A comparison of types of problems encountered by college students and psychiatric inpatients in social situations. Unpublished manuscript, Indiana University, 1973.

Shneidman, E. S., Farberow, N. L., & Litman, R. E. (Eds.), *The psychology of suicide*. New York: Jason Aronson, 1970.

Stern, S. Neurosis as disturbance in communication: A theoretical integration. Unpublished manuscript, University of Illinois, 1978.

Stevenson, I., & Wolpe, J. Recovery from sexual deviations through overcoming non-sexual neurotic responses. *American Journal of Psychiatry*, 1960, **116**, 737–742.

Stuart, R. B. Operant-interpersonal treatment for marital discord. *Journal of Consulting and Clinical Psychology*, 1969, **33**, 675–682(a).

Stuart, R. B. Token reinforcement in marital treatment. In R. D. Rubin & C. M. Franks (Eds.), *Advances in behavior therapy*. New York: Academic Press, 1969(b).

Sullivan, H. S. *The interpersonal theory of psychiatry*. New York: Norton, 1953.

Taylor, D. A. The development of interpersonal relationships: Social penetration processes. *Journal of Social Psychology*, 1968, **75**, 79–90.

Taylor, D. A., Altman, I., & Sorrentino, R. Interpersonal exchange as a function of rewards and costs and situational factors: Expectancy confirmation-disconfirmation. *Journal of Experimental Social Psychology*, 1969, **5**, 324–339.

Twentyman, C. T., & McFall, R. M. Behavioral training of social skills in shy males. *Journal of Consulting and Clinical Psychology*, 1975, **43**, 384–395.

Weiss, R. L., Birchler, G. R., & Vincent, J. P. Contractual models for negotiation training in marital dyads. *Journal of Marriage and the Family*, 1974, **36**, 321–331.

Weiss, R. L., Hops, H., & Patterson, G. R. A framework for conceptualizing marital conflict, a technology for altering it, some data for evaluating it. In L. A. Hamerlynck, L. C. Handy, & E. J. Mash (Eds.), *Behavior change: Methodology, concepts, and practice*. Champaign, Ill.: Research Press, 1973.

Willis, T. A., Weiss, R. L., & Patterson, J. R. A behavioral analysis of the determinants of marital satisfaction. *Journal of Consulting and Clinical Psychology*, 1974, **42**, 802–811.

Wolpe, J. *Psychotherapy by reciprocal inhibition*. Stanford, Calif.: Stanford University Press, 1958.

Wolpe, J. *The practice of behavior therapy*. Oxford: Pergamon Press, 1969.

Wolpe, J., & Lazarus, A. A. *Behavior therapy techniques*. New York: Pergamon Press, 1966.

ten

ANXIETY AND ITS MANAGEMENT

What is anxiety? What produces it? Where does it come from?

As W. H. Auden put it, we are living in the Age of Anxiety. His words are no mere poetic metaphor; indeed, they are a statement of fact, to which the vast and ever-increasing sales of Librium, Valium, and numerous other tranquilizers stand as an undeniable testament. Anxiety is the most frequent complaint with which mental health professionals are confronted. Indeed, anxiety has long been held by traditional theorists to be the foundation on which most psychological disorders are built. Pathological conditions aside, the experience of anxiety is one with which we are all familiar. This ubiquitousness, combined with the clinical importance of the problem, has resulted in its being one of the most widely studied of all psychological disorders.

Yet, with all the research into anxiety, we are still a long way from understanding what it is and how it evolves. Within the past twenty years, however, new ways of conceptualizing the disorder have proved exceedingly useful in the development of reliable and effective treatment methods. In fact, the treatment of anxiety has been one of behavior modification's triumphs. As we will see, the treatment technology now appears to be well ahead of the theorizing from which it sprang.

In this chapter we will examine behavioral approaches to the management of anxiety. We will begin by developing a working conceptualization of the complex emotion known as anxiety and considering the anxiety-related problems that lead people to seek clinical help. Next, we will present and evaluate some behavioral models of the development and maintenance of anxiety, including some recent thinking by one of the pioneers of the behavioral movement. Finally, we will turn our attention to the major anxiety-reduction procedures. In this discussion we will examine the theory underlying each procedure, what it really "looks like" when it is applied in a clinical setting, and the available evidence for its effectiveness.

Approaches to anxiety have undergone a fairly long and intricate development in comparison with many other areas of behavior modification, and any attempt to review the topic must necessarily reflect this fact. This is, in fact, the longest chapter in the book; it presents a variety of concepts and controversies, many of which are quite complex. But in the end we believe you will be rewarded with an understanding of one of the most important subjects in clinical behavior therapy.

WHAT IS ANXIETY?

Everyone thinks they know what they mean when they speak of being anxious or afraid, but this type of assumption causes difficulty in attempting to study any psychological experience objectively. In truth, considerable disagreement exists as to the nature of anxiety. Different theorists have variously used the term to refer to "a transient emotional/psychological *behavior* (i.e., 'He is anxious today'), a dispositional *trait* ('She is an anxious person'), and a cause or *explanation* of behavior (i.e., 'He overeats because of anxiety'; 'Her seductiveness is a defense against anxiety')" (Borkovec, Weerts, & Bernstein, 1977, p. 368). Perhaps the one thing on which most psychologists have come to agree is that anxiety is not a simple "thing" that an individual either has or does not have. Instead, it appears to be a complex response or set of responses that may be inferred from an individual's *self-report, physiological activity,* and/or *observable performance* in certain situations.

Although these three behavioral "channels" tend to covary to some extent, they often fail to correlate very highly with one another (Lang, 1968). Much of this inconsistency is the result of a variety of problems that can reduce the accuracy of measurements made in any of the channels (Borkovec, Weerts, & Bernstein, 1977; Lick & Katkin, 1976; Paul & Bernstein, 1973). It also seems clear that although the channels are related, they are also partially independent, and each is subject to modification in isolation from the others. For example, a young man who experiences a pounding heart and trembling hands at the sight of a harmless snake in the woods may claim he is not frightened so as not to appear "unmasculine" to the young woman he is with. Conversely, a bomb squad member may calmly approach a ticking shoebox and deftly perform the necessary operations to defuse the bomb inside, all the while insisting that he is terrified.

Although these problems make it difficult to define anxiety in any absolute terms, the feelings and behaviors most likely to evoke a label of anxiety in a clinical setting are easily described. Therefore, we will follow many others in using *anxiety* as a shorthand term for a complex, multidimensional pattern of response characterized by subjective feelings of apprehension and tension, accompanied by or associated with arousal of the sympathetic branch of the autonomic nervous system (Borkovec, Weerts, & Bernstein, 1977; Paul & Bernstein, 1973; Spielberger, 1966).

Physiology of Anxiety Reactions

Almost anyone who has experienced intense fear recognizes the rather striking internal sensations that accompany it: a pounding heart, quickening respiration, "butterflies" fluttering through the stomach, and so on. In extreme fear the responses may include involuntary trembling, urinary and fecal incontinence, and fainting. Such physiological consequences are under the control of the **autonomic nervous system (ANS)** (see Figure 10–1). The ANS (also known as the involuntary nervous system because it operates largely without our conscious effort) innervates the smooth muscle of the internal organs, and thus mediates changes in heart rate, gastric motility and secretion, distribution of blood flow throughout the body, sweat secretion, and glandular activity, to mention a few of the more important effects. The ANS is divided into two parts, known as the **sympathetic** and **parasympathetic** branches. As can be seen in Figure 10–1, most organs are innervated by both divisions of the ANS, and the relationship between the two is, for the most part, *mutually antagonistic;* that is, activity in one branch of the ANS produces an effect opposite that produced by activity in the other branch. In this way, sympathetic activity increases while parasympathetic activity decreases heart rate; sympathetic activity inhibits while parasympathetic activity stimulates gastric secretion; and so on.

Now let us observe what happens to the ANS when the person is placed under stress, as when he or she is presented with an anxiety-eliciting stimulus. You step into the street and, absorbed in the caramel corn you're munching, fail to notice a rapidly approaching bus. A horn blasts, brakes screech, and your nervous system goes into an "emergency reaction," which consists of a widespread discharge of the sympathetic branch of the ANS. Your heartbeat increases in strength and rate, and blood vessels in your arms and legs dilate to increase the blood supply necessary for evasive action. The adrenal medulla is stimulated to increase its secretion of the hormone epinephrine, which, besides enhancing other sympathetic effects, causes the release of stored sugar from the

① response to something in env: control we is fear. free floating

② physiological response of fear.

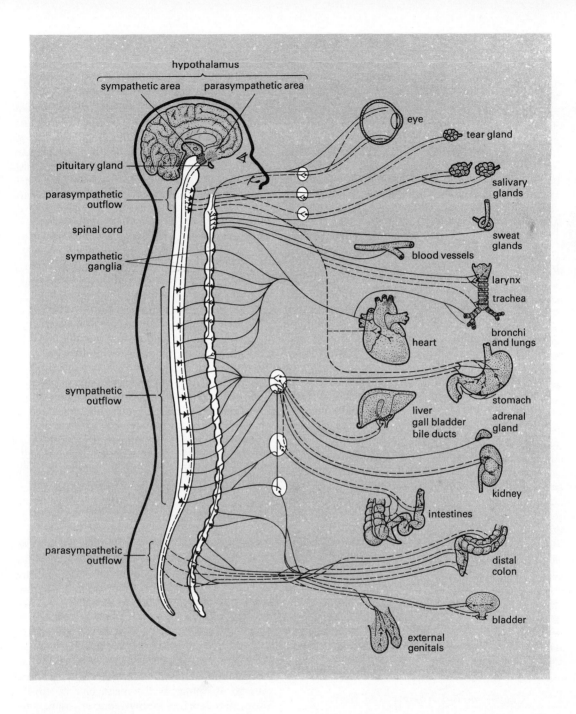

Figure 10–1. The autonomic nervous system (ANS). From *Elements of psychology*, Figure 22.3, p. 540, by David Krech, Richard S. Crutchfield, Norman Livson, with the collaboration of William A. Wilson, Jr. Copyright © 1974 by Alfred A. Knopf, Inc. Reprinted by permission of Alfred A. Knopf, Inc.

liver, making more energy available. Your respiration becomes deeper and faster to handle the increased oxygen delivery and carbon dioxide removal necessary during muscular movement. The pupils of your eyes dilate to allow more light in, and sweating begins on the palms of your hands and soles of your feet, probably to improve traction on these important surfaces. Digestion of your caramel corn, on the other hand, comes to an abrupt halt as the sympathetic wave overrides this parasympathetic activity. Gastric and salivary secretions shut down, intestinal motility is inhibited, and blood supply to your viscera is reduced by vasoconstriction in order to make more blood available for functions more relevant at that moment. This sympathetic discharge serves a very useful purpose—it mobilizes the body's resources for *fight* or *flight* (Cannon, 1932) and maximizes the chances for adaptive responding in times of danger. As a result of all this activity, you are able to execute a truly magnificent vertical leap, and the bus misses you.

What we have characterized as a purely sympathetic discharge is a bit of an oversimplification. The changes we have described might be typical of a startle reaction or an intense fear reaction. In these cases, the sympathetic nervous system tends to become activated *as a whole* (although poorly understood parasympathetic effects, such as fainting, stomach distress, and involuntary evacuation of the bowel and bladder may occur). At lower levels of arousal, as when an individual is moderately anxious or otherwise stressed, the sympathetic discharge may *fractionate* (Lacey, 1967). In these cases, only certain systems may react, or some systems may react much more than others. For example, a person may experience a violently pounding heart, while his palms remain dry and his respiration steady. But it is clear that in general the ANS tends toward sympathetic activation during anxiety.

Cognition and Anxiety Reactions

ANS activity does play an important role in the experience of anxiety, but it is not the whole story. The same type of massive internal changes elicited by fear-producing stimuli can be produced by vigorous exercise (Robinson, 1974) or injections of epinephrine (Wegner, Clemens, Darsie, Engel, Estess, & Sonnenschein, 1960) without an accompanying affective state reported as anxiety. Although some evidence indicates that different patterns of physiological response are associated with different emotional experiences (for example, Ax, 1953; Schachter, 1957), the major aspects of this response are the same across emotions, and it is unclear how much ANS patterns account for the differentiation of, for example, "anxiety" and "exhilaration."

Stanley Schachter and his colleagues (Schachter & Latane, 1964; Schachter & Singer, 1962; Schachter & Wheeler, 1962) have marshaled evidence suggesting that emotion, anxiety included, is the product of two factors: (1) an essentially undifferentiated state of physiological arousal and (2) a cognition, label, or interpretation of the meaning of that state of arousal. To illustrate this notion, consider the following:

> Imagine a man walking alone down a dark alley. A figure with a gun suddenly appears. The perception-cognition "figure with a gun" in some fashion initiates a state of physiological arousal; this state of arousal is interpreted in terms of knowledge about dark alleys and guns, and the state is labeled "fear." Similarly a student who unexpectedly learns that he has made Phi Beta Kappa may experience a state of arousal which he will label "joy." (Schachter & Singer, 1962, p. 380)

The direction such cognitions take appears to be a function of three factors. The context or setting in which the arousal is elicited is the first factor. The sensation of plummeting toward the ground may elicit quite different emotions when experienced on a roller coaster and on a commercial airliner. The second factor is the past learning history of the individual. Two individuals on the same roller coaster may experience quite different interpretations of their arousal if one of them once suffered an injury as the result of a severe fall. Third, the level of arousal elicited may affect whether the stimulus is experienced as pleasant or unpleasant. When someone sneaks up behind you and pokes you violently in the ribs, the startle reaction is of sufficient intensity to be labeled as bad, regardless of the laughter from the jokester.

Free Floating

Lesser degrees of arousal will be labeled according to the first two factors.

Schachter's hypothesis is appealing but raises some "chicken and egg" problems. It implies that autonomic arousal occurs before the cognition, and that the individual then evaluates the situation and labels the arousal accordingly. Frequently, however, cognitive activity *precedes* arousal, and is, in fact, *responsible for* it.

Several psychologists (for instance, Arnold, 1950, 1960; Lazarus & Averill, 1972) have emphasized the role of **cognitive appraisal** of stimuli in producing arousal and anxiety. Observing a rattlesnake in a glass case at the zoo may not elicit any particular arousal or fear, but observing the same rattlesnake in one's bed is quite another story. The difference obviously lies in the appraisal of the stimulus (the snake) as either threatening or nonthreatening. This appraisal process may not be objectively correct. For example, a person afraid of public speaking may appraise even a friendly audience as threatening, and may suffer physiological arousal and mental anguish more appropriate to the prospect of facing a lynch mob.

Maladaptive Anxiety: Clinical Problems

Anxiety can be a very useful emotion: it helps the individual recognize danger and react to it in an adaptive fashion. Few people seek clinical help for reduction of adaptive anxiety such as, "I get very anxious whenever I smell gas seeping into the living room. Can you help me?" Anxiety becomes a clinical problem when it is consistently evoked in the absence of a threat, or when its intensity or duration is entirely out of proportion to the degree of threat that is present. In these cases, anxiety is a maladaptive emotion.

Gordon Paul and Douglas Bernstein (1973, pp. 16–17) have discussed five major categories of clinical complaints in which maladaptive anxiety plays a central role. Although they deal specifically with problems related to conditioned anxiety (see below), their analysis applies to all anxiety-related problems. With the exception of this minor abridgment, the following descriptions of the problems (italicized portions) are taken directly from their presentation.

1. *Anxiety of sufficient duration or intensity to cause extreme subjective distress is elicited in the absence of objective danger or threat.* This describes the relatively "pure" anxiety reaction in which the experience of anxiety per se is the problem for which the client is seeking help. Included are unidimensional "phobias" (fears of specific stimuli or circumstances, such as dogs, flying, and small enclosed spaces) as well as more complex fears in which the stimuli may be broadly generalized and often difficult to specify ("free-floating" or "pervasive" anxiety). Intense stress reactions of psychotic proportions (commonly referred to as "nervous breakdowns") also fall under this category. *Physiological damage*

2. *The response pattern of anxiety becomes sufficiently specific to produce tissue change of the sort seen in so-called psychophysiological or psychosomatic disorders.* In problems of this type, the physiological arousal characteristic of anxiety has occurred with sufficient frequency, intensity, or duration to produce tissue damage or some relatively long-term alteration in bodily functioning. Such disorders as peptic ulcer, hypertension, and ulcerative colitis are examples of this class of anxiety-related difficulty. Often the initial intervention in such cases must necessarily be medical, but reduction of the underlying arousal is needed to prevent future problems. *Behavioral Problems*

3. *The current or prior intensity of anxiety results in the breakdown of efficient performance of complex behavior.* In this case, the client may not identify anxiety as the major problem, but may instead complain of difficulty in performing some motor or cognitive task. Anxiety of sufficient intensity can interfere with the efficient performance of almost any task, but complex tasks tend to be affected more severely than very simple tasks. Thus, complaints of inability to concentrate during examinations, disruption of piano playing during recitals, problems making short putts during golf tournaments, and stammering when talking with members of the opposite sex may well be the result of anxiety.

Sexual performance is one area frequently disrupted by the presence of anxiety. We will discuss this topic in Chapter 11. *Escape : avoidance*

4. *Adaptive behavior in the client's repertoire is inhibited to avoid inappropriate anxiety reactions.* In

problems of this type, the individual's performance of normal daily activities is disrupted by behaviors that have been developed to avoid anxiety-evoking stimuli. In this case (as opposed to item 5, below), the avoidance behavior per se is not problematic, as it is not bizarre or upsetting to others; however, the avoidance interferes with the person's "living effectively" and eliminates potential sources of reinforcement. An individual with test anxiety may quit school, a snake phobic may refrain from otherwise greatly enjoyed hikes in the woods, a person with interpersonal anxiety may find himself unable to attend parties or date, and so on. Whether a person seeks help for such a problem will be a function of how frequently the fear situation is encountered, how easily it is avoided, and the relative cost to the individual for continued avoidance. Maladaptive.

5. *Maladaptive behaviors are learned and maintained to alleviate or avoid inappropriate reactions.* Here again, the problem is produced by behaviors developed to escape or avoid anxiety. However, by virtue of being bizarre, offensive, and/or illegal, or because they interfere massively with the individual's daily functioning, these behaviors are themselves maladaptive. Examples are endless: compulsions, obsessions, amnesias, delusions, "conversion reactions," and the like may all function to escape, or to avoid contact with or perception of, anxiety-evoking stimuli. The anxiety-reducing nature of certain substances (alcohol, drugs, and in some instances food) and particular activities (masturbation, intercourse, sleep, and so on) may lead to their excessive and habitual use, often to the point of exclusivity. Sexual practices deemed "deviant" by society, such as homosexuality, fetishes, and exhibitionism, may sometimes result when more acceptable sexual outlets are avoided because they evoke inappropriate anxiety.

DEVELOPMENT AND MAINTENANCE OF ANXIETY REACTIONS

Although it is not necessary to know how anxiety reactions develop in order to find effective ways of reducing them, such an understanding does facili-

tate the intelligent application of treatment techniques. As we will see, certain treatments appear to be more appropriate for some anxiety reactions than others.

Several clinicians (Paul & Bernstein, 1973; Goldfried & Davison, 1976) have argued convincingly for distinguishing between anxiety that is *conditioned* to particular stimuli and that which is a *reaction* to some aspect of the person's overt or covert behavior. Let us look at each of these in turn.

Conditioned Anxiety

Many "simple phobias" and many components of more complex anxiety-based disorders appear to be examples of conditioned anxiety (Eysenck, 1960; Wolpe, 1958). **Conditioned anxiety** presumably arises through the process of respondent conditioning: an initially neutral stimulus comes to elicit anxiety after being associated with an aversive event that produced anxiety. The range of circumstances that can elicit strong anxiety and serve as the unconditioned stimulus (US) is enormous. Pain; sudden, violent changes in orientation or loss of support; extreme heat or cold—these are all well-known unconditioned stressors. But a large number of events, such as conflict situations, the sudden loss of customary reinforcers, loss of control over personally important aspects of one's life, unexpected changes in routine, social isolation, or criticisms, can also be potent sources of physiological arousal and subjective distress. Furthermore, it is not necessary for the individual to experience any of these stressors directly. The *threat* of their occurrence, especially if prolonged, is likely to induce anxiety, and stimuli consistently associated with this threat are sources for conditioning (compare Bridger & Mandel, 1964).

Development. There are three major processes by which conditioned anxiety is hypothesized to develop. The first of these, **traumatic single-trial conditioning,** is graphically illustrated by the following example (Wolpe, 1958). A young woman about to undergo a minor dental operation was given an injection of procaine, a local anesthetic. Unfortunately, the shot accidentally went into a vein instead of into the surrounding tissue. The injection produced convulsions, accelerated heart rate, nausea, hot and cold flashes, and partial loss of consciousness—obviously, a terrifying experience. By the next morning the woman had completely recovered, but when she sat down in a hairdresser's chair that afternoon she had an immediate anxiety reaction. The intense anxiety induced by the procaine had been conditioned to the feel of the dentist's chair and was then elicited by the tactile similarity of the hairdresser's chair. Although such examples of traumatic conditioning are obvious and dramatic, they probably account for a fairly small percentage of anxiety reactions.

Anxiety may become conditioned to a neutral stimulus if that stimulus has been associated with a **series of subtraumatic events** (Eysenck, 1960). Thus, a letter carrier who has repeatedly encountered unfriendly dogs may develop a strong conditioned anxiety response to dogs, even though he or she has never actually been bitten. Anxiety reactions may also be the result of **vicarious conditioning** (Bandura, 1965, 1969). Observation of someone undergoing a stressful experience or reacting to a stimulus with anxiety can result in the observer's acquiring a strong anxiety reaction to similar stimuli. Thus, a young child who is regularly treated to a display of her mother's distress about spiders may well develop her own fear of creepy-crawly things.

Once a CS for anxiety has been established, stimulus generalization may spread fear-evoking properties to other stimuli that are physically, functionally, or in some idiosyncratic way similar to the original CS. A fear of dogs may become a fear of all small animals; fear of blood or physical injury may spread to include fear of doctors, dentists, ambulances, cemeteries; and so on.

Maintenance. If anxiety has become conditioned to an innocuous stimulus, like an elevator, we might well expect this fear to extinguish as the individual finds that no disaster befalls him when he rides in elevators. But in fact, many conditioned anxiety responses do not undergo extinction, and instead persist at the same strength, or even become stronger, as years go by.

The "traditional" and still most widely accepted explanation for this is that stimuli which signal strong fear responses also give rise to **escape and avoidance behaviors,** which "protect" the anxiety responses from extinction. An elevator-phobic individual may try to use an elevator one day, find himself feeling very anxious, and get off just before the doors close. The relief and anxiety reduction he feels as he escapes the elevator negatively reinforce the escape behavior. In a short time, he may avoid riding in elevators at all; he may walk up twenty flights of stairs to avoid confinement in the elevator, or may even avoid tall buildings altogether no matter how important his business on the twentieth floor. This avoidance behavior is obviously self-defeating in two ways. First, it removes the opportunity for the individual to find that the stimulus is no longer associated with aversive events (that is, extinction cannot occur). Second, avoidance responses often interfere with adaptive behavior. Our elevator phobic may be forced to quit his job if his company rents office space on the ninety-seventh floor.

The protection or insulation of conditioned anxiety responses by escape and avoidance behavior may be the reason for the maintenance of maladaptive anxiety in some cases, but not in all. Some individuals regularly encounter feared stimuli and find that their anxiety *increases* with each exposure. The findings from animal studies (Napalkov, 1963; Rohrbaugh & Riccio, 1970; Rohrbaugh, Riccio, & Arthur, 1972) and some physiological data from human subjects (Campbell, Sanderson & Laverty, 1964; Stone & Borkovec, 1975) indicate that brief, unreinforced presentations of a CS for anxiety can enhance rather than extinguish fear, sometimes dramatically. Why does this happen?

Hans Eysenck (1968, 1975, 1976) has suggested the answer to the paradox lies in the fact that even in the absence of an external US, a CS for fear is *always* followed by aversive stimulation because the conditioned anxiety response is *itself aversive.* In this sense, a person presented with CS for fear (for example, a dog) that is not followed by a US (the dog does not bite) nevertheless experiences a CR (cognitive and physiological distress) that may be as noxious as any consequence the dog could have provided. In more technical terms, conditioned fear responses appear to be a

Incubation - vicious cycle

special case of classical conditioning in which the CS elicits a CR that *functions* as a US and *strengthens itself.* Eysenck refers to this vicious cycle as **incubation.**

The factor that seems most important in determining whether conditioned anxiety will undergo extinction or incubation with repeated unreinforced presentations of the CS is the duration of the individual's exposure to the CS. Brief exposures may favor incubation, whereas prolonged exposures produce extinction (Rohrbaugh & Riccio, 1970; Silvestri, Rohrbaugh, & Riccio, 1970; Stone & Borkovec, 1975). To pursue our example of the dog phobic, his or her encounters with dogs are all likely to be very brief—as brief as he or she can make them. Thus, during the entire time the dog is present, the individual will be fearful and aroused. In subsequent encounters, the person is likely to find that his or her fear has increased. If our phobic were to spend several hours with the dog, however, arousal and cognitive distress would probably abate as it became increasingly obvious that the animal was harmless. In this manner, a new response (comfort or relaxation) would begin to become associated with the dog, and future experiences with dogs might be considerably more pleasant. Thus, it can be seen that Eysenck's notion of incubation has important implications for anxiety reduction, as well as providing a conceptualization for anxiety enhancement. We will meet incubation theory again in our discussion of treatment procedures.

Problems with the Conditioning Model. The conditioning model of anxiety acquisition is attractive because of its theoretical simplicity and its clinical utility, but it should not be accepted uncritically. Clearly, there is much we do not understand. Laboratory investigations have confirmed the fact that human autonomic fear responses can be conditioned to innocuous stimuli (for example, Chatterjee & Ericksen, 1962; Bridger & Mandel, 1964, 1965), but with few exceptions (for example, Campbell, Sanderson, & Laverty, 1964), these responses have been of lesser magnitude, much more easily extinguished, and more subject to verbal-instructional modification than "real-life" anxiety reactions. Much of the discrepancy

between experimental findings and clinical observations may be due to fundamental differences between laboratory and real-world conditioning experiences.

The unconditioned stimuli in experimental fear conditioning (typically electric shock) are predictable, familiar, and under the control of the subjects (to the extent that they can halt the experiment when they want to). Typical college student subjects also know that the experimenter will not let any harm come to them. In the real world, however, aversive events tend to be unpredictable, unfamiliar, uncontrollable, and often potentially harmful. Put simply, aversive stimulation in the real world is much more stressful than that in the laboratory, and conditioned anxiety reactions can be expected to vary accordingly.

Perhaps most puzzling and troublesome from a conditioning point of view is why some people develop conditioned anxiety and others do not. Two people can fall from the same roof and sustain identical injuries, yet one may develop an intense fear of heights, whereas the other is unaffected. If the contiguous association of noxious events with a certain stimulus leads to fear of that stimulus, why is Evel Knievel not afraid of motorcycles? These are questions for which we do not yet have adequate answers. It seems likely that people differ with respect to their "conditionability." This may be due to congenital differences in nervous system stability or arousal level, or it may be the result of early learning experiences and "sensitizing" events. Perhaps the conditioning model is incomplete or just plain wrong. Research may eventually answer these questions, but for now, conditioning theory is the best available explanation of certain types of fear reactions, and demonstrably effective treatments have been derived from it. These are valid reasons to use conditioning theory until something better comes along.

Reactive Anxiety

Often anxiety is not an inappropriate conditioned response to a stimulus, but rather an appropriate response to a situation elicited by the individual's performance of inappropriate behavior or failure to perform appropriate behavior. In other words, the person does something, or fails to do something, that results in his being placed under stress and reacting with anxiety. We call this **reactive anxiety** (Paul & Bernstein, 1973).

Skills Deficits. People frequently find themselves in situations for which they do not have the necessary skills to function adequately. A nonswimmer in the deep end of a swimming pool epitomizes this situation. His lack of swimming skills has placed him under stress (that is, drowning) to which he is responding appropriately with anxiety. Treatment of this man's anxiety would not aim at eliminating his reaction to the stimuli associated with impeded respiration (thereby allowing him to drown in complete comfort); instead, it would consist of teaching him a set of skills (treading water, swimming, wearing styrofoam clothing) that he can use to cope with deep water. Clinical examples of reactive anxiety are usually a bit more subtle: a young woman may experience overwhelming anxiety when she is out on a date not because she has a conditioned fear of men, but because she lacks the necessary social skills to keep her date interested and to avoid subsequent rejection. A student can feel debilitated by anxiety during examinations because bad study habits leave him unprepared; he thus anticipates failing.

In addition to lacking requisite behaviors, a person may also be emitting behaviors that are inappropriate to the situation at hand, and that result in his being stressed. The person may, for example, possess an **aversive repertoire** that turns people off and leads to frequent social rejection. A funeral director who behaves like Don Rickles, a former drill instructor who maintains his armed forces demeanor with business associates, and a hypochondriacal housewife who monopolizes conversations with the details of her latest affliction may all suffer criticism, rejection, and anxiety as the result of their aversive repertoires. Social anxieties arising from skills deficits represent one of the largest classes of reactive anxiety. We have already discussed the genesis of such fears and their treatment by skills training procedures in Chapter 9.

Anxiety-Evoking Cognitions. One of the most common sources of reactive anxiety is the client's thought processes (Beck, 1976; Ellis, 1962; Meichenbaum, 1974). Results from laboratory research (May & Johnson, 1973; Velton, 1968), as well as everyday experiences, indicate that individuals' internal dialogues—the things they tell themselves about events—can be a strong determinant of their emotional state. In fact, identical objective circumstances can produce quite different subjective consequences, depending on the self-statements that people attach to what they see (Meichenbaum, 1974, p. 1):

> Picture the following scene. Two individuals, both of whom possess essentially the same speaking skills, are asked on separate occasions to present a public speech. The two individuals differ in their levels of speech anxiety: one has high speech-anxiety while the other has low speech-anxiety. During each speaker's presentation, some members of the audience walk out of the room. This exodus elicits quite different self-statements or appraisals from the high versus the low speech-anxiety individuals. The high speech-anxiety individual is likely to say to himself: "I must be boring. How much longer do I have to speak? I knew I never could give a speech," and so forth. These self-statements engender anxiety and become self-fulfilling prophecies. On the other hand, the low speech-anxiety individual is more likely to view the audience's departure as a sign of rudeness or to attribute their leaving to external considerations. He is likely to say something like: "They must have a class to catch. Too bad they have to leave; they will miss a good talk."

Anxiety-evoking cognitions may take a variety of forms. The individual may have a particular "automatic" thought that occurs to him in certain situations, such as: "That dog is going to bite me!" or "The plane will crash and we'll all be killed!" Or the person may be more deliberate in his distressing thinking: he may ruminate, repetitively elaborating and magnifying the negative aspects of some past, present, or future event (see Figure 10–2). This type of thinking has been graphically referred to as **catastrophizing** (Ellis, 1962). Anxious cognitions may be visual as well as verbal. For example, one woman experienced anxiety when driving over bridges because she held a mental image of her car breaking through

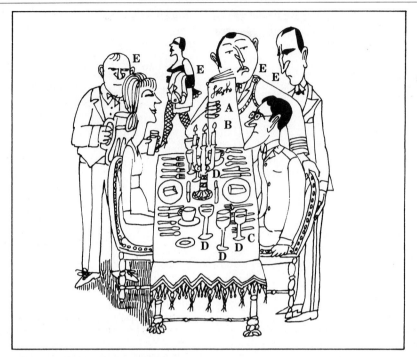

FIG. VI : BASIC WORRIES ABOUT DINING OUT

(A) The prices on the menu will be too high and you'll be embarrassed to get up and leave; **(B)** the dishes on the menu will be in a language you don't understand and you'll feel foolish asking for translations; **(C)** you won't know which fork to use; **(D)** you'll inadvertently knock over a glass and spill the contents all over or upset the candelabra and set your date on fire; **(E)** by tipping the person who gives you your coat and not the one who took it from you, or by tipping the waiter and not the captain, or by tipping the waiter and the captain but not the headwaiter, or by tipping all of the preceding too little or too much or by tipping someone you're not supposed to, you will prove yourself a clod.

Figure 10–2. The art of reactive rumination is humorously portrayed in the book *How to make yourself miserable* by Dan Greenburg and Marcia Jacobs. This all-too-truthful excerpt demonstrates the anxiety-evoking cognitive activity that may accompany simple situations like dining out. Copyright © 1966 by Random House, Inc., and Dan Greenburg. Reprinted by permission of Random House, Inc., and Dan Greenburg.

the guard rail and plummeting off the bridge (Beck, 1970).

Theoretically at least, reactive cognitions have the potential for conditioning anxiety to the stimuli that precede them (Russell & Brandsma, 1974).

In fact, this appears to be a problem with all long-standing reactive anxieties. Any stimulus that is repeatedly followed by the emission of stress-evoking (or the failure to perform stress-avoiding) overt behaviors, or a cognition that reliably elicits anxiety, should become a CS capable of evoking anxiety in the absence of these behaviors. It therefore becomes essential for the clinician to assess the extent to which a conditioned component has built up in anxiety reactions that appear reactive in nature. If a conditioned component exists, anxiety will likely remain even after the primary anxiety-evoking behaviors or thoughts have been eliminated.

Having presented behavioral conceptualizations of the origins of maladaptive anxiety, we now turn our attention to the procedures that have been developed to reduce fear. Although many such procedures can be identified, most do not yet enjoy a significant clinical history and/or experimental evaluation. Therefore, we will focus on a handful of techniques (and some variations) that we believe represent the core of most behavioral clinicians' fear-reduction arsenal. These techniques also illustrate the application of theories of fear reduction from which many other procedures were later derived.

RELAXATION TRAINING

The commonsense remedy of "relaxing" or "hanging loose" when feeling anxious has been the subject of much serious study. In fact, systematic training in muscle relaxation is now one of the most pervasive and useful tools of the behavior therapist. Muscle relaxation training is presumed to induce a state of parasympathetic dominance which, due to the nature of the ANS, is antagonistic to the sympathetic arousal characteristic of anxiety (Wolpe, 1958). Reducing sympathetic arousal should result in a corresponding decrease in the subjective experience of anxiety.

Training Methods

The most popular methods of brief relaxation training all stem from the work of physiologist Edmund Jacobson, who set down the basic procedures in his now classic book, *Progressive Relaxation* (1938). Jacobson's work went unrecognized until Wolpe (1958) assigned muscular relaxation a central role in his systematic desensitization and greatly abbreviated Jacobson's cumbersome training procedure. Other investigators have continued to refine Wolpe's procedures, and detailed instructional manuals for therapists are now available (for example, Bernstein & Borkovec, 1973).

Although there are some differences in the various training methods in use, enough commonalities exist to permit a general description of the procedure. The client is placed in a comfortable,

reclined position and asked to close his or her eyes. He or she is then instructed to concentrate on a particular muscle group and to tense those muscles by isometric contraction or by performing some movement (for instance, bending the arm, shrugging the shoulders). This contraction is held for about five to ten seconds as the therapist focuses the client's concentration on feelings of tension in the muscle group. Then, on cue from the therapist, the client abruptly releases the tension and allows the muscles to relax for about thirty seconds while the therapist directs his or her attention to the pleasant internal sensations caused by the relaxation of the muscles. This basic sequence of operations is known as a **tension-release cycle.** The therapist accompanies the exercises with a running "patter," which sounds like this:

All right Marsha, focus your attention on the muscles of your right hand and forearm. OK, I'd like you to tense those muscles now by making a tight fist. That's it. (With increasing tension in the voice) Feel the tension . . . notice where it is, notice what it feels like . . . hold it; OK—relax. (Now in a soothing monotone) Just attending to the pleasant sensations of relaxation in the muscles of your right hand and forearm. (Pause) No effort at all on your part, just focusing on those muscles as they become more and more relaxed. (Pause) Completely letting go. (Pause) OK, let's tense those muscles again. (With rising tension) Hold it now . . . Feel it pull across your knuckles and along the bottom of your forearm . . . Concentrate on the tension; and—relax. (Soothing voice again) Just focusing on the muscles of your right hand and forearm. You might notice a gentle warmth as those muscles relax. . . .

Notice that the therapist attempts to facilitate the client's relaxation by directing her attention to important internal sensations and by employing suggestions of warmth, relaxation, and pleasantness.

A particular muscle group receives at least two tension-release cycles. If the client then reports that there is still some tension in the group, another tension-release cycle is applied. Only when he or she reports the muscle group to be completely relaxed is the client allowed to progress to the next group in the series. The number of muscle groups dealt with during initial training sessions varies somewhat from method to method, but tension-release exercises are applied to a total of about sixteen muscle groups in the arms, face, neck, thorax, abdomen, and legs. The entire relaxation induction requires about thirty minutes.

The client is also asked to practice the exercises at home. As his or her skill at relaxation develops, muscle groups are combined into larger units to be tensed and relaxed in unison. Finally, when the client is well trained, tension-release exercises are dispensed with entirely. At this stage, called **relaxation by recall,** the client is presumably able to achieve complete relaxation simply by taking a deep breath, focusing on any residual tension in his or her muscles, and then exhaling slowly while remembering the familiar sensations associated with previous release cycles. At this point, the client can become completely relaxed in as little as four minutes.

A fairly new method of inducing deep relaxation has come from the use of **electromyographic (EMG) biofeedback** of muscle activity (Budzynski & Stoyva, 1969). This procedure involves the use of an instrument that records the electrical activity in a muscle and then converts that signal into a form clients can use. Typically, the instrument emits a tone that varies in pitch according to the muscle's activity (a high tone indicates an active, tense muscle, and drops in pitch indicate relaxation). Many clients can readily learn to lower the tone—that is, reduce tension in their muscles—by adopting personal relaxation strategies. The tone tells the individual whether a particular strategy (for instance, imagining one's arm becoming as limp as a noodle) is effective. In this way, most people can rapidly produce profound reductions in tension of the muscle being monitored.

Relaxation as an Active Coping Device

One of the most frequent uses of relaxation as an independent treatment is as a coping device that clients can employ to counter anxiety in daily living. To be useful as an on-the-spot coping process, relaxation must be made portable. Clients can rarely find a couch to run to whenever they are faced with anxiety-arousing stimuli—and even if they could, they would lose the all-important extinction effects produced by exposure to the stimuli. Two variants of relaxation training are typically employed to allow clients to carry on necessary activities while reducing arousal.

The first of these methods, **differential relaxation,** was also developed by Jacobson (1938). In differential relaxation, clients already skilled in recumbent relaxation procedures learn to scan their muscles mentally and identify any unnecessary tension. This tension can then be relieved by tension-release exercises of the appropriate muscle groups or, preferably, by "recall" in well-trained clients. Thus, a person who becomes anxious while driving at expressway speeds inventories his muscles and decides which ones need to be tensed and how much tension is necessary for the task at hand (driving). He then systematically relaxes all other muscles he finds needlessly involved. A person typically tense and anxious at parties maintains tension in his or her legs (to keep from falling down) and minimal tension in his or her right—or left—arm (to hold a drink), but releases any involuntary tension that has developed in the forehead, neck, shoulders, or abdomen.

Conditioned or **cue-controlled relaxation,** first introduced by Paul (1966a), is another method of in vivo relaxation. It is called cue-controlled relaxation because the client learns to associate a state of deep relaxation with a particular cue word like "calm-control" or "relax." Cue-controlled training consists of instructing a client who has been totally relaxed through one of the standard induction methods to focus his or her attention on breathing and think the word (for instance, "calm") with each exhalation. The therapist facilitates this by saying the word in synchrony with the client's exhalations several times, and then directing him or her to continue this for fifteen or twenty more breaths. After a period of weeks, with the client pairing the cue word with exhalations both in session and during home relaxation practice, an association between the cue word and relaxation should develop. In successful applications, the client can reduce his or her anxiety in problem situations by taking a deep breath and thinking "calm" on exhalation. Clients often report that the procedure brings on a "rush" of relaxation and a great reduction in anxiety.

Physiological Effects

Perhaps the most basic question that can be asked about relaxation training is, does it do what it is presumed to do? That is, does it reduce sympathetic arousal? Informal clinical observations and uncontrolled studies strongly suggest that reduced heart rate, respiration, and muscle tension are indeed produced by relaxation induction. In a controlled evaluation, Paul (1969c) found evidence of widespread reductions in sympathetic arousal during relaxation training. These effects were superior to those produced by "hypnotic" relaxation or by instructions to simply rest quietly. The impact of this otherwise excellent study is lessened by the fact that the subjects were all "normal" (that is, nonanxious) female undergraduates.

Irving Beiman, Eileen Israel, and Stephen Johnson (1978) replicated and extended Paul's findings with a group of subjects for whom tension was a serious problem and who had volunteered to participate in the study in order to gain some relief. Beiman and his colleagues also demonstrated that after training, subjects who had learned Paul's brief relaxation procedure were more successful at rapidly reducing arousal by themselves than were subjects who had been trained in biofeedback-assisted relaxation or who had practiced personal methods of tension reduction. The results of other investigations (for example, Edelman, 1970; Mathews & Gelder, 1969; Grossberg, 1965) have not clearly supported the efficacy of relaxation training in reducing physiological arousal. However, each of these studies relied heavily on the use of tape-recorded relaxation instructions, which have been shown to be clearly inferior to live instructions (Beiman, Israel, & Johnson, 1978; Paul & Trimble, 1970). Despite this experimental observation, the use of tape-recorded relaxation instructions is still a common clinical practice.

Data on the arousal-reducing properties of EMG biofeedback-assisted relaxation are few and unimpressive. Although many people undoubtedly can learn to reduce tension in the specific muscle from which the feedback signal is derived, this relaxation does not necessarily generalize to other muscles, to sympathetically activated systems, or

to the individual's subjective experience (Alexander, 1975; Beiman, Israel, & Johnson, 1978; Jessup & Neufeld, 1977; Shedivy & Kleinman, 1977). The physiological effects of such self-control techniques as differential and cue-controlled relaxation have not yet been studied.

Relaxation Training and Clinical Problems

Relaxation techniques have proven remarkably useful clinical tools even though we do not yet know exactly how these procedures produce their effects. Standard relaxation training is almost routinely applied as a component of treatment for anxiety-related problems. Its efficacy as an independent treatment procedure for a wide variety of anxiety- or tension-based problems is supported by considerable controlled-group and single-subject research. For example, such problems as insomnia (Borkovec & Fowles, 1973; Borkovec, Kaloupek, & Slama, 1975; Lick & Heffler, 1977), tension headaches (Cox, Freundlich, & Meyer, 1975; Haynes, Griffin, Mooney, & Parise, 1975), essential hypertension (Beiman, Graham, & Ciminero, in press; Taylor, Farquhar, Nelson, & Agras, 1977; Shoemaker & Tasto, 1975), and asthma (Alexander, Miklich, & Hershkoff, 1972) all respond favorably to the application of standard relaxation training techniques.

Biofeedback-induced muscle relaxation appears to be useful in limited contexts, primarily the treatment of tension headaches (Budzynski, Stoyva, Adler, & Mullaney, 1973; Wickramasekera, 1972). However, comparative outcome studies have indicated that standard tension-release relaxation procedures are as effective as feedback training in eliminating tension headache (Cox, Freundlich, & Meyer, 1975; Haynes, Griffen, Mooney, & Parise, 1975). This finding, combined with the lack of evidence for the general arousal-reducing effects of biofeedback-assisted relaxation training and the expensive equipment required for its application, make it a less attractive clinical tool than standard relaxation techniques.

The effects of self-control relaxation procedures have not been extensively studied. Case studies have suggested the usefulness of cue-controlled relaxation for dealing with anxiety in vivo (for instance, Russell & Matthews, 1975; Russell & Si-pich, 1973), but the only controlled investigation to date is weakened by an almost complete reliance on self-report measures of improvement (Russell, Miller, & June, 1975). A well-designed study by Marvin Goldfried and Christine Trier (1974) found in vivo differential relaxation to be effective in reducing the anxiety and improving the performance of subjects fearful of public speaking. However, on most outcome measures, differential relaxation was not clearly superior to standard relaxation training (which lacked specific instructions for in vivo application) or to a group discussion treatment. More study is necessary before the utility of in vivo relaxation procedures can be determined with confidence.

SYSTEMATIC DESENSITIZATION

Systematic desensitization is a procedure developed by Joseph Wolpe (1958) for the treatment of conditioned anxiety reactions. Basically, desensitization involves having a deeply relaxed client confront, in imagination, each of a series of increasingly potent anxiety-eliciting stimuli. When the client is successful at imagining a particular stimulus without having anxiety disturb his or her relaxed state, the client moves on to the next more disturbing stimulus. Eventually, the client is able to encounter even the most disturbing stimulus without having an anxiety reaction. The desensitization "package" consists of four distinct components: (1) relaxation training; (2) construction of a graded list of anxiety-evoking stimuli known as an anxiety hierarchy; (3) desensitization proper, in which the relaxed client is asked to imagine items from the anxiety hierarchy; and (4) transfer testing, in which the client confronts previously fear-evoking situations in real life.

The Role of Relaxation

Wolpe (1958) first introduced desensitization as one of a series of techniques based on a principle he called **reciprocal inhibition.** This imposing bit of jargon simply means that two incompatible behaviors cannot occur simultaneously; the stronger response will always win out and inhibit the weaker one. Wolpe noted that relaxation, among other responses, appeared to be incompatible with anxiety and capable of inhibiting it. The importance of this observation is conveyed in Wolpe's now classic statement (1958, p. 71):

> If a response antagonistic to anxiety can be made to occur in the presence of anxiety evoking stimuli so that it is accompanied by a complete or partial suppression of the anxiety responses, the bond between these stimuli and the anxiety responses will be weakened.

In other words, if relaxation can be used to prevent anxiety when a CS for anxiety is presented, that CS will be **deconditioned** or **counterconditioned** (the terms are used interchangeably) and will lose its ability to elicit an anxiety response.

The "reciprocal" part of "reciprocal inhibition" does present a problem at this point, however; just as relaxation can inhibit anxiety, so can anxiety inhibit relaxation—and the *stronger* response will predominate. Relaxation is a fairly fragile state compared to the type of intense anxiety that drives many people to seek professional help. How can relaxation be made stronger than anxiety? The answer is that it cannot. Instead, the strength of the anxiety response is reduced by "diluting" the eliciting stimulus. This is the function of the anxiety hierarchy.

Anxiety Hierarchies

Wolpe reasoned that if a stimulus elicits more anxiety than can be suppressed by relaxation, the stimulus can be broken down, or pushed away to a point where it elicits only a small amount of anxiety. Recall the procedure used by Mary Cover Jones (see Chapter 1) to treat a young child with a fear of rabbits: when the animal was close to the child, his anxiety was strong, and his distress interfered with his ability to eat (the incompatible response in this case). However, when the animal was moved to a greater distance, the child's eating resumed. The stimulus of a distant rabbit was then being paired with pleasurable eating, thus blocking anxiety and weakening the ability of the stimulus to evoke it. The animal was subsequently moved closer in careful steps, each just short of a point that would produce anxiety and inhibit the child's eating. The amount of anxiety deconditioned at each step can be thought of as being subtracted from the total amount elicited by the most disturbing stimulus (in this case, the rabbit at close range). In this way, what was an initially overwhelming fear is chipped away until it becomes a manageable one. The child was eventually able to play happily with the rabbit. Anxiety hierarchies make it possible to do in imagination what Jones did in actuality: reduce a powerful stimulus to a form in which it elicits an easily suppressed amount of anxiety.

In general, an anxiety hierarchy consists of a series of statements describing situations that elicit inappropriate conditioned anxiety in the client. Care must be taken that each statement be concise, yet contain enough personalized detail so that the client can readily visualize the intended time, place, and circumstances. Thus, an item like "the morning of your French exam" is not as effective as "You are in the bathroom brushing your teeth on the morning of your French exam."

Construction of the hierarchy often begins with the therapist asking the client to describe the *most* anxiety-arousing situation related to his or her maladaptive fear that he or she can imagine. This item serves as the top of the hierarchy, which must then be approached in gradual steps. The therapist will attempt to fix the starting point for the hierarchy—a related scene that causes only minor discomfort—by asking the client to imagine a situation that would cause the *first noticeable sensations* of anxiety and tension. Starting from this first item and working toward the most anxiety-arousing item, client and therapist collaborate to produce the items in between. The guiding principle is always that each hierarchy item should be judged by the client to produce a "just noticeable increase" in anxiety over the previous item.

Hierarchy length may vary considerably depending on the intensity of the client's fear, the complexity and range of stimuli that evoke it, and the size of the step the client chooses as a "just noticeable increase" between items. Most hierarchies for relatively straightforward, unidimensional fears (like animal phobias, fear of heights, water, and flying) require from ten to twenty-five items, but anxiety engendered by complex interpersonal situations (for instance, sexual anxieties)

can require hierarchies of eighty items or more. Although the clinician may shape the form and length of the hierarchy to some extent, it is important that the client control its ultimate appearance. Only the client knows what best represents his or her own fears.

Hierarchies may assume two general forms: spatial-temporal and thematic (Paul, 1969a). **Spatial-temporal hierarchies** consist of steps that approach some object or event in time and/or space. Thus, for a case of public-speaking anxiety, items may deal with events leading up to the presentation of a particular speech, such as waking on the morning of the speech, reciting the speech while dressing, approaching the auditorium, walking toward the podium, and finally giving the speech. **Thematic hierarchies,** on the other hand, consist of items that are members of a class of objects or events that share some basic theme. A thematic speech-anxiety hierarchy might have items such as telling a joke to several friends, making an announcement to a group of co-workers, speaking at a company banquet, and giving the main address at a stockholders' convention. Most hierarchies are a combination of these two types and are often composed of an increasing series of thematic items, some of which are approached in a spatial-temporal fashion (see Table 10-1).

Hierarchy construction is seldom easy and is frequently tedious work for the therapist. What is more, it may be distressing for the client, who may experience considerable anxiety as a result of having to conjure up detailed information about the things that frighten him or her most. In fact, this is a good sign, because it indicates that imagined stimuli affect the client in much the same way as real stimuli—a prerequisite for successful desensitization (see below). The client's discomfort can be greatly lessened if the therapist closes hierarchy construction sessions with a period of relaxation training, allowing the client to leave feeling at least as comfortable as on arrival.

Desensitization Proper

Once hierarchy construction is completed and relaxation training has progressed to a point where the client can reliably achieve a state of low arousal in session, desensitization itself can begin.

Table 10–1. An Anxiety Hierarchy for a Fear of Flying

1. Your boss tells you that, in 6 months, you'll have to fly out to the coast for a new account.
2. You're sitting in your living room, watching a football game on TV, and you hear a plane overhead.
3. A colleague at work tells you of the great plane trip he had to Florida.
4. Your wife asks you, a week before your trip, whether you'll be needing any formal clothes to take along.
5. You're up in the attic, looking for your two-suiter to take along on your trip to the coast.
6. As you look through your desk diary, you're reminded that the coast plane trip is coming up in two weeks.
7. The evening before the trip, you're folding socks and underwear into your suitcase.
8. The taxi is pulling off the expressway at the exit marked "Airport," on the way to your trip.
9. There are five people ahead of you in line at the Pan Am ticket counter, having their baggage checked and tickets validated.
10. You're walking down the ramp onto the plane, and the flight attendant asks for your boarding pass.
11. As you look out the window, you observe the plane just getting airborne, and you can see the Bay Bridge in the distance.
12. You've been flying for a couple of hours, the air gets choppy, and the captain has just put on the fasten-seat-belt sign.
13. The ride is quite bumpy, and you check to see that your seat belt is fastened.
14. You wake up the morning of your trip to the coast and say to yourself, "Today's the day I leave for the coast."

Note the mixture of spatial-temporal and thematic type items, and the fact that the highest item is temporally more distant from the feared event than many lower items but evokes more anxiety.

From M. R. Goldfried & G. C. Davison, *Clinical behavior therapy.* New York: Holt, Rinehart and Winston, 1976, pp. 121–122. Copyright © 1976 by Holt, Rinehart and Winston. Reprinted by permission of Holt, Rinehart and Winston.

Desensitization proper relies heavily on the client's imagery. The entire procedure is predicated on the assumption that an imagined fearful situation is equivalent to the real situation in its anxiety-evoking effects. Although this assumption has received consistent experimental support (for example, Grossberg & Wilson, 1968; Van Egeren, Feather, & Hein, 1971), clinical experience suggests that clients differ in their ability to visualize and react to hierarchy scenes (for example, Wolpe, 1958). If the client becomes visibly upset during hierarchy construction, the therapist can be assured that the client's imagery is adequate. If, on the other hand, no particular upset is observed, the client's imagery must be tested—usually by having him or her imagine an item high on the hierarchy without benefit of relaxation and monitoring the reaction. The absence of anxiety may indicate problems with visualization. Sometimes clients will purposely alter the scene in some way to make it less stressful, or they may *watch* themselves acting in the scene rather than really "being" there. Many such imagery problems can be corrected with special training, and desensitization can then proceed normally. On rare occasions, however, no training or procedural changes are successful in evoking anxiety. Clients with this difficulty presumably cannot benefit from the standard desensitization procedure.

Of the numerous variations in desensitization procedures that have been reported, Paul's (1966a, 1966b, personal communications) procedural guidelines are fairly typical. The client is first relaxed and instructed to signal (usually by means of lifting a finger) if he or she feels the slightest anxiety, tension, or other disturbance of relaxation. Then the first hierarchy item is presented: for example, "All right, Lowell, I'd like you to imagine that you are washing the walls in your kitchen one morning and you notice a small cobweb near the ceiling." The client is then allowed to imagine the scene for about ten seconds before the therapist terminates the presentation with, "OK, stop imagining that and just go on relaxing." If no anxiety was signaled by the client, the therapist allows a brief period of pure relaxation before re-presenting the same item. If anxiety is not signaled on this second visualization, another period of undisturbed relaxation is permitted before the next highest hierarchy item is attempted. Thus, each item that does not evoke anxiety is given two presentations before moving to the next hierarchy scene. If the hierarchy is perfect—that is, if the inter-item intervals are such that no step is so large it disturbs relaxation—then the entire hierarchy may be completed in this fashion.

It is more often the case that one or more hierarchy scenes evoke some anxiety in the client. When the client signals anxiety, the therapist immediately withdraws the scene and attempts to reinstate relaxation. Once the client reports again being completely relaxed, the therapist has three choices of how to proceed. (1) The therapist can re-present the same item, but withdraw it short of the point at which anxiety was signaled on the first presentation. If anxiety is not evoked by this shortened visualization, the item is repeated several times, each slightly longer than the last, until a full presentation of about twenty seconds can be achieved. (2) The therapist can re-present the previous hierarchy item on the assumption that it was not fully deconditioned before and is thus increasing the size of the step to the new item. (3) The therapist can invent a new item that appears to fall between the previous item and the trouble-some one. Thus, if the client was successfully desensitized to a scene of a spider ten feet away but was having considerable difficulty mastering the next item, a spider at a distance of one foot, the therapist might wish to present an intermediate scene with the spider at five feet before again attempting the one-foot item.

Since no strict guidelines dictate when to back up an item or when to create new items, decisions of this sort require considerable sensitivity. The therapist must judge from observations of the client during desensitization and knowledge of the client's problem what the best course of action is. Thus, although the mechanics of desensitization appear straightforward, clinical skill contributes significantly to its efficient and successful application.

Transfer

The actual desensitization is conducted in the therapist's office, but the purpose of the procedure is to reduce clients' fears in real-life situations. In order to evaluate the effectiveness of the procedure, at some point in treatment clients must confront in vivo those things to which they have been desensitized in imagination. Such encounters may be referred to as **transfer tests.**

The point at which transfer testing is begun depends on the nature of the client's fear. The rule of thumb is that a client should not be exposed to real stimuli more intense than those to which he or she has been desensitized. Thus, if the anxiety is such that the therapist and/or the client can devise situations in which a controlled stimulus presentation is possible (for example, climbing a certain distance on a ladder, standing or swimming in water of a specified depth), transfer testing can begin immediately. The client need only go no further in vivo than he or she has progressed in the desensitization hierarchy. Often, however, anxiety centers around situations that are largely beyond the control of the client or therapist (such as certain spontaneous interpersonal situations) and in which there is a real danger that stimuli well beyond the desensitization point may be encountered. Should this occur and the client experience an anxiety reaction, stimulus generalization may result in the *re*sensitization of successfully completed hierarchy items. Perhaps even more undesirable, the client may view such an occurrence as a "failure" of the treatment and develop negative expectations toward further therapy. In cases where the potential for this exists, it may be better to postpone transfer testing until desensitization is well along or completed.

It should be remembered that whereas imagined stimuli are apparently very similar to the real stimuli they represent, something is almost always lost in this translation. The real stimulus may contain certain elements the client has not included in his or her visualizations, and transfer of fear reduction to in vivo situations is often not perfect (Bandura, 1969). The client should be prepared to deal with the mild anxiety he or she may feel and to avoid elaborating it with reactive self-statements such as "Oh my God, I'm still afraid! The treatment hasn't worked at all!" Initial encounters with previously frightening stimuli are excellent times for the client to employ other skills, such as differential relaxation and task-oriented coping self-statements (see below), to deal with any residual anxiety.

If the transfer tests indicate that a significant amount of anxiety and/or avoidance behavior remains, the therapist must reassess to determine the source of the difficulty. Has there been an undisclosed problem in the client's imagery? Is the client "jacking himself up" with anxiety-eliciting self-statements? Do other sources of reactive anxiety remain? Such reassessment can lead to a modification of desensitization, or perhaps to institution of a different treatment procedure.

Effectiveness

The amount of research on systematic desensitization is massive, and we will make no attempt to review it here. Readers are urged to familiarize themselves with the fine early reviews by Albert Bandura (1969), Peter Lang (1969), and Gordon Paul (1969a, 1969b). The status of the desensitization literature at that time was captured by Paul (1969b, p. 159) when he said:

The findings were overwhelmingly positive and for the first time in the history of psychological treatments, a specific therapeutic package reliably produced measurable benefits for clients

across a broad range of distressing problems in which anxiety was of fundamental importance. "Relapse" and "symptom substitution" were notably lacking, although the majority of authors were attuned to these problems.

One of the major factors that made such an enthusiastic endorsement of systematic desensitization possible was a landmark comparative outcome study conducted by Paul (1966b; see also 1969b for elaboration). Paul's subjects were undergraduates faced with a mandatory speech course who were suffering from performance anxiety. Upon learning that a treatment program was available, 380 students requested help, and from these, the 96 most debilitated by anxiety were selected. The means of selection was a comprehensive screening procedure consisting of personal interviews and numerous psychometric tests. Considerable effort was made to select as subjects only those for whom interpersonal performance anxiety was an important life problem that was evident "in nearly every social, interpersonal, or evaluative situation and [that was] . . . most severe in a public speaking situation" (Paul, 1969b, p. 112).

Once the most anxious people were identified, all underwent pretreatment behavioral assessments. They were required to present a short, impromptu speech to an unfamiliar audience while three types of data were obtained. Cognitive aspects of anxiety as measured by an anxiety questionnaire and physiological measures (pulse rate and palmar sweat) were assessed moments before the speech was to be given. Then, during the speech, trained observers in the audience recorded visible signs of anxiety on an observational checklist. Following the stress speech, subjects were matched and randomly assigned to four carefully equated groups to receive (1) systematic desensitization, (2) insight-oriented psychotherapy, (3) a carefully contrived but presumably inert attention-placebo or "pseudotherapy" treatment during which subjects performed a supposedly stressful task while *believing* themselves to be under the influence of a tranquilizer, or (4) no treatment.

Five experienced therapists, each of whom expressed a decided preference for a neo-Freudian or Rogerian approach to therapy, and who had to be trained in the techniques of desensitization and "pseudotherapy," administered the treatments. Each was polled as to the number of sessions he or she felt would be adequate to eliminate anxiety in speech situations with his or her usual (that is, insight-oriented) procedures. After general agreement that five one-hour sessions would suffice, all treatment subjects received five hours of desensitization, insight therapy, or pseudotherapy. Control subjects received no treatment and were merely placed on a waiting list for later contact.

Following treatment, all therapy subjects and the waiting-list control subjects underwent another stress speech that was identical to the first and that employed the same cognitive, physiological, and observational measures. The results of this posttreatment assessment were striking: all treatment groups, including the attention-placebo group, showed significant reductions on cognitive and observational measures of anxiety over the no-treatment controls. However, the desensitization group showed significantly greater improvement on cognitive and observational measures than either the insight or attention-placebo groups, and was the only group to show a significant reduction in the physiological aspects of anxiety. Interestingly, the insight-oriented and attention-placebo groups tended to show the same magnitude of improvement across measures, raising a question as to whether the insight group was responding to anything more than the therapist's attention and a feeling of being in therapy.

Followup studies were conducted to evaluate the endurance of the changes and to assess for symptom substitution. At six weeks after treatment, the results were essentially the same, with the exception that the untreated waiting-list controls showed a slight improvement. No evidence of symptom substitution was found. On the assumption that a longer time period might reveal relapse in the desensitization and attention-placebo groups and further gains in the insight group, a two-year followup was undertaken (Paul, 1967). Although the relocation of many of the subjects made another stress assessment impossible, psychometric and questionnaire data indicated the continued superiority of the desensitization treatment over all other treatments without a single case of relapse or symptom substitution. The final score at the two-year followup in terms of percentage of subjects showing significant improvement from pretreatment was: desensitization—85 percent; insight-oriented psychotherapy—50 percent; attention-placebo pseudotherapy—50 percent; untreated controls—22 percent.

The absence of recent comprehensive and critical reviews of the desensitization literature undoubtedly reflects the fact that the field has grown unmanageably large. However, such a review would probably still find considerable empirical support for the efficacy of systematic desensitization as a treatment for many types of anxiety. There is little doubt that desensitization works; The overriding question today is *how*.

Explaining Desensitization's Effects

Although still widely accepted, Wolpe's "reciprocal inhibition" thesis and the notion of desensitization through counterconditioning have come under increasing criticism from theorists who maintain that other mechanisms better explain the workings of desensitization. Much research has focused on uncovering the "active ingredients" of the process. The theoretical controversies are extremely complex and beyond the scope of this book, but we will present two of the most prominent alternative hypotheses to enable readers to appreciate the confusion that currently exists.

Extinction. Much of the dissatisfaction over Wolpe's counterconditioning theory stems from studies that have questioned the necessity of the relaxation component of desensitization. A number of investigators have found that the desensitization procedure *without* relaxation is as effective as when relaxation is included (for example, Cooke, 1968; Craighead, 1973). Other studies have suggested just the opposite—that relaxation is necessary if desensitization is to be effective (for example, Davison, 1968; Lomont & Edwards, 1967). If the supposedly anxiety-inhibiting response of relaxation in fact contributes nothing to desensitization, then it seems unlikely counterconditioning is the active process in this form of fear reduction.

Consistent with this reasoning, James Lomont (1965) suggested that the fear reduction associated with desensitization represents extinction rather than counterconditioning. He argued that the therapist's instructions to the client to confront the anxiety-evoking stimulus for a period of time prevents the client from engaging in normal avoidance responses, and the repeated exposure eventually results in the extinction of the response. Even when the client signals anxiety, there is a momentary delay before the therapist can halt the scene, and this exposure also contributes to extinguishing the response.

More recently, Terrance Wilson and Gerald Davison (1971) reviewed animal research relevant to the counterconditioning versus extinction controversy and concluded that extinction was indeed the most likely mechanism, but added that relaxation (or other incompatible responses) appears to *facilitate* extinction, encouraging exposure to the CS by reducing the unpleasant responses it evokes.

To add to the controversy, Bandura (1969) has pointed out that counterconditioning plays a major role in extinction; that is, during extinction the animal or human eventually makes responses that compete with the conditioned response and weaken the stimulus-response bond. In extinction, the occurrence of these competing responses is left to chance; in counterconditioning, the competing response is preprogrammed, presumably making the process more efficient. Obviously, terminological and conceptual confusion has significantly clouded the issue, and the role of relaxation remains unclear.

Cognitive and Social Factors. Myriad alternative explanations for the effects of desensitization have centered around cognitive variables and the influence of the client-therapist relationship. Expectancy for improvement (Borkovec, 1972), feedback of success from progress through the hierarchy (Wilkins, 1971), therapist "warmth" (Morris & Suckerman, 1974), and praise for progress (Leitenberg, Agras, Barlow, & Oliveau, 1969) have all been suggested as the source of anxiety reduction in desensitization. Much of this research has yielded contradictory findings, leading Davison and Wilson (1973) to conclude that "presently available research into cognitive and social variables has thus far produced little by way of convincing evidence for explaining the effective

process mechanisms involved in SD [systematic desensitization]" (p. 16). Despite Davison and Wilson's dismissal, one of these hypotheses—expectancy for improvement—has assumed considerable significance.

Basically, the **expectancy hypothesis** states that the effects of systematic desensitization are due not to processes *specific* to the procedure (like counterconditioning or extinction), but rather to the *nonspecific* effects of clients' believing the treatment will help them. The expectancy effect is nonspecific in that it should hold for *any* procedure clients believe is an equally effective treatment—even those that involve no real active ingredients (such as an inert pill or a bogus therapeutic technique). In other words, if the expectancy hypothesis is correct, then desensitization is effective because its rationale and procedures make sense to clients and lead them to believe they will improve. And *any* hodgepodge of procedures that clients find equally credible will produce the same effects.

In a major review article, Alan Kazdın and Linda Wilcoxon (1976) have argued convincingly that expectancy of improvement remains a viable explanation for the effectiveness of systematic desensitization despite attempts by many investigators to devise studies which control for this factor. Let us refer again to the outcome study of Paul (1966b) to understand this contention. Some of Paul's subjects underwent an attention-placebo or pseudotherapy treatment in which they engaged in a "stressful task" (actually a monotonous signal-detection task) while under the influence of a "fast-acting tranquilizer" (actually a placebo). This procedure was presented to subjects as a means of increasing stress tolerance that had been used in the training of astronauts. Throughout the sessions, the therapist attempted to maintain the credibility of the procedure by periodically checking the subjects' pupillary responses and pulse rates (to determine their reactions to the "drug"), recording their responses to the signal-detection task, and assuring them that the treatment was going well. Thus, considerable effort was directed toward creating a believable treatment that would lead subjects to expect a change in their fear. And, as we mentioned, the desensitization treatment was superior, indicating that it offered some therapeutic element(s) over and above mere expectancy effects.

The problem is, the *assumption* that the pseudotherapy and desensitization were *equally credible* and created *equal expectancies* was not verified empirically. Years later, Thomas Borkovec and Sidney Nau (1972) had a group of college students read the rationales for both systematic desensitization and Paul's attention-placebo treatment and rate their credibility and the expectancy for improvement each would create. They found that the students perceived desensitization to be significantly more credible and potentially helpful than the pseudotherapy, suggesting that Paul's subjects may have been responding to a nonspecific expectancy effect rather than to an active ingredient specific to desensitization.

Kazdin and Wilcoxon (1976) have found that the failure to assess the credibility of expectancy control procedures is the rule, rather than the exception, in desensitization research. And, in the handful of investigations in which expectancies have been assessed and equated across conditions, the findings are contradictory, with studies indicating that desensitization is both superior to (for instance, Gelder, Bancroft, Gath, Johnston, Mathews, & Shaw, 1973) and no different from (for instance, McReynolds, Barnes, Brooks, & Rehagen, 1973) control procedures of comparable credibility. Kazdin and Wilcoxon (1976, p. 745) summarize their review of the latter research by stating:

> Overall, [these] studies do not support the proposition that desensitization includes a specific therapy ingredient beyond expectancies for improvement. The relative paucity of studies showing that desensitization is superior to an equally credible control group would seem to weaken the usual statements made about desensitization as a technique with specific therapeutic ingredients. The alternative explanation, that the therapeutic effects are due to nonspecific treatment effects, at least at the present time, cannot be ruled out.

It bears emphasizing that the efficacy of systematic desensitization as a fear-reduction procedure is *not* placed in doubt by arguments in favor of the expectancy hypothesis—only the process by which it achieves its effects is being questioned.

Support for the expectancy hypothesis is at present based more on what has *not* been proved than on what *has*. However, it is clear that expectancy for improvement is an important variable which future research must address if the mechanisms of desensitization, or any other procedure, are ever to be understood.

A complex process such as desensitization is likely to involve a complex interaction of mechanisms in producing anxiety reduction. Thus, the question "Is desensitization due to counterconditioning, or extinction, or some other process?" can probably be more profitably reformulated as "What are the relative contributions of each of these processes to the outcome of desensitization?" At present, we are unable to answer this question with certainty.

FLOODING AND IMPLOSION

Two other procedures that have been applied to conditioned anxiety problems are flooding (Boulougouris & Marks, 1962; Malleson, 1959) and implosion (Stampfl, 1967; Stampfl & Levis, 1967). In contrast to desensitization, where the emphasis is on suppression of arousal, flooding and implosion involve prolonged, traumatic exposure to high-intensity CS. All anxiety-reducing behaviors are prohibited, with the aim of maximizing the client's arousal. Over time, such exposure to the CS in the absence of external aversive consequences should result in the extinction of the anxiety response. Thus, flooding and implosion are like locking the claustrophobic in a dark closet—at least in his or her imagination.

Although flooding and implosion are quite similar in their basic approach to anxiety reduction (and the terms are sometimes used interchangeably), they do differ. In general, **flooding** simply refers to prolonged exposure to a high-strength CS either in imagination or in vivo. A typical flooding session might involve the therapist presenting a scene equivalent to the highest hierarchy item in desensitization, without having built up to it through the presentation of lower items. Relaxation would not be used; instead, an anxiety reaction would be allowed to occur, and the therapist would attempt to intensify the client's distress by elaborating frightening aspects of the scene and directing the client's attention to his or her extreme arousal. The process would continue until the client's anxiety dissipated. If the session ended before the client's arousal extinguished, the procedure would be repeated in the following sessions until presentation of the scene evoked no reaction. Flooding in vivo typically involves a prolonged encounter with actual phobic stimuli while avoidance responses (withdrawal, compulsive rituals, attempts to elicit sympathy, and so on) are prevented (for instance, Baum & Poser, 1971; see also Case Study 10–2).

In contrast, **implosion** represents a curious blend of psychoanalytic and behavioral theories. Anxiety is assumed to result essentially from traumatic conditioning, which invests cues (stimuli) associated with the original conditioning incident with anxiety-evoking potential. In addition, the processes of generalization and higher-order conditioning spread anxiety to a variety of other cues, which vary in strength according to their degree of association with the original conditioning incident. According to implosion theory, those cues associated with the psychoanalytic themes of sex, aggression, conscience, death, and so on are particularly susceptible to conditioning and generalization. Furthermore, these cues are so threatening that they are *repressed* by the individual and are no longer available to his or her awareness.

During assessment interviews, the implosive therapist attempts to identify the various cues that evoke anxiety in the client. These are then ordered along a generalization gradient stemming from the original traumatic event. Cues most closely associated with the trauma are thought to elicit more anxiety than cues further away on the generalization gradient. But the cues that are *most* stressful are presumed to be repressed, and the therapist must make educated guesses as to their nature based on psychoanalytic interpretations of the client's behavior. These cues comprise the very top of the cue hierarchy.

The implosion sessions themselves are startling. The client is instructed to totally involve himself or herself in imagining as the therapist begins to present the least anxiety-evoking cues in the form of an extended narrative. Every effort is made to elicit maximal anxiety in the client. The

therapist elaborates and vivifies each scene in a dramatic fashion, and the images are exaggerated to horrifying proportions. When the client shows evidence of complete distress, he or she is held at this point until he or she "implodes" (extinguishes) and experiences a significant drop in arousal. At this point, the therapist revises the narrative or begins anew, presenting scenes incorporating cues from the next hierarchy level. Eventually, cues symbolically representing the "repressed material" are woven into the presentation. A brief transcript of an actual implosion session can only begin to capture the experience (Hogan, 1968, p. 430):

> Can you see the snake out in front of you again? Reach out and pick it up. Put it up by your face, make it bite you. Feel that scared feeling? Put it closer to your face, let it bite your lips. Are you letting it? Put out your tongue. Let it bite your tongue. Now let loose of it. And it jumps down in your stomach. And it is down in your stomach and it is wiggling around down there. Feel it jumping around and biting in your stomach, and laying eggs, and now thousands of little snakes are in your stomach and they are crawling around, slimy and wiggly, feel them inside you. They are biting at your heart and your lungs. Feel them crawling up into your lungs, they are shredding your lungs and biting and ripping and they are swimming in the blood in your stomach, kind of swishing their tails around, uhhh—horrible little snakes, slimy, wormy, crawly, feel them. You are getting sick to your stomach, take a deep breath, feel them, inside you, wiggling around. Can you feel them down there? Biting at your heart, feel them biting and gnawing at your heart. Crawling in and out of your mouth now, feel them crawling in and out of you. They are inside and outside of you, biting you, all over your body, feel them, just destroying you, cutting you up in little pieces. Biting you, feel them biting you. Pick up that snake again now, out in front of you, make yourself reach out. He snaps at you. Pick it up anyhow, pick it up, put it up by your face. Put it up by your eyes, right up by your eyes; feel it gnaw and bite at your eyes. Do you get the scared feeling? Let it bite, squeeze it, make it bite, now let it loose, let it bite at your eyes. Uhh—Now it is wiggling around and it is coming by your ear. It has got

a little head, a little slimy head and it is putting its head in your ear. It is kind of wiggling inside of your head now. Feel it crawl in there and crawl around and it is biting at your brains, chewing and gnawing, and biting and ripping, feel it, inside of you. And now it is turning into a giant snake and it is slowly coiling around you, feel it coil around you and it is tightening; squeezing you; feel it squeezing you, uhhh—feel the bones crunching, biting at your face, and squeezing you. Just give up, quit fighting it. Can you feel it biting you?

The woman on the receiving end of this particular scene was a research subject. In clinical practice, the "symbolic" significance of the snake would probably have been exploited through the inclusion of sexual material, such as the snake exiting the woman's vagina. The shock and horror value of an implosive presentation is limited only by the therapist's imagination and theatrical abilities.

Effectiveness

In contrast to the more uniformly positive results of desensitization outcome research, the findings from studies of both flooding and implosion have been decidedly mixed. Reports of positive outcome (for instance, Boudewyns & Wilson, 1972; Hogan, 1966; Hogan & Kirchner, 1968; Wolpin & Raines, 1966) are opposed by a considerable number of negative results (for instance, Fazio, 1970, 1972; Orenstein & Carr, 1975; Rachman, 1966). Moreover, most studies in the area contain serious methodological flaws or are limited by the same analogue problems that plague desensitization research (Levis & Hare, 1977; Morganstern, 1973). Comparisons of flooding or implosion with systematic desensitization (for instance, Borkovec, 1970; Boulougouris, Marks, & Marset, 1971; Mealiea & Nawas, 1971; Smith & Nye, 1973) suffer from similar deficiencies, making it impossible to draw any meaningful conclusions about the relative efficacy of the procedures.

One of the greatest problems for clinicians and researchers alike is the fact that procedural guidelines for the standardized administration of flooding and implosion do not exist. This undoubtedly contributes to the lack of consistency seen in the research findings. Investigation of procedural parameters has, with few exceptions (for example,

Kotila, 1969; Miller & Levis, 1971), been ignored, so that the development of rules for the reliable and effective application of the techniques has not really occurred. Moreover, with regard to implosion, the psychodynamic assumptions on which much of the technique rests are unsupported, and the necessity or advisability of including cues that are symbolic of "unconscious" material has never been demonstrated.

In addition to the unimpressive track records of both flooding and implosion, there are indications that the two procedures may actually be dangerous. There are many reports of individuals whose conditions deteriorated following flooding or implosion in both clinical and experimental settings (Barrett, 1969; Fazio, 1970; Hogan, 1966; Kotila, 1969; Wolpe, 1969). This troublesome phenomenon may well result from the incubation effect discussed earlier. As we mentioned, a crucial factor in determining whether anxiety will undergo extinction or exacerbation is the length of exposure to the CS. Strong anxiety cannot continue indefinitely; extinction and/or fatigue will *eventually* reduce the anxiety of an individual being flooded or imploded. However, if fear reduction is to result, it seems important to continue the treatment uninterrupted until that point is reached. If flooding or implosion is terminated before the client's arousal drops (for instance, because the fifty-minute therapy hour is up, or the research design calls for two hours of treatment regardless of the subject's response), the experience may *strengthen* the person's fear of the stimulus—the incubation effect.

Consistent with this notion, the available data seem to suggest that the outcomes of flooding and implosion are more favorable in studies using exposure times of 100 minutes or more (see Levis & Hare, 1977). But from a clinical standpoint, the most important thing to recognize is that individuals differ tremendously in the speed at which their anxiety dissipates during forced extinction. For example, in one case report (Thomas & Rapp, 1977), a client underwent imaginal and in vivo flooding of her eye-patch phobia for *nine continuous hours* before her heart rate finally stabilized at an acceptably low level!

In summary, a number of strong arguments can be made against the use of flooding or implosion in the treatment of anxiety: (1) the evidence for their effectiveness is equivocal; (2) the procedures are poorly understood and potentially harmful; (3) even when skillfully applied, both techniques are exceedingly unpleasant and unnecessarily distressing for the client. Nevertheless, the techniques are not infrequently applied—a fact that adds a note of urgency to the need for further research.

PARTICIPANT MODELING

We have already discussed the use of modeling in the reduction of children's fears (Chapter 4). Modeling-based procedures used for anxiety reduction in adults are quite similar in technique. Also, research into the parameters and effectiveness of each of these approaches has been similar. Here we will provide only a brief description of how modeling is employed in clinical situations involving adults.

Symbolic modeling is seldom the treatment of choice in clinical encounters. Instead, both the therapist and client usually take a more active role in the procedure. The therapist models approach and coping responses toward the feared stimulus, and the client becomes involved with the stimulus under the therapist's instruction, encouragement, and reinforcement. Although this approach has been known by many names (including contact desensitization, demonstration plus participation, and guided participation), the term **participant modeling** probably best describes the procedure.

Participant modeling is built around one of the basic rules of behavior modification: graduated performance, or successive approximation. By way of example, consider a participant modeling approach to fear of snakes. Therapist and client enter a large room containing a caged, harmless snake. The client is encouraged to come as close to the cage as comfort will allow, while the therapist models a calm response and verbally creates a warm and comfortable atmosphere. Often, the client has received prior training in relaxation and is encouraged to use these skills to manage any anxiety he or she feels during the procedure.

The therapist gradually approaches the snake, often giving the client factual information to dispel any myths he might have. The client observes the therapist behaving nonfearfully toward the snake, sees that there are no adverse consequences, and should begin to experience a decrease in anxiety. As the client reports feeling more comfortable, the therapist encourages him or her to approach the cage and praises (reinforces) progress. Eventually, through this slow, stop-and-go procedure, the client may touch the therapist, who is now holding the snake; touch the snake as it is being held; and finally hold the snake on his own. At each stage, the client is likely to experience some increase in anxiety, but through extinction, active coping, and the support and guidance of the therapist, the anxiety should dissipate, thus allowing the next step to be made. The most important thing for the therapist to remember is not to push the client too hard, or participant modeling will rapidly deteriorate into in vivo flooding. The therapist must observe the client's reactions carefully in order to adjust his or her own actions and demands for approach to the client's fear. Ideally, the therapist should create an atmosphere in which the client feels a consistent presure to progress but recognizes he or she can stop whenever necessary and allow arousal to subside.

The results of research on participant modeling have been uniformly positive (for example, Rimm & Mahoney, 1969; Ritter, 1969). The inclusion of a client participation component makes the procedure significantly more effective than modeling alone (Blanchard, 1970). Participant modeling is also clearly superior to systematic desensitization (Bandura, Blanchard, & Ritter, 1969). The speed at which fear reduction typically occurs in participant modeling is remarkable. We have seen individuals who before treatment had literally broken into a sweat at the mention of the word "snake" playing comfortably with a five-foot king snake after only two to three hours of participant modeling. This is undoubtedly one of the most efficient anxiety-reduction techniques available to the clinician, and in our opinion is the treatment of choice whenever the situation permits. However, participant modeling can only be used for anxiety associated with concrete, manipulable stimuli, such as small animals, water, and heights. Fear of rejection, death, or other abstract themes are not easily dealt with in a participant modeling format. Other procedures such as desensitization and the cognitive strategies (see below) can be easily adapted for use with such abstract anxieties.

✗ COGNITIVE STRATEGIES

We turn now to methods for reducing anxiety associated with reactive cognitions. These techniques center on teaching clients to "talk" to themselves in new, nondistressing ways. The currently employed cognitive modification strategies are strongly indebted to Albert Ellis (1962), whose **rational-emotive therapy (RET)** is their conceptual and procedural core.

Rational-Emotive Therapy

Ellis contends that emotional reactions, anxiety included, are not the direct result of objective events, but rather are a product of the view an individual takes of them. This process of appraisal consists of thoughts, or self-statements, that mediate between perception of the event and the emotional experience. Self-statements that label an event as "good" in some sense yield the emotions of happiness, love, and so on. Self-statements that appraise a situation as "bad" in general lead to feelings of anger, sadness, guilt, and anxiety.

Ellis's treatise embraces a philosophical position similar to stoicism. He maintains that it is "irrational" to become terribly upset over virtually *anything*. Negative emotions—even strong ones —are fine, but the continued, debilitating experience of such distressing emotions as depression or anxiety is *never* justified, and is the result of "irrational" (read "self-defeating") thinking. We will have more to say about Ellis's irrational beliefs in Chapter 13.

In therapy, Ellis is extremely forceful. He directly attacks clients' anxiety-evoking self-statements and the beliefs underlying them. It is not unusual for him to label a client's way of thinking as stupid, foolish, or sick. He assails clients' assumptions with such energy that eventually, per-

haps out of desperation, they relent and try out Ellis's new, more rational way of viewing the world. His clients are also given "homework" assignments to engage in those things they fear most, all the while monitoring and disputing their distressing internal dialogue.

✗ Systematic Rational Restructuring

Rational restructuring (Goldfried, Decenteceo, & Weinberg, 1974; Goldfried & Goldfried, 1975) takes Ellis's RET as a starting point and then employs the behavioral techniques of successive approximation, modeling, and behavioral rehearsal to train clients in using anxiety-countering rational self-statements. Rational restructuring begins very much like RET. The client is introduced to the notion that his or her internal dialogues are responsible for the anxiety, and discussion centers on the types of self-statements that the client makes when faced with problem situations. The therapist then leads the client into a rational analysis of the beliefs giving rise to the anxiety-evoking thoughts. Where Ellis will forcefully attack the irrationality of a client's assumptions, the rational restructuring therapist will rely more on persuasion and attempt to draw the client into verbalizing more appropriate beliefs. Research on attitude change suggests that such an approach may be more successful than Ellis's "strong arm" tactics (Brehm & Cohen, 1962).

Once this phase of therapy has progressed to a point where the client feels comfortable with conceptualizing his or her problems in this new way and has accepted the inappropriateness of the self-defeating cognitions, rational restructuring departs from RET. The client is then trained in the use of rational reevaluation in specific anxiety-evoking situations. This training involves the use of a hierarchy similar to that employed in desensitization. Beginning with the least difficult items, the client confronts distressing situations in imagination and through role playing with the therapist. While the therapist models appropriate responses, the client is encouraged to verbalize his or her thoughts and to practice disputing and reformulating anxiety-evoking self-statements (Goldfried & Davison, 1976, pp. 172–174):

Therapist: I'd like you to close your eyes now and imagine yourself in the following situation: You are sitting on stage in the auditorium, together with the other school board members. It's a few minutes before you have to get up and give your report to the people in the audience. Between 0 and 100 percent tension, tell me how nervous you feel.

Client: About 50.

Therapist: (*Now to get into his head.*) So I'm feeling fairly tense. Let me think. What might I be telling myself that's making me upset?

Client: I'm nervous about reading my report in front of all these people.

Therapist: But why does that bother me?

Client: Well, I don't know if I'm going to come across all right. . . .

Therapist: (*He seems to be having trouble. More prompting on my part may be needed than I originally anticipated.*) But why should that upset me? That upsets me because . . .

Client: . . . because I want to make a good impression.

Therapist: And if I don't . . .

Client: . . . well, I don't know. I don't want people to think that I'm incompetent. I guess I'm afraid that I'll lose the respect of the people who thought I knew what I was doing.

Therapist: (*He seems to be getting closer.*) But why should that make me so upset?

Client: I don't know. I guess it shouldn't. Maybe I'm being overly concerned about other people's reactions to me.

Therapist: How might I be overly concerned?

Client: I think this may be one of those situations where I have to please everybody, and there are an awful lot of people in the audience. Chances are I'm not going to get everybody's approval, and maybe that's upsetting me. I want everyone to think I'm doing a good job.

Therapist: Now let me think for a moment to see how rational that is.

Client: To begin with, I don't think it really is likely that I'm going to completely blow it. After all, I have prepared in advance, and have

thought through what I want to say fairly clearly. I think I may be reacting as if I already have failed, even though it's very unlikely that I will.

Therapist: And even if I did mess up, how bad would that be?

Client: Well, I guess that really wouldn't be so terrible after all.

Therapist: (*I don't believe him for one moment. There is a definite hollow ring to his voice. He arrived at that conclusion much too quickly and presents it without much conviction.*) I say I don't think it'll upset me, but I don't really believe that.

Client: That's true. I would be upset if I failed. But actually, I really shouldn't be looking at this situation as being a failure.

Therapist: What would be a better way for me to look at the situation?

Client: Well, it's certainly not a do-or-die kind of thing. It's only a ridiculous committee report. A lot of people in the audience know who I am and what I'm capable of doing. And even if I don't give a sterling performance, I don't think they're going to change their opinion of me on the basis of a five-minute presentation.

Therapist: But what if some of them do?

Client: Even if some of them do think differently of me, that doesn't mean that I would be different. I would still be me no matter what they thought. It's ridiculous of me to base my self-worth on what other people think.

Therapist: (*I think he's come around as much as he can.*) We can terminate this scene now. With this new attitude toward the situation, how do you feel in percentage of anxiety?

Client: Oh, about 25 percent.

Therapist: OK, let's talk a little about some of the thoughts you had during that situation before trying it again.

Looking back over the transcript, you can see that the therapist is teaching the client a five-step procedure: (1) identifying feelings of anxiety; (2) identifying the thoughts that are producing the anxiety; (3) evaluating the rationality of the distressing thoughts; (4) emitting more rational anxiety-countering self-statements; (5) noting the resulting effects on anxiety. On successive rehearsal trials, the therapist fades his or her involvement until the client can execute the sequence unassisted. When the client has demonstrated skill in dealing with a particular situation, the next most difficult item in the hierarchy is attempted. As in desensitization, in vivo tests can follow, with the client reporting any problems that might necessitate modification of the procedures.

Self-Instructional Training and Stress Inoculation

Donald Meichenbaum (1974, 1975) has devised a slightly different strategy for the modification of anxiety-engendering cognitions. This procedure may be called **self-instructional training,** and like the other procedures, it begins with the client receiving a cognitive conceptualization of his or her anxiety. Some effort is directed toward uncovering the self-defeating internal statements that the client is currently making. At this point, however, self-instruction deviates from both RET and rational restructuring. Rather than spending a great deal of time discussing the irrationality of the client's beliefs and training him or her in the rational refutation of self-statements, self-instructional training simply provides the client with a "package" of task-oriented coping self-statements that can be used on encountering anxiety-evoking situations. The client then learns and rehearses these new self-statements so that they are readily available during times of stress. Table 10–2 illustrates the type of sentences the client learns and the phases of a stressful encounter for which they are appropriate. Self-instructional training is usually combined with differential or cue-controlled relaxation; thus, many of the instructional statements remind the client to use these relaxation skills.

For the purpose of making the self-instructional technique both more effective and more widely applicable, Meichenbaum and Roy Cameron (1973) have suggested exposing the client in therapy sessions to a variety of stressful situations, such as unpredictable electric shock, stress-inducing films, or various embarrassing situations. In this way, the client gains experience in implementing these newly acquired skills "under fire," increasing the

probability that he or she will apply them successfully outside the therapeutic environment. When this application phase of the training is added to the self-instructional procedure, the entire package is called **stress inoculation.**

Effectiveness of Cognitive Strategies

All research on the effectiveness of cognitive modification procedures is of fairly recent origin, but the results thus far are very impressive. Some of the strongest evidence for the utility of these techniques comes from the work of Meichenbaum and his colleagues. In one study (Meichenbaum, 1972), self-instructional training was combined with a "coping imagery" procedure that closely resembled systematic desensitization. However, instead of withdrawing a hierarchy scene when subjects signaled anxiety, subjects were asked to use their anxiety-countering self-statements and relaxation responses to reduce the disturbance elicited by the item. In this way, the desensitization procedure provided subjects with practice in coping with anxiety reactions through self-instruction.

Meichenbaum evaluated the procedure with a group of college students who reported high anxiety in test-taking situations. The modified desensitization treatment was just as effective as standard desensitization in improving subjects' performance in an analogue test situation. Furthermore, the new technique proved superior to standard desensitization in reducing the students' self-reported anxiety and in raising their grade-point averages (an indirect measure of test-taking performance).

Although this study demonstrates that modifying desensitization along self-instructional lines does improve the effectiveness of that procedure, the contribution of cognitive interventions alone remains unclear. A number of studies that have attempted to establish the efficacy of RET alone (for example, DiLoreto, 1971; Ellis, 1957; Karst & Trexler, 1970; Trexler & Karst, 1972) have yielded conflicting results; and all are flawed by methodological or interpretive shortcomings (Mahoney, 1974). However, an excellent study by Meichenbaum, Bernard Gilmore, and Al Fedoravicius (1971), closely modeled after Paul's (1966b)

Table 10–2. Examples of Coping Self-Statements

Preparing for a stressor

    What is it you have to do?

    You can develop a plan to deal with it.

    Just think about what you can do about it. That's better than getting anxious.

    No negative self-statements: just think rationally.

    Don't worry; worry won't help anything.

    Maybe what you think is anxiety is eagerness to confront the stressor.

Confronting and handling a stressor

    Just "psych" yourself up—you can meet this challenge.

    You can convince yourself to do it. You can reason your fear away.

    One step at a time; you can handle the situation.

    Don't think about fear; just think about what you have to do. Stay relevant.

    This anxiety is what the doctor said you would feel. It's a reminder to use your coping exercises.

    This tenseness can be an ally; a cue to cope.

    Relax; you're in control. Take a slow deep breath.

    Ah, good.

Coping with the feeling of being overwhelmed

    When fear comes, just pause.

    Keep the focus on the present, what is it you have to do?

    Label your fear from 0 to 10 and watch it change.

    You should expect your fear to rise.

    Don't try to eliminate fear totally; just keep it manageable.

Reinforcing self-statements

    It worked; you did it.

    Wait until you tell your therapist (or group) about this.

    It wasn't as bad as you expected.

    You made more out of your fear than it was worth.

    Your damn ideas—that's the problem. When you control them, you control your fear.

    It's getting better each time you use the procedures.

    You can be pleased with the progress you're making.

    You did it!

From D. Meichenbaum, Self-instructional methods. In F. H. Kanfer & A. P. Goldstein (Eds.), *Helping people change.* New York: Pergamon, 1975, p. 371, Table 11.2. By permission of Pergamon Press, Ltd.

outcome evaluation, compared an RET-like procedure with standard desensitization, a combination of RET and desensitization, an attention-placebo treatment, and a no-treatment condition. All treatments were carried out with groups of speech-anxious college students. On both behavioral and self-report measures of anxiety, both the RET and standard desensitization groups showed the greatest and approximately equal reductions in anxiety from pretreatment to posttreatment assessments. Curiously, the combined RET and desensitization group showed some improvement over attention-placebo and waiting-list control subjects, but this combination was not as consistently effective as either desensitization or RET applied in isolation.

The results of this study were replicated and extended in an impressive investigation by Kenneth Holroyd (1976), who compared the effects of RET, systematic desensitization, combined RET and desensitization, and a pseudotherapy control procedure on test-anxious college students. Subjects in all treatment groups, including pseudotherapy, improved significantly more than those in a waiting-list control condition. However, only the RET and the RET plus desensitization conditions significantly improved subjects' performance in an analogue test-taking situation. The RET alone program was superior to all other conditions in reducing subjects' reported anxiety during the analogue test and in improving their grade-point averages for the following semester. Thus, the cognitive therapy was more effective overall than either the systematic desensitization or pseudotherapy treatments.

One of the most important aspects of Holroyd's study is that he carefully assessed the credibility of all treatment conditions in an effort to control for expectancy effects. All conditions, including pseudotherapy (which consisted of "mental control" and "body awareness" exercises that were supposed to induce a mental state that could not be disturbed by anxiety), appeared to produce approximately equal expectancies for improvement. The finding that only RET was reliably superior to pseudotherapy suggests that this cognitive procedure contains some active ingredients beyond the subjects' expectancy for improvement. However, the fact that desensitization was not more effective than the equally credible nonspecific therapy lends weight to the hypothesis that desensitization's effectiveness is primarily an expectancy phenomenon.

The experimental evidence thus far unequivocally documents the effectiveness of cognitive approaches to anxiety management. However, as of this writing, controlled studies of systematic rational restructuring and stress inoculation training for fear reduction have not been published, and we do not yet know which of the various cognitive strategies is most effective. Future research will answer this question and also establish the generality of the findings from these promising early studies.

THE PROBLEM OF ANALOGUE RESEARCH

Although we hesitate to end the chapter on a slightly negative note, one important issue remains that has implications for much of the preceding discussion. That issue concerns the generalizability of the conclusions drawn from behavioral anxiety management research.

Much of our knowledge about the effects of behavioral treatment procedures comes from studies employing college student "clients" who volunteer to undergo an experimental treatment in order to alleviate some difficulty they are experiencing. Such **treatment analogues** are relatively convenient for the investigator. It is often hard to come by a large group of "real" clients who share some particular problem. However, an abundant supply of students is usually readily available to the academic researcher, and certain problems are common enough that a sizable subject population can be secured without great difficulty. The question then becomes: Do these research subjects resemble real-world clients closely enough to allow us to generalize findings from one group to the other? This is a crucial question, and a matter of considerable concern to behavioral researchers (Bernstein & Paul, 1971; Borkovec & O'Brien, 1976).

The issue is particularly important in the behavioral literature on fear-reduction procedures, since most of the experimentation has been of the analogue type. One problem has been that the criteria used to select subjects are often not rigorous enough to ensure that only individuals with a *clinically relevant* level of anxiety are accepted for treatment. Consequently, it is conceivable that much of our confidence in the efficacy of behavioral fear-reduction procedures is based on data from subjects who are only mildly fearful. Extrapolation of these results to clinical populations in which the relative levels of disturbance may be much greater is fraught with difficulties. Factors that may grossly influence therapeutic outcomes in mildly fearful subjects (expectancy effects, for example) *may* not be potent enough to have any appreciable effect on severely distressed clients. Conversely, procedures that seem indispensable with highly anxious clients (like the relaxation component in systematic desensitization) *may* contribute little to the reduction of weaker fears. We simply do not know.

This argument should not in any way be construed as an attempt to dismiss the accumulated labors of the many researchers who have conducted analogue investigations. Such studies have added immeasurably to our understanding of therapeutic processes. Moreover, many studies have been designed to increase the probability that analogue problems have been kept to an absolute minimum. Nevertheless, the fact remains that we cannot at present be certain of the extent to which our experimental achievements guaran-

tee our clinical effectiveness. The discrepancy between the laboratory and the real world may be very small; but it may also be quite large.

One of the laudable characteristics of the behavioral movement is its propensity for self-criticism and self-correction. Behavioral psychologists have responded to the problems posed by analogue research with studies aimed at increasing our understanding of these difficulties, and these investigations are resulting in more sophisticated methodologies that promise to increase the generalizability of experimental findings. We will soon know whether the confidence that has been placed in many behavioral treatment procedures is fully warranted.

SUMMARY

A useful way of conceptualizing anxiety is as a complex pattern of response involving both physiological and cognitive components. Anxiety serves a very useful purpose in alerting people to potential danger and preparing them to deal with it. But sometimes people experience anxiety that is out of proportion to the threat, or that occurs in the absence of any objective danger. In these cases, anxiety becomes a "problem," and clinical intervention may be appropriate.

Behaviorally oriented clinicians differentiate between anxiety that is conditioned to certain stimuli (conditioned anxiety), and that which is a reaction to some aspect of the individual's overt or covert behavior (reactive anxiety). Although these types of anxiety reactions appear to call for different treatment strategies, both can produce psychophysiological disorders, performance deficits, and troublesome or bizarre avoidance behavior in addition to problems of simple "fear."

Several fear-reduction procedures are derived from the conditioning model and are primarily aimed at eliminating the physiological arousal characteristic of anxiety. Relaxation training appears to combat arousal and can be used as a coping strategy that clients can employ in vivo. When relaxation is combined with graduated imaginal exposure to anxiety stimuli, the procedure is known as systematic desensitization. Although much theoretical debate centers on the subject, desensitization appears to be a counterconditioning procedure that employs relaxation to suppress conditioned anxiety responses. Flooding and implosion, on the other hand, aim at extinguishing anxiety responses through prolonged presentation of high-intensity anxiety stimuli. Flooding involves imaginal or in vivo exposure to realistic but potent stimuli without the actual or imagined experience of aversive consequences. Implosion—which is derived from both behavioral and psychoanalytic theories—makes use of exaggerated, horrific images that combine fear cues with catastrophic fantasized outcomes. Research findings clearly indicate the usefulness of relaxation training and systematic desensitization, but support for both flooding and implosion is somewhat equivocal at present, with indications that the procedures may be dangerous in certain instances.

Modeling-based anxiety-reduction techniques for adults differ little from those used with children. Participant modeling, the most frequently used method, casts the therapist in an active role—modeling, assisting, and reinforcing the client during in vivo encounters with the feared stimulus. Research clearly supports the effectiveness and remarkable efficiency of participant modeling, but practical considerations somewhat limit the range of problems to which it can be applied.

Cognitive behavior modification strategies seek to eliminate reactive self-statements that may engender or exacerbate anxiety. These procedures have roots in Ellis's rational-emotive therapy (RET), which teaches clients to actively dispute the irrational, self-defeating assumptions underlying their anxiety-evoking thoughts. Systematic rational restructuring closely resembles Ellis's technique, but employs graduated behavioral rehearsal to sharpen clients' skills at disputing their reactive self-statements. Self-instructional techniques bypass rational reconceptualization of clients' anxious thinking, and instead focus on teaching clients a general "package" of self-statements that are task-relevant, coping, and self-reinforcing in nature. Stress inoculation involves clients' practicing self-instruction while in an analogue stress situation before taking the procedure into the "real world." Experimental evidence for the effectiveness of cognitive strategies, while preliminary, is very impressive.

CASE STUDY 10–1

MacDONALD, M. L., & BERNSTEIN, D. A. TREATMENT OF A SPIDER PHOBIA BY *IN VIVO* AND IMAGINAL DESENSITIZATION. *JOURNAL OF BEHAVIOR THERAPY AND EXPERIMENTAL PSYCHIATRY*, 1974, **5,** 47–52.

The treatment techniques we have described in this chapter are seldom applied in isolation except for research purposes. An almost endless variation of effective programs can be derived by combining a few basic strategies like successive approximation and incompatible responses. The case study reported by MacDonald and Bernstein illustrates the use of varied techniques in combination.

The client was a twenty-four-year-old female graduate student with an intense fear of spiders. The origin of her fear was unclear, as she had been afraid as long as she could remember. But the problem reached intolerable proportions when she moved into a new apartment that was infested with spiders.

On actually encountering a spider, the client experienced physiological arousal. If no spiders were present, she ruminated about their possible appearance. Nightmares about spiders disturbed her sleep. The client had also begun to exhibit numerous escape and avoidance behaviors: she stayed away from rooms and drawers where spiders might lurk; she enlisted the aid of friends or neighbors to kill spiders in her apartment, and at times would even ask to sleep overnight with these people rather than stay with her uninvited roommates. In all other life areas the woman was functioning quite well, indicating that the spider fear was an isolated problem.

The treatment strategy devised by MacDonald and Bernstein combined imaginal systematic desensitization with a series of in vivo desensitization tasks. The in vivo tasks were introduced in a graded fashion (see Figure 10–3), with the stimuli and desired response components for each successive task more closely approximating those that would be involved in an actual encounter with a spider.

Treatment began with the client being trained in relaxation. Early in training, cue-controlled relaxation procedures were instituted to provide the client with an arousal-reducing coping response for use in subsequent in vivo tasks. At the same time, an anxiety hierarchy for imaginal desensitization was developed. The complete hierarchy consisted of 68 primarily spatial-temporal items ranging from "walking into your apartment at night" to "waking up and seeing a huge spider walk across the hand of your outstretched right arm." Desensitization proper was conducted over the following fourteen sessions.

The first in vivo task was actually a transfer test of desensitization, with the client instructed to use her conditioned relaxation skills to counter any anxiety remaining in hierarchy situations. This task was continuous; each week new items were desensitized and available for transfer testing.

The second in vivo procedure was designed both to extinguish the client's anxiety response to symbolic stimuli and to dispel any misconceptions about spiders she might have. The therapist, drawing from several texts, prepared a report containing factual information about spiders and their

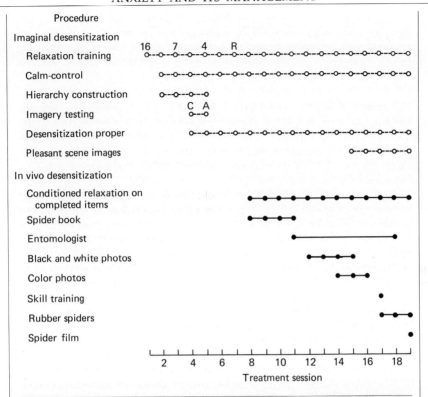

Figure 10–3. Summary of procedures used by MacDonald and Bernstein in treatment of a spider phobia. Numbers refer to muscle groups used in relaxation training; R means recall. The "imagery testing" item includes an assessment of image clarity (C) and an evaluation of whether an imaginal spider stimulus would elicit anxiety (A). From M. L. MacDonald and D. A. Bernstein, Treatment of a spider phobia by *in vivo* and imaginal desensitization. *Journal of Behavior Therapy and Experimental Psychiatry,* 1974, **5,** p. 48, Table 1. By permission of Pergamon Press, Ltd.

habits. No pictures or drawings were included. The sections of the report were organized in hierarchical fashion from least to most distressing based on information obtained during the assessment interviews. The client was to read portions of the report during her daily home-relaxation practice. If she became anxious, she was to stop reading, relax again, and then resume reading at a point prior to that which had elicited discomfort. She did report becoming anxious several times while reading the report, but this was easily managed with relaxation.

The third in vivo intervention built on the success of the spider report. A university entomologist agreed to meet with the client to give a minilecture on spiders. The entomologist did not try to frighten the client, but he also made no attempt to assuage her fears. Instead, he merely conveyed accurate and fascinating information about spiders and their habits as if he were speaking to a student. At times the client would interrupt to ask questions and was answered in a straightforward way. The client responded very favorably to this format, and reported feeling anxious only two or three times. Once again, conditioned relaxation removed her discomfort. There was also an additional benefit: she was quite pleased that she now knew a great deal more about spiders than the average person.

At the twelfth treatment session, the next in vivo procedure was initiated. The client was asked to rank 22 black and white photographs (ranging from a spider web to a large tarantula) from least to most distressing. She was then instructed to do the same with the pictures as she had with the spider report—that is, view them in order during home relaxation practice. Within two weeks, she reported being completely comfortable with each picture. A slight twist was introduced at this point to use the pictures in a way that more closely approximated what the client might actually face in reality. She was asked to place several of them around her apartment so that they would be in view as she moved through various rooms, and to change the pictures and rearrange their location every other day. Once again, conditioned relaxation was to be used whenever the sudden appearance of a spider picture caused her alarm. Within two weeks, the client was comfortable with this procedure, and a similar sequence was begun using color photos of spiders—the next closest step to the "real thing." In three weeks the client's anxiety to the color plates was extinguished.

In the seventeenth treatment session, the client's lack of skill at killing spiders was tackled. She was presented with a personalized "spider swatter" (note that humor is, in general, incompatible with anxiety) and was given practice in "killing" three lifelike rubber spiders. She was also asked to practice destroying the rubber spiders at home. As the client's skill improved, so did her reported confidence in her ability to deal decisively with the creepy-crawlers.

The next sequence of in vivo tasks was exceptionally realistic. First, the client was asked to place the rubber spiders in various conspicuous locations around her apartment, changing their positions each day. One week later, she was to enlist the aid of a friend to place the spiders in *unknown* locations in one particular room. Finally, the uncertainty of where the fake spider might be lurking was increased: the friend was given freedom to hide the spiders *anywhere* in the apartment. At the beginning of each phase, the client reported slight anxiety, but this rapidly extinguished and did not recur.

At the eighteenth treatment session, the entomologist was again contacted to aid in the client's first programmed contact with real spiders. The session began with the client viewing some large color plates of spiders while the entomologist discussed their habits. Next, both she and the therapist viewed twelve preserved spiders through a microscope. After viewing each spider, the instructor placed the specimen in the hand of the therapist, who examined it and handed it to the client. She reported only mild discomfort while looking at some of the color pictures; surprisingly, actually holding the spider specimens produced no anxiety at all. The client reported that watching the therapist handle the spider first added to her comfort. The participant modeling aspect of this phase is obvious.

The final in vivo procedure, which occurred on the nineteenth treatment contact, involved the viewing of an eighteen-minute color film about spiders. The client first relaxed, and then opened her eyes to view the film. Although she was instructed to signal any anxiety so that the film could be stopped and backed up, the client did not experience any and the film was shown uninterrupted.

During the final treatment session, the client was reminded to maintain her gains by continuing to practice relaxation and purposely exposing herself to spider stimuli (the pictures, the rubber spiders, spider sections of zoos) periodically. In terms of her real-life functioning, great improvements could be seen: By the twelfth session, she was confronting previously avoided drawers and rooms with complete calmness, and remained undisturbed after several encounters with spiders. At the end of treatment, the client's reactions to spiders of all sizes ranged from ignoring them outdoors to destroying them indoors. A six-month followup revealed the client had not experienced a return of her fears.

CASE STUDY 10–2

RAINEY, C. A. AN OBSESSIVE COMPULSIVE NEUROSIS TREATED BY FLOODING *IN VIVO. JOURNAL OF BEHAVIOR THERAPY AND EXPERIMENTAL PSYCHIATRY,* 1972, **3,** 117–121.

This case demonstrates the effective use of an in vivo flooding procedure with a client whose escape and avoidance behaviors had become so bizarre and pervasive that he had ceased to function effectively.

Mr. G was a twenty-five-year-old single man who had been troubled with obsessive-compulsive decontamination rituals for twelve years. At the time of his hospitalization, the rituals had become so distressing and time-consuming that suicide seemed to him the only solution.

Mr. G traced the onset of his disturbance to 1957 when he was in sixth grade. It was rumored that a girl in class had fleas, and the thought of this made him very uncomfortable. If he accidentally touched her, he was filled with disgust and would proceed to brush off the part of his body that had touched her. He would then blow the "contamination" off of the hand he had used to brush himself. Over the next two years his fear of contamination became so intense that he found himself unable to touch any of his classmates. When he made accidental contact with someone, he would rush to the bathroom to wash his hands repeatedly until his anxiety abated. The year 1957 acquired threatening significance, and objects or persons that were in any way associated with that year were also seen as contaminated and hence avoided.

The death of his mother several years later placed Mr. G under further stress, and his problems became more pronounced. At that time he was spending approximately two hours each day ritualistically decontaminating his surroundings. Soon he began to feel that his efforts were not sufficient —contamination was all around him. He confided in his father, who sought psychiatric help for his son, but Mr. G refused treatment on religious grounds. Within two years the problem had reached enormous proportions: he was spending sixteen hours a day washing himself and his environs. Handwashing alone required 1,000 strokes under the tap for successful decontamination. Finally, after one fifty-two-hour cleaning binge, Mr. G was hospitalized in a state of panic and exhaustion. Electroconvulsive treatment and two years of private psychiatric therapy resulted in some improvement, but soon the problem returned. He isolated himself in his apartment, leaving his sterile environment only when absolutely necessary. The company for which he worked purchased a piece of equipment manufactured in 1957, so he quit his job. He was even unable to open letters from his father because they were mailed from the town in which he had lived in 1957. Instead he would pick the letters out of his mailbox with Kleenex, burn them, and then scour the mailbox. At the time that Mr. G entered treatment

> The floors (of his apartment) were almost completely covered with newspapers, each piece having been carefully placed on an area of floor which had been ritualistically washed. Scattered around the room were 45 large cardboard containers filled with Kleenex tissues and 100 bowls of "contaminated water" which he had used to clean himself and objects in the room. Almost every waking hour was devoted to the

compulsive behavior. Because of the time involved in the painstaking ritual of cleaning each square inch of the shower, he had restricted this activity to once a month and had resorted to using copious amounts of sweet-smelling perfume and deodorant. Seldom a day passed that he did not entertain suicidal thoughts, and his mood fluctuated between deep depression and panic. (p. 118)

Mr. G was admitted to a day program at a mental health clinic. He appeared awkward, tense, and deficient in social skills, but was cooperative and motivated. For assessment purposes, Mr. G was asked to rate his anxiety, both before and after his compulsive behaviors, on a 5-point scale, where 1 = no anxiety and 5 = panic. Anxiety ratings made prior to the compulsive rituals were always higher than those made afterward, indicating the rituals functioned to reduce anxiety. It was also evident that in the week prior to the treatment, there was no improvement in Mr. G's overall anxiety level.

The anxiety evoked by objects associated with the date 1957 indicated their potential usefulness as in vivo flooding stimuli. Consequently, Mr. G was instructed to obtain a coin minted in 1957 to be carried with him at all times. He also recalled that in 1957 he had wanted to purchase a copy of a particular magazine, but had been unable to pick it up from the newsstand. Since back issues of the magazine were readily available, Mr. G was asked to purchase the relevant one. He secured both items immediately.

During the first week of flooding, Mr. G was prohibited from engaging in

Figure 10–4. Mean anxiety rating scores during first week of treatment. From C. A. Rainey, An obsessive compulsive neurosis treated by flooding *in vivo. Journal of Behavior Therapy and Experimental Psychiatry*, 1972, **3,** p. 120, Figure 2. By permission of Pergamon Press, Ltd.

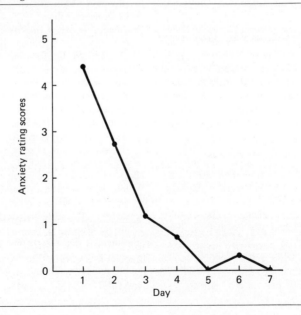

his compulsive rituals regardless of his anxiety level. Instead, his bathroom routine was restricted to that normally required for personal hygiene. He was instructed to touch the coin and read from the magazine as frequently as possible. Each time he did so, he was to rate his anxiety on the 5-point scale.

As can be seen in Figure 10–4, Mr. G's anxiety was near panic level for the first day of treatment, but it dropped off rapidly thereafter. He managed to resist powerful urges to wash himself, and by the end of the third day reported that the coin and the magazine had lost their terrible significance. By the end of the week, he had begun restoring his apartment to a more normal condition. Mr. G remained in the day hospital for an additional six weeks for interpersonal skill training. Eighteen months after treatment he was still free of his compulsive behaviors and was once again steadily employed.

REFERENCES

Alexander, A. B. An experimental test of assumptions relating to the use of electromyographic biofeedback as a general relaxation training technique. *Psychophysiology*, 1975, **12**, 119–123.

Alexander, A. B., Miklich, D. R., & Hershkoff, H. The immediate effects of systematic relaxation training on peak expiratory flow rates in asthmatic children. *Psychosomatic Medicine*, 1972, **34**, 388–394.

Arnold, M. B. An excitatory theory of emotion. In M. L. Reymert (Ed.), *Feelings and emotion*. New York: McGraw-Hill, 1950.

Arnold, M. B. *Emotion and personality*. Vol. 1, *Psychological aspects*. New York: Columbia University Press, 1960.

Ax, A. F. The physiological differentiation between fear and anger in humans. *Psychosomatic Medicine*, 1953, **15**, 433–442.

Bandura, A. Vicarious processes: A case of no-trial learning. In L. Berkowitz (Ed.), *Advances in experimental social psychology*, vol. 2. New York: Academic Press, 1965.

Bandura, A. *Principles of behavior modification*. New York: Holt, Rinehart and Winston, 1969.

Bandura, A., Blanchard, E. B., & Ritter, R. The relative efficacy of desensitization and modeling approaches for inducing behavioral, affective, and attitudinal changes. *Journal of Personality and Social Psychology*, 1969, **13**, 173–199.

Barrett, C. L. Systematic desensitization versus implosive therapy. *Journal of Abnormal Psychology*, 1969, **74**, 587–592.

Baum, M., & Poser, E. G. Comparison of flooding procedures in animals and man. *Behaviour Research and Therapy*, 1971, **9**, 249–254.

Beck, A. Cognitive therapy: Nature and relation to behavior therapy. *Behavior Therapy*, 1970, **1**, 184–200.

Beck, A. T. *Cognitive therapy and the emotional disorders*. New York: International Universities Press, 1976.

Beiman, I., Graham, L. E., & Ciminero, A. R. Self-control progressive relaxation training for essential hypertension: Therapeutic effects in the natural environment. *Behavior Therapy*, in press.

Beiman, I., Israel, E., & Johnson, S. A. During training and posttraining effects of live and taped extended progressive relaxation, self-relaxation, and electromyogram biofeedback. *Journal of Consulting and Clinical Psychology*, 1978, **46**, 314–321.

Bernstein, D. A., & Borkovec, T. D. *Progressive relaxation training: A manual for the helping professions*. Champaign, Ill.: Research Press, 1973.

Bernstein, D. A., & Paul, G. L. Some comments on therapy analogue research with small animal "phobias." *Journal of Behavior Therapy and Experimental Psychiatry*, 1971, **2**, 225–237.

Blanchard, E. B. The relative contributions of modeling, informational influences and physical contact in the extinction of phobic behavior. *Journal of Abnormal Psychology*, 1970, **76**, 55–61.

Borkovec, T. D. The comparative effectiveness of systematic desensitization and implosive therapy and the effect of expectancy manipulation on the elimination of fear. Unpublished doctoral dissertation, University of Illinois, 1970.

Borkovec, T. D. Effects of expectancy on the outcome of systematic desensitization and implosive treatment for analogue anxiety. *Behavior Therapy*, 1972, **3**, 29–40.

Borkovec, T. D., & Fowles, D. C. A controlled investigation of the effects of progressive and hypnotic relaxation on insomnia. *Journal of Abnormal Psychology,* 1973, **82,** 153–158.

Borkovec, T. D., Kaloupek, D. G., & Slama, K. M. The facilitative effect of muscle tension-release in the relaxation treatment of sleep disturbance. *Behavior Therapy,* 1975, **36,** 301–309.

Borkovec, T. D., & Nau, S. D. Credibility of analogue therapy rationales. *Journal of Behavior Therapy and Experimental Psychiatry,* 1972, **3,** 257–260.

Borkovec, T. D., & O'Brien, G. T. Methodological and target behavior issues in analogue therapy outcome research. In M. Hersen, R. M. Eisler, & P. M. Miller (Eds.), *Progress in behavior modification,* vol. 3. New York: Academic Press, 1976.

Borkovec, T. D., Weerts, T. C., & Bernstein, D. A. Assessment of anxiety. In A. R. Ciminero, K. S. Calhoun, & H. E. Adams (Eds.), *Handbook of behavioral assessment.* New York: Wiley, 1977.

Boudewyns, P. A., & Wilson, A. E. Implosive therapy and desensitization therapy using free association in the treatment of inpatients. *Journal of Abnormal Psychology,* 1972, **79,** 259–268.

Boulougouris, J. C., & Marks, I. M. Implosion (flooding): A new treatment for phobias. *British Medical Journal,* 1962, **2,** 721–723.

Boulougouris, J. C., Marks, I. M., & Marset, P. Superiority of flooding (implosion) to desensitization for reducing pathological fear. *Behaviour Research and Therapy,* 1971, **9,** 7–16.

Brehm, J. W., & Cohen, A. R. *Explorations in cognitive dissonance.* New York: Wiley, 1962.

Bridger, W. H., & Mandel, I. J. A comparison of GSR fear responses produced by threat and electric shock. *Journal of Psychiatric Research,* 1964, **2,** 31–40.

Bridger, W., & Mandel, I. Abolition of the PRE by instructions in GSR conditioning. *Journal of Experimental Psychology,* 1965, **69,** 476–482.

Budzynski, T. H., & Stoyva, J. M. An instrument for producing deep muscle relaxation by means of analogue information feedback. *Journal of Applied Behavior Analysis,* 1969, **2,** 231–237.

Budzynski, T. H., Stoyva, J. M., Adler, C. S., & Mullaney, D. J. EMG biofeedback and tension headache: A controlled outcome study. *Psychosomatic Medicine,* 1973, **35,** 484–496.

Campbell, D., Sanderson, R. E., & Laverty, S. A. Characteristics of a conditioned response in human subjects during extinction trials following a simple traumatic conditioning trial. *Journal of Abnormal and Social Psychology,* 1964, **68,** 627–693.

Cannon, W. B. *The wisdom of the body.* New York: Norton, 1932.

Chatterjee, B., & Eriksen, C. Cognitive factors in heart rate conditioning. *Journal of Experimental Psychology,* 1962, **64,** 272–279.

Cooke, G. Evaluation of the efficacy of the components of reciprocal inhibition psychotherapy. *Journal of Abnormal Psychology,* 1968, **73,** 464–467.

Cox, D. J., Freundlich, A., & Meyer, R. G. Differential effectiveness of electromyograph feedback, verbal relaxation instructions, and medication placebo with tension headaches. *Journal of Consulting and Clinical Psychology,* 1975, **43,** 892–898.

Craighead, W. E. The role of muscular relaxation in systematic desensitization. In R. D. Rubin, J. P. Brady, & J. D. Henderson (Eds.), *Advances in behavior therapy,* vol. 4. New York: Academic Press, 1973.

Davison, G. C. Systematic desensitization as a counterconditioning process. *Journal of Abnormal Psychology,* 1968, **73,** 91–99.

Davison, G. C., & Wilson, G. T. Processes of fear-reduction in systematic desensitization: Cognitive and social reinforcement factors in humans. *Behavior Therapy,* 1973, **4,** 1–21.

DiLoreto, A. O. *Comparative psychotherapy: An experimental analysis.* Chicago: Aldine-Atherton, 1971.

Edelman, R. I. Effects of progressive relaxation on autonomic processes. *Journal of Clinical Psychology,* 1970, **26,** 421–425.

Ellis, A. Outcome of employing three techniques of psychotherapy. *Journal of Clinical Psychology,* 1957, **13,** 344–350.

Ellis, A. *Reason and emotion in psychotherapy.* Secaucus, N.J.: Lyle Stuart, 1962.

Eysenck, H. J. (Ed.), *Behaviour therapy and the neuroses.* New York: Pergamon Press, 1960.

Eysenck, H. J. A theory of the incubation of anxiety/fear responses. *Behaviour Research and Therapy,* 1968, **6,** 309–322.

Eysenck, H. J. Anxiety and the history of neurosis. In C. D. Spielberger & I. G. Sarason (Eds.), *Stress and anxiety,* vol. 1. New York: Wiley, 1975.

Eysenck, H. J. The learning theory model of neurosis—a new approach. *Behaviour Research and Therapy,* 1976, **14,** 251–267.

Fazio, A. F. Treatment components in implosive therapy. *Journal of Abnormal Psychology,* 1970, **76,** 211–219.

Fazio, A. F. Implosive therapy with semiclinical phobias. *Journal of Abnormal Psychology,* 1972, **80,** 183–188.

Gelder, M. G., Bancroft, J. H. J., Gath, D. H., Johnston, D. W., Mathews, A. M., & Shaw, P. M. Specific and nonspecific factors in behaviour therapy. *British Journal of Psychiatry,* 1973, **123,** 445–462.

Goldfried, M. R., & Davison, G. C. *Clinical behavior*

292
APPLICATIONS: ADULTS

therapy. New York: Holt, Rinehart and Winston, 1976.

Goldfried, M. R., Decenteceo, E. T., & Weinberg, L. Systematic rational restructuring as a self-control technique. *Behavior Therapy,* 1974, **5,** 247–254.

Goldfried, M. R., & Goldfried, A. P. Cognitive change methods. In F. H. Kanfer & A. P. Goldstein (Eds.), *Helping people change.* New York: Pergamon Press, 1975.

Goldfried, M. R., & Trier, C. S. Effectiveness of relaxation as an active coping skill. *Journal of Abnormal Psychology,* 1974, **83,** 348–355.

Greenberg, D., & Jacobs, M. *How to make yourself miserable.* New York: Random House, 1966.

Grossberg, J. M. The physiological effectiveness of brief training in differential muscle relaxation. Technical Report No. 9. La Jolla, Calif.: Western Behavioral Sciences, 1965.

Grossberg, J. M., & Wilson, H. K. Physiological changes accompanying the visualization of fearful and neutral situations. *Journal of Personality and Social Psychology,* 1968, **10,** 124–133.

Haynes, S. N., Griffin, P., Mooney, D., & Parise, M. Electromyographic biofeedback and relaxation instructions in the treatment of muscle contraction headache. *Behavior Therapy,* 1975, **6,** 672–678.

Hogan, R. A. Implosive therapy in the short term treatment of psychotics. *Psychotherapy: Theory, Research and Practice,* 1966, **3,** 25–31.

Hogan, R. A. The implosive technique. *Behaviour Research and Therapy,* 1968, **6,** 423–431.

Hogan, R. A., & Kirchner, J. H. Implosive, eclectic verbal and bibliotherapy in the treatment of fears of snakes. *Behaviour Research and Therapy,* 1968, **6,** 167–171.

Holroyd, K. A. Cognition and desensitization in the group treatment of test anxiety. *Journal of Consulting and Clinical Psychology,* 1976, **44,** 991–1001.

Jacobson, E. *Progressive relaxation.* Chicago: University of Chicago Press, 1938.

Jessup, B. A., & Neufeld, R. W. J. Effects of biofeedback and "autogenic relaxation" techniques on physiological and subjective responses in psychiatric patients: A preliminary analysis. *Behavior Therapy,* 1977, **8,** 160–167.

Karst, T. O., & Trexler, L. D. Initial study using fixed-role and rational-emotive therapy in treating public speaking anxiety. *Journal of Consulting and Clinical Psychology,* 1970, **34,** 360–366.

Kazdin, A. E., & Wilcoxon, L. A. Systematic desensitization and nonspecific treatment effects: A methodological evaluation. *Psychological Bulletin,* 1976, **83,** 729–758.

Kotila, R. R. The effects of education and four varieties of implosive therapy on fear of snakes. Unpublished doctoral dissertation, Washington State University, 1969.

Lacey, J. I. Somatic response patterning and stress: Some revisions of activation theory. In M. H. Appley & R. Trumbull (Eds.), *Psychological stress.* New York: Appleton-Century-Crofts, 1967.

Lang, P. J. Fear reduction and fear behavior: Problems in treating a construct. In J. M. Shlien (Ed.), *Research in psychotherapy,* vol. 3. Washington, D.C.: American Psychological Association, 1968.

Lang, P. J. The mechanics of desensitization and the laboratory study of human fear. In C. M. Franks (Ed.), *Behavior therapy: Appraisal and status.* New York: McGraw-Hill, 1969.

Lazarus, R., & Averill, J. Emotion and cognition: With special reference to anxiety. In C. Spielberger (Ed.), *Anxiety: Current trends in theory and research,* vol. 2. New York: Academic Press, 1972.

Leitenberg, H., Agras, S., Barlow, D. H., & Oliveau, D. C. Contribution of selective positive reinforcement and therapeutic instructions to systematic desensitization therapy. *Journal of Abnormal Psychology,* 1969, **74,** 113–118.

Levis, D. J., & Hare, N. A review of the theoretical rationale and empirical support for the extinction approach of implosive (flooding) therapy. In M. Hersen, R. M. Eisler, & P. M. Miller (Eds.), *Progress in behavior modification,* vol. 4. New York: Academic Press, 1977.

Lick, J. R., & Heffler, D. Relaxation training and attention placebo in the treatment of severe insomnia. *Journal of Consulting and Clinical Psychology,* 1977, **45,** 153–161.

Lick, J. R., & Katkin, E. S. Assessment of anxiety and fear. In M. Hersen & A. S. Bellack (Eds.), *Behavioral assessment: A practical handbook.* New York: Pergamon Press, 1976.

Lomont, J. F. Reciprocal inhibition or extinction? *Behaviour Research and Therapy,* 1965, **3,** 209–219.

Lomont, J. F., & Edwards, J. E. The role of relaxation in systematic desensitization. *Behaviour Research and Therapy,* 1967, **5,** 11–25.

MacDonald, M. L., & Bernstein, D. A. Treatment of a spider phobia by *in vivo* and imaginal desensitization. *Journal of Behavior Therapy and Experimental Psychiatry,* 1974, **5,** 47–52.

Mahoney, M. J. *Cognition and behavior modification.* Cambridge, Mass.: Ballinger, 1974.

Malleson, N. Panic and phobia: A possible method of treatment. *Lancet,* 1959, **1,** 225–227.

Mathews, A. M., & Gelder, M. G. Psychophysiological

investigations of brief relaxation training. *Journal of Psychosomatic Research*, 1969, **13**, 1–12.

May, J. R., & Johnson, H. J. Physiological activity to internally elicited arousal and inhibitory thoughts. *Journal of Abnormal Psychology*, 1973, **82**, 239–245.

McReynolds, W. T., Barnes, A. R., Brooks, S., & Rehagen, N. J. The role of attention-placebo influences in the efficacy of systematic desensitization. *Journal of Consulting and Clinical Psychology*, 1973, **41**, 86–92.

Mealiea, W. L., & Nawas, M. M. The comparative effectiveness of systematic desensitization and implosive therapy in the treatment of snake phobia. *Journal of Behavior Therapy and Experimental Psychiatry*, 1971, **2**, 85–94.

Meichenbaum, D. H. Cognitive modification of test anxious college students. *Journal of Consulting and Clinical Psychology*, 1972, **39**, 370–380.

Meichenbaum, D. H. *Cognitive behavior modification.* Morristown, N.J.: General Learning Press, 1974.

Meichenbaum, D. H. Self-instructional methods. In F. H. Kanfer & A. P. Goldstein (Eds.), *Helping people change.* New York: Pergamon Press, 1975.

Meichenbaum, D. H., & Cameron, R. Stress inoculation: A skills training approach to anxiety management. Unpublished manuscript, University of Waterloo, 1973.

Meichenbaum, D. H., Gilmore, J. B., & Fedoravicius, A. Group insight versus group desensitization in treating speech anxiety. *Journal of Consulting and Clinical Psychology*, 1971, **36**, 410–421.

Miller, B. V., & Levis, D. J. The effects of varying short visual exposure times to a phobic test stimulus on subsequent avoidance behavior. *Behaviour Research and Therapy*, 1971, **9**, 17–21.

Morganstern, K. P. Implosive therapy and flooding procedures: A critical review. *Psychological Bulletin*, 1973, **79**, 318–334.

Morris, R. J., & Suckerman, K. R. The importance of the therapeutic relationship in systematic desensitization. *Journal of Consulting and Clinical Psychology*, 1974, **42**, 148.

Napalkov, A. V. Information process and the brain. In N. Wiener & J. C. Schade (Eds.), *Progress in brain research.* Vol. 2, *Nerve, brain and memory models.* Amsterdam: Elsevier, 1963.

Orenstein, H., & Carr, J. Implosion therapy by tape recording. *Behaviour Research and Therapy*, 1975, **13**, 177–182.

Paul, G. L. The specific control of anxiety: "Hypnosis" and "conditioning." Paper presented at the American Psychological Association symposium: Innovations in Therapeutic Interactions, 1966(a).

Paul, G. L. *Insight vs. desensitization in psychotherapy.*

Stanford, Calif.: Stanford University Press, 1966(b).

Paul, G. L. Insight vs. desensitization in psychotherapy two years after termination. *Journal of Consulting Psychology*, 1967, **31**, 333–348.

Paul, G. L. Outcome of systematic desensitization I: Background, procedures, and uncontrolled reports of individual treatment. In C. M. Franks (Ed.), *Behavior therapy: Appraisal and status.* New York: McGraw-Hill, 1969(a).

Paul, G. L. Outcome of systematic desensitization II: Controlled investigations of individual treatment, technique variations, and current status. In C. M. Franks (Ed.), *Behavior therapy: Appraisal and status.* New York: McGraw-Hill, 1969(b).

Paul, G. L. Physiological effects of relaxation training and hypnotic suggestion, *Journal of Abnormal Psychology*, 1969, **74**, 425–437(c).

Paul, G. L., & Bernstein, D. A. *Anxiety and clinical problems: Systematic desensitization and related techniques.* Morristown, N. J.: General Learning Press, 1973.

Paul, G. L., & Trimble, R. W. Recorded vs. "live" relaxation training and hypnotic suggestion: Comparative effectiveness for reducing physiological arousal and inhibiting stress response. *Behavior Therapy*, 1970, **1**, 285–302.

Rachman, S. Studies in desensitization, II: Flooding. *Behaviour Research and Therapy*, 1966, **4**, 1–6.

Rainey, C. A. An obsessive compulsive neurosis treated by flooding *in vivo. Journal of Behavior Therapy and Experimental Psychiatry*, 1972, **3**, 117–121.

Rimm, D. C., & Mahoney, M. J. The application of reinforcement and participant modeling procedures in the treatment of snake-phobic behavior. *Behaviour Research and Therapy*, 1969, **7**, 369–376.

Ritter, B. The use of contact desensitization, demonstration-plus-participation, and demonstration alone in the treatment of acrophobia. *Behaviour Research and Therapy*, 1969, **7**, 157–164.

Robinson, S. Physiology of muscular exercise. In V. B. Mountcastle (Ed.), *Medical physiology*, vol. 2. St. Louis: Mosby, 1974.

Rohrbaugh, M., & Riccio, D. V. Paradoxical enhancement of learned fear. *Journal of Abnormal Psychology*, 1970, **75**, 210–216.

Rohrbaugh, M., Riccio, D. V., & Arthur, S. Paradoxical enhancement of conditioned suppression. *Behaviour Research and Therapy*, 1972, **10**, 125–130.

Russell, P. L., & Brandsma, J. M. A theoretical and empirical integration of the rational-emotive and classical conditioning theories. *Journal of Consulting and Clinical Psychology*, 1974, **42**, 389–397.

Russell, R. K., & Matthews, C. O. Cue-controlled relaxation in *in vivo* desensitization of a snake phobia. *Journal of Behavior Therapy and Experimental Psychiatry*, 1975, **6**, 49–51.

Russell, R. K., Miller, D. E., & June, L. N. A comparison between systematic desensitization and cue-controlled relaxation in the treatment of test anxiety. *Behavior Therapy*, 1975, **6**, 172–177.

Russell, R. K., & Sipich, J. F. Cue-controlled relaxation in the treatment of test anxiety. *Journal of Behavior Therapy and Experimental Psychiatry*, 1973, **4**, 47–49.

Schachter, J. Pain, fear, and anger in hypertensives and normotensives. *Psychosomatic Medicine*, 1957, **19**, 17–29.

Schachter, S., & Latane, B. Crime, cognition and the autonomic nervous system. In D. Levine (Ed.), *Nebraska symposium on motivation*. Lincoln: University of Nebraska Press, 1964.

Schachter, S., & Singer, J. E. Cognitive, social, and physiological determinants of emotional state. *Psychological Review*, 1962, **69**, 379–399.

Schachter, S., & Wheeler, L. Epinephrine, chlorpromazine, and amusement. *Journal of Abnormal and Social Psychology*, 1962, **65**, 121–128.

Shedivy, D. I., & Kleinman, K. M. Lack of correlation between frontalis EMG and either neck EMG or verbal ratings of tension. *Psychophysiology*, 1977, **14**, 182–186.

Shoemaker, J. E., & Tasto, D. L. The effects of relaxation on blood pressure of essential hypertensives. *Behaviour Research and Therapy*, 1975, **13**, 29–43.

Silvestri, R., Rohrbaugh, M., & Riccio, D. Conditions influencing the retention of learned fear in young rats. *Developmental Psychology*, 1970, **2**, 389–395.

Smith, R. E., & Nye, S. L. A comparison of implosive therapy and systematic desensitization in the treatment of test anxiety. *Journal of Consulting and Clinical Psychiatry*, 1973, **41**, 37–47.

Spielberger, C. D. Theory and research on anxiety. In C. D. Spielberger (Ed.), *Anxiety and behavior*. New York: Academic Press, 1966.

Stampfl, T. G. Implosive therapy, Part I: The theory. In S. G. Armitage (Ed.), *Behavior modification techniques in the treatment of emotional disorders*. Battle Creek, Mich.: V. A. Publication, 1967.

Stampfl, T. G., & Levis, D. J. Essentials of implosive therapy: A learning-theory based psychodynamic behavioral therapy. *Journal of Abnormal Psychology*, 1967, **72**, 496–503.

Stone, N. M., & Borkovec, T. D. The paradoxical effect of brief CS exposure on analogue phobic subjects. *Behaviour Research and Therapy*, 1975, **13**, 51–54.

Taylor, C. B., Farquhar, J. W., Nelson, E., & Agras, S. Relaxation therapy and high blood pressure. *Archives of General Psychiatry*, 1977, **34**, 339–342.

Thomas, M. R., & Rapp, M. S. Physiological, behavioural and cognitive changes resulting from flooding in a monosymptomatic phobia. *Behaviour Research and Therapy*, 1977, **15**, 304–306.

Trexler, L. D., & Karst, T. O. Rational-emotive therapy, placebo, and no-treatment effect on public-speaking anxiety. *Journal of Abnormal Psychology*, 1972, **79**, 60–67.

Van Egeren, L. F., Feather, B. W., & Hein, P. L. Desensitization of phobias: Some psychophysiological propositions. *Psychophysiology*, 1971, **8**, 213–228.

Velton, E. A. A laboratory task for the induction of mood states. *Behaviour Research and Therapy*, 1968, **6**, 473–482.

Wegner, M. A., Clemens, T. L., Darsie, M. L., Engel, B. T., Estess, F. M., & Sonnenschein, R. R. Autonomic response patterns during intravenous infusion of epinephrine and norepinephrine. *Psychosomatic Medicine*, 1960, **22**, 294–307.

Wickramasekera, I. Electromyographic feedback training and tension headache: Preliminary observations. *American Journal of Clinical Hypnosis*, 1972, **15**, 83–85.

Wilkins, W. Desensitization: Social and cognitive factors underlying the effectiveness of Wolpe's procedure. *Psychological Bulletin*, 1971, **76**, 311–317.

Wilson, G. T., & Davison, G. C. Process of fear reduction in systematic desensitization: Animal studies. *Psychological Bulletin*, 1971, **76**, 1–14.

Wolpe, J. *Psychotherapy by reciprocal inhibition*. Stanford, Calif.: Stanford University Press, 1958.

Wolpe, J. *The practice of behavior therapy*. New York: Pergamon Press, 1969.

Wolpin, M., & Raines, J. Visual imagery, expected roles and extinction as possible factors in reducing fear and avoidance behavior. *Behaviour Research and Therapy*, 1966, **4**, 25–37.

eleven

SEXUAL DYSFUNCTIONS

We are in the midst of a "sexual revolution"—or at least we have been told so with such frequency that the phrase has become trite and annoying. Whether society is really undergoing a radical change in its patterns of sexual behavior or whether our sexuality is merely becoming more "visible" is a matter for debate. Undeniably, a real change has taken place in our consciousness of sexual matters. Information about sex (both good and bad) and sexual stimulation (at least of the vicarious sort) are more readily available than ever before.

Being inundated with sex has had a number of beneficial effects. Myths and misunderstandings born out of sexual ignorance are beginning to be replaced by fact and reason (although the level of sexual ignorance among both professionals and the general public is still appallingly high). We are continually asked to accept sexual variations and preferences as "normal," and gradually our society is becoming more tolerant of alternate life styles. Although all this is probably to the good, the "new sexuality" carries with it more than the assertion that sex is natural and good—sex has become *necessary*, even *mandatory*, for those who consider themselves "contemporary." Today we have enormous demands placed on us to be sexually competent. Our society's demand for fault-less sexual performance may be one of the greatest enemies of natural, pleasurable sexual functioning.

The desire of individuals with sexual problems to become more fully functioning has placed added pressure on clinicians to develop treatments for sexual problems. Traditionally, even the most common complaints, such as impotence or frigidity, were considered difficult if not impossible to correct, and existing treatment approaches were largely ineffective. William Masters and Virginia Johnson (1975, p. 548), the best-known pioneers in the field of sexology, summarize the situation this way:

In 1958, as we began to make plans for a clinical research program in the psychotherapy of human sexual dysfunction, we conducted a detailed review of existing methods and findings in the field. It was immediately apparent that the available research was fragmented and unsystematic, with a marked dichotomy between biological and behavioral data that reflected the scientific bias of the times. Clinical techniques were both time-consuming and unreliable, and there were many indications that these methods derived more from the therapist's personal investment in the psychotherapeutic process than from an objective knowledge of sexual function or a practical application of behavioral principles. Both published data and reports shared with us by people in the field clearly established the fact that health-care professionals were essentially ignorant not only of human sexual physiology but of the potential clinical application of such knowledge. It seemed that sexually dysfunctional patients were being treated with professional insight drawn either from the psychotherapist's own sexual experience—good, bad, or indifferent as it may have been—or from anecdotal material provided by previous patients.

Today the prognosis for most common sexual problems is good, owing to new treatment methods derived from fundamental behavioral principles. In this chapter we will examine behavior modification approaches to the treatment of sexual dysfunction. We will begin with an overview of the nature of sexual functioning and present a conceptualization of the development of sexual dysfunction. Next, we will take a broad look at behavioral sex therapy, drawing particularly on the strategy of Masters and Johnson (1970). After setting the stage with these general considerations, we will analyze in detail the specific treatment strategies employed for each of the common male and female sexual dysfunctions. We will close our discussion with an evaluation of behavioral approaches to the treatment of these problems. In Chapter 12 we will examine the issue of sexual variations.

NORMAL SEXUAL RESPONSE

Understanding sexual dysfunction requires some knowledge of normal sexual response. Although bits and pieces of such information have been available for some time, the greatest comprehensive study of sexual response was that conducted by Masters and Johnson (1966). One of their notable contributions was the description of human sexual response as consisting of four general phases. We will briefly examine the physiology of the sexual response cycle. Readers who are unfamiliar with sexual anatomy may find it helpful to refer to Figures 11–1 and 11–2.

Excitement

Excitement, the first stage of the sexual response cycle, signals the onset of erotic feelings in the man or woman. Of particular interest are the changes that take place in the sexual organs during the excitement phase. In the male, parasympa-

thetic activation causes arterioles in the penis to dilate, and blood enters caverns in the penis faster than it can be drained by venous outflow (a process known as **vasocongestion**); the penis, thus engorged with blood, becomes erect.

In the female, excitement is characterized by vasocongestion of a more diffuse sort. Externally, the labia, and, to some extent the clitoris, become engorged; internally, the tissue surrounding the vagina begins to swell, and a lubricating secretion forms on the walls of the vagina. Although the functioning of the ANS in female sexual response has not been extensively studied, it is probably safe to consider this vasocongestion/lubrication response to be parasympathetic in nature, as is erection in the male.

Plateau

If effective psychological and/or physiological stimulation is continued, the individual moves from the excitement phase to the plateau phase. At this point, the physiological changes that began during excitement reach their full proportions in preparation for orgasm. Erection in the male is at a maximum. In the female, vasocongestion has resulted in a further swelling of the lower third of the vagina, producing a structure known as the "orgasmic platform." As sexual response nears orgasm, the sympathetic nervous system begins to come into play. Widespread sympathetic effects begin to appear, such as increased respiration and heart rate.

Orgasm

The convulsive release of the sexual tension that has accumulated during the previous phases of the response cycle is known as orgasm. Orgasm in the male is a sympathetic reflex consisting of two stages. In the first stage, the prostate and the seminal vesicles pour their respective secretions into the prostatic urethra. This activity is accompanied by the clear sensation that ejaculation is imminent—in fact, once the ejaculatory sequence is begun, it cannot be stopped, and it will run through to completion regardless of changes in physical or psychological stimulation. The second stage of male orgasm—ejaculation—consists

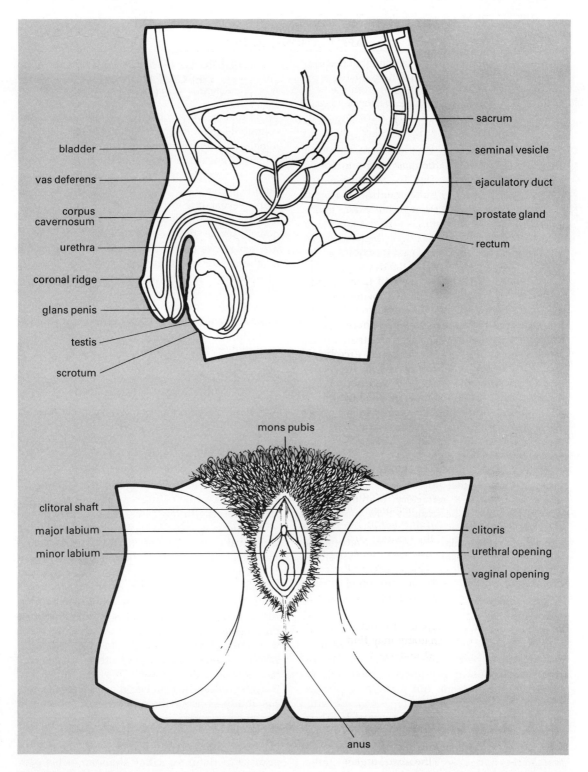

bladder

vas deferens

corpus
cavernosum

urethra

coronal ridge

glans penis

testis

scrotum

sacrum

seminal vesicle

ejaculatory duct

prostate gland

rectum

mons pubis

clitoral shaft

major labium

minor labium

clitoris

urethral opening

vaginal opening

anus

Figure 11–1. Male pelvic anatomy in cross section.

Figure 11–2. Female pelvic anatomy.

of pulsing contractions of the entire urethra, which propel the semen out of the penis with an exquisitely pleasurable sensation.

We may again assume by analogy that orgasm in the female is also a sympathetic phenomenon. Female orgasm appears to be a single-stage process, primarily involving rhythmic contractions of the orgasmic platform accompanied by intensely pleasurable sensations. The female orgasm, in contrast to the male's, can be interrupted once it has begun if adequate stimulation is not maintained.

Resolution

Resolution, the final phase of sexual response, involves a fairly rapid loss of the vasocongestion that characterized the previous phases. This **detumescence,** as it is called, has been traced in the male to sympathetic activity that constricts the arterioles supplying blood to the penis, thereby allowing the venous outflow to drain off the excess blood that caused the erection. The process in the female consists of the disappearance of the orgasmic platform, and a gradual detumescence of the external genitals. Again, we may speculate that the female resolution phase is sympathetic in nature as is the male's.

An important difference between male and female response is that immediately after orgasm males experience a **refractory period,** during which they cannot be stimulated to another orgasm. The duration of this refractory period varies from male to male, but for a period of some minutes after orgasm, further stimulation is usually experienced as unpleasurable, and for some men even as painful. Resolution then occurs and may return the male to a state of sexual quiescence; or this process may be interrupted *after* the refractory period by renewed stimulation, which may then produce another orgasm.

A refractory period does not exist in the female. Some women may prefer a single orgasm, followed by resolution; but many and perhaps all women are capable of *multiple orgasms* without interruption from a refractory period. Thus, whereas the man typically finds genital stimulation after orgasm neutral or unpleasant, the woman may find it very pleasurable and desirable.

SEXUAL DYSFUNCTIONS: DESCRIPTION AND CONCEPTUALIZATION

Six sexual dysfunctions, three for each sex, are commonly encountered in clinical practice. Physiologically and conceptually, two of the male dysfunctions have counterparts in the female (or vice versa, if you prefer), and each gender has one unique problem (see Table 11–1). Defining a particular sexual dysfunction is not as easy as it might appear. The highly individual nature of "adequate" sexual functioning means that what is problematic for one client or couple may not be for another. The variety of definitions that exist for each disorder are all inadequate. In the clinical situation, a dysfunction is jointly defined by the client(s) and therapist(s). We will attempt to avoid this confusion by describing in general the characteristic variations in sexual functioning that tend to draw specific labels.

Male Sexual Dysfunctions

The two most common male dysfunctions are erectile failure (less descriptively and more pejoratively known as "impotence") and premature ejaculation. In **erectile failure,** the man experiences difficulty in achieving or maintaining an erection, thus hindering or preventing him from having intercourse. Erectile failure may assume a great variety of forms. In rare cases, the man may be unable to achieve erection by any means (including masturbation). More often, the erectile failure may occur only at specific times (such as when attempting to penetrate his partner's vagina), under specific circumstances (such as when adopting a particular coital position), or with specific partners (such as his wife). Most males encounter erectile failure at one time or another as the result of fatigue, physical illness, excessive alcohol intake ("brewer's droop"), and other reasons, but such episodes do not result in a continuing dysfunction unless the man becomes concerned about his ability to achieve an erection in subsequent sexual encounters.

Premature ejaculation refers to a tendency to reach orgasm too rapidly for full enjoyment of the sexual experience by either the man or his part-

Table 11–1. Comparison of Male and Female Sexual Dysfunctions

Male Dysfunctions	Female Dysfunctions
No male counterpart.	*Vaginismus:* Involuntary constriction of the outer third of the vaginal barrel making penile penetration difficult or impossible. Conditioned avoidance response.
Erectile failure: Inability to achieve or maintain erection of sufficient strength or duration to allow for satisfactory intercourse. Sympathetic overarousal interferes with parasympathetic vasocongestion.	*Sexual arousal deficit:* Insufficient vaginal engorgement and lubrication making penetration difficult and/or unpleasant. Sympathetic overarousal interferes with parasympathetic vasocongestion.
Premature ejaculation: Ejaculation occurs "too quickly" or with minimal stimulation. Sympathetic overarousal hastens the ejaculatory reflex.	No female counterpart. Although rapid orgasm may occur due to sympathetic overarousal, the nature of female orgasmic capacity allows for the continuation of sexual stimulation. Thus, rapid orgasm is rarely identified as a problem.
Retarded ejaculation (ejaculatory incompetence): Ejaculation fails to occur or is very difficult to achieve despite prolonged stimulation. Inability to release orgasmic reflex from cortical control.	*Orgasmic dysfunction:* Orgasm fails to occur or is very difficult to achieve despite prolonged stimulation. Inability to release orgasmic reflex from cortical control.

ner. Here again there is great variation. Some men ejaculate when merely anticipating sexual opportunity. Ejaculation may occur during the preliminaries to intercourse (when such was not the intention of either party), or during attempts to insert the penis into the vagina. More often, the man is able to begin intercourse, but consistently ejaculates almost immediately, long before his partner has achieved satisfaction. The refractory period that follows the man's orgasm then often necessitates an interruption of intercourse, and may leave both partners feeling unfulfilled even if other means are used to bring the woman to orgasm.

A much rarer condition than either erectile failure or premature ejaculation is that of **retarded ejaculation** (also known as **ejaculatory incompetence**). The man with retarded ejaculation experiences difficulty in achieving ejaculation despite prolonged stimulation. Most often this ejaculatory problem is confined to intercourse: the male's orgasm may be very long in arriving, or it may not occur at all despite thirty to sixty minutes of con-

tinual thrusting. Usually, the male is capable of reaching orgasm through other types of stimulation, but cases have been reported of men who had *never* ejaculated, even during masturbation (for instance, Masters & Johnson, 1970; Newell, 1976). The line that separates the long-lasting "sexual athlete" from the retarded ejaculator is difficult to define, but the man who reports a persistent *inability* to ejaculate before he and his partner are forced to give up from soreness and exasperation is rarely proud of his stamina.

Female Sexual Dysfunctions

The most common disorders of female sexual function are those that have traditionally fallen under the humiliating label of "frigidity." Actually, at least two problems can be identified that receive this tag: Sexual arousal deficit and orgasmic dysfunction. **Sexual arousal deficit** may refer to an inhibition of the responses characteristic of the excitement phase of sexual response, most notably vasocongestion and lubrication. Great variation exists in the degree to which these responses may be impaired. The completely unresponsive woman—one who experiences no genital change during sexual stimulation—appears to be very rare. More common is the woman who does not lubricate sufficiently to allow comfortable penetration and coitus. This condition is usually but not always accompanied by subjective feelings of unresponsiveness to or displeasure with sexual activity. Although it must be stressed that women vary greatly in the amount of vaginal lubrication they produce, and that physical factors may impair this process, such arousal deficits are usually psychogenic in origin.

The most common female sexual problem is **orgasmic dysfunction,** which refers to an inability or difficulty in achieving orgasm. This problem may be general (the woman never or rarely reaches orgasm through any type of stimulation) or, more often, situational (the woman is inorgasmic during coitus, but not during oral stimulation or other kinds of stimulation). Coital inorgasmia is extraordinarily prevalent; for example, about 70 percent of the 3,000 women polled by Shere Hite (1976) reported difficulty achieving orgasm during intercourse. If, as these results suggest, a clear majority of women are not regularly orgasmic during intercourse, there is good reason to question whether coital inorgasmia can reasonably be thought of as a *dysfunction.* Some women are capable of experiencing orgasm through breast stimulation alone—but no one has suggested that the many women who cannot are dysfunctional. To automatically label coital inorgasmia a "problem" would seem to place an unnecessary burden of anxiety and doubt on the woman who is otherwise satisfied with her sexual functioning. We will return to this point later.

A much rarer condition is that of **vaginismus.** This refers to an involuntary spastic contraction of the outer third of the vagina, making penile penetration very difficult or impossible; attempts at intercourse are usually painful for the woman. Vaginismus usually occurs when penetration is attempted, and may be so severe that the vagina closes completely. Masters and Johnson (1970) have stressed the fact that vaginismus can be diagnosed positively only through a vaginal examination.

Conceptualizations

The factors that produce sexual dysfunction are as varied as the persons afflicted by them. Difficulties in the nonsexual aspects of the person's or couple's life, ignorance of sexual functioning and consequent technique difficulties, and preferences for alternate styles of sexual stimulation (for instance, homosexuality, fetishism) can all have an adverse effect on heterosexual responsiveness. But many experts feel that one of the greatest deterrents to natural sexual functioning is *anxiety* (Kaplan, 1974, 1975; Masters & Johnson, 1970; Wolpe, 1958, 1969; Wolpe & Lazarus, 1966).

Drawing on our understanding of anxiety from Chapter 10, we can see why anxiety might act as a deterrent. Remember that anxiety is accompanied by sympathetic activation, and that the sympathetic and parasympathetic branches of the ANS are mutually antagonistic. If anxiety is present during the excitement phase of sexual arousal, it may override the parasympathetic activation necessary for vasocongestion. Thus, the male may suffer an erectile failure, and the female may experience insufficient lubrication—that is, sexual arousal deficit. Increased sympathetic arousal due to anxiety has a different effect on the plateau level of sexual response. Since activation shifts from the parasympathetic to the sympathetic system as the response cycle moves from excitement to plateau, an excess of sympathetic involvement may serve to prematurely trigger orgasm, a sympathetic reflex. For the male, this produces premature ejaculation, and sexual stimulation must be discontinued until he recovers from his refractory period. In the woman, sympathetic overarousal may also produce a "premature" orgasm. But since she is able to continue and possibly experience other orgasms, this is not likely to be seen as a problem—in fact, it may even be seen as desirable.

A knowledge of nervous system functioning in anxiety and in sexual response thus provides us with a way of understanding erectile failure and premature ejaculation in the male, and arousal deficits in the female. However, the conceptualization is incomplete. We do not know why anxiety should produce excitement-phase problems in some persons and plateau-phase problems in others. We can only speculate that the parasympathetic activation during sexual excitement may be strong enough in some people to locally (that is, genitally) override sympathetic effects; but that sympathetic arousal then serves to speed the shift from excitement to plateau to orgasm.

Even more troublesome for our conceptualization are the problems of retarded ejaculation and orgasmic dysfunction. If these are indeed analogous dysfunctions, why is retarded ejaculation so rare and orgasmic dysfunction so common? One of the major reasons is that most of the commonly used coital positions, although highly stimulating to the man, are not very stimulating to the woman (Kaplan, 1975). Intercourse provides the woman with only indirect stimulation of the clitoris (Masters & Johnson, 1966; Sadock & Sadock, 1976), but most women prefer more direct stimulation of the clitoral area and seem far more easily orgasmic with such activity (Fisher, 1973; Hite, 1976; Masters & Johnson, 1966). Thus, most cases of "orgasmic dysfunction" may not be dysfunctions at all, but simply variations in sexual responsiveness. If we eliminate from consideration those women who are inorgasmic coitally, but are orgasmic through other means, the prevalence of true "orgasmic dysfunction" appears to be quite low.

How do we then explain the small proportion of men and women who have difficulty reaching orgasm despite "proper" stimulation? Anxiety and sympathetic arousal, although they may well be present, do not seem to be the key. It is clear that higher brain activity moderates sexual response, and both retarded ejaculation and true orgasmic dysfunction may be the result of higher-level psychological processes that override any other factors that may be in operation. Masters and Johnson (1970) found the early histories of men and women suffering from profound orgasmic inhibition to be dominated by extreme antisexual parental and/or religious training. Some individuals were severely punished for such activities as masturbation and nocturnal emission, or were continually assured of the terrifying personal and moral consequences of sexual pleasure. Additionally, a few men had consciously practiced ejaculatory control for contraceptive or other reasons,

only to find themselves unable to cast off the habit later on. Some individuals are uncomfortable about "losing control" and experiencing orgasm in the presence of their partners. Others actively "try for" an orgasm rather than simply allowing it to occur naturally.

The unifying theme in many of these cases appears to be that the individuals have developed a habit of closely monitoring their sexual response —so closely, in fact, that they unwittingly inhibit their orgasmic reflex (Kaplan, 1974, 1975). Other examples of the inability to release a reflex from cortical control are numerous: Have you ever tried so hard to swallow a pill that you could not do it (and the foul-tasting medicine dissolved in your mouth)? It is not unusual to find persons who concentrate so intently on urinating or defecating that they find themselves temporarily unable to do so. At this moment, if you concentrate on your breathing, you will find that it becomes irregular and feels unnatural. There are some things that the body does best when left alone, without conscious effort—orgasm is one of them.

Vaginismus usually seems to function as an avoidance response. Unfortunate circumstances in the woman's past have led her to fear sex—particularly coitus—and she develops a powerful involuntary vaginal spasm that prevents penetration. Strict religious training that induces apprehension about sexual activity appears to be a frequent precursor of vaginismus. Physical problems that produce painful intercourse, experience with males who are inexperienced or inept at making careful insertion, and acute sexual traumas like rape also appear to be prominent causes of vaginismus (Masters & Johnson, 1970).

Table 11–1 summarizes our discussion of some of the causes of sexual dysfunctions. Undoubtedly, our presentation oversimplifies the complexities of these problems. Furthermore, the data supporting these conceptualizations are inferential, correlational, and based on clinical observation rather than controlled experimentation. We have far to go before we can be very confident of our ability to understand sexual dysfunctions. However, these conceptualizations do provide us with a framework for understanding a number of therapeutic strategies, to which we turn next.

BEHAVIORAL SEX THERAPY

The traditional approach to the treatment of sexual dysfunction is exactly the same as the traditional approach to the treatment of every other psychological problem—the therapist talks with the client, delving into the "unconscious" origins of the problem and bringing them to consciousness. Eventually, the client has "insight" into the problem, and when the conflicts are fully "worked through," the sexual problem disappears. As we mentioned, traditional psychotherapeutic approaches have had little success with sexual difficulties.

Behaviorally oriented sexual therapy is much more active in nature. Discussions between the client(s) and therapist(s) are typically precursors to homework assignments that involve changes in sexual behavior. Except for the small percentage of cases in which physical factors are important, sexual problems are seen as resulting from anxiety, deficits in skills or communication, ignorance or misunderstanding of sexual functioning, or some combination of these. The overriding principle on which all therapy for sexual dysfunction is predicated is that of successive approximation. This principle is the theme of behavioral sex therapy, and almost all else is but a variation.

Although Joseph Wolpe's (1954, 1958; Wolpe & Lazarus, 1966) contribution as a pioneer in this area is rarely acknowledged, he laid the groundwork and developed many of the procedures that are now widely employed in the so-called new sex therapy (Kaplan, 1974; Masters & Johnson, 1975). Wolpe spoke of sexual dysfunctions as resulting from anxiety conditioned to sexual stimuli or sexual performance; he noted that sexual arousal, like relaxation responses, was capable of reciprocally inhibiting anxiety. His attempts to use sexual arousal to counter anxiety led him to develop strategies involving performance prohibitions and graduated sexual interactions that are now basic to Masters and Johnson's well-known approach. Wolpe was successfully using this approach before Masters launched his initial research into sexual functioning in 1954. In addition, Wolpe had other powerful anxiety-reducing techniques (for example, systematic desensitization) at his disposal that, as of yet, have not been incorporated into Masters-and-Johnson-type programs.

The Masters and Johnson Approach

Nevertheless, the most widely recognized and respected approach to sexual dysfunction is that expounded by Masters and Johnson in their important contribution *Human Sexual Inadequacy* (1970). The treatment program they developed, based on groundbreaking research into sexual response, is both rapid and intensive: the client or couple spend two weeks in daily contact with the therapists and in structured sexual experiences. At the core of the Masters and Johnson program are several basic concepts that, in their opinion, are inviolable in the conduct of sex therapy. The first of these concerns treating a sexual couple (married or otherwise) as a *unit*, even though it may be clear that only one member of the couple is experiencing difficulty. According to Masters and Johnson (1970), "there is no such thing as an uninvolved partner in any [relationship] in which there is some form of sexual inadequacy" (p. 2). This statement does not necessarily mean that the functional member of the couple has in some way caused or contributed to the dysfunctional member's problem (although this may well be the case). Rather, it means that since a sexual relationship is by nature interactional, a dysfunction in one member is a problem for *both*. It follows that the most effective treatment approach would involve both individuals.

Securing the cooperation of a partner was considered crucial by Masters and Johnson, and a number of dysfunctional men who were unmarried and unable to supply other partners were provided with **surrogate partners.** The surrogate partners were women who had volunteered for this assignment, who had passed extensive screening interviews, and with whom the therapists felt they could work comfortably. Wolpe and Lazarus (1966) had previously recommended enlisting the help of an intelligent and sympathetic prostitute when working with sexually deficient men. (The fact that providing male surrogates to females without partners is rarely if ever mentioned stands as a glaring double standard in a field that is otherwise fairly self-conscious with regard to sexism.) Although the use of surrogate partners is a popular concept among professionals who deal with sexual problems, the practice is not widespread (Jacobs, Thompson, & Truxaw, 1975; Malamuth, Wanderer, Sayner, & Durrell, 1976) primarily because of the legal questions that have been raised (LeRoy, 1971). Masters and Johnson decided to discontinue their surrogate program after becoming involved in a lawsuit.

A second basic concept of the Masters and Johnson approach is the use of a *dual-sex cotherapist team*. They assume that no man can ever fully understand and appreciate a woman's sexual experience, and vice versa; thus the dual-sex cotherapy format allows those directing treatment to more fully grasp the subjective sensations, concerns, and emotions of *both* members of the client couple. The use of male and female cotherapists also contributes to the clients' comfort and decreases the chance of the client who does not have a same-sex therapist feeling "ganged up on" by his or her partner and the therapist, a situation that may occur when therapy is conducted by a single therapist. Although other clinicians endorse the dual-sex cotherapist format (for instance, Lobitz & LoPiccolo, 1972; Fordney-Settlage, 1975), there is no convincing evidence that such a procedure is mandatory for successful treatment. The case reports of other professionals (for instance, Kaplan, 1974; Wolpe, 1958; Wolpe & Lazarus, 1966) as well as the personal experience of the authors indicate that a sensitive and informed clinician of either sex can closely approximate the facilitative atmosphere of the cotherapy process.

Masters and Johnson assert that sexual response is a *natural function*. Whereas sexual *behavior* is learned, sexual *responses* are reflexive in nature, although they can be moderated by countless psychological and physical factors. In fact, these factors can moderate sexual responses right out of existence. Sexual dysfunction is not the result of faulty learning of sexual responses; rather, it represents the inhibition of a natural process by incompatible emotions, or the failure of the reflexes due to ignorance of the ways in which they are stimulated (that is, skills deficits). Masters and Johnson write (1975, p. 549):

Many individuals seek counseling on the assumption that there are reliable methods of teaching sexual response. This is not quite accurate. What does exist is the possibility of identifying the obstacles to effective sexual functioning that have removed sex from its natural context and suggesting ways to alleviate and/or circumvent these obstacles. Similarly, attitudes, behavior, and emotional environments conducive to individual sexual response can be identified and encouraged. When this is done, natural function usually takes over with surprising ease.

It is important that the couple understand that sexual response is a natural function, and that they discard any erroneous or self-deprecating notions they may have about their problem. Thus, an important part of Masters and Johnson's intensive program is the *roundtable discussion* that takes place following the extensive medical and historical assessment of the clients. In the discussion, the cotherapists integrate all the diagnostic information and present to the couple a conceptualization of the origin and the current status of the problem. Clients are encouraged to question and correct the interpretation in order to have a complete understanding of the nature of their difficulty. The manner in which environmental, psychological, and, occasionally, physiological factors have conspired to interfere with sexual functioning is explained. The therapists emphasize again that the *relationship* itself is the client, not either individual. After the clients understand the therapists' conceptualization and feel comfortable with the general treatment strategy, therapeutic homework assignments are begun.

Performance Anxiety and Communication Deficits

Two factors that are invariably identified in the roundtable discussion as enemies of sexual functioning are **performance anxiety** and **communication deficits.** Performance anxiety typically becomes a problem when the individual "steps out" of the sexual interaction to observe and evaluate his or her own performance. Masters and Johnson (1970) call this "spectatoring." Instead of relaxing, becoming involved in the sexual stimulation, and allowing natural responses to take over, the person is distracted by apprehension and doubt: "Will I have an erection/orgasm?" "Do I look all right?" "How am I doing?" This barrage of questions engenders anxiety and also makes it difficult for the person to attend to any incoming sensual stimulation. The result is likely to be a dysfunction of some sort, like an erectile failure or an orgasmic dysfunction. Once a dysfunction has occurred, performance anxiety becomes a vicious cycle: the individual worries about the problem occurring, which increases the likelihood that it will, which creates even more worry next time, and so on.

Using the terminology introduced in Chapter 10, we may consider sexual anxiety to be of two general types: reactive and conditioned. Performance anxiety, as we have just described it, is clearly reactive in nature. The individual's constant self-evaluation; failure to relax and attend to his or her partner's stimulation; perception of sex as totally "goal oriented" (that is, orgasm) rather than enjoyable on a moment-to-moment basis; and lack of straightforward communication with his or her partner about likes and dislikes result in the sexual situation being stressful instead of pleasurable. Obviously, such a person would benefit greatly from learning a number of skills. However, performance anxiety may also have a conditioned component. The continued evocation of reactive anxiety in sexual situations may have conditioned anxiety to sexual performance, or to any of a variety of sexual stimuli. Or the conditioned anxiety may have its roots in some other aspect of the person's history. Sexual behavior—masturbation, for example—may have been severely punished in childhood, and anxiety is now elicited by sexual arousal itself.

No less a problem is that of deficient communication between sexual partners. Sexual stimulation is a highly individual matter, and "good technique" is more an ability to learn what feels pleasurable to one's partner than a memorized list of erogenous zones or a set of elaborate coital movements. Learning something about another's private experience requires communication. Often, however, people find explicit communication about sexual likes and dislikes far more difficult than sexual behavior itself, with the result that the experience is many times less enjoy-

able than it might be. Embarrassment or fear of rejection from a partner prevents many people from frankly expressing their sexual preferences. Requesting changes in a lover's stimulatory techniques is often made difficult by a fear of making the partner feel stupid or clumsy. Once a pattern of noncommunication or well-intentioned lying ("*Of course* I love the way you bite my nose . . .") is developed, it may be extremely hard to change.

Sensate Focus

When performance anxiety and/or communication deficits are present, the first step in treatment is usually an in vivo desensitization and communication training technique known as **sensate focus** (Masters & Johnson, 1970) or **pleasuring** (Kaplan, 1975). Wolpe (1958, 1969; Wolpe & Lazarus, 1966) first employed this approach in the treatment of sexual dysfunction, but Masters and Johnson (1970) elaborated and popularized it. Although the conduct of sensate focus varies somewhat from author to author (e.g., Kaplan, 1974, 1975; Masters & Johnson, 1970; Wolpe & Lazarus, 1966), the following can be considered a general strategy.

The couple, at some comfortable, quiet time, climb into bed together nude and begin to explore each other's bodies in whatever way they find pleasurable. To discourage a goal-oriented focus, and to eliminate any demand or expectations to "perform," specific sexual stimulation is prohibited. The woman's breasts and the genitals of both partners are "off limits" for the sensual massage, and intercourse is forbidden. Under these conditions, neither partner is under any pressure, either explicit or implicit, to become sexually aroused or to perform "adequately"; thus, anxiety about performance should be minimized. The couple's task is simply to give and receive pleasure, and to practice *communicating* clearly and affectionately about what they find pleasurable.

Very often the partners are asked to alternately assume the roles of "giver" and "receiver." The receiver's only responsibility is to focus on the sensations provided by the partner's caresses, and to communicate likes, dislikes, and suggestions to the giver. The receiver is to be totally "selfish" during his or her turn—to be concerned only with his or her own pleasure. The giver's sole task, on the other hand, is to experiment with ways of pleasuring the partner. He or she may stroke, massage, and nuzzle the partner in a variety of ways, while attending closely to the verbal and nonverbal feedback he or she receives. Both partners have one additional instruction: to stop whatever they are doing whenever they feel any anxiety, and to relax and wait for the tension to dissipate before resuming. This aspect of the process can be facilitated by training the client(s) in some form of relaxation that they can use in vivo.

Once the couple (particularly the dysfunctional member) reports feeling completely comfortable during these pleasuring sessions, and the therapist judges their communication to be sufficiently improved, the next phase of sensate focus is begun. At this point, the pleasuring exercises are broadened to include manual (and oral, if the clients enjoy this) stimulation of the genitals. Depending on the therapist's judgment of the clients' progress, orgasm may still be discouraged to reduce performance demand and to deemphasize orgasm as the goal of sexual interaction. The partners now gain practice in genital pleasuring and in the communication of specifically sexual feelings. The basic rule—stop and relax when feeling anxious—is still in effect. The giver and receiver roles may be maintained, or they may be abandoned in favor of more spontaneous, mutual stimulation. The specific exercises carried out may differ from couple to couple, depending on the nature and type of dysfunction present. We will examine these variations and the subsequent treatment sequences in the next section on specific dysfunctions. However, it is important to note that the initial sensate focus exercises that we have just described usually constitute the preface to *any* sexual treatment.

Although the sensate focus exercises are intended only as a preliminary strategy, they occasionally have a profound effect on sexual deficits. The performance prohibition often eliminates the dysfunctional individuals' tendency to monitor their sexual response, thereby allowing natural functioning to take over. It is not entirely unusual for couples to experience such an overwhelming return of sexual feelings and response that they "break training" and engage in intercourse

despite instructions to the contrary. This does not mean that treatment is successfully terminated at this point. Many of the lessons sensate focus was intended to teach have been short-circuited and still need to be taught if the dysfunction is not to return. Still, such an event usually has the very positive effect of providing the couple with a pleasurable and reassuring sexual experience—perhaps their first in years. It provides relief, and it instills confidence in the therapist(s) and motivation to continue with treatment. More often, of course, sensate focus does exactly what it was designed to do—it allows the couple to take that first, long step toward the return of pleasant, natural sexual functioning.

The sensate focus approach suffers from two major limitations. First, and most obvious, is the fact that it requires *two people* in order to work. The dysfunctional individual who is without a cooperative partner cannot benefit from sensate focus. Second, even the relatively low-level responses required in the initial phases of sensate focus may be far too anxiety-provoking for persons with strong conditioned reactions to sexual stimuli. In the case of such intense anxiety reactions, an in vivo desensitization program can be developed that begins well before the point of nude sex play. Handholding, kissing, and light petting while fully clothed are potentially more successful starting points.

However, when anxiety is this severe, imaginal systematic desensitization is often a more efficient strategy. Desensitization can then be augmented by structured sexual experience. The use of desensitization for anxiety too severe to be dealt with in vivo is illustrated by Wolpe (1969):

A . . . commonplace case was that of a woman who had from puberty had an anxious revulsion against sex. She had nevertheless married, and had borne four children in six years, because being pregnant was a "defense" against sex. She had been treated by various methods, including drugs and electro-shock treatment. Her psychiatrist, not a behavior therapist, had then decided to try systematic desensitization. This had been a fiasco, because the weakest item, the sight of naked female breasts, was far too anxiety-provoking. When he had presented this image to her it had produced such a severe anxiety reaction that it was impossible to go on with the treatment. When he referred her to me, I found it necessary to start at a much more remote point. The first scene I asked her to imagine was being at a swimming pool where there was only one male present, *50 yards away, with his bare chest exposed.* This man was later brought progressively closer. Next, we utilized, first at a distance of 50 yards and then closer, a completely nude male statue in a park. A later item in the hierarchy was seeing a little nude boy of four gambolling in a swimming pool. Eventually, after many steps, she was successfully desensitized to such images as dogs fornicating, French pictures of nude males, four-letter words, and, finally, personal coital contingencies. It became possible for her to indulge in and enjoy sexual intercourse with her husband. (p. 87, italics added)

MALE DYSFUNCTIONS: SPECIFIC TREATMENT STRATEGIES

Our discussion of problem-specific strategies for the treatment of both male and female dysfunctions is based on the programs of Masters and Johnson (1970). Modifications of their procedures that have been suggested by other authors and by our own clinical experience will be incorporated where relevant.

Erectile Failure

The early sensate focus exercises often result in considerable anxiety reduction in the dysfunctional man, and spontaneous erections may have already occurred. Regardless, when both partners feel completely comfortable with nongenital sensate focus, genital pleasuring is begun. Although the give-and-take concept is still in operation, the stimulation of the male is the aspect with which we are most concerned in this discussion. The couple assumes a relaxed position, and the woman experiments with various ways of stimulating the man's body and penis. Oils or other lubricants may be employed, and oral stimulation often proves extremely arousing to the male. The man is directed to immerse himself in the stimulation provided by his partner, but he is *not* to scrutinize his erectile response. If he re-

mains relaxed and merely enjoys his partner's fondling, erection will usually occur quite naturally.

Men who have been plagued by erectile failure are often only half relieved when they achieve an erection during genital pleasuring. An additional worry remains, namely, "What if I *lose* it?" This fear is dealt with paradoxically by deliberate attempts to *diminish* the erection. Once the man's penis becomes fully erect, the woman stops her pleasuring for several moments until the erection abates. Then she manipulates him to another erection. This "teasing" approach to stimulation is not only very erotic, but it teaches the man that an erection that disappears is not gone forever. Repetition of this stop-start procedure helps to reinstate the male's confidence. At this point, manual and/or oral genital pleasuring may be extended to orgasm for both partners so that the prolonged high levels of sexual tension do not make the exercises aversive.

When erection becomes a reliable phenomenon, and the couple feels ready to proceed, vaginal penetration in a **female superior position** (Figure 11–3) may be attempted. This position is used because it places minimal performance demands on the man, and allows the woman the freedom of movement necessary for subsequent procedures. The woman first straddles the man and manipulates him to a full erection. Then, in a nondemanding, unhurried fashion, she moves back on to the penis, guiding it into her vagina. The woman *always* handles the insertion process. Many an erection has been lost while a man sought the vaginal opening; the woman, on the other hand, knows precisely where the penis goes, and much anxiety is eliminated by her controlling this operation. Once insertion is completed, the woman rests quietly with the man inside her, moving only enough to enable the man to maintain his erection. Vigorous thrusting may be threatening to a man who is unsure of his erection, so this is delayed until he feels comfortable with vaginal containment. If the man loses full erection during insertion or containment, the woman simply dismounts, reinstates erection by gentle manual stimulation, and mounts again when a secure erection has been achieved.

If the man remains erect intravaginally, a stop-

Figure 11–3. Female superior coital position.

start procedure identical to that used in genital pleasuring is begun. The woman withdraws the penis after a short time and allows the erection to abate. She then restimulates the man and again inserts the penis. Only after this sequence has been successfully repeated several times is the couple allowed to proceed to orgasm. When intravaginal erection seems secure, the woman may gradually increase her thrusting to bring the man to orgasm. If she has not herself reached orgasm, noncoital sex play can be continued. If the man is having any erectile difficulty or has any hesitancy about ejaculating intravaginally, orgasm should be achieved by another means.

The final stages of treatment for erectile failure involve a gradual progression to more vigorous coital movements, with the man taking a more active role in thrusting as he becomes more confident about erectile security. Eventually, the fe-

male superior position may be abandoned in favor of other positions that place more demand on the male, although many couples continue to use the female superior position from time to time.

Premature Ejaculation

The treatment of premature ejaculation generally follows that of erectile failure, but with some important added features. We have conceptualized premature ejaculation as primarily a problem of anxiety. The preliminary sensate focus exercises serve to reduce some of this anxiety while building communication skills that will be valuable later in treatment. However, since the real problem seems to be the influence of anxiety at later stages of sexual performance, genital pleasuring may be included earlier in the treatment plan.

Genital pleasuring in the case of premature ejaculation aims at the establishment of ejaculatory control, and is somewhat different from that used in treating erectile failure. In the nondemand position, the woman masturbates the man while he concentrates on his sexual feelings and communicates these to her. When the man feels himself *nearing* the point of ejaculatory imminence, he tells his partner, and she stops her manipulation until his urge to ejaculate passes (Semans, 1956); then she resumes. This **stop-start procedure** is repeated four or five times before the man is allowed to ejaculate.

Masters and Johnson (1970) introduced a modification of stop-start known as the **squeeze technique** that is more reliable in inhibiting the ejaculatory reflex. When the man reports being close to orgasm, his partner stops her manipulation and firmly squeezes the penis just below the glans with her thumb and middle finger for three to four seconds (see Figure 11-4). This immediately abolishes the man's urge to ejaculate, and often results in a partial loss of erection. Stimulation is resumed fifteen to thirty seconds later, and the procedure is repeated several more times. (Note: the squeeze technique is only used when the male has a full erection. Its use at other times is very

painful and potentially injurious.) Continued practice of the stop-start and/or squeeze technique results in the man's developing an increasing tolerance of sexual stimulation, with his ejaculatory urge becoming more and more delayed. At this point, lubricants may be introduced into the sex play to more closely approximate the feel of the vaginal environment.

When extravaginal ejaculatory control has been established, female superior coitus is attempted. Thrusting is avoided at first, the object being for the man simply to become accustomed to the feel of vaginal insertion and containment. The woman dismounts and applies the squeeze whenever the man feels his ejaculatory control slipping. Eventually, an extended period of vaginal containment with complete ejaculatory control can be realized. On subsequent occasions, gentle movement is begun and ejaculation is delayed through stop-start and the squeeze. As the man's control becomes increasingly secure, more stimulating thrusting is encouraged. The man should always try to delay ejaculation until after an extended period (ten to twenty minutes) of coitus.

The final step in the alleviation of premature ejaculation involves a shift to the **lateral coital po-**

Figure 11–4. The "squeeze technique."

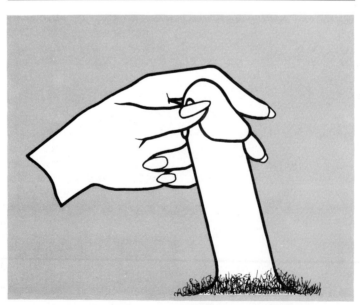

sition (Figure 11–5). In the lateral coital position, the man is free to thrust as much or as little as he wishes to maintain ejaculatory control without the very strong stimulation that is provided in the common male superior ("missionary") position. The woman too enjoys a unique freedom of movement, without the strain and restriction inherent in many other coital positions. Thus, she is able to carefully regulate her movements according to her partner's level of excitement. In the lateral coital position, the couple can gradually extend the male's ability to control ejaculation. When a satisfactory coital duration has been achieved in the lateral position, the partners may choose to experiment with other positions. However, Masters and Johnson (1970) found that most of the couples they introduced to the lateral position continued to prefer it after treatment was finished.

Retarded Ejaculation

As might be expected, the treatment of retarded ejaculation differs fundamentally from the strategies employed for erectile failure and premature ejaculation. After performance fears have been reduced, and communication increased by sensate focus exercises, the next goal in the treatment of the retarded ejaculator is the prompting of orgasm by some means. In most cases, a demanding masturbation of the male by the female using a lubricant will eventually produce the desired effect. In more obstinate cases the presence of the woman is an inhibitory factor, and the male may have to manipulate himself to orgasm, at first alone, and then with his partner gradually taking a more active role (Kaplan, 1975). In extreme cases, normal masturbatory excitation is insufficient, and the intense stimulation of an electric vibrator may be required (for instance, Newell, 1976; Schellen, 1968). It is important to note that there is no rush in producing ejaculation. Performance demands are to be avoided here as much as in other treatments. However, techniques that provide maximal stimulation are clearly favored. Once ejaculation is reliably established, the strength of the stimulation can gradually be cut back to more nominal levels. Eventually the male's orgasm should be readily produced by his partner's manual excitation.

Figure 11–5. The lateral coital position.

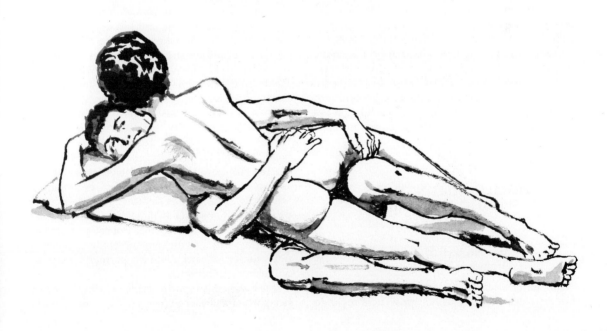

To the extent that the retarded ejaculator has a problem with monitoring his sexual response, it is often useful to find ways of distracting him during manipulation so that his ejaculatory reflex can take over normally (Kaplan, 1975). To this end, it may be useful to have the client immerse himself in what his *partner* is doing, or in an arousing fantasy while he is being stimulated. Erotic literature or photographs can even be employed. Later these aids can be withdrawn.

When the male's orgasm can be regularly achieved through his partner's manipulation, the next step is intravaginal ejaculation. Depending on the tenacity of the problem and the man's comfort, this step can be taken more or less slowly. In severe cases, it may be necessary for the woman to first manually bring the male to orgasm when his penis is near but still outside the vaginal entrance. Then the transition between extravaginal and intravaginal ejaculation is usually made by the woman's manually stimulating the male while astride him in the superior position. When the man indicates that his orgasm is imminent, his partner quickly guides him into her vagina and thrusts forcefully until he ejaculates. When this maneuver has successfully produced intravaginal ejaculations on several occasions, the amount of precoital manual stimulation provided by the woman is gradually reduced and insertion is accomplished slightly earlier on each subsequent occasion. As manual prestimulation assumes a lesser role, the couple may abandon the female superior position in favor of ones that provide more intense stimulation for the male (for instance, male superior with the female's legs held close together). These stimulation-enhancing techniques are gradually faded as intravaginal ejaculation becomes firmly established, until a more "normal" coital experience is sufficient to produce orgasm.

FEMALE DYSFUNCTIONS: SPECIFIC TREATMENT STRATEGIES

Sexual Arousal Deficits and Orgasmic Dysfunction

Although arousal deficits and orgasmic dysfunction may differ conceptually, few writers separate the two problems, and existing treatment procedures aim at both enhancing sexual arousal and establishing orgasmic response. We will therefore discuss a general approach to these problems, while stressing the procedural variations that seem appropriate to each.

For Masters and Johnson (1970), nongenital sensate focus is the first step in the treatment of the woman with an arousal deficit or an orgasmic dysfunction. However, other therapists find that a program of **directed masturbation** may be a useful precursor or adjunct to sensate focus. A systematic masturbation program can be a rich source of self-discovery to the dysfunctional woman and can allow her to become acquainted with her own sexual feelings in a "safe" atmosphere, away from the scrutiny of her partner. Joseph LoPiccolo and Charles Lobitz (1972) have developed just such a program. It begins with the client merely examining her body and genitals with the aid of a hand mirror. She is furnished with a set of diagrams of female pelvic anatomy and asked to identify various features on her own body. This exercise not only serves an educative function, it also allows the woman to become aware of any negative feelings she has about her body that might be playing a role in her unresponsiveness.

The next step in the program involves the client exploring herself tactually. To avoid performance demands, the client is not left with the expectation that she should become aroused during this self-exploration. She is asked merely to attend to the various sensations she produces and to identify areas that yield pleasurable feelings when stimulated. In the next phase, these areas are made the focus of increasingly intense stimulation. The woman is asked to masturbate until "something happens," or until she becomes tired or uncomfortable. If the woman does not experience orgasm through this activity, she is asked to use an electric vibrator. Even with the vibrator, achieving an orgasm may take time, but eventually it will occur. The woman's partner can then join the process as an observer so that the woman becomes desensitized to experiencing arousal and orgasm in his presence. At the same time, the man has an opportunity to learn about his partner's preferred stimulatory techniques.

If the woman's orgasm seems to be inhibited by her partner's presence, she may be asked to *role play an orgasm* (Lobitz & LoPiccolo, 1972). The purpose of this is not to deceive the male, since it is done with his knowledge and cooperation. Instead, the procedure is intended to reduce the woman's fears of "losing control" and displaying strong sexual arousal. The woman is asked to role play the wildest, most intense orgasm she can possibly imagine, replete with violent convulsions, gasps, moans, and screams. In this way, she gains some experience with losing control, while actually remaining very much in control.

With repetitions of the role play, the woman and her partner should lose their anxiety and instead begin to feel amusement or even boredom. The exaggerated nature of the ersatz orgasm makes the real thing comparatively less frightening. The realization that she could not possibly do anything as startling as she has already done can help the woman relax and abandon her controls when a real climax approaches. She may even be surprised by an honest-to-goodness orgasm in the midst of one of her rehearsals.

In cases in which the woman's goal is to be able to reach orgasm through coital stimulation, the directed masturbation exercises can be supplemented by the use of a dildo or any other safe penislike object (Zeiss, Rosen, & Zeiss, 1977). Using a dildo allows the woman to become familiar with the sensations of vaginal containment and thrusting without the anxiety that may be provoked by the presence of her partner. At first the woman should merely experiment with the feelings produced by insertion of the dildo. Later, she may bring herself to orgasm through her preferred masturbatory techniques while imitating penile thrusting with the dildo. This process permits the feelings of vaginal containment to become associated with increased arousal and orgasm. Eventually the woman can fade out other stimulation and rely increasingly on the movements of the dildo to produce orgasm. If the woman feels comfortable, the man can join the process as an observer. This provides him with an excellent opportunity to learn the type of penile movements that are most stimulating to his partner.

Eventually, the man takes an active role in his partner's stimulation, and here the independent masturbation program merges with the lovemaking exercises. The couple assumes a comfortable position, and the man stimulates the woman's breasts and genitals in the ways she finds pleasurable. If a dildo has been used previously, the man may now take control of it under the close direction of the woman. Role playing can be continued if the woman retains any inhibitions about having an orgasm through her partner's stimulation. Also, as in the case of the retarded ejaculator, the nonorgasmic woman may find some form of distraction helpful in preventing her from becoming a spectator to her own responses.

In time, with a relaxed, nondemanding approach, the woman should begin to respond with arousal and orgasm to her partner's manipulations. The couple can then experiment with intercourse. Following sufficient sex play for arousal in both partners, the woman mounts the man in the female superior position. At this point, therapeutic strategies may diverge, depending on the primary problem. If an arousal deficit is present, the woman may simply "play" with the penis in her vagina, moving slowly or simply resting quietly while concentrating on the sensations of penile containment. The penis is hers to enjoy in whatever manner she wishes. Her "selfishness" aids in the development of erotic sensation, and the nondemanding pace that she controls helps to relieve her anxiety. A stop-start approach may prove highly erotic to the woman, and certainly aids her partner in maintaining the prolonged ejaculatory control necessary for the procedure. The exercise continues until the woman has an orgasm, or until she tires and wants to stop. As the woman's arousal builds during repetitions of this procedure, the couple can begin to engage in more vigorous intercourse.

In the case of orgasmic dysfunction, the woman may decide that the pleasure she now derives from her partner's manual or oral stimulation is entirely satisfactory. However, she might also decide that coital orgasm is a reasonable and desirable goal. If this is true, and the woman's initial sexual arousal is unimpaired, a more stimulating coital procedure is usually employed. As in the treatment of the retarded ejaculator, the woman is brought to a high level of sexual excitement by her partner's manipulation, and coitus is begun only when her orgasm is imminent. The nature of the female orgasm makes this procedure somewhat less reliable than with the male; the woman's urge to have an orgasm or the orgasm itself may be lost during penile insertion. To facilitate this transition, manual clitoral stimulation can be continued by the man (or by the woman herself) *during* insertion and coital thrusting. In difficult cases, a vibrator may be used during intercourse to elevate clitoral sensation.

In every case, an attempt is made to discontinue the extra stimulation at the point of orgasmic inevitability, so that coital movements themselves actually trigger the orgasm. With increasing success, extra stimulation is halted gradually earlier and earlier during intercourse, and its intensity is slowly faded. If all goes well, the woman will eventually be able to reach orgasm during intercourse without directly augmenting the stimulation produced by penile thrusting. The purpose of this procedure is *not* to teach a "no hands" style of intercourse, but simply to make the woman more responsive to the specific stimulation provided by coital movements so that she can derive added pleasure from this form of sexual expression. Clearly, manual and oral stimulation, both before and during intercourse, remain extremely important to the maintenance of most women's (and men's) sexual enjoyment.

Vaginismus

Vaginismus may be a component of a more complex sexual problem, or it may be a relatively isolated response to attempts at vaginal penetration. Sensate focus and genital pleasuring can be useful in alleviating anticipatory anxiety that builds up during precoital lovemaking, but these procedures may well be unnecessary. Furthermore, when such strategies are indicated, it usually makes sense to apply them *after* the vaginal spasm has been relieved, rather than before. If the vaginal spasm is not eliminated first, its treatment will necessitate a costly interruption later in therapy. Thus, the treatment of vaginismus departs from the usual therapy sequence.

Vaginismus is treated in a straightforward successive approximation fashion. The woman is gradually taught to accommodate the insertion of very small objects into her vagina, and progressively larger objects are introduced as she becomes more comfortable with penetration. This process may be accomplished in several ways. If the vaginal spasm is severe and the woman is very fearful of penetration, she can begin treatment on her own. She may be supplied with a graduated series of smooth glass or rubber dilators that can be used in the privacy of her home. However, for convenience and for esthetic reasons, the client can use her own fingers in the dilation process (Kaplan, 1974, 1975). While observing her vaginal area in a mirror, the client gently inserts the tip of her little finger into the vaginal entrance. When she can do this comfortably, the entire finger is used. As treatment progresses, the woman repeats the process with her index finger, and later with two fingers.

At this point, the woman's partner can be included in the treatment. With the woman carefully guiding the man's hand, he follows the same sequence using his own fingers. Once the woman can experience the male's digital penetrations without anxiety or tension, penile insertion is attempted. A lubricant can be employed, and the woman controls penetration from the female superior position. When comfortable intercourse has been reliably established, further treatment for orgasmic problems can be undertaken in the usual manner, if necessary. In less severe cases of vaginismus, the woman's initial self-explorations may be unnecessary, and the male can be included in the treatment program from the beginning.

Problems in Implementation

Before turning to an evaluation of behavioral sex therapy, we must interject a note of caution regarding the treatment strategies just outlined. On paper, sex therapy appears to be simple and precise—almost mechanical in nature. In practice, this is rarely the case. Effective treatment of sexual dysfunction, like effective treatment of any other problem, requires all the skill and sensitivity the clinician can muster. Clients are not run through an inflexible "therapy machine." A particular treatment strategy must be tailored to meet the unique needs of each client. The rationale for each treatment component must be carefully explained, and the clients' feelings considered and explored. Procedures that may be embarrassing or offensive to some clients (masturbation, for example) might have to be modified, approached in small steps, or even abandoned and some substitute way of achieving the same goal found. When a problem in the clients' progress arises, the therapist must bring his or her technical skill and human understanding to bear to bring about a solution. The literature is deceptive: sex therapy is *not* easy. We have included an extended case report (Case Study 11–2) to give readers some idea of the complexity that is typical of such treatment.

EVALUATION OF BEHAVIORAL STRATEGIES

Masters and Johnson: Research

Masters and Johnson's approach to the treatment of sexual dysfunctions has been received with considerable enthusiasm, and a number of clinicians have reported success with programs based on their work (for instance, Kaplan, 1974; Lobitz, LoPiccolo, Lobitz, & Brockway, 1975; McGovern, Stewart, & LoPiccolo, 1975; see also Case Study 11–1). However, because developments in this area are of such recent origin, controlled outcome evaluations of Masters-and-Johnson-type retraining programs have not yet been published. The available data on the effectiveness of these methods consist of uncontrolled single- or multiple-case studies, some of which include measurement of treatment effects, but most of which are anecdotal in nature. This type of information does not allow for the establishment of cause-effect relationships between treatment procedures and therapeutic outcomes; instead, it permits only the formation of weak hypotheses about the effectiveness of the intervention (Paul, 1969).

Masters and Johnson (1970), for example, devote an entire chapter of their book to "Program Statistics." Table 11–2 summarizes the results of their intensive two-week treatment program, including data obtained on some of the subjects at five years' posttreatment. Although at first glance the data appear meaningful, numerous problems arise when attempts are made to interpret them. First, Masters and Johnson never specify the criteria by which a couple is considered to be a treatment

success or failure. With characteristic prolixity they state: "Initial failure is defined as indication that the two-week rapid treatment phase has failed to initiate reversal of the basic symptomatology of sexual dysfunction for which the unit was referred to the Foundation" (1970, pp. 352–353). But what constitutes sufficient "symptom reversal" to qualify as a success? How much symptom return must occur during followup for the couple to be considered overall failures? We should note that throughout their work, Masters and Johnson demonstrate a commendable tendency toward self-criticism and restraint, and the failure rates they cite are probably *overestimates*. Yet without an explanation of the criteria by which the therapeutic outcomes were evaluated, these percentages become almost meaningless.

Another significant problem is that readers are provided with only a gross description of the clients' complaints (such as "premature ejaculation" or "orgasmic dysfunction") rather than quantified data indicating just *how* dysfunctional these individuals were and *how much* they improved with treatment. The imprecise nature of Masters and Johnson's statistics places severe limitations on our understanding of the kinds of change (or lack of change) that took place in their couples.

Of course, the greatest difficulty with Masters and Johnson's data, and with all data of this type, is that the absence of crucial control groups makes it impossible to determine if the treatment was actually responsible for the improvements noted. Perhaps these individuals would have done just as well without any treatment—an unlikely, but nevertheless uncontrolled-for possibility. Or perhaps standard insight-oriented psychotherapy aimed specifically at the dysfunctional members of the dyads would have been equal or superior to the active retraining programs. Without proper control group comparisons, we cannot answer these questions with confidence, and the efficacy of the treatment approach remains very much in doubt.

Masters and Johnson: Anecdotal Support

Given the present lack of experimental support for the effectiveness of Masters and Johnson's methods, is there any reason to believe in the util-

Table 11–2. Summary of Masters and Johnson's Program Statistics

Dysfunction	Marital Units Referred for Treatment	Immediate Treatment Failure	Initial Failure Rate (%)	Treatment Reversal (Relapse)	Overall Failure Rate (%) Five-year Followup
Male					
Primary impotence (erectile failure in which vaginal penetration has never been accomplished)	32	13	40.6	0	40.6
Secondary impotence (erectile failure in which vaginal penetration has been successful on at least one occasion)	213	56	26.2	10	30.9
Premature ejaculation	186	4	2.2	1	2.7
Retarded ejaculation	17	3	17.6	0	17.6
Female					
Primary orgasmic dysfunction (orgasm has never been achieved by any means)	193	32	16.6	2	17.6
Situational orgasmic dysfunction (trouble achieving orgasm from specific type of stimulation, usually coital)	149	34	22.8	3	24.8
Vaginismus	29	0	0	—	—

Adapted from W. H. Masters & V. E. Johnson, *Human sexual inadequacy.* Boston: Little, Brown, 1970, p. 367. Used by permission of Little, Brown and the authors.

ity of these procedures? If viewed in a broader, less scientific, less hard-nosed perspective, *yes.* When we consider that as few as ten years ago, many sexual dysfunctions were considered almost intractable by existing therapeutic strategies, anecdotal reports of reasonably consistent treatment successes become quite impressive. Even the more optimistic reports of success from traditional approaches provide startling contrasts. For example, one survey of psychoanalytically oriented sex therapy reported a 77 percent "cure" rate for secondary impotence with *two years* of therapy, and that 25 percent of coitally inorgasmic women were "cured" after *three to five* years in treatment (O'Connor & Stern, 1972). Setting aside for the moment the question of the criteria for cure, these percentages are close to those produced by Mas-

ters and Johnson in only *two weeks of treatment!* The potential savings this represents in time, money, and human distress is incalculable. Of course, this kind of anecdotal support for therapeutic strategies cannot take the place of systematic experimental evaluation. But there is reason to look forward to the findings of future research with considerable optimism.

Improving the Approach

The basic Masters and Johnson strategies can undoubtedly be improved upon. Among the suggestions for revisions are the following:

1. The flexibility of the treatment procedures could be increased so that they could be more closely tailored to the particular needs of the cli-

ents. One way this can be facilitated is by viewing the treatment strategies within a general behavioral framework, rather than as a group of procedures unique unto themselves (Ascher & Clifford, 1976). In this way, when a certain aspect of the standard treatment program appears to be inappropriate for a particular client, the clinician can simply conceptualize the problem in behavioral terms and select a more appropriate procedure for dealing with it (for instance, substituting systematic desensitization for sensate focus in cases of extreme anxiety).

2. There does not appear to be any necessity for the clients and therapist to meet every day for two weeks. Although a daily meeting does provide an opportunity for immediate feedback, it also places pressure on the clients to carry out their therapeutic "homework" every night, whether they are in the mood to do so or not. Seeing the couple on a more nominal schedule (say once or twice a week) is usually more convenient for them. It also allows them some flexibility to engage in the treatment exercises when they are most likely to be maximally pleasurable and beneficial.

Placing a time limit on the length of treatment can have the paradoxical effect of increasing the very performance demands the treatment program seeks to minimize. The client who approaches the end of the two weeks of treatment without having experienced a return to full sexual functioning feels a pressure to "improve, and pronto!" Not all sexual dysfunctions will respond to two weeks of intensive treatment, and the length of therapy should be dictated by the clients' response, rather than vice versa.

3. Conversely, not all therapeutic programs require lengthy or intensive treatment. Rather than immediately beginning a comprehensive sexual retraining program, the clinician would be well advised to determine whether the dysfunction will respond to a simpler intervention. Jack Annon (1976), for example, has suggested four levels at which the therapist can approach sexual problems. In order of increasing complexity, these levels are (1) permission, (2) limited information, (3) specific suggestions, and (4) intensive therapy—PLISSIT for short.

At the permission level of treatment, the therapist attempts to allay fear or guilt by assuring the client(s) that some thought, feeling, or behavior they have is perfectly normal and not "wrong" or "sick." That is, the therapist gives the client(s) "permission" to think, feel, or behave in some particular way. For example, the woman who is nonorgasmic because her mother repeatedly told her that "decent women don't enjoy sex" may need nothing more than the therapist's permission to experience the sexual feelings she has been suppressing.

The limited information level of treatment is appropriate for concerns or dysfunctions that result from the client's ignorance of, or misinformation about, sexual functioning. Consider the case of a successful businessman who had not ejaculated during intercourse with his wife for a number of years (Hartman & Fithian, 1974, p. 199). He remarked that he would ejaculate if he could produce the right amount of seminal fluid. When the therapists asked him what he felt the proper amount was, he replied "about one quart of sperm." The therapists then informed him that a tablespoonful of fluid was more typical of the average ejaculatory emission, and the man's long-standing ejaculatory incompetence was "cured" without further treatment.

Problems of a somewhat more complex nature, in which limited retraining is called for, exemplify the specific suggestion level of treatment. Here the therapist advises the client(s) in the use of the specific techniques (such as the "squeeze" or directed masturbation) without involving them in a complete, multiprocedural treatment program.

Of course, some sexual dysfunctions are of such intensity, complexity, or tenacity that none of the above treatment levels will seem appropriate. These problems call for intensive therapy, of which the Masters and Johnson treatment programs are a prime example.

4. A greater focus should be placed on potential problems in the nonsexual relationship of the dysfunctional couple, since these frequently have a detrimental effect on sexual functioning. We have discussed behavioral approaches to such difficulties in Chapter 9.

5. An effort should be made to encourage the generalization and maintenance of gains made during sex therapy. One promising strategy sug-

gested by Lobitz and LoPiccolo (1972) is to gradually turn responsibility for treatment programming over to the clients themselves. Ideally, at the end of the regular treatment phase, the clients should be planning and executing their own therapeutic assignments and monitoring and correcting their own behavior. The therapists should gradually fade their influence and eventually function only as consultants to the couple. In this way, clients learn skills that will enable them to solve problems and prevent dysfunctions from recurring after treatment has ended.

Systematic Desensitization

Except for extensive retraining programs patterned after Masters and Johnson's work, systematic desensitization is the only behavioral technique to enjoy much use in the treatment of sexual dysfunctions. We have discussed desensitization at length in Chapter 10, so our remarks here will be brief.

Evidence for the effectiveness of desensitization in sexual problems comes from single and multiple case studies, and from a few controlled group evaluations (for reviews, see Ascher & Clifford, 1976; Caird & Wincze, 1977; Marks, 1976; Sotile & Kilman, 1977). Most of the controlled studies contain serious methodological or interpretive problems. Nevertheless, taken together, the available data suggest that desensitization used alone, or in conjunction with other treatment procedures, is useful in reducing a wide range of sexual dysfunctions in both males and females. Of course, more elegantly designed group evaluations are needed to strengthen this endorsement, but it does appear that desensitization can be an important tool in the elimination of sexual dysfunctions caused or exacerbated by anxiety.

SUMMARY

Changes in our society's sexual mores have placed an increasing demand for sexual competence on contemporary men and women. Traditionally, individuals with sexual dysfunctions were considered poor risks for psychotherapy, but the growth of behavioral approaches has changed this picture considerably.

Among the many variables that can adversely affect a couple's sexual functioning, performance anxiety and communication deficits are two of the most frequent and troublesome problems. The psychological and physiological effects of anxiety interfere with the normal sexual response cycle, producing such problems as erectile failure and premature ejaculation in men, and vaginismus and arousal deficits in women. Communication deficits prevent partners from understanding the sexual wants and needs of each other, and greatly reduce their ability to give or receive pleasure.

One of the precursors to most specific treatment strategies for sexual dysfunctions is the sensate focus procedure, which reduces performance anxiety and helps to build communication and cooperation in the dysfunctional unit. Once these requisite conditions have been established, a retraining program tailored to the specific problem(s) of the couple can be instituted. Each of the specific sequential strategies is developed around one basic rule: the terminal behavior is approached through successive approximations. A nondemanding atmosphere in which treatment progresses at a pace dictated by the clients' comfort is essential.

Numerous case studies and anecdotal reports exist attesting to the effectiveness of behavioral approaches to sexual dysfunction, but no controlled outcome investigations have been conducted yet. However, in light of the poor showing of traditional psychotherapy for the alleviation of sexual dysfunction, the preliminary findings for behavioral methods are indeed impressive.

CASE STUDY 11–1

LOPICCOLO, J., STEWART, R., & WATKINS, B. TREATMENT OF EREC-
TILE FAILURE AND EJACULATORY INCOMPETENCE OF HOMOSEX-
UAL ETIOLOGY. *JOURNAL OF BEHAVIOR THERAPY AND EXPERI-
MENTAL PSYCHIATRY,* 1972, **3,** 233–236.

The following case illustrates the use of a modified Masters and Johnson sexual retraining program to increase the heterosexual arousal of a male bisexual.

Two unmarried graduate students living together in a long-term relationship sought help because of the male's lack of sexual arousal to his partner. He was frequently unable to attain or keep an erection in their lovemaking. On those occasions when he could maintain his erection well enough to have intercourse, he was often unable to ejaculate.

It seemed clear that the male's problem stemmed from deficits in arousal to his female partner. He reported that he felt disgusted by the sight or touch of the female's genitals. The male client also had strong homosexual interests and had actively engaged in homosexual behavior since early adolescence. Although he had been involved in six or seven previous heterosexual relationships, each one was plagued by similar sexual problems and all ended for this reason. At the time the couple entered treatment, the male client was still homosexually active.

The female client was quite experienced sexually, having had more than forty sexual partners before the current relationship. She was aware of her partner's homosexuality, but had no objections to it. Her only concern was with his difficulty in sexual relations with her. In fact, both clients requested that the therapists do nothing to alter the male's homosexual interests; they only wanted to increase his heterosexual responsiveness. The therapists agreed to this; however, they requested that the male refrain from engaging in homosexual activity during the course of treatment. The elimination of this regular sexual outlet induced a state of deprivation aimed at increasing the sexual attractiveness of the female partner.

A male-female cotherapy team saw the couple weekly for a total of fifteen sessions. The performance anxiety which had built up in the male through his repeated sexual failures with women was approached by prohibiting sexual relations beyond those prescribed by the therapists. Sensate focus exercises were begun in the first week, and increasingly more demanding sexual behavior was allowed each week as the male became confident in his ability to perform. At first only kissing, caressing, and massage were allowed, with the female's breasts and the genitals of both partners to be avoided. In subsequent weeks, breast and genital caresses were allowed, followed by mutual masturbation without orgasm, penile insertion without thrusting, insertion with male movement only, mutual masturbation to orgasm, and finally, unrestricted intercourse to orgasm.

As the graduated sexual tasks were proceeding, the male's responsiveness to his female partner was further enhanced by a program of directed masturbation and orgasmic reconditioning (to be described more fully in Chapter 12). At the time treatment began, the male was masturbating several times a week to exclusively homosexual fantasies. He was instructed to continue masturbating using homosexual fantasies to become aroused and to approach orgasm, but to switch to a sexual fantasy of his mate at the brink of orgasm. On subsequent occasions he was to shift to the heterosexual fantasy earlier and earlier in masturbation. Since the client reported some difficulty in visualizing the necessary heterosexual stimuli, the couple was provided with a Polaroid camera with which the male could take sexually explicit pictures of the female to use during masturbation. This idea proved quite helpful, and toward the end of therapy the male found that he could fantasize about his mate without help from the photographs.

Fantasy substitution was also employed to increase the male's arousal during actual sex play. If he lost his arousal during lovemaking with his female partner, he was to briefly employ a homosexual fantasy to restore it. Then he was to shift his attention back to his mate and their sexual activity. In any event, his attention was always to be directed toward the ongoing sexual stimulation at the point of orgasm. As was the case with masturbation, the client at first relied heavily on homosexual fantasies, but later found himself highly aroused by the reality of heterosexual lovemaking.

As can be seen from the self-report data in Table 11–3, the male's arousal to heterosexual activities was markedly improved at the end of treatment and at a followup six months later. He was capable of obtaining and keeping erections through heterosexual activity and thoughts without resorting to homosexual fantasies, and could achieve sufficient arousal to ejaculate reliably during intercourse. These changes were very pleasing to both partners. The male's homosexual behavior, while infrequent at treatment termination, had returned to pretreatment levels by the time of the followup with no detrimental effect on his heterosexual functioning.

Table 11–3. Outcome Statistics

| | Time of Assessment | | |
Variable	Pre-treatment	Termination	Six-month Followup
1. Intercourse frequency	once/2 weeks	3 times weekly	twice weekly
2. Intercourse duration	1–5 min	11–15 min	11–15 min
3. Achieves erection—% of coital opportunities	25%	100%	100%
4. Achieves orgasm in intercourse, if erection achieved			
male	50%	100%	100%
female	50	75	75
5. Self-rating—satisfaction with sexual relationship (scale of 1–6)			
male	2	5	5
female	2	5	5

From J. LoPiccolo, R. Stewart & B. Watkins, Treatment of erectile failure and ejaculatory incompetence of Homosexual etiology. *Journal of Behavior Therapy and Experimental Psychiatry,* 1972, **3,** p. 235, Table 1. By permission of Pergamon Press, Ltd.

CASE STUDY 11–2

LOBITZ, W. C., LOPICCOLO, J., LOBITZ, G. K., & BROCKWAY, J.   A CLOSER LOOK AT "SIMPLISTIC" BEHAVIOR THERAPY FOR SEXUAL DYSFUNCTION: TWO CASE STUDIES.   IN H. J. EYSENCK (ED.), *CASE STUDIES IN BEHAVIOR THERAPY*.   LONDON: ROUTLEDGE & KEGAN PAUL, 1975.

Readers of the behavioral literature are often left with the impression that the treatment of sexual dysfunction is a straightforward, cut-and-dried procedure.   Practitioners of behavioral methods know that this is seldom the case.   The following highlights of a case reported by Charles Lobitz, Joseph LoPiccolo, and their colleagues illustrates some of the complexity typical in the conduct of behavioral sex therapy.

Mr. and Mrs. R, two university students in their twenties, sought treatment for Mrs. R's inability to achieve orgasm through any type of stimulation.   During the pretreatment assessment, Mrs. R revealed that she had never experienced orgasm, either through masturbation or sexual encounters.   Although her sexual experience prior to meeting her husband was not extensive, she had lived with one man for a period of six months.   He had been very concerned about her inability to achieve orgasm and she had begun faking it to please him.   When he finally discovered her deception, he terminated their relationship.

Although Mrs. R was mildly concerned about her difficulty, she felt that her sexual relationship with her husband was satisfactory.   Mr. R, however, was quite distressed by his wife's condition.   Pretreatment assessment suggested that Mr. R was insecure about his sexuality, and was possibly experiencing conflict over homosexual impulses.   Prior to meeting his wife he had engaged in sexual intercourse with over a dozen women and had established long-term relationships with three of them.   Despite his more extensive sexual experience, however, Mr. R felt guilty about masturbation, and did not enjoy being manually or orally stimulated by his partner.   Mr. R's insistence on his wife becoming orgasmic was seen by the therapists as an attempt to confirm his masculinity.

Mr. and Mrs. R were seen daily by a male and female cotherapy team for a total of fifteen one-hour sessions.   Assessment of their difficulties took two sessions, and implementation of treatment began in session three.

It was obvious to the therapists that the Rs had worked themselves into a performance anxiety spiral.   They had been having intercourse every day and were actively "trying for" Mrs. R's orgasm by employing a variety of foreplay techniques and coital positions.   As their efforts failed, they resolved to try even harder, and the accumulated performance demands and frustrations were beginning to take a toll on their relationship.   The therapists explained the destructive nature of this situation to the couple, and described a plan for breaking the spiral.   The initial strategy included prohibitions on intercourse and other attempts to reach orgasm, and the use of nongenital sensate focus exercises in which the object was to produce pleasure, not arousal.   Mrs. R was also given instructions on genital self-exploration as the first step in a masturbation program.

Although Mrs. R seemed pleased with the therapists' suggestions, Mr. R immediately wanted to know when they could resume intercourse and work on his wife's orgasm. The female therapist reacted by saying that if she were Mrs. R, such remarks would make her feel even more pressured to perform, and that what they both needed most at that moment was relief from pressure.

In the next session, the couple reported having had an enjoyable pleasuring session, but Mrs. R had been bothered by distracting thoughts about schoolwork and housework during her own genital exploration session. The female therapist assured her that this was a common problem and suggested that Mrs. R listen to music or read a romantic novel to help set the mood for self-exploration. The male therapist remarked that Mr. R might masturbate if he wished. The statement was designed as a permission rather than an assignment because of Mr. R's concern about masturbation.

In session five, the clients reported experiencing increased pleasure during the sensate focus exercises; and playing the radio had helped Mrs. R to maintain attention on her own sensations during her genital exploration. However, Mr. R appeared somewhat withdrawn. The therapists decided to separate the couple so that the male therapist might determine what was bothering Mr. R. He found that Mr. R was embarrassed to discuss his concerns about masturbation in front of his wife and the female therapist. For him, masturbation was all right for single men, but it was a sign of weakness in a married man.

The therapist replied by citing research reports indicating that masturbation is common even among married men. He also self-disclosed about his own masturbation. Mr. R appeared relieved. When he and the male therapist rejoined the women and shared their conversation, Mrs. R assured her husband that she would not think of him as unmanly if he masturbated. The Rs were sent home with the same instructions as before, except that breast stimulation was added to their pleasuring exercises.

In the following session, Mr. R reported becoming so aroused during the last sensate focus session that he remained with his wife and masturbated while she performed her self-pleasuring. Mrs. R reported intense pleasure from her own genital stimulation. In session seven she reported that she had almost had an orgasm while masturbating. The therapists again attempted to minimize performance demands by reminding her that at this point her task was to experience arousal, not orgasm. Genital stimulation was now added to the mutual pleasuring sessions.

Both clients were depressed when they appeared for the eighth session. They reported that genital stimulation during mutual pleasuring had started out well, but despite being extremely aroused, Mrs. R could not reach orgasm. The frustration felt by both partners had erupted in an argument. Mr. and Mrs. R were now quite discouraged. The therapists chose this time to discuss the problems that can be produced by carrying expectations into sexual situations. They disclosed that, for them, lovemaking went badly when they approached it with the notion that they or their partner *should* do this or that. The purpose of this discussion was twofold: first, to modify the clients' attitudes about the role of expectations in sexual relationships; and second, to help reduce their disappointment and anxiety by showing them that even sex therapists can have unpleasant sexual experiences now and then.

In a further attempt to reduce performance demands, the female therapist told Mrs. R that she was clearly experiencing the degree of arousal necessary for orgasm, but that she probably was not ready for one yet. She instructed her to purchase a hand-held vibrator and use it to stimulate various parts of her body, genitals included, during her self-pleasuring sessions. Most important, Mrs. R was told not to try for an orgasm, but simply to relax and enjoy the vibrator's stimulation.

Individual and mutual pleasuring continued to go well, but even though Mrs. R's arousal was extremely intense, she did not climax. In session ten, it became clear to the therapists that her problem was not one of insufficient arousal, but of "letting go." They therefore instructed Mrs. R *not to have an orgasm,* and instead to engage in an exaggerated role play of one. Mr. R was present when the assignment was made.

In session eleven, Mrs. R was happy but embarrassed to report that instead of role playing, she had experienced two real orgasms. One had been triggered by Mr. R's manual stimulation, and the other by her own masturbation with the vibrator. However, the reason for Mrs. R's embarrassment was that she had uncontrollably urinated during her orgasms. The therapists empathized with Mrs. R, but assured her that her problem was simply one of learning to release some bodily functions while maintaining control of others. Mr. R was quite supportive of his wife, and she was somewhat relieved. The therapists prescribed a program of exercises designed to increase tone and control in Mrs. R's pelvic muscles.

During this session, the therapists began shifting control of the treatment program to the Rs by asking them to suggest their next assignment. The couple felt that they were ready to move on to intercourse. The therapists consented, but instructed the Rs to maintain manual and vibrator stimulation during intercourse to aid in the transfer of Mrs. R's new orgasmic responsiveness.

Mrs. R did not immediately become orgasmic in intercourse, but did continue to experience orgasm during vibrator stimulation. Orgasm was still accompanied by urination. The therapists reassured her that the condition should diminish with time, and that a gynecological consultation could be arranged if the problem persisted. The clients continued to engage in intercourse supplemented by vibratory stimulation, and Mrs. R continued self-pleasuring to permit her to become familiar with the experience of orgasm.

In session thirteen, Mrs. R reported having had her first coital orgasm. The experience was not accompanied by urination, although this had occurred with another orgasm during masturbation. However, Mr. R was upset because he had, for the first time in his life, experienced an erectile failure during intercourse. He at first became quite anxious, and all attempts to regain the erection were failures. After relaxing for a few moments, however, Mrs. R was able to restimulate him, and intercourse resumed and culminated in orgasm for both of them. The therapists reassured Mr. R that such experiences are not uncommon or disastrous, and reminded the clients of their previous discussion about the dangers of anxieties and expectations.

The couple was then asked to outline a program for maintaining their treatment gains. They were to include a review of the treatment procedures they had learned, as well as a list of potential future problems and ways of dealing with them. This plan was reviewed in session fourteen. The therapists reinforced the clients' effort and amended their plan only by adding steps for fading vibratory stimulation out of both masturbation and intercourse. The vibrator could be used occasionally for variety thereafter.

In session fifteen, Mrs. R reported having orgasms during intercourse and masturbation, all with the aid of the vibrator. Her bladder control difficulties had ended. Both clients were pleased with their progress, and agreed with the therapists that their treatment goals had been reached. Treatment was terminated at this time.

However, two weeks later, Mr. R contacted the male therapist and reported that Mrs. R had told him that she had been faking orgasms during intercourse for the past week. Another meeting was scheduled with the couple, during which Mrs. R explained that her actions were in response to her husband's increasing pressure for her to achieve orgasm without the vibrator.

As Lobitz and his colleagues noted, this situation might have been avoided had the therapists attended more closely to some crucial information gathered during assessment—namely, Mr. R's sexual insecurities and Mrs. R's past history of feigning orgasm to please her partner. Together these factors should have suggested the possibility of the vibrator representing a threat to Mr. R's masculinity, and of Mrs. R resorting to old habits when placed under increasing pressure to meet her partner's expectations. Treatment should have been continued until Mr. and Mrs. R's new ways of responding were well established.

The therapists attempted to be empathic and supportive of both partners. They reflected that Mrs. R must have felt very pressured and that Mr. R must have felt threatened by his wife's enjoyment of the vibrator. The couple began to share their feelings with each other. With the therapists' assistance, they reached the conclusion that it would have been better if they had directly expressed their concerns and revised their maintenance program accordingly, rather than allowing anxieties and resentments to accumulate. With this, treatment contact was ended once again.

The couple was followed up for a total of twelve months after the termination of treatment. Their reports indicated that Mrs. R's orgasmic response to vibratory stimulation had successfully generalized to manual stimulation in both masturbation and intercourse. She was experiencing orgasm nearly 100 percent of the time, regardless of type of sexual activity. Both partners were extremely pleased, and reported increased happiness in their marriage.

REFERENCES

Annon, J. S. *Behavioral treatment of sexual problems: Brief therapy.* New York: Harper & Row, 1976.

Ascher, L. M., & Clifford, R. E. Behavioral considerations in the treatment of sexual dysfunction. In M. Hersen, R. M. Eisler, & P. M. Miller (Eds.), *Progress in behavior modification,* vol. 3. New York: Academic Press, 1976.

Caird, W., & Wincze, J. P. *Sex therapy: A behavioral approach.* New York: Harper & Row, 1977.

Fisher, S. *The female orgasm: Psychology, physiology, fantasy.* New York: Basic Books, 1973.

Fordney-Settlage, D. S. Heterosexual dysfunction: Evaluation of treatment procedures. *Archives of Sexual Behavior,* 1975, **4,** 367–387.

Hartman, W. E., & Fithian, M. A. *Treatment of sexual dysfunction: A bio-psycho-social approach.* New York: Aronson, 1974.

Hite, S. *The Hite report.* New York: Macmillan, 1976.

Jacobs, M., Thompson, L. A., & Truxaw, P. The use of sexual surrogates in counseling. *Counseling Psychologist,* 1975, **1,** 73–77.

Kaplan, H. S. *The new sex therapy: Active treatment of sexual dysfunctions.* New York: Brunner/Mazel, 1974.

Kaplan, H. S. *The illustrated manual of sex therapy.* New York: Quadrangle, 1975.

Kegel, A. H. Sexual functions of the pubococcygens muscle. *Western Journal of Surgery,* 1952, **60,** 521–524.

LeRoy, D. H. The potential criminal liability in human sex clinics and their patients. *St. Louis University Law Journal,* 1971, 586–603.

Lobitz, W. C., & LoPiccolo, J. New methods in the behavioral treatment of sexual dysfunction. *Journal of Behavior Therapy and Experimental Psychiatry,* 1972, **3,** 265–271.

Lobitz, W. C., LoPiccolo, J., Lobitz, G. K., & Brockway, J. A closer look at "simplistic" behavior therapy for sexual dysfunction: Two case studies. In H. J. Eysenck (Ed.), *Case studies in behavior therapy.* London: Routledge & Kegan Paul, 1975.

LoPiccolo, J., & Lobitz, W. C. The role of masturbation in the treatment of primary orgasmic dysfunction. *Archives of Sexual Behavior,* 1972, **2,** 163–171.

LoPiccolo, J., & Steger, J. C. The sexual interaction inventory: A new instrument for assessment of sexual dysfunction. *Archives of Sexual Behavior,* 1974, **3,** 585–595.

LoPiccolo, J., Stewart, R., & Watkins, B. Treatment of erectile failure and ejaculatory incompetence of homosexual etiology. *Journal of Behavior Therapy and Experimental Psychiatry,* 1972, **3,** 233–236.

Malamuth, N., Wanderer, Z. W., Sayner, R. B., & Durrell, D. Utilization of surrogate partners: A survey of health professions. *Journal of Behavior Therapy and Experimental Psychiatry,* 1976, **7,** 149–150.

Marks, I. Management of sexual disorders. In H. Leitenberg (Ed.), *Handbook of behavior modification and behavior therapy.* Englewood Cliffs, N.J.: Prentice-Hall, 1976.

Masters, W. H., & Johnson, V. E. *Human sexual response.* Boston: Little, Brown, 1966.

Masters, W. H., & Johnson, V. E. *Human sexual inadequacy.* Boston: Little, Brown, 1970.

Masters, W. H., & Johnson, V. E. Principles of the new sex therapy. *American Journal of Psychiatry,* 1975, **133,** 548–554.

McGovern, K. B., Stewart, R. C., & LoPiccolo, J. Secondary orgasmic dysfunction. I. Analysis and strategies for treatment. *Archives of Sexual Behavior,* 1975, **4,** 265–275.

Newell, A. G. A case of ejaculatory incompetence treated with a mechanical aid. *Journal of Behavior Therapy and Experimental Psychiatry,* 1976, **7,** 193–194.

O'Connor, J. F., & Stern, L. O. Results of treatment in functional sexual disorders. *New York State Journal of Medicine,* 1972, **72,** 1927–1934.

Paul, G. L. Behavior modification research: Design and tactics. In C. M. Franks (Ed.), *Behavior therapy: Appraisal and status.* New York: McGraw-Hill, 1969.

Sadock, B. J., & Sadock, V. A. Techniques of coitus. In B. J. Sadock, H. I. Kaplan, & A. M. Freedman (Eds.), *The sexual experience.* Baltimore: Williams & Wilkins, 1976.

Schellen, T. M. C. M. Induction of ejaculation by electrovibration. *Fertility and Sterility,* 1968, **19,** 566–569.

Semans, J. H. Premature ejaculation: A new approach. *Southern Medical Journal,* 1956, **49,** 353–357.

Sotile, W. M., & Kilman, P. R. Treatments of psychogenic female sexual dysfunction. *Psychological Bulletin,* 1977, **84,** 619–633.

Wolpe, J. Reciprocal inhibition as the main basis of psychotherapeutic effects. *Archives of Neurological Psychiatry,* 1954, **72,** 205–226.

Wolpe, J. *Psychotherapy by reciprocal inhibition.* Stanford, Calif.: Stanford University Press, 1958.

Wolpe, J. *The practice of behavior therapy.* New York: Pergamon Press, 1969.

Wolpe, J., & Lazarus, A. A. *Behavior therapy techniques.* Oxford: Pergamon Press, 1966.

Zeiss, A. M., Rosen, G. M., & Zeiss, R. A. Orgasm during intercourse: A treatment strategy for women. *Journal of Consulting and Clinical Psychology,* 1977, **45,** 891–895.

twelve

SEXUAL VARIATIONS

It is a sign of the times that the title for this chapter was chosen with more than the usual care and consideration. Not so long ago a discussion of this nature would have been introduced by such terms as deviance, aberrations, or even perversions. What's in a name? In this case, perhaps a great deal, because the difference between "variation" and "deviance"—or any other term that connotes pathology—represents a very real difference in the way behavioral and traditional clinicians view atypical sexual behavior.

In this chapter we will examine behavioral approaches to the sexual variations. We will begin by contrasting traditional and sociobehavioral views of the nature of atypical sexualities. This will lead us to a discussion of the ethical considerations that surround the treatment of individuals whose sexual preferences are in conflict with the standards of our culture. In the next portion of the chapter we will consider the component behaviors with which the clinician must deal in any effort to redirect a person's sexual behavior. Finally, we will critically examine the many and varied procedures that behavioral psychologists have developed to enable an individual to achieve this goal.

THE NATURE OF ATYPICAL
SEXUAL EXPRESSION

We have already alluded to the differences between traditional and behavioral views of sexual variation. Early psychoanalytic theory maintained that an exclusive orientation toward heterosexual intercourse was the natural outcome of healthy psychosexual development. Persistent interest in other sources or other activities for sexual gratification meant fixation at an early stage of development. Therefore, such variations were considered pathological. The extreme of this "disease model" is captured in a statement about one of the more common variations: "Homosexuality is not the 'way of life' these sick people gratuitously assume it to be, but a neurotic distortion of the total personality" (Bergler, 1956, p. 9). Although this viewpoint has generally undergone some "softening," many analytically trained psychologists still adhere to its basic tenets (compare Bieber, 1976; Bieber, Dain, Dince, Drellich, Grand, Gundlach, Kremer, Rifkin, Wilbur, & Bieber, 1962).

Behavioral conceptualizations of sexual variation begin with the assumption that there are no "normal" or "abnormal" sexual behaviors, except in the way society views those behaviors (Ullmann & Krasner, 1969). Human beings are born only with the anatomical and physiological prerequisites for sexuality; sexual orientation and focus are learned. That is, the ways in which we express our sexuality are determined by our unique learning histories. All learning in the biologically normal person involves the same processes, and "unusual" sexual behaviors are no exception. As the famous sexologist Alfred Kinsey (Kinsey, Pomeroy, Martin, & Gebhard, 1953, pp. 645–646) first put it:

Even some of the most extremely variant types of human sexual behavior may need no more explanation than is provided by our understanding of the processes of learning and conditioning. Behavior which may appear bizarre, perverse, or unthinkably unacceptable to some persons, and even to most persons, may have significance for other individuals because of the way in which they have been conditioned. . . . In rare instances some of the so-called aberrant types of behavior, meaning the less usual types of conditioned responses, may be definitely disadvantageous, but in most instances they are of no social concern. The prominence given to classification of behavior as normal or abnormal, and the long list of special terms used for classifying such behavior, usually represent moralistic classifications rather than any scientific attempt to discover the origins of such behavior, or to determine their real social significance.

The learning of unusual sexual feelings and behaviors may occur quite early in life. After reviewing several naturalistic studies, Bandura (1969) noted a number of consistencies in the histories of persons with atypical sexual interests. It appears that parents often model a particular sexual variation and prompt their children to behave similarly. When the children imitate the responses, they are heavily reinforced with affection or even physical stimulation. Once the atypical sexual behavior is established, other contingencies begin to play a role in its maintenance and strengthening. Continued direct and vicarious reinforcement by the parents is supplemented by **masturbatory conditioning** (McGuire, Carlisle, & Young, 1965). If the individual develops a pattern of masturbating while performing or fantasizing about the atypical activity, these stimuli tend to acquire strong erotic value through their repeated association with sexual arousal and orgasm. Eventually, engaging in the variation becomes reinforcing in itself, just as typical sexual behavior is, and the pattern of preference that is established may last a lifetime.

The learning process just outlined involves the same principles (modeling, prompting, reinforcement, and so on) as any other learning process. In this regard, it is perfectly *normal*. Deviance, then, appears to be defined by the standards of the society in which the behavior occurs. Cross-cultural studies have indicated that virtually all the sexual behaviors deemed deviant by our cultural standards are condoned and seen as normal in some other societies (Ford & Beach, 1951).

One can also see how value changes have affected the concept of deviance in our own society. For example, in April 1974, the American Psychiatric Association ruled that homosexuality would no longer be classified as a mental disorder in their *Diagnostic and Statistical Manual* (the "bible" of traditional diagnostic nomenclature). Instead, a new classification—"sexual orientation disturbance"—was created to accommodate only those individuals "whose sexual interests are directed primarily toward people of the same sex *and who are either disturbed by, in conflict with, or wish to change their sexual orientation*" (American Psychiatric Association, 1975, italics added). Thus, homosexual behavior is considered a disorder only for those individuals who are troubled by it. If we take seriously the psychoanalytic contention that homosexuality is inherently pathological, it is difficult to understand how it could be voted otherwise. Obviously, what is really being changed is a professional value judgment about homosexual behavior.

An Ethical Challenge

Certain benefits accrue from subscribing to a "pathology theory" of sexual variation. The time-honored approach to pathology of all kinds is *treatment*. Clearly, if a particular sexual behavior is actually considered "sick," then unquestionably therapy should be implemented to change the behavior. But viewing unusual sexual behavior as deviant only in that it is incompatible with cultural standards raises some knotty ethical questions. Why has so much effort been directed toward developing effective "treatments" for sexual variations if the real problem is our society's intolerance of alternate modes of expression? Worse yet, does not the very existence of techniques designed to reorient persons with atypical sexual preferences encourage the notion that these are "disorders" in need of cure? These questions are particularly troublesome for behavioral psychologists who, on the one hand, tend to align themselves with "normality" conceptualizations of sexual variations and, on the other hand, are responsible for more than their fair share of treatments for these "nonproblems."

These issues have most frequently been discussed in connection with the treatment of homosexual behavior. In a controversial presidential address to the Association for the Advancement of Behavior Therapy in 1974, Gerald Davison surprised his audience by calling for behavioral clinicians to stop offering sexual reorientation therapy to homosexuals, and to concentrate instead on helping homosexuals improve their interpersonal relationships and cope with the stress of being at odds with societal codes of conduct. Davison (1976, p. 161) later elaborated:

> By working so diligently on change techniques, particularly but not exclusively aversive procedures, I would ask whether we have not been saying that the prejudices and laws against certain sexual acts are in fact well founded. What are we really saying to our clients when, on the one hand, we assure them that they are not abnormal and on the other hand, present them with an array of techniques, some of them painful, which are aimed at eliminating that set of feelings and behaviors that we have just told them is okay? What is the real range of "free choice" available to homosexually oriented people who are racked with guilt, self-hate, and embarrassment, and who must endure the burden of societal prejudice and discrimination? What of the anxieties arising from this discrimination —how have we helped them with *these* problems?

Davison's position is thought-provoking, but it can be argued that denying homosexual individuals the means to change should they voluntarily decide to do so is equally wrong. In fact, this view was taken by Davison himself in an earlier paper with Terrance Wilson (Wilson & Davison, 1974). At that time, Wilson and Davison reemphasized Bandura's (1969) statement that the choice of goals in behavior therapy rests with the client. But is a client ever really responsible for the selection of therapeutic goals? For example, although the following analysis is aimed at traditional psychotherapy, it is applicable to behavioral intervention as well:

At first glance, a model of psychiatric practice based on the contention that people should just be helped to learn to do the things they want to do seems uncomplicated and desirable. But it is an unobtainable model. Unlike a technician, a psychiatrist cannot avoid communicating and at times imposing his own values upon his patients. The patient usually has considerable difficulty in finding the way in which he would wish to change his behavior, but as he talks to the psychiatrist his wants and needs become clearer. In the very process of defining his needs in the presence of a figure who is viewed as wise and authoritarian, the patient is profoundly influenced. He ends up wanting some of the things the psychiatrist thinks he should want. (Halleck, 1971, p. 19)

An even more fundamental issue is whether individuals ever really *freely* choose to change homosexual behavior:

> To suggest that a person comes voluntarily to change his sexual orientation is to ignore the powerful environmental stress, oppression if you will, that has been telling him for years that he should change. To grow up in a family where the word "homosexual" was whispered, to play in a playground and hear the words "faggot" and "queer," to go to church and hear of "sin" and then to college and hear of "illness," and finally to the counseling center that promises to "cure," is hardly to create an environment of freedom and voluntary choice. (Silverstein, 1972, p. 4)

Let us accept, for the moment, the notion that offering sexual reorientation treatment to the homosexual individual helps to perpetuate the kind of oppression just described. If we therefore terminate such programs, what have we to offer the distressed gay person? Davison's contention that behavioral clinicians have done little to help homosexually oriented people improve their interpersonal relationships and cope with cultural prejudice is probably accurate. However, it is important to recognize that the fault does not lie with the treatment technology, but in the way in which it has been applied.

For example, interpersonal (Chapter 9) and sexual (Chapter 11) relationship enhancement methods can certainly be modified to fit the problems encountered by same-sexed couples. Fortunately, it appears that behavioral clinicians are becoming more willing to use the methods in this manner. For example, Davison and Wilson (1973) surveyed behavior therapists and found that 87 percent of their sample claimed they would help homosexually oriented clients become happier and more comfortable in their life style. Reports of such cases, though rare, have begun to appear in the literature (Fensterheim, 1972; Herman & Prewett, 1974; see also Case Study 9–1), and researchers have begun to evaluate behavioral programs aimed at improving the functioning of gay persons (Russell & Winkler, 1977).

Nevertheless, many would still disagree with Davison and others (for example, Begelman, 1975) that therapists should, in effect, force homosexual individuals to attempt to adjust by eliminating one of the options presently available to them—sexual reorientation. It is our impression that many behaviorally oriented clinicians would argue that this all-important decision must ultimately rest with each client. Of course, the questions we have already raised about the client's "freedom to choose"—given the subtle influence of the therapist and the not-so-subtle pressure from society—cannot be ignored. The therapist must be aware of these pressures, and must do everything he or she can to attenuate their influence on the client (Halleck, 1976). This can be facilitated by informing the homosexual client of the *full range* of alternatives available to him or her, and the pros and cons of each course of action. The therapist can challenge the client's decision, be it to change or to adjust, and encourage him or her to consider other options. The clinician can refuse to treat the homosexual person who is under stress from extraordinary circumstances until the client's condition has normalized and he or she can think more clearly about what should be done. By presenting the *total* picture, and by arguing both sides of the issue, the therapist can encourage the client to make an informed, well-reasoned decision.

It should also be recognized that a homosexual individual who wants to become heterosexually responsive does not necessarily have to give up homosexual interests in the process. As we will see, the emphasis in behavioral treatment approaches is often on eliminating homosexual

arousal; relatively less effort has been directed toward the development of heterosexual arousal and skills (Barlow, 1973). However, there is no a priori reason why one sexual interest need be eliminated before another one can be developed. Conceptually, it may make sense to reduce a client's homosexual contacts during a course of treatment aimed at establishing heterosexual stimulus control of arousal; but arousal to homosexual stimuli need not be eradicated for heterosexual cues to become eroticized (see, for example, Case Study 11–1). Treatment strategies devised with this in mind have the advantage of facilitating homosexual clients' freedom of choice. Individuals may develop heterosexual interests for whatever reason they wish without their homosexual behavior being condemned by implication. Then they can choose whatever style of sexual expression they prefer.

In summary, it is our impression that the arguments of Davison and others have not convinced large numbers of behavioral clinicians to refuse sexual reorientation procedures to homosexual clients who request them. Nevertheless, their contributions are extremely important in making therapists more aware of the implications of their actions and in encouraging them to reevaluate the status quo. They have certainly given us reason to rethink our own position. We can conclude only that the issues are far more complex than is often acknowledged by those who debate them. Indeed, the controversy applies not only to homosexual behavior, but to all the sexual variations —and to a great many other clinical "problems" as well. It would seem that any "solutions" that come to us as inflexible and absolute rules must necessarily be *wrong* in some sense. Complex issues can seldom be reduced to black-and-white clarity. What is most important, however, is that the issues have been raised at all. It is always useful to consider the moral judgments involved in clinical work. Such "self-consciousness" can only benefit both client and clinician.

In the remainder of this chapter we will turn our attention to the process of sexual reorientation. It bears repeating that we do *not* believe that this is the treatment of choice for all individuals whose sexual interests are incompatible with what society has deemed acceptable. But we *do* believe that it can be a reasonable and legitimate goal for some clients, particularly those whose preferences lie so far beyond acceptability as to virtually guarantee them a life of conflict and misery should they remain unchanged. In the material that follows, we will occasionally use such terms as "inappropriate arousal," and refer to various sexual feelings and behaviors as "problems" or "difficulties." Readers should understand that we use these terms as they are defined in the context of treatment, and not in any moralistic sense.

COMPONENTS OF SEXUAL VARIATION

Traditionally, atypical sexual behavior has been categorized according to the *object chosen* and/or the *activity engaged in* for sexual gratification. For instance, homosexuality, fetishism and pedophilia involve the unconventional objects of a person of the same sex, an inanimate object or a part of the body, and a child, respectively. Examples of uncommon sexual activities include public exposure of the genitals, or exhibitionism; inflicting pain on another person, or sadism; and seeking pain from another person, or masochism. Some variations are harder to classify in this scheme. Transvestism involves dressing in the clothing of the opposite sex, and thus combines an unconventional object with an unconventional activity. Transsexualism, in which an individual actually feels that he or she is a member of the opposite sex who is trapped in the wrong body, demands its own category. This classification system provides us with useful shorthand labels for sexual variations, and the terminology is almost universally employed. However, labeling a person a fetishist or a transvestite really tells us very little about his or her behavior. The clinician needs information about a number of aspects of the client's functioning before devising a program to redirect sexual interests.

David Barlow (1974) has identified four general areas that must be assessed if the client wishes to abandon his or her variation in favor of a heterosexual preference. First, and perhaps most obvious, is **inappropriate sexual arousal**—those sexual feelings and behaviors that the client finds unac-

ceptable for some reason and wants to eliminate. In general, the traditional labels provide some information about this dimension; for example, homosexual clients are aroused by members of their own sex. However, the particular stimuli that produce sexual arousal, and the exact form that the arousal response takes, are as varied among homosexual individuals as they are among heterosexual individuals. Thus, a detailed functional analysis of the client's inappropriate arousal is necessary.

A second area to be assessed is the client's **heterosexual responsiveness.** All too often, behavioral treatments have focused on eliminating inappropriate arousal, and the development of heterosexual responsiveness has been left to chance. For example, consider this observation: "It is probable that if [underwear fetishists] can abstain from their deviant behavior for a sufficient period of time, normal outlets for the control of sexual arousal will develop" (Bond & Evans, 1967, p. 1162). Conversely, can we expect underwear fetishes to develop in heterosexual individuals who abstain from their preferred sexual activity? Hardly. The therapist must determine the extent to which the client is aroused by heterosexual stimuli and specifically attempt to develop such responsiveness if the client is deficient.

A third important factor is whether the client possesses the **heterosocial skills** that will be necessary for interacting with persons of the opposite sex. Sexual variations sometimes exist in individuals who have adequate heterosexual arousal, but who lack the necessary skills or are too anxious to initiate contacts with members of the opposite sex. For example, an individual who is accustomed to homosexual contacts and relationships may find the social cues and unwritten rules that govern heterosexual interactions very confusing and impossible to "read." In such cases, treatment must include building skills the client needs to function appropriately in a new life.

Finally, the client's **gender role behaviors** must be assessed. That is, does the individual look, speak, and behave like a member of his or her sex? Although by no means universal, some homosexual or transvestite clients adopt ways of standing, sitting, moving, speaking, and gesturing that are typical of the opposite sex. These behaviors may "turn off" people with whom they want to interact and may make them the butt of criticism and harassment. In transsexuals, gender role reversal is complete: these individuals consistently behave, feel, and think as members of the opposite sex, and are profoundly distressed by their anatomical gender, which they view as "wrong" (Green & Money, 1969). Such clients often request sex reassignment surgery.

Before turning our attention to the procedures that have been used to modify each of these components of sexual variation, we must note that virtually all clinical and experimental data on the efficacy of behavioral procedures in sexual reorientation come from male subjects. For example, one review found that females represented only 1.1 percent of the homosexual individuals in *all* published accounts of behavioral programs to that time (Adams & Sturgis, 1977). Accounts of the treatment of women with other sexual variations are essentially nonexistent as well. This lopsided state of affairs seems to support the contention of many clinicians that women seldom seek professional help in altering sexual preferences. Why this should be so is not clear; but it is clear that we have no way of knowing whether conclusions derived from observations of males undergoing sexual reorientation can legitimately be extended to females. Although it is not unreasonable to assume that the development and elimination of atypical sexual interest should be basically the same in women as they are in men, this is an *assumption* nonetheless. For convenience, we will describe sexual reorientation procedures as if this assumption were true; in essence, we believe that it probably is. Readers should remember, however, that our conclusions about these procedures, both positive and negative, may not necessarily hold for women who seek a change in their sexual preference.

DEVELOPING HETEROSEXUAL RESPONSIVENESS

Assuming the client has deficits in arousal to heterosexual stimuli, the clinician may choose this as the first target of a treatment program for a number of reasons. First, as we have already mentioned, it may prove unnecessary to eliminate inappropriate arousal if the client can become heterosexually responsive without doing so. Second, most of the procedures for development of heterosexual responsiveness depend initially on the existence of inappropriate arousal. Thus, if inappropriate arousal is removed first, many procedures for producing heterosexual arousal become useless. A related problem is that eliminating inappropriate arousal in a client who lacks heterosexual arousal leaves him or her with no sexual outlet until new responsiveness can be developed. At best, this is frustrating for the client; at worst, it is possible that the client will not respond to treatment, will suffer a "relapse," or even adopt some new, but equally problematic sexual preference. For all these reasons, it makes good sense to provide clients with new sexual interests before pulling the old ones out from under them.

It should be noted at this point that "spontaneous" increases in heterosexual arousal do sometimes occur during treatment aimed specifically at reducing inappropriate arousal (Bancroft, 1970; Barlow, Leitenberg, & Agras, 1969; Callahan & Leitenberg, 1973; Gelder & Marks, 1969). However, this phenomenon is infrequent and inconsistent, and the reasons that it occurs at all are not understood. It should certainly not be relied on.

Aversion Relief

A technique that has been widely used to increase heterosexual responsiveness is aversion relief (Feldman & MacCulloch, 1965, 1971; Thorpe, Schmidt, Brown, & Castell, 1964). **Aversion relief** is a respondent conditioning technique in which heterosexual stimuli (for example, words like "intercourse" and "heterosexual"; or pictures of appropriate-gender nudes) are paired with the termination of an aversive stimulus (usually electric shock). The feelings of relief that accompany termination of the noxious stimulus presumably become conditioned to the heterosexual stimuli. Note, however, that it is not sexual arousal that is being paired with the heterosexual stimuli, but relief and relaxation; thus, there is no reason to believe, even on theoretical grounds, that aversion relief procedures can aid in the development of appropriate arousal. Some researchers have maintained that the purpose of aversion relief is to reduce heterosexual anxiety (Feldman & MacCulloch, 1971), but there is no convincing experimental evidence to indicate that aversion relief procedures have an anxiety-reducing effect. Moreover, the fact that aversion relief procedures have been evaluated only in conjunction with aversive conditioning treatments aimed at reducing inappropriate arousal makes it impossible to determine whether aversion relief alone has any therapeutic value. All these factors prompted Barlow to comment in 1973 (p. 659):

> It is revealing that in the empirical field of behavior modification, the use of a therapeutic technique has now been reported in the literature on approximately 150 cases and continues to be employed clinically without any evidence that it is effective.

Although Barlow's comments about the technique remain valid, the number of cases in which aversion relief procedures have been used has continued to increase (for example, Pinard & Lamontagne, 1976; Rehm & Rozensky, 1974).

Explicit Exposure to Heterosexual Stimuli

One remarkably straightforward way of increasing appropriate arousal may be to expose the client to "intense" heterosexual themes. Steven Herman, David Barlow, and Stewart Agras (1971, 1974b) developed the **explicit exposure** technique after a "problem" developed in an investigation of a different procedure. In a control phase of this earlier experiment, a homosexual male subject watched what was expected to be a nonarousing movie of an attractive nude female assuming various sexual poses. Unexpectedly, the subject's electronically monitored erectile response began to increase sharply, indicating that perhaps all that was necessary to generate heterosexual arousal in homosexual subjects was a sufficiently "strong" heterosexual stimulus.

Herman, Barlow, and Agras (1971, 1974b) subsequently replicated this finding in three male homosexuals and a male homosexual pedophile using single-case experimental analyses. Both physiological and self-report measures indicated increases in heterosexual arousal following re-

peated viewing of a short film depicting a seductive nude woman assuming a number of sexual postures. Inappropriate arousal (that is, to homosexual stimuli) was not affected by the procedure. Moreover, although all subjects did attempt to increase their heterosexual behavior outside therapy, all encountered considerable difficulty.

Explicit exposure appears to be a promising technique for developing appropriate sexual arousal. But the generality of its effects and the mechanisms by which it works are presently unknown and await further investigation.

Orgasmic Reconditioning

We have already mentioned the presumed role of masturbatory conditioning in the development of unconventional sexual interests (Evans, 1968; McGuire, Carlisle, & Young, 1965). J. G. Thorpe, E. Schmidt, and D. Castell (1963) used the converse of this process—that is, masturbation to orgasm while engaging in *heterosexual* fantasies—in an attempt to establish heterosexual arousal in a homosexual individual. Since this first report, **orgasmic reconditioning** (Marquis, 1970) has been used in a number of case studies involving a variety of sexual variations including fetishism (Marshal, 1974b), pedophilia (Marshall, 1973), voyeurism (Jackson, 1969), and sadistic fantasies (Davison, 1968; Mees, 1966). In addition, there are numerous reports of its use with homosexual clients (for example, Blitch & Haynes, 1972; Marshall, 1973; Rehm & Rozensky, 1974).

Orgasmic reconditioning usually involves having the client masturbate to orgasm while attending to a heterosexual fantasy or a picture of a nude member of the opposite sex. However, since these stimuli are by their very nature unarousing to the client, it is usually necessary for him or her to use an inappropriate fantasy or stimulus to gain arousal. For example, a man with a leather fetish might begin masturbating to an image of a pair of women's boots. Just at the point of ejaculation, he is to switch to an appropriate heterosexual fantasy, or to a *Playboy*-type picture if he has difficulty in imagining the necessary stimulus. On subsequent occasions, the client can be asked either to switch to the appropriate stimulus progressively earlier in the masturbation sequence (Marquis, 1970), or to switch back and forth between inappropriate and appropriate stimuli, gradually increasing the time occupied by the heterosexual stimulus (Thorpe, Schmidt, Brown, & Castell, 1964). In either case, a heterosexual fantasy or stimulus should always be associated with orgasm.

Unfortunately, almost all the data on the effectiveness of orgasmic reorientation come from uncontrolled case reports in which the technique is used in conjunction with other procedures, such as aversive conditioning. Only two reports of controlled individual analysis investigations of the procedure have appeared to date, providing data on a total of five subjects. In the first of these studies (Abel, Barlow, & Blanchard, 1973), a male with sadistic fantasies experienced substantial increases in heterosexual arousal (as reflected in penile erection measures), and also decreases in inappropriate arousal, as the result of orgasmic reorientation treatment. The subject also reported changes in sexual urges and fantasies. However, the same team of investigators reported the failure of the procedure in four other cases of sexual variation (Abel & Blanchard, 1976).

In the second controlled study (Conrad & Wincze, 1976), four male homosexual subjects underwent orgasmic reconditioning. All four were eventually able to sustain masturbation totally with female pictural stimuli, and all four reported vague changes in their heterosexual interests. However, none of the subjects showed any change in sexual behavior, fantasies, or urges; and physiological measures of homosexual and heterosexual arousal remained unaffected by the treatment.

These conflicting results leave the real efficacy of orgasmic reconditioning in doubt, and encourage further study of the procedure.

Fading

If a heterosexual stimulus can be gradually "faded in" while an individual is experiencing sexual arousal to an inappropriate stimulus, it should eventually acquire stimulus control of sexual responsiveness. David Barlow and Stewart Agras (1973) developed a procedure called **fading** that is intended to produce this result. In the initial test of their procedure, a male homosexual watched a slide of an attractive nude man while his erectile response was monitored. Another slide of a nude female was then superimposed on the image of the male and slowly faded in while the slide of the male was faded out. This gradual transformation of the homosexual stimulus into a heterosexual stimulus continued as long as the subject maintained sexual arousal (defined as 75 percent of a full erection). Whenever there was any failure of arousal, fading was stopped until erection returned to the 75 percent criterion; then transformation of the stimulus picked up where it left off. Eventually, the individual was able to maintain arousal while viewing the female stimulus alone.

Barlow and Agras (1973) applied their fading procedure to three homosexual subjects in an individual analysis experimental design. Although their data are somewhat variable, it appears that all subjects increased their arousal to heterosexual stimuli. Furthermore, two of the three individuals established a pattern of heterosexual behavior in which they remained active at a nine-month followup.

On the other hand, a report describing the use of a fading procedure with two pedophilic individuals did not replicate the findings of Barlow and Agras (Laws, 1974). Although the subjects of this study reported some changes in sexual interest, objective measures showed little systematic change in their sexual arousal to appropriate stimuli. Thus, conclusions about the effectiveness of fading must await further study of the procedure.

Classical Conditioning

The classical conditioning procedure is somewhat unfortunately named, since it is not the only technique discussed here that involves classical conditioning—aversion relief, orgasmic reconditioning, and fading all presumably operate through such a process. This particular procedure simply involves the sequential presentation of a heterosexual stimulus and an inappropriate stimulus. The inappropriate stimulus functions as a US that elicits the UR, sexual arousal. Repeatedly preceding the inappropriate stimulus with the "neutral" heterosexual stimulus presumably establishes the latter as a CS for sexual arousal.

The clinical procedure closely follows a strategy

used by Stanley Rachman (1966; Rachman & Hodgson, 1968) to experimentally induce a "fetish" in normal male subjects. A slide picturing a pair of women's boots was repeatedly followed by slides of nude females. In a short time, increases in penile erection were elicited by presentation of the boots alone. The clinical use of the technique involves reversing this sequence: the heterosexual stimuli are presented first, followed closely by the inappropriate but arousing stimuli.

In one case study, this classical conditioning technique was used successfully to increase a male heterosexual pedophile's arousal to mature women (Beech, Watts, & Poole, 1971). However, another study employing penile erection measures showed no increase in appropriate sexual arousal in four individuals despite over 300 CS-US pairings (Marshall, 1974a).

The classical conditioning procedure has been experimentally evaluated only once in an individual analysis study of three homosexual males (Herman, Barlow, & Agras, 1974a). In two of the subjects, the procedure was effective in increasing heterosexual arousal. However, for one of these two individuals (the transsexual described in Case Study 12–1), the CS and US had to be presented simultaneously, rather than sequentially, before the procedure was effective. Thus, experimental support for this technique is meager at present.

BUILDING HETEROSOCIAL SKILLS

Once a client has developed some interest in members of the opposite sex, the next goal is to provide him or her with the skills necessary to establish a heterosexual relationship, initiate sexual behavior in that relationship, and maintain the relationship over a period of time (Barlow, Abel, Blanchard, Bristow, & Young, 1977). The importance of this step is highlighted by numerous reports of clients who became heterosexually responsive during treatment but had great difficulty in developing new patterns of sexual behavior because of skills deficits and anxiety about heterosexual interaction (for instance, Barlow & Agras, 1973; Herman, Barlow, & Agras, 1974a, 1974b).

The procedures for developing heterosocial skills and reducing anxiety in sexually reoriented

individuals are the same as those for any client with these problems. (These strategies are discussed in Chapters 9 and 10.) However, social retraining in cases of sexual variation has received distressingly little attention in the treatment and research literature. Even those individuals who have made important contributions in the development of the new procedures for establishing heterosexual arousal have often discharged reoriented clients prematurely, only to watch them flounder in their attempts to function heterosexually. Isolated reports do exist of the use of such procedures as behavioral rehearsal (Cautela & Wisocki, 1969), assertion training (Edwards, 1972; Stevenson & Wolpe, 1960), and systematic desensitization (LoPiccolo, 1971) to facilitate the client's shift to heterosexual behavior. There have also been a few papers describing the use of social retraining as a component of comprehensive programs for the treatment of sexual variation (for instance, Hanson & Adesso, 1972; Pinard & Lamontagne, 1976; Rehm & Rozensky, 1974; see also Case Study 12–2). Perhaps clinicians are beginning to recognize the importance of this area.

MODIFYING GENDER ROLE BEHAVIOR

An important aspect of general heterosocial retraining in some cases of sexual variation is the modification of interests and overt behaviors toward those that are more appropriate to the client's gender. Great variation exists in the extent to which clients behave like members of the opposite sex, and this is by no means a treatment target for all clients; but most transsexuals, and some transvestite and homosexual individuals, behave atypically enough to draw attention to themselves or to sabotage their efforts at heterosexual interaction.

Barlow and his co-workers have presented the only detailed account of modifying inappropriate gender role behavior to date in their treatment of an adolescent male transsexual (Barlow, Reynolds, & Agras, 1973). Their approach to this problem was to break complex masculine characteristics of, for example, sitting, standing, and walking into component parts, and then teach the client these behaviors piece by piece through modeling and rehearsal. Because the uniqueness and importance of this study warrant a closer look, we have presented it in some detail as Case Study 12–1.

Although a slight departure from our focus on adults, mention should be made of the utility of early intervention in cases of gender identity confusion. There is reason to believe that children who show severe and persistent deviations from appropriate gender role behavior at age five are at high risk for gender identity confusion in adulthood (Green, 1974; Green & Money, 1969). Adults with gender identity conflicts are often very distressed; severe depression and suicide attempts are not infrequent among such individuals, and genital self-mutilation (for example, self-castration) is sometimes reported (Pauly, 1965, 1969). The desire to prevent such misery is the primary justification for attempting to eliminate gender problems at an early age. (For an interesting analysis of the ethical issues surrounding this position, see Rosen, Rekers, & Bentler, in press).

George Rekers and his colleagues have pioneered behavioral approaches to the assessment and treatment of childhood gender disturbances (see Rekers, 1977, for a review). They have obtained excellent results using behavioral procedures to modify sex role behaviors in highly feminized young boys. Their program generally involves social or token reinforcement for masculine mannerisms, speech, play behavior, and so on, with extinction, response costs, or mild punishment for feminine behaviors. Of particular importance is the finding that treatment effects tend to be highly specific. That is, only those particular responses that are the focus of treatment contingencies show any change, and new behaviors fail to generalize beyond the stimuli (trainers, environments, contingencies, and so on) under which they were acquired. To increase generalization, treatment is typically administered not only by a therapist in a clinical setting, but also by the child's parents in the home, and sometimes even by a teacher in the boy's classroom. Followup data obtained from a few months to several years after treatment have consistently indicated that the behavior changes produced by the treatment are lasting ones. Rekers is currently engaged in following treated children longitudinally to ensure that early intervention does indeed prevent the development of adult gender disturbances.

DECREASING INAPPROPRIATE AROUSAL: AVERSION THERAPY

The task of reducing an individual's inappropriate sexual arousal and behavior has fallen almost exclusively to aversive conditioning procedures. Repeatedly associating inappropriate erotic stimuli with unpleasant events is intended to endow those stimuli with negative properties—or at least to eliminate their positive (arousing) properties. Three major types of aversion therapy have been applied to unconventional sexual interests: chemical aversion, electrical aversion, and covert sensitization.

Chemical Aversion

Chemical aversion therapy generally involves the use of a drug (typically apomorphine or emetine hydrochloride) that induces intense nausea and vomiting. These extremely unpleasant reactions are timed to occur in the presence of the inappropriate sexual stimuli. To illustrate the chemical aversion procedure, let us look briefly at the first report of its use in the treatment of sexual variation (Raymond, 1956).

The client was a thirty-three-year-old married man with a twenty-year history of sexual arousal to handbags and baby carriages. He obtained relief from sexual tension by physically attacking these objects, a habit that had resulted in several arrests and confinements in mental hospitals. Several previous courses of psychotherapy had proven ineffective. Aversion therapy was conducted by injecting the client with apomorphine, and then surrounding him with handbags, baby carriages, and colored photographs of these things just before he became nauseated. As soon as the client had finished vomiting, these stimuli were removed. This procedure was repeated every two hours, day and night, for a week, followed by a week's suspension, and then another nine days of treatment. At the end of this exhausting program the client reported that he was no longer attracted to handbags and baby carriages; in fact, the mere sight of them made him sick. Nineteen months later, he appeared to remain free of his unusual variation.

Although the procedures are rarely as intensive as those just described, chemical aversion has been applied to other variations, including homosexuality (Freund, 1960; McConaghy, 1969, 1970), fetishism (Cooper, 1963), and transvestism (Lavin, Thorpe, Barker, Blakemore, & Conway, 1961; Morgenstern, Pearce, & Rees, 1965). For a number of reasons, however, chemical aversion has fallen into disuse. (1) The procedure is highly unpleasant to administer and undergo, and there appear to be significant medical dangers associated with its use (for example, Barker, Thorpe, Blakemore, Lavin, & Conway, 1961). (2) Medical supervision is required, and the intensive nature of a chemical aversion program usually necessitates hospitalization of the client. (3) The effects of nausea-inducing agents are somewhat unpredictable, so that precise CS-US pairings are very difficult to achieve. (4) What little experimental evidence exists suggests that chemical aversion is no more effective in reducing inappropriate sexual arousal than is electrical aversion, which is far less problematic (McConaghy, 1969, 1970; McConaghy, Proctor, & Barr, 1972).

Electrical Aversion

The aim of electrical aversion is the same as that of chemical aversion, but painful shocks delivered to the hands, arms, or legs replace nausea and vomiting as the aversive US. The first successful use of electrical aversion in a case of sexual variation was reported in 1935 (Max, 1935). The client, a homosexual male, was given a series of painful shocks as he viewed pictures of nude men. This report was largely ignored for a quarter of a century, and it was not until 1961, when Rachman removed a man's buttock and bloomer fetish with a similar procedure, that electrical aversion gained prominence as a treatment for sexual variation.

M. P. Feldman and M. J. MacCulloch (1965, 1971) have developed a prototypical method for electrical aversion treatment of homosexual males called **anticipatory avoidance learning (AA).** The AA technique combines components of respondent conditioning, operant escape and avoidance learning, and aversion relief. The client watches a slide of a male as it is projected on a screen. Eight seconds later, he receives a painful electric shock through electrodes on his leg. The client can escape this by pressing a button that removes the male slide, replaces it with a slide of an attractive female, and terminates the shock—the female stimulus is always associated with aversion relief. On succeeding trials, the client is presented with slides of increasingly attractive men, each of which is followed eight seconds later by shock. He is asked to tolerate the shock for as long as he finds the stimulus attractive, before pressing the button that produces the female stimulus and stops the shock. Each trial ends with the therapist removing the female slide unless the client presses another button, which brings him an instant replay. Doing this buys the client a few seconds of relaxation (again associated with the heterosexual stimulus) before the next trial is begun.

As this process is repeated, and male stimuli are repeatedly associated with shock, we might expect the client to find them less attractive. This is apparently what happens in many cases: within a short time, the client begins pressing the reject button in the eight-second period *before* the shock comes on, thereby escaping it entirely and relaxing with a picture of an attractive woman. This is an anticipatory avoidance response.

When the client is reliably avoiding shock in this manner, the procedure is changed somewhat. Pressing the reject button in the eight-second preshock period now has one of three consequences that vary randomly with each trial: (1) *reinforced,* in which the avoidance response is immediately successful (as already described); (2) *delayed,* in which the male slide is not replaced by the female slide until just before the eight-second limit is up; or (3) *nonreinforced,* in which the button press has no effect and the male stimulus remains while the client sits out the eight-second delay and suffers a brief but painful shock. The purpose of including delayed and nonreinforced trials is to ensure that the client still occasionally experiences an aversive event tied to the male stimulus. In the delayed condition, the client presses the button and then "sweats it out," wondering whether the male slide will be replaced and shock will be avoided. In this way, the anxiety of not knowing whether the avoidance response will succeed is paired with the homosexual stimulus, and anxiety relief occurs when the female finally appears. Nonreinforced trials continued to pair the male stimuli with shock, presumably reducing their arousing value. The reinforced trials are designed to develop a response that will be valuable to the client in the real world—that is, avoiding males for the company of females.

Following the rather remarkable success obtained with the AA procedure in preliminary investigations (MacCulloch & Feldman, 1967), Feldman and MacCulloch (1971) undertook a controlled evaluation of the technique. They compared AA with a standard classical conditioning treatment (unavoidable shock paired with the homosexual stimuli) and a traditional psychotherapy condition. The study has been criticized for a number of design and measurement problems (for instance, Barlow, 1972b; MacDonough, 1972), which make interpretation of the findings extremely difficult. Nevertheless, it appears that both the AA and classical conditioning treatments were far more effective than psychotherapy in reducing homosexual behavior and interest and in establishing a heterosexual orientation. However, the AA and classical conditioning procedures proved to be *equally* effective, suggesting that the inclusion of avoidance procedures contributes little to the efficacy of AA.

Of considerable importance is Feldman and MacCulloch's (1971) finding that the variable which most effectively discriminated treatment successes from treatment failures was a *prior history of pleasurable heterosexual behavior.* In view of our previous discussion, this is not surprising. It merely indicates that those clients with some preexisting heterosexual skills were able to benefit from reductions in their homosexual interests. Clients lacking such skills did not magically acquire them by suffering through a series of electric shocks.

Another interesting account of electrical aversion in the treatment of sexual variation is provided by Isaac Marks and M. G. Gelder (1967). They treated five clients who had been troubled by fetishes or transvestism for at least twenty years.

An impressive feature of this study was the detailed assessment of self-report and physiological data throughout the course of treatment. Electrical aversion was carried out in two phases. Initially, clients received shocks just above pain threshold when they signaled they had obtained a clear fantasy involving their sexual variation. In the second phase, shocks were given while clients actually engaged in their inappropriate behavior, namely, fondling a fetishistic object or crossdressing.

One of the first findings was that with repeated exposure to contingent shock, clients had more and more difficulty conjuring up inappropriate fantasies. Marks and Gelder checked to be sure that simple repetition of the image was not the cause of this effect, but only when images were associated with shock did the client require increasingly longer periods to produce the fantasy. This effect was paralleled by penile erection measures. When treatment began, the clients produced strong and rapid erections in the presence of the inappropriate stimuli. As electrical aversion progressed, increasing periods of time were required before such stimuli produced erection, or the stimuli lost their ability to produce erection entirely. Figure 12–1 illustrates this effect in one client with multiple fetishes. Note also the tremendous specificity of the effects of the electrical aversion. Erections to particular fetishistic objects remained completely unaffected by aversion treatment of other items, and fell only when treatment was directed toward them. Heterosexual arousal was not damaged even when all inappropriate arousal had been removed.

At treatment termination, all clients were completely free of the inappropriate sexual behavior that had plagued them for many years. Within a year, however, two of the five had shown some treatment reversal. Another group of twenty-four transvestites, fetishists, sadomasochists, and transsexuals was treated by this same procedure and assessed in a two-year followup study (Marks, Gelder, & Bancroft, 1970). The results for all but the transsexuals were very encouraging. All clients were rated as either "improved" (significantly less inappropriate sexual behavior than before therapy) or "greatly improved" (sexual variation rare or nonexistent). Most of these cli-

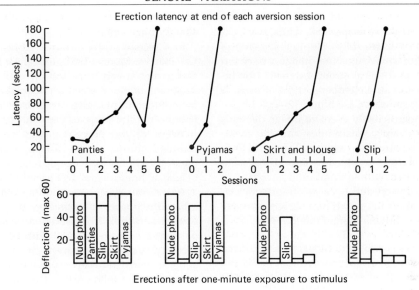

Figure 12–1. Increases in latency and decreases in amount of erections to fetishistic stimuli during electrical aversion treatment. From I. M. Marks & M. G. Gelder, Transvestitism and fetishism: Clinical and psychological changes during faradic aversion. *British Journal of Psychiatry*, 1967, **113,** p. 714, Figure 1. Copyright The British Journal of Psychiatry. Used by permission.

ents experienced little inappropriate arousal, and their attitudes toward their former variations remained "indifferent." The seven transsexual clients in the sample fared less well: all had returned to their previous behavior and interests within a few months after therapy. The refractoriness of transsexual behavior to aversive methods reflects the complexity of this variation, and it appears likely that only an intensive, multifaceted intervention program offers such individuals any hope of change (see Case Study 12–1).

Numerous other reports describe the effects of electrical aversion on sexual variations. Readers are encouraged to peruse one of the many interesting reviews available on this subject (for example, Barlow, 1972a; Hallam & Rachman, 1976; Marks, 1976; Rachman & Teasdale, 1969a, 1969b). Although electrical aversion undoubtedly suppresses inappropriate sexual arousal and leads to a change in sexual behavior in many cases, these ef-

fects are by no means reliable. We are not sure why electrical aversion helps some clients while leaving others unaffected. Furthermore, the contribution of such procedures as aversion relief to the efficacy of electrical aversion remains unclear. But, perhaps most important, we do not even understand the process(es) by which aversive procedures work, when they work at all. We will discuss this matter shortly.

Covert Sensitization

Aversive stimulation can also be administered "within the skin," that is, by way of the client's cognitive processes. The use of covert sensitization in the management of overeating and alcoholism was discussed in Chapter 8. Covert sensitization has also been applied to a number of sexual variations, including exhibitionism (Brownell & Barlow, 1976; Callahan & Leitenberg, 1973), pedophilia (Barlow, Leitenberg, & Agras, 1969), and homosexuality (Barlow, Agras, Leitenberg, Callahan, & Moore, 1972; Maletzky & George, 1973). As in the treatment of overeating and alcoholism, the procedure usually involves having the client imagine engaging in the undesirable behavior and becoming nauseated and violently ill. However, this format is not invariable; theoretically, at least, imaginally pairing the target stimuli with *any* aversive consequence should result in those stimuli acquiring negative properties. Thus, some clinicians have successfully employed anxiety-evoking, rather than disgusting, imagery in covert sensitization of atypical sexual interests (for instance, Callahan & Leitenberg, 1973; Curtis & Presley, 1972; see also Case Study 12–3).

Selecting a sufficiently aversive image depends on both the client's sensibilities and the therapist's creative flair. For example, Davison (1968) treated a young man troubled by sexual arousal to sadistic fantasies with a combined program of covert sensitization and orgasmic reorientation. Davison describes the search for the right aversive image in the following memorable passage:

> With his eyes closed, [the client] was instructed to imagine a typical sadistic scene, a pretty girl tied to stakes on the ground and struggling tearfully to extricate herself. While looking at the girl, he was asked to imagine someone bringing a branding iron toward his eyes, ultimately searing his eyebrows. A second image was attempted when this proved abortive, namely, being kicked in the groin by a ferocious-looking karate expert. When he reported himself indifferent to this image as well, the therapist depicted to him a large bowl of "soup," composed of steaming urine with reeking fecal boli bobbing around on top. His grimaces, contortions, and groans indicated that an effective image had been found, and the following five minutes were spent portraying his drinking from the bowl, with accompanying nausea, at all times while peering over the floating debris at the struggling girl (p. 86).

The efficacy of covert sensitization in the treatment of sexual variation has been evaluated in an interesting series of well-designed individual analysis experiments conducted by Barlow, Agras, Leitenberg, and their coworkers. In their first study (Barlow, Leitenberg, & Agras, 1969), covert sensitization successfully reduced self-reports of inappropriate arousal and sexual urges in both a male homosexual and a male pedophilic client. Once clear reductions in these measures had been obtained, covert sensitization treatment was discontinued for a control period, and reports of arousal and sexual urges returned to pretreatment levels. Covert sensitization was then reintro-

duced, and the unwanted sexual feelings declined sharply once again.

In a second study (Barlow, Agras, Leitenberg, Callahan, & Moore, 1972), four male homosexuals underwent covert sensitization with periodic assessment of their erectile responses to slides of male nudes to measure sexual arousal. The contribution of the subjects' expectancies to the effectiveness of the procedure was evaluated in a unique fashion. In the first phase of the experiment, the clients were deeply relaxed and asked to visualize homosexual scenes without imagining aversive consequences. Although this was really a baseline phase, subjects were told to expect reductions in their homosexual arousal due to the pairing of arousing stimuli with relaxation. The second stage involved covert sensitization, but the subjects were led to expect *increases* in homosexual arousal by the following instructions: "To obtain the best effects we are going to heighten the tension by pairing the sexually arousing scenes with images of vomiting. You will probably notice an increase in your sexual arousal to males and in your homosexual urges but don't be alarmed, this is part of the treatment" (Barlow, Agras, Leitenberg, Callahan, & Moore, 1972, pp. 412–413).

The third phase of the experiment was an extinction condition in which aversive scenes were removed from the imagery sessions, but subjects were told to expect a decline in inappropriate arousal. Finally, covert sensitization was reintroduced in phase four, with the "correct" expectation of reduction in arousal to the homosexual stimuli. In other words, in the first three phases of the study, subjects were led to expect exactly the opposite of what should really have resulted from the treatment conditions. Despite these counterdemand instructions, subjects' arousal to homosexual stimuli dropped during covert sensitization phases while remaining essentially unaffected by baseline and extinction conditions. These results are illustrated in Figure 12–2.

A third study (Callahan & Leitenberg, 1973) compared the effects of covert sensitization to electric shock delivered contingent on erectile responses to inappropriate stimuli. The six subjects for this study included homosexual, exhibitionistic, transvestite, and pedophilic males. Although some problems were encountered in

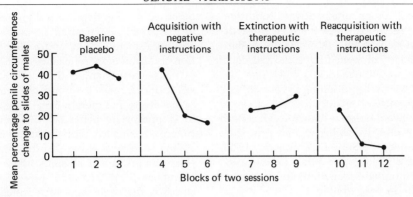

Figure 12–2. Changes in inappropriate sexual arousal during covert sensitization with counterdemand instructions. From D. H. Barlow, W. S. Agras, H. Leitenberg, E. J. Callahan, & R. C. Moore, The contribution of therapeutic instruction to covert sensitization. *Behaviour Research and Therapy*, 1972, **10,** p. 413, Figure 1. By permission of Pergamon Press, Ltd.

maintaining the original balanced experimental design, covert sensitization and electrical aversion appeared to be equally effective in reducing inappropriate arousal; however, covert sensitization was markedly superior in suppressing unconventional sexual fantasies and urges. Followup data obtained from four to eighteen months after treatment indicated that the combination of electrical aversion and covert sensitization procedures was highly effective in producing long-lasting behavioral changes.

An interesting variant of covert sensitization has been introduced by Barry Maletzky (1973, 1974; Maletzky & George, 1973). **Assisted covert sensitization** combines the visualization of a nauseating scene with inhalation of a noxious odor (for example, valeric acid). Maletzky's (1974) treatment of ten exhibitionists with assisted covert sensitization is of particular interest. In addition to assessing treatment outcome through self-report data and arrest records, Maletzky arranged for an ingenious (but ethically questionable) "temptation test" in which an attractive female was paid to stroll seductively past the clients' cars. A twelve-month followup assessment of these clients showed a complete absence of exhib-

iting, no instances of arrest, and no successful "temptations."

Taken together, the data on covert sensitization are impressive and suggest a cautious endorsement of the use of this method in the elimination of sexual variations (Mahoney, 1974). Further research is clearly called for. As with other aversive techniques, there is much about this procedure that we do not know. Not the least of our questions is *how does it work?*

How Does Aversion Therapy Work?

We are far from knowing how aversive procedures produce their results. However, from the manner in which aversive procedures are typically administered, it is quite obvious that classical conditioning is presumed to play a central role in the process. Nowhere in the field of behavior modification is a larger implicit "automaticity assumption" to be found (see Chapter 2). The repeated association of the inappropriate sexual stimuli with aversive consequences is presumed to automatically condition anxiety or revulsion to those stimuli, thus divesting them of their arousing properties. However, as we have pointed out in our discussion of conditioning theories of anxiety, there is little reason to believe that strong or lasting conditioned autonomic reactions of this type can be developed through conventional laboratory procedures. Moreover, several studies directly challenge conditioning explanations for both electrical aversion and covert sensitization. In one investigation, for example, forty-six homosexual males were treated by one of three electrical aversion procedures: classical conditioning, avoidance conditioning, or a backward conditioning treatment in which shock *preceded* presentation of homosexual stimuli (McConaghy & Barr, 1973). Subjects in all three groups showed equal improvements—quite remarkable when one considers that backward conditioning is very difficult to achieve. Similarly, outside the field of sexual variation, backward covert sensitization has been found to be as effective as the regular procedure (Ashem & Donner, 1968; Sachs & Ingram, 1972). If such data are replicated in other experiments, classical conditioning explanations for these procedures will be in deep trouble.

Bandura (1969) has proposed an alternative to straight conditioning accounts of aversion therapy. In his *aversive self-arousal hypothesis*, Bandura suggests that external stimuli—in this case, inappropriate sexual stimuli—acquire the capacity to trigger a redintegration of the unpleasantness experienced during aversive procedures. In other words, a pedophilic individual is reminded of his covert sensitization sessions whenever he sees an attractive child, and a moment's elaboration of this memory reinstates some of the feelings of nausea experienced during treatment. This self-induced nausea suppresses the individual's sexual desire and thereby breaks the chain leading to inappropriate behavior. Bandura notes that conceptualizing aversion therapy as a means of instilling such a self-control system moves the emphasis in treatment sessions away from precise timing of stimulus events toward explicitly instructing the client how to redintegrate aversive experiences at appropriate moments. Although Bandura's self-arousal model of aversion therapy has received little attention, other clinicians have pointed out the utility of providing the client with directions that help him or her extend aversive responses to the extratherapy environment (Denholtz, 1973).

SUMMARY

The alteration of unconventional sexual interests and behaviors is a topic that is somewhat difficult for the behavioral psychologist to deal with. On the one hand, behavioral theories of sexual variation emphasize their normal, nonpathological origins; on the other hand, behavior therapists have developed many "treatments" for the behaviors they have defined as normal. The ethical issues that arise from this logical contradiction are complex, and easy solutions are not to be found. Ultimately, the decision to change or not to change sexual orientation must rest with the client, problematic as this may be.

Until fairly recently, behavioral approaches to sexual reorientation have focused almost exclusively on decreasing inappropriate arousal. However, the tasks of increasing heterosexual arousal, building heterosocial skills, and modifying inappropriate gender role behaviors are equally if not more important. Procedures for increasing heterosexual arousal include aversion relief, explicit exposure, orgasmic reconditioning, fading, and classical conditioning. Because most of these techniques are in the preliminary stages of development, convincing evidence of their effectiveness does not yet exist. Building heterosocial skills in clients with sexual variations involves the same procedures used for any individual with social deficits. Altering gender role behavior involves breaking the appropriate responses into their component parts and teaching these components in a piece by piece fashion. Very little work has been done on these procedures.

The greatest attention has been directed toward reducing inappropriate arousal, and aversion therapy has been the procedure used almost exclusively for this task. Chemical aversion has had some popularity, but the many problems associated with its use have led to its abandonment. Electrical aversion has been widely employed with a fair amount of success, but the factors that determine its effectiveness are largely unknown. Finally, covert sensitization has accumulated an impressive record of preliminary findings and appears to be a promising alternative to electrical and chemical methods. Still, many fundamental questions remain unanswered about the workings of aversive procedures. A conditioning explanation does not fit the available data, and an aversive self-arousal model has been proposed to take its place. Future research may shed additional light on this area and allow us to apply aversive methods more intelligently and effectively.

CASE STUDY 12–1

BARLOW, D. H., REYNOLDS, J., & AGRAS, S. GENDER IDENTITY CHANGE IN A TRANSSEXUAL. *ARCHIVES OF GENERAL PSYCHIATRY,* 1973, **28,** 569–576.

This is a case report of the first known successful change of gender identity in a transsexual individual. The case superbly illustrates the sequential modification of each of the four components of sexual variation. As it is one of the few reports involving changes in gender role behavior, we will examine it in considerable detail.

The client was a seventeen-year-old-male. He was the last of five children, and a great disappointment to his mother, who had wanted a girl. He nevertheless became her favorite. The boy's father was rarely at home due to long working hours. The client had thought of himself as a female since his earliest recollection. Before the age of five he had begun cross-dressing spontaneously, and had developed interests in cooking, knitting, crocheting, and embroidering. The child's playmates were girls for the most part. When he developed sexual fantasies around age twelve, he imagined himself as a woman having intercourse with a man. The client reported masturbating during these fantasies, but at the time of the initial interview, he had never experienced an orgasm. When the client entered high school at age fifteen, his extremely effeminate manner earned him intense scorn and ridicule and led him to attempt suicide. He left school and consulted a psychiatrist, who hospitalized him and prescribed antidepressant and antipsychotic medication. When the client first came to Barlow and his colleagues, he was depressed and withdrawn, and was attending secretarial school, where he was the only male. He reported a strong desire to have a sex-change operation, but this could not be arranged because of his age. He thus consented to enter a treatment program to change his gender identity; surgery remained an option if therapy was unsuccessful.

Four measures of the client's gender identity were monitored: a self-report measure of transsexual attitudes, a daily diary of sexual urges and fantasies, penile circumference in response to slides of nude men and women, and an observational checklist of masculine and feminine behaviors which was employed later in treatment. Pretreatment baseline measures yielded a score of 32 out of a possible 40 on the attitude measure, indicating a strong transsexual orientation, and the client reported an average of seven homosexual urges a day. Sexual arousal to male slides was high, and there was no response to females.

Treatment began with a fading procedure designed to increase the client's heterosexual arousal, but eight sessions of this produced no measurable changes. Next, the client's dominant transsexual fantasy was chosen for electrical aversion therapy. The client was asked to engage in his fantasy and signal when he had a clear image. A painful electric shock was then delivered to his arm until he reported that the fantasy had ceased. This procedure also failed. Despite over 48 daily half-hour sessions, the client experienced no change in patterns of arousal or fantasy, and his latency to achieve the fantasy in session was unaffected.

At this point, Barlow and his co-workers decided that modification of the boy's gender role behaviors might be necessary before arousal and attitude change could be accomplished. To aid in assessing and implementing this program, an observational checklist of gender specific behaviors was developed by observing normal males and females in the natural environment. Four characteristics of walking, standing, and sitting behavior were chosen for each sex, and observers were trained to identify these characteristics reliably. Then, each day, an observer who was unaware of the treatment sequence surreptitiously rated the client's behavior when he entered the waiting room.

The therapists then began directly to modify the client's way of sitting through a painstaking daily modeling procedure using videotape feedback. The appropriate behavior was broken down, and each component was modeled by a male therapist and then imitated by the client. The therapist praised successes and delivered verbal and videotape feedback of errors. When the subject was sitting appropriately and feeling comfortable about it, the same procedure was applied to walking and later to standing. Figure 12–3 illustrates the independent observer's ratings of the behavioral changes produced by this treatment. Note that the client's behavior was initially quite feminine or decidedly mixed, and that, with the exception of standing, systematic change in a particular behavioral category did not occur until treatment was directed at that behavior.

Figure 12–3. Masculine and feminine behavioral components of sitting, walking, and standing during therapeutic attempts to increase masculine behavior in each category. From D. H. Barlow, J. Reynolds, & S. Agras, Gender identity change in a transsexual. *Archives of General Psychiatry*, 1973, **28,** p. 572, Figure 2. Copyright 1973, American Medical Association. Used by permission.

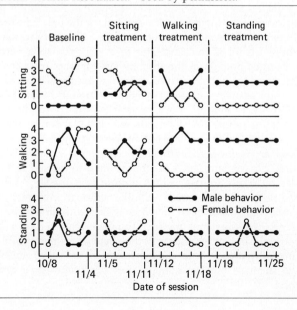

At this point, a similar program was begun to develop the client's hetero-social skills. A graded series of social situations involving both boys and girls was developed. The client then enacted a scene with a male and female therapist taking the part of peers, and the interaction was video-taped. On playback of the tape, the therapists delivered feedback and then taped the scene themselves, modeling appropriate behavior. This tape was then discussed, before the client rehearsed the scene once again. During this phase, the client's high-pitched, very precise manner of speaking was also modified in a masculine direction. He was taught to lower his voice by lowering his thyroid cartilage, which he monitored by placing his finger on his Adam's apple. A male therapist also modeled a less enunciated, more relaxed way of speaking using sentences with masculine content, like "A good looking woman really turns me on." Although no objective measures of voice change were recorded, significant differences were noted by the therapist, and the client reported with pride that several close acquaintances had failed to recognize his voice on the telephone.

At the end of this phase of treatment, the client was very pleased with his new masculine behavior. However, he still felt like a girl and still entertained transsexual fantasies. Arousal was still directed toward males, the transsexual attitude score remained at 32, and the client still expressed a desire for sexual reassignment surgery.

The next step in the treatment program was aimed at modifying transsexual cognitions. Since the client's most prevalent fantasy involved his having a female body and engaging in intercourse with a man, it was decided to develop a competing gender-appropriate fantasy. The client first chose pictures of a *Playboy* model who was least unattractive to him and then fantasized having sex with the woman in the picture. These fantasies were enriched by explicit descriptions of sexual activity given by a female therapist. The client was praised by the therapist for increasing the duration of his heterosexual fantasies. Not only did the length of the client's appropriate fantasies increase during this treatment, but for the first time other indications of transsexual ideation began to change. The transsexual attitude measure dropped from 32 to 4 and later to 0. Spontaneous heterosexual fantasies and urges outside of the therapy sessions occurred for the first time. At this point the client behaved, felt, and thought like a man. However, he was still sexually aroused by males, although his fantasies were now of homosexual content in which he retained his appropriate anatomical gender. At this point, the techniques which had failed to alter his pattern of sexual arousal almost a year before were attempted again.

Heterosexual arousal was strengthened first through a classical conditioning procedure. Unarousing slides of nude women were used as the CS and were followed by highly arousing slides of nude men, the US. Arousal was quickly conditioned to the female stimuli, although responses to male slides remained high. A reversal, in which the conditioning technique was withdrawn and then reinstated, produced a fall and then a rise in arousal to the female stimuli, indicating the procedure really was responsible for the changing arousal pattern. The client's heterosexual urges and fantasies continued to increase outside therapy, but his homosexual arousal remained strong.

The final treatment goal was the reduction of the client's homosexual arousal. A combination of electrical aversion and covert sensitization completely eliminated the client's arousal to male slides in 20 sessions, and his homosexual fantasies dropped significantly. Heterosexual arousal continued to grow. Gender-appropriate behaviors were still being monitored unobtrusively, and after leveling off following the first treatment phase eight months before, masculine components of sitting, standing, and walking underwent another sharp increase during the classical conditioning phase even though no further attempts had been made to modify these behaviors.

The major therapy effects are summarized in Figure 12–4. Formal treatment was terminated, but the client continued to meet with the therapist on a declining contact schedule for another year. Most of these meetings were

Figure 12–4. Major treatment effects as reflected in penile circumference change to heterosexual stimuli, transsexual attitude, and masculine motor behavior. From D. H. Barlow, J. Reynolds, & S. Agras, Gender identity change in a transsexual. *Archives of General Psychiatry*, 1973, **28,** p. 570, Figure 1. Copyright 1973, American Medical Association. Used by permission.

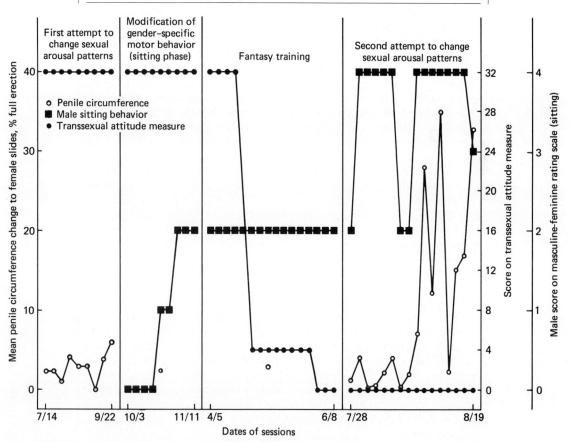

supportive and instructive in nature, although several sessions were devoted to aversion therapy for some lingering homosexual fantasies. Five months after termination, the client had his first orgasm while masturbating to a heterosexual fantasy. At nine months, the transsexual attitude measure was zero, indicating no gender confusion. Surreptitiously recorded masculine behavior remained at the high termination levels. The client was doing well in school, dating occasionally, and had lost all homosexual interests. At one year posttreatment, the client reported that he had a steady girlfriend with whom he had begun light petting. He was continuing to grow more comfortable with his new skills.

In a personal communication, Barlow (1977) reported that at five years posttreatment the client is still maintaining an exclusively heterosexual orientation. The young man, now twenty-two, is not married, but continues to date. Although he enjoys light petting, the client has not engaged in intercourse because of religious and personal opposition to premarital sex. His sexual fantasies during masturbation and at other times remain heterosexual in content. Barlow also reported the encouraging news that he and his co-workers have successfully treated two other transsexual individuals with behavioral techniques. A paper describing these cases is in preparation.

BLITCH, J. W., & HAYNES, S. N. MULTIPLE BEHAVIORAL TECH-
NIQUES IN A CASE OF FEMALE HOMOSEXUALITY. *JOURNAL OF BE-
HAVIOR THERAPY AND EXPERIMENTAL PSYCHIATRY*, 1972, **3,** 319–322.

There are a great many case reports of the treatment of male sexual variations in the behavioral literature. The research support for the various
treatment methods is also based entirely on investigations employing male
subjects. The extent to which behavioral approaches to sexual reorientation apply to females is an open question. The following case study is included because it is one of the very rare reports of the treatment of sexual
variation in a woman.

The client, Miss B, was an attractive twenty-two-year-old college student
who sought treatment for her homosexual interests. In the four months
prior to entering therapy, she had experienced eight or nine manual genital
contacts with three women. Though she was only rarely orgasmic during
these encounters, she derived considerable enjoyment from satisfying her
partner. Nevertheless, she was very upset by such activity, primarily because she felt that it indicated some underlying pathology.

Miss B had no apparent inappropriate gender role behaviors and was, in
fact, actively involved in heterosexual relationships. However, her primary motivation for these relationships was to prove to others that she was
not homosexual. She had engaged in intercourse about twenty times over
the preceding six months, mostly with the same man, but she had always
been anxious and upset on these occasions.

Miss B was seen twice weekly for a period of seven weeks. The first
thing the therapist did was to present her with a behavioral conceptualization of homosexual behavior. Miss B's stated goal was to rid herself of homosexual urges, but the therapist also explored other alternatives with her
(for example, becoming more comfortable with homosexual feelings) in
order to assess her motivation to change. The initial phases of therapy
were also devoted to identifying the specific behavioral and external stimuli
associated with Miss B's sexual encounters. For example, Miss B was instructed to discontinue the use of alcohol and marijuana for two months
and to stay off the bed of her most frequent female partner when it became
clear that these were important early stimuli in the chain leading to homosexual behavior.

Relaxation and systematic desensitization were used to reduce Miss B's
anxiety about sexual relations with men. Her training in relaxation was
supplemented by instructions on how to use it in vivo. Two hierarchies
were used for desensitization: one consisted of 14 items involving "touching" and the other of 10 items revolving around "being touched." The content of these hierarchies ranged from such low-anxiety activities as lip kissing to high-anxiety activities like mutual oral-genital stimulation to
orgasm.

An attempt was also made to improve Miss B's social skills—primarily in
the areas of communicating more effectively with new acquaintances, accepting compliments graciously, disagreeing with friends, and asserting
feelings. Role playing and behavioral rehearsal were used to sharpen Miss

B's skills. Generalization of her new behavior was facilitated by using psychology graduate students in certain role-playing assignments, and by conducting the role plays "on location" (in the campus student center) as well as in the therapist's office.

The final component of the treatment package consisted of changing Miss B's masturbation fantasies. She reported that she had been masturbating ten to fifteen times per week, and that the ratio of homosexual to heterosexual masturbation fantasies had been about five to one. Miss B was started on a standard orgasmic reconditioning program and asked to keep a daily record of the frequency of her masturbation and the nature of the images she used. This record indicated a steady increase in the frequency of heterosexual fantasies during masturbation.

At the end of the seven-week treatment period, Miss B reported that she had not engaged in any homosexual behavior since the second week. She had experienced one near contact but had avoided this by walking away. In social interactions, her heterosexual anxiety was decreasing and her self-confidence was increasing. She was dating and becoming involved in group activities more frequently. Two months after the termination of therapy, Miss B reported that she was happier and generally more at ease and that her interpersonal interactions were greatly improved. She was masturbating about eight times a week to exclusively heterosexual fantasies. Her homosexual behavior had not recurred, and she reported having a number of satisfying relationships with men.

CASE STUDY 12–3

BROWNELL, K. D., & BARLOW, D. H. MEASUREMENT AND TREATMENT OF TWO SEXUAL DEVIATIONS IN ONE PERSON. *JOURNAL OF BEHAVIOR THERAPY AND EXPERIMENTAL PSYCHIATRY*, 1976, **7**, 349–354.

The following case study illustrates the use of covert sensitization in the reduction of inappropriate arousal.

The client was a thirty-four-year-old male machinist who was hospitalized voluntarily after being caught exposing himself to a female neighbor. The client had been troubled by exhibitionistic urges for about a year and had actually exposed himself about a dozen times in the three months prior to his hospitalization. He also had a two-year history of experiencing intense sexual arousal toward his seventeen-year-old stepdaughter. On several occasions he had made blatant verbal or physical advances and had also made her the object of his self-exposure. The stepdaughter was horrified by each of these episodes. The client masturbated almost exclusively to sexual images of his stepdaughter and fantasized having intercourse with her during about 75 percent of his sexual relations with his wife. He also fantasized about exposing himself to various neighborhood women.

The client's history revealed a lack of parental warmth and a strict fundamentalist upbringing. His introduction to sex came at age nine when he observed his brother and sister having intercourse. He became sexually active at fifteen and by the time of his first marriage (at twenty-one) had accumulated considerable sexual experience. The client was unhappy with the frequency of sex with his first wife and became involved in numerous extramarital affairs. His first marriage produced two children and lasted eleven years. His two-year marriage to his second wife was more fulfilling sexually, but he still craved sex with other women, particularly his stepdaughter. The second marriage had already been interrupted by four separations, two of which involved the police. One of the separations was occasioned by the client's sexual advances on the stepdaughter and another by an exposure incident. The client entered treatment when the wife threatened divorce unless he changed his behavior dramatically.

In order to assess treatment effects, a card-sorting procedure was used. Five scenes were created in each of four categories: (1) exhibition incidents, (2) sexual contact with the stepdaughter, (3) nonsexual contact with the stepdaughter, and (4) sexual contact with the wife. Each of the twenty scenes was typed on a separate index card and presented to the client in random order. He was asked to obtain a vivid image of the scene and then to rate his sexual arousal by placing the card in one of five envelopes marked 0 (no desire) to 4 (very much desire). An arousal score for a given category of behavior was then obtained by totaling the ratings of the five cards from that category. The client was also asked to keep a running record of *all* urges to expose himself, or to have sexual contact with his stepdaughter, wife, or any other women.

After baseline measures of the subject's arousal had been obtained, covert sensitization was begun. The subject was asked to think of three scenes that were the worst possible things that could happen in connection with his inappropriate behaviors. He chose: (1) being caught by his wife and subsequently divorced, (2) being caught by his two children from his first marriage and losing the right to see them, and (3) being burned to death in the room where the inappropriate behaviors were taking place. Covert sensitization sessions were conducted once every two days. At the beginning of each session the client chose the scene that was most aversive to him at that particular time. Then the image was paired with each of the scenes from one category of the card sort, starting with the exhibition scenes. The client was asked to close his eyes, relax, and vividly imagine the scene being presented. For example:

> You are sitting in the kitchen waiting for the neighbor to come out and hang up her clothes. Finally you see her. You have the urge to expose yourself so you rush into the bedroom and take off your clothes. You open the window and stand there naked. As the neighbor sees you, you begin to play with yourself. You can feel your hand on your penis—how good it feels. Suddenly the door opens and your son and daughter walk in. They see you in front of the window and begin to cry hysterically. They run out of the house and you begin to feel the panic. You put on your clothes and begin to chase them but the police come to get you. You are in court and you are told that you may never see your children again. Later you hear that your children have to leave town because the other children are taunting them about having a perverted father. You feel empty inside and there is nothing worth living for. (pp. 350–351)

Each scene lasted about three minutes, with one minute between scenes. Six sessions were devoted to the exhibition scenes, followed by ten sessions involving both exhibition scenes and scenes of sexual contact with the stepdaughter. The client also received instruction in how to self-administer covert sensitization. He was discharged from the hospital midway through this second phase, and covert sensitization was continued twice weekly on an outpatient basis.

Following covert sensitization, the client and his wife were seen for marital therapy once each week. These sessions were aimed at improving communication in the marriage, and the client's sexual variations were not specifically dealt with. However, he did complete the card sort at the end of each session and also continued to monitor his sexual urges.

The effects of the covert sensitization are shown in Figure 12–5. As can be seen, self-reported arousal to both appropriate and inappropriate stimuli was very high during baseline (20 being the maximum possible card-sort score). In phase one, in which covert sensitization was directed toward exhibition scenes, arousal to these dropped precipitously. Note that arousal to *non*sexual scenes with the stepdaughter also dropped, while scenes depicting specifically sexual interactions with the stepdaughter remained potent sources of excitation. This appears to be a function of differential response strengths to the two types of stimuli. The client reported that the covert sensitization was making him more aware of the potential consequences of his inappropriate desires, and this was enough to dampen his arousal in situations that were not explicitly sexual.

In phase two, when sexually explicit scenes involving the stepdaughter were added to the covert sensitization sessions, these too began to lose their erotic potential. Stimuli involving exposure and nonsexual interaction with the stepdaughter continued to decline. To ensure that the cli-

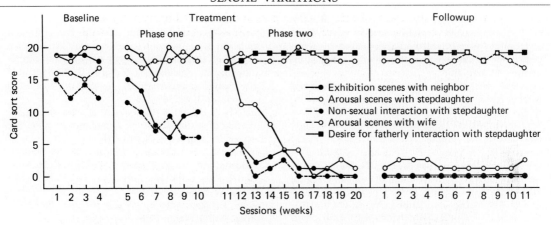

Figure 12–5. Card sort scores during baseline, treatment phase one (covert sensiti-zation for exhibitionism), phase two (covert sensitization for exhibitionism and arousal to stepdaughter), and followup. Ratings reflect degree of sexual arousal except for fatherly scenes with stepdaughter, in which ratings reflect desire to con-tinue such interaction. From K. D. Brownell & D. H. Barlow, Measurement and treatment of two sexual deviations in one person. *Journal of Behavior Therapy and Experimental Psychiatry,* 1976, **7,** p. 352, Figure 1. By permission of Pergamon Press, Ltd.

ent was not losing *all* interest in the stepdaughter, five scenes depicting ap-propriate fatherly interactions were added to the card sort, and the client was asked to rate them from 0 to 4 according to his desire to have such fa-therly contact. As can be seen in Figure 12–5, the client's reported interest in such interactions remained very high throughout treatment. Arousal to-ward the wife was unaffected by any treatment phase, and continued at a high level. During the eleven-week followup period, arousal was almost absent for all inappropriate stimuli, while sexual interest in the wife and fatherly interest in the stepdaughter were both strong.

The client had frequent sexual thoughts about other women during base-line, and few about his wife, his stepdaughter, or about exposing himself. The low level of the latter urges may have been due in part to the fact that the client was in the hospital rather than in his home environment. During treatment, the client began to experience more sexual thoughts about his wife and fewer about other women, and urges to expose himself or have sexual contact with his stepdaughter remained very low. This trend was maintained throughout the followup period.

The client reported that he did not expose himself or have sexual contact with his stepdaughter during treatment or followup, and this was con-firmed by his wife. The sexual relationship between the client and his wife improved considerably, and he did not fantasize about the stepdaughter during their lovemaking. Finally, the client's relationship with his step-daughter improved dramatically since he was no longer preoccupied with sexual thoughts when he was with her.

REFERENCES

Abel, G. G., Barlow, D. H., & Blanchard, E. B. *Developing heterosexual arousal by altering masturbatory fantasies: A controlled study.* Paper read at the Association for Advancement of Behavior Therapy Convention, Miami, 1973.

Abel, G. G., & Blanchard, E. B. The measurement and generation of sexual arousal in male sexual deviates. In M. Hersen, R. M. Eisler, & P. M. Miller (Eds.), *Progress in behavior modification*, vol. 2. New York: Academic Press, 1976.

Adams, H. E., & Sturgis, E. T. Status of behavioral reorientation techniques in the modification of homosexuality: A review. *Psychological Bulletin*, 1977, **84**, 1171–1188.

American Psychiatric Association. *Diagnostic and statistical manual of mental disorders (DSM-II)*, fifth printing. Washington, D.C., 1975.

Ashem, B., & Donner, L. Covert sensitization with alcoholics: A controlled replication. *Behaviour Research and Therapy*, 1968, **6**, 7–12.

Bancroft, J. A. A comparative study of aversion and desensitization in the treatment of homosexuality. In R. E. Burns & J. L. Worsley (Eds.), *Behaviour therapy in the 1970's*. Bristol, Eng.: Wright, 1970.

Bandura, A. *Principles of behavior modification.* New York: Holt, Rinehart and Winston, 1969.

Barker, J. C., Thorpe, J. G., Blakemore, C. B., Lavin, N. I., & Conway, C. G. Behaviour therapy in a case of transvestitism. *Lancet*, 1961, **1**, 510.

Barlow, D. H. Aversive procedures. In W. S. Agras (Ed.), *Behavior modification: Principles and clinical applications.* Boston: Little, Brown, 1972(a).

Barlow, D. H. Review of *Homosexual behaviour: Therapy and assessment*, by M. P. Feldman & M. J. MacCulloch. *Behavior Therapy*, 1972, **3**, 479–481(b).

Barlow, D. H. Increasing heterosexual responsiveness in the treatment of sexual deviation: A review of the clinical and experimental evidence. *Behavior Therapy*, 1973, **4**, 655–671.

Barlow, D. H. The treatment of sexual deviation: Toward a comprehensive behavioral approach. In K. S. Calhoun, H. E. Adams, & K. M. Mitchell (Eds.), *Innovative treatment methods in psychopathology.* New York: Wiley, 1974.

Barlow, D. H., Abel, G. G., Blanchard, E. B., Bristow, A. R., & Young, L. D. A heterosexual skills behavior checklist for males. *Behavior Therapy*, 1977, **8**, 229–239.

Barlow, D. H., & Agras, W. S. Fading to increase heterosexual responsiveness in homosexuals. *Journal of Applied Behavior Analysis*, 1973, **6**, 355–367.

Barlow, D. H., Agras, W. S., Leitenberg, H., Callahan, E. J., & Moore, R. C. The contribution of therapeutic instruction to covert sensitization. *Behaviour Research and Therapy*, 1972, **10**, 411–415.

Barlow, D. H., Leitenberg, H., & Agras, W. S. The experimental control of sexual deviation through manipulation of the noxious scene in covert sensitization. *Journal of Abnormal Psychology*, 1969, **74**, 596–601.

Barlow, D. H., Reynolds, J., & Agras, S. Gender identity change in a transsexual. *Archives of General Psychiatry*, 1973, **28**, 569–576.

Beech, H. R., Watts, F., & Poole, A. D. Classical conditioning of sexual deviation: A preliminary note. *Behavior Therapy*, 1971, **2**, 400–402.

Begelman, D. A. Ethical and legal issues of behavior modification. In M. Hersen, R. Eisler, & P. M. Miller (Eds.), *Progress in behavior modification*, vol. 1. New York: Academic Press, 1975.

Bergler, E. *Homosexuality: Disease or way of life?* New York: Hill & Wang, 1956.

Bieber, I. A discussion of "Homosexuality: The ethical challenge." *Journal of Consulting and Clinical Psychology*, 1976, **44**, 163–166.

Bieber, I., Dain, H. J., Dince, P. R., Drellich, M. G., Grand, H. G., Gundlach, R. H., Kremer, M. W., Rifkin, A. H., Wilbur, C. G., & Beiber, T. B. *Homosexuality: A psychoanalytical study.* New York: Random House, 1962.

Blitch, J. W., & Haynes, S. N. Multiple behavioral techniques in a case of female homosexuality. *Journal of Behavior Therapy and Experimental Psychiatry*, 1972, **3**, 319–322.

Bond, I., & Evans, D. Avoidance therapy: Its use in two cases of underwear fetishism. *Canadian Medical Association Journal*, 1967, **96**, 1160–1162.

Brownell, K. D., & Barlow, D. H. Measurement and treatment of two sexual deviations in one person. *Journal of Behavior Therapy and Experimental Psychiatry*, 1976, **7**, 349–354.

Callahan, E. J., & Leitenberg, H. Aversion therapy for sexual deviation: Contingent shock and covert sensitization. *Journal of Abnormal Psychology*, 1973, **81**, 60–73.

Cautela, J. R., & Wisocki, P. A. The use of male and female therapists in the treatment of homosexual behavior. In R. Rubin & C. Franks (Eds.), *Advances in behavior therapy, 1968.* New York: Academic Press, 1969.

Cautela, J. R., & Wisocki, P. A. Covert sensitization for the treatment of sexual deviations. *Psychological Record*, 1971, **21**, 37–48.

Conrad, S. R., & Wincze, J. P. Orgasmic reconditioning: A controlled study of its effects upon the sexual arousal and behavior of adult male homosexuals. *Behavior Therapy*, 1976, **7**, 155–166.

Cooper, A. J. A case of fetishism and impotence treated by behaviour therapy. *British Journal of Psychiatry*, 1963, **109**, 649–652.

Curtis, R. H., & Presley, A. S. The extinction of homosexual behavior by covert sensitization: A case study. *Behaviour Research and Therapy*, 1972, **10**, 81–84.

Davison, G. C. Elimination of a sadistic fantasy by a client-controlled counterconditioning technique: A case study. *Journal of Abnormal Psychology*, 1973, **81**, 60–73.

Davison, G. C. Homosexuality: The ethical challenge. *Journal of Consulting and Clinical Psychology*, 1976, **44**, 157–162.

Davison, G. C., & Wilson, G. T. Attitudes of behavior therapists toward homosexuality. *Behavior Therapy*, 1973, **4**, 686–696.

Denholtz, M. S. An extension of covert procedures in the treatment of male homosexuals. *Journal of Behavior Therapy and Experimental Psychiatry*, 1973, **4**, 305.

Edwards, N. B. Case conference: Assertive training in a case of homosexual pedophilia. *Journal of Behavior Therapy and Experimental Psychiatry*, 1972, **3**, 55–63.

Evans, D. R. Masturbatory fantasy and sexual deviation. *Behaviour Research and Therapy*, 1968, **6**, 17–19.

Feldman, M. P., & MacCulloch, M. J. The application of anticipatory avoidance learning to the treatment of homosexuality: I. Theory, technique and preliminary results. *Behaviour Research and Therapy*, 1965, **2**, 165–183.

Feldman, M. P., & MacCulloch, M. J. *Homosexual behaviour: Therapy and assessment.* Oxford: Pergamon Press, 1971.

Fensterheim, H. The initial interview. In A. A. Lazarus (Ed.), *Clinical behavior therapy.* New York: Brunner/Mazel, 1972.

Ford, C. S., & Beach, F. A. *Patterns of sexual behavior.* New York: Harper & Row, 1951.

Freund, K. Some problems in the treatment of homosexuality. In H. J. Eysenck (Ed.), *Behaviour therapy and the neuroses.* Oxford: Pergamon Press, 1960.

Gelder, M. G., & Marks, I. M. Aversion treatment in transvestitism and transsexualism. In R. Green & J. Money (Eds.), *Transsexualism and sex reassignment.* Baltimore: Johns Hopkins Press, 1969.

Green, R. *Sexual identity conflict in children and adults.* New York: Basic Books, 1974.

Green, R., & Money, J. (Eds.). *Transsexualism and sex reassignment.* Baltimore: Johns Hopkins Press, 1969.

Hallam, R. S., & Rachman, S. Some effects of aversion therapy on patients with sexual disorders. *Behaviour Research and Therapy*, 1972, **10**, 171–180.

Hallam, R. S., & Rachman, S. Current status of aversion therapy. In M. Hersen, R. M. Eisler, & P. M. Miller (Eds.), *Progress in behavior modification*, vol. 2. New York: Academic Press, 1976.

Halleck, S. L. *The politics of therapy.* New York: Science House, 1971.

Halleck, S. L. Another response to "Homosexuality:

The ethical challenge." *Journal of Consulting and Clinical Psychology*, 1976, **44**, 167–170.

Hanson, R. W., & Adesso, V. J. A multiple behavioral approach to male homosexual behavior: A case study. *Journal of Behavior Therapy and Experimental Psychiatry*, 1972, **3**, 323–326.

Herman, S. H., Barlow, D. H., & Agras, W. S. Exposure to heterosexual stimuli: An effective variable in treating homosexuality? *Proceedings of the 79th Annual Convention of the American Psychological Association,* 1971.

Herman, S. H., Barlow, D. H., & Agras, W. S. An experimental analysis of classical conditioning as a method of increasing heterosexual arousal in homosexuals. *Behavior Therapy*, 1974, **5**, 33–47(a).

Herman, S. H., Barlow, D. H., & Agras, W. S. An experimental analysis of exposure to "explicit" heterosexual stimuli as an effective variable in changing arousal patterns of homosexuals. *Behaviour Research and Therapy*, 1974, **12**, 335–345(b).

Herman, S. H., & Prewett, M. An experimental analysis of feedback to increase sexual arousal in a case of homo- and heterosexual impotence: A preliminary report. *Journal of Behavior Therapy and Experimental Psychiatry*, 1974, **5**, 271–274.

Jackson, B. A case of voyeurism treated by counterconditioning. *Behaviour Research and Therapy*, 1969, **7**, 133–134.

Kinsey, A. C., Pomeroy, W. B., Martin, C. E., & Gebhard, P. H. *Sexual behavior in the human female.* New York: Saunders, 1953.

Lavin, N., Thorpe, J., Barker, J., Blakemore, C., & Conway, C. Behavior therapy in a case of transvestitism. *Journal of Nervous and Mental Disease*, 1961, **133**, 346–353.

Laws, D. R. *Non-aversive treatment alternatives of hospitalized pedophiles: An automated fading procedure to alter sexual responsiveness.* Paper presented at the American Psychological Association Convention, New Orleans, 1974.

LoPiccolo, J. Case study: Systematic desensitization of homosexuality. *Behavior Therapy*, 1971, **2**, 394–399.

MacCulloch, M. J., & Feldman, M. P. Aversion therapy in the management of 43 homosexuals. *British Medical Journal*, 1967, **2**, 549–597.

MacDonough, T. S. A critique of the first Feldman and MacCulloch avoidance conditioning treatment for homosexuals. *Behavior Therapy*, 1972, **3**, 104–111.

Mahoney, M. J. *Cognition and behavior modification.* Cambridge, Mass.: Ballinger, 1974.

Maletzky, B. M. "Assisted" covert sensitization: A preliminary report. *Behavior Therapy*, 1973, **4**, 117–119.

Maletzky, B. M. "Assisted" covert sensitization in the treatment of exhibitionism. *Journal of Consulting and Clinical Psychology*, 1974, **42**, 34–40.

Maletzky, B. M., & George, F. S. The treatment of homosexuality by "assisted" covert sensitization. *Behaviour Research and Therapy*, 1973, **11**, 655–657.

Marks, I. M. Management of sexual disorders. In H. Leitenberg (Ed.), *Handbook of behavior modification and behavior therapy*. Englewood Cliffs, N.J.: Prentice-Hall, 1976.

Marks, I. M., & Gelder, M. G. Transvestitism and fetishism: Clinical and psychological changes during faradic aversion. *British Journal of Psychiatry*, 1967, **113**, 711–729.

Marks, I. M., Gelder, M. G., & Bancroft, J. Sexual deviants two years after electrical aversion. *British Journal of Psychiatry*, 1970, **117**, 73–85.

Marquis, J. N. Orgasmic reconditioning: Changing sexual object choice through controlling masturbation fantasies. *Journal of Behavior Therapy and Experimental Psychiatry*, 1970, **1**, 263–271.

Marshall, W. L. The modification of sexual fantasies: A combined treatment approach to the reduction of deviant sexual behavior. *Behaviour Research and Therapy*, 1973, **11**, 557–564.

Marshall, W. L. The classical conditioning of sexual attractiveness: A report of four therapeutic failures. *Behavior Therapy*, 1974, **5**, 298–299(a).

Marshall, W. L. A combined treatment approach to the reduction of multiple fetish-related behaviors. *Journal of Consulting and Clinical Psychology*, 1974, **42**, 613–616(b).

Max, L. W. Breaking up a homosexual fixation by the conditional reaction technique: A case study. *Psychological Bulletin*, 1935, **32**, 734.

McConaghy, N. Subjective and penile plethysmograph responses following aversion-relief and apomorphine aversion therapy for homosexual impulses. *British Journal of Psychiatry*, 1969, **115**, 723–730.

McConaghy, N. Subjective and penile plethysmograph responses to aversion therapy for homosexuality: A follow-up study. *British Journal of Psychiatry*, 1970, **117**, 555–560.

McConaghy, N., & Barr, R. Classical avoidance and backward conditioning treatments of homosexuality. *British Journal of Psychiatry*, 1973, **122**, 151–162.

McConaghy, N., Proctor, D., & Barr, R. Subjective and penile plethysmography responses to aversion therapy for homosexuality: A partial replication. *Archives of Sexual Behavior*, 1972, **2**, 65–78.

McGuire, R. J., Carlisle, J. M., & Young, B. G. Sexual deviations as conditioned behavior. *Behaviour Research and Therapy*, 1965, **2**, 185–190.

Mees, H. L. Sadistic fantasies modified by aversive conditioning and substitution: A case study. *Behaviour Research and Therapy*, 1966, **4**, 317–320.

Morgenstern, F. S., Pearce, J. F., & Rees, W. L. Predicting the outcome of behaviour therapy by psychological tests. *Behaviour Research and Therapy*, 1965, **2**, 191–200.

Pauly, I. Male psychosexual inversion: Transsexualism: A review of 100 cases. *Archives of General Psychiatry*, 1965, **13**, 172–181.

Pauly, I. Adult manifestations of male transsexualism. In R. Green & J. Money (Eds.), *Transsexualism and sex reassignment*. Baltimore: John Hopkins Press, 1969.

Pinard, G., & Lamontagne, Y. Electrical aversion, aversion relief and sexual retraining in treatment of fetishism with masochism. *Journal of Behavior Therapy and Experimental Psychiatry*, 1976, **7**, 71–74.

Rachman, S. Sexual disorders and behavior therapy. *American Journal of Psychiatry*, 1961, **118**, 235–240.

Rachman, S. Sexual fetishism: An experimental analogue. *The Psychological Record*, 1966, **16**, 293–296.

Rachman, S., & Hodgson, R. J. Experimentally induced "sexual fetishism": Replication and development. *The Psychological Record*, 1968, **18**, 25–27.

Rachman, S., & Teasdale, J. D. Aversion therapy: An appraisal. In C. M. Franks (Ed.), *Behavior therapy: Appraisal and status*. New York: McGraw-Hill, 1969(a).

Rachman, S., & Teasdale, J. *Aversion therapy and the behavior disorders*. Coral Gables: University of Miami Press, 1969(b).

Raymond, M. Case of fetishism treated by aversion therapy. *British Medical Journal*, 1956, 854–857.

Rehm, L. P., & Rozensky, R. H. Multiple behavior therapy techniques with a homosexual client: A case study. *Journal of Behavior Therapy and Experimental Psychiatry*, 1974, **5**, 53–58.

Rekers, G. A. Assessment and treatment of childhood gender problems. In B. B Lahey & A. E. Kazdin (Eds.), *Advances in child clinical psychology*, vol. 1. New York: Plenum, 1977.

Rekers, G. A., & Lovaas, O. I. *Treatment of cross-sex behavior in boys*. Paper presented at the 4th Annual Meeting of the Society for Psychotherapy Research, Philadelphia, June 1973.

Rekers, G. A., & Lovaas, O. I. Behavioral treatment of deviant sex-role behaviors in a male child. *Journal of Applied Behavior Analysis*, 1974, **7**, 173–190.

Rekers, G. A., Lovaas, O. I., & Low, B. P. The behavioral treatment of a "transsexual" preadolescent boy. *Journal of Abnormal Child Psychology*, 1974, **2**, 99–116.

Rosen, A. C., Rekers, G. A., & Bentler, P. M. Ethical issues in the treatment of children. *Journal of Social Issues*, in press, 1978.

Russell, A., & Winkler, R. Evaluation of assertive training and homosexual functioning. *Journal of Consulting and Clinical Psychology*, 1977, **45**, 1–13.

Sachs, L. B., & Ingram, G. L. Covert sensitization as a

treatment for weight control. *Psychological Reports,* 1972, **30,** 971–974.

Silverstein, C. *Behavior modification and the gay community.* Paper presented at the annual convention of the Association for Advancement of Behavior Therapy, New York, October 1972.

Stevenson, I., & Wolpe, J. Recovery from sexual deviations through overcoming non-sexual neurotic responses. *American Journal of Psychiatry,* 1960, **116,** 739–742.

Thorpe, J., Schmidt, E., Brown, P., & Castell, D. Aversion-relief therapy: A new method for general application. *Behaviour Research and Therapy,* 1964, **2,** 71–82.

Thorpe, J., Schmidt, E., & Castell, D. A comparison of positive and negative (aversive) conditioning in the treatment of homosexuality. *Behaviour Research and Therapy,* 1963, **1,** 357–362.

Ullmann, L. P., & Krasner, L. *A psychological approach to abnormal behavior.* Englewood Cliffs, N.J.: Prentice-Hall, 1969.

Wilson, G. T., & Davison, G. C. Behavior therapy and homosexuality: A critical perspective. *Behavior Therapy,* 1974, **5,** 16–28.

thirteen

DEPRESSION

We have all felt blue and down at one time or another. We often experience the feelings we call depression when we are exhausted and frustrated, when we fail at something important to us, or when a cherished relationship with a friend or lover ends. For most of us, depression only lasts a short while; it clouds our lives now and then, but soon passes. However, depression is not always a transient phenomenon. For many people, it seems to arise almost without cause, occurring with distressing frequency, or lingering for months or even years. The painful sadness can become intense. Some individuals come to view their lives as so unsatisfying and hopeless that suicide seems to be the only solution. Depression of this severity is a frequent complaint among individuals who seek psychological assistance.

The prevalence of depression in our society can only be estimated, but it is believed that 2 to 4 percent of the population—4 to 8 million Americans—are in need of treatment for depression. Unfortunately, not all who need treatment receive it. Approximately one in five depressed persons receives some treatment; one in fifty is hospitalized; and about one in two hundred actually takes his or her own life (Lehmann, 1971). The chance that a person will become "clinically depressed" sometime during a lifetime has been estimated to be 10 percent, but the odds for females may be about double that figure (Klerman & Barrett, 1973). Depression is clearly a problem of staggering magnitude.

Traditionally, psychoanalytic theory has provided the major psychological explanation for depression, or "melancholia" as Freud (1959) called it. Melancholia was characterized by three symptoms: lowered self-esteem, self-accusation, and a delusional need for self-punishment. The process by which melancholia arose was somewhat less than straightforward:

There is the loss of a love object (real or imagined) and the "withdrawal of libido" from the object. There follows unconscious rage at the object for leaving, an introjection (incorporation) of the object by the "ego," and a subsequent identification with the now introjected object. Now, libido is reattached to the introjected object and the rage originally felt toward the object for leaving is directed at part of the self. This results in the three cardinal symptoms of depression. (Schuyler, 1974, pp. 69–70)

The concept of depression as a physiological or disease process has also drawn tremendous interest, and biochemical studies have implicated dozens of nervous system chemicals as the culprits (see, for instance, Becker, 1974). Although biochemical theories of depression are a potentially fruitful area, they have been plagued by studies so unsophisticated in methodology and conceptualization that conclusions cannot yet be drawn (see critiques by Baldessarini, 1975; Beck, 1967).

Behavioral conceptualizations of depression and its treatment are relatively recent. Only

Table 13-1. Symptoms of Depression

Dysphoria	Behavioral Deficits	Behavioral Excesses	Somatic Symptoms	"Cognitive" Manifestations
Feelings dominated by sadness and blueness	Minimal social participation—"I do not like being with people."	Complaints about: Material problems—money, job, housing Material loss—money, property	Headaches	Low self-evaluation: feelings of failure, inadequacy, helplessness and powerlessness
Loss of gratification—"I no longer enjoy the things I used to."	Sits alone quietly, stays in bed much of time, does not communicate with others, does not enter into activities with others	The demands of others Noise Memory, inability to concentrate, confusion	Sleep disturbances: restless sleep, waking during night, complete wakefulness, early morning awakening	Negative expectation—"Things will always be bad for me."
Professes to have little or no feeling	Inability to do ordinary work	Lack of affection from others—"No one cares about me." Being lonely	Fatigue—"I get tired for no reason."	Self-blame and self-criticism—"People would despise me if they knew me."
Feels constantly fatigued—"Everything is an effort."	Decreased sexual activity	Expressed feelings of guilt and concern about: Making up wrongs to others Suffering caused to others	Gastrointestinal indigestion, constipation, weight loss	
Loss of interest in food, drink, sex, etc.	Psychomotor retardation: speech slow, volume of speech decreased, monotone speech, whispering; gait and general behavior retarded	Not assuming responsibilities Welfare of family and friends	Dizzy spells	
Feeling of apathy and boredom	Does not attend to grooming; neglect of personal appearance	Indecisiveness—"I can't make up my mind anymore."	Loss of libido	
	Lack of mirth response	Crying, weepy, screaming	Tachycardia	
		Suicidal behavior—"I wish I were dead." "I want to kill myself."	Chest sensations	
			Generalized pain	
			Urinary disturbances	

From P. M. Lewinsohn, The behavioral study and treatment of depression. In M. Hersen, R. M. Eisler, & P. M. Miller (Eds.), *Progress in behavior modification*, vol. 1. New York: Academic Press, 1975, p. 23, Table I. Used by permission of Academic Press and the author.

within the past decade has the problem received serious attention within the behavior modification literature, and the almost total lack of outcome evaluations of behavioral interventions is a source of consternation, to say the least. Behavioral clinicians have focused primarily on building "models" of depressive disorders and testing these models in both clinical and analogue settings. The treatment technology is in its infancy, with anecdotal case studies serving as the guidelines for clinical practice.

In this chapter, we will look at depression from a behavioral perspective. We will begin by trying to sort out what depression is—and isn't. Then we will critically examine several behavioral conceptualizations of the causes of depression. Finally, we will sample the wide range of techniques that have been applied to various "depressive behaviors," comparing and contrasting approaches where possible.

THE PROBLEM OF DEFINITION

The sheer familiarity of the term "depression" and the emotion it appears to represent might lead readers to think it would be easy to come by a definition of depression. This is quite true—in fact, there are virtually *dozens* of definitions, all different, yet all purporting to describe the same phenomenon. Depression variously refers to "a normal mood state, an abnormal mood state, a symptom, a symptom syndrome, as well as a disease process and possibly to a series of disease processes" (Lewinsohn, 1974, p. 63). Afflicted individuals may appear downcast or quite happy ("smiling depression"). They may report feeling sad and "blue," they may be verbally abusive and hostile, they may be incoherent, or they may be mute. They may show motor retardation, appearing to move in slow motion if at all, or they may be agitated and restless—constantly pacing, gesturing, and wringing their hands. All these behaviors and more are subsumed under the heading of depression (see Table 13–1). "Depression" tells the behavioral clinician as much about a client as "food" tells you about what you are having for dinner.

The inadequacy of the term "depression" as a

descriptive label has prompted many efforts to delineate subclassifications displaying more homogeneous characteristics. Most of these subclassifications seek to divide the depressive spectrum into two parts on the basis of some rational criterion. Thus, readers will frequently find such distinctions as endogenous versus exogenous, unipolar versus bipolar, primary versus secondary, agitated versus retarded, autonomous versus reactive, neurotic versus psychotic, and so on. More empirically based strategies define depressive subtypes on the basis of factor or cluster analyses of interview and observational data (for example, Grinker, Miller, Sabshin, Nunn, & Nunnally, 1961; Paykel, 1972), or on the basis of differential response to antidepressant medication (Overall, Hollister, Johnson, & Pennington, 1966). Each of these strategies has some value in dividing persons labeled depressed into groups sharing some feature or features. However, the characteristics within each group are still so varied, and the overlap between subclasses so great, that the refined labels still do little to transmit any useful information about what is wrong with a particular individual, how he or she got that way, and how he or she can be helped. Furthermore, clinicians using popular classification systems frequently disagree on the category in which a particular depressed individual belongs (for instance, Blinder, 1966).

Behaviorally oriented clinicians and theorists seem undecided as to how to view depression. Two general points of view can be identified (Lewinsohn, 1975a). The first derives from the functional-analytic approach, and tends to avoid conceptualizing depression as an entity or specific syndrome deserving of a special label. Instead, the particular behaviors exhibited by the "depressed" individual are examined and modified individually. In other words, "depression" is not treated as a unified entity. Rather, the antecedents and consequences of, for example, dysphoric verbalizations, negative self-statements, motor retardation or agitation, and so on, are determined independently, and each of these behaviors is modified through the application of an appropriate behavioral technique. The advantage of this viewpoint is that it requires no new assumptions about "depression" per se; instead, the component behaviors are understood within the framework of general principles of behavior.

The second approach assumes a common causal factor underlying all depressive behavior. From this view, depression is characterized by the occurrence of particular kinds of behavior, although persons display different combinations of these behaviors. Individual learning histories may modify the behavioral manifestations, but some common antecedent stands at the core of all depression. This viewpoint has the potential advantage of providing a framework around which to organize information about depressive behavior. It could lead to the discovery of a general therapeutic approach that would be of value in the treatment of all varieties of depression, and to assessment and treatment packages far more efficient than those derived from the functional-analytic approach.

Which of these positions is "correct"? At this point, we cannot answer this question, and clinicians differ as to the model to which they subscribe. A functional-analytic approach to assessment and treatment of "depressive behaviors" is probably most frequently employed among behavioral clinicians. However, the various models of depression often serve to focus clinicians' functional analyses in certain areas.

The point of this discussion is that there is no agreed-upon definition of the phenomenon (or phenomena) known as depression. Thus, each clinician takes an individual approach to the measurement and study of depression. Although many behaviorally oriented clinicians would like to dispense with the concept altogether, the fact remains that "clinicians daily are consulted by thousands of people who say they feel depressed" (Lazarus, 1968, p. 84). Therefore, readers should note that *we* will use the term *depression* specifically to denote *a condition characterized by self-report of a sad, dejected, dysphoric mood,* except in those instances where researchers or clinicians have provided us with their own operational definition. Behaviors or "symptoms" that commonly accompany a depressed mood, such as withdrawal, lethargy, and negative self-statements, will be explained and dealt with as individual entities where possible.

If readers find themselves somewhat perplexed, annoyed, or unsure of their footing at this point, they can take comfort in the fact that this is a feeling shared by many psychologists in the field. Rest assured that this is the proper mental set with which to approach the literature on depression.

BEHAVIORAL MODELS OF DEPRESSION

Extinction Models

The first, and by far the most widely recognized, behavioral conceptualization of depression views it as the result of an interruption in the positive reinforcement received by the individual. Put simply, a large number of behaviors in the person's repertoire, notably those involved in social interaction, are on extinction. Although Skinner (1953) alluded to this explanation in his classic book *Science and Human Behavior,* it was Charles Ferster (1965, 1966; also 1973, 1974 for updates) who first expounded an operant interpretation of depression.

Ferster sees a reduction in the frequency of behavior emitted by the person as the prominent feature of depression. Particularly affected are those behaviors that have been successful in eliciting positive reinforcement. According to Ferster, such a reduction in reinforceable behavior can arise from two general processes. (1) The person's incoming reinforcement has been directly reduced through some change in the environment. For example, the death of a loved one, the loss of a job, or a move to a new town are all situations that involve a disruption of customary sources of reinforcement. Persons with "all their eggs in one basket"—that is, persons with one or very few sources of reinforcement—are particularly vulnerable to such a loss. A classic example is the older, unmarried woman who becomes severely depressed following the death of a sister with whom she has lived for thirty years. (2) The individual's attempts to escape or avoid aversive stimulation have become so strong that they preempt responses which might produce positive reinforcement. In this case, depression is secondary to anxiety, which may be conditioned or reactive, realistic or unrealistic. For example, persons who are extremely anxious in interpersonal situations may withdraw from people to avoid discomfort and thereby cut themselves off from social reinforcement.

Arnold Lazarus (1968), who holds essentially the same view as Ferster, defines depression as a weakening of the individual's behavioral repertoire due to inadequate or insufficient reinforcement. For Lazarus, the development of depression is a two-stage process. First, loss of an important reinforcer throws the person into a state of "grief." This state is normally self-limiting, and disappears when the individual identifies and obtains other sources of reinforcement to make up for the loss. If the person has no other reinforcers and for some reason is unable to find and use other sources, "a chronic and/or acute nonreinforcing state of affairs can result in a condition where the person becomes relatively refractory to most stimuli and enters a state of 'depression'" (Lazarus, 1972, p. 249).

Peter Lewinsohn (1974) and his colleagues at the University of Oregon have worked extensively with the extinction model, refining and expanding earlier formulations, and are responsible for most of the experimental tests of the model's assumptions. Lewinsohn's (1974) version of the extinction model rests on three hypotheses: (1) A low rate of response-contingent positive reinforcement (RCPR) functions as an unconditioned stimulus for certain depressive behaviors, such as sad affect, fatigue, and other somatic symptoms. (2) A low rate of RCPR is responsible for other depressive symptoms, such as a low rate of behavior —the result of the person being on extinction. (3) The total amount of RCPR received by an individual is a joint function of three factors: (a) the number of activities and events the individual finds reinforcing (that is, enjoyable); (b) the availability of these reinforcing events in the person's environment; (c) the ability of the individual to obtain these reinforcers; that is, does the person possess the skills necessary for eliciting those things that he or she finds reinforcing? Lewinsohn's model is summarized in Figure 13–1.

One of the crucial features of Lewinsohn's formulation is the importance of *response-contingent*

positive reinforcement. Depression does not result simply from a reduction in pleasant input; rather, it is the extent to which the person's behavior is *responsible* for that input that is important. Thus, depression can arise from a deficit in the instrumental performance that leads to reinforcement, from a loss of reinforcement for that performance, *or* from continued noncontingent reinforcement. The last case is exemplified by the retired person who still receives a paycheck while "doing nothing."

Lewinsohn and many others (for instance, Burgess, 1969; Lazarus, 1968; Liberman & Raskin, 1971) have noted an additional problem faced by the depressed person: "he obtains frequent reinforcements as a consequence to the emission of depressive behaviors" (Burgess, 1969, p. 193). The depressed person may verbalize his or her distress and behave in ways that elicit attention, concern, and sympathy from others. These reactions are reinforcing to the individual, and so he or she increases such expressions of suffering. But in time, those in the depressive's immediate environment grow tired of the continual complaints and begin to avoid him or her for more cheerful surroundings, thus further decreasing the amount of reinforcement and exacerbating the depression (Lewinsohn, Weinstein, & Shaw, 1969). The adverse and repelling effect depressed persons' communications can have on those around them has been confirmed experimentally (Coyne, 1976). Normal individuals rate themselves as significantly more depressed, anxious, and hostile after talking with depressed persons than after talking with someone with a different psychological complaint. Furthermore, they report less willingness to interact again with the depressed individuals than with the nondepressed persons.

Lewinsohn and his coworkers have carried out an extensive research program on their extinction model. In their experiments, subjects are considered depressed if they meet predetermined criterion scores on selected scales of the Minnesota Multiphasic Personality Inventory and on a set of factors derived from a structured interview (Grinker, Miller, Sabshin, Nunn, & Nunnally, 1961; Lewinsohn & Libet, 1972). This effort is aimed at selecting a group of individuals with depression of clinical intensity that constitutes their

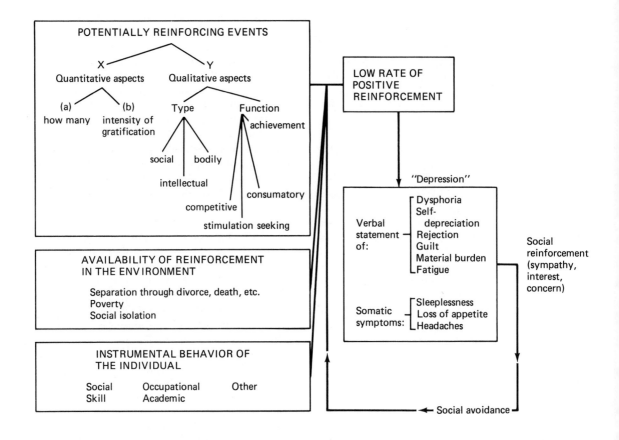

Figure 13–1. Schematic representation of the causation and maintenance of "depressive" behavior. From P. M. Lewinsohn, A behavioral approach to depression. In R. J. Friedman & M. M. Katz (Eds.), *The psychology of depression: Contemporary theory and research.* Washington, D.C.: Hemisphere Publishing Corporation, 1974, p. 159, Figure 1. Copyright 1974 Hemisphere Publishing Corporation. Used by permission.

primary psychological problem. The major findings of this research follow.

1. There is a significant relationship between an individual's mood and the number and kinds of pleasant activities and events in which he or she engages (Lewinsohn & Graf, 1973; Lewinsohn & Libet, 1972). In general, the more pleasant activities engaged in, the less depressed the mood, although large individual differences exist.

2. Depressed individuals find fewer activities pleasant, engage in pleasant activities less often, and consequently obtain less positive reinforcement than either normals or individuals with other psychiatric problems (MacPhillamy & Lewinsohn, 1974).

3. Depressed persons exhibit less social skill, and hence are less able to elicit positive reinforcement from others, than are nondepressed persons (Libet & Lewinsohn, 1973; Shaffer & Lewinsohn, 1971). Depressed individuals emit interpersonal behaviors at about half the rate of nondepressed persons; and male depressives tend to restrict the range of people with whom they interact in small-group situations. Depressed persons also emit fewer positive reactions toward others and are much slower to respond to others' verbalizations than nondepressed persons.

The findings of the research program conducted by Lewinsohn and his team have, in general, been consistent with the assumptions of their model. However, although the studies have shown an inverse relationship between depression and positive reinforcement (as both are defined by Lewinsohn), the *causal directionality* of this relationship cannot be determined from that research. Does a reduction in positive reinforcement cause depression, does depression cause a reduction in positive reinforcement, or do both simply occur together as the result of another, as yet unidentified, cause? The answer is not known.

A further difficulty with Lewinsohn's research is the failure to focus on the all-important response-contingent aspect of the individual's reinforcement. Although Lewinsohn maintains that it is not the rate of positive reinforcement per se, but the response-contingent nature of the reinforcement which is the important feature in depression, his research has centered only on the *amount* of reinforcement received by the individual. To the extent that the loss of response-contingent reinforcement stands as a foundation of Lewinsohn's position, the model remains untested.

A final problem is that some of Lewinsohn's basic assumptions are simply not in accord with what is known about behavior in response to low rates of reinforcement. Lewinsohn postulates that a low rate of RCPR accounts for the depressive's reduced behavior. However, animals that are bar-pressing for food on a very "thin" ratio schedule (say VR-100) typically work at a furious pace, because rapid responding will produce the rare reinforcement more quickly. We can only speculate on the animal's mood while working under this schedule—it may indeed be quite "depressed" about its situation, but its observable behavior runs counter to that suggested by Lewinsohn's analysis. Although there is a large difference between the animal in a Skinner box and a depressed human being, the extinction model of depression is predicated on principles derived to a great extent from observations of animal behavior. If the behavior the model is intended to explain is contrary to the observations from which the model was constructed, an explanation for the discrepancy is certainly in order. As yet, no explanation for this incongruity has been offered.

Variations of the Extinction Model. We can identify two points of view that agree with the basic notion that depression is an extinction phenomenon,

but that differ from the previous conceptualizations in terms of the presumed cause of the extinction. Charles Costello (1972), for example, has suggested that depression may result from a *loss of reinforcer effectiveness* rather than a loss of the reinforcer itself. Costello notes that depressed individuals often lose interest in formerly enjoyable activities such as eating and sex, even though these sources of pleasure are still available to them. In other words, the depressed person is no longer responsive to stimuli that were once reinforcing. Costello postulates that reinforcers may lose their effectiveness due to: (1) endogenous biochemical or physiological changes; and/or (2) the disruption of a chain of behaviors, such as the loss of one of the reinforcers in the chain.

For example, an undergraduate hoping to become a professor of biology may find a great many activities which contribute to that goal reinforcing (for instance, studying the field, getting good test grades, engaging in research, attending lectures). If one reinforcer in the chain—say, admission to graduate school—is removed, a great many related reinforcers may lose their effectiveness. Studying may become a drag, research boring, and so on. The reinforcement value of a whole network of activities disappears when one component in the chain is removed, and the "reason" (reinforcement) for much of the person's behavior is eliminated. The result is a pervasive reduction in behavior—that is, depression. It is important to note that although the biology student in this example has failed to receive one reinforcer (admission to graduate school), a great many of his or her customary reinforcers (studying, research, and so on) are still available. However, the removal of a "pivotal" reinforcer has led to a loss of effectiveness for many other reinforcers.

Lazarus (1972) has criticized Costello's position, saying that it is usually impossible to determine whether a loss of effectiveness of familiar reinforcers is an *effect* or a *cause* of depression. This question remains unsettled, but studies by Lewinsohn's group (Lewinsohn & MacPhillamy, 1974; MacPhillamy & Lewinsohn, 1973) have yielded data consistent with Costello's hypothesis. They found that whereas both nondepressed elderly and depressed individuals engaged less frequently in enjoyable activities, only the depressed individuals reported that those activities were also less enjoyable than they once had been. Thus, it would appear that a loss of the reinforcement value of previously pleasurable activities may be uniquely associated with depression. Whether this is the cause of depression, or merely a concomitant characteristic, remains to be demonstrated.

Although other extinction models, including Costello's, have focused entirely on external reinforcement contingencies, it has been suggested that a *low rate of internal, self-administered reinforcement* may also be a factor in some depressions. This position was originally proposed by Albert Marston (1964) and later echoed by Bandura (1969). Depressed individuals are hypothesized to evaluate themselves differently. Nondepressed individuals set reasonable and attainable goals, and readily reinforce themselves when they meet them. In contrast, depressed persons' standards for performance are unrealistic, perfectionistic, and largely unattainable. Thus, they frequently fail to reach their criteria for self-reinforcement, and instead of congratulating themselves, they end up feeling they have performed quite badly. The resulting low rate of self-reinforcement and high rate of self-punishment presumably have the same effects as those hypothesized for the other extinction models—namely, a low rate of behavior and depressive feelings.

The notion that depressed individuals differ from normals in the amount of self-reinforcement they emit has received some laboratory support. When asked to evaluate their performance on a memory task, high-depression subjects (as selected by a self-report inventory) administered significantly fewer self-reinforcements and significantly more self-punishments than did either low-depression or nondepressed subjects, even though all three groups actually made the same number of correct responses (Rozensky, Rehm, Pry, & Roth, 1977). Of course, the perennial question is, are these differences the *cause* or the *result* of the subjects' depression? At present, there is no way to know. However, as we will see, a treatment program derived in part from the self-reinforcement disturbance model is one of the few behavioral interventions proven useful in controlled research.

Learned Helplessness Model

Martin Seligman (1974, 1975, 1976) has proposed a model of depression based on a phenomenon known as **learned** or **conditioned helplessness** that was first observed in avoidance conditioning experiments with dogs (Overmeier & Seligman, 1967). An experimentally naive dog placed in a shuttlebox rapidly learns to escape, and eventually to avoid, painful electric shocks by jumping over a barrier between the shocked and the nonshocked compartments of the box. However, if the dog is first restrained in a harness and subjected to a series of shocks from which it is unable to escape, its subsequent unrestrained behavior in the shuttlebox is remarkably different. When the shock is turned on, it may briefly scramble about the shocked compartment, but it soon gives up, and sits or lies down, passively waiting for the shock to end. On trial after trial the dog may whine with pain, but continue to accept the shock passively rather than seek ways to prevent or escape it. Occasionally, one of these dogs accidentally tumbles into the nonshocked compartment and escapes the shock, but it seems unaware that its jumping the barrier had anything to do with relieving the pain. Whereas a naive dog will almost immediately "catch on" to the contingency and begin reliably jumping the barrier, the previously helpless dog reverts to enduring the escapable shock passively (Seligman, Maier, & Solomon, 1971). It has also been demonstrated that it is not the pain of the shock itself that causes the dog to act in this peculiar fashion; rather, the *uncontrollability* of that shock is the crucial factor (Maier, 1970; Seligman & Maier, 1967). The animal has apparently learned that relief from aversive stimulation is independent of its responding. It "believes" itself to be helpless.

According to Seligman, the belief in one's own helplessness is learned in the following manner. Consider Figure 13–2, which is a graph of response contingencies known as a "training space." On this graph, the outcome of a particular response in terms of the probability of its being reinforced can be described as a point in two-dimensional space. The X axis gives the probability of reinforcement for emitting the behavior in question from 0 (extinction) to 1.00 (con-

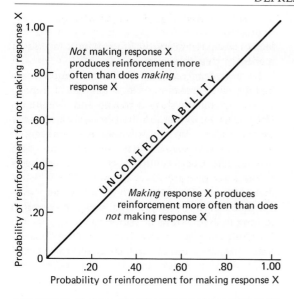

Within the figure:

Not making response X produces reinforcement more often than does *making* response X

UNCONTROLLABILITY

Making response X produces reinforcement more often than does *not* making response X

Y-axis: Probability of reinforcement for not making response X

X-axis: Probability of reinforcement for making response X

Figure 13–2. An instrumental training space showing the probabilities of receiving reinforcement for making and not making a particular response X. The diagonal line describes the points at which reinforcement is completely independent of responding; i.e., *not making* response X produces reinforcement just as often as *making* response X. At these points, reinforcement is uncontrollable and the organism is "helpless." From *Helplessness: On depression, development, and death*, by Martin P. Seligman, p. 17, Figure 2–3. W. H. Freeman and Company. Copyright © 1975.

tinuous reinforcement). The X axis is not the whole story, however, for there is also a certain probability of reinforcement being delivered should the response *not* be emitted. This probability is described by the Y axis. Thus, it is apparent that points falling below the diagonal describe contingency relationships in which performing the behavior will produce reinforcement more often than not performing the behavior, whereas points above the diagonal represent just the reverse. In either case, the contingency is learnable, and the animal or person can choose either to emit or not to emit a particular response, depending on the relative probabilities of producing reinforcement. Reinforcement is dependent to some extent on responding (or *not* responding, as the case may be), and the organism has control over the outcome.

Trouble arises for the organism when the contingencies are described by points falling along or near the diagonal itself. Here, responding or not responding with a particular behavior have equal probabilities of being reinforced. The organism can no longer determine whether responding or withholding a response will produce the most favorable outcome; reinforcement is now *independent* of response. What the organism does no longer affects the delivery of its reinforcement: it is helpless.

The phenomenon of learned helplessness is quite pervasive, and has been demonstrated in a wide variety of infrahuman species from the monkey, dog, and cat, down to the goldfish and even the lowly cockroach (see Seligman, 1975, for a review). Characteristics of learned helplessness have also been experimentally produced in human subjects following exposure to a wide range of uncontrollable aversive stimuli, including shock (MacDonald, 1946; Thornton & Jacobs, 1971), loud noise (Hiroto, 1974; Hiroto & Seligman, 1975; Miller & Seligman, 1975), and unsolvable discrimination problems (Hiroto & Seligman, 1975). Consistent with Seligman's assertion that the crucial variable is lack of control rather than the experience of noxious stimulation, investigators have also found the characteristics of learned helplessness in individuals exposed to positive but *noncontingent* reinforcement (Cohen, Rothbart, & Phillips, 1976; Hiroto & Seligman, 1975; Roth & Kubal, 1975). The relative ease with which the phenomenon can be produced in the laboratory encourages the speculation that learned helplessness may be a frequent natural occurrence.

Seligman (1974, 1975) has proposed naturally occurring learned helplessness as an explanation of depressive behavior. Depressed individuals are presumed to have been exposed to situations in which punishment or reinforcement was delivered independent of their responses, and they have come to believe they have no control over the things that happen to them. For example, the man whose every effort is faulted by his boss or wife may feel helpless to avoid aversive interactions. The woman who loses a child to leukemia is helpless to prevent the loss. The movie starlet who receives fame and fortune because of her physical attributes may feel helpless because her acting exerts no influence over those rewards. Seligman suggests that each of these individuals is learning "helplessness" (just as an animal who receives inescapable shock), and may later manifest symptoms of depression. As Seligman points out, numerous parallels exist between the behavior of helpless animals and that of depressed humans. Some of the more notable similarities follow.

1. *Passivity.* Helpless animals sit passively and accept punishment. Similarly, depressed persons are often withdrawn, lethargic, and apathetic, and may display profound deficits in instrumental behavior (compare "paralysis of the will" in Beck, 1967).

2. *Negative cognitive set.* The helpless animal behaves as if it believes its responding is useless. Even after an experience of "success" (that is, instrumentally terminating shock), it remains unconvinced of its ability to control its fate. Depressed individuals manifest a similar negative slant on their existence. Aaron Beck (1967), for example, has noted what he calls the "primary triad" in depression, consisting of a negative view of experience, a negative view of the self, and a negative view of the future. For depressives, life is a series of problems they feel incapable of dealing with, and for which no end is in sight.

Consistent with this clinical observation, it has been shown that mildly depressed subjects (as defined by scores on a depression inventory) are less positively affected by succeeding at a task of skill than nondepressed subjects (Miller & Seligman, 1973). When the task involves luck, success experiences affect both groups equally. But succeeding in the skilled task does not raise expectations of future success in depressed subjects the way it does in nondepressed subjects. Another study confirmed that depressed individuals are relatively unresponsive to success (Hammen & Krantz, 1976). However, when faced with failure, depressed subjects respond by evaluating themselves and their future performance in a highly negative fashion. In contrast, the self-evaluations of nondepressed subjects are relatively unaffected by a failure experience.

3. *Time course.* Learned helplessness tends to dissipate with time. Its duration appears to depend on the number and spacing of the inescap-

able shocks received by the animal. Likewise, depression is self-limiting in most cases, but the factors that determine whether it will last days, months, or years are not known.

4. *Lack of aggression.* Helpless animals seem devoid of aggression. Dogs who have experienced controllable shock will bark and run and resist being removed from their home cages by the experimenter. "In contrast, helpless dogs seem to wilt; they passively sink to the bottom of the cage, occasionally even rolling over and adopting a submissive posture; they do not resist" (Seligman, 1975, p. 25). Although by no means a universal observation, depressed persons are often lacking in expressions of aggression or hostility to a striking degree. In fact, it is interesting to speculate that the profound lack of aggression seen in many depressed persons led Freud and his followers to invent a concept (introjected hostility) to account for it.

5. *Loss of interest in food and sex.* Helpless animals often reduce their intake of food and lose weight. They also display deficits in sexual arousal and performance. Loss of appetite, weight loss, and reduced interest and enjoyment of sex are frequent complaints of depressed individuals.

As Lewinsohn (1975a) has pointed out, the learned helplessness paradigm has two major strengths. First, it provides a possible explanation of how aversive events can cause depression. This area is not adequately dealt with by extinction models. Second, it produces testable hypotheses about depressive behavior. Thus, whether Seligman's model is right or wrong, it adds to our understanding of depression.

The learned helplessness model also has its shortcomings, the greatest of which is the fact that its relevance to human depression is based almost entirely on its resemblance to a phenomenon seen in laboratory animals. Seligman's group has begun direct study of depression in humans (Klein, Fencil-Morse, & Seligman, 1976; Miller & Seligman, 1973, 1975), and the results in general indicate that depressed individuals and subjects exposed to situations that produce helplessness perform similarly in various laboratory tasks. However, convincing evidence that uncontrollable aversive stimulation or noncontingent positive reinforcement *causes* depression in humans does not yet exist.

Cognitive Distortion Model

Aaron Beck (1967, 1974, 1976) has been the leading proponent of the cognitive distortion model of depression. Although Beck is not necessarily to be considered a member of the "behavioral camp," his writings have done much to influence behavioral clinicians, and his clinical theory and technique have much in common with behavior therapy (Beck, 1970).

Beck views depression as a problem of distorted thinking. Depressed individuals' feelings and behaviors result from their negative perceptions and self-verbalizations. As mentioned earlier, Beck (1967) believes that the depressive's cognitive set can be described as a triad involving negative views of experience, the self, and the future. In everyday terms, depressed persons are uncompromising pessimists.

According to Beck, depressed individuals have suffered an early sensitizing event (for instance, loss of a parent) or have been subject to some more longstanding unfavorable life circumstances that predispose them to overreact to problems later on. Depressed persons typically develop distorted cognitive "styles" that lead them to misinterpret the things that happen to them. Beck (1963, 1976) has identified several of these distorted thinking styles:

1. **Polarized reasoning.** The person tends to see things in extremes. A particular event is either great or terrible; he or she is either saintly or despicable; things are either black or white. Beck (1976) gives the example of a college basketball player who thought "I'm a failure" if he scored fewer than eight points a game, or "I'm really a great player" if he exceeded eight points.

2. **Magnification.** The colloquial term is "making mountains out of molehills." The individual exaggerates each problem until it seems catastrophic. The usually straight-A student may get a B in a course and think, "This is terrible! How will I ever succeed?"

3. **Minimization.** This cognitive set often goes with magnification. Here the person constantly discounts positive things that occur and devalues his or her own talents. A woman might react to preparing a gourmet meal by thinking, "Anybody could have made this if they had had the recipe." A student receiving an excellent grade on an exam thinks, "This is a really Mickey Mouse course."

4. **Overgeneralization.** This refers to a tendency to jump to conclusions on the basis of only a few experiences. A woman who learns that her lover is seeing another woman concludes, "Men can't be trusted." A patient whose physician is unable to cure his cold thinks, "Doctors are all a bunch of quacks." Perhaps the most frequent overgeneralization among depressed persons is their conviction that "My life is ruined; I'm worthless."

Albert Ellis (1962, 1973) also sees negative self-statements as the cause of depression. He believes depressed persons view a world distorted by their own irrational beliefs and attitudes. These beliefs are not congruent with the way the world really is; and due to their often impossibly demanding character, they set depressed individuals up for continual disappointments that serve as the basis for negative ruminations. Of the dozen or so irrational beliefs identified by Ellis, perhaps the following three are the most prevalent and devastating:

1. The belief that one should be loved by everyone for everything one does—as opposed to the more realistic notion that each person is unique and that one can be a worthwhile individual even if only certain people recognize one's assets.
2. The idea that one should be thoroughly competent in all aspects of life—as opposed to the realization that everyone has limitations.
3. The idea that it is catastrophic when things are not exactly the way one might want them to be—instead of accepting the reality of life and striving to improve situations rather than agonizing over their imperfections.

Perhaps the following statement best summarizes the cognitive activity of the depressed individual:

Given the mildest opportunity to become preoccupied, particularly when external task demands are low, many depressives will entertain thoughts of self-degradation and negative outcomes, mulling over past events in an apparent attempt to find further fault. While these high-rate thoughts tinkle away in the background like MUZAK they have a dysphoric effect on mood and appear to mediate avoidance behavior and leave less time to maintain concentration on adaptive behavior. (McLean, 1976, p. 83)

At first glance, the cognitive distortion model may appear quite different from Seligman's learned helplessness model. However, on closer inspection, similarities between the models become clear. Both postulate the development of a negative, pessimistic set of attitudes and expectancies as a result of repeated or severe personal adversities. This cognitive set leads to feelings of helplessness and depression and alters the person's behavior in the direction of minimal, ineffectual interaction. As we will also see, Seligman's recommendations for the treatment of depression are quite similar to the strategy employed by Beck.

To the extent that Beck's model is similar to Seligman's, it also suffers from the same problems. Although it is an almost universal clinical and experimental finding that depressed persons frequently engage in gloomy, pessimistic, negative thinking, it has not been demonstrated that this way of thinking is the *cause* of the related feelings and behaviors called "depressive."

Wolpe's Anxiety Hypothesis

Joseph Wolpe (1971) contends that there is no single antecedent to depression; rather, it can result from a variety of causes. To the list of causes, Wolpe adds prolonged and severe anxiety. Take, for example, a man whose wife is suddenly hospitalized with a severe illness and hangs on the brink of death for weeks. Countless times he is called to the hospital in the dead of night as she goes through a crisis, but on each occasion her condition stabilizes. After several weeks of living like this, perhaps just when his wife begins to recover, the man sinks into a retarded depression. He refuses to rise from bed in the morning. His behavior is lethargic and withdrawn; his speech labored or absent—he talks only of feeling sad, fatigued, and giving up.

In cases such as this, depression appears to follow a prolonged period of stress. A possible explanation for this phenomenon comes from the observation that organisms subjected to continuous stress eventually reach a point of exhaustion and collapse (Selye, 1952). The hormones that have supported chronic arousal become depleted, and the physiological system is forced to give up. Individuals who show "retarded" depression look and act much the same. They appear to be "burnt out" from a continual bout with stress. Research has shown that such individuals may indeed be *underaroused* (Lader, 1975), as would be expected following hormone depletion. In contrast, "agitated" depressives display motor restlessness and physiological overarousal characteristic of ongoing anxiety, but their verbalizations are of dysphoria rather than fear. In either case, it would appear that an effective treatment strategy would be directed toward first removing the anxiety and reducing stress.

Status of the Models

Perhaps the most important contribution of the various behavioral models of depression is the extent to which they generate testable hypotheses about the nature of depression. Most notable in this regard are the models proposed by Lewinsohn and Seligman. Although many basic assumptions of the various behavioral theories of depression remain untested, they are, nonetheless, there to test. This represents an enormous improvement over psychoanalytic conceptualizations of depression. Also important is the extent to which these models suggest effective treatment strategies. Unfortunately, the critical tests of treatment effectiveness have not yet been conducted.

The weaknesses of the behavioral conceptualizations are many. As we mentioned at the outset, we cannot even be sure that the various models are focusing on the same phenomenon (phenomena). Behavioral researchers have done little to alleviate the confusion surrounding the term "depression." Equally frustrating is the fact that the models are so broadly formulated that many empirical findings can be taken as support for *each* of them. One example is the research on the relationship of stressful life events to depression (Paykel, Myers, Deinelt, Klerman, Lindenthal, & Pepper, 1969). In the six months preceding the onset of their symptoms, depressed clients experienced three times the number of stressful events as a group of matched normal control subjects. For these depressed persons, most of the events entailed some sort of loss (for instance, divorce, death in the family). Clearly, then, these events produce a loss of reinforcers, and hence support the extinction model. However, are they not also the type of uncontrolled aversive stimuli that produce learned helplessness? Are they not the kind of events that could serve as the basis for catastrophic, distorted ruminations? And couldn't these occurrences also place the person under the kind of continual stress and anxiety that leads to a burnt-out depression? If every piece of data fits equally well within each model, it is impossible to choose among them. Until the models are refined to the point where specific and contrasting predictions can be drawn from each, it is impossible to evaluate their validity.

Of course, a very real possibility exists that no single model is adequate to account for all depressive behavior. Some depressions may have a biochemical basis, whereas others may result from a loss of reinforcers, uncontrollable events, cognitive distortions, and so on. Several theorists have already tackled the ambitious task of integrating the various behavioral models with each other (Eastman, 1976) and with psychoanalytic and biochemical theories (Akiskal & McKinney, 1975) to produce comprehensive theories of depression. It is far too early to evaluate the success of these integrations, but they clearly represent the next logical step on the road to understanding the complexities of depressive behavior.

BEHAVIORAL TREATMENTS

General Considerations

As in all behavioral treatment programs, the functional analysis is the basis for tailoring a program to the client's needs. Lewinsohn (1975a) suggests that the therapist should clearly explain to the client that the initial phase of treatment will involve assessment. Once the therapist has obtained the information necessary to understand the problem and devise a treatment plan, therapist and client discuss how the therapist conceptualizes the problem and what treatment plan seems the most appropriate. A verbal or written contract is established that specifies the goals, procedures, and responsibilities of those involved in treatment.

Several clinicians (Lewinsohn, 1975a; McLean, 1976) recommend that treatment for depression be time-limited, and three months seems to be the most popular duration. Limiting the course of therapy provides an extra incentive to both client and therapist to work hard and produce change. Clients are encouraged to avoid resisting and backsliding when they know that the length of treatment is limited. But because depressed individuals are known particularly for their inertia and apathy, additional motivators may have to be employed. For example, therapy time may be made contingent on the client's completing extrasession tasks (Lewinsohn, Biglan, & Zeiss, 1976).

Reestablishing Instrumental Behavior

The primary difficulty in the early phases of treatment with many depressive individuals is to get them moving and doing things incompatible with their dysphoric ruminations and that bring them positive reinforcement. The incredible reluctance of some depressed individuals to break out of a pattern of inactivity and passivity has a parallel in Seligman's helplessness experiments. In their attempt to "cure" helplessness in dogs, Seligman and his co-workers (Seligman, Maier, & Geer, 1968) found the animals unresponsive to a wide range of prompts and incentives to leave the shocked compartment. Only by removing the barrier and forcibly dragging the animals out of shock into the nonshocked compartment could they get the dogs to move. Furthermore, it took repeated trials in which the experimenters dragged the dogs out of the shock compartment before the dogs began to be cooperative. Eventually, the dogs began to move on their own and were finally rid of their helpless behavior.

These observations of the dogs' passivity and

reluctance led Seligman to suggest that depressed persons must be directed to engage in progressively more difficult tasks, until the experiences of success convince them that they are not helpless. This *graded-task approach* has been widely endorsed as a treatment for depression (Beck, 1976; Burgess, 1969; Lazarus, 1974; McLean, 1976). Initial task assignments are quite simple and easily within the person's decreased capabilities in order to ensure that he or she will experience the reinforcement of success. For example, a depressed student may be asked to read five pages of a text, or simply to make a phone call. A depressed homemaker may be asked to boil an egg in preparation for the day she will again cook an entire meal. Successful completion of these tasks is met with praise from the therapist and, it is hoped, from significant others. The client is encouraged to focus on his or her accomplishment and to avoid minimizing it. Once the client has completed the first assigned task, more demanding ones can be attempted.

Based on his research on the relationship between mood and participation in pleasurable activities (Lewinsohn & Graf, 1973), Lewinsohn suggests that depressed individuals be instructed to engage in particular pleasurable activities. With the aid of the therapist, the client identifies personally enjoyable events from an extensive list of potentially reinforcing activities. Then, in order to increase the client's exposure to positive reinforcement, the therapist explicitly instructs him or her to engage in the selected activities.

As a means of ensuring that clients are involved in some meaningful activity, Lazarus (1974) finds it useful to become involved in their daily lives. When confronted with an inactive and resistive client, the therapist may drive to the client's house, get the person out of bed, and lead him or her into potentially reinforcing activities. Lazarus reports having clients "shadow" him as he taught classes and met with students. Sometimes they performed office chores for him.

As yet, no controlled research has been done showing that increasing activities, pleasant or otherwise, is effective in alleviating depression. In fact, in one study depressed subjects who engaged in more self-selected pleasant activities experienced no greater elevation of their mood than did subjects who received no treatment (Hammen & Glass, 1975). Lewinsohn (1975b) has criticized several aspects of this study, but his most important point is that the subjects did not meet two necessary preconditions for successful treatment by this procedure. First, they did not show a low base rate of pleasant activity. Second, there was no attempt to determine whether these individuals demonstrated an association between their activity level and their mood. (Remember that there are vast individual differences in the extent to which mood varies with the amount of pleasurable activity.) In conducting his defense, Lewinsohn has pushed his theory perilously close to being unacceptable as an explanation for depression. As one reviewer has noted: "A theory cannot be said to explain much if it merely claims that there is a relation between mood and activity level in those individuals in whom there is a relation between mood and activity level and that this relation exists only with regard to those events that are mood related" (Blaney, 1977). However, Lewinsohn's assertions still have meaning for the clinician. They reemphasize the importance of conducting a functional analysis to determine whether the client's depression results from a lack of pleasant activities or from some other factor.

Of course, it remains to be shown that increasing pleasurable activities reduces depression in anyone—even those individuals who do show a relation between mood and enjoyable activities. Remember that the fact that a relation exists between these two variables does not tell us which one is the causal agent; indeed, neither may be causal, and the relation may be the product of a third variable (such as a biochemical disturbance) which affects both mood and activity level.

Inducing Incompatible Affects

Lazarus (1968) has suggested that a number of emotions, such as amusement, affection, anger, and sexual arousal, are basically incompatible with depressive affect, and that the deliberate stimulation of these could be of therapeutic value. Naturally, if the therapist can get a depressed client to laugh, he or she is doing quite well, but this is often next to impossible.

A systematic approach to the induction of incompatible affects in depressed hospital patients has been reported (Taulbee & Wright, 1971). These individuals were placed in an "antidepression room" where a staff member continually supervised them as they performed some boring task, such as mopping floors, counting tiny sea shells in a large pile, or sanding a small block of wood. The staff member kindly but incessantly criticized the patient's performance: "You're sanding against the grain. Now you're sanding too hard. Why don't you sand the other side a bit?" Sooner or later, the formerly depressed patient got angry and blew up at the staff member. This aggressive outburst was reinforced by acceptance, and the patient was released from the room to pursue more pleasant activities on the ward. From a theoretical perspective, the patient not only experienced an emotional state incompatible with depression, but he also began to break his helplessness by emitting a response that successfully removed aversive stimulation. Several pilot investigations suggest that the procedure had some efficacy in relieving depressed mood, but application is obviously limited to inpatient populations.

Lazarus (1968, 1971) reports another method called **time projection with positive reinforcement.** This is an imagery technique designed to elicit positive emotions. Through the use of hypnotic induction, the client is imaginally projected into the future to a time where he or she is no longer troubled by depression. The therapist vividly describes the client engaging in a number of pleasurable activities and enjoying them to the fullest. Once the client has attained some relief from depression and experienced positive feelings in the imaginal state, he or she is brought back through time with suggestions to retain the pleasant feelings. Lazarus believes the procedure can provide the client with positive experiences and expectations that can help break the depressive cycle and encourage him or her to become active and enjoy life. Unfortunately, no experimental analyses of the technique exist.

Changing Negative Cognitive Sets

The distorted perception of the depressed individual can be dealt with in a number of ways. One important step is getting the client to become aware of the good things that happen (Beck, 1976; Rush, Khatami, & Beck, 1975). To this end, it is sometimes useful to have the client keep a diary of daily activities along with notes of feelings experienced in connection with those activities. Whenever possible, it is also helpful to have some significant other (a spouse or a friend) who is with the client much of the time keep a parallel diary of events in the client's life. It is often surprising to the client to look back over the week and see how many things happened about which he or she had some good feelings. A comparison of the client's diary with that of the companion may also reveal many experiences that the client interprets as negative but that are seen by the other person as quite positive. With the therapist's prompting and encouragement, the client can begin to become aware of this distortion of daily events and discover that life is not *all* bad.

RET. A somewhat more direct attempt to change cognitive set is through the use of rational-emotive therapy (RET) (Ellis, 1962), or some related technique (for instance, Beck, 1976). In RET, the therapist seeks to make the client aware of the irrational beliefs and associated negative self-statements that he or she produces and responds to with dejection. The client is then taught how to change his or her thinking by silently disputing self-defeating thoughts and substituting more realistic, less depressive thoughts in their place. The process of RET is best described by example. What follows is a transcript of part of an RET session with a student who was depressed over his "average" grades (Rimm & Masters, 1974, pp. 422 –424).

Therapist: I'd like to point out that you're competing against some of the best students in the country, and they don't care very much about grading on the curve there. An average performance among outstanding people isn't really average, after all, is it?

Client: I know what you are getting at, but that doesn't help too much. Any decent medical school requires at least a B+ average, and I've got to get into medical school. That's been my goal ever since I was a kid.

Therapist: Now, wait a minute! You say you *have* to go to medical school. Sounds like you think not going to medical school is against the law. Is that so?

Client: Well, not exactly. You know what I mean.

Therapist: I'm not sure. Do you really mean that you want very much to go to medical school? Because that is very different from believing that you *must* go to medical school. If you think you have to go to medical school, you are going to treat it like it's a life or death thing, which it isn't. But you believe that it is and that is likely to be a major reason why you're depressed.

Client: I can see your point, but even if I agreed with you, there's my family. They wouldn't agree with you.

Therapist: What do you mean?

Client: They are big on my being successful. All my life my parents have been telling me that the whole family is counting on my being a doctor.

Therapist: O.K., but that is their belief. Does it have to be yours?

Client: I just can't let them down.

Therapist: What would happen if you did?

Client: They'd be hurt and disappointed. Sometimes I almost think they wouldn't like me any more. That would be awful!

Therapist: Well, the worst possible thing that could happen if you don't go to medical school is that your father and mother wouldn't like you, and might even reject you. You aren't even sure this would happen. But, even if they did, does it follow that it would be awful? Could you prove that, logically, I mean?

Client: It's lousy when your own family rejects you.

Therapist: I still can't see the logical connection between their rejecting you and things being awful or even lousy. I would agree that it wouldn't exactly be a pleasant state of affairs. You are equating rejecting with catastrophe, and I'd like you to try and convince me one follows from the other.

Client: They wouldn't even want me around . . . like I was a worthless shit. And that would be rotten.

Therapist: Well, there you go again, telling yourself that because they would reject you, which means they wouldn't want you around, you are a worthless shit. Again, I don't see the logic.

Client: It would make me feel that way.

Therapist: No, I emphatically disagree . . . it's *you* who would make you feel that way. By saying those same things to yourself.

Client: But I believe it's true.

Therapist: I'm still waiting for some logical basis for your belief that rejection means you are worthless, or not going to medical school means you're a shit.

Client: O.K., I agree about the medical school bit. I don't *have* to go. But about my parents . . . that's heavy. As far as reasons are concerned . . . (long pause) . . . I started to say I need them for emotional support but, as I think about it, I get a hell of a lot more from a couple of good buddies here at school than I ever got from them. They are pretty cold, especially Mom.

Therapist: O.K. . . . What else might be terrible about being rejected by your parents?

Client: I was thinking . . . where would I go over the holidays? But I don't spend that much time at home anyway, come to think of it. But, there is money . . . this place is damned expensive, and I don't have a scholarship. If they cut off funds, that would be a disaster.

Therapist: There you go again . . . catastrophizing. Prove to me that it would be a disaster.

Client: Well, maybe I was exaggerating a bit. It would be tough, though I suppose I could apply for support, or get a job maybe. In fact, I know I could. But then it would take longer to get through school, and that would be shitty.

Therapist: Now you are beginning to make a lot of sense. I agree that it would be shitty . . . but certainly not terrible.

Client: You know, for the first time in weeks I think I feel a little better. Kind of like there is a load off my mind. Is that possible?

Therapist: I don't see why not, but I'm wondering what would happen if you'd start feeling depressed tonight or tomorrow . . . how would you deal with it?

The efficacy of RET in the treatment of depression has not yet been demonstrated in controlled experimentation.

Coverant Control. In an effort to directly increase the rate of positive self-statements emitted by depressed clients, some clinicians have used the **coverant control procedure** developed by Lloyd Homme (1965). Homme extended Premack's differential probability principle (see Chapter 2) to include coverants (*covert* op*erants*), or thoughts. According to Homme's hypothesis, a freely chosen high-probability *behavior* can be used to reinforce a low-probability *thought*. Thus, if the depressed person seldom has a positive thought about him or herself, it should be possible to increase the frequency of such thoughts by following them with some high-probability behavior.

Several case studies illustrate the successful application of this procedure using such high-frequency behaviors as urination (Johnson, 1971) and smoking (Mahoney, 1971) as reinforcers for positive self-statements (see Case Study 13–1 for one such report). However, it has been pointed out that some who have applied Homme's technique have made the common error of confusing a high-frequency behavior with a *freely selected* high-frequency behavior (Mahoney, 1974). Since presumably only the latter functions as a reinforcer, there is doubt as to the real explanation of the effects of Homme's procedure. One reasonable hypothesis is that the behavior chosen to follow the target thought does not serve a reinforcing function, but rather a *cueing function* (Danaher, 1974). That is, the individual is reminded to think a positive thought each time he or she performs or thinks about performing a certain behavior. Consistent with this notion, tying the positive thought to a particular behavior may not even be necessary if the client can respond reliably to other cues, like the passage of time (Vasta, 1975).

However, remembering to associate a positive self-statement with a particular activity may be easier for the client than trying to emit a certain number of such thoughts per unit of time.

Such speculations are perhaps premature. Despite its promising showing in case studies, the use of Homme's coverant control procedure in cases of depression has not yet been experimentally evaluated.

Improving Social Interactions

Often depressed individuals are withdrawn and isolated, and thus cut off from social reinforcement. Or, they may be part of a family, but engaged in minimal (Lewinsohn & Atwood, 1969; Lewinsohn & Shaffer, 1971) or aversive (McLean, Ogston, & Grauer, 1973) social interactions. In either case, some sort of intervention in such persons' social environment is mandatory.

One of the first steps is to determine the client's social skills; that is, how effective is the individual in evoking reinforcing interactions from others in the environment? If such skills appear lacking, the therapist can embark on a program of social skills training (see Chapter 9). Likewise, if there is evidence that the individual is isolated because of anxiety about interpersonal relations, an appropriate technique can be applied to eliminate this barrier (see Chapter 10). Once skills have been sharpened and anxieties reduced, the client can begin to rebuild his or her social environment.

If the client is socially withdrawn, it is often helpful to enlist the aid of some significant other (a close friend or relative) to accompany the client on initial social outings (McLean, 1976). This reentry into social interaction is also approached in a graduated fashion. The client may at first be asked merely to question a department store employee on the location of some item, and work from there to more complex and intimate social relations.

Peter McLean, K. Ogston, and L. Grauer (1973) conducted one of the few controlled treatment evaluations to be found in the behavioral literature on depression. Working with married couples in which one member was depressed, these investigators used communication training and reciprocal behavioral contracts (see Chapter 10) to reduce marital strife. A comparison group of subjects received a variety of more traditional treatments, such as psychotherapy and antidepressant medication. Results showed a significant change in problem behaviors, depressed mood, and communication style within the experimental group, but not in the control group. However, the efficacy of other components of social skills training, such as assertion, feeling-talk, and graded social interactions, has not been subjected to experimental evaluation with depressed individuals.

A Self-Control Treatment Package

Carilyn Fuchs and Lynn Rehm (1977) have contributed an important study to the almost nonexistent literature on controlled evaluations of behavioral treatments for depression. (We present their work under a separate heading because the multifaceted treatment program they developed and researched does not fit neatly into any of the aforementioned categories.) Fuchs and Rehm adhere to the self-reinforcement variant of the extinction model of depression discussed earlier. Their treatment package is centered on the three components of self-control proposed by Kanfer (see Chapter 8): self-monitoring, self-evaluation, and self-reinforcement.

The subjects for their study were depressed women, ages eighteen to sixty, who responded to newspaper announcements of an experimental therapy program for depression. Thirty-six of the respondents were selected on the basis of MMPI scores and their responses to screening questionnaires and interviews. The women were randomly assigned to one of two group treatments or to a waiting-list control group. The two therapy groups received either self-control therapy, which we will describe below, or nonspecific therapy based on the principles of nondirective, client-centered counseling. Subjects in each of the therapy groups met for six weekly two-hour sessions to receive their respective treatments. Subjects in the waiting-list group were informed that they had been accepted for treatment but that the present therapy groups were filled, necessitating an eight-week delay. They did not receive treatment until the study was completed.

The self-control therapy had three phases, each devoted to a different aspect of Kanfer's model. In the first session, the subjects were introduced to the self-control rationale for the therapeutic program. Then they received instruction in *self-monitoring*. They were asked to keep an "activities log" in which they were to write one-line descriptions of each of their day's pleasant activities. They were also requested to rate their mood after each activity from 0 (most miserable feelings ever experienced) to 10 (most elated feelings ever experienced). Subjects were also given graphs on which to plot their average daily mood and the total number of pleasant activities. The second session and all subsequent treatment sessions began with the therapist and group reviewing each individual's log. Subjects were encouraged to look for patterns in their data, like a greater than expected number of positive activities or an association between their mood and the number of positive activities they engaged in. They were also asked to identify particular types of activity that were very important and enjoyable to them, but that they engaged in only infrequently.

The third session marked the beginning of the *self-evaluation* phase of the treatment program. The importance of setting realistic goals and making accurate self-evaluations was emphasized. A terminal goal was designated; it was to increase the desirable but low-frequency classes of behavior that each subject had identified from her activity log. Then, with the therapist's direction, the subjects wrote out three to five subgoals for each of the activities they had chosen. For example, one woman's terminal goal was to pursue her interest in cats as a hobby. One of the subgoals on her list was "going to the library for a book about cats." Subjects were also given the homework assignment of refining and attempting to accomplish some of their subgoals.

In the fourth session, a point system for rating the subgoals was introduced. The subjects were asked to assign a weight from 1 to 5 to their subgoals, according to the subjective importance or difficulty of achieving each one. During the following week's self-monitoring, subjects also recorded in their activity logs the point values of the subgoals they reached.

In the fifth session, the *self-reinforcement* phase

of the program was initiated. The therapist explained the general principles of reinforcement. Self-reinforcement and its relationship to depression were also described. Subjects were then asked to construct personal "reward menus." These were lists of immediate and freely available treats or reinforcing activities to which particular "point prices" were assigned. Subjects were to use the points they accumulated by reaching subgoals on their lists to "purchase" items from their reward menus. The therapist encouraged the subjects to set point prices low initially to ensure that they would receive plenty of self-reinforcement. Reward menu prices could be raised later on if the subjects were making good progress toward their terminal goals. In the sixth and last session, the entire treatment program was reviewed. Subjects were encouraged to continue using the self-control procedures after the experiment was over.

A comprehensive battery of self-report inventories and psychometric tests plus naturalistic observations of the subjects' activity levels within their therapy groups were used to assess pretreatment to posttreatment changes. In general, subjects in both therapy groups changed significantly more than waiting-list controls, but the self-control treatment proved to be significantly and consistently superior to the nonspecific therapy. Self-control subjects showed less self-rated depression, greater increases in interpersonal interaction within their therapy group, and greater improvement in MMPI indications of overall pathology than did nonspecific subjects. A followup assessment showed a reduction in some of these differences at six weeks. However, this was attributable primarily to the fact that almost all the nonspecific treatment subjects sought further therapy after the experiment. In contrast, self-control subjects maintained their original treatment gains, and none became involved in additional treatment over the followup period.

As Fuchs and Rehm readily acknowledge, the multifaceted nature of their self-control program makes it impossible to determine the active ingredients responsible for the treatment effects. Subjects received training in self-reinforcement, but the program also included other presumably therapeutic components, notably graded tasks and increases in pleasant, personally significant behaviors. This does not in any way represent a fault in Fuchs and Rehm's study—their program works and works well, and given the paucity of solid outcome research in this area, is a significant accomplishment. Perhaps future investigations will determine whether a specific component or combination of components make the Fuchs and Rehm package work as it does. For now, it is encouraging to know that behavioral clinicians have discovered something useful in their search for effective treatments.

Status of Behavioral Treatments

Although behavioral clinicians and researchers take pride in the extent to which their treatment techniques in general have survived rigorous experimental tests, such an attitude is not yet justified with reference to the treatment of depression. Considerable effort has been expended in theorizing about the nature of depression, but experimentally controlled evaluation of the proposed means of alleviating the disorder has been almost totally ignored. The treatments appear to have much to recommend them in terms of an active, systematic way of dealing with the depressed individual's many difficulties, and the results of several case studies and preliminary controlled research are encouraging. Perhaps in the future more research will be directed toward determining whether behavior modification approaches have anything worthwhile to offer the depressed person. At present, they offer mostly promises.

SUMMARY

The deceptively familiar concept of depression has proven remarkably difficult to define. Both researchers and clinicians disagree on the characteristics of the disorder, with the result that scientific study of the phenomenon (or phenomena) of depression has been severely hampered. Behavioral clinicians also seem undecided as to how to view depression. One approach considers each aspect of the depressive spectrum as an individual entity; an alternative assumes that all "depressive behavior" arises from a common cause or antecedent condition.

With regard to this "common cause" notion, a number of models of depressive behavior have been developed. The extinction model treats depression as essentially a pervasive reduction in the individual's instrumental behavior due to a reduced rate of positive reinforcement. The learned helplessness model assumes that depression is caused by the individual's believing himself or herself to be lacking control over punishing or reinforcing stimuli. The cognitive distortion model views depressive emotions and behaviors to be the result of a distorted cognitive set which causes the person to perceive the environment, the future, and his or her own abilities in negative ways. Finally, the anxiety hypothesis regards prolonged anxiety and stress to be one precusor of depression.

On the whole, behavioral models have proven useful in generating testable hypotheses regarding the nature and treatment of depression. However, many problems remain, including a lack of specificity in definitions of depression, a failure to determine the direction of cause-effect relationships, and an overlap in predictions derived from the models.

Most behavioral treatments for depression have not been experimentally evaluated, and anecdotal case reports are the basic guidelines for clinical practice. Techniques have been devised to break the depressive cycle. These include the reestablishment of instrumental behavior, induction of incompatible affects, alteration of negative cognitive sets, and improvements in quality and quantity of social interactions. The paucity of research on treatment strategies does not allow for meaningful conclusions regarding the effectiveness of behavioral approaches to depression.

CASE STUDY 13-1

TODD, F. J. COVERANT CONTROL OF SELF-EVALUATIVE RESPONSES IN THE TREATMENT OF DEPRESSION: A NEW USE FOR AN OLD PRINCIPLE. *BEHAVIOR THERAPY*, 1972, **3,** 91–94.

Todd describes the treatment of a woman with complex problems through the use of multiple behavioral techniques. Of particular interest is Todd's application of Homme's extension of the Premack principle to alter the woman's self-evaluative statements and reduce her depression.

Mrs. M was a forty-year-old physician's wife who sought treatment for numerous problems, including general tension, several phobias, and a host of psychosomatic complaints. Of central concern, however, was her chronic depression, which periodically became so severe that she had made three suicide attempts. Three and a half years of psychotherapy, one brief hospitalization, and a two-month trial of antidepressant medication had all proved of little benefit.

Following detailed assessment, a comprehensive treatment program was outlined which included desensitization for her phobias and conditioned relaxation for some of the physiological difficulties. Attempts to increase Mrs. M's social activities consisted of assertive training and behavioral rehearsal, followed by graded-task assignments, the completion of which was reinforced by therapy time. Marital therapy was also indicated. However, the therapist judged that the program could not be successfully implemented given Mrs. M's current severe depression; the depression would have to be dealt with first.

It was apparent that much of Mrs. M's depression stemmed from the self-deprecating thoughts she entertained. When asked to describe herself, she could find only negative things to say. The therapist pointed out the relationship between her negative self-statements and her feelings of depression, and suggested the substitution of positive statements as a way of alleviating her unhappiness. With considerable prompting and encouragement, Mrs. M finally managed to produce six positive statements about herself. These statements were then systematically cued and reinforced using one of Mrs. M's higher-frequency behaviors—cigarette smoking—in the following way:

The six positive statements were printed on a sheet of paper and on a small card. Mrs. M was told to slip the card under the cellophane wrapper of her cigarette package and to place the package on the larger sheet every time she put her cigarettes down. Whenever Mrs. M had an urge to smoke, she was to read one or two of the six positive statements *before* smoking the cigarette. She was to do this every time she smoked, without exception. She was also asked to add new positive items to the list as they occurred to her.

Within a week of faithfully following the instructions, Mrs. M's mood had improved markedly; and she had added eight more positive self-statements to her list. In another week, the list had grown to twenty-one items, and Mrs. M was reporting feeling better than she had in several years. At this point, positive thoughts were beginning to occur to her spontaneously even when she was not about to smoke. Mrs. M's depression had lifted enough that the comprehensive treatment program could be instituted.

Mrs. M received a total of thirty-five individual sessions, and was seen with her husband for an additional six sessions. Over the three-year posttherapy period, Mrs. M encountered no instances of serious depression and considered herself to be quite happy. She had become active in volunteer work and had developed a wide circle of friends. During occasional "down" periods, Mrs. M coped by focusing on positive thoughts, but had not found it necessary to reapply the Homme technique.

CASE STUDY 13–2

JACKSON, B. TREATMENT OF DEPRESSION BY SELF-REINFORCE-MENT. *BEHAVIOR THERAPY*, 1972, **3**, 298–307.

This case study illustrates the treatment of a woman's depression using procedures derived from the self-reinforcement disturbance model. The client, L.M., was a twenty-two-year-old married homemaker who had suffered from feelings of depression, worthlessness, and periods of inactivity for two years. She had consulted several therapists for the problems, each of whom had emphasized the importance of her understanding why she was depressed and becoming active again. These treatments usually reduced the depression temporarily, but it always returned.

As an only child, L.M. had been the target of frequent lectures from her mother on her lack of love and respect. She often found herself being negatively compared with other children her own age. Her father was a kind man, but he made no effort to intervene in his wife's tirades against the child. In school, L.M.'s performance was consistently above average, and she earned a B.A. in sociology. Her husband reported that she was an excellent housekeeper and cook; nevertheless he tended to be critical of her performance.

Not surprisingly, L.M. was also very hard on herself. Although she "objectively" realized that she did some things better than most of her peers, she tended to focus only on those performances that were not up to her standards. She rarely rewarded herself for anything, claiming that to do so would go against her upbringing. About the only positive reinforcement she received was from others in her environment, but she had developed the habit of negating compliments by making some self-deprecating comment.

Treatment began by selecting a task that L.M. performed frequently and which she considered important to use as a target for self-reinforcement. She chose housekeeping as the first such task. A ten-day period of baseline observations was initiated during which L.M. was asked to monitor the number of times she rewarded herself for doing her housework each day. A reward was defined as praising herself, doing something she enjoyed, or feeling contented as a consequence of her housekeeping. She was also asked to keep a daily record of her depression on a 10-point scale, with 10 being "very depressed." As Figure 13–3 illustrates, L.M. administered no self-reinforcements during the baseline period, and her depression remained quite severe.

During the second interview, L.M. was introduced to a self-reinforcement conceptualization of her depression, and a program to alleviate her distress was initiated. She was asked to take each individual task that made up her housework and to specify exactly what she wanted to accomplish on each task and the amount of time she thought necessary to reach that goal. As L.M. had a tendency to set unrealistic goals, it was necessary for the therapist to lower her expectations to ensure that she would meet with success. Each goal was specified and written down. After completing a task, L.M. was to refer to her list of goals and evaluate her performance in light of what she had wanted to accomplish. If she achieved what she

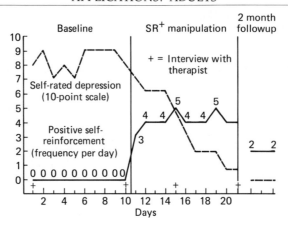

Figure 13–3. Daily records of depression and frequency of positive self-reinforcement (SR⁺). From B. Jackson, Treatment of depression by self-reinforcement. *Behavior Therapy*, 1972, **3,** p. 303, Figure 1. By permission of Academic Press and the author.

had set out to, she was to immediately reward herself with a compliment, a cigarette or some brief, enjoyable activity. To make the self-reinforcement more tangible and to prompt her to carry out the procedure, L.M. was also supplied with a box of poker chips and asked to take as many as she thought she had earned up to a maximum of ten. The whole process was modeled by the therapist and rehearsed by L.M. before she was sent out to try the procedure at home.

As shown by Figure 13–3, L.M. immediately began to emit self-reinforcements and her depression started to dissipate rapidly. She reported spending less time doing housework because she was doing it more efficiently and had a more easygoing attitude about it. She also, on her own initiative, applied self-reinforcement to other areas, such as socializing. For example, when serving as a hostess, she decided exactly how she wanted to behave beforehand and later evaluated her performance and rewarded herself. Within three weeks of the first interview, L.M.'s depression had been almost entirely eliminated. She continued to use self-reinforcement, and at a two-month followup reported no depression at all. Self-reinforcement at that time took the form of contentment with her behavior—an attitude which contrasted sharply with her previous self-criticism.

REFERENCES

Akiskal, H. S., & McKinney, W. T. Overview of recent research in depression: Integration of ten conceptual models into a comprehensive clinical frame. *Archives of General Psychiatry*, 1975, **32**, 285–305.

Baldessarini, R. J. The basis for amine hypotheses in affective disorders. *Archives of General Psychiatry*, 1975, **32**, 1087–1093.

Bandura, A. *Principles of behavior modification.* New York: Holt, Rinehart and Winston, 1969.

Beck, A. T. Thinking and depression. *Archives of General Psychiatry*, 1963, **9**, 324–333.

Beck, A. T. *Depression: Causes and treatment.* Philadelphia: University of Pennsylvania Press, 1967.

Beck, A. T. Cognitive therapy: Nature and relation to behavior therapy. *Behavior Therapy*, 1970, **1**, 184–200.

Beck, A. T. The development of depression: A cognitive model. In R. J. Friedman & M. M. Katz (Eds.), *The psychology of depression: Contemporary theory and research.* New York: Wiley, 1974.

Beck, A. T. *Cognitive therapy and the emotional disorders.* New York: International Universities Press, 1976.

Becker, J. *Depression: Theory and research.* New York: Wiley, 1974.

Blaney, P. H. Contemporary theories of depression: Critique and comparison. *Journal of Abnormal Psychology*, 1977, **86**, 203–223.

Blinder, M. G. The pragmatic classification of depression. *American Journal of Psychiatry*, 1966, **123**, 259–269.

Burgess, E. P. The modification of depressive behaviors. In R. D. Rubin & C. M. Franks (Eds.), *Advances in behavior therapy, 1968.* New York: Academic Press, 1969.

Cohen, S., Rothbart, M., & Phillips, S. Locus of control and the generality of learned helplessness in humans. *Journal of Personality and Social Psychology*, 1976, **34**, 1049–1056.

Costello, C. G. Depression: Loss of reinforcers or loss of reinforcer effectiveness? *Behavior Therapy*, 1972, **3**, 240–247.

Coyne, J. C. Depression and the response of others. *Journal of Abnormal Psychology*, 1976, **85**, 186–193.

Danaher, B. G. Theoretical foundations and clinical applications of the Premack principle: Review and critique. *Behavior Therapy*, 1974, **5**, 307–324.

Eastman, C. Behavioral formulations of depression. *Psychological Review*, 1976, **83**, 277–291.

Ellis, A. *Reason and emotion in psychotherapy.* Secaucus, N.J.: Lyle Stuart, 1962.

Ellis, A. *Humanistic psychotherapy: The rational-emotive approach.* New York: McGraw-Hill, 1973.

Ferster, C. B. Classification of behavioral pathology. In L. Krasner & C. P. Ullmann (Eds.), *Research in behavior therapy.* New York: Holt, Rinehart and Winston, 1965.

Ferster, C. B. Animal behavior and mental illness. *Psychological Record*, 1966, **16**, 345–356.

Ferster, C. B. A functional analysis of depression. *American Psychologist*, 1973, **28**, 857–870.

Ferster, C. B. Behavioral approaches to depression. In R. J. Friedman & M. M. Katz (Eds.), *The psychology of depression: Contemporary theory and research.* New York: Wiley, 1974.

Freud, S. Mourning and melancholia. In E. Jones (Ed.), *The collected papers of Sigmund Freud.* New York: Basic Books, 1959.

Fuchs, C. Z., & Rehm, L. P. A self-control behavior therapy program for depression. *Journal of Consulting and Clinical Psychology*, 1977, **45**, 206–215.

Grinker, R. R., Miller, J., Sabshin, M., Nunn, R., & Nunnally, J. C. *The phenomena of depression.* New York: Harper & Row, 1961.

Hammen, C. L., & Glass, D. R., Jr. Depression, activity, and evaluation of reinforcement. *Journal of Abnormal Psychology*, 1975, **84**, 718–721.

Hammen, C. L., & Krantz, S. Effect of success and failure on depressive cognitions. *Journal of Abnormal Psychology*, 1976, **85**, 577–586.

Hiroto, D. S. Learned helplessness, and locus of control. *Journal of Experimental Psychology*, 1974, **102**, 187–193.

Hiroto, D. S., & Seligman, M. E. P. Generality of learned helplessness in man. *Journal of Personality and Social Psychology*, 1975, **31**, 311–327.

Homme, L. E. Perspectives in psychology, XXIV: Control of coverants, the operants of the mind. *Psychological Record*, 1965, **15**, 501–511.

Jackson, B. Treatment of depression by self-reinforcement. *Behavior Therapy*, 1972, **3**, 298–307.

Johnson, W. G. Some applications of Homme's coverant control therapy: Two case studies. *Behavior Therapy*, 1971, **2**, 240–248.

Klein, D. C., Fencil-Morse, E., & Seligman, M. E. P. Learned helplessness, depression, and the attribution of failure. *Journal of Personality and Social Psychology*, 1976, **33**, 508–516.

Klerman, G. L., & Barrett, J. E. The affective disorders: Clinical and epidemiological aspects. In S. Gershon & B. Shopsin (Eds.), *Lithium: Its role in psychiatric treatment and research.* New York: Plenum Press, 1973.

Lader, M. The psychophysiology of anxious and depressed patients. In D. C. Fowles (Ed.), *Clinical applications of psychophysiology.* New York: Columbia University Press, 1975.

Lazarus, A. A. Learning theory and the treatment of

depression. *Behaviour Research and Therapy*, 1968, **6**, 83–89.

Lazarus, A. A. *Behavior therapy and beyond.* New York: McGraw-Hill, 1971.

Lazarus, A. A. Some reactions to Costello's paper on depression. *Behavior Therapy*, 1972, **3**, 248–250.

Lazarus, A. A. Multimodal behavioral treatment of depression. *Behavior Therapy*, 1974, **5**, 549–554.

Lehmann, H. E. Epidemiology of depressive disorders. In R. R. Fieve (Ed.), *Depression in the 70's: Modern theory and research.* Princeton, N.J.: Excerpta Medica, 1971.

Lewinsohn, P. M. A behavioral approach to depression. In R. J. Friedman & M. M. Katz (Eds.), *The psychology of depression: Contemporary theory and research.* New York: Wiley, 1974.

Lewinsohn, P. M. The behavioral study and treatment of depression. In M. Hersen, R. M. Eisler, & P. M. Miller (Eds.), *Progress in behavior modification*, vol. 1. New York: Academic Press, 1975(a).

Lewinsohn, P. M. Engagement in pleasant activities and depression level. *Journal of Abnormal Psychology*, 1975, **84**, 729–731(b).

Lewinsohn, P. M., & Atwood, G. E. Depression: A clinical-research approach. *Psychotherapy: Theory, Research and Practice*, 1969, **3**, 166–171.

Lewinsohn, P. M., Biglan, A., & Zeiss, A. M. Behavioral treatment of depression. In P. O. Davison (Ed.), *The behavioral management of anxiety, depression and pain.* New York: Brunner/Mazel, 1976.

Lewinsohn, P. M., & Graf, M. Pleasant activities and depression. *Journal of Consulting and Clinical Psychology*, 1973, **41**, 261–268.

Lewinsohn, P. M., & Libet, J. Pleasant events, activity schedules, and depression. *Journal of Abnormal Psychology*, 1972, **79**, 291–295.

Lewinsohn, P. M., & MacPhillamy, D. J. The relationship between age and engagement in pleasant activities. *Journal of Gerontology*, 1974, **29**, 290–294.

Lewinsohn, P. M., & Shaffer, M. Use of home observations as an integral part of the treatment of depression: Preliminary report and case studies. *Journal of Consulting and Clinical Psychology*, 1971, **37**, 87–94.

Lewinsohn, P. M., Weinstein, M. S., & Shaw, D. A. Depression: A clinical-research approach. In R. D. Rubin & C. M. Franks (Eds.), *Advances in behavior therapy, 1968.* New York: Academic Press, 1969.

Liberman, R. P., & Raskin, D. E. Depression: A behavioral formulation. *Archives of General Psychiatry*, 1971, **24**, 515–523.

Libet, J., & Lewinsohn, P. M. The concept of social skill with special references to the behavior of depressed persons. *Journal of Consulting and Clinical Psychology*, 1973, **40**, 304–312.

MacDonald, A. Effects of adaptation to the unconditioned stimulus upon the formation of conditioned avoidance responses. *Journal of Experimental Psychology*, 1946, **36**, 1–12.

MacPhillamy, D. J., & Lewinsohn, P. M. Studies on the measurement of human reinforcement and the relationship between positive reinforcement and depression. Unpublished manuscript, University of Oregon, 1973.

MacPhillamy, D. J., & Lewinsohn, P. M. Depression as a function of levels of desired and obtained pleasure. *Journal of Abnormal Psychology*, 1974, **83**, 651–657.

Mahoney, M. J. The self-management of covert behavior: A case study. *Behavior Therapy*, 1971, **2**, 575–578.

Mahoney, M. J. *Cognition and behavior modification.* Cambridge, Mass.: Ballinger, 1974.

Maier, S. F. Failure to escape traumatic shock: Incompatible skeletal motor responses or learned helplessness? *Learning and Motivation*, 1970, **1**, 157–170.

Marston, A. R. Personality variables related to self-reinforcement. *Journal of Psychology*, 1964, **58**, 169–175.

McLean, P. Therapeutic decision-making in the behavioral treatment of depression. In P. O. Davidson, (Ed.), *The behavioral management of anxiety, depression and pain.* New York: Brunner/Mazel, 1976.

McLean, P. D., Ogston, K., & Grauer, L. A behavioral approach to the treatment of depression. *Journal of Behavior Therapy and Experimental Psychiatry*, 1973, **4**, 323–330.

Miller, W. R., & Seligman, M. E. P. Depression and the perception of reinforcement. *Journal of Abnormal Psychology*, 1973, **82**, 62–73.

Miller, W. R., & Seligman, M. E. P. Depression and learned helplessness in man. *Journal of Abnormal Psychology*, 1975, **84**, 228–238.

Overall, J. E., Hollister, L. E., Johnson, M., & Pennington, V. Nosology of depression and differential response to drugs. *Journal of the American Medical Association*, 1966, **195**, 946–948.

Overmeier, J. B., & Seligman, M. E. P. Effects of inescapable shock upon subsequent escape and avoidance learning. *Journal of Comparative and Physiological Psychology*, 1967, **63**, 23–33.

Paykel, E. S. Correlates of a depressive typology. *Archives of General Psychiatry*, 1972, **27**, 203–210.

Paykel, E. S., Myers, J. K., Dienelt, M. W., Klerman, G. L., Lindenthal, J. J., & Pepper, M. P. Life events and depression: A controlled study. *Archives of General Psychiatry*, 1969, **21**, 753–760.

Rimm, D. C., & Masters, J. C. *Behavior therapy: Techniques and empirical findings.* New York: Academic Press, 1974.

Roth, S., & Kubal, L. Effects of noncontingent reinforcement on tasks of differing importance: Facilitation and learned helplessness. *Journal of Personality and Social Psychology*, 1975, **32,** 680–691.

Rozensky, R. H., Rehm, L. P., Pry, G., & Roth, D. Depression and self-reinforcement behavior in hospitalized patients. *Journal of Behavior Therapy and Experimental Psychiatry*, 1977, **8,** 31–34.

Rush, A. J., Khatami, M., & Beck, A. T. Cognitive and behavioral therapy in chronic depression. *Behavior Therapy*, 1975, **6,** 398–404.

Salter, A. *Conditioned reflex therapy.* New York: Creative Age Press, 1949.

Schuyler, D. *The depressive spectrum.* New York: Aronson, 1974.

Seligman, M. E. P. Depression and learned helplessness. In R. J. Friedman & M. M. Katz (Eds.), *The psychology of depression: Contemporary theory and research.* New York: Halstead-Wiley, 1974.

Seligman, M. E. P. *Helplessness: On depression, development, and death.* San Francisco: Freeman, 1975.

Seligman, M. E. P. Learned helplessness and depression in animals and men. In J. T. Spence, R. C. Carson, & J. W. Thibaut (Eds.), *Behavioral approaches to therapy.* Morristown, N.J.: General Learning Press, 1976.

Seligman, M. E. P., & Maier, S. F. Failure to escape traumatic shock. *Journal of Experimental Psychology*, 1967, **74,** 1–9.

Seligman, M. E. P., Maier, S. F., & Geer, J. The alleviation of learned helplessness in the dog. *Journal of Abnormal and Social Psychology*, 1968, **73,** 256–262.

Seligman, M. E. P., Maier, S. F., & Solomon, R. L. Unpredictable and uncontrollable aversive events. In F. R. Brush (Ed.), *Aversive conditioning and learning.* New York: Academic Press, 1971.

Selye, H. *The story of the adaptation syndrome.* Montreal: Acta, 1952.

Shaffer, M., & Lewinsohn, P. M. *Interpersonal behaviors in the home of depressed vs. nondepressed psychiatric and normal controls: A test of several hypotheses.* Paper presented at the meeting of the Western Psychological Association, April 1971.

Skinner, B. F. *Science and human behavior.* New York: Macmillan, 1953.

Taulbee, E. S., & Wright, H. W. A psychosocial-behavioral model for therapeutic intervention. In C. D. Spielberger (Ed.), *Current topics in clinical and community psychology*, vol. 3. New York: Academic Press, 1971.

Thornton, J. W., & Jacobs, P. D. Learned helplessness in human subjects. *Journal of Experimental Psychology*, 1971, **87,** 369–372.

Vasta, R. Coverant control of self-evaluations through temporal cueing. *Journal of Behavior Therapy and Experimental Psychiatry*, 1975, **7,** 35–37.

Wolpe, J. Neurotic depression: Experimental analog, clinical syndromes, and treatment. *American Journal of Psychotherapy*, 1971, **25,** 362–368.

Wolpe, J., & Lazarus, A. A. *Behavior therapy techniques.* Oxford: Pergamon Press, 1966.

fourteen

SEVERELY DISORDERED BEHAVIOR: "SCHIZOPHRENIA"

According to a major psychiatric text (Freedman, Kaplan, & Sadock, 1976), approximately 180,000 individuals are hospitalized for "schizophrenia" in the United States each year. Projections of the number of undiagnosed, untreated cases put this country's schizophrenic population at close to half a million. Schizophrenia costs us an estimated $14 billion annually. Worldwide, there may be more than 2 million new cases of schizophrenia each year, and the total number of schizophrenics is thought to be near 10 million.

"Schizophrenia" is not the only category of severely disordered or psychotic behavior, but it is by far the most important. Persons diagnosed as schizophrenic constitute about two-thirds of the resident population of the nation's mental hospitals. As the preceding paragraph shows, the problem is of awesome proportions. It is little wonder that schizophrenia is the most studied psychopathological condition of all time. More research time, effort, and money; more pages of professional publications; and more hours of lecture, discussion, debate, and argument have focused on the etiology, nature, and treatment of schizophrenia than on any other psychological disorder. It has rightfully been called "modern psychiatry's greatest challenge" (Romano, 1967, p. 1).

Behavioral contributions to the problem of schizophrenia are in some ways the mirror image of what we found in depression; that is, compara-

tively little effort has been directed toward developing conceptualizations of "schizophrenic behavior," but a widely applied treatment technology exists. In this chapter, we will examine behavioral approaches to the treatment of the severely disorganized behaviors subsumed by the label of schizophrenia. First we will look at the diagnostic category itself and at the problem it presents. Then we will overview the major conceptual orientations that have been applied to schizophrenic behavior—focusing, of course, on the behavioral position. Next, we will briefly examine the care and treatment traditionally provided individuals hospitalized as schizophrenic. Finally, we will discuss in detail behavioral strategies for the treatment of severely disorganzed behavior.

THE CONCEPT OF SCHIZOPHRENIA

Despite the vast amount of research on schizophrenia, it remains one of the most poorly understood of all psychological disorders. Indeed, one of the major issues yet to be resolved is whether schizophrenia even *exists*; or, more precisely, whether the diagnostic label describes a particular, unitary, identifiable entity of some sort. We can begin to understand why so basic a question is still the subject of hot debate by looking at the bewildering assortment of behavioral characteristics to be found in individuals supposedly suffering from schizophrenia. Such persons may hold delusional beliefs of all descriptions. They may have hallucinations in any of the sensory modalities, although auditory hallucinations appear to predominate. Their verbal behavior may range from nonexistence (muteness) to mumbling, swearing, screaming, and varying degrees of nonsensicalness. The emotions of "schizophrenics" are often flattened or blunted—but they may also be euphoric, depressed, grossly inappropriate, or extremely labile. Speech and performance on cognitive tasks often indicate some impairment of attention or thought processes, the extent of which varies considerably from person to person. In the area of motoric behavior, schizophrenics have been known to freeze in strange positions for hours or days; display incessant agitation; perform bizarre, stereotyped movements; posture; grimace; talk to themselves or to unseen companions; stare blankly; or act in ways that are not unusual in themselves, but that are inappropriate given the time, place, or circumstances under which they occur (for example, masturbating at the dinner table, or breaking into laughter when asked the time of day).

This description covers a lot of ground, yet all these characteristics—and many more—can be found in persons receiving a diagnosis of "schizophrenia." Obviously, we are traveling a road we have been on before, in our discussion of depression. Indeed, the problems encountered in attempting to define and delimit a category called "schizophrenia" are the same, or perhaps worse, than those which plague depression. The inadequacy of schizophrenia as a descriptive label, and of the traditional diagnostic nomenclature as a whole, has been recognized for a very long time (Ash, 1949; Beck, 1962; Schmidt & Fonda, 1956; Zigler & Phillips, 1961). Moreover, the situation has not improved in recent years (Blashfield, 1973; Helzer, Clayton, Pambakian, Reich, Woodruff, & Reveley, 1977). We will not bother to repeat these well-known deficiencies. For this discussion, Gordon Paul's (1974) summary of the situation will suffice:

> "[S]chizophrenia" does not mean the same thing to different people at the same point in time, nor to the same people at different points

in time. As used in either research or practice, the label neither consistently excludes any particular set of behaviors or inclusively describes any set of behaviors which do not occur outside the classification. . . . That is, the concept lacks reliability, and since, by definition, validity coefficients cannot exceed the square-root of reliability coefficients, the concept as currently applied cannot be very useful. (p. 196)

Given this bewildering state of affairs, it is important that we take a moment to clarify the terminology we will use in our discussion of this perplexing topic. Thus far, we have periodically set the word "schizophrenia" in quotation marks to call attention to its controversial status. We will not rely on this practice, as the point has been made. For the most part, we will avoid the term in favor of describing the particular behavioral excesses or deficits under consideration at that moment. Similarly, it is important to recognize that behavioral clinicians deal not with schizophrenia, but with those behaviors that interfere with an individual's functioning and preclude his or her acceptance by society—*the behaviors that earned him or her the label of schizophrenic.* To return to our dilemma: for convenience and economy, it will sometimes be necessary for us to speak of such behaviors *as if* they comprised a group of some sort. Exclusive use of some phrase such as "severely disordered behavior" would be fairly noncontroversial, but it would also be awkward and annoying. We will therefore refer to schizophrenic behavior, *by which we mean no more than behavior that is grossly inappropriate or dysfunctional in some way and/or that is likely to earn an individual a diagnosis of "schizophrenia" in a typical psychiatric setting.* With this understanding, we can begin.

CONCEPTUAL PERSPECTIVES

A great many theories have been proposed regarding the etiology of schizophrenic behavior. Among the most prominent have been psychodynamic theories (Freeman, Cameron, & McGhie, 1966), humanistic-existential theories (Laing, 1964), interpersonal-familial theories (Bateson, Jackson, Haley, & Weakland, 1956; Lidz, 1973), genetic theories (Gottesman & Shields, 1972; Rosenthal & Kety, 1968), biochemical theories (*Schizophrenia Bulletin*, 1976, Vol. 2, No. 1), and behavioral theories. It is beyond the scope of this chapter to review each of these conceptualizations. But it is safe to say that the major theories of the origin of schizophrenic behavior are of three types: (1) those that assume the cause is experiential (such as a stressful familial environment); (2) those that assume the cause is biological (such as a genetic abnormality in the functioning of the nervous system); and (3) those that assume the cause is an interaction between biological and experiential factors.

Diathesis-Stress Theory

Of the three theoretical perspectives, an interaction between a genetic predisposition and environmental stress is probably the most widely accepted explanation for the development of schizophrenic behavior. This is known as **diathesis-stress theory.** Numerous versions of the diathesis-stress theory exist, but perhaps the most cogent is that proposed by Paul Meehl (1962). Meehl suggests that an individual is placed at risk for the development of "clinical schizophrenia" (which, for Meehl, is characterized primarily by a thought disorder) by inheriting an "integrative neural defect" which he calls **schizotaxia.** Meehl advances several hypotheses about the nature of this defect, but for our discussion it is sufficient to view schizotaxia as a genetically determined dysfunction of the central nervous system. Schizotaxia does not in itself lead to schizophrenic behavior; instead, it causes the individual to respond to socialization by developing a personality organization known as **schizotypy.** Schizotypy is characterized by a mild degree of "cognitive slippage" (disordered thinking) and affective disturbance, but if the individual has an otherwise sound constitution and a relatively benign social learning history, he or she will live a fairly normal life. But if the person is particularly vulnerable to stress, or if his or her developmental environment has been aversive, schizotypy will give way to schizophrenic behavior.

Support for the diathesis-stress interpretation of schizophrenic behavior is mostly indirect. There is a growing body of evidence for a genetic factor operating in at least some cases of schizophrenic behavior (see Keith, Gunderson, Reifman, Buchsbaum, & Mosher, 1976, for a review of recent research), and most genetic theorists agree that the data do lend themselves to a diathesis-stress interpretation (Mosher & Gunderson, 1973). The indication of a genetic factor has stimulated an enormous amount of biochemical research aimed at identifying the inherited defect (the schizotaxia, if you will), but until recently, these efforts have been almost comical. Dozens of "breakthroughs" have been announced, only to be dismissed later because of poor experimental methodology (Farina, 1972). Biochemical studies are becoming increasingly sophisticated and appear to hold considerable promise, but the hypothesized physiological basis for the diathesis has yet to be found.

Behavioral Conceptualizations

As we mentioned, behavioral psychologists have contributed little to the conceptualization of schizophrenic behavior—at least in terms of comprehensive models that have been subjected to empirical evaluation. Of course, readers can surmise that any behavioral conceptualization is likely to hold experiential factors as being most important, and this is exactly the case. For example, Albert Bandura (1969) reviewed some of the data regarding the families of individuals diagnosed as schizophrenic and concluded: "[They] provide ample evidence that delusions, suspiciousness, grandiosity, extreme denial of reality, and other forms of schizophrenic behavior are frequently learned through direct reinforcement and transmitted by parental modeling of unusually deviant behavior patterns" (p. 295). In other words, bizarre behavior is thought to be learned early in life according to the same principles that produce other, more normal behavior.

Perhaps the most well-known behavioral conceptualization is that advanced by Leonard Ullmann and Leonard Krasner (1969, 1975), who suggest that unlearning or failing to learn may be more pertinent to the development of severely disordered behavior. They see schizophrenic behavior as arising primarily from "the extinction of attention to social stimuli to which 'normal' people respond" (Ullmann & Krasner, 1975, p. 357). The individual who undergoes this extinction of attentional responses presumably stops responding to the cues that guide everyone else's behavior, and instead begins to focus on idiosyncratic stimuli of which others are unaware. This makes the individual appear withdrawn and "strange," and people may begin to avoid him or her, which leads to even greater reduction in reinforcement for attention to social stimuli, and so on.

Ullmann and Krasner believe that this vicious cycle functionally detaches the person from his or her social environment and sets the stage for the development of many schizophrenic behaviors. Since the person is preoccupied with stimuli that are irrelevant to others, he or she may respond to questions in an inappropriate, disjointed fashion, and thus appear to have a thought disorder. In attempting to think through the things that happen to him or her, the individual may reach unusual conclusions (such as "People are out to get me"), which without corrective input from others, may become fixed and elaborated as delusional beliefs. If social isolation becomes complete enough, the person may begin talking to himself or herself or engaging in vivid fantasies sheerly for the stimulation these activities provide. Over time, the individual may come to regard these internally generated stimuli as every bit as important as external stimuli. Indeed, it may become difficult for him or her to tell whether the voices and images originate from within or without.

Ullmann and Krasner also view the traditional mental hospital as playing a significant role in the individual's deterioration. Once hospitalized, the individual quickly learns to "play the role of being mentally ill." The hospital environment is bland and unstimulating, and offers little to restore the patient's waning attention to external stimuli. The new patient is surrounded by other patients who model a variety of bizarre behaviors and staff members who believe the individual to be "sick" and treat him or her accordingly. Energetic, assertive responses—indeed, interpersonal behaviors in general—often go unreinforced by staff who value patients who are quiet, clean, and nondemanding. Withdrawn, apathetic behavior is thus shaped by the very environment intended to rehabilitate the individual.

As support for their view that schizophrenic behavior is produced through the mechanisms of learning, Ullmann and Krasner rely primarily on research and clinical observation indicating that severely disorganized patients are often a lot more "with it" than they are believed to be. Such patients often seem to become more or less "schizophrenic" depending on which holds the greater promise of some sort of payoff. Although these observations are consistent with the conceptualization that schizophrenia is largely a social role, they are at variance with the notion that mental patients are suffering from an extinction of attention to social stimuli. Another inadequacy in the conceptualization is that Ullmann and Krasner fail to explain exactly what causes an individual to undergo this peculiar type of extinction in the first place. It is difficult to imagine a social environment devoid of any kind of reinforcement for appropriate attentional responses. At present there is no evidence that severely disturbed individuals develop in such remarkable vacuums.

Moreover, to accept the hypothesis that schizophrenic behavior results from learning alone requires that we reject the compelling genetic evidence. Many behavioral psychologists, unwilling to do this, align themselves with the traditional view that schizophrenic behavior is at least in part the result of a genetically based biochemical disorder (for example, Eysenck & Rachman, 1965; Nathan & Jackson, 1976; Wolpe, 1969). We agree that a strict learning-theory conceptualization of schizophrenic behavior is overly simplistic and does not account for the available data. Nevertheless, the role of learning in the development of such behavior is undoubtedly quite large. More important, however, is the effectiveness of learning-based procedures in treating severe disturbances no matter what their origin.

HOSPITALIZATION AND THE PROBLEM OF CHRONICITY

Individuals who display behaviors that seriously interfere with their daily functioning, or that annoy, concern, or frighten those around them, usually find themselves hospitalized. In the past, such hospital visits frequently stretched into extended stays, but this is somewhat less the case today. Since the mid-1960s, there has been a shift away from institutionalization toward returning severely disorganized individuals to the community, where they can be provided with broad-spectrum treatment through the outpatient services of community mental health centers. This approach has, in part, been responsible for accelerating the decline in the numbers of institutional residents that began in the mid-1950s with the introduction of psychoactive drugs. However, the decline has been accompanied by a discouraging phenomenon: hospital *readmissions* have increased to such an extent that the psychiatric hospital has been characterized as a "revolving door." Individuals who undergo "multiple admissions" often stay a bit longer on each successive occasion and may eventually remain in the hospital permanently. They become *chronic mental patients* (see Paul, 1969, and Paul & Lentz, 1977).

As already mentioned, the predominant characteristic of the environment in which institutionalized chronic patients find themselves is dullness. They have lots of time and very little to do. Although most hospitals have improved a great deal in the amount of "treatment" given chronic patients, the various activity therapies, group therapies, occupational therapies, and so on usually make up a very small portion of the patients' lives in the institution. As long as patients are quiet and cause the aides and nurses little trouble, they will likely be left to themselves. The majority of their time will probably be spent in the institution's large dayroom, sitting and staring blankly at the walls or at the television set that blares on endlessly. The stupor and withdrawal this situation creates further debilitate patients, and each day they become a bit less able to function independently.

By far the most widely applied "treatment" given institutionalized mental patients is drug therapy. The drugs typically employed are of the phenothiazine family, often referred to as the "major tranquilizers." Once patients are started on medication, their continued need for it is only

rarely, if ever, reviewed. Patients typically wind up taking a daily "maintenance dose," which is frequently arrived at by increasing the dosage level to a point at which the drug's side effects start becoming a major problem, and then backing off a bit.

Although there is little doubt that the major tranquilizers can help suppress the bizarre behavior of acutely disturbed individuals and enable them to regain their composure and reenter the community, the value of phenothiazines for the maintenance of chronic patients is the subject of a raging debate. Medically oriented clinicians have reviewed the drug treatment literature and concluded that long-term use of phenothiazines is necessary to ensure the chronic patient's optimal functioning, and that discontinuation leads to a return of florid psychotic symptoms (Klein & Davis, 1969; Prien & Klett, 1972). Behavioral psychologists have reviewed the same literature and found most studies to suffer from such methodological inadequacies that their results cannot be accepted (Marholin & Phillips, 1976; Tobias & MacDonald, 1974). The fact is that withdrawing medication from even severely debilitated chronic patients has no detrimental consequences if the patients are involved in an active and effective treatment program (Paul, Tobias, & Holly, 1972). Let us now look at what behavioral psychologists have done to build such programs.

BEHAVIOR-SPECIFIC INTERVENTIONS

The most widely employed comprehensive behavioral approach to the treatment of severely disordered behavior is the token economy, which we will examine in detail later. In this section we will look at some of the component behaviors and deficits frequently found among individuals labeled schizophrenic, and some of the treatment procedures applied to each. Many of these procedures do not depend on the existence of an ongoing token economy, and can be used independently or to supplement a token economy. We have selected for this review those behaviors that have been given most attention in the literature.

Mutism

A fair number of chronic mental patients never utter a sound, even though there is no indication of organic impairment of crucial brain centers or of the vocal apparatus. The first successful attempt to reinstate verbal behavior in such chronic patients was reported by Wayne Isaacs, James Thomas, and Israel Goldiamond (1960), who used a shaping procedure to evoke speech in two men who had been mute for nineteen and fourteen years, respectively. For one man, chewing gum reinforcement was delivered initially when he merely focused his eyes on it. Next, a succession of facial movements, mouth movements, and finally croaks were required before the patient got the gum. The experimenter then unsuccessfully prompted the man to say "gum" for several sessions. However, in the middle of one training session the man suddenly said, "Gum, please," and thereafter was able to answer simple questions put to him by the experimenter. Still, the patient's new verbal behavior did not generalize to other ward personnel until they were instructed not to interpret his nonverbal requests as they had done in the past. The unusual "all-at-once" manner in which the patient's speech returned has also been noted by other researchers (for instance, Sherman, 1963).

As has been the case in language training with "autistic" children (see Chapter 6), establishing a general nonverbal imitation response is sometimes helpful as a first step with chronic patients who cannot be prompted into *any* verbal behavior at all (Sherman, 1965). Getting such individuals to imitate simple motor movements reliably can "start things rolling" by acquainting them with response-contingent reinforcement that may provide motivation to imitate the trainer's other behaviors. A long chain of approximations can then be used to change the unrelated imitative response into something closer and closer to verbalization.

Since the earliest reports, a number of investigators have proved the usefulness of modeling, shaping, and reinforcement procedures for reinstating speech in mute or near-mute chronic patients (Baker, 1971; Sabatasso & Jacobson, 1970). However, as we have often pointed out in other contexts, maintenance of the new verbal behavior beyond the training setting is not assured (Sherman, 1965; Wilson & Walters, 1966), and specific attempts to foster generalization should be built into the program.

Delusional and Hallucinatory Behavior

As traditionally defined, a delusion is a false belief an individual maintains despite considerable evidence to the contrary. A hallucination is a perceptual experience in the absence of an appropriate sensory stimulus. Delusions and hallucinations have generally been regarded as "mental" phenomena—that is, they exist in the individual's private experience (in the person's "mind," if you will). But both are recognizable to others only through observable behavior. Thus, if an individual walks about with his hand thrust inside the lapel of his coat, muttering "Waterloo will be my greatest victory," we say he has a delusion that he is Napoleon (and his predictions about the battle aren't so great either). Or, if we observe an individual diving behind pieces of furniture with cries of "Look out! Somebody get that guy's license number!" we conclude that he or she has hallucinated an automobile speeding through the room.

One of the approaches behavioral psychologists have taken in cases of delusion or hallucination has been to view the observable behaviors as "the problem" and to apply straightforward operant procedures to eliminate them. An early example of this strategy comes from a report by Teodoro Ayllon and Jack Michael (1959) of a female mental patient who refused to eat, apparently because she believed her food had been poisoned. Ward nurses had to spoon-feed her in order to get her to take any nourishment. Allyon and Michael observed that one of the woman's greatest pleasures seemed to be in keeping neat and clean. They decided to use this reinforcer in a unique way to get her to feed herself. The nurses who spoon-fed the woman were instructed to be intentionally messy and to drop food on the woman's clothing as they attempted to feed her. This proved to be quite unpleasant to the woman, and within two months she had taken to feeding herself in order to keep her clothing tidy. Thus, the observable delusional behavior—refusing to eat until coaxed—was eliminated without ever dealing with the poisoning belief.

Another example of this approach involved reducing a chronic patient's high rate of delusional statements (Rickard, Dignam, & Horner, 1960). An experimenter spoke with the patient in an interview situation. Whenever the patient said something like, "I have a fractured head and a broken nose because of spinal pressure," or "Stars have metal bottoms and exert a magnetic pressure on the earth," the interviewer turned away, looked at his watch or out the window, or otherwise withdrew attention from the patient. However, when the patient's conversation was coherent and relevant, the interviewer showed great interest by smiling, nodding, and interacting with him. This timeout and DRO procedure appeared to decrease the patient's delusional expressions and greatly increase "rational" speech, and gains appeared to be maintained at a two-year followup (Rickard & Dinoff, 1962).

Since these early investigations, a host of reports have appeared in which overt delusional and/or hallucinatory behaviors have been met with extinction or response costs (such as timeout, and loss of tokens or privileges), while rational behavior was differentially reinforced (Ayllon & Haughton, 1964; Haynes & Geddy, 1973; Liberman, 1972; Liberman, Teigen, Patterson, & Baker, 1973; Richardson, Karkalas, & Lal, 1972; Wincze, Leitenberg, & Agras, 1972). Many of these reports were of the controlled, individual analysis type, and taken together they offer fairly convincing evidence for the usefulness of operant procedures in reducing these overt behaviors. Not so convincing, however, is an assumption that appears to underlie many of these studies. That assumption is clearly stated in the following excerpt from a report of the reduction of hallucinatory expressions in a young man (Nydegger, 1972, p. 227).

> [I]t is interesting to record the reactions of some members of the staff. They asserted that the patient had not been purged of his hallucinations, but had merely been taught not to speak of them. Thus it could not be said that he was not hallucinating. When I asked the critics how they knew that [the patient] had hallucinated in the first place, they promptly reeled off these behavioral indicators: he talks to himself; "listens" to things no one else hears; withdraws to isolated corners; and says that he hallucinates. I then pointed out that all of these indicators were observable behavior—a point which they reluctantly conceded. I then asserted that since none of the indicative behaviors existed any longer, it could be maintained that [the patient] no longer hallucinated.

This bit of "reasoning" represents a throwback to radical behaviorism. Using this same logic, you can try relieving your next headache by not mentioning it to anyone, and not moaning, wincing, holding your head, or otherwise indicating your distress. If others cannot see that you are in pain, it can be maintained that you are not in pain, right? Wrong.

As several behavioral writers have pointed out, patients who are timed-out, lose tokens or privileges, or are otherwise punished whenever they express an unshared belief or an unusual sensory experience will probably learn to keep their mouths shut even if their private experiences remain unchanged (Davison, 1969; Stahl & Leitenberg, 1976). It seems irresponsible not to assess for an experiential basis for unusual behavior instead of simply punishing the behavior itself out of existence. It may even be dangerous in certain cases. Individuals have been known to commit acts of violence on the basis of bizarre beliefs or experiences no one knew they had. This is not to say that the operant procedures in the investigations just reviewed did not, in fact, eliminate the *internal* delusional or hallucinatory experiences along with their external manifestations; but in most cases researchers did not bother to question their subjects about any such changes. Self-report may have its problems, but it is potentially the most direct means available of gaining an understanding of another person's conscious experience. Of course, it is possible that the individuals in these studies never *had* delusions or hallucinations, and only performed their outward indications to gain attention or for some other reason—but how can we be sure of this?

Some clinicians have reacted to this dilemma by approaching delusions from a more cognitive perspective. For example, Gerald Davison (1966) reported the case of a forty-four-year-old male who was hospitalized with a diagnosis of paranoid schizophrenia. The man seemed to be most concerned about "pressure points" over his right eye that were caused by a spirit who helped him make decisions. Rather than punishing delusional expressions, Davison looked for ways to restructure the man's beliefs. Treatment consisted of giving the client another way of interpreting the "pressure points" above his eye. Davison demonstrated that they were really muscle contractions brought on by tense situations. He showed the client that he could produce similar pressure points in his hand and arm by making a fist and bending his wrist. He also proved that tense situations (such as a game of blackjack with the therapist) produced the pressure points the client had experienced at other times. Finally, Davison taught the client to reduce the pressure points through relaxation exercises. As the man became convinced of the truth of Davison's alternative explanation for the pressure points, he stopped referring to spirits and appeared increasingly less paranoid. The client left the hospital minus his delusion, and nine months later reported that he was employed, coping well with daily pressures, and only infrequently bothered by pressure points, which he could easily control (Davison, 1969).

In a similar vein, Fraser Watts, Graham Powell, and S. Austin (1973) developed a systematic procedure for altering paranoid beliefs. Following preliminary interviews, the therapist compiles a list of problematic beliefs which the patient is asked to rate on a five-point scale according to how strongly he or she holds each one. The assumption is that beliefs which are least strongly held will be easiest to alter and will evoke the least resistance. Starting with the lowest-ranked item, the therapist questions the patient about his or her reasons for believing it. Each piece of evidence the patient presents is challenged by the therapist through counterevidence and alternative explanations. The belief itself is not discussed— only the evidence on which it is based. To avoid a direct confrontation that might lead the patient to strengthen the belief in defiance (Brehm, 1966), the therapist makes it clear that the counterarguments are raised only for the patient's considera-

tion; the patient's opinions need not be abandoned in favor of those of the therapist. Nevertheless, as many lines of argument as possible are presented against the patient's position, and he or she is also encouraged to try to come up with some reinterpretations of the evidence.

Pilot studies with three male mental patients, each of whom harbored a false belief that their appearance was "odd" or feminine, indicated that this procedure produced considerable reduction in the strength of the beliefs. Furthermore, the effects did not appear to stem from placebo or "nonspecific" factors alone. However, controlled research on the technique has not yet been published.

In summary, two strategies seem to have emerged from behavioral work on delusional and hallucinatory behavior. The first—straightforward operant manipulation of the observable behaviors—has its roots in Watsonian behaviorism and assumes that the internal experience of the individual is unobservable and hence irrelevant. The second is a cognitive restructuring approach that clearly reflects the growing interest of behavioral clinicians in the way persons construe their world. We are reminded at this point of an interesting question posed to us by a colleague of a different clinical orientation. He wondered whether a chronic patient in a behavioral program would earn or lose social and/or token reinforcement for saying, "Excuse me, doctor. I know this sounds very unusual and that it can't really be happening, but I honestly hear a clear voice urging me to kill myself for my many sins." This hypothetical patient is telling us in a very appropriate manner about an internal experience that is bizarre and maladaptive. If we reinforce the person, what have we reinforced? And if we turn away or put the patient in a timeout room, what have we punished? We cannot answer these questions.

Thought Disorder

Ever since the term "schizophrenia" was introduced by Eugen Bleuler in 1911, a thought disturbance has been held to be central to the disorder. Indeed, many mental patients present deficits that appear to result from disorganized thinking. One very common observation is that such persons often show disturbances in their association of words or ideas. For example, given the word "light" in a word-association test, the "normal" individual would likely respond with a common association, such as "dark" or perhaps "bulb." The psychotic patient is much less likely to give a common association to the word, and may instead say "cup" or "boat" or some other word that appears to bear no relation to the stimulus word.

The first attempt to alter the associations of "schizophrenics" through behavioral procedures was reported by Robert Sommer, Gwynneth Witney, and Humphry Osmond (1962). They used cigarettes to reinforce patients every time they gave a common association to the stimulus word in an association test. A control group of hospitalized alcoholics underwent the same procedure. Cigarette reinforcement significantly increased the number of common associations given by both groups, but the alcoholics responded much more rapidly and showed much greater improvement than the mental patients. Furthermore, the alcoholics showed more generalization of their associational skill to a new list of stimulus words. These findings were replicated by another team of investigators who used social reinforcement rather than cigarettes (Ullmann, Krasner, & Edinger, 1964). However, although the results of both investigations are of academic interest, the very slight improvements obtained cast doubt on the usefulness of such procedures in the rehabilitation of chronic patients.

Another area of mental functioning in which many severely disordered individuals show profound deficits is *abstract reasoning*. For example, persons diagnosed as schizophrenic often have great difficulty interpreting the abstract, larger meaning of a simple proverb, such as "You don't miss the water until the well has run dry." Instead, they give a literal, overly concrete interpretation, such as "A dry well has no water," or "Everyone needs water."

In a beautifully designed and comprehensive series of investigations, Donald Meichenbaum has studied the use of operant procedures to increase the level of abstraction in hospitalized mental patients. In the first study (Meichenbaum, 1966), equated groups of mental patients were subjected to four different reinforcement conditions as they interpreted proverbs presented to them. The patients in the first group received contingent social reinforcement (a smile, a nod or a word of praise) whenever they gave an appropriate abstract interpretation. The second group received the same amount of social reinforcement, but it was delivered randomly and was not contingent on a particular type of response. The third group received mild social punishment (a frown, a shake of the head, and a word of discouragement, like "poor") contingent on ridiculous or overly concrete interpretations. Finally, a fourth group received no feedback at all during the task and served as controls. Subjects receiving contingent social reinforcement significantly increased their appropriate abstract interpretations over the other three groups, which did not differ from each other. Furthermore, this group's superiority *generalized* to an entirely different test of abstraction, the Similarities subtest of the Wechsler Adult Intelligence Scales (which contains questions such as "In what way are a coat and a dress alike?" ". . . a poem and a statue?" ". . . a fly and a tree?").

These findings were replicated and extended in a second investigation (Meichenbaum, 1969). Although the study is too complex to discuss in detail here, several important findings emerged. (1) "Schizophrenic" patients given either social or token reinforcement for increasing abstractness on a proverbs test also displayed reductions in nonsensical or bizarre verbalizations ("sick talk") in a separate test. Conversely, patients whose percentage of "straight talk" had been increased through identical procedures also increased their level of abstraction on the proverbs task. (2) Patients in both these training conditions maintained their improvements in a one-week followup interview with the experimenter, and in a posttest interview conducted by another patient who was a confederate of the experimenter. (3) After training, the proverb responses of the mental patients were *indistinguishable from those given by a group of normal medical patients*. Thus, Meichenbaum's remarkable findings clearly support the use of social and token reinforcement techniques for reducing verbal indices of disorganized thinking. Both the magnitude of the improvements and the considerable evidence for generalization of the treatment effects underscore the practical value of Meichenbaum's procedure for rehabilitative programs.

A casual observation made during the course of the previous study provided the impetus for a third important experiment. Meichenbaum noted that patients who had undergone the training to increase straight talk often spontaneously repeated the instructions "be coherent, be relevant, give healthy talk" to themselves when facing generalization tasks such as proverb interpretation. This was the seed from which **self-instructional training** was born. Meichenbaum and Roy Cameron (1973) set out to see if "schizophrenics" could be taught to reduce their cognitive disorganization by emitting task-relevant self-statements. The self-instructional training Meichenbaum and Cameron gave the mental patients was almost identical to that used with impulsive children (described in Chapter 5). Basically, the trainer modeled appropriate self-statements while working at a task. Later, the patient tried the task while imitating the trainer's verbalizations out loud. On subsequent trials, the patient learned to self-instruct more and more quietly, and eventually to do it in thought alone. For example, when working on the Similarities subtest of the Wechsler Adult Intelligence Scales, the trainer modeled these self-instructions (Meichenbaum & Cameron, 1973, p. 525):

> I have to figure out how a fly and a tree are alike. A fly and a tree? (pause). A fly is small and a tree is big. I got it, the fly can carry germs to the tree . . . (pause). No, that doesn't make sense. That doesn't tell me how they are alike. Go slowly and think this one out. Don't just say the first thing that comes to mind. (Pause while the model thinks.) I want to give the best answer I can. Let me imagine in my mind the objects . . . fly, tree . . . out in the sunshine. They both need sunshine to live. That is it, they are both living things! Good, I figured it out. If I take my time and just think about how the two objects are alike, I can do it.

Patients began training working with simple sensorimotor tasks (finger mazes, and so on), and progressed through more demanding cognitive tasks. A tape recorder was also used to add distracting sounds the patients had to learn to tune out. Finally, the last phase of training involved teaching the patients to monitor the reactions of others for cues as to the appropriateness of their own behavior. A strange look from someone the patient was talking with was to prompt the patient to evaluate what he or she was doing or saying to elicit such a response and use self-instruction to get his or her behavior under control again. Patients were also taught to use such phrases as "I'm not making myself clear; let me try again," to keep others in contact while they got back on track.

The results of the study indicate that self-instructional training was very effective in decreasing patients' "sick talk" and improving their performance on a variety of cognitive tasks. In almost every task, self-instruction subjects significantly outperformed other patients who had been given equal practice at the various tasks, but who had not received training in self-instruction. Their skills also generalized to new tasks, and they maintained their improvements impressively at a three-week followup.

A case report (Meyers, Mercatoris, & Sirota, 1976) in which self-instructional training was used to control a mental patient's irrelevant and rambling speech further supports the clinical usefulness of the technique. However, one team of investigators has been unable to replicate the findings of Meichenbaum and Cameron (Margolis & Shemberg, 1976). Until the reason for this discrepancy has been accounted for, an unqualified endorsement of the procedure cannot be given.

Apathy and Withdrawal

The most frequently encountered problems in chronically hospitalized mental patients are apathy and withdrawal. Such individuals often appear almost totally unresponsive to their environment. Their emotional responses may be flattened to the extent that they become zombie-like in appearance. Along with these qualities, the chronic patient often avoids human contact, preferring instead to sit alone in a corner and stare blankly. Whether such characteristics are a product of the "disorder" or the chronic hospitalization is not clear. Most likely these behaviors represent an interaction between the patient's deficits and the dehumanizing, deadening atmosphere of many institutions. What *is* clear is that these problems must be overcome if any rehabilitative effort is to be successful.

One way chronic patients can appear apathetic and emotionally blunted is by failing to express their feelings (see Chapter 9). It should come as no great surprise to find that verbal conditioning procedures can produce an increase in self-referred affective statements (that is, "I feel . . .") (Salzinger & Pisoni, 1958, 1960, 1961; Salzinger & Portnoy, 1964; Salzinger, Portnoy, & Feldman, 1964) and in emotionally toned words (Ullmann, Weiss, & Krasner, 1963; Weiss, Krasner, & Ullmann, 1963); and that patients can be conditioned to emit words reflecting more "pleasant" emotion (Ullmann, Krasner, & Gelfand, 1963). The usefulness of these data is questionable. Some of the conditioning effects were so minimal that high-powered (and questionable) statistical techniques were necessary to find them (Ullmann, Krasner, & Gelfand, 1963). Others extinguished very rapidly when reinforcement was withdrawn (Salzinger & Pisoni, 1960). Studies attempting to relate verbal-emotional conditioning to such supposedly meaningful measures as "perceptual defensiveness" (strangely enough, a psychoanalytic concept) (Ullmann, Weis, & Krasner, 1963) or global ratings of patients' behavior in group therapy (Ullmann, Krasner, & Collins, 1961) have been poorly controlled and are open to alternative explanations. Finally, the issue we raised in our discussion of delusions and hallucinations is also relevant here: a change in a patient's verbal-affective responses under reinforcement contingencies says nothing about the way he or she really *feels*. Here again, no one seems to have thought about *asking* the patient whether the conditioning procedure has really changed his or her emotional responses in any useful fashion.

Several methods have been used to encourage withdrawn patients to take more interest in their environment and to begin interacting with other people once again. One of the most unusual but successful methods was described in an early report by Gerald King, Stewart Armitage, and John Tilton (1960). Their procedure, called the **operant-interpersonal method,** made use of a machine not unlike a complex, human-sized Skinner box. Extremely withdrawn chronic patients who had proved unresponsive to a variety of other treatments were initially shaped into simple lever-pulling responses that produced reinforcers such as Hershey's candy kisses or cigarettes. During training, a therapist stood by to model, prompt, and instruct the patient, and to praise appropriate responses. When the patient was reliably performing the simple operant responses, more complex lever movements (for instance, a cross) were required to produce reinforcement. The increasing difficulty of the tasks created a situation in which the therapist could attempt to communicate with the patient in an effort to help him solve the problem (for example, "What will your first move be?" "Now, where do you go next?"). Verbal interaction was faded in slowly over a period of weeks.

After a minimum level of communication was established between therapist and patient, something new was added to the procedure: A second lever was introduced, and it was explained to the patient that both he and the therapist had to operate the levers in some sequential fashion to earn the reinforcer. Thus, a situation was established in which the patient was motivated to interact with the therapist in order to solve the lever problem. Verbal interaction, such as "Who does what next?" was emphasized. Occasionally, the therapist would intentionally make a mistake, leaving it up to the patient to point it out and correct him. Finally, when all patients were fairly skilled at solving the lever problems with the therapist, patients were given a chance to work the machine together while the therapist looked on. Other patients were allowed to observe the cooperating team and encouraged to offer their ideas about solving the lever problems. Eventually, every patient was given an opportunity to work with every other patient.

Improvement in patients undergoing the operant-interpersonal treatment was compared with that achieved by matched patients involved in (1) verbal therapy (in which the therapist carried on a monologue on various topics punctuated with "hopeful pauses" during which the patient could speak), (2) recreational therapy (during which patients were encouraged to join in dancing, games, and other social activities), or (3) no treatment (during which patients continued in the usual hospital routine).

The operant-interpersonal method emerged as clearly superior to all other treatments. In summarizing the data from their comprehensive battery, King, Armitage, and Tilton (1960, p. 286) note:

> The operant-interpersonal method was more effective than all the control methods in promoting clinical improvement, based on both ward observations and interview assessments. Comparison on the following variables also yielded differences in favor of the operant-interpersonal method: level of verbalization, motivation to leave the ward, resistance to therapy, more interest in occupational therapy, decreased enuresis, and transfers to better wards. The patients undergoing verbal therapy became worse in some ways (e.g., verbal withdrawal).

A six-month followup of subjects from all but the recreational therapy group indicated patients who had undergone operant-interpersonal therapy were still functioning significantly better than subjects from the verbal therapy and no-treatment groups. Important anecdotal data also supported the use of the operant-interpersonal method. Of greatest interest was the observation that patients seemed to be genuinely interested in the tasks in which they were involved. More than a month after the termination of the study, patients were still asking ward personnel when they would have a chance to participate again. Evoking such expressions of interest from apathetic and withdrawn individuals is itself significant. Despite these very encouraging findings, however, the operant-interpersonal method has not made a reappearance in the literature.

A more recent approach to replacing psychiatric patients' apathetic and withdrawn behavior with interactive, prosocial responses involves the use of **social-skills training packages** much like those used with interpersonally anxious individuals (Chapter 9). Arnold Goldstein (1973) reports that his research group has used such procedures with both acute and chronic patients, most of whom were diagnosed "schizophrenic" (Gutride, Goldstein, & Hunter, 1972, 1973). They used videotapes that portrayed a model involved in increasingly complex social interactions. For

example, one set of tapes depicted several variants of each of the following themes: (1) a model interacting with another individual who approaches; (2) a model initiating an interaction with another person; (3) a model initiating interactions with a group of people; and (4) a model resuming relations with relatives, friends, and other individuals outside the hospital. The tapes also contained a number of other features designed to enhance their effectiveness. Several differing models were used on the tapes, although all were similar to the patients in age, sex, and status. This maximized the chance of each patient finding a model with whom he or she could identify. The tapes included an introduction and summary by a prestigious narrator (such as a hospital superintendent) who attempted to underscore the concrete social behaviors depicted by the models. Finally, the models received frequent and obvious reinforcement from their interactions, in the hope that this would provide the patients who observed them with a reason to imitate their behavior.

While showing each tape to groups of five to eight patients, a trainer frequently drew their attention to critical behaviors. Occasionally, he would turn off the sound to emphasize the nonverbal components of effective social behavior. Following the tape, a group discussion was held relating the model's behaviors to each patient's problems and experiences. Finally the taped scenes were reenacted in role-plays that were themselves videotaped and replayed for discussion, reinforcement, and corrective feedback. As the patients became more involved in this process, the trainer gradually faded his influence.

The evaluative data for the training package are far too complex to report in detail. In general, rating scales completed by the patients and observational assessments of their responses in both contrived and naturally occurring social situations confirmed that the training improved patients' interpersonal skills. Unfortunately, the procedure had little effect on patients' self-reported desire to seek or to be sought out for social interaction. This finding is disappointing in view of the goal of getting withdrawn patients "out of their shells" and back into active social participation. However, in view of the preliminary nature of this work and of the efforts of other investigators who are exploring similar procedures (for example, Goldsmith & McFall, 1975; Hersen & Bellack, 1976), it would be a mistake to overvalue either positive or negative findings. The approach shows promise and deserves further study.

COMPREHENSIVE TREATMENT ENVIRONMENTS

One of the milestones in the history of behavior modification was the development of wardwide token economies and incentive systems for chronic mental patients. These programs grew from the premise that most institutional environments foster withdrawal and apathy by relieving individuals of all responsibility for their own welfare. To correct this problem, efforts were made to develop treatment environments in which patients' adaptive, prosocial behavior was heavily reinforced, and maladaptive behavior was ignored or punished.

Three early projects had a profound impact on the development of comprehensive behavioral interventions for chronic mental patients. These are (1) the token economy ward established at Anna State Hospital (Illinois) by Teodoro Ayllon and Nathan Azrin, (2) a similar program which operated at the Menlo Park Veterans' Administration Hospital (California) under the direction of John Atthowe and Leonard Krasner, and (3) the program developed by George Fairweather at the Palo Alto Veterans' Administration Hospital (California). The hallmark of each of these projects was the replacement of the "warehouse" environment of the traditional institution with conditions aimed at encouraging normalized functioning.

Since the mid-1960s, similar programs have spread rapidly and now can be found in institutions everywhere. With the proliferation of this treatment approach has come a flood of research reports pertaining to its various aspects and outcomes. There exist a number of encyclopedic reviews of this extensive literature (for example, Davison, 1969; Kazdin, 1977; Stahl & Leitenberg, 1976). Rather than presenting an overview of this material, we will take an approach we believe will make behavioral interventions with chronic men-

tal patients "come alive" for readers. After providing a historical perspective by briefly summarizing the three seminal programs mentioned above, we will examine one "state of the art" rehabilitation project in considerable detail. This discussion should enable readers to appreciate the complexity involved in expanding basic token economy principles (see Chapter 5) to form sophisticated treatment environments. It will also illustrate the procedural and ethical difficulties that arise in working with severely debilitated persons.

Three Pioneering Projects

Ayllon and Azrin's Program. Ayllon and Azrin (1965, 1968) are responsible for the first true token economy. Their program was instituted on a closed ward for female mental patients at Anna State Hospital. The goal of their program was straightforward: they sought to eliminate the syndrome of withdrawal, dependence, and apathy that characterized most of their patients. Prior to the onset of the token economy, the patients remained idle most of the time. Ayllon and Azrin changed that by giving the women tokens for successful performance of various ward duties, off-ward work assignments, and reductions in particular kinds of maladaptive behavior.

As in the procedure for classroom token economies we described in Chapter 5, staff members dispensed tokens (plastic chips and cards) contingent on the patients' emitting specified adaptive behaviors. Since the programs were individualized, the specific requirements for reinforcement depended upon a patient's level of functioning. The requirements for each patient were gradually increased as she progressed in the program. Thus, a patient might begin by receiving tokens for getting out of bed when called. Then, as she improved and was reliably earning her token for getting up, reinforcement criteria would be increased so that she might have to get up, make her bed, and get dressed, all within twenty minutes, to receive her tokens.

The tokens could be redeemed for six kinds of backup reinforcers: (1) more privacy, (2) passes to leave the ward, (3) private consultation with particular staff members, (4) extra religious services,

(5) recreational activities, and (6) items from the hospital commissary. These backups were arrived at through a Premack principle analysis of how patients chose to spend their time.

In a series of six studies spanning a period of three years, Ayllon and Azrin obtained data on the effectiveness of tokens and the use of verbal instructions and prompts to change the patients' behavior. Figure 14–1 demonstrates the reinforcing power of contingent tokens. Participation in rehabilitation activities remained high as long as it led to token reinforcement. But when tokens were made available noncontingently, participa-

tion decreased rapidly. Although this procedure was generally effective, Ayllon and Azrin reported that the behavior of 8 of the 48 patients did not change. These "nonresponders" did not differ from the other patients in terms of psychiatric diagnosis, IQ, age, or length of hospitalization. Ayllon and Azrin concluded that the absence of effective reinforcers accounts for these failures. That is, they felt all the patients could have been affected if they had found strong enough reinforcers. This interpretation of their failures has been criticized as narrow (Davison, 1969); it is quite possible that a token program was not appropriate for these individuals.

Atthowe and Krasner's Program. The goals and procedures of the Atthowe-Krasner (1965, 1968) program at the Menlo Park VA were very similar to those of Ayllon and Azrin. The Menlo Park VA program involved sixty males who had been institutionalized for an average of twenty-four years. Like Ayllon and Azrin's patients, these men were severely disorganized and apathetic. The aim of the program was to establish adequate self-care and social skills. As with the Anna State program, tokens were backed up with items such as television and special privileges. Atthowe and Krasner also introduced a **step system.** After a patient had maintained a predetermined higher level of function for a certain length of time, he advanced to the next step-level in the program. Moving to a higher step-level earned the patient additional freedoms and privileges. Each subsequent step-level more closely approximated the real world, both in terms of the level of functioning the patient had to demonstrate to make the step and the reinforcers that were made available to him when he did. To reach the top level, the patient was expected to function in a basically independent fashion. In return, he was graduated from the token system and was given a "carte blanche" with which to secure desired backups.

Although hospital discharge was not the goal of the Menlo Park VA program, the discharge rate for the patients on the token ward was twice that of the patients on other wards. Unfortunately, eleven of the twenty-four patients who were discharged were rehospitalized within nine months.

Figure 14–1. Total number of hours the group of forty-four patients participated in rehabilitation when token reinforcers were dispensed contingently and noncontingently. From Teodoro Ayllon & Nathan Azrin, *The token economy: A motivational system for therapy and rehabilitation,* © 1968, p. 252. Reprinted by permission of Prentice-Hall, Inc., Englewood Cliffs, New Jersey.

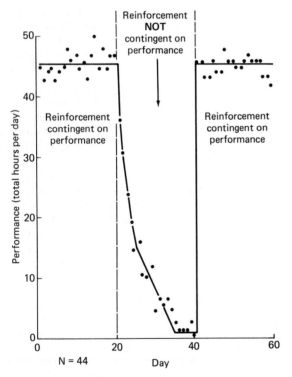

In their discussion of their project, Atthowe and Krasner (1968) reported that the token system did not have an appreciable effect on approximately 10 percent of the patients.

Fairweather's Lodge Program. Although Fairweather's (1964) project did not involve a token economy, its underlying philosophy, its goals, and many of its methods were similar to those of the Anna State and Menlo Park VA programs. Fairweather worked with a group of male patients who were, on the whole, not as severely debilitated as the patients in the aforementioned studies. He attempted to counter the dependency fostered by traditional hospital care by forming the patients into small, self-governing, task-oriented groups that functioned with only minimal staff supervision. The groups were responsible for regulating their own activities, maintaining their personal areas, and evaluating their own members' progress and suitability for transfer. According to Fairweather, the greatest source of positive influence on the patients was the social pressure from other group members. The ward staff functioned more in the role of consultants than as direct supervisors. A step system was also part of the program; staff dispensed money and privileges according to the step-level of individual patients and the functioning of the group as a whole. In this way, staff maintained an element of control while at the same time allowing patients greater autonomy and responsibility.

Fairweather's program was successful in many ways. When compared with a matched group of patients on a traditional ward, the patients in the experimental program did significantly better on a variety of measures. They spent less time in the hospital, stayed in the community longer following discharge, and had better employment records than control patients. However, the program had no effect on long-term rates of recidivism. As suggested by the findings of Atthowe and Krasner, the patients appeared to need some form of continuing social support after leaving the program.

In an effort to improve discharged patients' community tenure, Fairweather and his colleagues (Fairweather, Sanders, Maynard, & Cressler, 1969), devised an experimental program in which patients moved from the in-hospital program to a group "lodge" in the community. Patients participated in running the lodge, and in developing their own small business (a janitorial service). They were permitted to leave the lodge to live independently whenever they wished.

Patients in the lodge program were compared to matched patients who received the hospital's traditional aftercare program (which consisted primarily of drug maintenance and periodic outpatient counseling). Over the forty months that data were collected, the recidivism rate for lodge residents was one-quarter that shown by the comparison group. Lodge residents were involved in full-time employment about 40 percent of the time, whereas there was almost no full-time employment among members of the control group. However, patients who left the lodge in an effort to function independently were rarely able to find work.

The Value of the Pioneering Projects. Before moving to our next topic, we wish to emphasize the contribution made by these and other early programs. As examples of well-controlled research, all have their faults (see Davison, 1969; Paul & Lentz, 1977); but their value in establishing a viable alternative to traditional hospital care for chronic mental patients cannot be overstated. They represent a radical departure from prevailing psychiatric theory and practice. The projects also give some indication of the speed with which applied behavioral psychology was advancing during that period. Readers will recall from our discussion in Chapter 1 that only a decade earlier researchers were concerned with the basic question of whether the behavior of psychotic individuals was affected by simple reinforcement contingencies. In contrast, these projects involved the broad-scale manipulation of such contingencies to bring about changes in the functioning of chronically hospitalized individuals. In summary, readers should not overlook the theoretical and social significance of this early work. It is not an exaggeration to consider it a landmark in the history of clinical psychology.

PAUL'S COMPARATIVE REHABILITATION PROJECT

The remainder of this chapter will be devoted to an examination of a comparative study of treatments for chronically institutionalized mental patients conducted by Gordon Paul and his colleagues at the University of Illinois. A massive report on the study has recently been prepared by Paul and Robert Lentz, the project's research director (Paul & Lentz, 1977). We will devote a great deal of attention to this study because, to put it simply, the Paul project is the most ambitious, rigorously controlled, closely documented, and discretely analyzed long-term comparative study of psychological treatments ever conducted. In many respects, it represents the "state of the art" —a culmination of the work begun by Ayllon and Azrin, Atthowe and Krasner, Fairweather, and others. The Paul study is a model of experimental sophistication, and an excellent example of a well-designed, tightly executed treatment program derived from behavioral principles. As such, we feel that it is an eminently suitable framework within which to understand behavioral approaches to the treatment of chronic mental patients. The treatment procedures employed also raise important legal and ethical questions that will be addressed at length in the next chapter.

Inception

Let us first examine how the project was conceived. In 1965, while working as a consultant to the public mental hospitals in Illinois, Paul became impressed with the enormous problem presented by the forgotten individuals who spent the better part of their lives languishing in the back wards of institutions. It also became apparent to him that his efforts as a consultant were of little value, since weekly contacts could have no significant impact on the functioning of individuals who spent their entire lives in the numbing institutional "sameness." These facts, combined with the distressing lack of data on the effectiveness of almost all institutional interventions, led Paul to a study of the "chronic problem" (Paul, 1969). The work culminated in plans for a comparative evalu-

ation of comprehensive treatment programs for chronic mental patients.

The original plan was to focus on the typical chronic patient. However, at the time a movement to decentralize Illinois' mental hospital services was in full swing, with the result that all chronic patients in the state hospitals who met certain minimal criteria of adequate functioning were being placed in private extended-care facilities in the community. By the time federal funds for the comparative rehabilitation project were finally made available in the fall of 1968, the only patients remaining in the institutions from which Paul could draw experimental subjects were those who were so dysfunctional or bizarre they had been rejected for shelter-care placement. Thus, the individuals actually selected for treatment were the most severely debilitated population yet subjected to systematic study. All were eighteen to fifty years of age, carried a diagnosis of "schizophrenia," and had been institutionalized for at least two years (averaging about seventeen years hospitalization as a group).

Three groups of twenty-eight patients each (fourteen males and fourteen females per group) were drawn from this unique pool and equated on a variety of relevant dimensions. Two of the groups were housed in identical adjacent units of a relatively new mental health center in central Illinois; the members of the third group remained at or were transferred to a single state hospital. Each group received a different treatment program. Two experimental programs, which a review of the treatment literature had indicated held the most promise for helping chronically institutionalized patients, were conducted in the adjacent units of the new facility. These two programs (described below) were conducted by the same highly trained treatment staff, who rotated between the two units daily to control for the effects of treatment personnel. The third group of patients, who were residing at the state hospital, received the usual institutional care from regular hospital staff.

All three programs had as their goal the release of patients to relatively independent living (that is, with support from a "significant other") in the community. Releasing patients to shelter-care facilities (which in most respects are somewhat less restrictive "institutions in the community") was *not* an acceptable objective when the project began, except in the event that the project terminated before patients were capable of independent functioning. The criteria used to determine that a patient was capable of relatively independent functioning were highly specific and were identical for all programs. The original plan called for the intramural treatment programs to be in operation for a total of three years, with each patient who achieved release being provided with aftercare consultation, first from project staff and later from existing community agencies. As we will see, problems arising during the course of the project changed this plan considerably. Most notable, perhaps, is the fact that the intramural phase of the project remained in operation for four and a half years. All patients were followed up for a minimum of eighteen months after the project was terminated.

Overview of the Treatment Programs

The Paul project involved the comparison of three treatment approaches: traditional hospital care, and two experimental programs, referred to collectively as the *psychosocial programs*. The state hospital ward that housed Paul's control subjects exemplified what we have already said about traditional mental hospitals. Treatment consisted primarily of administering high dosages of phenothiazines and custodial care. Patients spent the vast amount of their time essentially wasting away, *not* involved in any form of rehabilitation. Although the physician in charge of the ward painted a picture of a multifaceted treatment environment (which included industrial therapy, recreational therapy, individual and group therapy, social activities, ward meetings, and so on), on the scene observational assessment revealed the ward to be something less than a flurry of activity. Figure 14–2 shows the striking difference in the amount of time devoted to structured therapeutic activities in the state hospital and in the psychosocial programs. Most of this discrepancy was due to the increased percentage of time psychosocial patients spent in classes and similar activities. However, note that the psychosocial programs also used patients' rising times, bed times,

and meal periods to teach self-care skills and table manners, rather than allowing these natural opportunities to go to waste.

Perhaps the most crucial comparison was that between the two psychosocial programs, one of which was based on the principles of **milieu therapy,** the other of which was based on **social learning** (behavioral) principles. We will describe the assumptions and procedures that differentiated these two programs below. First, however, let us consider their commonalities.

Every effort was made to instill in the psychosocial staff the attitude that the people they were dealing with were not "sick," but rather had learned inappropriate behaviors and failed to learn or had forgotten behaviors that would allow them to function independently outside the institution. Consistent with this rejection of the "disease model" of disordered behavior, a hospital atmosphere was avoided on the psychosocial units. Treatment subjects were referred to as "residents" rather than "patients." Professional and aide-level staff dressed informally and related on a first-name basis with residents and with each other. Staff also ate their meals with the residents, rather than in a separate dining area. Most important, open, clear communication between staff and residents was encouraged, and staff members were expected to act immediately on every legitimate request made by a resident. In return for being treated like reasonable adults, residents were expected to assume certain responsibilities, which were summarized and posted in the form of Ten Basic Rules (Paul & Lentz, 1977, p. 47):

As a resident of the Rehabilitation Unit, you are expected to:
(1) Care for yourself and present a desirable appearance.
(2) Perform your own housekeeping chores and share in those of the unit.
(3) Think, talk and act straight (in ways which make sense to others).
(4) Show gentlemanly or ladylike behavior.
(5) Show respect for the rights of others, for yourself and for property.
(6) Interact cooperatively and actively with residents, staff and others.
(7) Attend and participate in all scheduled activities (be where you're supposed to be).

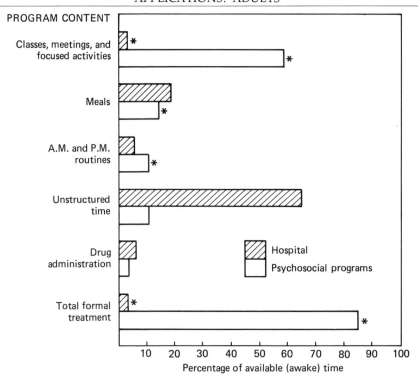

PROGRAM CONTENT

Classes, meetings, and focused activities

Meals

A.M. and P.M. routines

Unstructured time

Drug administration

Hospital

Psychosocial programs

Total formal treatment

10 20 30 40 50 60 70 80 90 100

Percentage of available (awake) time

Figure 14–2. Weekly percentages of time spent in various activities for the average resident in the state hospital and psychosocial programs. Bars marked with an asterisk represent periods during which specific therapeutic activities were conducted. Drawn from data in G. L. Paul and R. J. Lentz, *Psychosocial treatment of chronic mental patients.* Cambridge, Mass.: Harvard University Press, 1977. Used by permission.

(8) Acquire and demonstrate work habits and skills that will provide for an income after you leave.

(9) Move through the four steps of the program and return permanently to the outside community.

(10) *NOT* act "crazy"!!!

Rule 9 refers to a very important procedural similarity between the milieu and social learning programs—a step system. To progress through the four steps of the programs, a resident had to behave increasingly responsibly and systematically

acquire the skills necessary for independent functioning. In return for meeting these increased demands, the resident was granted greater privileges, such as accompanied and unaccompanied passes around the center and into the community. Each step was cumulative in that it required the resident to maintain the level of functioning demanded in the previous steps in addition to making further gains. The privileges afforded at each step were cumulative as well. Step-level requirements and privileges were posted and residents were familiarized with the system. This allowed residents to always know exactly where they were, how far they had to go, and exactly what they had to do in order to be released from the institution.

Residents in both programs were helped toward their goal of release by attending classes conducted on each unit. Instruction was devoted to establishing self-care and housekeeping skills, and to basic reading, writing, and math. Better-functioning residents in the upper step-levels were given practical vocational training. These residents also attended prerelease planning sessions where they learned such things as how to fill out a job application and handle an interview. An important aspect of the resocialization of residents in the psychosocial programs involved "informal interaction periods." During these times, residents had access to games, television, and craft materials, and they were encouraged to involve themselves in "normal" social interactions in order to develop the social skills which would be crucial to their independent functioning.

We will now turn our attention to the assumptions and procedures that characterized each of the psychosocial programs. Although our primary interest is in the social learning program (which will be examined in detail below), the significance of its effects cannot be appreciated without some understanding of the milieu program, which we will examine first.

The Milieu Program

The concepts underlying the milieu approach were introduced by Maxwell Jones (1953), and have been applied to chronic populations by a number of investigators. Milieu therapy "is characterized by increased social interaction and group activities, expectancies and group pressure directed toward 'normal' functioning, more informal patient status, focus on goal-directed communication, freedom of movement, and treatment of patients as responsible human beings rather than custodial 'cases'" (Paul & Lentz, 1977, p. 7). The descriptions of milieu therapy available at the time the comparative project was being developed were quite general and vague. No one had detailed the procedures involved. To remedy this situation, Paul and his team combed the literature and consulted with major practitioners of milieu therapy. The assumptions and principles they gathered were then translated into a concrete set of rules and procedures for the conduct of milieu therapy.

The major therapeutic vehicle of the milieu program was the *therapeutic community*. The residents on the unit constituted a miniature community, and like a community they were entrusted with the responsibility of governing themselves

(within the guidelines established by the basic rules). The *community group* as a whole was divided into three *living groups* of nine or ten members each. These living groups were responsible for decisions affecting only themselves and for the behavior of their own members, whereas the community group met to make unitwide decisions. An elected *executive council* of residents was responsible for identifying issues in need of discussion and solution. The staff communicated respect for the residents' competence by following through on all decisions that did not violate basic rules. Although some of the council's decisions were "crazy," they were honored just the same. The residents thus reaped what they sowed and learned firsthand the consequences of their actions. Poorly handled situations were allowed to go uncorrected by staff until the pressure of an impending crisis forced the group into effective problem solving.

Treatment staff always worked to maximize residents' responsibility taking. They never did anything for residents that they could do for themselves. Instead, a staff member helped the resident clarify the problem and the possible solutions; for example, "How could you go about this?" Whenever possible, the staff member would attempt to enlist the help of other members of the residents' living group. Staff *never* made decisions for residents.

Treatment staff also used the living group structure to foster group cohesiveness and an esprit de corps that could be therapeutically useful. For example, a staff member might note that "Living group A has fewer members at Step I than any other group" in order to bring group pressure to bear on the lower-functioning members in the other groups. Or a resident might be told, "Gee, Charlie, you're really letting your group down by looking so sloppy," and so on.

Staff also attempted to influence residents' behavior directly through their spoken communications. Appropriate behaviors were established and maintained by statements that communicated a *positive expectancy,* such as "Wouldn't you like to join them in the game?" or "I'm sure you'll remember to wash your hair tomorrow morning." When appropriate behaviors occurred, the staff provided *positive feedback* in the form of praise, compliments, or comments about the appropriateness of the response. Inappropriate behaviors were never ignored. Instead, they were met with *negative feedback,* including an expectancy the behavior would not occur again; for instance, "Mary, you know you don't make any sense when you talk crazy like that. We'll have to let your living group know about this and see what they want to do if you continue to babble." A staff member was never to leave a resident who was performing an inappropriate behavior, but was to continue giving negative feedback and positive statements for appropriate behavior until the inappropriate behavior stopped. *Intolerable behaviors,* those that were offensive or that interfered with the rights of others, such as assaults, throwing feces, and screaming, were met with expulsion from the community. Expelled residents were placed in small, unfurnished rooms and released after some specified period. Residents who had been expelled were also reported to the living and community groups, and were subjected to whatever sanctions the groups wished to impose.

This thumbnail sketch gives the reader an idea of the operation of the milieu program. We will now examine the social learning program.

The Social Learning Program

The social learning program was organized around the basic principles of operant and respondent learning. The two control vehicles for producing change were: (1) systematic manipulation of social reinforcement, and (2) a token economy. Appropriate behaviors were elicited from the residents by prompting, instructing, modeling, and shaping, and maintained through contingent social reinforcement and delivery of tokens. Inappropriate behaviors were met with ignoring by staff and losing the chance to earn tokens in most cases, but intolerable behaviors were met with token fines and "timeout." Although readers are familiar with this general approach, particularly the manipulation of social reinforcers, the actual mechanics of this complex social and token reinforcement system might better be brought to life by examining staff and resident interactions in a sampling of important daily activities.

Morning Routine. The residents' day began with a staff member turning on the lights in their rooms and awakening them with a single prompt— "Time to get up!" Five minutes after lights on, the staff member returned to the room and passed out tokens and praise to those who were out of bed. Residents who were not yet up were told, for example, "You don't get a token, Fran, because you didn't get up on time. If you get up right on time tomorrow, you'll earn your token then. Hurry and get up now so you don't miss your personal appearance token." Notice that the staff member's communication specified the reason the token was missed and prompted the resident to perform behaviors that would earn tokens in the future.

Residents had about a half hour to dress, groom themselves, and put their rooms in order before breakfast. During this period, the staff member helped residents who could not perform the necessary behaviors using the now familiar prompt, shape, reinforce (socially, in this case), and fade formula. Then the residents were to present themselves for an appearance check. Each stood before a mirror while a staff member checked to see that his or her appearance met certain criteria, given in Table 14–1. Initially many residents were unable to meet these criteria, so they were given a token and praise for any positive aspects to their appearance, and prompted for a specific improvement. The staff's job of shaping the residents' appearance was simple because the items in the list of appearance criteria were arranged from those easiest to accomplish immediately to those that were difficult. Thus, if a male resident came to appearance check with only his fingernails clean, his hair combed, all appropriate clothing on and buttoned, zipped, or tucked, the staff member might say, "Here's your appearance token for this morning, Fred; but you haven't brushed your teeth" (the lowest unmet criterion). "You'll have to look as good as you do now *plus* brush your teeth to earn your token at the next appearance check." A note was made of what was expected of Fred so that the staff member at the next appearance check could decide either to deny him a token, or to reward him and prompt the next criterion; for example, "Great, Fred, you've got your teeth brushed now—here's your appearance token. At the next appearance check you'll need to look as good as you do now, *plus* have a clean shirt on (the next criterion) to earn your token."

Appearance checks were held three times a day, so residents had ample opportunity to improve their appearance and earn tokens. Following the appearance check, the residents' sleeping areas were checked for neatness (using a list of criteria similar to that for the appearance check), and tokens and prompts disbursed before proceeding to breakfast.

Meals. Residents were expected to attend meals when they were announced and to purchase them with their token earnings. Each meal period was divided into an "early meal" and a "regular meal." The early meal cost more tokens, but allowed the resident thirty minutes to eat, rather than the regular twenty. Staff lined up to get their food, ate with residents, and interacted freely with them as long as they were talking and acting reasonably.

Residents could earn a token at each meal by displaying appropriate table manners. If a resident began behaving inappropriately—eating

---

Table 14–1 Hierarchically Arranged Appearance Criteria Checked Three Times Each Day

---

Appearance Criteria

---

1. Proper use of makeup
2. Clean fingernails
3. Hair combed
4. Teeth brushed
5. All appropriate clothing on
6. Clothing buttoned, zipped, tucked
7. Clothing clean and neat
8. Body clean
9. No odor
10. Shaven
11. Hair cut appropriately (males)

From G. L. Paul & R. J. Lentz, *Psychosocial treatment of chronic mental patients.* Cambridge, Mass.: Harvard University Press, 1977, p. 64. Copyright © 1977 by the President and Fellows of Harvard College. By permission of Harvard University Press and Gordon Paul.

with his hands or grabbing food off of his neighbor's plate, for example—a staff member would deliver a single prompt, reminding the resident that he might not earn his token. When the meal was over, staff would deliver tokens and praise to deserving residents, prompting for improvements when terminal behavior had not been reached.

Residents who did not show up after meals were announced or who did not have the tokens necessary to purchase a meal initially did not eat, but they were immediately placed under scrutiny to ensure they received enough food to remain healthy. If residents missed enough meals that their health was threatened, they were escorted to the dining area at mealtimes and supervised to ensure that they ate. However, their food consisted of a concoction known as the "medical meal," which was made up of all the elements of a regular dinner run through a blender, turned grayish purple with food coloring, and served in a single container. Thus, although the residents were assured of the same nutrition as their meal-earning companions, the unappetizing nature of their food was an inducement to participate in the program and earn enough tokens to buy the regular meals.

Class Periods and Work Assignments. Residents on the first two step-levels spent most of their weekday mornings attending classes, each containing no more than ten residents. Content of the classes varied depending upon the needs of the residents, and instruction focused on self-care skills and home economics, as well as elementary reading, writing, speaking, and arithmetic.

Residents had the opportunity to earn two tokens during class periods: one given for attendance as they arrived, and the other delivered at the end of class to those residents who had actively participated. Plastic chips known as *shaping chips* were used to bridge the gap between in-class participation and after-class token reinforcement. When a resident made an effort to participate in class or work independently on assignments, he or she was given a shaping chip that could be redeemed for the participation token at the end of class. The criteria residents had to achieve for a shaping chip were systematically increased as time went on.

Some residents were functioning at such a low level that they were unresponsive to token and social reinforcement. These individuals attended special *shaping classes* in which bites of food were used as reinforcers. The content of shaping classes varied according to residents' needs. For some, food was given for learning to follow simple instructions, such as "sit down," whereas for others, food was used to reinforce behaviors like those required in the regular classes. Shaping chips and tokens were used in conjunction with food in an effort to establish them as conditioned reinforcers. As they gained reinforcing power, food reinforcement was faded, and the residents were gradually eased out of the shaping class and into regular classes.

Residents on Step II were required to assume afternoon vocational training assignments, and those on Steps III and IV spent both mornings and afternoons working. All were provided with real work experiences such as janitorial, dietary, clerical, or carpentry assistants. However, tokens for satisfactory performance on the assignments were delivered at a weekly "payday," rather than at the time the work was completed. In this way, residents were introduced to another slice of the outside world—delayed reinforcement.

Informal Interaction Periods. The primary purpose of the three to five informal interaction periods scheduled each day was to provide an opportunity for appropriate social interaction between residents and with staff. During these periods all the recreational facilities on the unit (such as various arts and crafts, television, radios, a lounge area) were available to residents in exchange for small token fees. Games or activities requiring two or more people were provided without charge to encourage interaction. Staff members circulated, reinforcing residents with shaping chips for appropriate social interactions and for independent activities such as reading or writing letters. The shaping chips could be exchanged for an interaction token at the end of the period.

Canteen Time. As we have noted, backup reinforcers for tokens were available to residents throughout the day in the form of meals and privileges; but additional backups could be acquired each evening at the unit canteen. The canteen was stocked with a wide variety of items including cigarettes, snacks, cosmetics, soaps, and inexpensive clothing. A number of other items were available for overnight rental (for example, privacy screens to put around beds, bedside stands, and chairs), and residents could also order certain items from a mail order catalogue by paying half the purchase price (in tokens, of course) at the time the order was placed and the remainder when the item arrived.

The type of sleeping accommodations the resident would have for the next week was also determined during canteen time at the beginning of each week. Free accommodations were available in the form of six-bed dormitories, but these were not particularly pleasant to stay in. For one thing, all incontinent residents were required to sleep in these rooms, and everyone's sleep was disturbed several times each night by staff members awakening the incontinent residents and escorting them to the bathroom. The six-bed dorms were also devoid of all furniture except beds, and lacked even drapes to shut out the morning sun. However, residents could use their tokens to secure better accommodations: four-bed dorms with drapes (and without the nightly bathroom patrol); two-bed rooms with the same features; or private rooms, which were also equipped with a bedside stand and a chair. The token rental varied according to the desirability of the rooms.

Dealing with Intolerable Behavior. As we have pointed out, treatment staff reacted to most of the residents' inappropriate or crazy behavior by prompting them to stop, mentioning the tokens they would fail to earn if they did not, and then ignoring them until they did. However, high-intensity intolerable behaviors could not be ignored because of their aggressive and disruptive nature. There were three mechanisms for dealing with such behaviors: (1) *token fines,* by which the offending resident either lost tokens already earned or else incurred a debt; a resident with such a debt could purchase nothing but a regular lunch until the debt was repaid; (2) *timeout,* which at the beginning of the project was identical to "expulsion" for milieu residents; (3) *overcorrection,* which was not used until late in the project.

These procedures underwent a number of changes over the course of the project, and some of the most interesting and controversial developments arose from their use. We will defer further discussion until our description of the effects of the treatment program.

Although our overview of the social learning program only touches on the complexity that was involved, readers should now have a sense of the type of moment-to-moment interactions by which it operated. Before turning our attention to the course of the treatment project itself, we must examine one final aspect of its operation—program evaluation.

Evaluation of the Treatment Programs

The most impressive aspect of Paul's study is the comprehensive, detailed, and meaningful data that were collected to evaluate the treatment programs. It is well beyond the scope of this discussion to do justice to the complete data collection system, so we will merely attempt to give the reader an overview of some of its major components.

Basically, two types of data were obtained. The first was based on structured interview and ward rating scales completed by treatment staff at regular six-month assessments. This group of rating scales, known as the Inpatient Assessment Battery (IAB), yielded a composite score that reflected each resident's overall level of functioning at the time of assessment. IAB data were collected on both psychosocial units and at the state hospital.

The second type of data was based on continuous objective assessments on the psychosocial units only. These ongoing data came from two sources. First, a detailed recordkeeping system known as the Clinical Frequencies allowed staff to record residents' responses to virtually every aspect of the treatment programs. The clinical frequencies served as one measure of the effects of the programs; but more important, they provided the type of moment-to-moment monitoring necessary to enable the staff to tailor the programs to the needs of individual residents. For example, the clinical frequencies form used for appearance checks on the social learning unit told staff at a glance what each resident's status had been at the previous check, whether he or she had earned a token, and what the resident had been prompted to do for the current check. Thus, a staff member could decide whether to reinforce the resident for meeting the last prompt, and could record the criteria met and prompts delivered at the current check for comparison at the next one. Similar clinical frequencies forms existed for almost every aspect of program operation.

The other source of continuous assessment was observational. A group of full-time professional observers was trained in the use of two observational instruments, the Time-Sample Behavior Checklist (TSBC) and the Staff-Resident Interaction Chronograph (SRIC), which were developed by Paul and his coworkers specifically for use with institutional programs (see Paul, in press). The observers' major responsibilities were the use of the TSBC and the SRIC, and they were trained to make observations with extraordinary reliability (the average interobserver reliability usually exceeded .99 on both instruments during the entire project). Observers were almost always on the units, but they were forbidden to interact in any way with residents or treatment staff so that their presence would not affect ongoing activities. They were trained to appear "as pieces of furniture" and to function as cameras—documenting every detail of the residents' behavior and the staff's application of the treatment programs.

The TSBC was a rich source of information on resident behavior. Each resident was observed once every hour of every waking day. For each observation, the observer checked appropriate items from a list of 71 descriptors which covered the resident's location, physical position, awake or asleep status, facial expression, social orientation, and any "normal" or "crazy" behaviors he or she was performing at the instant the observation was made. Grouping different TSBC categories together made it possible to obtain a number of indexes that reflected such things as the degree of hostility and belligerence, indications of a thought disorder, and so on.

The SRIC, on the other hand, provided detailed information on the nature of staff-resident interactions. Five different classes of resident behavior were crossed with 21 different types of staff responses, resulting in a matrix describing 97 different types of interactions between staff members and residents. One of the most important functions of the SRIC was to enable the directors of the comparative project to monitor staff's "on the floor" performance to ensure they were interacting with residents in ways appropriate to the content of the treatment programs. For example, a SRIC observation that indicated a staff member had reacted to a resident's bizarre behavior by suggesting alternative ways to behave was interpreted differently depending on the unit on which the observation was made. On the milieu unit, the staff member's response would have been consistent with program procedures (in this case, the use of positive expectancies). On the social learning unit, however, the staff member would have been committing an error, since he or she should be *ignoring* crazy behavior. In the latter case, the staff member would have been prompted to avoid such a mistake in the future.

An almost limitless amount of information can be gleaned from SRIC recordings. Most important to our discussion is the fact that the SRIC revealed that treatment staff conducted each psychosocial program in an essentially flawless fashion. Now that readers are familiar with the objectives, design, procedures, and evaluation methodology of Paul's project, we are ready to discuss what happened.

The Course of the Treatment Project

The First Six Months. The project began with a brief "settling in" period during which residents were acquainted with their new surroundings on the psychosocial units. Then, a week of baseline was introduced. Unit rules were posted and schedules were in effect, but outside of announcing regular activities and telling residents where they were supposed to be at various times, no specific program procedures were put into operation. Instead, staff functioned primarily in a custodial fashion. Data collection was begun during baseline, providing reliable and stable pretreatment measures against which treatment effects could be compared. At the end of the baseline week, the full psychosocial programs were put in effect.

We have already mentioned that these individuals were the most severely debilitated of any group ever subjected to systematic study, but this statement does not really convey with any impact the level at which these residents were functioning during the early weeks of the treatment project. The psychosocial units were not places where anyone with a weak stomach would have wanted to be. Many residents were incontinent day and night, and an overpowering stench emanated from the units and extended quite some distance down the hall on which they were located. On the units, the scene was grim: observational data indicated that *at any given instant, 90 percent of the residents were engaging in bizarre behavior.* Particularly common were strange postures, blank staring, repetitive movements, and other bizarre motor behaviors. Some residents were given to episodes of screaming or swearing, whereas others were entirely mute. A few residents even ate their own feces, or threw them at staff or other residents; the walls and ceilings outside the lavatories were virtually painted with stains of fecal material. Inappropriate sexual displays were common. Residents' behavior at meals was clearly inappropriate. Many ate with their hands or buried their faces in their food. Although physical assaults did not become a major problem until later, they began early in the study. While conducting the very first social learning group meeting, a staff member narrowly avoided a naked female resident who leaped over a planter in an attempt to stab him with a knife she had stolen from the kitchen. (She was angry at him for chopping her husband up with a power mower and feeding him to the cats.) One staff member aptly summarized the level at which the residents were functioning by noting that the most difficult aspect of conducting treatment was keeping in mind the basic psychosocial philosophy—that these were responsible *human beings.*

By the end of the first six months of operation, both programs had significantly reduced bizarre and inappropriate behavior, while significantly improving residents' interpersonal, vocational, housekeeping, and self-care skills. The social learning program had already proven itself to be significantly more effective than the milieu program in several respects. Figure 14–3 shows the

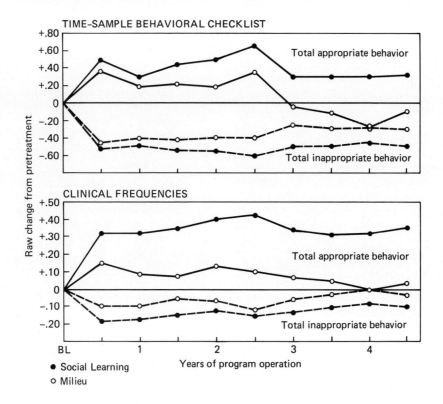

TIME-SAMPLE BEHAVIORAL CHECKLIST

Total appropriate behavior

Total inappropriate behavior

CLINICAL FREQUENCIES

Total appropriate behavior

Total inappropriate behavior

Raw change from pretreatment

BL   1   2   3   4

• Social Learning
○ Milieu

Years of program operation

overall level of functioning of milieu and social learning residents as reflected in the TSBC and clinical frequencies measures.

The Next Two Years. For the most part, both programs continued to run smoothly, and observational assessments indicated that treatment staff discharged their responsibilities with extraordinary accuracy. A major problem developed within the first year of operation when assaults committed by residents began to increase, particularly on the milieu unit. Most of the assaults involved simple punches or kicks aimed at other residents or at staff, but many were more serious. One staff member sustained a broken leg. Another staff member was seized by a burly resident and literally thrown over a counter some ten feet away.

On the social learning unit, the positive, rewarding aspects of the program and the one-hour maximum timeout with token fines that removed the offending resident's ability to gain other reinforcers had held the line against large increases in assaultiveness. Still, a few residents had severely

Figure 14–3. Changes in overall appropriate and inappropriate behaviors as reflected in the TSBC and Clinical Frequencies over the course of the comparative study. Adapted from G. L. Paul & R. J. Lentz, *Psychosocial treatment of chronic mental patients.* Cambridge, Mass.: Harvard University Press, 1977. Used by permission.

injured staff or other residents. High-dosage phenothiazines introduced as "chemical straight-jackets" had also not been sufficient to restrain these aggressive individuals. It appeared that being sent to timeout even served as a reinforcer for some residents, since by committing an intolerable act they were removed from the demands placed on them by the program and could use the timeout room to sleep in for an hour. In an attempt to make the timeout room less attractive to these few residents, staff members intermittently blasted an aerosol air horn or aimed a spray of cold water through a high window to prevent inhabitants from dozing. Another timeout room was equipped with a room heater and a vaporizer that could be used to make the interior unpleasantly

409

hot and humid if necessary. Thus, timeout actually became *aversive segregation* (our term) on occasion.

On the milieu unit, the ever-increasing danger of serious assault prompted the community group into action. Since one hour of expulsion had not curbed such attacks, the residents voted to increase the length of expulsion to a maximum of seventy-two hours in cases of assault. Aversive procedures, being contrary to milieu therapy principles, were not added to expulsion. However, the seventy-two-hour maximum segregation for residents committing assaults was put into effect on both milieu and social learning units after being cleared through the necessary state review committees. Within three months, the milieu community voted to reduce the limit to forty-eight hours, and this standard was then adopted by both programs for the remainder of the two-year period.

The extension of expulsion had an immediate effect on the milieu unit: assaults dropped to pretreatment levels and residents displayed less bizarre behavior, perhaps as a result of being less anxious about being injured. However, assaults soon began to rise again despite the expulsion rule, increasing from 23 at six months to 60.5 assaults per week by the end of two and a half years. The social learning program, however, maintained better control, increasing only from 6 to 11.25 in the same period.

For all these reasons and more, milieu residents essentially "stalled" and made very few additional gains over the two-year period. Social learning residents, however, continued to improve significantly in both adaptive and maladaptive behavior (see Figure 14–3).

The Next Year and a Half. As the first two and a half years of the comparative project were drawing to a close, project personnel had good reason to be pleased with their efforts: residents' functioning had been increased to the extent that many of them were on their way to becoming pleasant human beings once again. The increasing assaultiveness, while a problem, had not become unmanageable, and the new aversive segregation and expulsion rules seemed to be keeping a lid on resident outbursts. Then, just prior to the two-

and-a-half year mark, the Illinois Department of Mental Health, in reaction to gross abuses of restraint procedures at another institution, cut the allowable time for seclusion to *two hours*. Thus, the maximum penalty for a resident committing an assault on either unit dropped suddenly from forty-eight hours of expulsion or aversive segregation to two hours.

The consequences of this externally imposed change were disastrous. The rate of assaultiveness climbed dramatically on both units. By the end of four years of program operation, assaults were occurring on the milieu unit at the average of over *320 per week!* Social learning residents were also affected adversely, but the program was far more effective in controlling assaults, which rose to only about one-third the level reached on the milieu unit.

The tense atmosphere of the psychosocial units had a powerful detrimental effect on the functioning of both groups. The milieu program was hardest hit; maladaptive behavior increased and treatment gains for adaptive behavior were completely reversed, so much so that the milieu residents looked like they had during baseline. The social learning program, while displaying overall losses, showed more ability to maintain itself in the face of adversity, and all classes of adaptive and maladaptive behavior remained significantly improved over pretreatment levels (see Figure 14–3).

When it became clear that residents' functioning had undergone a significant deterioration over the period, a decision was made to extend intramural treatment in an effort to prepare residents for placement in private shelter-care facilities.

The Last Six Months. For the last six months of intramural operations, the emphasis was on stemming the tide of violence on the units and recouping the previous treatment gains. In most respects, the procedures for each program remained as before, but permission was finally gained from the state of Illinois to experimentally increase the length of expulsion and aversive segregation in cases of assault "from the instance of the assault until 5:30 A.M. the following morning." With the reintroduction of stiffer penalties, assaults on both units dropped precipitously to approximately 125 per week for milieu and 50 per week for social learning by the end of program operations. The trends of the previous eighteen months were reversed, and the overall functioning of residents on both units increased. Once again, the social learning program was clearly superior to the milieu program in producing overall improvements (Figure 14–3).

As the intramural phase of the comparative project drew to a close, the focus of the treatment programs shifted somewhat. More of the staff's time was devoted to eliminating the critical intolerable behaviors remaining in some residents that alone might preclude their placement in community extended-care facilities. In the social learning program, the extended segregation period was replaced by an **overcorrection** procedure for intolerable behavior. For example, one resident was fond of stuffing entire rolls of bathroom tissue down the toilet, causing it to back up and send water pouring out onto the unit. Overcorrection for this individual consisted of requiring her to unplug the toilet and clean it up, clean *every* toilet in the lavatory until it was spotless inside and out, and mop up the water that had spilled onto the floor. A staff member stood by to ensure the job was done right, to the point of using *physical direction*, if necessary, to get the resident to complete the overcorrection assignment. Residents of the milieu therapy program who were still committing intolerable behaviors at the end of the program were transferred to the social learning unit to undergo active overcorrection to put them in shape for community placement. This treatment strategy proved to be very effective.

Findings and Followup. It would be impossible to distill the voluminous outcome data gleaned from Paul's study and present them in any meaningful fashion. However, a few particularly important measures should indicate the relative efficacy of the treatments studied.

The original goal of the treatment project was to increase residents' level of functioning to such an extent that they could leave the institution and live "relatively independently" in the community. The steady climb in the functioning of social learning residents for the first two and a half years of intramural treatment made this goal appear reasonable. Unfortunately, the great reversal of treatment gains that occurred when the state reduced the consequences that could be brought to bear in cases of assault put this goal out of reach. In the end, only three social learning and two milieu residents ever achieved release to independent functioning. No patients in the hospital comparison group met this goal.

When the psychosocial programs were terminated, all residents who were functioning at an acceptable level, including those in the hospital comparison group, were placed in shelter-care facilities in the community. Of the twenty-eight individuals in each of the original equated treatment groups, twenty-seven from the social learning program, nineteen from the milieu program, and only thirteen of the hospital comparison group were accepted for extended-care placement and remained in the community at the time of an eighteen-month posttreatment followup. Thus, both in terms of improving relative levels of functioning in the institution, and preparing residents for release to community living in shelter-care homes, the social learning approach emerged as the superior treatment for this severely debilitated group of chronic mental patients.

It is especially noteworthy that the psychosocial programs produced improvements without relying heavily on drugs. When the comparison study was initiated, approximately 92 percent of the patients were on medication. By the end of the study, only 17.9 percent of the milieu and 10.7 percent of the social learning residents were receiving drugs. Only one resident in the psychosocial programs (a milieu group member) was being given a high dosage of medication. In contrast, fully 100 percent of the patients in the hospital comparison group were on drugs at the end of the project; over half of these were receiving high dosages.

Finally, it is interesting to note, as Paul and Lentz (1977) do, that if extended-care community placement had been the *original* treatment goal, it would have been realized with remarkable speed. This group of back ward patients who had been hospitalized for most of their lives, and who, statistically, had *zero* chance of ever being released from the institution, first achieved a level of functioning sufficient for extended-care placement after only *twenty-six to thirty weeks in the social learning program*. Whether this climb in performance would have continued if the consequences for assaultiveness had not undergone the crucial changes that they did is a matter for speculation, but the rapidity with which these "incurable" individuals responded to the program is amazing, to say the least.

Final Comment

It is difficult to overstate the importance of Paul's study. In many respects, it is definitive. It clearly establishes the social learning program based on behavioral principles to be the most effective treatment presently available for severely debilitated chronic mental patients.

We have had much praise for Paul's study thus far, but some aspects of the comparative project also warrant criticism. Most questionable from our viewpoint is the original extension of the duration of "timeout" to three days—and its later stabilization at two days—for instances of assaultive behavior. Leaving ethical concerns aside, it does not appear to us that such lengthy segregation is justified by the data presented by Paul and Lentz, or for that matter, by any other data. The reason for implementing the extension is unclear in the first place. The milieu residents had voted to increase the length of expulsion in an effort to suppress the rapidly escalating incidence of violence on their unit. However, the social learning unit was *not* at that time experiencing any significant problem with assaultiveness. Indeed, it appears that the positive aspects of the program in combination with brief "aversive segregation" and token fines were quite effective in keeping assaultiveness in check on the social learning unit. The reason for automatically extending segregation to match the length of expulsion chosen by the milieu community is never explained. Was this an attempt to maintain equation between the programs? If so, equation of what? The manner

in which the two programs dealt with intolerable behavior would seem to have been a genuine difference in need of comparative evaluation rather than equation. The somewhat arbitrary nature of the extension for the social learning residents seems uncalled for and unnecessarily punitive.

Even more than this, it is entirely possible that the extension was in some ways *responsible for* the devastating increases in violence that later occurred when external agencies eased the consequences for assault. The state reduced segregation to a length that was *approximately double what the social learning program had previously found effective*, yet assaults climbed dramatically—clearly suggesting a "positive contrast" effect that might not have occurred had segregation never been lengthened in the first place. Had a reduction in segregation never occurred, it is likely that assaults would have remained at a low level. But the question remains, was such a punitive procedure *necessary* for the social learning residents? In our opinion, the data do not indicate that it was.

We should also point out that important ethical and legal questions surround the use of powerful incentive systems such as the one employed by Paul. The issue is essentially one of means and ends. There is no question that making appetizing food, privacy, comfortable sleeping accommodations, recreational activities, and the like *contingent* on an individual's compliance with therapeutic demands is an effective way to produce change. Some would suggest, however, that the individual's basic *human* and/or *legal rights* are violated in the process. This concern is particularly relevant in the case of persons who are involuntarily enrolled in therapeutic programs. Thus, the issue appears to have three aspects: empirical, legal, and ethical. Paul's investigation addresses the empirical aspect, the next chapter explores the legal aspect, and the ethical question we leave to our readers.

SUMMARY

There is no one accepted theory of the cause of schizophrenia or, for that matter, what schizophrenia is. Many behavioral psychologists argue that the bizarre behaviors that result in a person being labeled "schizophrenic" are learned, or more precisely, result from a combination of learning, unlearning, and failing to learn. However, a number of behaviorally oriented researchers and clinicians do not accept a strict learning explanation for severely disordered behavior. Instead, they tend to align themselves with the more traditional view that schizophrenic behaviors are at least in part a manifestation of some type of disease process in which genetic predisposition may play a role. Although evidence to support the latter position has increased, definitive data are not yet available.

Behavioral treatment of severely disturbed individuals in general relies very heavily on straightforward operant conditioning procedures. Rather than aiming to cure "schizophrenia," the behavioral clinician attempts to modify the individual component excesses and deficits that interfere with the person's functioning. A number of such problems, including mutism, hallucinations, delusions, thought disorders, apathy, and withdrawal have been the focus of specific procedures.

One of the real milestones in the history of behavior modification was the advent of wardwide token-economy-based treatment programs for chronic mental patients. The first such program was instituted by Ayllon and Azrin in 1965. Since that time, token economies have become quite popular and can now be found in many mental health facilities across the nation and around the world. Along with the proliferation of token programs has come a flood of research reports evaluating their effects. By far the most ambitious of these is a comparative outcome evaluation of milieu and social learning treatments conducted by Gordon Paul and his colleagues at the University of Illinois. The Paul study provides a wealth of information on the establishment, operation, and evaluation of a comprehensive social learning program for chronic mental patients. It also demonstrates the superiority of social learning treatment over milieu therapy and traditional institutional care for these individuals. Even so, the problems that were encountered during the course of the program, and the failure to achieve its goal of returning chronic patients to permanent independent functioning, underscore the fact that behavioral approaches have not yet solved the problem of "schizophrenia."

CASE STUDY 14-1

AYLLON, T. INTENSIVE TREATMENT OF PSYCHOTIC BEHAVIOUR BY STIMULUS SATIATION AND FOOD REINFORCEMENT. *BEHAVIOUR RESEARCH AND THERAPY*, 1963, **1**, 53–61.

This classic study demonstrates the use of negative punishment, positive reinforcement, and stimulus satiation in the elimination of bizarre behavior. The patient was a forty-seven-year-old woman committed to the Saskatchewan Mental Hospital in Canada. After having been treated on a traditional ward for more than nine years, she was transferred to a special behavior modification unit at the hospital. The staff immediately focused on a number of bizarre behaviors which they felt contributed to her poor social adjustment. One of the most annoying problems was her habit of stealing food from other residents and from the ward cafeteria. The nursing staff had tried various methods to eliminate this behavior, but nothing seemed to work. The second behavior problem was her towel hoarding. Whenever staff personnel went into her room they would find bath towels stored in various places; they often found towels under her mattress, beneath her bed, and in her closet. Despite the efforts of nursing staff to stop her, between 19 and 29 towels were found in her room each day baseline observations were conducted. The third problem was related to the second and involved the woman wearing excessive amounts of clothing. At any one time she might be wearing several dresses, dozens of pairs of stockings, and three or four sweaters. It was also not unlike her to carry a bundle of miscellaneous garments in one hand and two or three coffee cups in the other. Each of these behaviors (stealing, hoarding, and wearing excessive amounts of clothing) was treated separately.

1. *Stealing food.* After collecting baseline data, the staff instituted a straightforward response-cost procedure to eliminate the food stealing. That is, whenever she approached someone else's tray or grabbed for extra food, she was escorted out of the dining room and missed the remainder of the meal. Nursing staff were specifically instructed not to try to coax, persuade, or coerce her. This procedure was quite effective. Within two weeks food stealing was eliminated. What's more, the woman started losing excess weight. During the first seven months after her stealing ceased, she lost 20 pounds, and after fourteen months her weight had fallen another 50 pounds (from 230 to 180). The staff physician was very pleased with the weight loss and at that time regarded her physical condition as excellent.

2. *Towel hoarding.* After reviewing previous attempts to eliminate her hoarding behavior, Ayllon decided to eliminate towel hoarding by reducing the reinforcement value of towels through a satiation procedure. Staff simply brought the woman as many towels as she wanted and let her use them as she wished. At first she was delighted. But after she had collected 625 towels in her room, she seemed to start finding them aversive and proceeded to rid herself of them. The following quotes from the patient show the shift in her response to towels:

First week: As the nurse entered the patient's room carrying a towel, the patient would smile and say, "Oh, you found it for me, thank you." Second week: When the number of towels given to patient increased rapidly, she told the nurses, "Don't give me no more towels. I've got enough." Third week: "Take them towels away. . . . I can't sit here all night and fold towels." Fourth and fifth weeks: "Get these dirty towels out of here." Sixth week: After she had started taking the towels out of her room, she remarked to the nurse, "I can't drag any more of these towels, I just can't do it." (p. 57)

Observations during weeks seven to twenty showed an average of 1.5 towels in the woman's room, indicating that towel hoarding had been eliminated.

3. *Wearing excessive clothing.* The overdressing problem was handled by a mealtime contingency: In order to enter the dining room the woman had to meet a predetermined weight requirement (her weight plus a specific number of pounds of clothing). She was weighed before each meal. If she met the contingency she got her meal—if she were overweight she had to wait until the next time. When she exceeded the requirements it was carefully explained why she could not have her meal. Initially the requirement was set so that the woman was allowed twenty-three pounds of clothing (two pounds lower than her usual "excessively dressed" weight). At the end of each week the requirement was lowered a few pounds. Within fourteen weeks she was regularly meeting a requirement which allowed her to wear only three pounds of clothing. In the course of the three-and-a-half-month program she had shed twenty-one pounds of clothing. Nurses reported that she appeared to adjust to the program without protest.

The woman's family was extremely pleased with her progress and decided to take her home for a visit (the first one in nine years). She did very well; in fact so well that they asked the hospital staff if she could stay. Ayllon and his colleagues felt the woman could make the adjustment and agreed to release her. A followup evaluation five years later revealed that the woman was successfully meeting the demands of community life. She now lives with her extended family on a farm in rural Canada and has not been rehospitalized or needed psychiatric services of any kind since her discharge (Ayllon, personal communication, 1977).

CASE STUDY 14–2

PAUL, G. L., & LENTZ, R. J. THE CASE OF BOBBI F. IN *PSYCHOSO-CIAL TREATMENT OF CHRONIC MENTAL PATIENTS.* CAMBRIDGE, MASS.: HARVARD UNIVERSITY PRESS, 1977.

We have selected this case from Paul and Lentz's report of the social learning program because it provides a clear example of the kind of improvement many of their residents made. Bobbi F. was a fifty-two-year-old former housewife who had been hospitalized for more than fourteen years before being transferred to their program. Her behavior was representative of the large group of residents who had come from locked wards of state mental hospitals. When she was observed before being admitted to the social learning unit, she was running around the hospital ward nude, climbing over furniture. During the week prior to entering the program she made twenty-three physical assaults on staff members and other patients. She also showed signs of hallucinations and delusions, often shouting things like, "There is a vampire on the wall," and "They are going to kill Princess Grace." In terms of appropriate behavior such as bathing, maintaining her personal appearance, and interacting with others, she was totally deficient.

Bobbi showed rapid improvement in the program. Within eighteen weeks her frequency of disruptive behavior had dropped from an average of 23 incidents per week to 5 and by the end of the first six months she had dropped to an average of .5 per week. Her bizarre verbalizations also decreased markedly. Although initially she was uncooperative and refused to attend training and rehabilitation classes, after eight weeks in the program she was active in the educational programs. Observation of her on the unit showed that she participated in 60 percent of all classes offered. During the first six-month period she also showed great improvement in her self-care skills and in her relationships with others.

Unfortunately, like several other residents of the social learning program, Bobbi's behavior showed marked deterioration when, in accordance with changes in state regulations, the length of segregation was limited to two hours. This deterioration began with a decrease in appropriate behavior, followed by an increase in bizarre motoric behaviors and social withdrawal. Observational data indicated that during this period Bobbi actively avoided other residents over 87 percent of her waking hours. Within ten weeks after the new segregation restriction was instituted, Bobbi's assaultiveness increased dramatically, rising from an average of .5 per week (during the first six months of the program) to 7 per week. Interestingly, during this period there was no change in Bobbi's cognitive behavior. Her hallucinations and delusions did not return.

When the state finally granted permission for the length of timeout to be increased once again, Bobbi's behavior began to improve. Within four weeks Bobbi regained her earlier levels of functioning. The frequency of her bizarre behavior dropped to less than 18 percent of pretreatment levels and her adaptive behavior doubled. On 60 percent of the observations made at the end of the intramural treatment program, Bobbi's behavior was indistinguishable from what would be expected from the normal "woman on the street." In the words of Paul and Lentz, "Bobbie had literally changed from functioning as a savage animal to a pleasant human being, with quite a sense of humor."

After the social learning program was terminated, Bobbi was transferred to a shelter-care home in the community, where she lived for over two and a half years until her death of natural causes in June 1977. Although it is unlikely that Bobbi would ever have been able to live without supervision, she functioned well in the community home. She cared for herself, helped with housework, and was free to go out into the community whenever she wished. The aides who work at the home reported that Bobbi had made a good adjustment. She was well liked and did not display the bizarre behaviors that once characterized her (Lentz, personal communication, 1977).

REFERENCES

Ash, P. The reliability of psychiatric diagnosis. *Journal of Abnormal and Social Psychology*, 1949, **44**, 272–276.

Atthowe, J. M., Jr., & Krasner, L. *The systematic application of contingent reinforcement procedures (token economy) in a large social setting: A psychiatric ward.* Paper presented at the annual meeting of the American Psychological Association, Chicago, 1965.

Atthowe, J. M., Jr., & Krasner, L. A preliminary report on the application of contingent reinforcement procedures (token economy) on a "chronic" psychiatric ward. *Journal of Abnormal Psychology*, 1968, **73**, 37–43.

Ayllon, T., & Azrin, N. H. The measurement and reinforcement of behavior of psychotics. *Journal of the Experimental Analysis of Behavior*, 1965, **8**, 357–383.

Ayllon, T., & Azrin, N. H. *The token economy.* New York: Appleton-Century-Crofts, 1968.

Ayllon, T., & Haughton, E. Modification of symptomatic verbal behavior of mental patients. *Behaviour Research and Therapy*, 1964, **2**, 87–97.

Ayllon, T., & Michael, J. The psychiatric nurse as a behavioral engineer. *Journal of the Experimental Analysis of Behavior*, 1959, **2**, 323–334.

Baker, R. The use of operant conditioning to reinstate speech in mute schizophrenics. *Behaviour Research and Therapy*, 1971, **9**, 329–336.

Bandura, A. *Principles of behavior modification.* New York: Holt, Rinehart and Winston, 1969.

Bateson, G., Jackson, D., Haley, J., & Weakland, J. Toward a theory of schizophrenia. *Behavioral Science,* 1956, **1**, 251–264.

Beck, A. T. Reliability of psychiatric diagnoses: I. A critique of systematic studies. *American Journal of Psychiatry*, 1962, **119**, 210–216.

Blashfield, R. An evaluation of the DSM-II classification of schizophrenia as a nomenclature. *Journal of Abnormal Psychology*, 1973, **82**, 382–389.

Brehm, J. W. *A theory of psychological reactance.* New York: Academic Press, 1966.

Davison, G. C. Differential relaxation and cognitive restructuring in therapy with a "paranoid schizophrenic" or "paranoid state." *Proceedings of the Seventy-fourth Annual Convention of the American Psychological Association*, 1966, **2**, 177–178.

Davison, G. C. Appraisal of behavior modification techniques with adults in institutional settings. In C. M. Franks (Ed.), *Behavior therapy: Appraisal and status.* New York: McGraw-Hill, 1969.

Eysenck, H. J., & Rachman, S. *Causes and cures of neurosis.* London: Routledge & Kegan Paul, 1965.

Fairweather, G. W. (Ed.). *Social psychology in treating mental illness.* New York: Wiley, 1964.

Fairweather, G. W., Sanders, D. H., Maynard, H., &

Cressler, D. L. *Community life for the mentally ill: An alternative to institutional care.* New York: Aldine, 1969.

Farina, A. *Schizophrenia.* Morristown, N.J.: General Learning Press, 1972.

Freedman, A. M., Kaplan, H. I., & Sadock, B. J. *Modern synopsis of comprehensive textbook of psychiatry/II.* 2nd ed. Baltimore: Williams & Wilkins, 1976.

Freeman, T., Cameron, J. L., & McGhie, A. *Studies on psychosis.* New York: International Universities Press, 1966.

Goldsmith, J. B., & McFall, R. M. Development and evaluation of an interpersonal skill-training program for psychiatric inpatients. *Journal of Abnormal Psychology*, 1975, **84**, 51–58.

Goldstein, A. P. *Structured learning therapy.* New York: Academic Press, 1973.

Gottesman, I. I., & Shields, J. *Schizophrenia and genetics: A twin study vantage point.* New York: Academic Press, 1972.

Gutride, M., Goldstein, A. P., & Hunter, G. F. *Structured learning therapy for increasing social interaction skills.* Unpublished manuscript, Syracuse University, 1972.

Gutride, M., Goldstein, A. P., & Hunter, G. F. The use of modeling and role playing to increase social interactions among schizophrenic patients. *Journal of Consulting and Clinical Psychology*, 1973, **40**, 408–415.

Haynes, S. N., & Geddy, P. Suppression of psychotic hallucinations through timeout. *Behavior Therapy,* 1973, **4**, 123–127.

Helzer, J. E., Clayton, P. J., Pambakian, R., Reich, T. R., Woodruff, R. A., & Reveley, M. A. Reliability of psychiatric diagnosis II. The test/retest reliability of diagnostic classification. *Archives of General Psychiatry*, 1977, **34**, 136–141.

Hersen, M., & Bellack, A. S. A multiple-baseline analysis of social-skills training in chronic schizophrenics. *Journal of Applied Behavior Analysis*, 1976, **9**, 239–245.

Isaacs, W., Thomas, J., & Goldiamond, I. Application of operant conditioning to reinstate verbal behavior in psychotics. *Journal of Speech and Hearing Disorders,* 1960, **25**, 8–12.

Jones, M. *The therapeutic community.* New York: Basic Books, 1953.

Kazdin, A. E. *The token economy.* New York: Plenum Press, 1977.

Keith, S. J., Gunderson, J. G., Reifman, A., Buchsbaum, S., & Mosher, L. R. Special report: Schizophrenia, 1976. *Schizophrenia Bulletin*, 1976, **2**, 509–565.

King, G. F., Armitage, S. G., & Tilton, J. R. A therapeutic approach to schizophrenics of extreme pathology: An operant-interpersonal method. *Journal of Abnormal and Social Psychology*, 1960, **61**, 276–286.

Klein, D., & Davis, J. *Diagnosis and drug treatment of psychiatric disorders.* Baltimore: Williams & Wilkins, 1969.

Laing, R. D. Is schizophrenia a disease? *International Journal of Social Psychiatry*, 1964, **10**, 184–193.

Liberman, R. P. Behavior modification of schizophrenia: A review. *Schizophrenia Bulletin*, 1972, **6**, 37–48.

Liberman, R. P., Teigen, J., Patterson, R., & Baker, V. Reducing delusional speech in chronic paranoid schizophrenics. *Journal of Applied Behavior Analysis*, 1973, **6**, 57–64.

Lidz, T. *The origin and treatment of schizophrenic disorders.* New York: Basic Books, 1973.

Margolis, R. B., & Shemberg, K. M. Cognitive self-instruction in process and reactive schizophrenics: A failure to replicate. *Behavior Therapy*, 1976, **7**, 668–671.

Marholin, D., & Phillips, D. Methodological issues in psychopharmacological research: Chlorpromazine—a case in point. *American Journal of Orthopsychiatry*, 1976, **46**, 477–495.

Meehl, P. Schizotaxia, schizotypy, schizophrenia. *American Psychologist*, 1962, **17**, 827–838.

Meichenbaum, D. Effects of social reinforcement on the level of abstraction in schizophrenics. *Journal of Abnormal and Social Psychology*, 1966, **71**, 354–362.

Meichenbaum, D. The effects of instructions and reinforcement on thinking and language behavior of schizophrenics. *Behaviour Research and Therapy*, 1969, **7**, 101–114.

Meichenbaum, D., & Cameron, R. Training schizophrenics to talk to themselves: A means of developing attentional controls. *Behavior Therapy*, 1973, **4**, 515–534.

Meltzer, H. Y., & Stahl, S. M. The dopamine hypothesis of schizophrenia: A review. *Schizophrenia Bulletin*, 1976, **2**, 19–76.

Meyers, A., Mercatoris, M., & Sirota, A. Use of covert self-instruction for the elimination of psychotic speech. *Journal of Consulting and Clinical Psychology*, 1976, **44**, 480–482.

Mosher, L. R., & Gunderson, J. G. Special report: Schizophrenia, 1972. *Schizophrenia Bulletin*, 1973, **1**, 12–52.

Nathan, P. E., & Jackson, A. D. Behavior modification. In I. Weiner (Ed.), *Clinical methods in psychology.* New York: Wiley, 1976.

Nydegger, R. V. The elimination of hallucinatory and delusional behavior by verbal conditioning and assertive training: A case study. *Journal of Behavior Therapy and Experimental Psychiatry*, 1972, **3**, 225–228.

Paul, G. L. Chronic mental patient: Current status—future directions. *Psychological Bulletin*, 1969, **71**, 81–94.

Paul, G. L. Experimental-behavioral approaches to "schizophrenia." In R. Cancro, N. Fox, & L. Shapiro (Eds.), *Strategic intervention in schizophrenia: Current development in treatment.* New York: Behavioral Publications, 1974.

Paul, G. L. (Ed.). *Observational assessment instrumentation for institutional research and treatment.* Cambridge, Mass.: Harvard University Press, in press.

Paul, G. L., & Lentz, R. J. *Psychosocial treatment of chronic mental patients.* Cambridge, Mass.: Harvard University Press, 1977.

Paul, G., Tobias, L., & Holly, B. Maintenance psychotropic drugs in the presence of active treatment programs. *Archives of General Psychiatry*, 1972, **27**, 106–115.

Prien, R. F., & Klett, C. J. An appraisal of the long-term use of tranquilizing medication with hospitalized chronic schizophrenics: A review of the drug discontinuation literature. *Schizophrenia Bulletin*, 1972, **1**, 64–71.

Richardson, R., Karkalas, Y., & Lal, H. Application of operant procedures in treatment of hallucinations in chronic patients. In R. D. Rubin, H. Fensterheim, J. D. Henderson, & L. P. Ullmann (Eds.), *Advances in behavior therapy.* New York: Academic Press, 1972.

Rickard, H. C., Dignam, P. J., & Horner, R. F. Verbal manipulations in a psychotherapeutic relationship. *Journal of Clinical Psychology*, 1960, **16**, 364–367.

Rickard, H. C., & Dinoff, M. A follow-up note on "verbal manipulation in a psychotherapeutic relationship." *Psychological Reports*, 1962, **11**, 506.

Romano, J. (Ed.). *The origins of schizophrenia.* Amsterdam: Excerpta Medica Foundation, 1967.

Rosenthal, D., & Kety, S. S. (Eds.). *The transmission of schizophrenia.* Oxford: Pergamon Press, 1968.

Sabatasso, A. P., & Jacobson, L. J. Use of behavioral therapy in the reinstatement of verbal behavior in a mute psychotic with chronic brain syndrome: A case study. *Journal of Abnormal Psychology*, 1970, **76**, 322–324.

Salzinger, K., & Pisoni, S. Reinforcement of affect responses of schizophrenics during the clinical interview. *Journal of Abnormal and Social Psychology*, 1958, **57**, 84–90.

Salzinger, K., & Pisoni, S. Reinforcement of verbal affect responses of normal subjects during the interview. *Journal of Abnormal and Social Psychology*, 1960, **60**, 127–130.

Salzinger, K., & Pisoni, S. Some parameters of the conditioning of verbal affect responses in schizophrenic subjects. *Journal of Abnormal and Social Psychology*, 1961, **63**, 511–516.

Salzinger, K., & Portnoy, S. Verbal conditioning in interviews: Application to chronic schizophrenics and relationship to prognosis for acute schizophrenics. *Journal of Psychiatric Research*, 1964, **2**, 129.

Salzinger, K., Portnoy, S., & Feldman, R. S. Experimental manipulation of continuous speech in schizophrenic patients. *Journal of Abnormal and Social Psychology*, 1964, **68**, 508–516.

Schizophrenia Bulletin, 1976, **2**, No. 1.

Schmidt, H. O., & Fonda, C. P. The reliability of psychiatric diagnosis: A new look. *Journal of Abnormal and Social Psychology*, 1956, **52**, 262–267.

Sherman, J. A. Reinstatement of verbal behavior in a psychotic by reinforcement methods. *Journal of Speech and Hearing Disorders*, 1963, **28**, 398–401.

Sherman, J. A. Use of reinforcement and imitation to reinstate verbal behavior in mute psychotics. *Journal of Abnormal Psychology*, 1965, **70**, 155–164.

Sommer, R., Witney, G., & Osmond, H. Teaching common associations to schizophrenics. *Journal of Abnormal and Social Psychology*, 1962, **65**, 58–61.

Stahl, J. R., & Leitenberg, H. Behavioral treatment of the chronic mental hospital patient. In H. Leitenberg (Ed.), *Handbook of behavior modification and behavior therapy*. Englewood Cliffs, N.J.: Prentice-Hall, 1976.

Tobias, L., & MacDonald, M. Withdrawal of maintenance drugs with long-term hospitalized mental patients: A critical review. *Psychological Bulletin*, 1974, **81**, 107–125.

Ullmann, L. P., & Krasner, L. *A psychological approach to abnormal behavior*. Englewood Cliffs, N.J.: Prentice-Hall, 1969.

Ullmann, L. P., & Krasner, L. *A psychological approach to abnormal behavior*. 2nd ed. Englewood Cliffs, N.J.: Prentice-Hall, 1975.

Ullmann, L. P., Krasner, L., & Collins, B. J. Modification of behavior through verbal conditioning: Effects in group therapy. *Journal of Abnormal and Social Psychology*, 1961, **62**, 128–132.

Ullmann, L. P., Krasner, L., & Edinger, R. L. Verbal conditioning of common associations in long-term schizophrenic patients. *Behaviour Research and Therapy*, 1964, **2**, 15–18.

Ullmann, L. P., Krasner, L., & Gelfand, D. M. Changed content within a reinforced response class. *Psychological Reports*, 1963, **12**, 819–829.

Ullmann, L. P., Weiss, R. L., & Krasner, L. The effect of verbal conditioning of emotional words on recognition of threatening stimuli. *Journal of Clinical Psychology*, 1963, **19**, 182–183.

Watts, F. N., Powell, G. E., & Austin, S. V. The modification of abnormal beliefs. *British Journal of Medical Psychology*, 1973, **46**, 359–363.

Weiss, R. L., Krasner, L., & Ullmann, L. P. Responsivity of psychiatric patients to verbal conditioning: "Success" and "failure" conditions and pattern of reinforced trials. *Psychological Reports*, 1963, **12**, 423–426.

Wilson, F. S., & Walters, R. H. Modification of speech output of near-mute schizophrenics through social-learning procedures. *Behaviour Research and Therapy*, 1966, **4**, 59–67.

Wincze, J. P., Leitenberg, H., & Agras, W. S. The effects of token reinforcement and feedback on the delusional verbal behavior of chronic paranoid schizophrenics. *Journal of Applied Behavior Analysis*, 1972, **5**, 247–262.

Wolpe, J. *The practice of behavior therapy*. New York: Pergamon Press, 1969.

Zigler, E., & Phillips, L. Psychiatric diagnosis: A critique. *Journal of Abnormal and Social Psychology*, 1961, **63**, 607–618.

PART IV

LEGAL ISSUES AND NEW DIRECTIONS

fifteen

MENTAL HEALTH LAW AND BEHAVIORAL INTERVENTIONS

Society historically has shown little real concern for the powerless and the weak—the aged, the imprisoned, the "mentally ill," and the mentally retarded. Aside from the occasional interest generated by a press exposé of inhumane conditions at some public institution, these people have largely been forgotten. There have been few advocates concerned with their health, treatment, or safety. Relatives have often been frustrated in their efforts to secure better conditions. Courts have preferred to leave the matter to "professionals" with their presumed expertise in treatment while they themselves attended to the disposition of the powerless individual's property rather than to his or her person.

More recently, however, public concern has shifted, and improvements in institutional care are slowly occurring. One notable reason for this turnaround is the declining hesitancy of legal authorities to articulate the legal rights of institutional residents. Within the last ten years, the number of cases prefaced by "Right to . . ." (right to education, right to treatment, right to education/treatment in the least restrictive setting, right to refuse treatment, and so forth) has increased dramatically. Indeed, the current trend in legal reform is toward the specification of broad individual protections, particularly for institutionalized populations.

One outcome from the legal efforts is an increased questioning and subsequent regulation of all forms of treatment and research in clinical settings. Many people feel, however, that behavioral techniques and research practices have been, in some sense, singled out for extra scrutiny (Friedman, 1975; Goldiamond, 1975; Paul & Lentz, 1977; Brown, Wienckowski, & Stoltz, 1976). This has occurred for a variety of reasons. One is that great confusion surrounds the term "behavior modification," which is often interpreted literally to include virtually *any* operation that changes behavior. The result is that behavioral techniques are often inappropriately associated with controversial medical procedures such as psychosurgery, electroconvulsive shock, and chemotherapy. Such naïveté is evidenced in the report prepared by the U.S. Senate Committee on the Judiciary set up to investigate individual rights and the federal role in behavior modification. In that report, the aim of behavior modification was described as "to restructure personality and the methods range from gold-star-type rewards to psychosurgery" (Committee on the Judiciary, 1974, p. 1). Even in the popular press, examples of "behavior mod" are linked to a *1984* or *A Clockwork Orange* mind-controlling treatment mentality. This misunderstanding, coupled with a few highly publicized reports of outrageous "treatment" and "rehabilitation" programs, has led to a push for the legal control of behavior modification techniques.

In addition to misinformation about behavioral

interventions from individuals who either do not understand the principles or misapply the technology, other factors have contributed to behavior modification's vulnerability to criticism. The specific nature of the methods and objectives of behavioral approaches are concrete and therefore can be attacked more easily than the vague goals and operations of many other therapeutic approaches. Describing human problems in terms of specific behaviors and using such terms as "stimulus" and "response" have contributed to public notions of behavior therapy as being less humanistic or sensitive and more mechanistic than other approaches. Finally, because behavior therapists emphasize direct alteration of the environmental stimuli that change human behavior, they are subject to more criticism for manipulation or control than are other clinicians, who confine their interventions to the therapeutic hour (Roos, 1974).

Thus, for a variety of reasons, behavioral researchers and clinicians must become sensitive to judicial rulings and legal notions of human rights, particularly when relatively powerless individuals are clients or research subjects. Since we have dealt with various ethical issues throughout the book, we will limit this discussion to three general legal concerns that cut across most areas of behavior modification but are particularly important to the treatment of institutionalized adults. First, we will examine the selection of treatment goals and the special problem this poses for individuals confined in institutions and unable to make such decisions. Second, we will review the latest legal decisions regarding institutional treatment and look at the ways these rulings might affect the future operation of behavioral treatment programs. Third, we will consider the most legally controversial behavioral procedure: the use of aversive stimuli to alter behavior.

GOAL DEFINITION AND CLIENT DECISION MAKING

Albert Bandura (1969) has aptly summarized the behavioral position that decisions regarding the goals of therapy are rightfully the client's, whereas the choice of appropriate procedures necessary to produce change is reserved for the therapist. Although many behavioral psychologists would agree that this is an ideal strategy, numerous circumstances can limit its applicability. A client may make treatment requests that a therapist could not possibly honor because they are potentially harmful to other individuals or to the client. A more frequent difficulty, particularly for institutionalized populations, is the limited ability of clients (either because of their problems or the constraints of the institution) to establish goals and make decisions. In light of this, a number of proposals have now been offered to facilitate client involvement in this all-important process.

Relevance of Client Status

A client's "bargaining power" in considering treatment options can be influenced by a variety of factors. For example, whether a client receives treatment on an inpatient or outpatient basis is important. An individual seeing a therapist once a week for one hour has considerably more latitude in decision making than the individual confined in a mental institution twenty-four hours a day. Some court decisions (*Kaimowitz* v. *Michigan Department of Mental Health*) have gone so far as to state that institutional atmospheres are inherently coercive in that the lack of meaningful alternatives from which patients may choose when considering a treatment proposal may make it virtually impossible for them to make an *informed* decision (see below) regarding their treatment. To some extent, the individual's autonomy in decision making depends on the legal standard for his or her confinement. Those who sign themselves into the hospital (voluntary admission) may have more control over treatment options, since they can also, at least theoretically, sign themselves out if they want to discontinue treatment or seek services elsewhere.

Involuntary patients (those individuals committed by the court for an indefinite period) must remain in the institutional program until the staff make plans for discharge. The legal standard for involuntary confinement (the individual is "dangerous to others," "dangerous to himself," or "in need of care and/or treatment") may provide an additional rationale for hospital authorities to make more frequent or encompassing treatment decisions. For instance, a "dangerous to others" commitment, which presumably *protects society* from the violent acts of others, may provide greater cause for the hospital to make *all* treatment decisions than a "dangerous to self" commitment *protecting the particular individual*. Thus, the central problem from a legal standpoint is "to reconcile the desire of the individual to avoid unnecessary deprivation of liberty with the desire of the state to provide protection for the community and the mentally ill individual" (Riesner, 1977, p. 1).

Despite the existence of legal distinctions regarding voluntary versus involuntary status and the various standards for commitment, in reality there may actually be few possibilities for decision making for *any* individual confined in an institution. Many persons classified as "voluntary" often arrive at the institution under some form of escort, such as a parent or spouse threatening them with involuntary proceedings if they do not sign in "voluntarily." Similar pressures can be exerted on individuals to accept the available treatment once they are in the hospital. Thus, voluntary patients may functionally have no more control than those who are involuntarily confined.

Finally, many clients, particularly long-stay institutional residents, may be so debilitated that their decision-making ability is seriously hampered. After years of little more than custodial care and few opportunities to take on even minor responsibilities, some institutional residents may be in a precarious position to make decisions in their own best interests.

Proposals for Ensuring Client Involvement in Treatment Decisions

The Consensual Model. Many of the administrative regulations and court guidelines being developed to protect the rights of clients in treatment settings and participants in treatment-relevant research are centered around the concept of **informed consent** (Schwitzgebel, 1974a, 1974b). The idea of requiring consent for experimentation arose following the Nazi war crimes trials. The disclosure of the diabolical "medical" experiments (for example, injections of live typhus into individuals to provide a "home" for the virus and to

maintain the strain; intravenous injections of gasoline or forced ingestion of sea water to discover the subject's length of survival) in *United States* v. *Brandt* led to development of the Nuremberg Code, which outlined ten principles for conducting research with humans. Since that time, the importance of informed consent has extended beyond purely experimental or medical contexts into nonmedical research and treatment settings.

In the legal sense, informed consent consists of at least three elements. First, the consenting individual must be judged legally *competent*. That is, the person must be able to make decisions regarding his or her own care without the assistance of a legally appointed guardian. Second, any consent must be a *knowing* one: any information relevant to the decision-making process must be presented to the individual for consideration. This includes such information as the desired outcome(s) of the treatment, the likelihood of successful outcome(s), the nature of any risks, and the availability of alternative treatments. Third, any consent must be given *voluntarily*. Participation in treatment programs should not be obtained through coercive means; unfair or unreasonable pressures must not be exerted on the individual to accept treatment proposals, and he or she must be permitted to withdraw consent at any time.

In the context of treatment, operating along a consensual model has potential advantages and disadvantages. Probably the clearest advantage is that it specifies goals, risks, benefits, and procedures for the individual to consider. Rather than having every decision made for him or her, the client becomes a decision maker, and also has all the available information to make the best decision.

The difficulties with the consensual model stem from two sources. One concerns the purely legal conceptualization of competency that is often used. Many individuals in institutions have never been declared "incompetent" and thus remain "competent" in the eyes of the law, yet they may be functionally unable to make important treatment decisions. Obtaining signatures from these people on treatment consent forms is as ethically questionable as obtaining no consent at all. The problem is that legal and functional definitions of competence do not necessarily coincide. Even if they did, the problem would still remain of deciding who should take responsibility for the incompetent individual's decisions regarding treatment. Relatives are an obvious choice. They often provide adequate advocacy, but they may also, on occasion, wish to ensure the continued confinement of the person as a convenience to themselves. To avoid this, some type of independent committee (to be discussed shortly) may be in a better position to evaluate, negotiate, and approve treatment programs in the best interests of the client.

The second source of difficulty with the consensual model stems from the numerous practical problems in implementation. The possibility of making a "knowing" decision is limited in the sense that risks, benefits, and outcomes of many procedures are not presently known. Although behavior therapy is more empirically based than many other types, most specific techniques have only just begun to be demonstrated as reliable and valid treatments. However, if interpreted in the strict sense, the knowingness requirement is a Catch-22 that precludes the use and development of any new experimental procedure. It requires factual information on the benefits, risks, and outcomes of new treatments before they can be applied—but it is necessary to apply the treatments in order to obtain these facts. If the requirement is interpreted in a "softer" form, the client need only be informed of all the *available* information about a treatment, including the fact that it *is* experimental and that its potential risks, benefits, and outcomes are not yet fully known. This formulation is the only one that will allow experimentation with treatment procedures. (Interestingly, in *Kaimowitz* v. *Michigan Department of Mental Health*, the court chose to adopt the strict version of the knowingness requirement when an involuntary patient's consent for experimental psychosurgery was reviewed.)

The question of the "voluntary" nature of a client's consent will always arise as long as individuals receive treatment at the request or dictate of other individuals (relatives, friends, judges) or agencies (courts, prisons, and so forth). Finally, many researchers and clinicians have expressed the concern that the option of revocable consent would functionally sap any program of its motivational components (Paul & Lentz, 1977; Wexler,

1975); any time the "going got rough" the client might abandon all his or her goals and give up. Due to these concerns with the consensual model, consideration of alternatives is necessary.

The Contractual Model. The relationship between therapist and client or between experimenter and subject can also be viewed in terms of a *contract*. In the legal sense, a contractual arrangement consists of a legally binding agreement (either expressed or implied) between parties regarding an exchange of services. A simple therapeutic contract may state, for example, that the therapist will treat the patient with the degree of care that similar therapists would exercise under similar circumstances, and that the client will follow instructions and pay the therapist the reasonable value for these professional services (Schwitzgebel, 1974a). Other contracts might also specify treatment goals, risks, expected outcomes, methods and procedures, and/or treatment time limits. Such contracts would conceivably be as binding for the client as for the therapist, and would offer an opportunity for input by the client while at the same time specifying the nature of the therapist's accountability.

Unfortunately, many of the difficulties inherent in the consensual model are also problematic in the contractual model, largely because informed consent is also required for contracts. Courts have voided contracts when the bargaining power between parties was unequal (that is, when the weaker party had no meaningful choice or real alternative). Thus, the issues of knowledge, competency, and voluntariness are just as relevant under a contractual model of therapy as under a consensual one. If the elements of informed consent can be fulfilled, however, then the client has a legally binding agreement with the therapist and possibly a recourse for action (that is, suit for breach of contract) if the contract is not fulfilled. Similarly, the time-defined nature of many contracts necessitates a commitment from clients to stay with the program, which need not be the case with some consensual agreements.

Advocacy Committees. Since the integrity of either consensual or contractual agreements can easily be open to question due to the potential for inequity in "bargaining power," independent committees with authority to make treatment decisions for clients have been suggested (Brown, Wienckowski, & Stoltz, 1976; Friedman, 1975; Paul & Lentz, 1977). The committee could act either as an exclusive representative for a client or as an institutional review body for treatment proposals for a group of clients. In either case, committee membership would probably include lawyers specializing in mental health law and civil liberties and experienced clinicians with adequate training to evaluate treatment proposals. The advantage of an exclusive client representative committee is that it need not have any ties with the provider of service and thus avoids possible conflict of interests. This would not be the case for institutional review committees, which often include such members as institutional administrative and/or treatment staff. Although a committee could evaluate the adequacy of the treatment proposed to the client, it is unlikely that this body could then make an objective decision for the client regarding acceptance or rejection of the proposal. Institutional review committees can, however, perform an extremely useful function in terms of continually monitoring all treatment proposals and evaluating the outcome of treatment implementation.

As the reader can see, the problem of ensuring client input into the treatment decision-making process has no easy solution. As with many issues, the best proposal probably consists of a combination of the three we have discussed. In this manner, a balance might be found between means and ends and the short- and long-term effects of various treatments proposed in the client's best interests.

RIGHT TO TREATMENT

The notion that individuals involuntarily committed to mental institutions have a "right to treatment" was first proposed in the early 1960s. This term is something of a misnomer since it suggests that such a right is explicitly stated in the Constitution. Rather, the **right to treatment** has come to be a "shorthand way of describing that package of rights which the involuntarily confined

mental patient is guaranteed by the due process and equal protection clauses, and the cruel and unusual punishment prohibition" in the U.S. Constitution (Friedman & Halpern, 1973, p. 280).

The right to treatment cases that have come before the courts during the last fifteen years have sought remedies for specific instances of abuse against mentally disabled or retarded institutional residents or provisions for at least *minimal standards of treatment* within institutions previously offering only marginal levels of custodial care. In their rulings, courts have outlined the principles for remedy and established monitoring structures to ensure against any problems in the future. Courts have also, on occasion, gone one step further and specified or limited the use of certain treatment procedures.

These rulings have potentially conflicting implications for all therapies, but particularly for behavior modification (Budd & Baer, 1976). Ironically, findings in right to treatment cases can potentially limit the application of some behavior modification techniques. However, acceptance of a right to *effective* treatment could also result in a wider application of behavioral programs. Thus, it appears that in the future, the legal status of behavioral techniques may become as relevant to their application as to their empirical status.

History of the Concept

One starting point for examining the relationship of behavior modification and the law is to examine how the right to treatment concept has evolved and how it is reflected in case findings. The idea of a right to treatment first gained the attention of the courts in 1966 in *Rouse* v. *Cameron*. After spending four years in St. Elizabeth's Hospital in Washington, D.C., Charles Rouse petitioned for his release on grounds that he was receiving no treatment and that the reason for treatment ("insanity") no longer existed. After hearing the case on appeal, Judge David Bazelon noted that without treatment, mental institutions essentially become prisons where a person can be held indefinitely without ever being convicted of an offense. Bazelon ordered St. Elizabeth's to provide a treatment program designed to cure or improve Rouse's condition; the program also had to be individually suited to Rouse's needs and adequate in terms of the present knowledge about treatment.

The next major development of the right to treatment concept came with the case of *Wyatt* v. *Stickney*, in which the state of Alabama was charged with failure to provide adequate treatment for every individual confined in the state institutions for the mentally disabled or mentally retarded. Conditions in the two institutions where the case originated were outrageous. At Bryce, a large facility for the mentally disabled, there was one psychologist for every 1,670 patients and one physician for every 200 patients. Staffing ratios were even worse at Partlow, a facility for the retarded, where unpaid residents on some wards prepared all the meals and fed their fellow inmates. Alabama spent less than fifty cents per day for food for each inmate; in fact, food was used more as punishment by starvation than as nutrition. A court expert in *Wyatt* v. *Stickney* aptly summarized the problem:

> The situation which exists and obviously has existed in Partlow for a long time is one of storage, of persons. I am using that word because I would not use care, which involves—has a certain qualitative character, and I would not even use the word, "custodial," because custody, in my term, means safekeeping. And, as is visible to the visitor at the present time, employees at Partlow are not in a position to effect safekeeping, considering the number of people they have to take care of; so I would say it is a storage problem at the moment. (Testimony of Dr. Gunnar Dybwad, Hearing III at 13)

Due to the gross inadequacies in the Alabama hospitals, the court established three principles to guide all future treatment programming in Alabama institutions. Institutions must provide: (1) a humane psychological and physical environment, (2) qualified staff in numbers sufficient to administer adequate treatment, and (3) individualized treatment programs for each resident. The court then specified some of the minimal standards for implementing each principle of treatment. Many of the standards outlined in *Wyatt* have direct relevance to behavior modification, even though they were not originally intended to either limit or extend the use of behavioral treat-

ment techniques. (We will discuss specific examples of standards in the next section.) The original intent of the *Wyatt* court rulings was to force the state of Alabama to take positive steps toward providing some form of treatment, not to regulate the use of behavioral techniques in institutions.

Current Status of the Law

Despite the sweeping nature of the *Wyatt* standards, the right to treatment issue has hardly "come of age" either as a constitutional principle or as a practical reality. In the only right to treatment case to come before the Supreme Court (*O'Connor* v. *Donaldson*) the issue of treatment was largely avoided. Instead, the Court focused specifically on an individual's right to liberty, which it said is violated if an institution confines an individual when he or she is (1) not dangerous to self or others, (2) capable of surviving in the community with the help of family and/or friends, and (3) not provided with treatment while in the institution. The concurring opinion by Chief Justice Warren Burger in *O'Connor* also shot some rather large holes in several of the right to treatment theories litigators have relied on (Lottman, 1977). Perhaps of greater practical importance is the fact that efforts to provide the funds necessary to implement right to treatment standards have not been forthcoming from most state legislatures (Morris, 1974). Laws still portray "the mental patient as one who is likely to be permanently confined in an institution and who is and will continue to be devoid of all ability to comprehend or exercise any rights" (Morris, 1974, p. 967). There seems little value to establishing judicially a right to treatment if it is not supported legislatively.

Standards for Treatment

We can only speculate on the ultimate implications of the right to treatment concept for institutional patients. Nevertheless, we can examine the various principles and standards that have been included under the right to treatment rubric and how their implementation might limit or extend the use of behavioral programs in institutional settings. It is important to remember, however, that legal doctrine *evolves*, just as conceptualizations of human behavior and empirical findings evolve. Current legal rulings will become future standards only to the extent that similar circumstances exist. Furthermore, the judicial level (district court, appeals, Supreme Court, and so on) at which a decision is reached also has a bearing on the degree of importance of a case. It is extremely important for behavioral researchers and clinicians to be aware of these factors when evaluating the treatment case law.

Individualized Treatment Plan. The *Wyatt* decision specified guidelines as to how treatment plans are to be devised for each resident. Most of the requirements are consistent with the criteria of responsible behavior modification we discussed in Chapter 3. According to *Wyatt,* each resident must have a treatment plan that includes the following:

1. A statement of the nature of the specific problems and specific needs of the patient;
2. A statement of the least restrictive treatment conditions necessary to achieve the purposes of commitment;
3. A description of intermediate and long-range treatment goals, with a projected timetable for their attainment;
4. A statement and rationale of the treatment plan for achieving these intermediate and long-range goals;
5. A specification of staff responsibility and a description of proposed staff involvement with the patient in order to attain these treatment goals;
6. Continuous review and modification of the plan if necessary;
7. Criteria for release to less restrictive conditions, and criteria for discharge. (*Wyatt* v. *Stickney,* 1972, p. 384)

In many respects, the *Wyatt* standards were tailor-made to fit the philosophy and strategies of behavioral intervention. Explicitly defining areas of intervention and treatment goals, individualizing treatment procedures, and continually monitoring the client's progress to determine the effectiveness of the program are all hallmarks of the behavioral approach.

The standards also require certain treatment components not routinely included in behavioral intervention programs. One such component involves consideration of least restrictive conditions for treatment (see below). Another makes a step toward limiting the duration of treatment. This provision establishes a built-in mechanism for guaranteeing an individual's release before the benefits of institutional care are outweighed by its problems, thereby preventing individuals from routinely slipping into chronic patient status. Behavioral psychologists would prefer treatment duration based on goal attainment rather than simply the passage of time, but the *Wyatt* standards may make this criterion impossible in the future.

Maintenance of a Humane Environment. Unless residents have previously been in prison, the institutional environment they enter probably does not resemble anything they have ever experienced. First, they may lose access to all their personal possessions and not even be allowed to wear their own clothes. All private activities, such as using the toilet, bathing, and sleeping, are done en masse. Rather than moving freely, they are confined and must obtain permission to leave the wards. Finally, contact with the "outside"—telephone calls, mail service, and visitor privileges—is often strictly regulated. These conditions are commonplace in many institutions. Although some of them may be necessary for security or for therapeutic reasons, most of them are imposed to maintain control or for the convenience of staff.

The *Wyatt* principle of providing treatment in a humane psychological and physical environment attempts to eliminate those aspects of institutional life that arbitrarily or unnecessarily restrict residents' rights. A partial listing of the minimal rights and standards set forth in *Wyatt* includes the following:

1. Patients have a right to privacy and dignity.
2. An opportunity must exist for voluntary religious worship on a nondiscriminating basis.
3. Dietary menus must be satisfying and nutritionally adequate to provide the Recommended Daily Dietary Allowances. Denial of a nutritionally adequate diet must not be used as punishment.
4. Within multi-patient sleeping rooms, screens or curtains must be provided to ensure privacy. Each patient must be furnished with a comfortable bed, a closet or locker for personal belongings, a chair, and a bedside table.

5. Toilets must be installed in separate stalls to ensure privacy. If a central bathing area is provided, each shower must be divided by curtains to ensure privacy.

6. Patients have a right to wear their own clothes and to keep and use their own personal possessions.*

7. Patients have the same rights to visitation and telephone communications as patients at other public hospitals.*

8. Patients have unrestricted right to send mail. Patients also have a right to receive mail.*

9. Patients have a right to regular physical exercise several times a week as well as a right to be out of doors at regular and frequent intervals.

10. An opportunity must exist for interaction with members of the opposite sex.

* Denotes items or activities which may be restricted by a qualified mental health professional who is responsible for the formulation of an individual's treatment plan. This usually requires a written order which is subject to periodic review. (*Wyatt* v. *Stickney*, 1972, pp. 379–383)

The *Wyatt* standards, and similar provisions in other cases (*Barnes, et al.* v. *Robb, et al.; Inmates of Boys Training School* v. *Affleck; Morales* v. *Turman*), have special relevance for behavioral treatment techniques, particularly those involving reinforcement programs. Virtually all the items and activities (such as privacy, religious services, food, extra baths, clothes, off-unit passes, beds, and room furnishings) mentioned above as *rights* have been provided as reinforcers (*contingent rights*) in one or more institutional token economy programs (for instance, Atthowe & Krasner, 1968; Ayllon & Azrin, 1968; Paul & Lentz, 1977). Thus, implementation of the *Wyatt* standards might mean that certain items and activities could no longer be withheld as part of a token system, but would instead have to be made available noncontingently.

This issue has generated some concern among behavioral psychologists, many of whom have noted that the number of "things" that serve as powerful reinforcers for severely debilitated or withdrawn individuals is extremely limited (Ayllon & Azrin, 1968; Bandura, 1969; Lovaas & Newsom, 1976). For such individuals, contingency programs begin with primary reinforcers, with the aim of later using secondary reinforcers such as praise or tokens. According to *Wyatt*, however, residents must be provided with many primary and secondary reinforcers, regardless of their behavior. It would certainly be ironic if, in an attempt to restore and protect individual rights, the courts were to restrict an available and promising treatment approach (Wexler, 1975).

Before behavioral psychologists give up in frustration and proclaim that token economies and similar contingency programs are doomed, a few factors need to be elaborated. First, the seeming dilemma that current judicial attempts to protect client rights poses to behavior modification illustrates the difficulties inherent in any attempt to balance human rights and individual freedoms with conditions for the best, most effective treatment within an institutional setting.

Second, the courts are attempting to change decades, perhaps centuries, of ideas and treatment practices concerning the "mentally ill." In some respects, courts are trying to eliminate in one motion all the areas of neglect and abuse that have created the institutional environments that exist today. As the courts take on such a monumental task, some of their rulings may possibly "cost" more than they "benefit." Third, the wording of legal rulings (for instance, "it shall be ordered," "it is decreed") gives the impression that the findings are, in some sense, forever binding. However, in opinions such as *Wyatt*, considerable leeway does exist. Some rights, such as receiving mail or holding personal possessions, can be altered by decisions of the treatment staff. For other rights, the wording is sufficiently open-ended to allow interpretations to vary depending on the circumstances to which they are applied.

Finally, it may be possible to meet standards such as those outlined in *Wyatt* without forfeiting the benefits associated with the use of primary reinforcers in behavioral programs. Thus, a resident might receive basic necessities noncontingently and more "attractive" basic necessities as reinforcers (for instance, a "plain" meal versus a "fancy" meal). However, it remains to be seen whether or not these "elaborations" of basic necessities would function as reinforcers for severely debilitated populations.

Protections Regarding Institutional Labor. For years, institutions have used large numbers of residents as a supplementary labor force. Residents have typically assisted in such areas as janitorial work, laundry, kitchen detail, farm work, and/or the care of other residents. Some residents have even performed so well that their discharges have been held up because the regular staff felt they could not do without their help. In exchange for their labor, residents usually receive some extra privilege, extra food, or possibly a monthly allowance; however, this in no way adequately compensates for the forty, fifty, or even sixty hours a week the residents might work. This widespread practice of employing institutionalized persons to perform productive labor associated with the maintenance of the institution without adequate compensation has been referred to as **institutional peonage.**

The thrust of the *Wyatt* standards and subsequent rulings (*Souder, et al.* v. *Brennan, et al.; Townsend* v. *Treadway*) is to end the involuntary labor of institutional residents while providing adequate compensation for any voluntary work they might do. The *Wyatt* court defined the following classes of work: (1) labor involving the operation and maintenance of the institution or labor for which the institution is under contract with an outside organization; (2) therapeutic tasks not involving institutional maintenance; and (3) personal housekeeping such as making one's own bed. The court ruled that no resident shall be *required* to perform institution-maintaining labor. If, however, an individual *volunteers* for this type of labor, the job must be an integrated part of the treatment program and the individual must receive minimum-wage compensation. In either case, a resident's privileges or release must not be dependent on the performance of institution-maintaining labor. Therapeutic tasks and personal housekeeping tasks, on the other hand, may be required of the resident, provided they are an integrated part of the treatment program.

The *Wyatt* court was clearly attempting to eliminate all traces of one-sided institutional benefits from peonage systems. Many behavioral psychologists have expressed the concern that the ruling prohibits using institutional work as a target response for earning reinforcers or as mandatory on-the-job experience prior to discharge. Discharge from an institution should not depend totally on a person's work skills, but it would seem that work performance on *some* job, whether involving institutional maintenance or not, should be considered (Budd & Baer, 1976; Paul, 1969).

Right to Least Restrictive Setting for Treatment. The idea of "least restrictive alternative" did not originate with the *Wyatt* court or with the right to treatment movement. In fact, the principle has traditionally been applied in the area of federal, state, or local legislation rather than in the sphere of constitutionally protected rights. The principle of **least restrictive alternative** states that when government has a legitimate goal to pursue that affects everyone's interests, it should act through means that least curtail individual freedom. Thus, government must find an alternative that achieves its goal and is least restrictive of individual freedoms. For example, one goal of many governmental restrictions of the "mentally ill" is to protect society from individuals who are presumably less able to control themselves. This most restrictive form of action—commitment to a mental institution—will nearly always maximize the protection of society, but it may also unnecessarily restrict the individual's rights, especially if there are other alternatives available.

In the context of mental health litigation, the least restrictive alternative doctrine has been applied in three areas (Chambers, 1973). First, courts have held that commitment to an institution is appropriate only when less restrictive alternatives are not available (*Covington* v. *Harris; Dixon* v. *Attorney General; Lake* v. *Cameron; Lessard* v. *Schmidt; Wyatt* v. *Stickney*). Second, for those individuals already confined, the court, in the case of *Covington* v. *Harris,* has held that the principle of least restrictive alternative is equally applicable to alternative settings *within* the institution. Judge David Bazelon, writing the opinion of the court, stated:

> It makes little sense to guard zealously against the possibility of unwarranted deprivations [of liberty] prior to hospitalization, only to abandon the watch once the patient disappears behind hospital doors. The range of possible dispositions of a mentally ill person within a

hospital, from maximum security to outpatient status, is almost as wide as that of dispositions without. The commitment statute no more authorizes unnecessary restrictions within the former range than it does within the latter. (*Covington* v. *Harris*, 1969, pp. 623–624)

Finally, the doctrine of least restrictive alternative has recently been interpreted as a component of the right to treatment (*Dixon* v. *Weinberger*), and the court has ordered the development of a hierarchy of treatment alternatives (for example, nursing homes, halfway houses, foster-care homes) less restrictive than mental institutions.

To date, behavior modification has not been directly affected by the least restrictive alternative court rulings. But if the principle is extended to specific treatment programs or procedures, the impact could be considerable. For instance, a token economy program that allows residents to leave the ward for specified periods only after they purchase passes with their token earnings would probably be regarded as considerably more restrictive than a different program where passes are freely available. It is difficult to determine which program ultimately involves a greater restriction of individual freedom; one that involves extensive restrictions yet produces rapid "improvement," or one that is less restrictive but is proportionately less effective or efficient.

AVERSIVE PROCEDURES: LEGAL REGULATIONS

The use of punishment and aversive conditioning to eliminate maladaptive behaviors in severely disturbed individuals has come under close scrutiny as courts have examined the adequacy of institutional programs. In fact, much of the scathing criticism that has been directed toward behavior modification has been in large part a reaction to the use of aversive procedures. At the risk of emphasizing the aversive components that may play an important yet limited role in behavioral interventions, we will now consider recent court rulings and the effects they may have on the future of these procedures. Although we will discuss the procedures as distinct entities, we remind readers that aversive procedures should *not* be used alone, but in conjunction with positive rein-

forcement methods designed to strengthen adaptive incompatible behaviors in the context of a total treatment program.

Aversive Conditioning Procedures

Treatments following a classical conditioning paradigm have generated the greatest controversy. This is largely due to the exposé of two prison programs purportedly using "aversion type therapy based on Pavlovian conditioning" (*Knecht* v. *Gillman*). One program was operated at the California Medical Facility in Vacaville, where inmates were given the respiration-inhibiting drug Scoline (without their consent) to reduce aggression, suicide attempts, or destruction of property (*Mackey* v. *Procunier*). The other program was carried out at the Iowa Security Medical Facility. There, nausea-inducing drugs were used as punishment for such behaviors as not getting up on time, giving cigarettes away, talking, swearing, or lying (*Knecht* v. *Gillman*). As with Vacaville, prisoners were not informed as to the effects of the drugs or the purpose of the procedures before they were introduced. Despite the label used to describe these procedures, readers will immediately recognize that they bear no resemblance to classical aversive conditioning. They were no more than torture and were without either moral or empirical justification. The existence of these two programs generated a great deal of misunderstanding among legal authorities about the nature of behavioral procedures, with the result that behavior modification programs in institutions came under close scrutiny.

Although aversive conditioning procedures (such as those discussed in Chapters 8 and 12) have not been used extensively in institutional settings, this has not prevented courts from regulating their future use. For instance, in its first ruling, the *Wyatt* court stated that "patients have a right not to be subjected to treatment procedures such as . . . aversive reinforcement conditioning [sic]" (*Wyatt* v. *Stickney*, 1972, p. 380), despite the fact that the procedures had never been used in Alabama institutions. Later *Wyatt* rulings specified in detail the safeguards (for instance, approval of institutional review committees, client informed consent) that were necessary before the procedures could ever be used (*Wyatt* v. *Hardin*).

In this later ruling, the court was not evaluating the appropriateness of aversive conditioning; rather, the only purpose was to ensure that the procedures were applied responsibly. If the courts were to rule on the appropriateness of the procedure for institutional treatment, basing their decision on empirical evidence, chances are that aversive conditioning procedures would not fare very well. When evaluated as an overall treatment program, results have been mixed (see Chapters 8 and 12). If aversive conditioning procedures were evaluated as one component of comprehensive treatment programs involving the strengthening of adaptive behavior as well as the reduction of maladaptive behavior, their use might be regarded more favorably. Nonetheless, such rulings would not affect the use of aversive conditioning with noninstitutionalized individuals.

Punishment: Contingent Application of Aversive Stimuli

Many behavior modification programs use contingently applied aversive stimuli to reduce problem behaviors. The choice of the particular aversive stimulus is determined by such variables as whether the problem behavior must be immediately reduced, the prior effectiveness of the stimulus in reducing similar problem behaviors, and so on. The stimulus that has come under the closest legal scrutiny is electric shock, which has often been used to reduce self-injurious behavior in children.

Electric shock punishment has come under many of the same restrictions as have been applied to aversive conditioning procedures. For instance, along with establishing procedural safeguards, the *Wyatt* court ruled:

> Electric shock devices shall be considered a research technique for the purpose of these standards. Such devices shall only be used in extraordinary circumstances to prevent self-mutilation leading to repeated and possibly permanent physical damage to the resident and only after alternative techniques have failed. (*Wyatt* v. *Stickney*, 1972, pp. 400–401)

This type of standard is potentially problematic in two respects. By limiting the use of shock only

to cases involving self-injurious behavior, the possibility of controlling other intolerable problem behaviors, such as assaultiveness, is severely limited. Also, when dealing with self-injurious individuals, the rule that shock can be employed "only after alternative techniques have failed" may be extremely *dangerous*. Individuals might kill themselves or do irreversible damage before the therapist has finished testing out other procedures. For example, a child's self-destruction treated by extinction procedures (which most courts would probably regard as less aversive and intrusive) could *easily* subject a child to considerable, life-threatening danger. These are the kinds of problems that can arise when courts prescribe and proscribe specific procedures rather than establish safeguards to ensure their responsible use.

Punishment: Timeout

Perhaps the most common behavioral technique used to decrease maladaptive behavior is timeout. Timeout procedures may range from simply turning away from the individual to placing him or her alone in a barren room. Despite the misapplication of the term by some psychologists, timeout does *not* include the addition of aversive stimulation.

As a treatment procedure, timeout has come under a surprising degree of regulation. Possibly one reason for this is the seemingly close correspondence the court often sees between timeout rooms and prison solitary confinement; the latter has been applied in the past purely as punishment with little concern for its effectiveness (Budd & Baer, 1976). Another reason may be the fear that institutional staff will simply lock a person in a timeout room for days. For these reasons, courts have either included numerous safeguards when they have allowed the use of timeout (*Morales* v. *Turman, Wyatt* v. *Stickney*) or have prohibited its use entirely (*Horacek* v. *Exon, New York Association for Retarded Children* v. *Carey, Wyatt* v. *Stickney*).

The prohibitions against timeout procedures seem unusually harsh for several reasons. First, the effectiveness of timeout in reducing problematic behaviors when implemented consistently and responsibly has been clearly demonstrated. Second, timeout can be viewed as less intrusive than many other treatment methods (for example, drugs and restraint) that might be used. Finally, it is ironic that courts have been considerably less restrictive of institutions' use of physical restraints. This traditional manner of restricting an individual's movements has *never* been the subject of evaluation. It is quite difficult to conceive of an individual preserving a semblance of dignity when tied spread-eagle to a bed in the middle of a ward. In contrast, brief timeout seclusion appears to preserve more of the individual's freedom and dignity.

SUMMARY

Many of the administrative regulations and court guidelines being developed to protect the rights of clients in treatment settings and participants in treatment-relevant research center around the concept of informed consent, which, in the legal sense, consists of at least three elements: (1) the consenting individual must be legally judged competent (must be able to make decisions regarding his or her own care without the assistance of a legally appointed guardian); (2) any consent must be a knowing one (any information relevant to the decision-making process must be presented to the individual for consideration); (3) any consent must be voluntarily given (participation in treatment programs should not be obtained through coercive means).

Various strategies in addition to informed consent have been suggested for ensuring that the client's rights are protected. One is to establish a contract between the therapist and the client in which all procedures and options are clearly outlined. Another is to set up an advocacy committee including lawyers specializing in mental health law and civil liberties and experienced clinicians with adequate training to evaluate treatment proposals. This committee would be charged with making decisions that the client is unable to make. Each of these options has its pros and cons; clearly, no easy solution exists for the problem of ensuring client input into the treatment decision-making process.

Another concept that has emerged to protect the rights of institutionalized individuals has come to be known as the right to treatment. The right to treatment cases that have come before the courts during the last fifteen years have sought remedies for specific instances of abuse against mentally disabled or retarded residents or provisions for at least minimal standards of treatment within institutions previously offering only marginal levels of custodial care. In their rulings, courts have outlined the principles of remedy and established monitoring structures to ensure against problems in the future. Courts have also, on occasion, gone one step further and specified or limited the use of certain treatment procedures.

The major decisions regarding right to treatment have come from the case of *Wyatt* v. *Stickney*. According to the court's rulings, institutional residents must have (1) a humane psychological and physical environment; (2) qualified staff in sufficient numbers to administer adequate treatment; and

(3) an individualized treatment plan. These rulings have potentially conflicting implications for all therapies, but particularly for behavior modification. Findings in right to treatment cases can potentially limit the application of some behavior modification techniques. However, acceptance of a right to *effective* treatment could also result in a wider application of behavioral programs. Thus, it appears that in the future, the legal status of behavioral techniques may become as relevant to their application as their empirical status.

The use of punishment and aversive conditioning procedures to eliminate maladaptive behaviors in severely disturbed individuals has come under close scrutiny as courts have examined the adequacy of institutional programs. Although the courts are clearly attempting to protect the institutionalized person from abuse, it would be ironic if their rulings were to prohibit the responsible use of aversive procedures that could be in the individual's best interest. Furthermore, the techniques that could be used if certain mild punishment procedures (such as timeout) were to be prohibited would appear to do greater damage to the individual's freedom and dignity than the techniques they would replace.

REFERENCES

Atthowe, J. M., & Krasner, L. A preliminary report on the application of contingent reinforcement procedures (token economy) on a "chronic" psychiatric ward. *Journal of Abnormal Psychology*, 1968, **73**, 37–43.

Ayllon, T., & Azrin, N. *The token economy.* New York: Appleton-Century-Crofts, 1968.

Bandura, A. *Principles of behavior modification.* New York: Holt, Rinehart and Winston, 1969.

Barnes, et al. v. Robb, et al. C.A. 75 CV87-C (W.D. Mo., Central Division).

Brown, B. S., Wienckowski, L. A., & Stoltz, S. B. *Behavior modification: Perspective on a current issue.* Rockville, Md.: U.S. Department of Health, Education, and Welfare, 1976.

Budd, K. S., & Baer, D. M. Behavior modification and the law: Implications of recent judicial decisions. *Journal of Psychiatry and Law*, 1976, **4**, 171–244.

Chambers, D. Right to the least restrictive alternative setting for treatment. In B. Ennis & P. Friedman (Eds.), *Legal rights of the mentally handicapped*, vol. 2. New York: Practicing Law Institute, the Mental Health Law Project, 1973.

Committee on the Judiciary. U.S. Senate. *Individual rights and the federal role in behavior modification.* Washington, D.C.: U.S. Government Printing Office, 1974.

Covington v. Harris, 419 F. 2d 617 (D.C. Cir. 1969).

Dixon v. Attorney General, 325 F. Supp. 966 (M.D. Pa. 1971).

Dixon v. Weinberger, 405 F. Supp. 974 (D.D.C. 1975).

Friedman, P. R. Legal regulation of applied behavior analysis in mental institutions and prisons. *Arizona Law Review*, 1975, **17**, 39–104.

Friedman, P. R., & Halpern, C. R. The right of treatment. In B. J. Ennis & P. R. Friedman (Eds.), *Legal rights of the mentally handicapped*, vol. 1. New York: Practicing Law Institute, the Mental Health Law Project, 1973.

Goldiamond, I. Singling out behavior modification for legal regulation: Some effects on patient care, psychotherapy and research in general. *Arizona Law Review*, 1975, **17**, 103–126.

Horacek v. Exon, C.A. 72–L–299 (D. Neb.), Order and Decree of August 6, 1975.

Inmates of Boys' Training School v. Affleck, 346 F. Supp. 1354 (D.R. I. 1972).

Kaimowitz v. Michigan Department of Mental Health, 42 U.S.L.W. 2063 (C.A. 73-19434-AW, Cir. Ct. Wayne County, Mich., July 10, 1973).

Knecht v. Gillman, 488 F. 2d 1136 (8th Cir. 1973).

Lake v. Cameron, 364 F. 2d 657 (D.C. Cir. 1966).

Lessard v. Schmidt, 349 F. Supp. 1078 (E.D. Wis. 1972).

Lottman, M. S. Whatever happened to Kenneth Donaldson? *Mental Disability Law Reporter*, 1977, **1**, 288–293.

Lovaas, O. I., & Newsom, C. D. Behavior modification with psychotic children. In H. Leitenberg (Ed.), *Handbook of behavior modification and behavior therapy*. Englewood Cliffs, N.J.: Prentice-Hall, 1976.

Mackey v. *Procunier*, 477 F. 2d 877 (9th Cir. 1973).

Morales v. *Turman*, 364 F. Supp. 166 (E.D. Texas 1973).

Morris, G. H. Institutionalizing the rights of mental patients: Committing the legislature. *California Law Review*, 1974, **62**, 957–1024.

New York State Association for Retarded Children v. *Carey*, C.A. 72–356 & 72–357 (May 5, 1975).

O'Connor v. *Donaldson*, 422 U. S. 563 (1975).

Paul, G. L. Chronic mental patient: Current status—future directions. *Psychological Bulletin*, 1969, **71**, 81–94.

Paul, G. L., & Lentz, R. J. *Psychosocial treatment of chronic mental patients: Milieu versus social-learning programs*. Cambridge, Mass.: Harvard University Press, 1977.

Riesner, R. Materials on law and psychology. Unpublished manuscript, University of Illinois, 1977.

Roos, P. Human rights and behavior modification. *Mental Retardation*, 1974, **12**, 3–6.

Rouse v. *Cameron*, 373 F. 2d 451 (D.C. Cir. 1966).

Schwitzgebel, R. K. *A contractual model for the protection of the rights of institutionalized patients and prisoners*. Paper presented at American Psychological Association Convention, 1974(a).

Schwitzgebel, R. K. The right to effective mental treatment. *California Law Review*, 1974, **62**, 936–956(b).

Souder, et al. v. *Brennan, et al.*, 367 F. Supp. 808 (U.S. D. Ct., D.C. 1973).

Townsend v. *Treadway*, C.A. 6500 (U.S. D. Ct., M.D., Tenn.), decided September 21, 1973.

United States v. *Brandt, 2 Trials of War Criminals Before the Nuremberg Military Tribunals* (The Medical Case) 181–182 (Military Tribunal I, 1947).

Wexler, D. B. Reflections on the legal regulation of behavior modification in institutional settings. *Arizona Law Review*, 1975, **17**, 132–143.

Wyatt v. *Hardin*, No. 3195-N (M.D. Ala., February 28, 1975, modified July 1, 1975).

Wyatt v. *Stickney*, 344 F. Supp. 373, 344 F. Supp. 387 (M.D. Ala. 1972), affirmed sub nom. *Wyatt* v. *Aderholt*, 503 F. 2d. 1305 (5th Cir. 1974).

sixteen
NEW DIRECTIONS

Since we do not presume to be able to predict the future, we will approach the question of the future of behavior modification by reviewing some of the areas behavioral psychologists have begun to explore. It is clear that behavior modification has joined the mainstream of clinical psychology and is now moving into other areas of social science. There is much interest in the analysis of societal and ecological problems in terms of behavioral principles. Also, a great deal of enthusiasm accompanies the possibility of using behavior modification to alleviate certain types of physical (that is, medical) problems. Most of the research in these areas is still at the preliminary stage; thus, we are unable to evaluate the long-term impact of these new applications. But this work holds great promise and merits our careful consideration.

We will first discuss the application of behavior modification in health care, focusing primarily on recent developments in biofeedback. In addition, we will consider the emerging role of behavior modification in business and personnel management. Another issue we will review is the contribution of behavioral psychologists to ecological programs such as energy conservation, maintenance of public facilities, recycling materials, and the use of mass transportation. Our goal is to make readers aware of the advancing behavioral technology.

CONTRIBUTIONS TO HEALTH CARE

Psychology and medicine have stood in a symbiotic relationship ever since the realization that behavior affects biology just as biology affects behavior. In the past, however, psychology has often made only a minimal contribution to this relationship since traditional therapeutic techniques have been neither effective nor reliable enough to change behavior in any medically significant way. The growth of behavioral technology promises to change this picture.

From time to time throughout this book, we have touched on the application of behavioral procedures to medical problems. In this section we will extend that coverage by discussing three behavioral innovations in health care service: (1) the learned control of physiological functioning through biofeedback; (2) operant approaches to the management of chronic pain; and (3) the reduction of anxiety regarding certain medical procedures.

Clinical Applications of Biofeedback

The lay public has been deluged by magazine articles and books about the miracle of biofeedback. Most of these reports view biofeedback as a panacea; and each seems to contain speculations that biofeedback will someday replace conventional medicine as the treatment of choice for most human illnesses. Although such extremism has caused many professionals to ignore the real potential of biofeedback procedures, a large body of clinical literature has accumulated that suggests that this approach may have a great deal to offer.

Basically, biofeedback training involves providing individuals with relatively immediate information (feedback) about some physiological process of which they are generally unaware. This feedback can often enable people to exercise voluntary control over responses that they would otherwise be unable to regulate in a systematic fashion. For example, if you were asked right now to increase the blood flow in your right hand, chances are you would have great difficulty—primarily because you have no way of knowing when you have successfully increased the blood flow. However, if sensitive thermistors were placed on your hand and attached to a dial that provided you with an immediate display of minute changes in skin temperature, it is likely that you could learn to increase blood flow to your right hand in a fairly short time. In this instance, you would have accomplished the conscious regulation of a typically automatic, "involuntary" response through biofeedback.

Nearly any physiological system for which measurement and recording devices exist can be the focus of biofeedback training, but some systems have been more popular targets than others. Some of the more frequently encountered types of biofeedback include electromyographic (EMG) monitoring of neuromuscular activity, electroencephalographic (EEG) monitoring of electrical activity in the brain, heart rate monitoring, blood pressure monitoring, and a variety of measures of blood flow in various areas, of which skin temperature is the most popular. The information fed back to the individual is usually of a quantitative sort, except in the case of EEG feedback, in which the individual is told what type of brainwave is being produced in a certain area of the cortex. The feedback itself may be either visual or auditory. Visual feedback, typically in the form of dial, meter, or oscilloscope displays, is most often used for heart rate, blood pressure, and blood flow monitoring. Auditory feedback is usually employed for EEG and EMG monitoring. The feedback cue for EEG is a tone that sounds when a particular brainwave pattern is present; for EMG, a tone that varies in pitch according to the amount of muscle tension in a particular area is often used.

The underlying mechanisms by which individuals learn to exert conscious control over their physiological processes are not yet known. Indeed, many people who are successful at biofeedback regulation find it very difficult to describe exactly how they accomplished the feat. Typically, subjects in a biofeedback training situation are given few instructions beyond "Try to lower the meter reading" or "Try to make the tone come on." They are then left to their own strategies to accomplish the task. The feedback that subjects receive rewards effective strategies and punishes ineffective ones. In successful applications, subjects learn a personally effective way of reliably producing the desired response.

Although the field is still very young, a great many reports of the application of biofeedback procedures to medical problems have already appeared. Biofeedback has been used in the treatment of cardiac problems (for instance, Engel & Bleecker, 1974; Weiss & Engel, 1970, 1971a, 1971b, 1975), hypertension (for instance, Benson, Shapiro, Tursky, & Schwartz, 1971; Kristt & Engel, 1975), tension headaches (for instance, Budzynski, Stoyva, & Adler, 1970; Cox, Freundlich, & Meyer, 1975; Epstein & Abel, 1977), epileptic seizures (Johnson & Meyer, 1974; Rouse, Peterson, & Shapiro, 1974), circulatory disorders (Blanchard & Haynes, 1975; Schwartz, 1972; Surwit, 1973), and a number of other conditions. As is the case with pioneering efforts in most of the social and life sciences, much of the preliminary work with clinical biofeedback is lacking in experimental rigor, and few conclusions can be drawn at this time. It is beyond the scope of this chapter to provide comprehensive coverage of the area to date, and readers are urged to avail themselves of the excellent critical reviews written by Edward Blanchard and his colleagues Larry Young (1973, 1974) and Leonard Epstein (1977).

To give readers an appreciation of the potential of biofeedback training, we will examine one application in which it has shown considerable promise—physical rehabilitation. Another application—migraine headache reduction—has received considerable attention in the popular press, and although the research to date does not justify the wild enthusiasm the procedure seems to have generated, there are consistent indications that biofeedback may be a viable treatment for migraine. We will also examine these data.

Physical Rehabilitation. When a person loses the use of a muscle or muscle group due to the effects of stroke, disease, or accident, the road to recovery is often torturous. Traditional physiotherapy aims at reeducating the person in the use of the dysfunctional muscle through graduated exercises, but this slow process is frequently disheartening to the patient. Particularly frustrating are the early stages of treatment when the patient is trying to learn to move a paralyzed muscle. The individual has little way of knowing whether his or her efforts are fruitful until some movement can actually be seen or felt in the afflicted area, and this breakthrough may be a long time in coming. Electrical activity in the motor neurons is the precursor to actual muscular contraction. But since this cannot be sensed, the patient does not know when he or she has responded in a way that, if continued, will lead to muscular movement. If the patient could be made aware of the occurrence of this electrical activity, he or she could learn to strengthen it, and eventually to move the muscle.

EMG biofeedback has been used to provide this type of information to patients with a variety of neuromuscular disorders (Marinacci & Horande, 1960). An interesting example of this approach is J. M. Andrews's (1964) report of retraining twenty hemiplegic patients to use the muscles in their upper arms. These patients had been paralyzed from one to fourteen years. None had shown any return of functioning since the onset of paralysis despite intensive traditional rehabilitation programs. Andrews's biofeedback training followed a clear behavioral format. First, fine needle electrodes were placed in the muscle of the patient's functional arm, and he or she was asked to bend the arm while observing a screen that displayed the accompanying bursts of electrical activity. In this way, he or she modeled the target behavior.

Next, electrodes were placed in the muscle of the paralyzed arm, and the patient was asked to try to move it. If the person's effort produced no electrical activity, the therapist moved the arm passively and asked the patient to try to "follow through" with the movement. As soon as any electrical bursts were noted, the patient was asked to repeat whatever he or she had done to produce the activity. The EMG biofeedback training was incredibly successful: seventeen of the twenty patients developed strong, voluntary, controlled movement of the arm within *five minutes of training!* Of the remaining three patients, one required an additional ten minutes of feedback to regain movement. Thus, only two of the twenty patients derived no benefit from the procedure. Andrews's report lacks the control factors that would classify it as a true experiment, but we cannot discount the overwhelming improvement produced after years of traditional neuromuscular reeducation had proven fruitless. In an interesting aside, Andrews cautioned therapists about the intense emotional reactions that often accompany the return of functioning to a limb the patient had given up for lost. This comment eloquently captures the real significance of the results.

Another particularly interesting case of physical rehabilitation accomplished by EMG feedback has been reported by H. E. Booker, R. T. Rubow, and P. J. Coleman (1969). Their patient was a woman whose left facial nerve had been severed in an automobile accident. As a result, that side of her face was expressionless and slack. She was unable to even blink her eye. In an effort to reinnervate the left side of the woman's face, physicians had surgically connected some nerves from her left shoulder to the damaged facial nerve. However, attempts to train the woman to move her facial muscles by increasing shoulder tension had failed. She could produce some left facial changes by making exaggerated shoulder movements, but the results were difficult to control and cosmetically unacceptable. The failure of this training left the woman in a state of depression.

Booker and his co-workers then designed a complex computer-assisted EMG feedback system to teach the woman to control the left side of her face. In the first phase of training, she watched an oscilloscope with two dots of light, one above the other. The top dot rose or fell according to a preprogrammed computer signal; the bottom dot rose or fell according to the strength of EMG activity the woman produced. The patient's task was to track the top signal with the bottom signal. If the upper dot climbed, she had to increase the EMG activity (that is, the tension) in the muscle being monitored to follow it with the lower dot, and so on. At first, EMG signals from the left facial muscles were very weak, so recordings were instead made from the left shoulder, whose nerves were now also driving the unresponsive facial region.

As the woman gained control in the dot-chasing task, the concomitant activity in her facial muscles increased its strength, and the electrodes were then moved to this region as training continued. Initially, the patient needed to move her shoulder to generate enough EMG signal to keep the spot on target; but as training progressed, she learned to restrict the movement. In several days, she had learned to track the dot—and produce facial movement—by holding her shoulder still and merely contracting the muscles isometrically. She also began to think in terms of facial rather than shoulder movement, and shoulder muscle tension began to become an integrated, automatic response.

At this point, the patient's resting appearance was fine; the left side of her face no longer drooped, and she could once again blink her left eye. However, whenever she spoke or smiled, the left side of her face would not follow the right side, producing a disconcerting asymmetry. To correct this problem, a second feedback procedure was developed. The woman again watched an oscilloscope, which this time displayed two side-by-side spots of light—one generated by EMG signals from the right side of her face, and the other by EMG signals from the left. Two additional computer-generated signals oscillated in unison above the facial signals, and the woman was asked to try to track both of these simultaneously. To do this, she had to move both sides of her face symmetrically.

When she was successful at this tracking task, the computer targets were removed from the screen, and the woman practiced a variety of facial expressions and speech sounds while attempting to keep the facial signals aligned as they rose and fell with the muscle tension. Biofeedback sessions were supplemented with homework in which the woman practiced making coordinated facial expressions in front of a mirror. The frequency of biofeedback sessions was gradually reduced as the patient improved. She left treatment with excellent control over the left side of her face. Four months later she had lost a little of her facial symmetry, but three days of EMG feedback practice restored her appearance once again.

Other clinicians have also used EMG biofeedback procedures to good effect in the treatment of paralytic conditions (for instance, Brundy, Korein, Levidow, Grynbaum, Lieberman, & Friedman, 1974; Johnson & Garton, 1973). As with the two studies just discussed, control procedures have been lacking, but the fact that all studies have reported remarkable success with individuals who have been disabled for long periods and who have not improved during standard rehabilitation programs adds to the importance of their findings. In addition, one controlled outcome study has shown the effects of EMG biofeedback to be about twice as great as those produced by standard physical therapy in cases involving paralysis of the lower leg muscles (Basmajian, Kukulka, Narayan, & Takebe, 1975). Taken together, these studies clearly establish EMG biofeedback as an important breakthrough in the rehabilitation of patients with neuromuscular problems.

Migraine Headache Control. Estimates indicate that between 5 and 10 percent of the U.S. population suffers from migraine headaches. Unlike the simple tension headache that most of us experience from time to time, and that is the subject of innumerable aspirin commercials, a migraine attack can be extremely debilitating. The headache is frequently preceded by a warning phase, during which the individual experiences scintillating blind spots in vision, sensitivity to light, and often nausea. These manifestations are replaced a short time later by a deep, throbbing pain in the head, usually on one side. The pain is typically very severe, and the afflicted individual is often unable to do anything but lie down in a darkened room and wait for the headache to ease. Intense nausea and vomiting may accompany the attack.

It is not unusual for the headache to last twelve to twenty-four hours or more, and its aftereffects may be felt for several days. Worst of all, when the pain finally abates, the migraine sufferer knows that it will happen again days, weeks, or months later.

The cause of migraine is not yet clear, but it seems that the headache may be the result of a vascular disturbance in the head (Bakal, 1975; Dalessio, 1970). The warning phase that precedes the headache is associated with an intense constriction of the cranial arteries, which diminishes the cerebral blood flow. The headache itself follows as this process reverses itself and the arteries distend painfully. Current research and theory suggest that a combination of highly sensitive cranial vasculature and a general instability of the autonomic nervous system may be to blame for these vasomotor reactions (Bakal, 1975). Several investigators (for instance, Graham & Wolff, 1938; Herburg, 1967; Rao & Pearce, 1971) regard the hypothalamus—the point of origin of the autonomic nervous system and the center of vasomotor control—as the focus of the disturbance, but this is still a matter of conjecture.

The autonomic responses in migraine sufferers do not appear to be limited to blood vessels in the head. It has been noted that individuals in the throes of a migraine attack often have cold hands and feet (Wolff, 1963), possibly indicating a widespread sympathetic discharge. In fact, the casual observation that migraines are accompanied by cold extremities served as the jumping-off point for a biofeedback treatment approach. At the Menninger Foundation in Topeka, Kansas, Joseph Sargent, Dale Walters, and Elmer Green (1973) were conducting pilot research on migraine. One day they were monitoring the finger temperature of a woman who was at that moment suffering from a migraine. During the observation, the woman's headache happened to fade away, but as it did, the temperature of her hands rose 10°F within a two-minute period. Word of this unusual coincidence spread rapidly through their laboratory, and soon two staff members with migraines volunteered to be trained in hand warming to see if it might affect their headaches. The training all but eliminated the headaches in one subject, and helped the other subject gain some

control over their intensity and frequency. Biofeedback treatment of migraine was born.

The technique the Menninger group devised is known as **autogenic feedback training.** Thermistors are attached to the headache sufferer's forehead and right index finger. The individual then watches a dial that indicates the difference in temperature between the two locations. The subject's task is to increase the temperature of the hands relative to that of the forehead. Although this can be accomplished by reducing forehead temperature, positive responses are almost entirely the result of increases in hand temperature (that is, blood flow) (Sargent, Walters, & Green, 1973). The subject is aided in the hand-warming task by thinking a series of autogenic phrases (Schultz & Luthe, 1969). These are simple self-suggestions aimed at inducing relaxation and regulating physiological functioning; for example, "I am beginning to feel quite relaxed. . . My arms and hands are heavy and warm . . . Warmth is flowing into my hands. . . ." Temperature feedback training is continued until the individual develops a keen awareness of the sensations that are associated with increased blood flow in the hands. At this point, the biofeedback can be faded out, and the client can continue to practice hand warming on his or her own and attempt to use the response to prevent or abort migraine attacks.

The Menninger group conducted several preliminary investigations of the technique (Sargent, Green, & Walters, 1972, 1973) and reported success rates ranging from 63 to 74 percent with migrainous subjects. Unfortunately, none of the studies employed even the most minimal control procedures, and the reports are so poorly presented that it is impossible to evaluate the real significance of the data (see critiques by Blanchard & Young, 1973; Blanchard & Epstein, 1977). Perhaps most troubling from an evaluative standpoint is the fact that the treatment procedure is a combination of autogenic training and temperature biofeedback. There is some indication that autogenic training alone may be effective in the reduction of migraine (Schultz & Luthe, 1969), leaving the contribution of biofeedback in doubt.

The preliminary work of the Menninger group was influential if nothing else. Temperature feedback training devices were marketed immediately, and migraine clinics using the apparatus sprang up across the country. Other investigators also began reporting successful applications of the procedure in uncontrolled case studies (for example, Peper, 1973; Peper & Grossman, 1974; Weinstock, 1972). Ian Wickramasekera (1973) conducted the first systematic case study in which temperature feedback alone was used to treat two clients with long (fifteen plus years) histories of migraines. Both clients had undergone extensive training in EMG-assisted relaxation without experiencing a significant reduction in either the frequency or intensity of their migraine attacks. After a three-week baseline period, hand-warming biofeedback training was begun. The clients also practiced their hand-warming skill at home without feedback. As can be seen in Figure 16–1, headache activity in both clients declined steadily as the hand-warming skill was acquired. A three-month followup indicated the gains were maintained.

William Johnson and Alan Turin (Johnson & Turin, 1975; Turin & Johnson, 1976) reported on the effects of temperature training on seven clients with two- to fifty-year histories of migraine attacks. Included in the reports are data on three subjects who underwent a control procedure in which they were told that learning to *decrease* the temperature of their hands through biofeedback would reduce their headaches. Cooling their hands was apparently quite difficult for all three subjects, and none derived any benefit from the training. In fact, one subject's migraines increased during hand-cooling training. When switched to hand-warming training, all three subjects improved, as did the four other subjects. A perusal of Turin and Johnson's (1976) data reveals that subjects' responses to treatment were extremely variable, with some showing great reduction in the frequency and duration of headaches and others showing only minimal effects. The subjects' need for medication following training also varied greatly.

A controlled outcome evaluation has been conducted that compared autogenic feedback training with EEG feedback of alpha waves (brain waves associated with a state of relaxation and unfocused attention) and self-hypnosis/relaxation (Andreychuk & Skriver, 1974). Results indicated that all

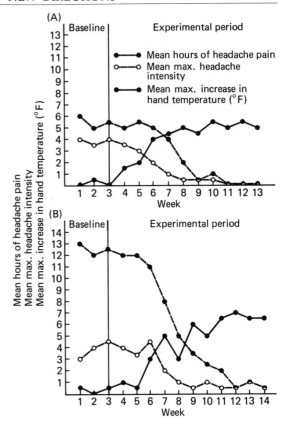

Figure 16–1. Effects of temperature feedback on migraine attacks in two subjects, A and B. Changes in headache duration, intensity, and absolute hand temperature. From I. Wickramasekera, Temperature feedback for the control of migraine. *Journal of Behavior Therapy and Experimental Psychiatry*, 1973, **4**, p. 344, Figures 1, 2. By permission of Pergamon Press, Ltd.

three procedures were equally effective in producing significant reductions in the subjects' migraines. Most interesting was the finding of a significantly greater improvement in those subjects who scored higher on measures of hypnotic susceptibility. Unfortunately, the autogenic feedback training group contained more of these highly suggestible subjects than did the other groups, indicating a possible source of bias working for the biofeedback condition.

Finally, Linda Friar and Jackson Beatty (1976) have conducted a controlled evaluation of yet another biofeedback treatment for migraine. Migraine sufferers in the experimental group were provided with visual feedback of the pulse amplitude in their temporal arteries. A reduction in the amplitude of the temporal pulse is indicative of constriction in the cranial arteries. It was assumed that if subjects could learn to produce this constriction, it would prove useful in opposing the intense cranial vasodilation that caused their headaches. Migraine subjects in the placebo control group were given this same rationale, but they received feedback training in decreasing pulse amplitude in their hands, while being led to believe that the vasoconstrictive response would generalize to arteries in their heads.

Both groups were successful in learning to decrease pulse amplitude at the trained site and could produce the effect even without the feedback. They were instructed to use this skill at the onset of their migraines. The major finding was that subjects in the experimental group experienced fewer major (that is, over three hours) headache attacks in the month following training than in the month before training. The experimental group underwent a greater reduction in major headache attacks than did the control group, which essentially showed no change. However, both within- and between-group treatment effects achieved only marginal statistical significance, probably owing to wide variance within the relatively small treatment groups (nineteen subjects in all). Thus, the study is interesting, but inconclusive.

What conclusions can be reached from these reports? Temperature biofeedback treatment is probably successful in reducing migraine headaches for many individuals. Why it works is not known, but it seems fairly certain that the act of simply maneuvering blood into the hands has nothing to do with the effects. If this were the case, migraine sufferers could obtain relief from their headaches by simply dunking their hands in warm water, but anecdotal reports indicate that this is rarely if ever of any benefit (for example, Sargent, Green, & Walters, 1973). The active ingredient in temperature training may well be reduction of sympathetic arousal, of which in-

creased blood flow to the hands and feet is one indication (Sargent, Green, & Walters, 1973; Wickramasekera, 1973). Thus, the individual undergoing this training may merely be learning to relax; and if this is the case, then other relaxation-inducing procedures should also be effective in reducing migraine.

Treatment packages incorporating a variety of arousal-reducing techniques including relaxation training (Hay & Madders, 1971; Lutker, 1971; Mitchell & White, 1977), EEG alpha enhancement (Andreychuk & Skriver, 1974), desensitization of tension-eliciting stimuli (Mitchell, 1971; Mitchell & Mitchell, 1971), and even transcendental meditation (Benson, Malvea, & Graham, 1973) have all been used with some success to reduce migraine, although conflicting reports also exist (for example, Wickramasekera, 1973). In general, these data suggest that the relaxation induced during successful temperature feedback training may account for the procedure's (variable) effects, and that the expensive equipment necessary for biofeedback treatment could possibly be dispensed with in favor of simpler, more reliable arousal-reducing techniques. What is certainly necessary are well-controlled comparative outcome studies to identify the most effective procedure. In view of the present research, it is clearly premature to herald biofeedback as a cure for migraine headache.

Operant Approaches to Chronic Pain

Pain and Pain Behavior. Pain has always been conceptualized as primarily a medical problem. It is generally viewed as a symptom of some disease process or physical trauma, and treatment typically involves removing this underlying cause. In cases where the cause of the pain cannot be remedied, narcotic or analgesic medication is usually given to reduce the pain itself.

Pain is also a behavior or response. Part of this response is purely experiential—only the individual experiencing the pain can know how it feels—but another part of the response is a complex set of observable behaviors. The pain sufferer may moan, grimace, or wince; talk about the pain; or move in a manner that indicates discomfort, such as limping or moving gingerly. In these ways, the individual communicates his or her experience to others. If we were to think about these behaviors in psychological terms, we would probably conclude that they were *respondents,* in that they appear to be elicited by the stimuli that precede them; that is, the mechanical or chemical conditions that activate the pain receptors. In most cases, we would be correct in this view, and a physician would probably be able to identify the underlying cause of the pain response—perhaps a sprained ankle or an infection of some sort. However, in many cases, no medical reason for the report of pain can be found. Assuming that the medical assessment is valid, how can we now account for the maintenance of pain behavior?

Wilbert Fordyce and his colleagues (Fordyce, 1973, 1976a, 1976b; Fordyce, Fowler, Lehmann, DeLateur, Sand, & Trieschmann, 1973) have suggested that pain behaviors may function as *operants* as well as respondents and thus be maintained by their consequences. Individuals' expressions of pain, whether verbal or nonverbal, often bring them considerable reinforcement; family, friends, and medical professionals react with attention and concern, and a great deal of effort may be directed at easing the discomfort. Relief from pain is generally contingent on sufferers' complaints, since medication is given only when they request it. The medication itself may produce pleasurable feelings apart from its analgesic properties. Pain behaviors may receive further negative reinforcement if individuals escape or avoid unpleasant situations and responsibilities because of them. The drudgery of going to work may be replaced by rest, relaxation, and the ministrations of a concerned spouse.

Certainly, most of us would not find the life of a pain sufferer reinforcing for very long. We would be anxious to be up and about, pursuing other interests as soon as our distress had eased. For many individuals, however, the benefits provided by the "sick role" may be preferable to the dull and undistinguished lives they normally lead. The attention, the relief from responsibility, and the varied and frequent contacts with the medical community may provide reinforcements that maintain a person's expressions of pain long after the original cause of the discomfort has been corrected. It is conceivable that these reinforcers

might even contribute to the continued experience of pain itself.

Reduction of Pain Behavior. From this conceptualization, Fordyce and his team have developed an operant-conditioning-based treatment program for use in selected cases of debilitating chronic pain. Their strategy is aimed at dissociating pain behaviors from reinforcement, and rewarding behavior that is incompatible with the sick role instead. The initial phases of the program are conducted while the handicapped individual is an inpatient. First, a detailed physical and psychological assessment of the individual is made. Only those patients with a longstanding pain problem who have failed to respond to traditional treatments, who are physically capable of walking, and who appear to be manifesting "operant pain," based on the relationship between their pain behavior and environmental consequences, are selected for the program.

Patients (and spouses where possible) who agree to participate in the program are fully briefed on the treatment procedures and their rationale. Specific goals are established for each patient regarding those pain behaviors to be eliminated, and those activities to be increased. Baseline measurements are then taken on medication and activity levels. Medication is given as needed during baseline, and a careful record is made of what the patient takes and when. The amount of time the patient spends standing and walking is noted. Samples are also taken of the patient's ability to perform prescribed therapeutic exercises, such as sit-ups in cases of back pain. The patient is asked to engage in uninterrupted exercise until he or she feels pain or fatigue, and the duration of this exercise is recorded.

Reinforcement is dissociated from pain behavior in several ways. When treatment begins, pain medication is no longer delivered on the customary "as needed" schedule, which negatively reinforces reports of pain by providing relief. Instead, medication is given around the clock on a fixed-time interval that is shorter than the interval observed during baseline. Thus, if the patient had requested medication on the average every six hours during baseline, a four-hour fixed interval might be chosen for treatment. Medication is always delivered in a "pain cocktail" consisting of the analgesic ingredient and a substance that disguises the taste, color, and amount of the medication being given. In this manner, medication is given in anticipation of the patient's need, rather than contingent on reports of pain. The pain cocktail allows the physician to manipulate the medication dose without the patient's knowledge. As treatment progresses, the dosage is gradually reduced, and in most cases eventually eliminated, without the patient experiencing withdrawal or discomfort.

A similar procedure is adopted for increasing physical activity. In most cases, the patient's customary practice has been to "work to tolerance"; that is, the patient exercised until feeling pain, and then stopped to rest. Thus, rest has been contingent on the experience of pain. During treatment, working to tolerance is replaced by "working to quota." The quota is set at just slightly below the lowest exercise duration recorded during baseline—an amount that the patient should be able to attain without significant discomfort. Rest then becomes contingent on completing a specified quantity of work, rather than on reporting pain. As the patient grows stronger, the exercise quota is gradually increased, eventually surpassing the original tolerance limit. Once again, the gain is achieved with a minimum of discomfort to the patient.

The behavior of the patient's spouse and family and the hospital staff are crucial to the implementation of this program. They must be trained to be unresponsive to the patient's pain behavior, and to lavish praise and attention on the patient when he or she engages in therapeutic tasks or other behaviors that are incompatible with pain. For example, pain medication is never delivered on request, and failures to meet exercise quotas are met with no comment. On the other hand, being up and around and not complaining about pain earns the patient a great deal of positive social reinforcement. Although readers may feel somewhat uncomfortable about this strategy, remember that only those patients who appear to be displaying an operant type of pain are subjected to these contingencies. Furthermore, the patient volunteers for the treatment and fully understands the "rules of the game."

The strongest justification for the program lies in the data on its effectiveness (Fordyce, Fowler, Lehmann, DeLateur, Sand, & Trieschmann, 1973). Thirty-six patients who were suffering primarily from chronic back pain and who met the previously stated criteria for inclusion in the program were studied. All had been bothered by pain for between four and a half and thirty years. None had been able to do full-time work for an average of three and a half years. The inpatient phase of their treatment averaged seven weeks, with some individuals continuing treatment as outpatients for up to twenty-four weeks (the average was 3.13 weeks). Figures 16–2 and 16–3 illustrate some of the gains made during the inpatient program. Medication consumption was reduced significantly, and the hours of "uptime"—time spent doing something other than reclining in bed —increased significantly. Patients' ability to perform prescribed exercises also showed a dramatic and significant increase. A followup questionnaire completed an average of twenty-two months after the last outpatient contact indicated that many of the patients maintained their gains and even improved in some areas. Patients also reported significantly less interference in daily activities from pain, and more hours spent up and around, than before treatment. In addition, patients rated themselves as having significantly less pain than they had had on admission to the program. However, these ratings are dubious since they required individuals to recall their physical status from many months before.

This study lacks necessary controls and thus can be considered only suggestive. Nonetheless, the observed improvements are impressive when one considers the subjects' long histories of pain that had proved refractory to standard medical treatments. We must await further investigations by Fordyce and his team or by other researchers before drawing firm conclusions. Still, it appears that the concept of operant pain may be useful in many cases, and that some selected chronic pain sufferers can benefit from the Fordyce program.

Reducing Anxiety about Medical Procedures

We all know individuals who are afraid to go to a physician or dentist. Such anxiety is a familiar

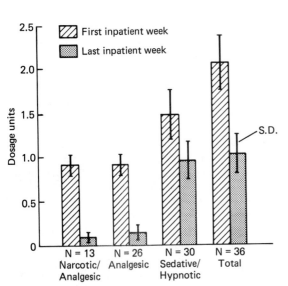

Figure 16–2. Changes in medications during inpatient treatment. From W. E. Fordyce, R. S. Fowler, J. F. Lehmann, B. J. DeLateur, P. L. Sand, & R. B. Trieschmann, Operant conditioning in the treatment of chronic pain. *Archives of Physical Medicine and Rehabilitation*, 1973, **54,** p. 406, Figure 2. Reprinted by permission of Archives of Physical Medicine and Rehabilitation.

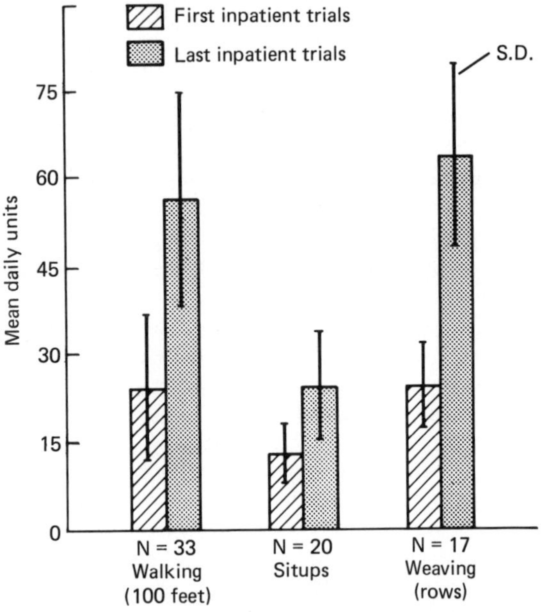

Figure 16–3. Changes in performance of most frequently prescribed activities during treatment. From W. E. Fordyce, R. S. Fowler, J. F. Lehmann, B. J. DeLateur, P. L. Sand, & R. B. Trieschmann, Operant conditioning in the treatment of chronic pain. *Archives of Physical Medicine and Rehabilitation,* 1973, **54,** p. 405, Figure 1. Reprinted by permission of Archives of Physical Medicine and Rehabilitation.

phenomenon and a significant problem to health care professionals. Fear of medical procedures can lead people to avoid services that may be important to their well-being; or the anxiety can make performance of those services many times more difficult and unpleasant for both the patient and doctor.

Children are particularly susceptible to such fears, and many professionals believe that psychological preparation for significant medical or dental treatment is mandatory (Cherches & Blackman, 1963; Dimock, 1960). With the success of behavioral approaches to anxiety reduction (see Chapters 4 and 10), it is not surprising to find these procedures being used effectively in the treatment of children's fears of medical procedures.

Dentistry. Although systematic desensitization has been used successfully to reduce children's

fears of dental treatment, a simpler, less time-consuming procedure is symbolic modeling (Machen & Johnson, 1974). Barbara Melamed and her colleagues (Melamed, 1976; Melamed, Hawes, Heiby, & Glick, 1975; Melamed, Weinstein, Hawes, & Katin-Borland, 1975) have conducted a series of investigations using filmed modeling to prepare children for trips to the dentist. All the studies used inner-city children who ranged from four to eleven years old, many of whom had no prior dental experience.

In the first study (Melamed, Weinstein, Hawes, & Katin-Borland, 1975), each of fourteen children made three visits to a dental clinic. The first two visits involved examination and cleaning of the child's teeth; the third trip involved injection of a local anesthetic and the filling of one or two cavities. All children were treated alike during the first two visits. However, on the third trip, half the children viewed a short videotape portraying a four-year-old black youngster coping with his anxiety during a session with the dentist. The rest of the children were allowed to draw pictures for the same interval. Trained observers recorded instances of anxious and disruptive behavior during each of the treatment sessions. These observations indicated no significant differences between the groups during the first two examinations, but the children who had no opportunity to view the modeling film before facing the anesthetic injection and filling placement showed more than a 120 percent increase in anxious/disruptive behavior in the final treatment session. Experimental children showed no increase in these behaviors. The observers' data were paralleled by ratings of the children's anxiety made by both their mothers and the dentist.

The second investigation (Melamed, Hawes, Heiby, & Glick, 1975) duplicated the first, with the exception that children in the control group viewed a short film portraying a black child engaging in activities unrelated to dentistry. The addition of this control factor had no effect on the results, which were essentially the same as those in the initial study.

A third investigation (Melamed, 1976) attempted to isolate some of the effective components of the modeling procedure. The format of the study was the same as before, but this time the children were divided into five groups, each of which saw a different film. Two of the films were modeling films, showing a black child at the dentist's office. One of these films demonstrated all aspects of the dental restorative treatment; the other was shorter and only showed the child receiving the anesthetic injection and an examination. Two other films were demonstration films that paralleled each of the modeling films in content, but a dentist and an assistant merely described the procedures without a child in the dentist's chair. The last film showed a black youngster doing things unrelated to dentistry. In contrast to the previous studies, all groups demonstrated a significant increase in anxious/disruptive behaviors over the three treatment sessions, but children who viewed the modeling films did significantly better than those who viewed the demonstration films. (Curiously, no data are given for children who saw the unrelated film.) In

addition, children viewing the long films depicting the entire dental procedure rated themselves as significantly less anxious immediately prior to the final treatment session than did children who viewed the shorter films.

Taken together, these data clearly point to the efficacy of symbolic modeling in the reduction of children's fears of dentistry. Although there is some indication that longer, more comprehensive preparation is preferable to briefer treatments (Melamed, 1976), the costs to the dentist or hygienist in time and effort seem minimal compared to the benefit of less anxious, more cooperative children.

Surgery. A consensus seems to exist in the literature that all children facing hospitalization need some kind of preparation for the experience, particularly when surgery is involved. Traditionally, preoperative preparation has consisted of (1) providing the child with information, (2) encouraging emotional expression, and (3) establishing a trusting relationship between the child and hospital staff (Vernon, Foley, Sipowicz, & Schulman, 1965). As in treatment of dental fears, behavioral techniques can help to optimize hospitals' preoperative preparation of children.

Melamed and her colleagues (Melamed, 1977; Melamed & Siegel, 1975; Melamed, Meyer, Gee, & Soule, in press) have examined the efficacy of filmed modeling to reduce children's surgical anxieties. The approach is similar to that taken for dental preparation, except that the children view a film called *Ethan Has an Operation* (Health Sciences Communication Center, Case Western Reserve University, Cleveland, Ohio 44106) depicting a seven-year-old white male who has been hospitalized for a hernia operation. The movie shows Ethan coping with most of the events the children will encounter in their hospital stay, including having a blood test, leaving the mother, and being in the operating and recovery rooms. Throughout the movie, hospital staff explain the various procedures while Ethan, the narrator, discusses his feelings and experiences along the way. Ethan displays some anxiety in the film, but he repeatedly demonstrates his ability to cope with it. In this way, children can both identify with Ethan and learn coping behaviors from him.

Melamed's studies with children undergoing routine elective surgery (such as a tonsillectomy) have indicated that filmed modeling is a useful anxiety-reducing procedure when used in conjunction with, or in the absence of, normal hospital preoperative preparation. Self-report as well as observational and physiological indices of anxiety reveal that children who view models display significantly less preoperative and postoperative fear arousal than do children who view a control film unrelated to surgery (Melamed & Siegel, 1975). Parents report significantly fewer postdischarge behavior problems in children in the modeling group. Some findings indicate that the timing of the modeling preparation is crucial and depends on the age of the child. Older children benefit most from seeing the film a week or so in advance of their hospitalization, whereas younger children respond better when preparation is closer to the time of their surgery (Melamed, Meyer, Gee, & Soule, in press).

As was true in the case of preparation for dental treatment, symbolic modeling appears to be extremely useful in the reduction of children's surgical and medical fears. Further research should guarantee a place for filmed modeling in the preparatory programs of many health care services.

APPLICATIONS TO PERSONNEL MANAGEMENT

Within the last five years there has been growing enthusiasm within the business community regarding the possibilities of applying behavior modification principles to increase work productivity and efficiency. The major interest has been in personnel management: specifically, how to get workers to work harder and managers to manage better.

Recent advances in behavioral research and theory have led to an increased emphasis on the importance of recognition, praise, and feedback in improving both productivity and employee satisfaction. Interestingly, behavioral principles have not been used to devise more elaborate forms of piece-rate wages. This does not mean that those in management do not recognize the reinforcing value of money: fixed-ratio reinforcement was used in business long before Skinner's time.

However, union agreements and labor laws prohibit management's dispensing wages directly according to work output. Another reason that industry is focusing on social reinforcement is that, in certain cases, money is not the crucial factor. Many management experts have observed that job satisfaction and recognition by peers and superiors are often equally important. Although business executives have not conducted controlled experiments comparing effects of praise and monetary rewards on output and job satisfaction, they have instituted social reinforcement programs that they believe have led to increased profits and greater employee satisfaction.

Social Reinforcement Programs

The use of behavior modification techniques in business was first introduced at Emery Air Freight by Edward Feeney (vice-president in charge of systems performance) (Business Week, 1972; Hamner & Hamner, 1976; Hilts, 1974; Cherns, 1973). Feeney's pioneer program dealt with the behavior of loading-dock personnel—specifically, their use of large shipping containers to hold a number of small packages going to the same location. Rather than moving many small packages, loaders could handle one large container, resulting in considerable savings. A performance audit indicated that the dock loaders only used the large containers 45 percent of the time, which cost Emery valuable time and money. After this assessment, dock foremen were instructed to keep charts on the dock bulletin board showing container use. In addition to recording the loaders' behavior, the foremen were also told to praise them for improved performance. The foremen cooperated and container use increased to 95 percent.

This simple change in procedures was so successful that it was instituted at Emery offices throughout the country; according to Feeney's figures, the company saved approximately $520,000 in one year. Moreover, the effects were not transient. The program has been in operation for three years, and substantial savings are still being observed.

In the course of his work, Feeney devised a staff training program in which Emery managers and supervisors learn how to dispense social reinforcers effectively (through public recognition, award luncheons, assignment of greater decision-making duties) and how to give constructive feedback. According to an Emery official, the positive reinforcement program is flourishing (R. Michael Swift, 1977, personal communication).

Although these results are indeed impressive, cautious optimism is advised. Without the existence of controlled outcome research on the effectiveness of the Emery Air Freight program, we cannot conclude that the savings and increased profits observed were a direct function of the behavior modification program. Other factors may have been operating at the same time. What is more, the long-term success rate of the social reinforcement program is quite unusual. In a large number of laboratory and applied studies, it has been found that the gains made by programs using social reinforcement are often short-lived unless strong reinforcers (such as money or food) are used to back up the praise and social reinforcement. At Emery, however, no backup reinforcers were used, yet the program appeared to be successful. It is clear that carefully controlled research on the effectiveness of social reinforcement programs in personnel management is needed.

Since his pioneering work at Emery, Feeney has gone on to establish a management consulting firm specializing in behavioral intervention. Following an intervention strategy similar to the one outlined in Chapter 3, Feeney and his associates begin with a detailed assessment of the personnel practices of the company. This **performance improvement analysis** (Feeney, 1976) involves firsthand observation and recording of the output of individual employees, supervisors' instructions and feedback to workers, and the physical design of work areas. During this baseline period, the dollar value of performance is determined. Then Feeney works with management and labor to establish realistic goals that can be objectively measured. The focus is on clearly observable behaviors.

Social Skills Training

During the last five years, other major corporations (for instance, Michigan Bell and B. F. Goodrich Chemical Company) (Hamner & Hamner, 1976) have introduced behavior modification prin-

ciples into personnel policies. Although the goal of most programs is to increase supervisors' use of positive reinforcement, the training program instituted by psychologist Melvin Sorcher at General Electric also focuses on general social skills training (Goldstein & Sorcher, 1976). Sorcher makes extensive use of videotapes, participant modeling, and role playing in his training program. During each of the ten one- to two-hour training sessions, supervisors watch a video recording and then practice the behaviors demonstrated. Situations that are modeled on the tapes include: (1) introducing a new employee to the work situation, (2) motivating a worker whose performance is below what is expected, (3) overcoming resistance to change, (4) recognizing and reinforcing good work, and (5) dealing with employees who have poor work habits, such as excessive absenteeism. During role playing, the instructor stresses the importance of: (1) being specific when providing feedback, (2) focusing on the problem rather than the employee, (3) resolving conflict via negotiation, and (4) establishing procedures that will encourage follow-through. The instructor also discusses specific problems supervisors are having in their work and suggests how behavioral principles might be applied to correct them.

Sorcher has subjected his program to experimental evaluation. In a controlled study, he compared the work productivity and efficiency of 100 employees whose supervisors had participated in the skills training program with 100 employees whose supervisors had not been so trained. Thus, rather than measuring the supervisors' behavior directly, Sorcher assessed the impact of the supervisors' behavior on the work of the employees they oversee. Sorcher found that the level of work productivity was significantly higher for workers who were supervised by "trained" foremen. Anecdotal reports also indicated that job satisfaction for both supervisors and workers improved as a result of the training program. Similar programs instituted in other corporations have met with equal success (for instance, Luthans & Lyman, 1972–1973; Wexley & Nemeroff, 1975).

Monetary Reinforcement Programs

As we have pointed out earlier, most behavior modification programs in business have relied on social reinforcement; however, at least a half-dozen programs have involved monetary reinforcement in the form of bonuses. Two of the more interesting programs involved the Detroit garbage collectors (Hamner & Hamner, 1976) and employees at a Michigan-based distribution center (Pedalino & Gamboa, 1974). In their labor negotiations with city officials, Detroit garbage collectors signed an agreement whereby the collectors would share with the city all savings gained through increased productivity. That is, any money saved as a result of reduction in paid man-hours of overtime per ton of refuse collected, increased percentage of routes completed on schedule, and improved quality of services were shared on a fifty-fifty basis. During the first year of the new contract, the city saved $1,654,000, and each garbage collector received an average of $350 in bonuses. In addition, complaints by the city's customers decreased significantly.

Another interesting monetary reinforcement program involved a lottery system designed to reduce absenteeism (Pedalino & Gamboa, 1974). Each day that an employee arrived at work on time, the employee was allowed to choose a card from a deck of playing cards. On Friday of each week the employee in each department with the highest poker hand won twenty dollars. Using an ABA reversal design in which work attendance during the periods before and after the four-month intervention were compared with attendance during the intervention, the researchers found that the lottery system resulted in a significant 18.27 percent reduction in absenteeism. During the same intervention period, a matched comparison group that was not on the lottery system showed a 13.79 percent *increase* in absenteeism. Similar results are reported by researchers working for the Mexican subsidiary of American Standard (Hermann, de Montes, Dominguez, Montes, & Hopkins, 1973). Absenteeism was significantly reduced when employees received daily bonuses for being punctual.

The available reports seem to indicate that these programs have yielded benefits for all those involved. From a relatively superficial perusal they do not appear to be exploitive. However, as we pointed out in Chapter 1, behavior modification techniques are powerful and can be easily abused. The senior author recalls a particularly exploitive bonus system he encountered one summer when he worked in a bottling plant. Accidents in the plant were not uncommon; bottles frequently exploded and workers were often cut. Management decided to institute a program whereby workers would receive a twenty-five-dollar bonus at Christmas if they did not have an accident during the preceding year. Since the hourly wage was less than $1.20, the bonus was a real incentive. However, accidents could not be avoided, so what the workers did was not report their accidents. If they were hurt in some way, they would bandage their wounds with anything they could find and keep on working. They did not want to lose their bonus. This was fine with management. By having only a few accident claims on their insurance policy, they kept their premiums low and saved a great deal of money—far more than what they had to pay out in bonuses. The bonus system reinforced employees for not *reporting* accidents, but it did not affect the occurrence of accidents.

The major problem with programs using positive reinforcement is that, because the control is "pleasant," those who are affected by it do not resist. Candy-coated coercion feels good, so we do not fight it, even though in the end it might be harmful. In *About Behaviorism* (1974), B. F. Skinner points out that many state governments have become aware of the advantages of positive control:

> The fact that positive reinforcement does not breed countercontrol has not gone unnoticed by would-be controllers, who have simply shifted to positive means. Here is an example: A government must raise money. If it does so through taxation, its citizens must pay or be punished, and they may escape from this aversive control by putting another party in power at the next election. As an alternative, the government organizes a lottery, and instead of being *forced* to pay taxes, the citizens *voluntarily* buy tickets. The result is the same: the citizens give the government money, but they feel free and do not protest in the second case. Nevertheless they are being controlled, as powerfully as by a threat of punishment, by that particularly powerful (variable-ratio) schedule of reinforcement. (p. 198)

Skinner was appalled when he learned of the Illinois instant lottery, in which players buy the opportunity to be reinforced immediately. Players buy a ticket, wet the back side, and know right away whether they have the winning ticket. It is much more enticing than the regular weekly or monthly lotteries. In southern Illinois, ticket sales jumped 1,000 percent when the system switched from weekly to immediate payoffs.

We are not saying that bonus systems, lotteries, and the like are necessarily evil. Our only point is that such programs must be carefully monitored by someone who does not have conflicting interests. The welfare of all those involved must be protected.

Response Costs Used in Business

In contrast to the use of positive reinforcement is the use of fines and penalties to reduce poor performance. As we have discussed throughout the book, behavioral psychologists are often opposed to the use of aversive consequences to modify behavior, and psychologists working in business are no exception.

In our review of the literature we found only one example of the use of response costs in personnel management. The program was designed to reduce daily cash register shortages in a small retail business, a pizza parlor (Marholin & Gray, 1976). The procedure designed by psychologist David Marholin and his colleague Deanne Gray was relatively simple. After the owner of the restaurant recorded losses for a five-day assessment period, the employees were told that shortages would be taken out of their weekly salaries. Then, if any single day's cash shortage equaled or exceeded 1 percent of the day's receipts, the total shortage, divided by the number of employees working on that day, was subtracted from each cashier's salary. The program was immediately effective. The average daily shortage was 4.02 percent of receipts during the assessment period and .43 percent during the period in which the response-costs contingency was in effect. In order to determine the full impact of the program, the contingency was removed after twelve days and the employees were told that the program was no longer in effect. Cash register shortages im-

mediately increased to 3.73 percent of daily receipts—nearly a ninefold increase. When the response cost was reintroduced, shortages dropped again to an average of .04 percent of the daily receipts.

Although the program did save the owner of the pizza parlor money, there is no way of knowing whether the employees became more careful, more honest, or just started short-changing the customers rather than the owner. Marholin and Gray recognized this problem and suggested that better methods of monitoring cash shortages were needed. Another problem that the authors pointed out is that the group contingency might have resulted in one employee's being fined for the errors of others. This possibility could have been avoided by giving each cashier his or her own cash drawer. As with any powerful technique, safeguards must be integrated into the system.

ECOLOGICAL PROBLEMS

During the last three years, interest in the application of behavior modification principles to improve the relationship between people and the environment has grown. At least fifty studies in the area have already been published. At the present time, the major emphasis has been on energy conservation, litter control, and use of public transportation. The strategy proposed by most behavioral "engineers" is quite simple—rearrange reinforcement contingencies so that people will find it reinforcing to conserve—and it has proved to be very effective. All the research reported has been relatively successful in modifying ecology-related behavior. Most of the programs have involved positive reinforcement procedures in which the desired behavior is prompted by instructions and reminders and is reinforced through contingency contracts, lotteries, prizes, and immediate feedback (Tuso & Geller, 1976).

Energy Conservation

The federal government, public utility companies, and various citizen groups are currently waging a campaign to get people to conserve electricity, gas, and oil. They have used television commercials, pamphlets, and free seminars on energy use. Although these programs are certainly appealing, researchers have found that the techniques are not successful in reducing consumption (Hayes & Cone, in press; Kohlenberg, Phillips, & Proctor, in press; Winett & Nietzel, 1975). Every study reported in the literature dealing with methods for prompting energy conservation, reminding people to conserve, telling them how to cut back, and even giving them feedback on their own consumption has had a minimal effect. The only procedure that has been found to be effective is paying people when they conserve. For example, in one study (Winett & Nietzel, 1975) involving the electricity consumption of households in Lexington, Kentucky, usage was reduced by 20 percent when families received monetary reinforcement for conserving. Families who only received information regarding energy conservation reduced consumption by less than 5 percent. In another study involving residents of a married student housing complex at the University of West Virginia (Hayes & Cone, in press), weekly monetary bonuses for conserving electricity (three dollars for 10 to 19 percent reduction; six dollars for 20 to 29 percent reduction; nine dollars for 30 to 39 percent reduction; and so on) resulted in reductions ranging between 26 and 46 percent, with a mean of 33 percent.

These results are indeed encouraging, but a number of questions must be answered before we can conclude that we have found an effective means of getting people to conserve: Was the energy saved by the programs greater than the energy consumed in carrying them out? How much paper, gasoline, electricity, and so on, was required to provide the feedback? Was the amount of money used as reinforcers less than the money saved as a result of the families' conserving? If a program costs more than it saves, it is obviously not viable. Another issue concerns the people who participated in these pilot projects. Since they were volunteers and were not selected from the population at random, it is quite possible they are not representative of the general population of energy consumers. If this is the case, we cannot be sure the programs would be successful on a large scale.

Finally, it is important that researchers evaluate programs carried out for extended periods of time, because it is possible the **Hawthorne effect** was operating in the studies reported. In this case, the fact that the people knew they were participating in a study of energy conservation might have made them more aware of their wastefulness and thereby resulted in a temporary reduction in consumption. But no one knows what might happen after the novelty wears off. For two of the three published studies (Hayes & Cone, in press; Kohlenberg, Phillips, & Proctor, in press), results are based on programs lasting only two weeks. And in the third study (Winett & Nietzel, 1975), intervention lasted four weeks. The current research in the area of energy conservation has certainly provided important guidelines for how to begin an effective conservation program. Now what is needed is an evaluation of the proposals implemented on a broad scale.

Litter Control

Telling people to "Keep America Clean" helps, but only a little (Kazdin, 1977; Kohlenberg & Phillips, 1973). If people are explicitly told where to dispose of trash, and if trash containers are strategically situated, then some people will not litter (Marler, 1970; Geller, Witmer, & Tuso, in press). As with energy conservation, effective methods of controlling people's littering behavior have involved clear contingencies of positive reinforcement. To date, no fewer than six experimental studies have been conducted that show that the rate of littering can be significantly reduced by the introduction of monetary reinforcement for placing trash in appropriate containers (Burgess, Clark, & Hendee, 1971; Chapman & Risley, 1974; Clark, Burgess, & Hendee, 1972; Hayes, Johnson, & Cone, 1975; Kohlenberg & Phillips, 1973; Powers, Osborne, & Anderson, 1973). These programs use a variety of procedures, ranging from immediate financial reward for depositing trash in proper receptacles to the opportunity to participate in a lottery. In all the cases reported, reinforcement programs have been successful in reducing litter.

Although these studies have yielded encouraging results, certain practical issues must be considered in implementing incentive programs on a large scale. One issue is the cost of the program.

In addition to the cost of material rewards, personnel must be hired to monitor behavior and dispense reinforcers. Another issue concerns the quality of work being reinforced (Kazdin, 1977). That is, how well do the participants pick up trash? If reinforcers are dispensed contingent upon an individual's placing debris in an appropriate container, there is no way to ensure that the trash deposited is the same trash that litters our public areas. Certainly, these issues must be examined before we can conclude that behavioral programs offer a viable solution to the problem of litter control.

Recycling

Although recycling has not received as much attention by behavioral psychologists as littering, the two behavioral programs dealing with the issue have reported success (Geller, Chaffee, & Ingram, 1975; Geller, Wylie, & Farris, in press). The most impressive behavioral program designed to increase recycling is the response-cost/reinforcement program in Oregon. The program is quite simple: (1) heavy fines are imposed for anyone littering the landscape; (2) all beverage containers require a substantial deposit that is refunded upon return of the container; and (3) one-way bottles and cans are not sold in the state. Despite initial complaints from some merchants, all reports indicate that the program has been highly successful. A research study conducted by the Oregon Environmental Council (*Oregon's Bottle Bill, the 1977 Report*, 1977) showed that the program resulted in a significant reduction in the amount of litter in public areas such as parks and highways. Moreover, the council reported that the energy saved by not producing throwaway bottles and then having to dispose of them was substantial. During the first year alone, 1.4 trillion BTU's were saved—equivalent to the amount required to supply the annual heating needs of 50,000 Oregonians. Oregon's program has generated much interest across the country, and similar bills are now being considered by other states.

Public Transportation

During the last decade, millions of dollars have been allocated for mass transportation. Federal and city governments have expended great effort in researching various systems and in trying to determine efficient designs that also provide maximal passenger comfort. However, even the most modern systems are not being used to capacity. To encourage greater usage, many cities have devised incentive systems. For example, without the assistance of behavior analysts, the city of Pittsburgh has implemented what is called the "Big Buck" program to encourage bus ridership (Cone & Hayes, 1977; Everett, 1977). The Big Buck pass entitles a family of four unlimited use of the transit system for an entire weekend for one dollar. The Central New York Regional Transportation Authority offers free coupons good at local restaurants when customers purchase bus tokens in multiples (Everett, 1977). The rationale is that if people have extra bus tokens in hand they will be more likely to use them. Both programs have been successful. Ridership in Pittsburgh showed a large jump following the implementation of the Big Buck program, and in central New York there was an immediate 86 percent increase in the number of bus tokens purchased when the incentive system was introduced.

The only systematic behavioral research on use of public transportation has been conducted by Peter Everett and his colleagues at the Pennsylvania State University (Deslauriers & Everett, in press; Everett, Deslauriers, Newsom, & Anderson, in press; Everett & Hayward, 1974; Everett, Hayward, & Meyers, 1974). Everett's research has focused on relatively simple reinforcement programs to encourage bus ridership. Conducting his research in a small university community, Everett has found that dispensing tokens redeemable for merchandise in local stores results in a significant increase in ridership. Interestingly, dispensing tokens on an irregular basis (VR-3) was just as effective as continuous reinforcement. Of course, the advantage of the variable-ratio incentive program is that it costs the city less. In order to implement such incentive programs on a large scale, costs must be kept low. Everett's strategy is to use higher ratios of reinforcement and to enlist the financial backing of local merchants, but chances are that such a program will ultimately require government subsidy.

Automobile Use

Since the oil crisis of 1973, a great deal of controversy has surrounded the use of the private automobile. Gasoline rationing, special privileges for those riding in car pools, and higher taxes on cars that use gas inefficiently have been suggested as ways to alter our consumption of gasoline for driving. One proposal is to levy higher taxes on gasoline (as much as sixty cents per gallon) at the pump and then to return the revenue collected through federal tax rebates. This proposal represents an ingenious application of behavioral principles. Gas consumption would be punished via an immediate response-cost procedure (the sixty-cent tax) but presumably would not be an economic hardship because the tax would be returned (when federal income taxes are paid).

What is especially fascinating about this proposal is that, if it works, the tax would function as a punishment without any long-term aversive economic consequences. This represents an application of the principles of immediate versus delayed consequences. If the proposal is enacted and is effective, then our behavior would be modified at no cost to us and at limited cost to the government. However, as is evident from the increased sales of big cars that are expensive to operate, all these programs are fighting a powerful reinforcer —the luxury of living room comfort on the highway. Gasoline rationing and gas-guzzler taxes may not be sufficient. It seems we will have to resort to more extreme methods of behavior modification to break the people's love affair with the American dream machine.

SUMMARY

Behavior modification methods have been refined and made more sophisticated during the last five years. In this chapter we have attempted to give the reader an appreciation of how this expansion might progress in the next few years.

One important recent contribution of behavioral psychologists is in the area of health care, including work on the control of physiological functioning through biofeedback, the operant control of chronic pain, and the reduction of anxiety related to certain medical procedures.

Biofeedback training involves providing an individual with relatively immediate information (feedback) regarding physiological processes of which he or she is usually unaware. This feedback can often enable the person to exercise voluntary control over responses he or she would otherwise be unable to regulate in any systematic fashion. The resultant voluntary control of certain physiological processes can aid in the remediation of certain serious medical problems. Although the field is still in its infancy, some success in treating certain chronic problems has been reported. The area of physical rehabilitation shows considerable promise. Also, biofeedback training may be a viable method for treating migraine headaches; however, research to date does not justify the wild enthusiasm that the procedure has generated in the popular press.

The major contribution of behavior modification in the treatment of chronic pain has centered around the elimination of "operant pain behaviors" via relatively straightforward programs involving the extinction of observable expressions of pain (for example, complaints) and differentially reinforcing incompatible behavior (for example, therapeutic activities). These programs must be carried out in conjunction with careful medical monitoring to ensure that respondent pain behavior is recognized as a symptom of physical disease or injury. Preliminary research indicates that, in certain cases, contingency programs have resulted in large reductions of chronically debilitating pain.

The treatment of anxiety related to certain medical procedures has also benefited from modern behavioral technology. In this research, filmed modeling treatments have been used to reduce children's fears of dental and surgical procedures. The results thus far appear to justify including this as a standard component in the routine preparatory programs conducted by medical professionals.

Another new thrust is the application of behavior modification principles in business. The major emphasis has been in the area of personnel management: getting workers to work harder and managers to manage more effectively. The focus has been the importance of recognition, praise, and feedback in improving productivity and employee satisfaction.

Another strategy that has been successfully used is social skills training with direct line management. Again, the focus has been on teaching foremen to give constructive feedback and praise to workers. Psychologists have introduced training programs that have led to great job satisfaction and increased productivity for workers as well as increased profits for stockholders.

The third strategy used to improve business operations has been special monetary bonus systems. These have involved the use of, for example, lottery tickets and cash as reinforcers for punctuality and increased work efficiency. Preliminary findings as well as anecdotal statements from labor indicate that such programs have been effective.

The third area that has been explored is the application of behavior modification to ecological problems such as energy conservation, recycling, and litter control. Almost all these programs have used straightforward reinforcement procedures to encourage desirable behavior. Although pilot projects have been extremely successful, the cost-benefit ratios such programs would have if carried out on a broad scale for an extended period of time have not been evaluated.

REFERENCES

Andrews, J. M. Neuromuscular re-education of the hemiplegic with the aid of the electromyograph. *Archives of Physical Medicine and Rehabilitation*, 1964, **45**, 530–532.

Andreychuk, T., & Skriver, C. *Hypnosis and biofeedback in the treatment of migraine headache.* Paper read at the Biofeedback Research Society, Colorado Springs, Colorado, February 1974.

Bakal, D. A. Headache: A biopsychological perspective. *Psychological Bulletin*, 1975, **82**, 369–382.

Basmajian, J. V., Kukulka, C. G., Narayan, M. G., & Takebe, K. Biofeedback treatment of foot-drop compared with standard rehabilitation techniques: Effects on voluntary control and strength. *Archives of Physical Medicine and Rehabilitation*, 1975, **56**, 231–236.

Benson, H., Malvea, B. A., & Graham, J. R. Physiological correlates of meditation and their clinical effect in headache: An ongoing investigation. *Headache*, 1973, **13**, 23–24.

Benson, H., Shapiro, D., Tursky, B., & Schwartz, G. E. Decreased systolic blood pressure through operant conditioning techniques with essential hypertension. *Science*, 1971, **173**, 740–742.

Blanchard, E. B., & Epstein, L. H. The clinical usefulness of biofeedback. In M. Hersen, R. M. Eisler, & P. M. Miller (Eds.), *Progress in behavior modification*, vol. 4. New York: Academic Press, 1977.

Blanchard, E. B., & Haynes, M. R. Biofeedback treatment of a case of Raynaud's disease. *Journal of Behavior Therapy and Experimental Psychiatry*, 1975, **6**, 230–234.

Blanchard, E. B., & Young, L. D. Self-control of cardiac functioning: A promise as yet unfulfilled. *Psychological Bulletin*, 1973, **79**, 145–163.

Blanchard, E. B., & Young, L. D. Clinical applications of biofeedback training: A review of the evidence. *Archives of General Psychiatry*, 1974, **30**, 530–589.

Booker, H. E., Rubow, R. T., & Coleman, P. J. Simplified feedback in neuromuscular retraining: An automated approach using electromyographic signals. *Archives of Physical Medicine and Rehabilitation*, 1969, **50**, 621–675.

Brundy, J., Korein, J., Levidow, L., Grynbaum, B. B., Leiberman, A., & Friedman, C. W. Sensory feedback therapy as a modality of treatment in central nervous system disorders of voluntary movement. *Neurology*, 1974, **24**, 925–932.

Budzynski, T., Stoyva, J., & Adler, C. Feedback-induced muscle relaxation: Application to tension headache. *Journal of Behavior Therapy and Experimental Psychiatry*, 1970, **1**, 205–211.

Burgess, R. L., Clark, R. V., & Hendee, J. C. An experimental analysis of anti-litter procedures. *Journal of Applied Behavior Analysis*, 1971, **4**, 71–75.

Business Week. "Where Skinner's theories work." December 2, 1972, pp. 64–65.

Chapman, C., & Risley, T. R. Anti-littering procedures in an urban high-density area. *Journal of Applied Behavior Analysis*, 1974, **7**, 377–383.

Cherches, M. L., & Blackman, S. Alleviating the anxiety of children in dental treatment. *Journal of the American Dental Association*, 1963, **66**, 824–826.

Cherns, A. B. At Emery Air Freight: Positive reinforcement boosts performance. *Organizational Dynamics*, 1973, **2**, 41–50.

Clark, R. N., Burgess, R. L., & Hendee, J. C. The development of anti-litter behavior in a forest campground. *Journal of Applied Behavior Analysis*, 1972, **5**, 1–5.

Cone, J. D., & Hayes, S. C. Applied behavior analysis and the solution of environmental problems. In J. F. Wohlwill & I. Altman (Eds.), *Human behavior and environment: Advances in theory and research*, vol. 2. New York: Plenum, 1977.

Cox, D. J., Freundlich, A., & Meyer, R. G. Differential effectiveness of electromyograph feedback, verbal relaxation instructions, and medication placebo with tension headaches. *Journal of Consulting and Clinical Psychology*, 1975, **43**, 892–898.

Dalessio, D. J. Headache. In C. G. Costello (Ed.), *Symptoms of psychopathology.* New York: Wiley, 1970.

Deslauriers, B. C., & Everett, P. B. The effects of intermittent and continuous token reinforcement on bus ridership. *Journal of Applied Psychology*, 1977, **62**, 369–375.

Dimock, H. G. *The child in hospital: A study of his emotional and social well-being.* Philadelphia: Davis, 1960.

Engel, B. T., & Bleecker, E. R. Application of operant conditioning techniques to the control of cardiac arrhythmias. In P. A. Obrist, A. H. Black, J. Brener, & L. V. DiCara (Eds.), *Cardiovascular psychophysiology*, Chicago: Aldine, 1974.

Epstein, C. H., & Abel, G. G. An analysis of biofeedback training effects for tension headache patients. *Behavior Therapy*, 1977, **8**, 37–47.

Everett, P. B. A behavior science approach to transportation systems management. Unpublished manuscript, Pennsylvania State University, 1977.

Everett, P. B., Deslauriers, B. C., Newsom, T., & Anderson, V. B. Increasing the effectiveness of free transit. *Transportation Research*, 1978 (in press).

Everett, P. B., & Hayward, S. C. Behavioral technology—An essential design component of transportation systems. *High Speed Ground Transportation Journal*, 1974, **8**, (2).

Everett, P. B., Hayward, S. C., & Meyers, A. W. Effects of a token reinforcement procedure on bus ridership. *Journal of Applied Behavior Analysis*, 1974, **7**, 1–9.

Feeney, E. J. *ACDC reaches new levels in productivity.*

Ridgefield, Conn.: Feeney Associates, 1976.

Fordyce, W. E. An operant conditioning method for managing chronic pain. *Postgraduate Medicine,* 1973, **53,** 123–134.

Fordyce, W. E. *Behavioral methods for chronic pain and illness.* St. Louis: Mosby, 1976a.

Fordyce, W. E. Behavioral concepts in chronic pain and illness. In P. O. Davidson (Ed.), *The behavioral management of anxiety, depression and pain.* New York: Brunner/Mazel, 1976b.

Fordyce, W. E., Fowler, R. S., Lehmann, J. F., DeLateur, B. J., Sand, P. L., & Trieschmann, R. B. Operant conditioning in the treatment of chronic pain. *Archives of Physical Medicine and Rehabilitation,* 1973, **54,** 399–408.

Friar, L. R., & Beatty, J. Migraine: Management by trained control of vasoconstriction. *Journal of Consulting and Clinical Psychology,* 1976, **44,** 46–53.

Geller, E. S., Chaffee, J. L., & Ingram, R. E. Prompting paper recycling on a university campus. *Journal of Environmental Systems,* 1975, **5,** 39–57.

Geller, E. S., Witmer, J. F., & Tuso, M. A. Environmental interventions in litter control. *Journal of Applied Psychology,* 1977 (in press).

Geller, E. S., Wylie, R. G., & Farris, J. C. An attempt at applying prompting and reinforcement toward pollution control. *Proceedings of the Seventy-ninth Annual Convention of the American Psychological Association,* 1971, **6,** 701–702.

Goldstein, A. P., & Sorcher, M. *Changing supervisor behavior.* New York: Pergamon Press, 1976.

Graham, J. R., & Wolff, H. G. The mechanism of the migraine headache and the action of ergotamine tartrate. *Archives of Neurological Psychiatry,* 1938, **39,** 737.

Hamner, W. C., & Hamner, E. P. Behavior modification and the bottom line. *Organizational Dynamics,* 1976, **4,** 2–21.

Hay, K. M., & Madders, J. Migraine treated by relaxation therapy. *Journal of the Royal College of General Practitioners,* 1971, **21,** 664–669.

Hayes, S. C., & Cone, J. D. Reducing residential electrical energy use: Payments, information, and feedback. *Journal of Applied Behavior Analysis,* 1978 (in press).

Hayes, S. C., Johnson, V. S., & Cone, J. D. The marked item technique: A practical procedure for litter control. *Journal of Applied Behavior Analysis,* 1975, **8,** 381–386.

Herburg, L. J. The hypothalamus and the aetiology of migraine. In R. Smith (Ed.), *Background to migraine.* London: Heinemann, 1967.

Hermann, J. A., de Montes, A. E., Dominguez, B., Montes, F., & Hopkins, B. L. Effects of bonuses for punctuality on the tardiness of industrial workers. *Journal of Applied Behavior Analysis,* 1973, **6,** 563–570.

Hilts, P. J. *Behavior Mod.* New York: Harper's Magazine Press, 1974.

Johnson, H. E., & Garton, W. H. Muscle re-education in hemiplegia by use of EMG device. *Archives of Physical Medicine and Rehabilitation,* 1973, **54,** 320–325.

Johnson, R. K., & Meyer, R. G. Phased biofeedback approach for epileptic seizure control. *Journal of Behavior Therapy and Experimental Psychiatry,* 1974, **5,** 185–187.

Johnson, W. G., & Turin, A. Biofeedback treatment of migraine headache: A systematic case study. *Behavior Therapy,* 1975, **6,** 394–397.

Kazdin, A. E. Extensions of reinforcement techniques to socially and environmentally relevant behaviors. In R. M. Eisler and P. M. Miller (Eds.), *Progress in behavior modification,* vol. 4. New York: Academic Press, 1977.

Kohlenberg, R., & Phillips, T. Reinforcement and rate of litter depositing. *Journal of Applied Behavior Analysis,* 1973, **6,** 391–396.

Kohlenberg, R., Phillips, T., & Proctor, W. A behavioral analysis of peaking in residential electrical energy consumers. *Journal of Applied Behavior Analysis,* 1978 (in press).

Kristt, D. A., & Engel, B. T. Learned control of blood pressure in patients with high blood pressure. *Circulation,* 1975, **51,** 370–378.

Luthans, F., & Lyman, D. Training supervisors to use organizational behavior modification. *Personnel,* 1972–1973, **29–30,** 38–44.

Lutker, E. R. Treatment of migraine headache by conditioned relaxation: A case study. *Behavior Therapy,* 1971, **2,** 592–593.

Ma, J. B., & Johnson, R. Desensitization, model learning and the dental behavior of children. *Journal of Dental Research,* 1974, **58,** 83.

Marholin, D., & Gray, D. Effects of group response-costs procedures on cash shortages in a small business. *Journal of Applied Behavior Analysis,* 1976, **9,** 25–30.

Marinacci, A. A., & Horande, M. Electromyogram in neuromuscular re-education. *Bulletin of the Los Angeles Neurological Society,* 1960, **25,** 57–71.

Marler, L. A study of anti-litter messages. *Journal of Environmental Education,* 1970, **3,** 52–53.

Melamed, B. G. *Peer modeled fear behaviors during local anesthesia and its influence on children's dental treatment behavior.* Paper read at the Tenth Annual Convention of the Association for Advancement of Behavior Therapy, New York, December 1976.

Melamed, B. G. Psychological preparation for hospitalization. In S. Rachman (Ed.), *Contributions in medical psychology.* Oxford: Pergamon Press, 1977.

Melamed, B. G., Hawes, R. R., Heiby, E., & Glick, J. The use of filmed modeling to reduce uncooperative behavior of children during dental treatment. *Journal of Dental Research,* 1975, **54,** 797–801.

Melamed, B. G., Meyer, R., Gee, C., & Soule, L. The influence of time and type of preparation on children's adjustment to hospitalization. *Journal of Pediatric Psychology,* 1978 (in press).

Melamed, B. G., & Siegel, L. J. Reduction of anxiety in children facing surgery by modeling. *Journal of Consulting and Clinical Psychology,* 1975, **43,** 511–521.

Melamed, B., Weinstein, D., Hawes, R., & Katin-Borland, M. Reduction of fear-related dental management problems with the use of filmed modeling. *Journal of the American Dental Association,* 1975, **90,** 822–826.

Mitchell, K. R. Note on treatment of migraine using behavior therapy techniques. *Psychological Reports,* 1971, **28,** 171–172.

Mitchell, K. R., & Mitchell, D. M. Migraine: An exploratory treatment application of programmed behavior therapy techniques. *Journal of Psychosomatic Research,* 1971, **15,** 137–157.

Mitchell, K. R., & White, R. G. Behavioral self-management: An application to the problems of migraine headaches. *Behavior Therapy,* 1977, **8,** 213–221.

Oregon's bottle bill, the 1977 report. State of Oregon Department of Environmental Quality.

Pedalino, E., & Gamboa, V. U. Behavior modification and absenteeism: Intervention in one industrial setting. *Journal of Applied Psychology,* 1974, **59,** 694–698.

Peper, E. Frontiers of clinical biofeedback. In L. Birk (Ed.), *Seminars in psychiatry,* vol. 5. New York: Grune & Stratton, 1973.

Peper, E., & Grossman, E. R. *Preliminary observation of thermal biofeedback training in children with migraine.* Paper read at the Biofeedback Research Society meeting, Colorado Springs, February 1974.

Powers, R. B., Osborne, J. G., & Anderson, E. G. Positive reinforcement of litter removal in the natural environment. *Journal of Applied Behavior Analysis,* 1973, **6,** 579–586.

Rao, L. W., & Pearce, J. Hypothalamic-pituitary-adrenal axis studies in migraine with special reference to insulin sensitivity. *Brain,* 1971, **94,** 289–298.

Rouse, L., Peterson, J., & Shapiro, G. *EEG alpha entrainment reaction within the biofeedback setting and some possible effects on epilepsy.* Paper read at the Biofeedback Research Society, Colorado Springs, February 1974.

Sargent, J. D., Green, E. E., & Walters, E. D. The use of autogenic feedback training in a study of migraine and tension headaches. *Headache,* 1972, **12,** 120–124.

Sargent, J. D., Green, E. E., & Walters, E. D. Preliminary report on the use of autogenic feedback training in the treatment of migraine and tension headaches. *Psychosomatic Medicine,* 1973, **35,** 129–135.

Sargent, J. D., Walters, E. D., & Green, E. E. Psychosomatic self-regulation of migraine headaches. *Seminars in Psychiatry,* 1973, **5,** 415–428.

Schultz, J. H., & Luthe, W. *Autogenic therapy,* vol. 1. New York: Grune & Stratton, 1969.

Schwartz, G. E. Clinical applications of biofeedback: Some theoretical issues. In D. Upper & D. S. Goodenough (Eds.), *Behavior modification with the individual patient: Proceedings of third annual Brockton Symposium on behavior therapy.* Nutley, N.J.: Roche, 1972.

Skinner, B. F. *About behaviorism.* New York: Knopf, 1974.

Surwit, R. S. Biofeedback: A possible treatment for Raynaud's disease. In L. Birk (Ed.), *Biofeedback: Behavioral medicine.* New York: Grune & Stratton, 1973.

Turin, A., & Johnson, W. G. Biofeedback therapy for migraine headaches. *Archives of General Psychiatry,* 1976, **33,** 517–519.

Tuso, M. A., & Geller, E. S. Behavior analysis applied to environmental/ecological problems: A review. *Journal of Applied Behavior Analysis,* 1976, **9,** 526–527.

Vernon, D. T. A., Foley, J. M., Sipowicz, R. R., & Schulman, J. L. *The psychological responses of children to hospitalization and illness.* Springfield, Ill.: Thomas, 1965.

Weinstock, S. A. A tentative procedure for the control of pain: Migraine and tension headaches. In D. Shapiro, T. X. Barber, L. V. DiCara, J. Kamiya, N. E. Miller, & J. Stoyva (Eds.), *Biofeedback and self-control.* Chicago: Aldine, 1972.

Weiss, T., & Engel, B. T. Voluntary control of premature ventricular contractions in patients. *American Journal of Cardiology,* 1970, **26,** 666.

Weiss, T., & Engel, B. T. Operant conditioning of heart rate in patients with premature ventricular contractions. *Psychophysiology,* 1971, **8,** 262–264 (abstract)(a).

Weiss, T., & Engel, B. T. Operant conditioning of heart rate in patients with premature ventricular contractions. *Psychosomatic Medicine,* 1971, **33,** 301–321(b).

Weiss, T., & Engel, B. T. Evaluation of intracardiac limit of learned heart rate control. *Psychophysiology,* 1975, **12,** 310–312.

Wexley, K. N., & Nemeroff, W. F. Effectiveness of positive reinforcement and goal setting as methods of management development. *Journal of Applied Psychology,* 1975, **60,** 446–450.

Wickramasekera, I. Temperature feedback for the control of migraine. *Journal of Behavior Therapy and Experimental Psychiatry,* 1973, **4,** 343–345.

Winett, R. A., & Nietzel, M. T. Behavioral ecology: Contingency management of consumer energy use. *American Journal of Community Psychology,* 1975, **3,** 123–133.

Wolff, H. G. *Headache and other pain.* New York: Oxford University Press, 1963.

EPILOGUE

As we reflect on the task we have just completed, our reactions are many and varied. We are aware more than ever before that behavior modification is a field of subtle complexity. Entire books could be—and have been—written on many of the topics we address only briefly. In fact, during the final revision of our work, we found ourselves having to suppress (not always successfully) an urge to expand discussions. Although there are many issues we would like to explore more fully, there is one so basic to the enterprise of behavior modification as to warrant further comment: namely, the struggle within behavior modification to be scientific. We end our book with a few personal observations on this issue.

More than any other approach to human problems, behavior modification embraces the scientific method as *the* basis for knowledge. Whereas other treatment approaches originated in the clinic and then moved hesitantly, if at all, into the laboratory, behavior modification is an invention of the laboratory and has carried its scientific heritage into the clinic. The result has been a truly staggering accumulation of data. There is no question that behavior modification has made extensive use of the scientific method—but how relevant are the data to what goes on in the real world of clinical intervention? Too often, the answer is "not very."

The discrepancy between research and practice is sometimes striking. In the clinic, the behavioral psychologist must work with individuals whose pain or unhappiness is considerable; but the procedures in which the clinician will place his or her faith are often based on research with mildly distressed college student volunteers. In the clinic, the behavioral psychologist will conduct a painstaking functional analysis before selecting a treatment program and carefully tailoring it to the unique needs of the client. In the laboratory, however, the functional analysis is often dispensed with, and the researcher will, for purposes of experimental control, apply a standardized approximation of the clinician's procedure to a group of individuals who may have little in common besides some acquaintance with the target problem. In the analysis of the research, the subjects' individual differences will disappear in the statistical mean, and little attempt may be made to identify meaningful differences between subjects who responded to the treatment and those who did not. The clinician, however, must make crucial treatment decisions based on the client's individual characteristics.

There are many reasons for this dissociation between "the experiment" and the "real world." Part of the problem is inherent in the scientific method. To achieve experimental control, one must restrict the conditions under which a phenomenon is studied. To do so often places limitations on the "external validity"—the real-world relevance—of one's observations. The task in science is always to optimize this control/relevance relationship. This requires time and patience.

Time and patience are clearly working against the achievement of relevance in behavioral research. We are impatient with our progress in producing treatments to reduce human discomfort, and we must research complex questions in an academic system that values high productivity and positive findings. Our natural response to these pressures is to oversimplify our subject matter and overgeneralize our findings. Although much has been learned about human behavior change from our scientific endeavors, it seems clear that we do not know as much as we might sometimes suppose.

Behavior modification is the first therapeutic strategy to draw heavily on scientific methodology in the study of human behavior change. It is inevitable that there should be some problems in such a pioneering effort. But there is every reason to believe that behavioral clinicians and researchers are aware of and responsive to these problems. Behavioral approaches are clearly evolving toward an increasing appreciation of the complexity of human behavior, and an increasing sophistication in the methodology with which it is studied. We find the prospect of a self-correcting, evolving science of behavior change exciting indeed.

GLOSSARY

ABAB reversal design. Method used to evaluate treatment programs: after stable measures of the client's behavior under normal (nontreatment) conditions are obtained (A), treatment is introduced and data collection continues until stable measures are obtained (B), baseline conditions are reestablished until stability is again achieved (A), and finally treatment is reinstituted (B). Treatment is demonstrated to be effective if behavior changes in the desired direction during each B phase and returns to pretreatment levels during each A phase.

Adaptive behavior measures. Instruments used to assess an individual's functioning in such basic areas as ambulation, self-care, communication, and social development.

Alpha control. Term used in Kanfer's model of self-control to refer to the impact of environmental variables on behavior.

Anticipatory avoidance learning (AA). A procedure for the sexual reorientation of homosexual individuals in which homosexual stimuli are paired with electric shock that can be escaped or avoided by the client's pressing a button that produces a heterosexual stimulus.

Anxiety. A shorthand term for a complex, multidimensional pattern of response characterized by subjective feelings of apprehension and tension accompanied by or associated with arousal of the sympathetic branch of the autonomic nervous system.

Anxiety hierarchy. In systematic desensitization, a list of stimulus scenes arranged according to the degree of anxiety the client experiences in relation to each. The scenes may be arranged along a spatial-temporal dimension (each successive scene being closer in time or space to the most anxiety-evoking stimulus), a thematic dimension (each successive scene being a more stressful representative of the class of feared stimuli), or a combination of the two.

Assertion training. Procedure used to teach people how to express their positive and negative feelings and to stand up for their rights in ways that will not alienate others.

Assisted covert sensitization. A variation of covert sensitization in which the imagined aversive stimulus (a scene involving nausea and vomiting) is enhanced by the inhalation of a noxious odor.

Autism. A diagnostic label applied to children who very early in life exhibit such characteristics as profound deficits in communication, inability to relate to their surroundings, and frequently a preoccupation with stereotypic or self-stimulatory behavior.

Autogenic feedback training. A procedure for the control of migraine headaches developed by Joseph Sargent and his co-workers. It combines skin temperature feedback and self-suggestions aimed at reducing the cerebral vasodilation characteristic of the disorder.

Automaticity assumption. The notion that conditioning is automatic and involuntary, with thoughts and attitudes having little or no effect on the process.

Autonomic nervous system (ANS). A part of the nervous system originating in the hypothalamus and innervating the smooth muscle of the internal organs and the glands. The ANS is divided into two branches (sympathetic and parasympathetic) and is responsible for the regulation of many physiological processes.

Aversion relief. A respondent conditioning technique in which a stimulus is repeatedly paired with the termination of aversive stimulation (usually electric shock) so as to associate the stimulus with positive feelings.

Aversion therapy. Any treatment aimed at reducing the attractiveness of a stimulus or a behavior by repeatedly pairing it with aversive stimulation of a real or imaginal nature.

Aversive repertoire. Any pattern of interpersonal behaviors an individual may display which are unpleasant to others and result in their alienation.

Avoidance behavior. Any response directed toward preventing anticipated aversive stimulation.

Avoidance conditioning. Learning paradigm in which an individual acquires a response that prevents the presentation of an aversive stimulus.

Backup reinforcer. Any event or commodity that can be purchased with a token; such items are used to "back up" tokens. *See also* token economy.

Baseline. A period prior to the introduction of a treatment procedure during which the frequency, duration, intensity, and/or latency of the target behavior is measured for comparison to treatment or posttreatment periods.

Behavior analysis model. A Project Follow-Through program developed by Donald Bushell and Eugene Ramp which combined programmed materials and a classroom token economy.

Behavior modification. The systematic application of behavioral principles to human problems, including childrearing, education, psychotherapy, vocational preparation, business, and social concerns.

Behavior therapy. A special case of behavior modification referring to the application of behavioral principles to psychological problems in adults and children.

Behavioral contract. *See* contingency contract.

Behavioral deficit. Term used in behavioral assessment; behavior that is judged to be problematic because it occurs at too low a frequency, intensity, or duration.

Behavioral excess. Term used in behavioral assessment; behavior that is judged to be problematic because it occurs at too great a frequency, intensity, or duration.

Behavioral programming. In Kanfer's model of self-control, an individual's self-administration of reinforcement and/or punishment to influence his or her own behavior.

Beta control. Term used in Kanfer's model of self-control to refer to the effect of an individual's self-evaluation, self-reinforcement, and self-punishment on his or her behavior.

Biofeedback training. Providing an individual with relatively immediate information about some normally subliminal aspect of physiological functioning so that he or she might learn to exercise voluntary control over this functioning.

Catastrophizing. Ruminating about and exaggerating the possible negative aspects of a situation; same as *magnification*.

Chemical aversion. A form of aversion therapy in which the aversive stimulus is a chemical agent.

Classical conditioning. *See* respondent conditioning.

Conditioned anxiety. An anxiety reaction that develops immediately and automatically upon presentation of a stimulus previously associated with aversive stimulation; to be contrasted with *reactive anxiety*.

Conditioned reinforcer. Stimulus that acquires reinforcing value as a result of learning; examples include grades, money, praise, and fame.

Conditioned (cue-controlled) relaxation. A procedure in which the individual learns to associate a state of low arousal with a particular cue word (such as "calm") by repeatedly subvocalizing the word in synchrony with breathing while in a state of complete relaxation. Over time, the cue word comes to function as a CS for relaxation and can then be used to counter anxiety reactions in vivo.

Conditioned response (CR). A response, closely resembling the unconditioned response, elicited by a conditioned stimulus.

Conditioned stimulus (CS). An initially neutral stimulus which, through repeated pairing with an unconditioned stimulus, comes to elicit an approximation of the unconditioned response called the conditioned response.

Constructive feedback. Assertive statement that includes an expression of disapproval of another's behavior as well as recommendations as to what the individual might do to correct the problem.

Contingency contract. An agreement between two or more individuals that specifies a behavior change which is to take place in one or more of the individuals, and the positive and negative consequences that will result if the agreement is or is not honored.

Continuous reinforcement (CRF). A schedule of reinforcement in which reinforcers are delivered following every occurrence of a response; also known as *FR-1* (fixed ratio 1).

Controlling response. Term used in the self-control literature to refer to a response emitted by an individual which alters critical features of the environment that, in turn, alter the probability of the individual performing some undesirable behavior (for example, putting a time lock on the refrigerator door).

Counterconditioning. *See* deconditioning.

Coverants. A contraction of the term *covert operants*, referring to thoughts that one attempts to modify by means of operant conditioning procedures.

Covert sensitization. A form of aversion therapy in which the aversive stimulus is a mental image of an unpleasant event.

Covington v. *Harris.* A case in which the court held that the principle of least restrictive alternative is equally applicable to alternative settings within an institution.

CR. *See* conditioned response.

CRF. *See* continuous reinforcement.

CS. *See* conditioned stimulus.

Cue-controlled relaxation. *See* conditioned relaxation.

Deconditioning (counterconditioning). The principle that if a response which competes with and suppresses a CR can be repeatedly made to occur in the presence of the CS, the CS will eventually lose its ability to elicit the CR. The CS becomes *deconditioned* (or *counterconditioned*).

Delusion. A false belief maintained in the face of negative evidence.

Desensitization proper. In systematic desensitization, the actual presentation of hierarchy items to the relaxed client.

Detumescence. The subsidence of any swelling, such as that resulting from *vasocongestion.*

Diathesis-stress theory. Any theory that postulates the origin of a psychological disorder to be an interaction between a genetically determined susceptibility to the disorder (a *diathesis*) and an environment which potentiates that susceptibility (a *stress*).

Differential reinforcement of other behavior (DRO). Reinforcement of behavior incompatible with a problem behavior so as to reduce the occurrence of the problem.

Differential relaxation. An in vivo relaxation procedure in which the individual uses tension-release exercises or relaxation by recall to reduce tension in only those muscles not involved in some ongoing task.

Direct instruction model. A Project Follow-Through program developed by Siegfried Engelman and Wesley Becker that involved specially developed instructional materials and a highly structured format for teacher-student interaction.

Directed masturbation. Systematic exercises in genital self-stimulation used in sex therapy to facilitate sexual responsiveness.

Discrimative stimulus (S^D). A stimulus which signals that reinforcement is available contingent on a particular response. Through repeated associations of an S^D and a particular reinforcement contingency, the S^D will come to evoke the previously reinforced behavior.

DRO. *See* differential reinforcement of other behavior.

Dry-bed training. Multifaceted procedure used in the treatment of enuresis which includes the bell-pad alarm, hourly awakenings with reinforcement of correct toileting, and full cleanliness training.

Electromyographic (EMG) biofeedback. A biofeedback procedure in which the subject hears a tone whose pitch varies directly with the amount of electrical activity (and tension) in a certain muscle. This procedure can be used to teach the subject to relax or, in physical rehabilitation, to increase the activity of the muscle.

Emotive imagery. Fear reduction procedure used with children. The therapist narrates a story in which the leading character (the child) is brought progressively closer to some feared stimulus in the context of fear-suppressing stimuli, such as the child's favorite storybook characters.

Empathic assertion. Assertive statement that includes an acknowledgment of the listener's feelings and rights.

Encopresis. Fecal incontinence often associated with constipation.

Enuresis. Involuntary release of urine in the absence of organic pathology after the age at which a child is expected to be toilet trained. *Nocturnal enuresis* refers to bedwetting.

Environmental planning. Concept derived from Skinner's model of self-control involving an individual's altering the surrounding environment in such a way as to influence his or her own behavior.

Erectile failure. The inability to achieve or maintain a penile erection of sufficient strength or duration to allow for satisfactory intercourse.

Escalation. In assertion training, the introduction of progressively stronger assertions when weaker ones prove to be ineffective.

Escape behavior. Any response directed toward terminating or lessening ongoing aversive stimulation.

Escape conditioning. Learning paradigm in which the individual acquires a response that terminates an aversive stimulus.

Exhibitionism. Public exposure of the genitals under socially unsanctioned circumstances.

Expectancy hypothesis. The hypothesis that any positive change which occurs during a treatment results from the subjects' expectations or beliefs that the procedure will help them, rather than from any specific therapeutic ingredients in the treatment itself.

Explicit exposure to heterosexual stimuli. A procedure for increasing heterosexual responsiveness by exposing an individual to a short film of a nude member of the opposite sex behaving in a seductive manner.

Extinction. In respondent conditioning, the weakening and eventual cessation of a conditioned response upon repeated presentation of the conditioned stimulus without the unconditioned stimulus. In operant conditioning, the gradual return of a previously reinforced response to its operant level upon the withdrawal of reinforcement for its occurrence.

Fading. (1) The gradual withdrawal of aids used in training (prompts, artificial S^{D}s, artificial reinforcers, and so on) so that the trained response is eventually brought under the control of naturally occurring stimuli and reinforcers. (2) A procedure for increasing heterosexual arousal that involves gradually replacing an inappropriate sexual stimulus being viewed by the client with a superimposed heterosexual stimulus so that the arousal generated by the former becomes associated with the latter.

Female superior position. A coital position in which the female is on top of the male.

Fetishism. A sexual interest in a specific part of the body or an inanimate object (typically an item of apparel) more or less independent of the context in which this stimulus occurs.

Fixed interval (FI) reinforcement. A schedule of reinforcement in which reinforcers are delivered for the first emission of a response after a fixed period of time has elapsed since the last response.

Fixed ratio (FR) reinforcement. A schedule of reinforcement in which reinforcers are delivered following the emission of a fixed number of responses.

Flooding. A treatment procedure in which an individual's anxiety is extinguished by prolonged imaginal or in vivo exposure to high-intensity feared stimuli.

Full cleanliness training. Overcorrection procedure used in the treatment of enuresis. The child is required to change clothes and bedsheets and bathe thoroughly following each incident of bedwetting.

Functional analysis. A detailed examination of the relationship between an individual's behavior, and the antecedent stimuli, setting events, and consequences that affect it.

Gamma control. Term used in Kanfer's model of self-control to refer to the impact of an individual's biological system on his or her behavior.

Gender identity confusion. The state of being uncomfortable with one's anatomical gender; in extreme form, also known as *transsexualism.*

Gender role behaviors. Those behaviors that are characteristic of and can be used to differentiate members of each sex within a particular society.

Good faith contract. A contingency contract in which each of two individuals agrees to change certain behavior(s) in exchange for specified reinforcers that are under the control of the other.

Group contingency. A contingency in which each member of a group receives consequences determined by the behavior of either the group as a whole or a specific individual within the group.

Hallucination. A perceptual experience in the absence of appropriate sensory stimulation.

Hawthorne effect. A temporary positive change in behavior following an environmental manipulation which has no real functional relationship to that behavior; similar to a placebo effect.

Hemiplegia. Paralysis of one side of the body.

Heterosexual responsiveness. The extent to which an individual is capable of sexual arousal to adults of the opposite sex.

Heterosocial skills. Those interpersonal behaviors necessary to initiate, develop, and maintain an intimate relationship with a member of the opposite sex.

Hyperactivity. A diagnostic label used to describe schoolchildren exhibiting such problems as short attention span, impulsivity, and emotional lability.

Implosion. An anxiety-reduction procedure similar to *flooding* involving prolonged exposure to fantastic and horrific imagery. Material employed in implosion scenes is often derived from psychoanalytic theory.

Inappropriate sexual arousal. Sexual arousal evoked by stimuli or activities deemed unacceptable by the client and/or some segment of society, which is to be reduced by treatment.

Inappropriate stimulus control. In behavioral assessment, a term used to describe behavior that is problematic because it occurs at the wrong time, in the wrong place, or under inappropriate circumstances.

Incubation. A paradoxical strengthening of a conditioned anxiety response that sometimes occurs following an unreinforced presentation of the conditioned stimulus.

Informed consent. The principle that if an individual is to consent to a procedure or treatment, then he or she must be legally competent to make such decisions; all information relevant to the decision must be known to the individual; and his or her consent must be given voluntarily.

Institutional peonage. The widespread practice of employing institutionalized persons to perform productive labor associated with the maintenance of the institution without adequate compensation.

Instrumental conditioning. *See* operant conditioning.

Involuntary admission. A court-ordered confinement of an individual in a residential mental health facility on the basis that the person is dangerous to himself or herself, dangerous to others, and/or in need of care or treatment.

Lateral coital position. A coital position in which the individuals lie face to face on their sides; often employed in sex therapy for the freedom of movement it affords both partners.

Law of effect. The assertion that the probability that a response will be emitted is a function of the consequences it has produced in the past. Behaviors that produce pleasurable consequences will be repeated; behaviors that produce aversive consequences will cease.

Learned helplessness. A lack of goal-directed responding and passive acceptance of avoidable aversive stimulation seen in organisms previously exposed to aversive stimulation or positive reinforcement that was beyond their control.

Learning disability. Generic term referring to a variety of perceptual and performance problems that may interfere with a child's academic achievement.

Least restrictive alternative. A legal principle which states that when government has a legitimate goal to pursue that affects everyone's interests, it should act in the manner that least curtails individual freedoms.

Legal contract. A legally binding agreement between parties regarding an exchange of services.

Magnification. *See* catastrophizing.

Masochism. Obtaining sexual pleasure by suffering pain, torment, or humiliation.

Masturbatory conditioning. The association of sexual arousal to a stimulus by an individual repeatedly masturbating to orgasm while imagining or viewing the stimulus.

Migraine. A recurrent, typically unilateral headache, vascular in origin and varying in intensity, frequency, and duration. Such headaches are often associated with nausea and vomiting, and may be preceded by sensory, motor, or mood disturbances.

Milieu therapy. A treatment approach introduced by Maxwell Jones in which mental patients form an essentially self-governing therapeutic community whose members are expected to assume responsibility for their behavior.

Minimal effective response. In assertiveness training, assertion strong enough to achieve the individual's goal but not so strong as to evoke a negative reaction in the listener.

Minimization. A way of thinking characterized by devaluation of positive events or personal attributes.

Modeling. Method of instruction which involves an individual (the model) demonstrating the behavior to be acquired by the observer.

Multiple baseline design. Method used to evaluate treatment programs: After stable baseline measures are obtained for three or more behaviors or individuals, the treatment program is introduced with one behavior/individual and measurement continues. After stable measures for the "targeted" behavior/individual are obtained, the treatment program is extended to a second behavior/individual; and so on for all remaining behaviors or individuals. If there is a sequential improvement in the behaviors/individuals when treatment is directed toward each, it can be concluded that the treatment is effective.

Mutual antagonism. The relationship between the sympathetic and parasympathetic divisions of the autonomic nervous system. Activity in one branch produces physiological effects opposite those produced by activity in the other branch.

Negative punishment. The withdrawal of a stimulus contingent on a response to decrease the frequency of that response.

Negative reinforcement. The withdrawal of an aversive stimulus contingent on a response to increase the frequency of that response.

Negative reinforcer. A stimulus whose withdrawal contingent upon the occurrence of a response increases the frequency of that response.

Normalization. A treatment programming strategy in which a "real world" milieu is established to encourage "normal" behavior rather than regressed or dependent behavior.

O'Connor* v. *Donaldson. A Florida case in which the Supreme Court ruled on an individual's "right to liberty," which it said is violated if an institution confines an individual when he or she is not dangerous to self or others, is capable of surviving in the community with the help of family or friends, and is not provided with treatment while in the institution.

Operant conditioning. Increasing and decreasing the frequency of a response by manipulating events that follow its occurrence.

Operant-interpersonal method. A treatment for withdrawn mental patients which was introduced by G. King and co-workers. Patients were involved in lever-manipulation problems, the correct solution of which resulted in a consumable reinforcer. Communication and cooperation between patient and therapist or patient and patient was necessary in order to solve some of the problems.

Orgasm. The intensely pleasurable release of accumulated sexual tension characterized by ejaculation in the male and by rhythmic contractions of the orgasmic platform in the female.

Orgasmic dysfunction. A sexual dysfunction in which the female's orgasm fails to occur or is very difficult to achieve despite prolonged stimulation.

Orgasmic platform. The outer third of the vaginal barrel when this tissue is in a state of vasocongestion.

Orgasmic reconditioning. A procedure for increasing heterosexual arousal by pairing fantasies of heterosexual activity with masturbation and orgasm.

Overcorrection. A method of punishment in which the individual is required to correct the environment following an undesirable behavior (e.g., cleaning up the mess created by the misbehavior) and to practice the correct behavior many times.

Overgeneralization. A way of thinking characterized by drawing broad conclusions on the basis of insufficient evidence.

Parasympathetic activity. Activity in the parasympathetic division of the autonomic nervous system that, in general, is associated with a physiological state of quiescence and relaxation.

Participant modeling. An anxiety-reduction procedure in which the therapist takes an active role in encouraging and guiding the client in interaction with a fear-evoking stimulus.

Pavlovian conditioning. *See* respondent conditioning.

Pedophilia. Sexual desire directed toward children.

Performance anxiety. Anxiety experienced in conjunction with an individual's belief that his or her behavior is being critically evaluated by others; also known as *evaluation anxiety.*

Personalized system of instruction (PSI). A classroom teaching format combining elements of programmed instruction with reinforcement principles.

Pleasuring. *See* sensate focus.

Polarized reasoning. A predisposition to interpret events in an extreme, black or white fashion.

Positive practice. An aspect of overcorrection involving the individual's repeating the correct form of the behavior many times.

Positive punishment. The presentation of an aversive stimulus contingent on a response to decrease the frequency of that response.

Positive reinforcement. The presentation of a stimulus contingent on a response to increase the frequency of that response.

Positive reinforcer. A stimulus whose presentation contingent upon the occurrence of a response increases the frequency of that response.

Premack principle. The observation that, given the free availability of a number of behaviors, the opportunity to engage in a behavior that occurs more frequently can be used as a reinforcer for a less frequently occurring behavior.

Premature ejaculation. A sexual dysfunction in which the male's ejaculation occurs too rapidly or with minimal stimulation and thus interferes with his or his partner's full sexual enjoyment.

Primary reinforcer. *See* unconditioned reinforcer.

Psychophysiological disorder. Physiological damage or dysfunction produced by intense or prolonged psychological stress.

Psychosomatic disorders. *See* psychophysiological disorder.

Psychosurgery. Cortical surgery intended to alleviate psychological disorders.

Quid pro quo contract. A contingency contract in which each of two individuals agrees to change certain behavior(s) if the other individual changes some behavior(s). The agreement is reciprocal in that each person's change serves as a reinforcer for the other's change.

Rapid smoking. Aversive conditioning procedure in which the client (under therapist supervision) inhales cigarette smoke at a rapid rate until he or she can no longer tolerate it.

Rational-emotive therapy (RET). A cognitively oriented psychotherapy in which the therapist seeks to change the client's irrational beliefs by argument, persuasion, and rational reevaluation, and by teaching the client to counter self-defeating thinking with new, nondistressing self-statements.

Reactive anxiety. Anxiety that results when an individual performs inappropriate, stress-producing behavior, or fails to perform appropriate, stress-avoiding behavior. The anxiety is thus a reaction to the individual's behavior, rather than an automatic reaction to a particular stimulus. To be contrasted with *conditioned anxiety.*

Recidivism. Reinstitutionalization or reimprisonment following reoccurrence of disordered or criminal behavior.

Reciprocal inhibition. The principle that two incompatible responses cannot occur simultaneously. The stronger of the two responses at a given moment will be expressed and will inhibit the weaker one.

Refractory period. The period immediately following orgasm during which the man cannot be stimulated to another orgasm; not present in female.

Relaxation by recall. The final stage of training in some relaxation procedures. Tension-release exercises are dispensed with, and the individual relaxes by simply remembering the sensations associated with previous releases of each muscle group.

Relaxation training. Generic term referring to any systematic procedure whose aim is the reduction of muscular tension, sympathetic arousal, and/or feelings of apprehension or tension. The most popular relaxation training methods in behavior therapy are variants of *progressive relaxation,* introduced by Edmund Jacobson.

Respondent conditioning. Process of learning in which a neutral stimulus (CS) that is repeatedly presented immediately before the onset of stimulus which naturally elicits a response (UCR) comes to elicit a response (CR) which is similar to the UCR.

Response costs. Withdrawal or loss of positive reinforcers contingent upon the occurrence of a behavior.

Response differentiation. Gradual modification of the form and/or intensity of existing behavior by reinforcing successive approximations of the desired behavior. Reinforcers are given only when the behavior meets certain requirements.

Retarded ejaculation. A sexual dysfunction in which the male's ejaculation fails to occur or is difficult to achieve despite prolonged stimulation.

Retention control technique. Direct reinforcement of an individual's holding his or her urine for progressively longer periods of time; used in the treatment of enuresis.

Right to treatment. A broad term describing the rights believed to be guaranteed to involuntarily confined mental patients by the due process, equal protection, and cruel and unusual punishment clauses of the Constitution.

Role playing. Reenactment of a life experience or a hypothetical situation in which significant psychological issues should emerge. Role playing can be used in both behavioral assessment and treatment.

Rouse v. Cameron. An early case in which an appeals court held that a District of Columbia act established a statutory "right to treatment."

Sadism. Obtaining sexual pleasure by inflicting pain, torment, or humiliation.

S$^\Delta$. S delta, stimulus which signals that reinforcement is unavailable.

S^D. *See* discriminative stimulus.

Schedule of reinforcement. The rules governing the delivery of reinforcers.

Schizotaxia. A hypothetical defect in the central nervous system postulated by Paul Meehl to be the diathesis for schizophrenia.

Schizotypy. A personality organization characterized by mild cognitive and affective disturbances. Postulated by Paul Meehl to be a manifestation of *schizotaxia.*

Secondary reinforcers. *See* conditioned reinforcer.

Self-instructional training. A cognitive behavior modification procedure in which the client learns to covertly emit a set of task-relevant self-instructions that guide behavior and that can help reduce anxiety and increase problem-solving ability.

Self-stimulatory behavior. *See* stereotypic behavior.

Sensate focus. An in vivo desensitization and communication-enhancement procedure used in sex therapy that involves a couple providing each other with pleasurable sensory stimulation through a structured body massage; also known as *pleasuring.*

Setting event (setting condition). Conditions of the organism or of the environment in which the organism functions that affect the function of antecedent and consequent events.

Sexual arousal deficit. A sexual dysfunction in which the woman produces insufficient vaginal lubrication for comfortable penile penetration. The condition may be accompanied by subjective feelings of unresponsiveness.

Shaping. Method used to train a new behavior by prompting and reinforcing successive approximations of the desired behavior.

Simultaneous communication. An innovation in language training that combines manually signed English and spoken language.

Social imitation. Term coined by Mary Cover Jones in her treatment of children's fears; refers to *modeling.*

Spatial-temporal hierarchy. *See* anxiety hierarchy.

Squeeze technique. A procedure for delaying ejaculation in which the female places two fingers on either side of the coronal ridge of the erect penis, her thumb on the underside opposite the fingers, and squeezes the penis for several seconds until the male's urge to ejaculate passes.

Step system. An incentive system used with institutionalized patients involving a clearly specified hierarchy of functional levels (steps) through which the patient is expected to progress. The higher the functional level attained by the patient, the more privileges and freedoms he or she is afforded.

Stereotypic behavior. Any repetitive movement that seems to serve no function other than possibly to provide an individual with sensory stimulation.

Stimulus control. Control of behavior exerted by an S^D or a CS.

Stimulus overselectivity. The hypothesis that autistic children presented with a stimulus complex with auditory, visual, and tactile components will attend to only one component and ignore the others.

Stress inoculation. An extension of *self-instructional training* for use in cases of anxiety, pain, and anger control. The client practices self-instruction while under some controlled, artificially produced stress, thereby gaining experience in using his or her new skills under conditions approximating those expected in the real world.

Surrogate partner. In sex therapy, an individual who works in conjunction with the therapist and serves as a sexual partner for a dysfunctional individual.

Sympathetic activity (or arousal). Activity in the sympathetic division of the autonomic nervous system that, in general, is associated with a physiological readiness to defend against or flee from physical danger. Sympathetic arousal is a prominent characteristic of anxiety reactions.

Symptom substitution. Hypothesis that a novel problem behavior (symptom) will develop following the elimination of an existing problem behavior if the underlying causes of the symptoms have not been resolved.

Systematic desensitization. A procedure for the reduction of conditioned anxiety that involves having a deeply relaxed individual confront, in imagination, each of a series of increasingly potent anxiety-eliciting stimuli.

Systematic rational restructuring. A variant of rational-emotive therapy in which the techniques of successive approximation, modeling, and behavioral rehearsal are employed in training the client to use nondistressing self-statements.

Tension-release cycle. A basic procedure used in many forms of relaxation training. The individual tightens and then releases each muscle group. It is presumed that the muscle will relax more deeply if it is first tensed. The sequential experience of tension and relaxation also helps the subject learn to discriminate these sensations.

Thematic hierarchy. *See* anxiety hierarchy.

Timeout (timeout from positive reinforcement). Removal of the opportunity to obtain positive reinforcement; used as a negative punisher.

Time projection with positive reinforcement. A procedure used by Arnold Lazarus in the treatment of depression. By means of a hypnotic induction, the client is imaginally projected to a future time in which the depression has lifted, and is then brought back to the present with suggestions to maintain the positive feelings.

Token. Any object (such as plastic chip, star, or check mark) used as a generalized conditioned reinforcer in a *token economy*. Tokens can be exchanged for any available backup reinforcer such as food, clothing, or privileges.

Token economy. An intervention environment in which an individual or individuals receive tokens as reinforcement for performing specified behaviors. The tokens function as currency within the environment, and can be exchanged for desired goods, services, or privileges.

Transfer (generalization) tests. The client's posttreatment contacts with environments or situations in which he or she previously responded in an undesirable fashion.

Transsexualism. A sexual variation in which the individual finds his or her anatomical gender repugnant and identifies completely with the opposite sex.

Transvestism. Obtaining sexual pleasure by dressing in clothing characteristic of the opposite sex.

Traumatic single-trial conditioning. The development of conditioned anxiety through a single pairing of a neutral stimulus with intense aversive stimulation.

UCR. *See* unconditioned response.

UCS. *See* unconditioned stimulus.

Unconditioned reinforcer. A stimulus that naturally functions as a reinforcer without conditioning. Examples include food, water, and air.

Unconditioned response (UCR). A response elicited by an unconditioned stimulus.

Unconditioned stimulus (UCS). A stimulus that naturally elicits a response without conditioning.

Vaginismus. A sexual dysfunction in which the outer third of the vagina undergoes an involuntary constriction, making penile penetration difficult or impossible.

Variable interval reinforcement (VI). A schedule of reinforcement for the contingent delivering of reinforcer(s) after a variable period of time has elapsed since the last response.

Variable ratio reinforcement (VR). A schedule of reinforcement for the delivery of reinforcer(s) contingent upon the subject's emitting a variable number of responses.

Vasocongestion. A localized swelling resulting from an increase in blood flow to and/or a decrease in blood flow from tissue. Observed in the genitalia during sexual excitement.

Vicarious conditioning. Development of a conditioned response in an individual who merely observes someone else undergoing conditioning or emitting a conditioned response.

Voluntary admission. A self-initiated entry into a residential mental health facility.

Voyeurism. The obtaining of sexual pleasure from observing people perform intimate acts, such as undressing, urinating, defecating, or engaging in sexual activity.

Wyatt v. *Stickney*. A landmark right-to-treatment case in which the court ruled that Alabama state mental institutions must provide a humane psychological and physical environment, qualified staff in numbers sufficient to administer adequate treatment, and individualized treatment programs for each resident.

INDEX

469

ABOUT THE AUTHORS

WILLIAM H. REDD received his Ph.D. in psychology at the University of North Carolina at Chapel Hill and is now associate professor of psychology at the University of Illinois at Urbana-Champaign. Before joining the clinical psychology faculty at Illinois, he worked as a clinician and researcher at the Fernald School and at Massachusetts General Hospital in Boston. During that period, Professor Redd held teaching appointments at Harvard College, Harvard Medical School, and Boston University. His primary research contributions have been in the areas of adult-child social interaction and generalization of treatment effects following behavioral intervention. In addition to teaching an undergraduate course in behavior modification, he conducts a graduate seminar in clinical-child psychology and undergraduate practica in behavior modification. Professor Redd is a fellow of the Behavior Therapy and Research Society.

ALBERT L. PORTERFIELD is a Ph.D. candidate in clinical psychology at the University of Illinois at Urbana-Champaign. Although his publications have been in the area of physiological psychology, his major interests now include anxiety, depression, and sexual difficulties in adults. Mr. Porterfield's clinical experience has primarily involved treatment of adult outpatients through the University of Illinois Psychological Clinic and the Psychological and Counseling Center.

BARBARA L. ANDERSEN is a Ph.D. candidate in clinical psychology at the University of Illinois at Urbana-Champaign. Her research has been in the area of educational intervention with severely disturbed and academically unsuccessful children. One of her primary interests is in mental health law, particularly as it relates to children and institutionalized individuals. Ms. Andersen's clinical experience has been with children and adults seen on an outpatient basis. She has also spent one year working in an institutional program for psychotic adults.